Rhineland Radicals

Rhineland Radicals

THE DEMOCRATIC MOVEMENT AND THE REVOLUTION OF 1848–1849

Jonathan Sperber

PRINCETON UNIVERSITY PRESS

PRINCETON, NEW JERSEY

Library of Congress Cataloging-in-Publication Data

Sperber, Jonathan, 1952–
Rhineland radicals : the democratic movement and the revolution
of 1848–1849 / Jonathan Sperber.
p.   cm.
Includes bibliographical references and index.
1. Rhineland (Germany)—History. 2. Germany—History—Revolution,
1848–1849. I. Title.
DD801.R682S64   1991
943′.4—dc20   91–127

ISBN 0-691-03172-X

ISBN 0-691-00866-3 (pbk.)

First Princeton Paperback printing, 1993

This book has been composed in Linotron Times Roman

Princeton University Press books are printed on
acid-free paper, and meet the guidelines for permanence
and durability of the Committee on Production Guidelines for
Book Longevity of the Council on Library Resources

Printed in the United States of America

10   9   8   7   6   5   4   3   2

FOR MY WIFE, NANCY KATZMAN

For all the happiness she has brought into my life

Contents

Tables

Preface

LIKE MANY works of scholarship, this book grew out of a previous one. In the course of working on a study of religion, politics, and society in western Germany in the middle decades of the nineteenth century, I came across a speech given in 1873 by a Catholic priest in the lower Rhine manufacturing town of Krefeld. In it, he condemned the liberals as "men who once wanted to wade up to their ankles in the blood of tyrants." It seemed an odd reference, not what would first come to mind in attacking the politically moderate, almost conservative National Liberals of Bismarckian Germany.

I did find it interesting that the speaker should have bothered to make a veiled reference to the revolution of 1848–1849, an event occurring a quarter-century in the past. As I continued my investigations into post-1850 politics, I found many similarly veiled references to the events of 1848–1849, mostly in negative or hostile fashion. The frequency with which the memory of the revolutionary events kept turning up seemed out of character with the dominant scholarly image of the revolution as a failed uprising, which was never a very serious challenge to the existing order in the first place.

Continuing my researches in a different sphere, I uncovered much evidence about the unruliness of German society in the two decades before 1848, the period commonly known as the *Vormärz*, the "pre-March [revolution of 1848]." Yet this unruly character of prerevolutionary German society rarely seemed to enter much into accounts of the revolution. Consequently, I resolved to write my own study, one which would take the revolution as seriously as contemporaries did, and link it to the strains and tensions of the *Vormärz* socioeconomic, political, and cultural order. After some years spent squinting into microfilm readers, peering at almost indecipherable handwritings, and staring into a video display terminal, the current book emerged. That it finally did emerge is in great part due to the substantial assistance I received from many organizations and individuals.

Most of the primary research for the book was done in Germany during the academic year 1987–1988. I was then a fellow of the Alexander von Humboldt Stiftung, an agency whose generosity and assistance to foreign scholars cannot be praised enough. An equally generous fellowship of the John Simon Guggenheim Memorial Foundation enabled me to produce a manuscript while the research was still fresh in my mind. Preliminary investigations were funded by smaller grants from the National Endowment for the Humanities, the Deutscher Akademischer Austauschdienst, and the University of Missouri Faculty Research Council.

As a Humboldt fellow, I was affiliated with the seminar of Professor Otto Dann of the University of Cologne. Professor Dann and his students, particularly Elisabeth Friese, Matthias Kitsche, Sabine Riem, and Marcel Seypel, were incisive critics and friendly and accommodating hosts. The hours of detailed research into the finer aspects of Rhenish culture at *Keldenich* will long remain a pleasant memory. Two of Otto Dann's Cologne colleagues, Professors Jost Dülffer and Dieter Düding, were also friendly and helpful, the latter generously providing suggestions from his store of knowledge of *Vormärz* Germany.

The current center of studies on the revolution of 1848–1849 in the Federal Republic of Germany is at the University of Tübingen, and I always came away from my visits to Tübingen with some suggestion or insight of substantial value for my work. For this, I am indebted to Professor Dieter Langewiesche, Wolfram Siemann, Carola Lipp, and especially to Friedrich Lenger, an acute scholar and amiable host.

My colleagues in the department of history at the University of Missouri have put much effort into making possible the practice of scholarship, in spite of severe financial constraints. My thanks to all of them, but particularly to Susan Porter Benson, Kerby Miller, and David Roediger, who took on themselves the onerous task of reading the manuscript and making critical comments. At various institutions and repositories in the United States, the Federal Republic of Germany, and the former German Democratic Republic, I have met archivists and librarians whose advice and patient assistance substantially eased the difficulties of research. I hope that none will be offended if I just mention one of them by name, Ms. Anne Edwards, Geography-History-Philosophy librarian at the University of Missouri. Over the years, Professors John Boyer, Margaret Anderson, and Vernon Lidtke have taken a sustained interest in my career, and offered advice and encouragement. Like everyone else mentioned above, they have a substantial share in any positive aspects of this book; its mistakes and failures are my sole responsibility.

A Note on the Translations

SINCE government agencies and offices appear frequently in the text and, in spite of relatively similar administrative systems, the individual offices had different designations in each of the three Rhenish Provinces under study, I have included the translations in advance. I have referred to the chief of the administration of the three Rhenish provinces—known in Rhenish Prussia as *Oberpräsident*, in the Palatinate as the *Regierungspräsident*, and in Rhine-Hessen under a variety of different names—as the "provincial governor." I have translated the main administrative subdivision of the Prussian Rhine Province, the *Regierungsbezirk*, as "district," and referred to its chief official as "district governor." The provinces of Rhine-Hessen and the Palatinate had no such administrative subdivisions, which is not surprising, since they were each about the size of one of the five districts of the Prussian Rhineland.

The next unit down, in Rhenish Prussia and Rhine-Hessen, the *Kreis*, in the Palatinate, the *Landkomissariatsbezirk*, I have translated as "county," and I have translated the title of its chief administrator—*Landrat*, *Kreisrat*, and *Landkomissär*, respectively—as "county commissioner." In Rhine-Hessen and the Palatinate, counties were subdivided into cantons, which, however, had no presiding administrative official. The comparable administrative unit in Rhenish Prussia was the *Landbürgermeisterei*, which I have translated as "magistracy," with the title of its presiding official, *Landbürgermeister*, translated as "magistrate."

With regard to communal affairs, the urban offices were common to all three provinces. I have translated *Bürgermeister* or *Oberbürgermeister* as "mayor" and *Stadtrat* as "city council." In the countryside, the elected head of village government administration in Rhine-Hessen and the Palatinate was called the *Bürgermeister*. In Rhenish Prussia, this official was the *Gemeinde-vorsteher* or *Ortsvorsteher*; the term *Bürgermeister* was reserved for the magistrate. I have translated the office of all these rustic officials as "village mayor."

Most nonofficial terms are more consistent and easier to render in English consistently. Whenever a translation from German into English might appear unclear, or involve a less than literal rendition to preserve its meaning, I have included the German original in brackets. Two phrases might be noted here. One is *Verein*, which can be translated into English as "club," "association," or "society." I have used all three, translating *Demokratischer Verein* as

"Democratic Club," *Arbeiterverein* as "Workers' Association," and *Turnverein* as "Gymnastics Society." The other is *Bürgerwehr*, which could be translated as "bourgeois militia," "civic guard," or "citizens' defense force." I have opted for the second, but the word, and the institution it named, combined all three meanings.

Abbreviations Used in the Footnotes

AfHGA	*Archiv für Hessische Geschichte und Altertumskunde*
AHVN	*Annalen des Historischen Vereins für den Niederrhein*
Anklag-Akte	*Anklag-Akte, errichtet durch die K. General Staatsprokurator der Pfalz . . . gegen Martin Reichard . . . und 332 Consorten wegegn bewaffneter Rebellion. . . . Hoch- und Staatsverraths & c.*
BAF	Bundesarchiv Außenstelle Frankfurt a. Main
BfPK	*Blätter für Pfälzischen Kirchengeschichte*
BHSTAM	Bayerisches Hauptstaatsarchiv München
FA	*Freiheit, Arbeit*
FBA	*Freiheit, Brüderlichkeit, Arbeit*
HSTAD	Hauptstaatsarchiv Düsseldorf
JbwL	*Jahrbuch für westdeutsche Landesgeschichte*
KA	Kriegs-Archiv
KnZ	*Kölnische Zeitung*
Kr.	Kreis
LAK	Landeshauptarchiv Koblenz
LAS	Landesarchiv Speyer
LK	Landkommissär
LR	Landrat
MfEKR	*Monatshefte für Evangelische Kirchengeschichte des Rheinlandes*
MHVP	*Mitteilungen des Historischen Vereins der Pfalz*
MInn	Ministerium des Innern
MZ	*Mainzer Zeitung*
NKZ	*Neue Kölnische Zeitung*
NRhZ	*Neue Rheinische Zeitung*
NSZ	*Neue Speyerer Zeitung*
Pr	Präsidialregistratur
RA	Regierung Aachen
RD	Regierung Düsseldorf
RhBA	*Rheinische Briefe und Akten zur Geschichte der politischen Bewegung*
RhG	*Rheinsche Geschichte*
RhVjBl	*Rheinische Vierteljahrsblätter*
RK	Regierung Köln
RP	Regierung der Pfalz

StdT	Stadtarchiv Trier
Vbl	*Volksblatt*
VdB	*Verfolger der Bosheit*
Vhdl	*Die Verhandlungen des rheinhessischen Hochverrathsprozesses von 1850*
ZAVK	*Zeitung des Arbeitervereins zu Köln*
ZGO	*Zeitschrift für die Geschichte des Oberrheins*
ZSTAM	Zentrales Staatsarchiv der DDR, Dienststelle Merseburg

Rhineland Radicals

Introduction

IN THE CYCLE of European revolutions, running from the taking of the Bastille to the storming of the Winter Palace, those of 1848 stand out for their conspicuous lack of success. The revolutionaries of that year were unable to seize and hold state power, yielding their positions, after a shorter or longer interval, to representatives of the previously established regimes. Nowhere was this failure more ignominious than in central Europe, and the German Revolution of 1848 has often been portrayed in a series of comic vignettes: Germany's first attempt at democracy leading merely to confusion; the professors of the Frankfurt Parliament, endlessly talking, while events moved past them; the parliamentarians finally resolving to act and naming the king of Prussia emperor, only to discover that he had no interest in such an office. The comic series usually ends more soberly, with Bismarck announcing fifteen years later that the great issues of the day are not resolved with parliamentary speeches as was attempted in 1848, but with blood and iron.

While not totally false, such a view is one-sided in the extreme, ignoring the extent to which the mid-nineteenth-century revolution was a remarkable mass movement. Germany's first experiment with democracy did not just take place among a few hundred parliamentarians, but involved millions of participants in elections, mass meetings, and the sessions of political clubs. In 1848–1849, the recourse to blood and iron was not solely the prerogative of the Prussian army, but was exercised by insurgents on the barricades and rioters in the streets and in the forests. Whether or not the revolution was successful, its widespread ramifications make it worthy of investigation for its own sake.

The year 1848 was also halfway between 1789 and 1917, a nodal point in European political and social history. In that year, peasants rioted against feudal lords, while urban artisans were demanding the abolition of capitalism. Political radicalism in the mid-century revolution sometimes took the form of an early socialism, but also—and this is too often forgotten—of a revived, popular Jacobinism. However, it would distort the politics of 1848 to understand them exclusively as a successor to past revolutions or a precursor to future ones. They were also distinct and characteristic of the social and political tensions of mid-nineteenth-century Europe, arising from a social order differing from both the corporate society of the eighteenth-century old regime, and the industrial-capitalist world of the late nineteenth and early twentieth centuries.

It might have been expected that the development of social history over the last several decades would have led to a different view of the 1848 revolution, one incorporating some of these perspectives. The use of the techniques of social history to investigate events in central Europe has usually not had this result; rather, it has tended to reinforce from a different direction the picture of the failed revolution. Social conflict, historians have argued, led toward political passivity or even to the support of counterrevolution. The year 1848 was, in this interpretation, a sort of self-canceling revolution.[1]

This viewpoint is also too narrow, although in a different way from the traditional one. It suffers from a problem not limited to the historiography of the revolution of 1848, the segregation of the study of prerevolutionary society from that of the revolution itself. Long-term accounts of the development of social conflict in Germany during the first half of the nineteenth century usually stop at or before March–April 1848, leaving unconsidered the further course of the revolution, from the elections to the Frankfurt National Assembly in May 1848 onwards. Doing so neglects the process of politicization, the interaction of spontaneous popular movements with organized political radicalism. Conversely, social histories of the year of revolution often start out with only a vague notion of prerevolutionary society and the conflicts inherent to it, sometimes filling in the gap with generalizations derived from sociological modernization theory or Marxist-Leninist models of class conflict.[2]

To put it differently, the tensions of prerevolutionary society were not expressed once and for all in the spring of 1848, nor did the revolution as mass movement come to an end then. Rather, both continued but were transformed, a process apparent in the growth of a democratic movement, and its campaigns of organization and agitation, in the results of further elections held in the fall of 1848 and the winter of 1849, and in numerous localized uprisings, culminating in the widespread insurrections of May 1849. Any interpretation of the revolution that cannot explain this year-long period of conflict and crisis—cannot explain a revolution of 1848–1849, not just 1848—and understand its roots in prerevolutionary society is simply incomplete.

---

[1] The first social-historical studies on 1848, such as Rudolf Stadelmann, *Social and Political History of the Revolution of 1848/49*, trans. James Chastain (Athens, Ohio: Ohio University Press, 1975) [original German edition published in 1948], or Theodore Hamerow, *Restoration, Revolution, Reaction: Economics and Politics in Central Europe, 1815–1871* (Princeton: Princeton University, 1958), pioneered this interpretation. The essays on 1848 in the recent *Sozialer Protest: Studien zu traditioneller Resistenz und kollektiver Gewalt in Deutschland vom Vormärz bis zur Reichsgründung*, ed. Heinrich Volkmann and Jürgen Bergmann (Opladen: Westdeutscher Verlag, 1984), show its continued influence.

[2] Two recent otherwise excellent works on social conflict that pull up short in the spring of 1848 are Rainer Wirtz, *"Widersetzlichkeit, Excesse, Crawalle, Tumulte und Skandale": Soziale Bewegung und gewalthafter sozialer Protest in Baden 1815–1848* (Frankfurt, West Berlin, and Vienna: Ullstein, 1981), and Gerd Husung *Protest und Repression im Vormärz. Norddeutschland zwischen Restauration und Revolution* (Göttingen: Vandenhoeck & Ruprecht, 1983). Problems with the use of modernization theory or Marxism-Leninism in the study of the 1848–1849 revolution will be considered in the conclusion.

In this book, I will attempt such a comprehensive study, analyzing the structures of pre-1848 German society, considering the conflicts that arose from them, and discussing the radical activists who attempted to politicize them, both before and during the year of revolution. The interaction mentioned above between popular movements and organized democratic radicalism will serve as a guiding thread throughout the twists and turns of the analysis and the narrative. Because the subject is so complex, any attempt to do it justice, especially one working primarily from manuscript sources, must be in some way restricted. I have chosen to write a regional study about the Rhineland, on Germany's western border.

Many aspects of Rhenish society and politics were not typical of central Europe, but at a time when there were still considerable limitations on communications, transport, and the market, when there was no national state to create a common framework of political experience, no one region could be called "typical." It was, instead, the "exceptional" features of the Rhineland that caught my attention and made a study of the 1848 revolution there seem like a particularly rewarding scholarly enterprise. Three features in particular deserve mention, since they have helped shape the nature of this work.

First, the Rhineland was one of the major centers of the democratic movement during the revolution, an area rich in radical political activity of both a violent and a peaceful nature. It might have been possible to write a history of the democratic movement in Pomerania or Lower Bavaria; such a work, however, would have been excessively short and more was to be gained by considering an area where left-wing activists came to enjoy an above-average measure of popular support.

The second aspect is perhaps a little peripheral but worth considering nonetheless. The year 1848 is a long way off, and most of the events of the revolution and the people who played a leading role in them are today only known to specialists. This is certainly true of prominent Rhenish democrats. Nikolaus Schmitt, Ludwig Blenker, Franz Raveaux, and Mathilde Franziska Anneke are not exactly household words, even in historians' households. Two of their number, namely Karl Marx and Friedrich Engels, went on to a more permanent renown. The events of 1848–1849 provide a chance to recapture Marx and Engels's character as revolutionaries, an increasingly unfamiliar role for them in the late twentieth century, when they have been frozen into cultural icons, or recast as academic social theorists.

The third, important feature for this work was the nature of the Rhineland as a region. It was extraordinarily diverse, and its varied economic, social, religious, political, and, of course, geographic landscapes make it a useful subject for comparative historical investigation. Coexisting with this diversity, however, was a common historical experience, a revolutionary heritage particularly appropriate to the study of 1848. Of all the regions of central Europe, the Rhineland had been most deeply affected by the *Ur*-revolution, the great French Revolution of 1789.

The major part of the Rhineland had belonged to the French First Republic and Napoleonic Empire for two full decades; most of the rest had been under the rule of one of the Napoleonic satellite states and so had had its share of revolutionary experience. This revolutionary period remained a living memory during the first half of the nineteenth century. Inhabitants of Rhaunen, on the banks of the Moselle River, could still point out the tree of liberty, planted fifty years previously in their village. The iron Phrygian cap, placed by the Jacobins on the spire of St. Augustine's church in Landau, remained there for decades, even after the church had been converted into an armory, and the city of Landau into a fortress of the German Confederation, designed to prevent any recurrence of military expansion by a newly revolutionary France.

Every year, Cologne's surviving veterans of Napoleon's army met and marched to church, to hear a mass for the souls of their deceased comrades. The veterans would gather on Appelhofplatz (Appeals Court Square), seat of the court of appeals for that portion of the Prussian Rhine Province—about 90 percent of it—in which the Napoleonic Code was still legally valid, as it was in all of the Rhenish possessions of the Kingdom of Bavaria and the Grand Duchy of Hessen-Darmstadt. Many of the jurists employed at the court of appeals were among the two hundred Cologne notables who crossed the Rhine on July 14, 1841, to join a Bastille Day banquet in a suburban restaurant, the festivities presided over by a high Prussian official.

This heritage was both an advantage for the mid-century Rhenish democrats and a challenge to them. It was an advantage, since they could act among a population familiar with the idiom of revolution. It was a challenge, because by the 1840s this idiom had become increasingly foreign. Just as Hegel boasted of having taught philosophy to speak German, the Rhineland radicals had to find ways of converting the Jacobin ideals of the 1790s into the nationalist language of nineteenth-century politics.

This last consideration points to one of several ways in which this regional study can be seen in a broader context. It is in part a modest historical contribution to the bicentenary of the French Revolution, but quite different in tenor from the negative, often downright hostile, scholarly evaluations of the revolution, which have been so common on its two-hundredth anniversary. Rather, this work suggests the continuing significance of the revolutionary ideals, and the possibility of their transformation to meet changed social and political conditions in another time and place.

In a rare coincidence for an historian of the nineteenth century, contemporary events have reinforced this viewpoint. As I was completing a preliminary draft of this book in the fall of 1989, the heritage of the French Revolution was being reaffirmed once more throughout central and eastern Europe. As Alexander Dubcek said of these events, "Two hundred years have gone by since the French Revolution . . . but its ideals, its ideas of Equality, Liberty, Fraternity, have survived until today and in many parts of the world are waiting to become reality." What was true in 1989 was even more the case 140 years previously.[3]

The book can also be situated in the context of another interpretation of the mid-century German revolution. Unlike the two approaches mentioned above, this version stresses the significance of conflicts within prerevolutionary society, the importance of popular political participation, and the continuation of the revolutionary movement beyond the spring of 1848. While not new, this approach has long been found primarily in relatively obscure regional studies, whose results have remained outside the scholarly mainstream. In recent years, historians and folklorists at the University of Tübingen have emphasized in more systematic fashion these features of the revolution. Although independently conceived, my work has many similarities with theirs, both in the way the problem is approached and in the conclusions drawn from studying it.[4]

Finally, I have conceived the work as an example of the study of society and politics "from below." I have attempted to ascertain the significance of the events of 1848–1849 for the common people of the mid-nineteenth-century Rhineland. What, after all, did the revolution mean to a baker in Cologne, a scissors-smith of Höhscheid, a market-wife of Bretzenheim, a vintner in Flemmlingen? The answer to such a question can never be given with the exactitude possible in a comparable study of the wealthy and powerful, since the lower classes lacked the education, the practiced and precise articulation

[3] Dubcek's statement is from an interview in *Die Zeit*, Nr. 8, 23 Feb. 1990.

[4] Relevant regional studies include Wilhelm Schulte, *Volk und Staat. Westfalen im Vormärz und in der Revolution von 1848/49* (Münster: Aschendorff, 1954); Dietmar Nickel, *Die Revolution 1848/49 in Augsburg und Bayerisch-Schwaben* (Augsburg: Michael Seitz, 1965); Rolf Weber, *Die Revolution in Sachsen 1848/49* (East Berlin: Akademie-Verlag, 1970). Among the works of the Tübingen scholars are Dieter Langewiesche, *Liberalismus und Demokratie in Württemberg von der Revolution bis zur Reichsgründung* (Düsseldorf: Droste, 1974); by the same author, the important interpretative article "Republik, Monarchie und 'Sozial Frage.' Grundprobleme der deutschen Revolution von 1848," *Historische Zeitschrift* 230 (1980): 529–48; Wolfgang Kaschuba and Carola Lipp, *1848—Provinz und Revolution. Kultureller Wandel und soziale Bewegung im Königreich Württemberg* (Tübingen: Tübinger Vereinigung für Volkskunde e.V. Schloss, 1979); and their "Wasser und Brot. Politische Kultur im Alltag des Vormärz—und Revolutionsjahre," *Geschichte und Gesellschaft* 10 (1984): 320–51; Friedrich Lenger, *Zwischen Kleinbürgertum und Proletariat. Sozialgeschichte der Düsseldorfer Handwerker im 19. Jahrhundert* (Göttingen: Vandenhoeck & Ruprecht, 1986), esp. pp. 150–87; and the best general history of the revolution, Wolfram Siemann, *Die deutsche Revolution von 1848/49* (Frankfurt a.M.: Suhrkamp, 1985). The most recent work of this school, the very fine dissertation of Langewiesche's student Michael Wettengel, *Die Revolution von 1848/49 im Rhein-Main-Raum. Politische Vereine und Revolutionsalltag im Großherzogtum Hessen, Herzogtum Nassau und in der Freien Stadt Frankfurt* (Wiesbaden: Selbstverlag der Historischen Kommission für Nassau, 1989) was only available to me as I was completing the manuscript, so I was not able to incorporate fully all the results of the work into my text. Readers of both books will note the many points of agreement.

of ideas, and the access to the printed word available to elite groups. Nevertheless, it is hard to imagine studying a mass political movement such as a revolution without at least trying to understand the popular experience of it.

Over the last several decades, this genre of historical study has become increasingly common in French and Anglo-American scholarship, so much so that a reaction to it has emerged as the latest trend. Prominent among the critics have been the partisans of the "linguistic turn" of historical scholarship. Drawing on developments in semiotics, poststructuralist literary criticism, and cultural anthropology, they have argued that social and political struggles are contained in and determined by symbolic structures that are linguistic and textual in nature. The very idea of a separate popular experience vanishes, since it, like all others is determined by a "discourse," a self-referential linguistic structure conceptually prior to human individuals or social groups.

This linguistic/symbolic approach offers substantial possibilities to expand the study of social history. In particular, I find useful the idea that collective action presupposes shared symbolic structures, so that a study of the symbolism of social or political action becomes an important means of understanding it. However, the main theme of this approach and of its criticism of the previous practice of social history, the linguistic construction of social reality, seems to me to confuse literature with society. Critics can deconstruct literary texts as they please, but to determine social and political change, discourses must be expressed by individuals or social groups with differing and varying kinds of access to the power to express publicly such discourses and to impose them on others. Even a common discourse can be used and understood in different ways by different social groups. Symbolic structures ought to be understood as part of social reality rather than as constituting it.[5]

Ironically, the same study of history from below, which is increasingly passé in French and Anglo-American circles, remains new and contentious in central European historiography. German historians have pointed to a quite different problem with this approach, a tendency toward the reification of popular experience, treating it as a thing in itself, unconnected to national events or to the organized currents of politics. This is an apt criticism, which can be met by emphasizing the extent to which popular experience was the product

[5] A vehement criticism of social history by a prominent partisan of the linguistic turn can be found in Dominick LaCapra, *History and Criticism* (Ithaca and London: Cornell University, 1985), esp. the essay "Is Everyone a *Mentalité* Case? Transference and the Culture Concept," pp. 71–94. An equally vehement defense of social history can be found in Bryan Palmer, *Descent into Discourse: the Reification of Language and the Writing of Social History* (Philadelphia: Temple University Press, 1990). For a good example of an acute lingustic criticism of an accepted viewpoint and a thoughtful rejoinder, see Gareth Stedman-Jones, "Rethinking Chartism," in his *Languages of Class: Studies in English Working Class History 1832–1982* (Cambridge: Cambridge University Press, 1983), pp. 90–178, and Paul Pickering, "Class Without Words: Symbolic Communication in the Chartist Movement," *Past and Present* 112 (1986): 144–62.

of political mobilization, that is, of the interaction between spontaneous, largely unselfconscious social movements and organized, self-consciously political actors. The development of this interaction, and the transformation of both elements in it by their encounter with each other, made up the democratic movement, the subject of this book.[6]

The work is divided into three parts, each dealing with a different phase of this interaction. Beginning with a description of the Rhineland near the middle of the nineteenth century, the first part goes on to analyze the nature of social tensions there in the two decades before the 1848 revolution. It describes those activists who sought to politicize these tensions, and explains how the authoritarian nature of the German states set limits to their activity.

The second part is about the encounter between the masses and radical political activists in the freer atmosphere prevailing after the initial and partial victories of revolution in March 1848. Its starting point is the disjunction between the widespread and frequently violent expressions of popular grievances at the onset of the revolution, and the modest political influence exerted by the democrats. Most of this second part is devoted to exploring how leftists tried to change this situation. It details the forms of agitation and organization they used to gain and consolidate popular support, and the way different social and religious groups responded to these efforts. A final chapter in this section looks at major political events in the Rhineland between June 1848 and March 1849, in the light of the democrats' drive to organize a broad base of supporters.

The third part considers the revolutionary struggles of April–June 1849. In most accounts they appear as a sort of political afterthought, since historians usually assert that the revolution was over before these struggles began. Seen in terms of the interaction between popular movements and organized radicalism, however, they were the climax of the mid-century revolution. During these months, leftists mobilized the popular following they had won over the previous year to attempt a second, far more radical, democratic and republican revolution.

---

[6] A good, if admittedly partisan, account of the discussion among German historians on this topic, with useful comparisons to the situation in other countries, can be found in Hans Medick, " 'Missionare im Ruderboot'? Ethnologische Erkenntnissen als Herausforderung an die Sozialgeschichte," *Geschichte und Gesellschaft* 10 (1984): 295–319.

PART ONE

Before the Storm

"[T]he word of honor of a burgher of Cologne is worth every bit as much as that of a Prussian lieutenant, even one ostensibly from the nobility."
—Remark made by a certain Hisberg, during the Big St. Martin's parish fair riot in Cologne, August 4, 1846.

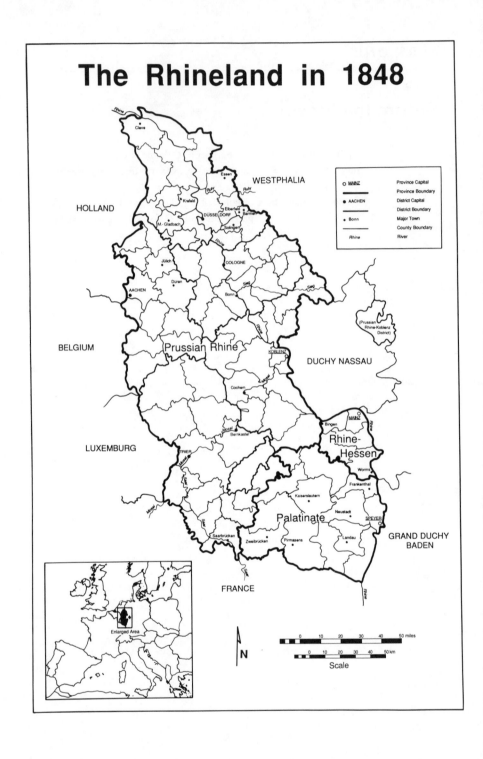

The Rhineland in 1848

Cleve

WESTPHALIA

HOLLAND

Krefeld
Ruhr
Ruhr
Essen
Elberfeld
Barmen
DÜSSELDORF
M.-Gladbach
Solingen

Jülich
COLOGNE
Sieg
Sieg
Düren
AACHEN
Bonn

Prussian Rhine

BELGIUM

(Prussian
Rhine-Koblenz
District)

KOBLENZ

DUCHY NASSAU

Cochem

MAINZ
Bingen
Bernkastel
Rhine-
Hessen

LUXEMBURG

TRIER
Worms
Frankenthal

Kaiserslautern

Palatinate
Neustadt
SPEYER

Saarbrücken
Zweibrücken
Pirmasens
Landau

GRAND DUCHY
BADEN

FRANCE

	Province Capital
MAINZ	
	Province Boundary
AACHEN	District Capital
	District Boundary
Bonn	Major Town
	County Boundary
Rhine	River

Enlarged Area

N

0 10 20 30 40 50 miles

0 10 20 30 40 50 km

Scale

CHAPTER ONE

The Rhinelands

RIVER, VALLEY, HILLS, AND PLAIN

Like many things in life, the region of the Rhine Valley is best understood by starting in the middle. A traveler on the romantic, touristy stretch of the river between Mainz and Koblenz cannot help but notice the contrast between the narrow river valley, the towns just one or two streets wide, and the enroaching steep cliffs, leading up to a terrain of hills and forest. This contrast between valley and uplands is also found on the Rhine's left bank (western) tributaries, the Ahr, Moselle, Saar, and Nahe. Geographers distinguish two separate upland regions, the Eifel and the Hunsrück, respectively, north and south of the Moselle, but they are both alike in alternating high plateau with hilly, forested peaks, rising to a maximum height of some 2,200 feet.

South of Bingen, two-thirds of the way from Koblenz to Mainz, the hills become gentler and more rolling. Upstream of Mainz they retreat westward, the intervening land forming the upper Rhine plain, a flat area, rather swampy on the banks of the river, but generally rich and fertile. If one continues twenty miles inland from Speyer, however, one meets the up-country again, at first the hilly Haardt "mountains" and, to their south and west, the more genuinely mountainous Vosges, along the border with France. Together, these uplands make up the western Palatinate, or Westrich, sharply distinguished from the "forward Palatinate" [Vorderpfalz] of the upper Rhine plains.

There is a similar development to the north, on the lower Rhine. Starting near Bonn, the hills flatten and retreat to the west. When the river takes its bend around Cologne, where, in Heinrich Böll's charming phrase, the "wine-drinking Rhine becomes the Schnapps-drinking Rhine," they vanish altogether. The hilly country, the "Bergisches Land," continues further on the right bank, up to the confluence of the Rhine and Ruhr rivers at Duisburg. There it also gives way to the flatlands, part of the great northern European plain stretching from the English Channel to the Urals.[1]

In the mid-nineteenth century, when natural phenomena played a much more directly shaping role in human affairs than in the industrial era, these geographic contrasts were immediately apparent in society and economy, even in personality. Contemporaries easily distinguished between the "greater im-

---

[1] On the geography of the Rhine basin, see Étienne Juillard, *L'Europe rhénane. Géographie d'un grand éspace*, (Paris: Armand Colin, 1968). Curiously, there is no modern, German-language Rhineland geography.

mobility, simplicity in life and hence contentment with current conditions" of the peasants of the uplands and the "mobility, the relations of trade and transport, the many and varied requirements" of the residents of the valley, this quotation contrasting the inhabitants of the Hunsrück and the dwellers on the banks of the Moselle near Bernkastel. When this geographical difference was combined with a difference in religion, as was the case with the Roman Catholics of the Rhine Valley between Cologne and Düsseldorf, and the Protestants of the Bergisches Land and Wuppertal directly to the east of them, observers had the impression of entering a foreign country in going just a few miles from one area to the next. Even today, in spite of (post)industrialization, urbanization, and the massive population movements of the later nineteenth and the twentieth centuries, the distinction between the voluble and lively, if somewhat unreliable inhabitants of the Rhine Valley, and the soberer, indeed moroser, if more determined dwellers of the surrounding uplands has by no means disappeared.[2]

RYE, POTATOES, AND WINE

Agriculture remained by far the most prevalent occupation in the mid-nineteenth-century Rhineland. Even in the Düsseldorf District of the Prussian Rhine Province, one of the leading manufacturing regions on the European continent, the 1849 census counted some 40 percent of the inhabitants as making a living from agricultural pursuits. In the more agrarian southern districts of the Prussian province, and further south in Rhine-Hessen and the Palatinate, between 50 and 70 percent of the population were farmers, farm tenants, farm servants, farm laborers, and their dependents.[3]

Rhenish agriculture of the time can be divided into three distinct types, corresponding approximately to the three geographic areas of valley, hills, and plain, each with its distinctive social structure and economic prospects. The plains of the upper and lower Rhine were well suited to grain growing, mostly

---

[2] Quotation from LAK 442 Nr. 6659 pp. 91–96. For other examples of contemporary observation of this contrast, see Hermann Joseph Aloys Körner, *Lebenskämpfe in der Alten und Neuen Welt*, 2 vols., (New York: L. W. Schmidt, 1865–1866), 1:251–52; Hans Wegener, "Elberfeld in den vierziger Jahren des 19. Jahrhunderts," *MBGV* 20 (1913): 1–15, 21–35, 41–49, 61–66, 81–91, 102–111, 125–31, 141–58, here p. 11; *NRhZ*, 2 Feb. 1849; August Becker, *Die Pfalz und die Pfälzer* (Kaiserslautern: E. Lincks-Crusius, 1961), reprint of the first edition of 1858, pp. 14–18; a twentieth-century version, Albert Becker, *Pfälzer Volkskunde* (Bonn and Leipzig: Kurt Schroeder, 1925), pp. 90–92.

[3] *Tabellen und amtliche Nachrichten über den Preussischen Staat für das Jahr 1849*, 6 vols. (Berlin: A. W. Heyn, 1852–1855), 1:276 and 5:821; *Beiträge zur Statistik des Grossherzogtums Hessen* 3 (1864): 24–25; 1852 Palatine census returns in LAS H3, Nr. 220b–220m. Just to say it once and for all, these censuses are neither completely compatible, nor perfectly internally consistent, but they will do for the broad approximations used here.

rye, along with oats and potatoes. Animal husbandry centered on cattle and sheep raising.[4]

By and large, the agriculture of this region was successful and prosperous in the middle decades of the nineteenth century. Farmers adopted the most modern agricultural methods, introducing root crops and the associated complex systems of crop rotation, consigning to the past the old three-field system, gradually eliminating fallow and dividing the village common lands. First attempts at the cultivation of market-oriented crops, such as sugar beets, and the practice of distilling potatoes into potent spirits provided additional income. Output, taking the usual fluctuations into account, seems to have been climbing. Returns to seed on rye of 10–15 to 1, occasionally even higher, marked farmers on the plains of the lower Rhine as world-class agriculturalists, producing in the same league as their Flemish, English, or North American counterparts.[5]

Flanking and encouraging these developments were movements in agricultural prices. Although older accounts describe the first half of the nineteenth century as a deflationary period, this is only true for some times and some products. To be sure, after the high prices of the Napoleonic Wars and the famine year of 1817, grain prices fell sharply in the first half of the 1820s, but then began a long and steady rise. Average rye prices in the Prussian Rhine Province rose some 29 percent between the five-year periods 1825–1829 and 1840–1844, that is, even before the doubling of prices caused by the harvest failures of 1845 and 1846. Oat and potato prices also climbed around 20 percent in the interval, bringing up with them the price for meat and the overall

---

[4] Nineteenth-century Rhenish agriculture is little studied; a good preliminary survey is Georg Droege, "Zur Lage der rheinischen Landwirtschaft in der ersten Hälfte des 19. Jahrhunderts," in *Landschaft und Geschichte. Festschrift für Franz Petri zu seinem 65. Geburtstag am 22 Feb. 1968*, ed. Georg Droege (Bonn: Röhrscheid, 1970), pp. 143–56; also useful is the older work of Adolf Müller, "Die Grundlage der pfälzischen Landwirtschaft und die Entwicklung ihrer Produktion im 19. Jahrhundert bis zur Gegenwart" (Rechts- und Staatswiss. Diss., Würzburg, 1911). Hans Heukeshofen, "Die wirtschaftliche Entwicklung des Jülicher Landes seit seiner Zugehörigkeit zu Preußen unter besonderer Berücksichtigung des Kreises Jülich" (Wirt.- und Sozialwiss. Diss., Cologne, 1933) is a helpful account of a grain-growing region on the plains of the lower Rhine. T. C. Banfield, *Industry of the Rhine. Series I. Agriculture* (London: Charles Knight & Co., 1846) is an interesting traveler's account, with the biases one might expect from an Englishman of the time.

[5] See the yearly market reports for the late 1820s and early 1830s in HSTAD RA Nr. 1757 and LAK 403 Nr. 180. At least some of the authorities seem to have taken some care with these figures and even did some cross-checking (cf. LA Kr., Düren to RA, 30 May 1829, HSTAD RA Nr. 1758a), so they be regarded as least approximately correct. Regrettably, the Prussian authorities stopped systematically collecting these figures in 1835 (scattered material on the early 1840s, HSTAD RD Pr. Nr. 1329 ff. 175–77, 192, shows similar results), and comparable statistics from Hessen or Bavaria were never gathered. The English observer T. C. Banfield had praise for lower Rhine agriculture, which he found almost as good as England's. *Industry of the Rhine . . . Agriculture*, pp. 56–75.

cost of foodstuffs to the consumer. Farmers with a surplus to market, on the other hand, could count on a rising income and a growing prosperity. The only problem arose for tenants. Tenantry was particularly common in the vicinity of Cologne and in the especially fertile area around Jülich, where rents tended to rise even faster than grain prices, siphoning off revenue into the hands of absentee landlords.[6]

This prosperity was accompanied by an inegalitarian social structure, especially in the area of impartible inheritance customary on the lower Rhine north of a line running roughly from Mönchengladbach to Düsseldorf. Families of agricultural proprietors and tenants were outnumbered by day laborers' families and farm servants. The latter did not share in the former's prosperity, the growing number of propertyless rural inhabitants exceeding the demand for agricultural laborers, forcing the rural lower classes to supplement their income with wood theft and smuggling. On the other side of the social scale, there were even a fair number of noble estate owners on the plains of the lower Rhine. Some of the aristocratic families there, unlike their counterparts further south in the Rhineland, had survived the storms of the French revolutionary period by retreating to their estates.[7]

On the plains of the upper Rhine, the practice of equal inheritance led to a more egalitarian social structure. Areas with many day laborers, such as Frankenthal County on the northern border of the Palatinate, contrasted with those dominated by smallholders, such as Germersheim County on its southern end. In these areas, and throughout the Palatinate and the southern Rhineland, most of the day laborers also owned a small amount of landed property, enabling them to marry and set up their own households. For this reason, farm servants were much less common in the southern Rhineland than on the lower Rhine.[8]

---

[6] Price figures calculated from Ernst Engel, "Die Getreidepreise, die Ernteerträge und der Getreidehandel im preussischen Staate," *Zeitschrift des Könglich Preusssichen Statistischen Bureaus* 1 (1861): 249–89. Figures on regional developments, in HSTAD RA Nr. 12758 (the Aachen marketplace); and LAK 442 Nr. 2298 (Trier market), show a similar trend. On generally increasing food prices, see Pierre Ayçoberry, "Histoire sociale de la ville de Cologne (1815–1875)," 2 vols. (Thèse, Univ. de Paris, 1977), 1:115 (the published version of this work, *Cologne enter Napoléon et Bismarck: le croissance d'une ville rhénane* [Paris: Aubier-Montaigne, 1981] is far less detailed and lacks all scholarly apparatus, but is more easily available, so I will cite from it when possible). Broader trends throughout Germany show a similar picture. Hans-Ulrich Wehler, *Deutsche Gesellschaftsgeschichte*, 2 vols. to date (Munich: Beck, 1987–), 2:27–33. On tenantry, cf. Heukeshofen, "Entwicklung des Jülicher Landes," p. 17; Ayçoberry, *Cologne*, pp. 27–30, 132–33; Droege, "Lage der rheinischen Landwirtschaft," 149, 151–52.

[7] Droege, "Lage der rheinischen Landwirtschaft," pp. 147, 152; HSTAD RD Pr. Nr. 1470 ff. 19, 274–75; Pr. Nr. 1462 ff. 308–9, 331–333; Pr. Nr. 1463 ff. 27–28. The line between areas of equal and impartible inheritance also divided regions of nucleated villages and those of isolated farms. On the presence of the nobility, see K. Reinhold Weitz, "Die Preussische Rheinprovinz als Adelslandschaft," *RhVjBl* 38 (1974): 332–54.

[8] Assertions about social structure are based on the census returns, comparing the number of agricultural proprietors' and tenants' families, with the number of day laborers' families and the

Ever since Roman legionnaires introduced the grapevine into the Rhineland, viticulture has been one of the region's most characteristic features. The vineyards extend along the Rhine from Koblenz to Worms, in the valleys of the Ahr, Nahe, Moselle, and Saar and, farther south, where the plain meets the hills, at the feet of the Haardt mountains. Wine is the very epitome of a market crop, and vintners were of all the Rhenish peasants the ones most deeply involved in and most dependent on the market and the most subject to its often violent fluctuations. Winegrowers had both to sell and to buy in the agricultural market, since even in a good harvest year they were not self-sufficient in grains and potatoes.[9]

In spite of this extreme market dependence it is not easy for the historian and was not easy for contemporaries to ascertain wine prices. Wine is not a homogeneous crop like rye or oats; differences in quality were much greater in the early nineteenth century than they are today. There were equally substantial price differentials between the finest vintages, bought by senior government officials and leading manufacturers, and ''day laborers' wine,'' produced from grapes that would otherwise have been used to make vinegar. Furthermore, the public market in wines was little developed; most wine was sold privately from cellars or even from vineyards before the grapes were harvested.[10]

Nonetheless, approximate price series for mediocre-quality wines, the sort produced by ordinary, smallholding winegrowers, can be devised. They show how sharp the fluctuations in wine prices could be, and how they could vary from one winegrowing region to the next, often moving in opposite directions.

---

number of (almost always unmarried) farm servants. Prussian statistics just give proprietors/tenants and dependents combined, so I have calculated the number of families by assuming that an average farm family had five members. They also just give the number of day laborers, by sex, and I have assumed that day laborers' families were equal to the number of male day laborers. This procedure misses families headed by female day laborers, but since not all male day laborers worked in agriculture, the two errors may cancel each other out. The ratios of proprietor and tenant families to laborers' families and servants for Geldern and Kleve counties, on the plains of the lower Rhine are 0.67 and 0.59 respectively; for Frankenthal county, 0.88, for Germersheim county, 1.48. *Tabellen und amtliche Nachrichten*, 5:629–30, 660–61; LAS H3 Nr. 220c–d.

[9] Although there is no recent work on the modern history of Rhenish viticulture, there are several very helpful older studies: Friedrich Bassermann-Jordan, *Geschichte des Weinbaus unter besonderer Berücksichtigung der Bayerischen Rheinpfalz*, 3 vols. (Frankfurt a.M.: Heinrich Keller, 1907); Felix Meyer, ''Zur Entwicklung des Moselweinbaues und Weinhandels im 19en Jahrhundert'' (Wirt.- und Sozialwiss Diss., Cologne, 1922); Wilhelm Kriege, *Der Ahrweinbau, seine Geschichte und wirtschaftliche Lage in der Gegenwart* (Trier: Paulus-Druckerei, 1912). On grain needs for viticultural regions, see LAS H1 Nr. 1396, ff. 153–55; LR Kr. Wittlich to RT, 1 Dec. 1828, LAK 442 Nr. 3441.

[10] Bassermann-Jordan, *Geschichte des Weinbaus*, pp. 611–15, 826–27; reports of the tax inspectors in Trier and Mülheim to RT, 9 Feb. and 9 Mar. 1841; excerpt from *Zeitungsbericht* of LR Kr. Berncastel, May 1841, all in LAK 442 Nr. 2298; LR Kr. Trier to RT, 2 Jan., 1829, LAK 442 Nr. 3441; LAK 441 Nr. 1304 pp. 13–19. In the Ahr Valley, public auctions only became the rule with the creation of a vintners' cooperative in the 1860s. Kriege, *Ahrweinbau*, pp. 47–48.

Wholesale wine prices in Neustadt a.d.W., center of the Palatine wine trade, totally collapsed in the 1820s, falling about 70 percent in the decade. From there, prices climbed back up again, although very unsteadily (no higher in the years 1835–1839 than in 1825–1829), doubling by the mid-1840s and surpassing the levels of the early 1820s. Price developments in winegrowing regions of the Prussian Rhineland were less favorable to vintners. They started well, with prices of ordinary Rhine or Moselle wine in the Koblenz wholesale market about twice the level in Neustadt during the first half of the 1820s. Prices declined somewhat in the second half of the decade but then plunged disastrously during the following ten to fifteen years, falling about 50 percent between 1825–1829 and 1840–1844 (another price series shows a drop of 60 percent in this period), in other words, moving in the exact opposite direction of Palatine wine prices.[11]

The usual explanation for this development is the opening of the Prussian market to south German wines, following the Prussian-Hessian tariff agreement of 1828, and its successor, the German tariff union (the celebrated *Zollverein*) of 1834. However, competition from the upper Rhine cannot be the whole explanation of the collapse in Moselle wine prices before 1850, since this competition did not prevent prices from climbing modestly in the early 1850s and then quite sharply after 1857. Rather, the steady rise in the price of basic foodstuffs from 1825 onwards cut back the demand for those mediocre-quality vintages grown by small vintners and destined for popular consumption. These circumstances encouraged the lower classes to switch to cheaper alcoholic alternatives, such as potato spirits, thus making it impossible to raise wine prices, a severe blow to the vintners, who had to pay ever more for bread and potatoes. Overall wine price levels remained depressed in the second quarter of the nineteenth century: For all the success of the Palatine vintners in conquering the Prussian market, Neustadt wine prices in the early 1840s were still only two-thirds of what they had been in the Moselle Valley during the glory days of the early 1820s.[12]

[11] This paragraph is based on the following price series: wholesale prices of ordinary Palatine wines in Neustadt a.d.W., Bassermann-Jordan, *Geschichte des Weinbaus*, pp. 797–800; wholesale wine prices in Koblenz, reported monthly in the *Amtsblatt der Königlichen Regierung zu Coblenz*; prices paid to the vintner Adam Scheer in Zeltingen, Meyer, "Entwicklung des Moselweinbaues," Anlage 7.

[12] On pre-1850 conditions, see Meyer, "Entwicklung des Moselweinbaues," secs. II/3–4 (the work is unpaginated), as well as the similar arguments advanced by the contemporaries cited in note 10, above. The usual explanation for better conditions in Moselle viticulture after mid-century is a switch from quantity to quality in grape growing (Meyer, "Entwicklung des Moselweinbaues," sec. II/5). A look at the offical statistics shows, however, that both output and yields were falling with prices in the 1830s, and the yield of the vintage of 1857, the *anno mirabilis* of Moselle viticulture, was about a third higher than during that depressed decade. Ernst Engel, "Der Weinbau im preussischen Staate vom 1819 bis mit 1860," *Zeitschrift des Königlich Preussischen Statistischen Bureaus* 1 (1861): 303–06.

Declining wine prices were just the beginning of the winegrowers' problems with the market. Viticulture was impossible without wood for stakes and barrels, which made up, according to contemporary estimates, between one-third and one-half a vintner's expenses. Wood was becoming steadily more expensive in this period, increasing in price 28 percent in the Trier marketplace between 1834 and 1844. Complaints about rising wood prices were a staple of public discussion of the problems of vintners; to take the most famous example, they provided Karl Marx's first encounter with the social question in 1842. The discourse of the educated public was flanked by the peasants' direct action, as they simply expropriated the ever more expensive wood they needed for their livelihood.[13]

One final market problem made vintners' lives miserable, and this was the credit market. All peasants could and did have unpleasant encounters with usurers in the first half of the nineteenth century, but since vintners were not self-sufficient in foodstuffs they needed to contract annual "bread-debts," as contemporaries called them. The erratic nature of viticulture, with an occasional wonderful and highly profitable vintage's making up for years of mediocre ones, only compounded the debt problem. Storing a harvested vintage in the cellar to improve its value with age, or simply to outwait low prices, meant still more debt. In this context, a series of bad years, as happened in the 1820s and 1830s, made the debt burden simply unbearable. Vintners were delivered into the hands of their creditors and wine merchants. The winegrowers' debts forced them to unload their grapes right after picking them, or even to sell them while still on the vine, when prices were at their lowest. If a vintner needed more money, he would have to sell vineyard land in a glutted market, only reducing prices and increasing his colleagues' misery further.[14]

If there was any consolation for the vintners it was that they lived in a rela-

---

[13] Wood prices according to Trier market statistics in LAK 442 Nr. 2298. Cf. Banfield, *Industry of the Rhine I. Agriculture*, p. 99. Cost estimates: LR Kr. Wittlich to RT, 1 Dec. 1828; LR Kr. Berncastel to RT, 4 Jan. 1829, both in LAK 442 Nr. 3441. Complaints about high wood prices and wood theft: Bassermann-Jordan, *Geschichte des Weinbaus*, pp. 168–69; memos of J. M. Czach, executive secretary of Association for the Improvement of Mosel Viticulture in Trier, 24 Apr. 1840, and of Zeltingen wine dealer Sebastian Breuning, 12 July 1840, in LAK 442 Nr. 3441; LAK 441 Nr. 1308 pp. 35–43; Nr. 1314 pp. 83–97. All biographies of Marx mention the articles he wrote on the topic in 1842, and usually discuss the context in which they appeared. Cf. Oscar J. Hammen, *The Red '48ers: Karl Marx and Friedrich Engels* (New York: Charles Scribner's Sons, 1969), pp. 55–57. The best and most detailed account is Hans Pelger, "Karl Marx und die rheinpreussische Weinkrise," *Archiv für Sozialgeschichte* 13 (1973): 309–75.

[14] Müller, "Grundlagen," pp. 102–03; Bassermann-Jordan, *Geschichte des Weinbaus*, p. 826; Kriege, *Ahrweinbau*, p. 49; Meyer, "Entwicklung des Moselweinbaues," sec. II/4/a; memos cited in note 13; LAK 441 Nr. 1304 pp.13–19; Nr. 1306 pp. 163–75; Nr. 1309 pp. 13–16; Nr. 1310 pp. 17–23, 47–57; Nr. 1312 pp. 75–89; Nr. 1318 pp. 11–15; Nr. 1320 pp. 89–102; Nr. 1323 pp. 11–19. (The latter are the monthly reports of the county commissioners from winegrowing areas on the Ahr, Moselle, and Rhine during the early 1840s, which provide a very plastic picture of the vintners' economic difficulties.)

tively egalitarian rural environment. Day laborers and farm servants were few in viticultural regions; most families had at least a small piece of land, which, if all else failed, could be sold to pay for a one-way ticket to the United States—provided, of course, that the property was not too encumbered with debt and that vineyard prices had not fallen through the cellar. The one wine-growing region with a somewhat different social structure was the mid-Haardt mountains, between the towns of Neustadt a.d.W. and Bad Dürkheim, center of the most advanced Rhenish viticulture, where very wealthy large proprietors produced expensive, high-quality vintages with the help of many day laborers. Even there, however, the day laborers were themselves mostly small vineyard proprietors supplementing the returns on their holdings, as can be seen by a form of compensation common on the Haardt in the nineteenth century: The estate owner paid his laborers in part by agreeing to purchase the product of their vineyards.[15]

The vintners' social equality was an equality of poverty in the period between 1820 and 1850, a secular low point in the long history of Rhenish viticulture. A few good years, such as the first half of the 1820s in the Prussian Rhineland, or the first half of the 1840s in the Palatinate, were set out against longer periods of low prices for wine, high prices for wood and grains, evergreater dependence on creditors and merchants. More than other Rhenish peasants, winegrowers were in and of the market, experiencing all its negative aspects and few of its positive ones.

Inhabitants of the uplands comprised the single largest group of the Rhenish peasantry in the middle of the nineteenth century. They lived in the hills on the right bank of the Rhine across the river from Cologne, in the Eifel and Hunsrück, stretching along the left bank between the valley of the river and the border with Belgium and Luxembourg, and the mountains and forest of the western Palatinate on the French border. Poor soil and a harsh climate left the uplands ill suited to grain growing. Even in a good year, returns on seed to rye were unlikely to exceed 5–6 to 1 and in a bad year could drop to a Stone Age 3.5 to 1. Subsistence farming, mostly of oats and potatoes, the staple of the diet of the poor, provided a meager harvest, which, with luck, might just suffice to feed a family.[16]

[15] Bassermann-Jordan, *Geschichte des Weinbaus*, pp. 122–26, 824–25. Calculating the ratio of tenants/proprietors to day laborers and farm servants (cf. note 7) yields 1.63 for Ahrweiler County, in the Ahr Valley; 1.78 for Bernkastel County, in the heart of the Moselle wine country; and 1.23 and 1.54, respectively, for Landau and Bergzabern counties, on the southern end of the Haardt Mountains; but only 0.61 for Neustadt County. However, according to the 1852 census, 74 percent of the agricultural day laborers there were also property owners. *Tabellen und amtliche Nachrichten* 5:704–05; LAS H3 Nr. 220b, 220i–j.

[16] Harvest statistics for the Koblenz District in LAK 441 Nr. 11466. On subsistence agriculture in the uplands, cf. Droege, "Lage der rheinischen Landwirtschaft," p. 153; LAK 403 Nr. 17961 pp. 101–18; LR Kr. Malmedy to RA, 4 Sept. 1845; LR Kr. Schleiden to RA, 25 Nov. 1845, HSTAD RA Nr. 1775; LAK 403 Nr. 2398 pp. 569–75; RP to MInn, 22 Jan. 1847, BHSTAM

Since the upland peasants needed cash for taxes, debt payments, and purchases of manufactured goods, they turned to animal husbandry, raising some cattle but especially swine. Purchasers from urbanized Belgium or the Netherlands came to the St. Martin's Day pig market in the Eifel town of Adenau. But the dismal climate and soil conditions and the primitive agricultural techniques of the mountain country stood in the way of a profitable animal husbandry. If the harvest barely sufficed to feed the people, how could the livestock consume it as well?[17]

The answer to this question and the key to survival for the upland peasantry in the first half of the nineteenth century lay in the poor family's cornucopia, the forest. Important for all Rhenish peasants and the small-town lower classes generally, the forest and the mountain heath and wasteland were crucial to the farmers living on the hills and high plateaus. Oaks provided acorns for swine; heath and underbrush, grazing for cattle. There was woodcutting and hauling work to be performed in the forest for a little extra cash income; oak bark to be stripped for tanneries; wood to be burned for charcoal used in the forges and iron mills situated on streams throughout the uplands, both of these industries also providing some seasonal employment.[18]

Yet no matter how hard they worked or how ingeniously they found ways to squeeze subsistence out of an unfavorable environment, the expedients of the upland peasantry simply did not suffice to provide a living for their growing numbers. Seasonal migration to the fertile lands or manufacturing districts on the lower Rhine or to France, permanent emigration to North America, or poaching, theft, and begging, the last sometimes engaged in individually and pathetically, or menacingly, in groups, were the last resorts before starvation. Its specter haunted the Rhenish uplands throughout the first half of the nineteenth century. Even before the potato famine of 1845–1846, mediocre harvests, such as that of 1842, created spot shortages of bread and required mobilization of public resources to avoid starvation. The mountain peasants were at least as badly off as the vintners; if anything, their condition was probably worse, but the cause of their difficulties was the opposite of that of the winegrowers' problems. The latter were oppressed by excessive involvement in the market; the former, by their exclusion from it, by the lack of possibilities for earning a living.[19]

MInn Nr. 46240; 1844/45 property tax returns in LAS H1 Nr. 501; Joachim Kermann, "Die gesundheitliche, soziale, und wirtschaftliche Lage der pfälzischen Landbevölkerung in der Mitte des 19. Jahrhunderts nach Berichten der Kantonärzte und des Kreismedizinalrates," *MHVP* 74 (1976): 101–29, esp. pp. 118–20.

[17] Besides the sources cited in the previous note, see LAK 441 Nr. 1312 pp. 1–10; Nr. 1314 pp. 1–13.

[18] On ironworks and tanneries, cf. HSTAD RA Nr. 1577; LAK 403 Nr. 8558 pp. 9–16, 197–206; LAK 441 Nr. 6042–43. For a detailed discussion of the forest and conflicts concerning it, see Chapter Two.

[19] Besides the sources cited in notes 15 and 16, see LAK 403 Nr. 2415 pp. 1–12, 203–04, 219–

The distribution of rural property in the uplands varied more widely than in the valley or the plains. There were areas with many day laborers, such as mountainous and forested Kaiserslautern County in the Palatinate; others, such as the neighboring Kusel County, an area of high plateaus, were predominantly smallholding. The Prussian Eifel districts, in what was probably the most typical pattern of the uplands, held a middling position, with agricultural proprietors and their families about equal in number to day laborers' families and farm servants. Of course, owning a small piece of unfertile, hilly terrain was no road to riches; property distribution in the uplands was overshadowed by the general poverty and underemployment prevalent in the area.[20]

INDUSTRY AND MANUFACTURES

Although not hitting full stride until the 1850s, industrialization was already under way in the Rhineland during the two previous decades. The chief industrial center was the city of Aachen and its vicinity, on the Prussian Rhine Province's border with Belgium. As early as the mid-1830s, the city's woolens manufacturers were striving to end the system of outworking and centralize all branches of production in large, mechanized workshops. By mid-century, virtually every textile manufacturing establishment in the city possessed at least one steam engine, suggesting that the manufacturers had made substantial progress toward their goal. This development encouraged the creation of machine shops, which began by producing textile machinery but were soon building railroad parts and steam engines. The city was the center of a broader industrial region, with industrialized woolens manufacture in the nearby towns of Eupen (today part of Belgium) and Monschau, and coal mining and metallurgy in Aachen's suburbs of Eschweiler, Burtscheid, and Stolberg. Some of the metallurgical establishments, including machine shops, ironworks, and zincworks, seem to have been very large, employing hundreds of workers.[21]

By the decade following mid-century, the Ruhr industrial area would grow far beyond its rival in Aachen, but before 1850 it was hardly comparable, counting some 1,350 workers in textiles and 2,300 in metallurgy against some 17,800 textile and almost 3,000 metallurgical workers (all these figures in-

---

20, 277–78, 301–03; Nr. 17960 pp. 557–59; Nr. 17961 pp. 111–18; LAK 441 Nr. 1303 pp. 113, 219–37; Nr. 1305 pp. 1–12; Nr. 1306 pp. 111–32; 441 Nr. 1312 pp. 1–10; Nr. 1313 pp. 155–62; Nr. 1315 pp. 1–7; Nr. 1317 pp. 1–11; *KnZ*, 1 Apr. 1842; 23 May 1843 (Beilage); Becker, *Pfälzer Volkskunde*, p. 274.

[20] Calculating the ratio between proprietors'/tenants' families and day laborers' families plus farm servants, discussed in notes 7 and 15, gives 0.68 for Kaiserslautern County, 2.28 for Kusel County, and 1.08 and 0.98 for Prüm and Bitburg Counties, respectively. *Tabellen und amtliche Nachrichten* 5:704–07; LAS H3, Nrs. 220f and 220h.

[21] *Der gewerblich-industrielle Zustand der Rheinprovinz*, pp. 93, 119; *Tabellen und amtliche Nachrichten* 6:900–03, 1174. T. C. Banfield, *Industry of the Rhine. Series II. Manufactures* (London: C. Cox, 1848), p. 245; HSTAD RA Nr. 1578 ff. 40–50.

clude both factory proletarians and outworkers) in and around Aachen. Most of the industry and coal mining of the Ruhr Valley was then concentrated in small towns and villages on the Ruhr River. The city of Essen, in spite of Friedrich Krupp's steelworks, was still predominantly a burgher and market town. Duisburg, the largest city of the region, located at the confluence of the Rhine and Ruhr, was above all a river port. Its chief "industry" was the craft of cigarmaking, in which some 570 workers were employed at mid-century.[22]

Outside these two regions, however, factory industry and an industrial proletariat were hard to find. Even in the 1840s, coke-fired blast furnaces were unknown in the Rhineland, iron and steel being reduced from ore exclusively with charcoal. Most ironworks and forges were relatively small affairs, employing under a hundred workers. They were usually located in the uplands near the wood needed to reduce the ore, which was sent along the Rhine or Moselle to the nearest river port and then laboriously carted into the hills. Coal was used primarily for heating and that only in the immediate vicinity of the mines and the river valleys where it could be brought by water. The railroad net was still skeletal, and without it, extended overland transportation of such a physically heavy and bulky commodity was uneconomical. Coal mining was carried out in the Ruhr, Saar, and Aachen basins under direct state supervision; coal miners were state employees with guaranteed jobs, positions that were more relics of the mercantilist eighteenth century than exemplars of the laissez-faire and industrial nineteenth.[23]

Cologne, the Rhenish metropolis, was a river port and commercial and financial center; its one main industry was sugar refining. Tanning was also important, but it was carried out in large craft workshops with twenty or thirty workers each. Mainz, although with less than half Cologne's population, far and away the largest city on the middle and upper Rhine, had developed a number of speciality crafts in the first half of the nineteenth century, including the manufacture of fine furniture, umbrellas, and straw hats. These were carried out sometimes in medium-sized craft workshops, more commonly as outworking.[24]

[22] *Tabellen und amtliche Nachrichten* 6:794–800; Friedrich Meisenburg, "Die Stadt Essen in den Revolutionsjahren 1848–1849," *Beiträge zur Geschichte von Stadt und Stift Essen* 59 (1940): 12–274, esp. pp. 101–94. Conditions in the Saar Basin of the southern Rhineland were not so different. Richard Noack, "Die Revolutionsbewegung 1848/49 in der Saargegend" (Diss. phil., Frankfurt, 1927), published as Nr. 18 (1929) of *Mitteilungen des Historischen Vereins für die Saargegend in Saarbrücken*, pp. 7–11.

[23] On up-country ironworks, see HSTAD RA Nr. 1577 ff. 50–61; Nr. 1578 ff. 19–22, 203–206; LAK 441 Nrs. 6050–51, esp. Nr. 6051 pp. 157–86; LAK 403 Nr. 6583 ff. 288–91; *RhG*, 3:35, 221. On coal mining, coal miners, and coal consumption, see Klaus Tenfelde, *Sozialgeschichte der Bergarbeiterschaft an der Ruhr im 19. Jahrhundert* (Bonn-Bad Godesberg: Neue Gesellschaft, 1977), pp. 63–131; Alois Nießner, *Aachen während der Sturmjahre 1848/49: Stimmungsbilder aus der deutschen Revolution* (Aachen: Gustav Schmidt, 1906), p. 26; *RhG* 3:223; RP to MInn, 20 Nov. 1838, BHSTAM MInn Nr. 46247.

[24] Ayçoberry, *Cologne*, pp. 143–47; Dietrich Gessner, "Metallgewerbe, Maschinenbau und

The rest of Rhine-Hessen and the Palatinate was overwhelmingly rural and agricultural; the small towns were almost exclusively market and administrative centers. Manufacturing establishments were few and far between: a few paper mills and the wool weavers' village of Lambrecht-Grevenhausen in the valleys to the west and uphill of the busy town Neustadt a.d.W., which owed its economic importance to the wine trade; ironworks in St. Ingbert, in the corner of the Saar basin extending into the Palatinate; and Dingler's machine works in Zweibrücken, an all-purpose mechanical workshop that built steam engines, but also printing presses and transmission belts for water mills. In the late nineteenth century, the mountain town of Pirmasens on the French border would become Germany's shoe city, but before the 1860s, shoemaking was a form of migrant labor, the wives and daughters of the shoemakers leaving their impoverished upcountry surroundings to hawk their men's wares throughout central Europe.[25]

Steam engines and large workshops occupied just small niches in the Rhenish manufacturing economy toward the middle of the nineteenth century. Far more common was production by outworkers, described in an account of the labor process in the Wuppertal silk industry, written in 1842: The weavers, "work on the material given them by the manufacturers [Fabrikanten] in their own apartments and on their own looms at a wage determined in advance." The same was true for the dyeing of the silk cloth:

[A]lmost all master dyers, both in the city of Elberfeld and elsewhere in the county, dye for wages, [but] independently, the cloth given to them by a manufacturing establishment [Fabrik]. . . . Twisters of the thread [Spuler der Garn] twist the thread given them on their own spinning wheels for a predetermined wage. . . . [Virtually all] finishers, pressers, fabric gluers [Gummirer] ribbon weavers, cloth printing form makers [Formenstecher] and cloth printers . . . practice their trade in their own dwellings; that is, they prepare for a wage the material given them by one or even many manufacturers.[26]

This description shows the three main characteristics of outworking. Manufacturers did not themselves direct the production of the material in their own workshops, but acted as merchant manufacturers, contracting out production to nominally independent master craftsmen, who might not even live in the

---

Waggonbau am Mittelrhein und Untermain (1800–1860/65)," *AfHGA*, n.s., 38 (1980): 287–338; id., " 'Industrialisiertes Handwerk' in der Frühindustrialisierung. Ein Beitrag zu den Anfängen der Industrie am Mittelrhein und Untermain 1790 bis 1865," *AfHGA*, n.s., 40 (1982): 231–301.

[25] *RhG* 3:245–64; Becker, *Die Pfalz und die Pfälzer*, pp. 537–39; Bernd Schwarzwälder, "Die Ursachen der Reichsverfassungskampagne in der Pfalz 1849: politische Bewegung in Neustadt an der Haardt" (Wissenschaftliche Hausarbeit, Univ. Munich, 1982), pp. 123–26 (a copy of this work is in the Landesbibliothek der Pfalz in Speyer). During the rule of the insurrectionary government in the Palatinate, May–June 1849, Dingler's machine shop proved to be the only establishment in the entire province that could bore cannon barrels. LAS J1 Nr. 277 (alt) ff. 401–04.

[26] HSTAD RD Nr. 2178 ff. 193–203.

same city. While the relationship between manufacturer and master was nominally a free contract between two businessmen, the masters were employed for a wage; they were really workers dependent on the manufacturer. The exact degree of dependence varied, being determined by several factors: whether or not the master worked for one manufacturer or more than one; whether he owned his own tools (in the Kempen-Krefeld silk-weaving district, in contrast to the Wuppertal, the looms were owned by the manufacturers, tying the weaver to the manufacturer who rented him his loom); how deeply indebted the master was to the manufacturer[s] he worked for. Finally, the workers in this system were themselves masters, small craftsmen who might employ a journeyman or apprentice in turn. The 1849 census returns showed 12,237 master silk weavers in the Düsseldorf District, along with 12,455 journeymen and apprentices. In various forms and degrees, this system of outworking existed in all the lower Rhine textile districts: silk weaving in the Wuppertal, the Kempen-Krefeld area, and Cologne's suburb Mülheim a. Rhein; cotton textiles in the vicinity of Rheydt and Mönchengladbach; woolens in and around Aachen, in the Bergisches Land near Lennep, and in the Ruhr Valley, around Werden and Kettwig.[27]

The introduction of mechanization, usually in the form of steam-powered spinning mills, did not destroy this system but enhanced it. Cotton spinning was increasingly mechanized before 1850, but the rapidly growing output of cotton thread created an intensified demand for handloom weavers, with the number of handlooms in the Düsseldorf District rising from 5,876 in 1822 to 12,520 in 1849. A similar process occurred in the manufacture of woolen textiles, although some of the growing demand in that branch may have been met in the 1840s by the construction of mechanical weaving mills. Craft outworkers far outnumbered factory workers at mid-century: Some 60,000–63,000 handloom weavers in the Prussian Rhine Province were counted by the census in 1849, against 12,000–15,000 workers in spinning and weaving mills. The disparity was even greater for adult males, since half the labor force in mechanized spinning mills consisted of children under the age of fourteen and women.[28]

---

[27] The lower Rhine textile industry has been well studied. Among other works, see Hermann Ringel, *Bergische Wirtschaft zwischen 1790 und 1860* (Neustadt a.d. Aisch: Ph.C.W. Schmidt, 1966), pp. 59, 65, 91–92; Hermann Herberts, *Alles ist Kirche und Handel . . . Wirtschaft und Gesellschaft des Wuppertals im Vormärz und in der Revolution 1848/49* (Neutsadt a.d. Aisch, Ph.C.W. Schmidt, 1980), pp. 49–51; Wolfgang Köllmann, *Sozialgeschichte der Stadt Barmen im 19. Jahrhundert* (Tübingen: J.C.B. Mohr, 1960), pp. 14–26, 37–43; Hae-Bon Chung, "Das Krefelder Seidengewerbe im 19. Jahrhundert (ca. 1815–1880)," (Diss. phil., Bonn, 1974); Ayçoberry, *Cologne*, p. 141; Gerhard Adelmann, "Die ländlichen Textilgewerben des Rheinlandes vor der Industrialisierung," *RhVjBl* 43 (1979): 260–88. Census figures from *Tabellen und amtliche Nachrichten* 5:971.

[28] Figures for 1822 from "Neues von der historischen Wirtschaftskarte der Rheinlande," *RhVjBl* 30 (1965): 334–45; 1849 figures from *Tabellen und amtliche Nachrichten* 6:970–72. It is

After textiles, metalworking was the most important branch of manufacturing in the mid-nineteenth-century Rhineland, but outworking was prevalent there as well. Certainly the most famous example was the Solingen-Remscheid steel wares industry, whose merchant manufacturers coordinated the labor of several thousand highly skilled outworkers in the villages of the Bergisches Land: smiths who hammered raw steel into knives, files, scissors, cutlery, and razor blades; grinders who honed the material to a fine edge; and finishers who put on a final polish. A peculiarity of this branch was that it was outworking without being home industry. The grinders in particular worked together in workshops on the banks of the swiftly flowing Wupper River, which provided the power for their grinding wheels. These workshops were not factories under central direction but establishments where grinders worked as independent contractors for merchant manufacturers. Each grinder rented a workspace along the stream that powered his grinding wheel, a highly expensive tool, which he usually owned. The manufacture of nails and sewing needles in Aachen and vicinity was a simpler and less skilled trade than Solingen steel wares, but it was organized along the same outworking lines. Outworkers in this trade and in woolen textiles lived alongside factory workers in Aachen and its suburbs.[29]

Outworking remained the dominant form of production in Rhenish manufactures before 1850. If anything, it was increasing in extent, continuing a development begun around the middle of the eighteenth century. The first beginnings of industrialization were tending to reinforce rather than to undermine its position. The typical factory worker [Fabrikarbeiter] in the mid-nineteenth-century Rhineland was not a classic propertyless industrial proletarian, but a nominally independent small producer working under the direction of and usually in debt to a mercantile capitalist.

---

unclear from the census figures how many weavers worked in mechanized weaving mills, and the information the census does offer is contradictory, showing, for instance, twenty-one steam engines employed for weaving in the Aachen District, but no mechanical looms in woolens, the area's textile speciality (Ibid. 5:982 and 6:973–76). My figures are based on the (probably exaggerated) assumption that between one-fourth and one-half of all wool weavers worked in factories. For figures for child labor, see ibid. 6:1146–47. Women and children made up one-third the labor force in weaving (ibid.), presumably concentrated in mechanized weaving mills.

[29] Previous works on the Solingen steel wares industry have been superseded by the remarkable study of Rudolf Boch, *Handwerker-Sozialisten gegen Fabrikgesellschaft. Lokale Fachvereine, Massengewerkschaft und industrielle Rationalisiserung in Solingen 1870 bis 1914* (Göttingen: Vandenhoeck & Ruprecht, 1985). Pp. 66–69, 81–89, deal with the period before 1850. On outworking in Aachen and vicinity, cf. *Der gewerblich-industrielle Zustand der Rheinprovinz im Jahre 1836*, ed. Gerhard Adelmann (Bonn: Röhrscheid, 1967), p. 101; HSTAD RA Nr. 1577, Bl. 43–59; Nr. 1578 Bl. 29–37, 186–91; and the sources cited in note 21. Regrettably, the work of Clemens Bruckner, *Zur Wirtschaftsgeschichte des Regierungsbezirks Aachen* (Cologne: Selbstverlag Rheinisch-Westfälisches Wirtschaftsarchiv zu Köln e.V., 1967) does not meet even modest scholarly standards.

MANUFACTURES AND CRAFTS

While the products of Krefeld silk weavers and Solingen scissors grinders were sold in a European or worldwide market, the products of butchers, bakers, tailors, shoemakers, cabinetmakers, smiths, and construction workers, the most common crafts, were largely marketed locally. There were 175,000 such artisans working for the local market in the Prussian Rhine Province in 1849, as against 132,000 manufacturing and factory workers. The latter group was numerically dominant only in the Düsseldorf and Aachen districts; in the southern part of the Prussian province and even more so in Rhine-Hessen and the Palatinate, with their largely agrarian and commerical economies, small-scale craftsmen outnumbered them three and four to one.[30]

The condition of crafts and craftsmen varied enormously, influenced by a large number of factors. Among the most important were whether the trade was uncommon, or one of the "mass crafts"; whether it was a secure and well-paying occupation, or an insecure and impoverished one; and whether the craftsman was an independent master—and if so, a large or small one—or a journeyman or apprentice. However, there were economic developments common to the crafts throughout Germany, creating a common situation, or at least a common background for the situations of the different crafts. Because of unique legal circumstances, these developments took a special form in the Rhineland.

Artisans' numbers and their representation in the labor force had been growing throughout Germany since the mid-eighteenth century. This tendency is usually attributed to a farming population's increasing faster than the capability of agricultural techniques to support it, leading the excess to seek a living in the crafts. In most of central Europe this development was opposed, hampered, and slowed down, at least to some extent, by the guilds. These artisans' corporations, still existing in the 1840s, in spite of decades of bureaucratic hostility, possessed the right to approve entrants into their trades. They did their best to limit the number of artisans in general, and independent master craftsmen in particular.[31]

In the Rhineland, though, the French had introduced the revolutionary eco-

[30] *Tabellen und amtliche Nachrichten* 5:918 and 6:970–95 (official definitions of *Fabrik* and *Fabrikarbeiter*, ibid. 6:1, were not always applied consistently, so the figures I cite are only approximate, but they give a good general impression). For Rhine-Hessen and the Palatinate, see note 32. The best general work on the artisanate in nineteenth- (and twentieth-) century Germany is Friedrich Lenger, *Sozialgeschichte der deutschen Handwerker seit 1800* (Frankfurt a. M.: Surkahmp, 1988).

[31] On long-term tendencies in the development of the German artisanate, cf. Wehler, *Deutsche Gesellschaftsgeschichte* 1:90–94, 2:54–64; Lenger, *Sozialgeschichte der deutschen Handwerker*, pp. 13–63; Andreas Grießinger, *Das symbolische Kapitel der Ehre. Streikbewegungen und kollektives Bewußtsein deutscher Handwerksgesellen im 18. Jahrhundert* (Frankfurt, West Berlin, and Vienna: Ullstein, 1981), pp. 302–05 and passim.

nomic legislation abolishing guilds and instituting laissez-faire, which remained valid even after the French withdrawal in 1814. By the 1840s, occupational freedom had been established in the region for a good half-century. Without any guild barriers to stop them, a disproportionately large number of Rhinelanders entered the crafts, and of these a disproportionate number went into business for themselves. Prussian statistics showed that craftsmen not working in manufacturing made up 6.2 percent of the Rhine Province's population toward the middle of the nineteenth century, as against 5.8 percent for the state as a whole. According to the 1849 census, just fifty-nine of these Rhenish artisans were journeymen and apprentices for each hundred masters as against seventy-six journeymen and apprentices per hundred masters in the whole state. Hessian and Bavarian statistics are not as detailed as the Prussian ones, but they suggest that the situation was even more lopsided in the southern Rhineland. In 1849, the province of Rhine-Hessen counted 15,941 independent proprietors in commerce, industry, and crafts, as against 1,513 manufacturing workers (including outworkers) and 8,189 journeymen and apprentices; roughly comparable figures for the Palatinate show some 25,000 independent proprietors in these three sectors, but only 8,900 male journeymen, apprentices, and clerks.[32]

The wide spread of such small, independent craft workshops was no guarantee of prosperity, or even of genuine economic independence. Particularly in the "mass crafts," shoemaking, tailoring, and cabinetmaking, just the opposite was the case. Their trades were, as contemporaries said, "overcrowded," too many masters chasing too few paying customers. Detailed local studies exist only for larger urban centers, such as Cologne, Düsseldorf, and the twin cities of the Wuppertal, Barmen and Elberfeld, but they show that most master craftsmen in these trades led an impoverished existence, earning perhaps one hundred taler a year, no better than the wages of an unskilled day laborer. Additionally, it was precisely in these crafts that the practice of outworking was becoming increasingly dominant. Master shoemakers and tailors were losing direct connection with their customers, working instead under the direction of a merchant who provided them with their raw material and took their finished product, usually lending them money to finance the whole operation. Such outworkers' status as master craftsmen was increasingly illusory: Neither their yearly income nor their control over the production process were any better than those of a journeyman artisan.[33]

---

[32] *Tabellen und amtliche Nachrichten* 5:918; *Beiträge zur Statistik des Großheroztums Hessen* 3 (1864): 24–25; LAS H3 Nr. 220b–m. On the legal bases for these developments, see the section on Rhenish law, below.

[33] Ayçoberry, *Cologne*, pp. 168–81; Lenger, *Zwischen Kleinbürgertum und Proletariat*, pp. 36–64; id. "Polarisierung und Verlag: Schuhmacher, Schneider und Schreiner in Düsseldorf 1816–1861," in *Handwerker in der Industrialisierung: Lage, Kultur und Politik vom späten 18. bis ins frühe 20. Jahrhundert* (Stuttgart: Klett-Cotta, 1984), pp. 127–45; Klara Wittgenstein,

The historian Friedrich Lenger has argued that this development, which he defines as a double process of "polarization and outworking," is the key to understanding the economic condition and the social stratification of the Rhenish artisanate in the nineteenth century. One group of master craftsmen worked without assistants, was, in many crafts, increasingly dependent on outwork merchants, and generally lived at a proletarian level. A second group successfully made the transition from guild master to small businessman, employed all the journeymen, enjoyed direct access to customers, and maintained a solidly lower-middle-class standard of living. What divided the different artisan trades was the extent of this successful group. It was smallest in the "mass crafts" of shoemaking, tailoring, and cabinetmaking. Lenger estimates it for Düsseldorf in the 1840s at between 10 and 20 percent. The affluent group was more sizable in the food trades, butchering, baking, and brewing, where some two-thirds fell into this category, although often only by running a tavern or restaurant in addition to their craft shops. All of Düsseldorf's master artisans in the construction trade were among the more prosperous, but in these crafts, masters made up only a small percentage of the total labor force. The average master carpenter or mason employed three to six journeymen, while in most other crafts it was unusual for this ratio of masters to journeymen to exceed one or one and a half to one.[34]

In 1841 an industrial hall [Industriehalle] was opened in Mainz, where craftsmen of the town might display their wares for sale to the public. The newspaper correspondent reporting on this new institution noted with enthusiasm that "Masters who have been obliged, from lack of markets [wegen Mangels an Absatz] to work for others will be placed by this industrial hall on the same level as the most renowned manufacturers [Fabrikanten] and through it be dramatically lifted out of [gerissen] their dependent condition." Similar institutions, particularly favored by tailors and cabinetmakers, two of the impoverished "mass crafts" where outworking had made considerable inroads, were planned or actually set up in the course of the decade in Worms, Trier, Cologne, Aachen, Düsseldorf, Speyer, and Simmern.[35]

"Die Entstehung der sozialen Frage und Bewegung im Wuppertal in den vierziger Jahren des 19. Jahrhunderts und ihre wirtschaftlichen Grundlagen," *ZBGV* 49 (1923/24): 118–89, esp. pp. 149–54.

[34] Lenger's works, as in the previous note; similar, if differently expressed, observations in the studies of Ayçoberry and Wittgenstein. The extent to which these conditions existed in smaller towns and the southern Rhineland is unclear, given the lack of similarly detailed studies, but cf. StdT Tb 33/179 ff. 12–13; LAS J1 Nr. 228 (alt) ff. 274–75; and sources cited in note 37.

[35] *KnZ*, 25 Apr. 1841; 19 May 1845 (Beilage); 22 Sept. 1845; Ayçoberry, *Cologne*, pp. 177–78; Nießner, *Aachen*, pp. 141–42; Lenger, *Zwischen Kleinbürgertum und Proletariat*, p. 183; Helmut Renner, "Der Bericht des Regierungspräsidenten von Zenetti über die politische Bewegung in der Pfalz 1848/49," *MHVP* 59 (1961): 138–78, esp. p. 147. LAK 441 Nr. 1330 pp. 407–11; statutes of the cooperative sales hall of the united master furnituremakers [Tischlermeister] of Trier, 4 Oct. 1845, StdT Tb 15/849.

The correspondent's quote is a revealing explication of the social structure of the Rhenish artisanate in the first half of the nineteenth century. What counted, what differentiated a simple craftsman from a "renowned manufacturer," was not formal economic independence, or possession of the means of production, but direct and favorable access to the market. Differences between employers and employees, that is, between masters and journeymen, certainly existed, and memories of the old guild system, with its united front of all corporate artisans against any threat from the outside world, had by no means disappeared. Nonetheless, the main distinction within the ranks of craftsmen was between that successful minority of masters enjoying direct and favorable access to the market and the journeymen and impoverished majority of masters, cut off from the market by dependence on outwork merchants or forced to chase after customers on highly unfavorable terms. In this respect, most craftsmen working for a local market were in a similar situation to that of manufacturing outworkers, whose products were sold on a European or worldwide scale. The problems of the legally independent but economically dependent small producer lay at the center of the Rhenish crafts and manufacturing population in the first half of the nineteenth century.

UP AND DOWN THE RIVER

Since the days of the Roman Empire, the Rhine has been a major artery of transport and commerce in Europe. In the mid-nineteenth century, river traffic was the third main element of the commercial economy of the region, along with agriculture and manufacturing. The wholesale merchants, at whose command goods moved up and down the river, comprised an important segment of the regional elite, besides the manufacturers of the lower Rhine and the vineyard owners of the upper Rhine. The Rhine boatmen, dock laborers, waterfront artisans, and towmen were "regarded from olden times to the present as an especially tumultuous and undisciplined element" of the lower-class population of the riverside towns. Changing economic circumstances and legal conditions were imposing a painful transition on the waterfront economy and the waterfront population in the decades before 1850. In view of the centrality of the river to the region, it was a development with repercussions for all Rhinelanders.[36]

Clauses of the Treaty of Vienna, finally implemented in 1831 after prolonged diplomatic wrangling, established free navigation on the river. Old regime staple rights of Mainz and Cologne—that is, the requirement that goods be off-loaded and offered for sale there—were abolished, as was the corporation of boatmen, created by Napoleon to regulate shipping schedules and

---

[36] Quote from Ludwig Bamberger, "Erlebnisse aus der Pfälzer Erhebung," in *Gesammelte Schriften*, 4 vols. (Berlin: Rosenbaum & Hart, 1895), 3:59–158, here pp. 73–74; a similar description of the waterfront population of Speyer, in LAS J1 Nr. 252 (alt) ff. 192–94.

freight rates. About the same time, the first steamboats appeared on the river, initially limited to passenger transport and tourism. They were impractical for carrying freight, since the combined weight of the engine and any substantial cargo made the boats ride too deeply for the shallow riverbed. In the early 1840s, steamboat companies found a way around this limitation on freight transport by building ironclad barges, tugged by their boats. In these years, the first railroad lines in the area were completed, and the introduction of steam power to land and water transportation greatly heightened the effects of the implementation of free navigation a decade earlier.[37]

In the long run enormously beneficial to Rhine commerce, the new transportation regime was at first highly disruptive. Relieved of the necessity to off-load in Mainz or Cologne, shippers simply bypassed the cities. Tonnage moving through the former harbor declined by one-third between 1829 and 1832, and that through the latter, by one-half between 1834 and 1840. The increase in railroad freight coming into Cologne following the construction of the Antwerp-Cologne line in 1843 did not compensate for the decline in the tonnage of goods reaching Cologne by water. In theory, railroads running at right angles to the river, unlike Antwerp-Cologne, which was more or less parallel to it, ought to have increased harbor traffic. The first such feeder line, opened in 1840 from Frankfurt west along the Main to Mainz, had the opposite effect. The rails ended on the eastern side of the river, in theory accessible to Mainz's right bank suburb, Kastel, but in practice more favorable to the competing harbor in nearby Biebrich.[38]

Those most threatened by the new arrangements were the boatmen and towmen, who could move cargo upstream only at a far slower pace and an increasingly less competitive price than could the steam tugs. Within a few years of the introduction of these tugs, contemporaries were already predicting the demise of their nonmechanical competition. While prospects were indeed bleak for the laborers who towed the upstream boats through the cities of Cologne and Mainz, or the inhabitants of the riverain villages who had the rather easier task of leading horses doing the same, this was by no means the case for the boatmen.

The very substantial downstream trade remained in their hands for decades, over 80 percent of total tonnage as late as the mid-1860s. Technological change did not entirely shut them out of the upstream business. Commerce on the Rhine grew very rapidly, tonnage increasing by some 75 percent between the late 1830s and early 1840s. The famine years 1845–1846, elsewhere an

[37] On Rhine navigation, see the three older but very useful studies, Christian Eckert, *Rheinschiffahrt im XIX Jahrhundert* (Leipzig: Duncker & Humblot, 1900); Eberhard Gothein, *Geschichtliche Entwicklung der Rheinschiffahrt im XIX Jahrhundert* (Leipzig: Duncker & Humblot, 1903); Edwin J. Clapp, *The Navigable Rhine* (Boston and New York: Houghton Mifflin, 1911).

[38] Ayçoberry, *Cologne*, pp. 112–16; Hans Döhn, "Eisenbahnpolitik und Eisenbahnbau in Rheinhessen 1835–1914" (Diss. phil., Mainz, 1957), p. 42.

economic disaster, were a boon to waterborne commerce as hundreds of thousands of tons of grain were imported from the Baltic and North America and shipped up the river. Small loads and short, local trips offered market niches to the boatmen. In addition, steamboats could also tow the boatmen's ships as easily as they could ironclad tugs. Even in the mid-1860s, about 60 percent of the upstream traffic (the exact amount varied at different points on the river) was carried by sailboats in these two ways; the number of boatmen on the Rhine, far from having declined since the 1840s, had increased substantially. As with manufactures, the real economic issue was not so much technological change as small producers' (or in this case transporters') access to the market. The boatmen needed to find ways to maintain their chances to move cargo in spite of the freight forwarders who arranged the transfer of goods from rail to water and the wholesale merchants who were the majority stockholders in the steamship companies.[39]

A THOROUGHLY BOURGEOIS SOCIETY

Rhenish society in the first half of the nineteenth century was structured around access to the market. The characteristic member of the lower classes was a nominally independent small producer, whose relation to the market was controlled, or at least influenced, by the possessors of mercantile and financial capital. This group of small producers was not at all homogeneous. Some of its members were clearly more affluent, like the Solingen knife grinder, proud practitioner of a highly skilled craft, or the Cologne master mason, who took a flier in constructing houses on his own account with borrowed money and was wiped out in the real estate crash of 1846. Others, the majority, were less well off: the Düsseldorf or Mainz tailor, sewing in a garret for a merchant contractor, earning, even with the help of all his family members, no more than a day laborer did; a Barmen silk weaver, living under similar circumstances; the Moselle or Ahr Valley vintner, his cellars full of wine, but no one willing to offer him a price sufficient to buy bread; the Eifel or Westrich peasant, unable to grow enough potatoes on his infertile small plot to feed his family and unable to find paying employment to supplement his meager harvest. For all the differences in affluence—and they would be considerably reduced by the years of famine and commercial crisis, 1845–1849—the mediated, dependent relationship to the market remained a common attribute of their social condition.

Closely related to the small producers were journeymen artisans. Because of the lack of guild restraints, they were a smaller group in the Rhineland than

---

[39] Figures from Eckert, *Rheinschiffahrt*, pp. 285–88, 332–33, 342–43. In general, cf. ibid., pp. 250–63; Gothein, *Geschichtliche Entwicklung*, pp. 206–68; Clapp, *Navigable Rhine*, pp. 23–29. For some contemporary views, besides those cited in these books, cf. LAS H3 Nr. 193 ff. 7–30; LAK 441 Nr. 1316 pp. 75–89.

elsewhere in Germany. They had every reason to expect that they might easily accede to the status of master craftsman and every reason to see that doing so would not be much of an improvement in their position. The third major element of the Rhenish lower classes was comprised of day laborers, especially on the Rhine waterfront and in grain-growing areas of the upper and lower Rhine plains. As a rule, their earnings did not suffice to support a family, and they were dependent on outside income, from small plots, theft, smuggling, or begging, to make ends meet. Compared with these groups, factory workers, the prototypical late nineteenth century proletarians, were far less significant.

A vague and indeterminate line separated the lower classes from the middling groups of society. Once again, access to the market provided the chief determining factor: The grain-growing peasant on the plains of the lower Rhine, or in the *Gau*, the southeastern Palatinate between Landau and Germersheim, enjoying a favorable price trend for his chief crop; the master tanner selling more of his product and hiring more journeymen; the master baker combining his shop with a tavern, doubling the income he made on the sale of bread. Some might hope to accede to the ranks of estate-owners or small manufacturers; others, especially in the poorer upland regions, where someone who "just got along" [in den guten Jahren sein Auskommen hat], was counted part of the middle segment of society and could easily be set back. Bad harvests, business downturns—the 1840s were rich in such events—would burden them with debt, and leave many of the middling social groups still nominally independent, but in a lower-class condition of unfavorable access to the market.[40]

At the summit of Rhenish society were those who controlled the market, coordinating and directing the activities of small producers: merchant manufacturers of Barmen or Krefeld employing hundreds or even thousands of outworking weavers; the bankers who provided the manufacturers with their capital; wholesale merchants in Cologne and Mainz, at whose command grain and wine moved down the Rhine while coffee and sugar moved upstream; rentiers and estate owners collecting payments from their agricultural tenants; lawyers and notaries, who guided, registered, and financed the distribution and redistribution of landed property. Some of the upper classes, like the owners of Lennep textile mills, Cologne sugar refineries, Eifel ironworks, or large-scale vineyards in the Palatinate, were directly in charge of production, but, like the industrial proletariat among the lower classes, they were the exception rather than the rule.

It was a thoroughly bourgeois social order, with ownership of property in a free market the main criterion of social stratification. Guilds were nonexistent; the nobility, when not replaced with a "bourgeois aristocracy" of estate own-

---

[40] Quote, LAK 441 Nr. 1327 pp. 93–100; similarly, Nr. 1303 pp. 97–102; Nr. 1306 pp. 73–80.

ers, as in the Palatinate, was little different from its commoner counterpart. The lower classes, even most of those contemporaries called factory workers or the proletariat, were part of this system as well, consisting primarily of households of nominally independent small producers. In this respect, the Rhineland was one of a kind with mid-nineteenth-century western Europe and North America. It had a social order similar to that of France under the July Monarchy, those areas and economic sectors of England not yet affected by the course of the industrial revolution, or even New York City circa 1840, whose economy was characterized by what historian Sean Wilentz has called "metropolitan industrialization"—by which he means the subordination of outworking producers to merchant capitalists.[41]

PROGRESS AND POVERTY

Economic indicators, as near as the primitive statistics of the day permit, produce a mixed picture of the Rhenish economy in the three decades before 1850. Economic growth was clearly considerable: output of textiles, pig iron, metallurgical products, coal, leather, refined sugar, and specialty crafts all increasing; productivity and output of grain on the rise; river commerce growing strongly, even as a railroad net was being put in place. Contemporaries, while noting all this progress, seemed more impressed by the increasing numbers of poor and the declining conditions of the lower classes.[42]

Some figures seem to bear out their impressions. Throughout the first half of the nineteenth century, a minimum of 17 percent of Cologne's inhabitants were recipients of poor relief, the proportion rising to one-third in years of harvest failure or commercial crisis, such as 1817, 1830, and 1846–1849. Another group showing a comparable trend is the number of people in the Düsseldorf District exempt by reason of poverty from paying the Prussian government's graduated poll tax [Klassensteuer]. Since the minimum rate was just one taler, paid in twelve monthly installments, they were poor indeed. In 1855, 12.7 percent of the district's inhabitants were exempted. The proportion declined ever so slightly to 12.2 percent by 1844, only to rise to 14.9 percent

[41] William H. Sewell, Jr., *Work and Revolution in France: The Language of Labor from the Old Regime to 1848* (Cambridge: Cambridge University Press, 1980), pp. 154–61; Sean Wilentz, *Chants Democratic: New York City and the Rise of the American Working Class, 1788–1850* (Oxford and New York: Oxford University Press, 1984), pp. 107–42; a most interesting comparison is the little essay of Friedrich Lenger, "Die handwerkliche Phase der Arbeiterbewegung in England, Frankreich, Deutschland und den USA—Plädoyer für einen Vergleich," *Geschichte und Gesellschaft* 13 (1987): 232–43.

[42] An excellent summary of the scholarly and contemporary literature on "pauperization," as it was known at the time, is in Wehler, *Deutsche Gesellschaftsgeschichte* 2:281–96; the Rhenish variant of the debate is summarized by Karl Georg Faber, *Die Rheinlande zwischen Restauration und Revolution. Probleme der rheinischen Gesdchichte von 1814 bis 1848 im Spiegel der zeitgenössischen Publizistik* (Wiesbaden: Franz Steiner, 1966), pp. 247–62.

in 1848. In the neighboring Aachen District, the trend was the same, the proportion somewhat higher: 17.4 percent of those eligible exempted for poverty in 1842; 20.3 percent in 1847.[43]

These areas were among the more prosperous in the Rhineland, centers of manufacture, commerce, and market agriculture. The residents of the uplands were undoubtedly much poorer. Comparable tax statistics are lacking, but arrest records of the gendarmerie show some two to six times as many arrests made for begging in relation to the population of the Koblenz and Trier districts of the Prussian Rhine Province—mostly agricultural, largely uplands and winegrowing valleys—than in the lower Rhine districts, Aachen, Düsseldorf, and Cologne. The district poorhouse [Landesarmenhaus] in Trier was a notorious snake pit, where orphaned children bathed in the same room with syphilitics—exposure of the conditions there would create a major scandal in 1849—but the number of residents grew from 300 in 1822 to 839 in 1842, and many seeking admission were turned away for lack of space.[44]

Wage figures, whether for day laborers, journeymen artisans, or manufacturing outworkers, are scanty, incomplete, and endlessly varied, but they tend to show either a very small increase between the 1820s and the 1840s, perhaps 5 percent, or an actual decline. Considering the rising food prices of these years, it is hard to avoid the conclusion that in the long run real wages and working people's standards of living were falling—especially as these figures do not take into account the very real problems of unemployment—even before the catastrophic effects of the famine years in the mid-1840s. Food consumption statistics bear this out, per capita meat consumption in the cities of the Prussian Rhine Province declining from ninety-two pounds in 1838 through eighty-four in 1840 to a low of sixty-seven in 1848.[45]

Contemporaries described the mass impoverishment as pauperization, and they offered two main explanations for it, which have usually been seconded by historians taking up the issue. One argument asserts that the chief cause was the increase in capitalist exploitation, while a counterexplanation sees the

[43] Ayçoberry, *Cologne*, pp. 98–99, 186; HSTAD RD Pr Nr. 1474 ff. 14–15; Pr. Nr. 1475 f. 16; Pr. Nr. 1476 f. 350; Pr. Nr. 1477 f. 130; HSTAD RA Pr. Nr. 475 ff. 328–33. These figures exclude the inhabitants of the walled cities Wesel, Düsseldorf, Aachen, and Jülich, all of whom were exempt from the poll tax, since they paid the more demanding grain and meat octroi.

[44] LAK 403 Nr. 2195 p. 7; Emil Zenz, *Geschichte der Stadt Trier im 19. Jahrhundert*, 2 vols. (Trier: Spee, 1979), 1:90–91. A similar difference obtained in the Palatinate, where 11 percent of the residents of upland Pirmasens County were "registered paupers" in 1846, as against a provincial average of 4.3 percent. Werner Weidmann, "Die wirtschaftlich-sozialen Hintergründe der Pfälzer Revolution von 1849 und die sozialrevolutionären Umsturzversuche," *JGStLK* 22/23 (1984/85): 19–58, esp. pp. 27–28.

[45] Bassermann-Jordan, *Geschichte des Weinbaues*, pp. 606–07; Heinrich Rubens, *Forstgeschichte im Zeitalter der industriellen Revolution* (Berlin: Dunckler & Humboldt, 1967), p. 162; Lenger, *Zwischen Kleinbürgertum und Proletariat*, pp. 40–41; Ayçoberry, "Cologne," 2:24–25; Köllmann, *Stadt Barmen*, pp. 138–39.

impoverishment as a consequence of a Malthusian expansion of the population beyond economic resources, which could only be resolved by capitalism, by factories and industrialization. Evidence can be found in support of both positions, but so can conditions that fit neither of them.[46]

The upland peasantry was a group clearly caught in a Malthusian squeeze between growing population and static resources. Peasants of the Hunsrück or Palatine Westrich would undoubtedly have benefited from some capitalist exploitation, since their main economic problem was lacking cash, being shut out of marketplace opportunities to earn it. The resolution of their problems, however, would not be found in industrialization, but in mass emigration to North America.

Conditions in the city of Aachen, the most industrialized in the Rhineland, hardly suggest that factory industry was, before 1850 at least, a blessing to the working class. Child labor flourished—half the school-age children there did not attend school in spite of Prussia's strict compulsory education laws—but adult male employment languished. The growing metallurgical industry employed just 632 workers in 1846, an increase of 100 since 1835, more than offset by declines in employment in the traditional craft of needlemaking. Low adult male wages made child labor a necessity, preventing young people from going to school or taking up an apprenticeship and thus perpetuating a cycle of poverty. Even in economically good years, one Aachener in seven received poor relief and mendicants were an everyday sight in the city. Affluent travelers going from the railroad station to the spa and casino had to run a gauntlet of beggars. Industrialization in Germany seemed to have produced not a replication of English prosperity but a strange mixture of Manchester and Naples.[47]

The majority of the Rhenish lower classes were neither upland peasants nor factory workers, but artisans, manufacturing outworkers, vintners, watermen, day laborers, and small peasants in the grain-growing plains of the upper and lower Rhine. They lived in a fully capitalist but nonindustrial environment, characterized by an increasing lower-class population, declining real wages, falling consumer purchasing power, ever-greater dependence on and indebtedness to the possessors of mercantile and financial capital. Before mid-century, it seemed that the disruptive effects of the spread of the market on the lower classes outweighed the wealth it created, perhaps because the most

[46] On the debate over "pauperization," fired up in the 1950s, by cold war polemics between East and West German historians, see sources cited in note 42.

[47] LAK 403 Nr. 8082 pp. 279–84, 422–33; HSTAD RA Nr. 1577 ff. 34–39, Nr. 1578 ff. 19–22; Pr. Nr. 472 f. 179; Nießner, Aachen, pp. 59, 96. Both the Protestant-liberal and Catholic-clerical wings of the Aachen bourgeoisie were known for their charitable good works; yet, curiously enough, in spite of the savings banks and St. Vincent de Paul societies they founded, they showed no particular interest in the education of working-class children.

money could be made by exploiting the Malthusian situation of population's outstripping economic resources rather than alleviating it.

For example, in Cologne, the Rhenish financial center, by far the most profitable and popular investment in the decades before 1850 was real estate speculation. While in the 1820s and 1830s, the action was in purchasing rural land and splitting it into small lots for sale to the peasantry, by the 1840s, it was in the sale and resale of urban property. Pierre Ayçoberry, Cologne's social historian, has shown that the city's bourgeoisie put more capital into real estate in 1845, the peak year of the speculative boom, than its bankers provided for all of Rhenish industry throughout the entire period before mid-century.[48]

It would be an exaggeration to see the years 1820–1850 as one long Golgotha of the Rhenish lower classes. The second half of the 1830s was a period of rich harvests and low food prices. Employment opportunities were good, with boom conditions in outworking and the construction of the first railroads and mechanical textile mills. Inhabitants of Rhine-Hessen and the forward Palatinate, areas of a mild climate, fertile soil, and widespread ownership of at least a little landed property, were probably in general better off than their counterparts in the uplands or on the lower Rhine. Over the long run, however, the stagnant or declining economic condition of the lower classes stood in strange contrast to the signs of commercial, manufacturing, and agricultural expansion—even before the harvest failures of 1845–1846 and the commercial crisis of 1847–1848 created an economic emergency.

THREE STATES; ONE LAWBOOK

At the Congress of Vienna, the bulk of the Rhineland had been parceled out among three German states, the Kingdom of Prussia, the Grand Duchy of Hessen-Darmstadt, and the Kingdom of Bavaria. Like so many of the Congress's efforts to restore stability and order to Europe after a quarter-century of upheaval, this territorial rearrangement was a problematic one. Any attempt to integrate the new Rhenish possessions into the three core states faced substantial difficulties, since most Rhinelanders had no traditional, dynastic loyalties to the their new, trans-Rhenan rulers but shared instead a common, almost two-decades-long past of direct or indirect domination by the French revolutionary and Napoleonic regimes. The social, economic, and legal institutions created by these regimes had taken root in the Rhineland; their continued existence was yet another stumbling block to the provinces' integration into their respective states.

These Rhenish Institutions, as they were known, were, in effect, a codifi-

[48] Ayçoberry, *Cologne*, pp. 27–30, 132–33, 158–63. More broadly, on the nature of profitable investment in this period, see ibid., pp. 146–52; Richard Tilly, "Zur Entwicklung des Kapitalmarkts im 19. Jahrhundert unter besonderer Berücksichtigung Deutschlands," *Vierteljahrsschrift für Wirtschafts- und Sozialgelschichte* 60 (1973): 145–61.

cation of the achievements of the French Revolution. They included the abolition of the guilds, feudal tenures, and other restrictions on a free market in land, labor, and capital; equality before the law and the abolition of any special privileges of the nobility; a uniform communal administrative system making no distinction between town and country; and civil registration of vital events. Above all, there was "Rhenish law" [Rheinisches Recht], a circumlocution for the Napoleonic Codes of civil, commercial, and criminal law. The first, with its regulation of property relations, confirmed the social and economic transformations of the revolution (and remained valid in the Rhineland until the introduction of the all-German civil code of 1901); the last, with its guarantee of public, oral, and jury trials for felony charges, was a major prop of civil liberties in an age with few other supports for them.[49]

Of the three states, Prussia had the most difficulty in absorbing and integrating its Rhenish possessions. Social structures, governmental institutions, confessional allegiances, and political traditions of the old provinces east of the Elbe were just too different from those of the new one along the Rhine. A largely rural East Elbia was dominated by the landed nobility, the famous Junkers, who were in the process of losing their seigneurial privileges in the first half of the nineteenth century, but nonetheless maintained a dominant position in state and society. Arriving in the new Rhenish province as military officers and civil administrators, or pondering its problems in Berlin court circles, they confronted a society that was more urbanized, or, to be more precise, where differences between city and country were smaller; where the nobility were few in number, enjoyed, at best, local influence, had little social cachet and no legal privilege; where the tone was set by a bourgeois elite of bankers, merchants, manufacturers, rentiers, lawyers, and notaries. Social differences were compounded by confessional ones. Most of the inhabitants, the ruling house, and socially elite groups of Old Prussia were Protestants, while a large majority of the kingdom's Rhenish subjects were adherents of the Catholic confession. The new ruling dynasty always found more sympathizers and supporters among the Protestant minority of the Rhinelanders than among the Catholic majority.[50]

---

[49] On the Rhenish Institutions, see, above all, the major work of Karl Georg Faber, *Die Rheinlande zwischen Restauration und Revolution*, pp. 110–18 and passim. While all areas on the left bank of the Rhine enjoyed these institutions, not all of those on the right bank in the Prussian Rhine Province did. The counties of Duisburg and Rees, which had been part of Prussia during the old regime, were governed by the Prussian General Code of 1795; the counties of Altenkirchen, Wetzlar, and Neuwied were governed by the old German common law; and the remaining right bank counties, while subject to the Napoleonic Code, had not quite eliminated all feudal tenures. See Carl Wilhelm Kockerols, *Das Rheinische Recht, seine zeitliche und räumliche Begrenzung* (Hannover: Helwingsche Verlagsbuchhandlung, 1902).

[50] Cf. Wehler, *Deutsche Gesllschaftsgeschichte* 2:320; Friedrich Keinemann, *Das Kölner Ereignis, sein Widerhall in der Rheinprovinz und in Westfalen*, 2 vols. (Münster: Aschendorff,

Along with legally trained commoners, the Junker nobility staffed the Prussian state service. Regarding themselves as the guardians of social progress, Prussian bureaucrats had developed in the early nineteenth century a program of social and political modernization for the kingdom to bring it closer to the more advanced nations of western Europe. This may have been all well and good for the society of East Elbian Prussia, although in practice it led to clashes with the more traditionally minded nobility. When transferred to the Rhineland, it ran up against a bourgeoisie that saw itself as part of the advanced society of western Europe and regarded itself as perfectly capable of running its own—and society's—affairs without bureaucratic direction and as possessing in the Rhenish Institutions a distinctive legal blueprint for an up-to-date social and economic order.[51]

These differences were well expressed in the endless wrangling over law codes and local government that filled the decades before 1850. Officials in Berlin wished to replace the Napoleonic Code in the Rhineland with the Prussian General Code of 1795, a proposal that met with the obstinate refusal of the vast majority of the educated public. Berlin also wanted to recast Rhenish municipal administration along the lines of the reforms of 1807, but as this would have meant accepting legal differences between city and country, the Rhinelanders would not go along. The Prussian authorities responded by refusing to permit municipal elections under the French system of administration, and the conflict was not resolved or municipal elections held until 1846.[52]

Exacerbating these differences was the lack of any real form of parliamentary representation for the king of Prussia's subjects. Reforming officials' plans for a constitution and a representative assembly were defeated in the early 1820s by the reactionary court camarilla. Under its influence, the king ordered the creation of a system of Provincial Estates [Landtage, usually translated into English as Diets]. The Rhenish version of these Diets was composed of four orders, two for the nobility and one each for the towns and country. With thirty of the eighty seats in the Diet, the noble deputies possessed de facto veto power, since important decisions required a two-thirds' majority. This massive noble overrepresentation stood in direct contradiction to the Rhenish Institutions and their principle of equality before the law, as well as being totally unreflective of the minor role of the nobility in Rhenish society.

1974), 1:33–37; Faber, *Die Rheinlande*, pp. 348–49; *RhBA* 1:530 n.2; Carl Schurz, *Sturmjahre. Lebenserinnerungen 1829–1852* (East Berlin: Verlag der Nation, 1973), p. 88.

[51] The classic work on Prussia and its bureaucracy in the first half of the nineteenth century, Reinhart Koselleck, *Preußen zwischen Reform und Revolution*, 3d ed. (Stuttgart: Klett-Cotta, 1982) tends to neglect the social differences between the older, eastern provinces of the monarchy and its new possessions in the west, thus leading to an insufficiently differentiated appraisal of the effects of the bureaucracy's actions. Cf. Jonathan Sperber, "State and Civil Society in Prussia: Thoughts on a New Edition of Reinhart Koselleck's *Preussen zwischen Reform und Revolution*," *Journal of Modern History* 57 (1985): 278–96.

[52] *RhG* 2:513–18; Faber, *Die Rheinlande*, pp. 118–86, 192–208.

In a sense, though, the predominance of the nobility made little difference, since the Diets had no lawmaking or revenue-approving powers of any kind. They were not much of a representative body either: Until the 1840s their deliberations were secret, and publication of the proceedings was prohibited by censorship. The Prussian authorities hoped the Diets would renounce any legislative efforts, or attempts to represent public opinion and instead become involved in "provincial self-administration," including such tasks as supervising the running of the Provincial Insane Asylum in Siegburg or the introduction of compulsory fire insurance for homeowners.[53]

The Provincial Diet could avoid being a farce only by engaging in activities that lay beyond its sphere of competence, at least as it was defined by the state authorities. To some extent, it would do just that, but the decades in which it provided the only form of even quasi-political representation for the inhabitants of the Prussian Rhine Province created a serious deficit in political activity there, a lack of familiarity with elections and political organization that would become apparent in 1848.

Although the smallest and the least populous of the three Rhenish provinces, Rhine-Hessen had the greatest weight in the state to which it belonged. While the population of the Prussian Rhineland and the Bavarian Palatinate each made up about one-eighth of their respective states, Hessen-Darmstadt's Rhenish possessions held a quarter of the Grand Duchy's inhabitants. The provincial capital, Mainz, with a population of some 40,000, was the largest city in the entire state. Unlike most of the German states of the day, including Prussia and Bavaria, Hessen-Darmstadt was geographically contiguous. The Rhine Province was just across the river from the rest of the Grand Duchy; the capital, Darmstadt, was an easy day trip by railroad from Mainz.

The great contrasts between East Elbian and Rhenish Prussia were not to be found between Hessen's two provinces east of the Rhine and the one to the west of it. All provinces of the Grand Duchy were inhabited mainly by small-holding peasants and the residents of market towns, although those living on the east bank of the Rhine were noticeably poorer than those to the west of the river. The Hessian nobility was largely a class of rentiers, not large landowners cultivating their own estates, as was the case in East Elbian Prussia. The ruling princely house and a majority of the inhabitants were Lutheran in the trans-Rhenan provinces, while Catholics and Protestants were present in roughly equal numbers in Rhine-Hessen. Sharp confessional differences between the core state and its Rhenish province, so important in Prussia, were thus lacking in Hessen-Darmstadt.

Hessen-Darmstadt's constitution, granted by the grand duke in 1820, pro-

---

[53] *RhG* 2:487–507; Faber, *Die Rheinlande*, pp. 264–305; above all, and superseding all previous works on the Prussian "constitutional struggle" of the years 1815–1820, its reactionary outcome, and the system of Provincial Diets, Herbert Obenaus, *Anfänge des Parlamentarismus in Preußen* (Düsseldorf: Droste, 1984), pp. 55–209 and passim.

vided for a bicameral legislature, with the lower house elected by an almost universal, yet highly plutocratic manhood franchise. Voters chose electors, who then chose a second set of electors, and it was these second electors who actually selected the parliamentary deputies. At each stage of the process, a stiffer property qualification was imposed, so that while most adult males could be voters, there were sometimes difficulties in finding enough candidates eligible for election to the Hessian parliament. For all the problems of the system, parliamentary elections did provide a continuing basis for political activity, at least among the more affluent inhabitants of Rhine-Hessen during the three decades before mid-century. Municipal elections, which also were held continuously throughout this period, provided another opportunity for a regular political life.

Compared with Prussia, the relationship of trans-Rhenan core state and Rhenish province in Hessen-Darmstadt was much less strained. Conflicts, though, were far from lacking, over such issues as interprovincial equity in taxation and the expenditure of government revenues, the introduction of an all-Hessian criminal code in the early 1830s, and the planned introduction of a new civil code in 1846. If the Rhine-Hessians were better integrated into their state than their Prussian counterparts, the distinctive nature of the Rhenish province, and a certain distance of its inhabitants from the state to which it belonged, was still quite noticeable.[54]

Conditions in the Palatinate, the southernmost of the three Rhenish provinces, and its relationship to the Bavarian state, showed elements of both Prussian and Hessian conditions. Like Hessen-Darmstadt, Bavaria was a constitutional state with a bicameral legislature possessing limited lawmaking and budgetary powers; the deputies to the lower house were elected at large from each province by estates. Unlike Prussia, Bavaria did not attempt to impose noble privileges on its Rhenish provinces. Palatine deputies represented, respectively, property-owning townsmen, rural landowners, and the Protestant and the Catholic clergy. This system of indirect and at-large elections encouraged a supralocal organization of political life, regularly bringing together notables from different parts of the province to elect deputies, leading them to discuss candidates and political platforms in common.[55]

While Bavarian rule in the Palatinate proceeded along similarly constitutional lines to that of Hessian rule in its Rhenish province, the distance and

[54] On Hessen-Darmstadt and its Rhenish province, see esp. Siegfried Büttner, *Die Anfänge des Parlamentarismus in Hessen-Darmstadt und das du Thilsche System* (Darmstadt: Selbstverlag des Historischen Vereins für Hessen, 1969); also, Friedrich Schütz, "Der Vormärz in Mainz und Rheinhessen," in *Hambach 1832: Anstöße und Folgen*, ed. Alois Gerlich (Wiesbaden: Franz Steiner, 1984), pp. 77–99; Faber, *Die Rheinlande*, pp. 308–11.

[55] *Handbuch der Bayerischen Geschichte*, ed. Max Spindler, 4 vols. in 5 (Munich: Beck, 1968–1975), 4, pt. 1, pp. 79–81; on elections in the Palatinate before 1848, BHSTAM MInn Nr. 44354; Nr. 44357; Nr. 44362; Nr. 45605.

isolation of the Palatinate from the the the rest of the Bavarian state was, if any-thing, even greater than that of the Prussian Rhine Province. Bordering the Prussian Rhineland on the east was the Prussian province of Westphalia, the two western provinces forming a unit of sorts, although cut off from the rest of the monarchy by the intervening states of Hanover and Hessen-Kassel. The Palatinate, however, was quite alone on the left bank of the Rhine, surrounded in all four directions by non-Bavarian territory. Until 1830, there did not even exist a customs union between the Palatinate and trans–Rhenan Bavaria, Pal-atine products being charged tariff duties, like those of foreign countries.[56]

Statesmen seriously debated whether Bavaria would be better off without its distant, unassimilable Rhenish province. Dynastic sentiment spoke against such a course. The Bavarian royal family did not originate in the Alpine regions that made up the core of the state, but in the old regime Palatinate, which, unlike its nineteenth-century successor, existed on both sides of the Rhine. King Ludwig I would spend hours looking at a map, muttering, "The Palatinate! The Palatinate! If I only had the [whole] Palatinate back!" Policy was not shaped just by the whims of eccentric rulers—of which Bavaria has had more than its share—but by considerations of power politics as well. The monarchy's statesmen had never entirely given up their long-term aspirations toward a Greater Bavaria that would be in the first rank among the European powers. Throughout the first half of the nineteenth century, they sought con-tinuously for some way to annex all or part of the intervening Grand Duchy of Baden and create a land bridge between contiguous, trans-Rhenan Bavaria and its Rhenish possession.[57]

As in Prussia, social and political differences amplified geographic ones. The reforming bureaucrats who created the modern Bavarian state in the first decades of the nineteenth century had envisaged recasting its socioeconomic and political structures along Napoleonic lines, which would have fit the Pa-latinate well, in spite of its distance from Munich. However, in the 1820s conservative court circles gained an ever-increasing influence over state pol-icy, turning it toward the preservation of the guilds, seigneurial privilege, and other old regime social distinctions, against public, jury trials, and toward an enhancement of the position of the Catholic Church as the official state reli-gion. None of this went over particularly well in the Palatinate, whose inhab-itants, besides sharing their fellow-Rhinelanders' attachment to the Rhenish Institutions, were also predominantly Protestant. The development of the Pa-

[56] Werner Weidmann, "Wirtschaftliche Probleme und sozialrevolutionäre Ansätze im Unfeld des Hambacher Ereignisses von 1832," *MHVP* 80 (1982): 23–67, here pp. 29–30.

[57] *Handbuch der Bayerischen Geschichte* 4, pt. 1, pp. 160–63; Kurt Baumann, "Die bayer-ische Oberrheinpolitik vom Wiener Kongress bis zum Ersten Weltkrieg," in *Von Geschichte und Menschen der Pfalz. Ausgewählte Aufsätze von Kurt Baumann*, ed. Kurt Andermann (Speyer: Verlag der Pfälzischen Gesellschaft zur Forderung der Wissenschaften in Speyer, 1984), pp. 215–25.

latinate's position within the Bavarian state shows that geography is not destiny, but when mixed with public policy it can become so.[58]

Bavarian rule in the Palatinate paralleled in many ways Prussian rule in its Rhine Province: geographical isolation of the western possessions from the core state in the east; sharply differing social, economic, and legal institutions between Rhenish territories and the rest of the state; confessional differences between the dynasty and the majority of the Rhenish population. In another sense, it was Bavarian and Hessian rule that had the most in common, since those two states had a constitution and elected legislature before 1848, while Prussia did not. To be sure, the power of these legislatures was minimal. They lacked the right of initiative or authority over nontax revenue. The elected lower houses were checked by upper houses composed of nobility, clergy, and government appointees; the monarch could refuse to give any elected civil servant (and lawyers were defined as such) leave to sit in the legislature and, above all, possessed the power to prorogue legislative sessions should opposition to the royal will gain the upper hand. The Darmstadt liberal Wilhelm Schulz noted in 1846 that the difference between an organic body and a German representative body was that the former dissolved when it showed no signs of life; the latter was dissolved as soon as it showed any.[59]

If election to such legislatures did not allow the voters much influence on affairs of state, it did provide them with an arena of participation in public life. At least the more affluent inhabitants of Rhine-Hessen and the Palatinate met regularly to consider candidates, hear their promises, and vote them into office. They could then follow in the newspapers the proceedings of their respective legislatures, thus enjoying an apprenticeship in organized politics. The Prussian system of Provincial Diets was designed to prevent this from happening and did in fact prevent it, leaving the inhabitants of the Prussian Rhine Province far less familiar with a structured political life than their counterparts in the southern Rhineland.

GOD AND SOCIETY ON THE RHINE

Religion was a powerful influence on public life and one of the major forms of group identification in western Germany during the first half of the nineteenth century. Confessional allegiances were significant for their own sake, but also for the ways they underscored or undercut dynastic loyalties and

[58] Werner K. Blessing, *Staat und Kirche in der Gesellschaft. Institutionelle Autorität und mentaler Wandel in Bayern wärend des 19. Jahrhunderts* (Göttingen: Vandenhoeck & Ruprecht, 1982), pp. 23–109; Heiner Haan, "Die bayerische Personalpolitik in der Pfalz von 1816/18 bis 1849," *JbwL* 3 (1977): 351–94; cf. Becker, *Die Pfalz und die Pfälzer*, pp. 31–32; Georg Friedrich Kolb, *Lebenserinnerungen eines liberalen Demokraten 1808–1884*, ed. Ludwig Merckle (Freiburg: Rombach, 1976), pp. 38–43.

[59] Büttner, *Parlamentarismus in Hessen*, p. 68.

helped shape nationalist sentiment. Social structure and, to an even greater extent, social conflict, were strongly influenced by religious antagonisms. Intraconfessional differences were no less important, and the structures and conflicts arising from them overlapped and acted at cross-purposes to those stemming from interconfessional differences. Religion was significant everywhere: either visibly or directly, or in hidden, mediated fashion.

Of the 3.65 million mid-century inhabitants of the three Rhenish provinces, about three-eighths were Protestants, slightly under five-eighths were Roman Catholics, and some 1.5 percent were Jews. The confessions were far from uniformly distributed. That portion of Rhenish Prussia lying on the right bank of the river was a predominantly Protestant region, in some areas just by a relatively narrow majority, in the Wuppertal and the Bergisches Land by as much as 70 percent. Only in the immediate Rhine Valley, around Emmerich, Düsseldorf, and the right bank Cologne suburbs, were there Catholic majorities. Just the opposite was the case for Prussia's possessions on the left bank of the Rhine. The areas around Kleve and Moers that had belonged to the monarchy even under the old regime formed a Protestant enclave on the far north of the left bank. Another such enclave existed in the extreme south of the province, in the Hunsrück and the Nahe Valley. Most of the area to the left of the river was overwhelmingly Catholic, with Catholic majorities reaching their peak in the Aachen district, where the 1849 census counted 96 percent of the population belonging to that confession.

The Protestant population of the left bank of the Rhine increased as one went south, making up some 46 percent of the inhabitants of Rhine-Hessen and 56 percent of those of the Palatinate at mid-century. The northeastern part of Rhine-Hessen, along the Rhine between Mainz and Bingen, was mostly Catholic, as were the southern and western portions of the Palatinate, on or near the border with France. The intervening area, crossing nineteenth-century political boundaries and testifying to the confessionally shaping effects of old regime governments, was predominantly Protestant. These confessional distinctions were nowhere near so sharp on the upper Rhine as further north. The population was confessionally much more mixed: Villages of different confessions lay right next to each other; villages whose inhabitants included substantial numbers of each Christian confession were common. All the chief towns of the Palatinate, however, no matter what the leading confession of the surrounding countryside, were predominantly Protestant.

The Jewish population of the lower Rhine was small, even for a small minority group, amounting to less than 1 percent at mid-century. This proportion was only slightly higher in the southern districts of the Prussian Rhineland, but was more substantial in Rhine-Hessen, at 4.3 percent of the population, declining further south to 2.6 percent in the Palatinate. The two cities with substantial Jewish minorities, Mainz and Worms, were both in Rhine-Hessen.

Jews made up 6.5 percent and 8.3 percent of their respective populations, according to the 1861 census.[60]

These statistics say nothing about intensity or direction of religious life. It followed two main currents, found in varying degrees in all three confessions. These were rationalism, drawing on its Enlightenment antecedents, sometimes with a trace of French revolutionary-era anticlericalism thrown in; and neoorthodoxy, in part a continuation of pre-Enlightenment religious traditions, in part reflecting the beginning influences of the great nineteenth-century religious revivals.

The contrast was strongest among Rhenish Protestants. Those living on the lower and middle Rhine were far more likely to be adherents of a severe piety, especially in the Wuppertal and the Bergisches Land, where a strict Calvinism, in all its seventeenth-century rigidity, set the religious tone. Often attributed to a climate that is unusually gloomy and sunless, even by central European standards, the doctrinaire piety practiced there has earned the area an unflattering nickname it preserves even today: not the Wuppertal, in English, the "Valley of the Wupper River," but the Muckertal, that is, the "Valley of the Bigots." Protestant rationalists were a beleaguered minority; the main alternative to Calvinism was found among the adherents of the "Awakening," who rejected predestination, holding that the lost sheep were not damned forever, and advocating revival meetings, Bible study groups, and abstinence societies to bring them back into the fold. One prominent supporter of this tendency was the Barmen manufacturer Friedrich Engels, Sr., father of the godless revolutionary, who, like most freethinkers, found the religious atmosphere of the Wuppertal completely unbearable.[61]

Circumstances were quite different in Rhine-Hessen and the Palatinate. Religious rationalism had put down broad roots there and commanded the allegiance of most Protestants. Prominent pastors denied the divinity of Jesus, with the enthusiastic support of their congregations and even peasants decorated their churches with enlightened slogans. One revivalist noted in horror

[60] Confessional statistics from *Tabellen und amtliche Nachrichten* 1; *Beiträge zur Statistik des Grossherzogtums Hessen* 3 (1864): 24–25, 244–51; LAS H3 Nr. 220b–m; *Verzeichniß der Beamten und Angestellten im Staats- und Gemeindedienste der . . . Pfalz nebst . . . einer Gemeindestatistik der Pfalz* (Speyer: Daniel Kranzbühler, 1857), pt. 2, pp. 2–50.

[61] Herberts, *Alles ist Kirche und Handel*, pp. 92–102; Siegfried Quandt, "Eduard Colsman (1812–1876). Ein Beitrag zur Geschichte der sozialen und politischen Auswirkungen der rheinischen Erweckungsbewegung des 19. Jahrhunderts," *ZBGV* 85 (1970/71): 129–69; Klaus Goebel, "Der rheinische Friedrich Engels," *MfEKR* 22 (1973): 131–60. Readers may note the similarity of the "awakened," with adherents of the contemporaneous American Second Great Awakening. Some examples of contemporary freethinkers' opinions of the Wuppertal's piety include Wegener, "Elberfeld," pp. 3, 9–11; Körner, *Lebenskämpfe* 1:284–92; *Lebenserinnerungen von Dr. med. C. H. Alexander Pagenstecher*, ed. Alexander Pagenstecher, 3 vols. in 1 (Leipzig: R. Voigtländer, 1913), 2:79, 3:37. On the minority status of rationalists among Protestants on the lower and middle Rhine, cf. LAK 403 Nr. 13710

that the farmers of Gerhardsbrunn had posted a sign above the church door reading "In honor of the All Mighty. Wanderer look about you: this house shall teach loyalty, truth, love and light." Although German Calvinism had begun in the Palatinate, that doctrinal orthodoxy which still held sway in the Wuppertal and Bergisches Land had long since given way to rationalism; enemies of Protestant religious Enlightenment on the upper Rhine had to base themselves on some rural bastions of traditional Lutheranism or a revivalist neoorthodoxy imported from Franconia.[62]

Organizationally, there were neither Lutheran nor Calvinist churches along the Rhine in the nineteenth century, following their merger in the Protestant "Union" of 1818. The circumstances and results of the Union were very different in the three Rhenish provinces, revealing a good deal about the differing nature of the Protestant churches and their relations with the respective states. In Rhine-Hessen and especially the Palatinate, the merger of the two churches had been a mass movement, emerging spontaneously from the celebrations of the Reformation tricentenary. Many of the local activists came from families of former Jacobin revolutionaries, whose descendants would be democratic leaders in 1848–1849, the campaign for a Protestant Union bridging several generations of radical politics. The catechisms of the union churches were strongly rationalist, espousing Enlightenment and praising freedom of conscience. Opposition came from devout Lutherans, such as the villagers of Altstadt, near Homburg in the Palatinate, who boycotted communion from 1818 until 1844, and from the state authorities, who found the whole movement doctrinally and politically suspicious.

In Prussia, on the other hand, the Union was imposed by the authorities on the special wish of the king. Its chief supporters were Lutherans, especially in those areas on the lower Rhine that had been part of Prussia under the old regime. The Calvinists of the Wuppertal and the Bergisches Land were vehemently opposed, fearing state interference with their presbyterial church organization, and condemning the government's proposed liturgy, similar to that of the High Anglicans, as crypto-Papist or even pagan. One young candidate for the position of pastor in an Elberfeld congregation tried using the new liturgy in services he conducted, and was tartly asked by a parishioner if he was planning to sacrifice goats and calves as well. The Union in the Prussian Rhineland remained primarily organizational: There was neither a common confession of faith nor a common liturgy, and individual congregations continued to be Calvinist, Lutheran, or adherents of the Union, as they still are today.[63]

---

[62] Bernhard H. Bonkhoff, *Geschichte der vereinigten protestantisch-evangelisch-christlichen Kirche der Pfalz* (Munich: C. H. Beck, 1986), pp. 42–43, 73, and passim; Hans Fenske, "Rationalismus und Orthodoxie. Zu den Kämpfen der pfälzischen Landeskirche im 19. Jahrhundert," *ZGO* 132 (1984): 239–69; Blessing, *Staat und Kirche*, pp. 54–55; Wilhelm Hoffmann, *Rheinhessische Volkskunde* (Bonn and Cologne: Ludwig Röhrscheid, 1932), pp. 109–10.

[63] Bonkhoff, *Kirche der Pfalz*, pp. 29–34; Fenske, "Rationalismus und Orthodoxie," pp. 240–

A similar opposition between rationalism and neoorthodoxy ran through Rhenish Catholicism in the first half of the nineteenth century, although with the characteristic difference that the rationalist tendency was weaker and enjoyed less popular support than among Protestants. Its adherents wished to see a German-language mass and the abolition of "superstitious" practices and institutions, such as the rosary, pilgrimages, processions, and religious brotherhoods and sodalities. Clerical partisans of this point of view underlined their convictions by dressing in frock coats instead of cassocks. They were skeptical of papal authority and cultivated a friendlier attitude toward Protestants, playing down doctrinal differences and not opposing mixed marriages. A more radical wing, which dominated the Trier seminary through the 1830s and was supported by some priests in the southern Rhineland, looked toward the abolition of individual confessions and clerical celibacy.

Their opponents, usually referred to by contemporaries as ultramontanists, which indicates clearly enough their attitude toward papal authority, had a quite different program for the church. Instead of abolishing "superstitious" practices, they wished to encourage and extend them, reviving the saying of the rosary, or creating new Marianic sodalities and pilgrimages. While the leading Catholic rationalist theologian, the Bonn professor Georg Hermes, had attempted to reconcile Kantianism with Catholic dogma, his neoorthodox opponents, who were successful in convincing the Pope to place Hermes's works on the Index, looked toward a theology based either on idealist romanticism or, increasingly, on a revival of Thomist philosophy. Hostility toward and mistrust of Protestantism was a rallying point for Catholic neoorthodoxy, especially in its popular form, opposition to religiously mixed marriages, one of its main public issues.[64]

The distinction between a strongly neoorthodox Prussian Rhineland and a more rationalist Rhine-Hessen and Palatinate, very pronounced among Protestants, was present in more attenuated form among Catholics. The north-

41; Karl Scherer, "Zur pfälzischen Kirchengeschichte des 19. Jahrhunderts. Theologischer Rationalismus und politischer Liberalismus im pfälzischen Vormärz," *BfPK* 32 (1965): 146–74, esp. p. 148 n.6; *RhG* 3:423; Erwin Mühlhaupt, "Die Union ihre Freunde und ihre Gegner im Bergischen Land und am Niederrhein im 19. Jahrhundert," *MfEKR* 14 (1965): 45–59; Manfred Wickelhaus, "Einheit und Freiheit im preußischen Kirchenkampf des 19. Jahrhunderts. Die Elberfelder Kirchenspaltung 1847," *MfEKR* 25 (1976): 33–64; Albert Rosenkranz, *Kurze Geschichte der Evangelischen Kirche im Rheinland bis 1945*, 2d ed. (Neukirchen-Vluyn: Neukirchen Verlag, 1975), pp. 102–04.

[64] This description of Catholicism owes a good deal to the work of Christoph Weber, especially his *Aufklärung und Orthodoxie am Mittelrhein 1820–1850* (Paderborn: Ferdinand Schöningh, 1973); see also *RhG* 3:338–42; Heinrich Schroers, "Hermesianische Pfarrer," *AHVN* 103 (1919): 76–183; Alfons Hoffmann, "Franz Tafel als Mensch und Priester (1799–1869)," *Archiv für mittelrheinische Kirchengeschichte* 15 (1963): 180–207; LAK 403 Nr. 4069 (on the Trier seminary and movements against celibacy among the Trier clergy in the early 1830s); Ayçoberry, *Cologne*, pp. 79–83, 213–22; Jonathan Sperber, *Popular Catholicism in Nineteenth Century Germany* (Princeton: Princeton University Press, 1984), pp. 10–28.

south contrast was less of a doctrinal matter, since both rationalist and neoorthodox theologians were active throughout the region. One of the strongholds of Catholic rationalism was the theological faculty of the University of Bonn, while the Mainz theological seminary was the chief center of neoorthodoxy. Rather, the difference lay in the degree of enthusiasm with which the two theological programs were received.

Both clergy and laity on the upper Rhine, although certainly less given to rationalist religion than their Protestant neighbors, displayed a somewhat greater skepticism toward the neoorthodox revivals of ostentatious public devotion than did their coreligionists further north, a difference in attitude discernible even in the early twentieth century. There was nothing in the Palatinate or Rhine-Hessen to compare with the factory town of Aachen, a sort of Roman Catholic Wuppertal, where clergy and pious merchants and manufacturers joined to promote the saying of the rosary, establish St. Vincent de Paul societies, and pronounce anathemas on Protestants, or on Catholics who wanted to marry one. Mainz was a predominantly Roman Catholic city and, with its seminary and monthly periodical, *Der Katholik*, a center of Rhenish neoorthodoxy, but many of its inhabitants were influenced by rationalist and anticlerical ideas, as would become clear in 1848. Militant Catholic circles there were careful not to provoke a confrontation with the Protestant Hessian state, unlike their counterparts further north, who took on the Prussian authorities with verve and energy.[65]

Differences between religious rationalists and the neoorthodox were just as pronounced among Rhenish Jews as among their Christian neighbors. Advocates of a "Reformed" Jewish religion wished to introduce German-language synagogue services, organ accompaniment to religious songs, sexually integrated synagogue seating, and an end to what they regarded as backward and superstitious practices, such as swaying while saying prayers or bidding for the right to read from the Torah. Radicals among them wished to go further and abolish ritual circumcision and move the main day of worship to Sundays. Their opponents, while occasionally acknowledging the need for some changes, emphasized the retention of the bulk of the orthodox religion as it had existed in the ghettos of the old regime.

Intraconfessional religious differences among Jews have not been well studied, but it does seem that a rationalist, reformed religion had its strongest adherents in the southern Rhineland—Worms and Alzey being centers of the movement—although equally strong adherents of a traditionalist orthodoxy could be found there as well. The much smaller Jewish population on the

---

[65] Besides the sources cited in the previous note, cf. Becker, *Pfälzer Volkskunde*, p. 111; Hoffmann, *Rheinhessische Volkskunde*, pp. 109–10; Erwin Gatz, "Kaplan Josef Istas und der Aachener Karitakskreis," *RhVjBl* 36 (1972): 207–28; Friedrich Keinemann, *Das Kölner Ereignis* 1:37–39, 99–103; *RhBA* 1, Nr. 47; Schütz, "Vormärz in Mainz," pp. 79–80; *NSZ*, 30 Jan., 12–13, 16, 24 Feb., 11 Mar., 13 Apr. 1848.

lower Rhine played a less visible role in the controversy, but the one appearance lower Rhine Jews made was on the traditionalist side, when two Bonn rabbis signed an 1846 rabbinical declaration condemning the reform movement.[66]

Separation of church and state was, and is, unknown in Germany, but connections between the two were especially close in the period before mid-century, something that was rather a mixed blessing for organized religion. The Rhenish Institution of civil marriage deprived the church of a role of considerable importance elsewhere in central Europe, so public education became the main field for the exercise of state-sanctioned clerical influence. There were no private, parochial schools because the public school system was religiously segregated, each Christian confession having its own schools. The Catholic priest or Protestant pastor was ex officio chairman of the local school board of his confession; district school inspectors were invariably clergymen. Not only were teachers under direct clerical supervision but their job included a whole series of church-related duties: organist and choir director, in addition, usually janitor and bell ringer.[67]

Senior church officials were either directly appointed by the government, or the authorities retained an influence over their appointment, being able, for instance, to veto a cathedral chapter's choice of bishop. This provided an opportunity for the government to become involved in the conflicts between adherents of rationalism and neoorthodoxy, either on its own initiative, or at the request of one or both of the religious factions. Such intervention could and did exacerbate interconfessional tension, when the governments of Prussia or Hessian-Darmstadt, Protestant dynasties with predominantly Protestant bureaucracies, became involved in the affairs of the Catholic Church, or when the Catholic government and ruling house of Bavaria became enmeshed in Protestant affairs.

Even more to the point, German states of the early nineteenth century were not confessionally neutral. It was expected that they would favor the confession of the ruling house, which they did, often in stupid and tactless ways. Requiring Catholic recruits in the Prussian army to attend Protestant Sunday services and demanding that Protestant Bavarian soldiers or members of the militia [Landwehr] kneel during processions when the sacrament was carried through the streets were decisions guaranteed to stir up discontent among the

[66] Steven M. Lowenstein, "The 1840s and the Creation of the German-Jewish Religious Reform Movement," in *Revolution and Evolution 1848 in German-Jewish History*, ed. Werner E. Mosse, Arnold Paucker, and Reinhard Rürup (Tübingen: Mohr, 1981), pp. 256–97; cf. LAS J1 Nr. 206 ff. 141–42; Dorothea Uhrig, "Worms und die Revolution von 1848/49" (Diss. phil., Frankfurt/M., 1934), pp. 46–47.

[67] *RhG* 3:359; Hermann Schneider, "Die Schule im Spannungsfeld zwischen Kirche, Staat und Gesellschaft im 19. Jahrhundert, dargestellt am Problem der Simultanschule in der Pfalz," *BfPK* 35 (1968): 253–63. For more on schoolteachers and their place in society, see Chapter Two.

minority confession in the state—which was, in these cases, the majority confession in the respective Rhenish provinces.[68]

As one might expect, Jews were the religious group that bore the greatest burden of discrimination. Compared with their coreligionists elsewhere in Germany, the legal position of Jews in the Rhineland was relatively good, a function of the emancipatory effects of the French Revolution. Jews could move about and settle freely, could practice any trade or profession, paid no special, discriminatory taxes, and enjoyed the dubious right to be drafted into the armed forces, just like their Christian neighbors. The institution of civil marriage meant that neither marriage among Jews nor between Jews and Christians presented the special legal problems it did elsewhere.

The Jews of Rhenish Prussia could not vote in elections for the Provincial Diets, sit as elected officals (insofar as such positions existed), or hold posts in the state administration involving the exercise of judicial or executive functions. In both Rhine-Hessen and the Palatinate, on the other hand, Jews possessed the franchise and the right to hold municipal office, which they did occasionally, but were banned from sitting in the legislatures of Hessen-Darmstadt or Bavaria, where seats were reserved for members of the Christian confessions.

Two forms of discrimination existed everywhere in the Rhineland and impinged directly on everyday life. To testify in court, Jews had to take a special "Jews' oath," degradingly formulated to imply that they had a pronounced inclination toward perjury. Even worse was Napoleon's "infamous decree" of 1808, which required that Jews engaging in a commercial occupation obtain a certificate of moral good conduct each year from the local authorities. Both these discriminatory practices were largely symbolic in nature, since the certificates of good conduct were rarely if ever denied, but in a society which took both the law and the free exercise of commerce very seriously, they were a galling reminder of an inferior status.[69]

Confession was no less intertwined with social structure than it was with the state. Decades before Max Weber formulated the idea in his tortured prose, Rhinelanders were well aware that the upper classes were disproportionately

[68] On these two examples, see Keinemann, *Das Kölner Ereignis*, 1:45–46; and *Handbuch der Bayerischen Geschichte* 4, pt. 1, pp. 201–02. The sources cited in notes 61–64 contain more general accounts of these problems.

[69] H. S. Schulte, "Die Rechtslage der Juden in Köln und am Niederrhein 1815–1847," in *Köln und das rheinische Judentum. Festschrift Germania Judaica 1959–1984*, ed. Jutta-Bohnke Kollwitz, Willebad Paul Eckert, Frank Golczewski, and Hermann Greive (Cologne: J. P. Bachem, 1984), pp. 95–101; Jacob Toury, *Die politischen Orientierungen der Juden in Deutschland. Von Jena bis Weimar* (Tübingen: J.C.B. Mohr, 1966), p. 4; Helga Karch, "Die politische Partizipation der Juden in der Pfalz," in *Juden in der Provinz: Beiträge zur Geschichte der Juden in der Pfalz zwischen Emanzipation und Vernichtung* (Neustadt a.d.W.: Pfälzische Post, 1988), pp. 49–64, esp. pp. 49–50. On practice with regard to the certificates of good conduct, see LAS H3 Nr. 189 ff. 39–55.

Protestant. Protestantism and a bourgeois upper class went together, in both predominantly Catholic cities, such as Cologne, Aachen, Mainz, and Mönchengladbach, and predominantly Protestant ones, such as Elberfeld, Lennep, and Duisburg. Protestants were present in disproportionate numbers among the leading figures of manufacturing, commerce, and even large-scale wine-growing. Some were strict Calvinists, such as the manufacturers of the Wuppertal, others, freethinking rationalists, such as the "bourgeois aristocracy of the Palatinate," the vineyard owners of the Haardt mountains, but they were all Protestants. A Catholic bourgeoisie certainly existed, containing a strong manufacturing element in the city of Aachen, elsewhere mostly wholesalers and professionals, but it was everywhere less affluent, less influential, and a disproportionately smaller share of the population than its Protestant counterparts.[70]

The small Jewish population of the lower Rhine was also disproportionately bourgeois, concentrated in wholesale commerce and banking. Most Jews, however, lived in small towns and villages of the southern Rhineland, earning their living as cattle dealers, property brokers, peddlers—the line between this occupation and begging was not always easy to draw—and petty moneylenders. Needless to say, neither all nor even most Jews or Protestants were rich, but they were a large and influential element among the bourgeoisie, the dominant group of Rhenish society.[71]

Just counting the number of people adhering to each confession creates substantial complexities: the relationship among the composition of the confessional majorities in the trans-Rhenan core state, that in its Rhenish province, and that among the bourgeoisie of the province was different in all three provinces under consideration. In addition to this, there need to be considered doctrinal differences within confessions, which could be as great or even greater than those between confessions, the impact of state influence on religious life, and the extent to which religion was caught up in broader questions, such as the relationship between Rhenish law and the law codes of the trans-Rhenan core states. Religious belief and confessional identity were independent, autonomous factors influencing social and political life, but this influence could only be brought to bear within the context of the social and legal institutions of Rhenish society.

[70] Wehler, *Deutsche Gesellschaftsgeschichte* 2:195–97; Ayçoberry, *Cologne*, pp. 116–17; *RhBA* 1, Nr. 47; Scherer, "Zur pfälzischen Kirchengeschichte," p. 158.

[71] Alwin Müller, "Das Sozialprofil der Juden in Köln (1808–1850)," and Klaus H. S. Schulte, "Zur gewerblichen Betätigung der Juden in Köln und im ländlichen Rheinland," both in *Festschrift Germania Judaica*, pp. 102–06 and 125–40, respectively; Herbert Strauss, "Pre-Emancipation Prussian Policies towards the Jews," *Leo Baeck Institute Yearbook* 11 (1966): 105–36, esp. pp. 119–20; Avraham Barkai, "The German Jews at the Start of Industrialisation: Structural Change and Mobility 1835–1860," in *Revolution and Evolution*, pp. 123–49, esp. p. 137; LAS H3 Nr. 187, esp. ff. 62–63, 79 (occcupational census of the Jewish population of the Palatinate, 1846).

THE RHINELANDS

A river does not make a society, and it is certainly legitimate to wonder whether a common social order existed along the entire length of the Rhine, from Kleve in the north, near the Dutch border, to Germersheim, in the south, near the border with France. There is no difficulty in pointing to enormous differences. The manufacturers of the Wuppertal hurried through the narrow streets of their factory towns, walking bolt upright, while keeping their eyes fixed to the ground, never raising their voices except when speaking the words "market price," "exchange rate," or "protective tariff." The vineyard owners of the Haardt mountains, verbose and jovial like most inhabitants of the forward Palatinate, met over wine at the Four Seasons hotel in Bad Dürkheim or across the river in Mannheim, to discuss, loudly and heatedly, religion, politics, and wine prices. They hardly seemed to inhabit the same world—yet they were both part of the Protestant bourgeoisie, having more in common with each other than they did with members of the lower classes of either confession or with Roman Catholics of all social classes.[72]

It is with such geographic, confessional, and class differences in mind, that I used the plural to describe the region in the chapter title, following contemporaries, who commonly spoke of the "lands on the Rhine" or "the Rhinelands" [die Rheinlande]. Behind all this diversity lay a common social order: a society composed primarily of households of proprietors/independent producers, equal before the law, but in practice differentiated by their access to the market, unhampered but also unprotected by such restraints on the market as the guild system or feudal agricultural tenures. This social order was concretely guaranteed and expressed by "Rhenish law," which differentiated the Rhinelands from the rest of central Europe, including the three core states to which the region belonged.[73]

Economic developments took place and social and confessional tensions were expressed within this social order guaranteed by a code of law, making it both an object of political struggles and a framework for them. The river did not create a region, but it flowed through one created by the impact of past historical events, above all those of the era of the French Revolution.

[72] These descriptions are borrowed from Körner, *Lebesnkämpfe*, 1:251–52; Becker, *Die Pfalz und die Pfälzer*, pp. 215–20; and LAS H1 Nr. 1017 ff. 2–3.

[73] On the use of the expression *the Rhinelands*, see Karl-Georg Faber, "Rheinlande und Rheinländer 1814–1848. Umrisse einer politischen Landschaft," in *Landschaft und Geschichte. Festschrift für Franz Petri zu seinem 65. Geburtstag am 22. Februar 1968* (Bonn: Ludwig Röhrscheid, 1970), pp. 194–210. Those right bank counties of Neuwied, Altenkirchen, and Wetzlar, in the Prussian Rhine Province, where Rhenish law did not obtain and both guilds and feudal tenures were widespread, were quite different from the rest of the Rhineland, and will play a marginal role in this study.

CHAPTER TWO

Social Conflict during the *Vormärz*

A SOCIETY AND ITS CONFLICTS

In the decades before 1850, conflict was endemic to the social order of the Rhineland, arising over conditions of access to the market, around the exercise of state power, and from differences between and within confessions. Whether consisting of peasants confronting forestry officials while chopping down spruce trees, manufacturers and outworking weavers disagreeing about proper payment for a piece of cloth, or Protestants and Catholics brawling in the streets, all such conflicts involved, at least implicitly, the structure of power and domination within that social order. They were, in other words, political. Before 1848, however, the transition from the implicitly to the explicitly political was a difficult one. Public expression of political ideas was bound by the decrees of the German Confederation, the league of central European states created by the Treaty of Vienna in 1815, and set on an authoritarian course by the Prussian and Austrian monarchies, which dominated it. The press was subject to prior censorship; there was no right of peaceful assembly or of collective petition; officially unsanctioned meetings were regularly broken up by the police or, if neccesary, the army. Political associations were prohibited and other forms of voluntary association subject to state approval. The franchise was restricted, and such representative bodies as were elected had little or no power.[1]

In such circumstances, conflicts tended to remain individual, isolated events without broader implications, as public knowledge of them was limited, and public discussion of them abortive or nonexistent. There was a substantial public interested in such political issues: especially intellectuals and members of the legal profession, more broadly, members of the bourgeoisie, even more broadly, the class of newspaper readers. These people could not openly articulate their opinions about politics, but were forced to keep their ideas to themselves or to discuss them in small, private circles. If they wanted to make them public, they had to do so in indirect, roundabout ways.

This separation or imperfect connection of social conflict and popular politics was characteristic of the historical period called the *Vormärz*, literally the "pre-March," the two or so decades before the revolutionary uprisings of

---

[1] A good survey of the system of the German Confederation, with extensive references to the literature is in Wehler, *Deutsche Gesellschaftsgeschichte* 2:322–69.

March 1848. The outbreak and initial successes of revolution in central Europe would abolish this separation, allowing political agitation over social conflicts to be carried out openly, but both the conflicts themselves and those who would politicize them stemmed from the prerevolutionary period.

CONFLICTS IN THE MARKET

Market conflicts typically pitted against each other the protagonists of production: nominally independent small producers and their actual employers, the possessors of mercantile and financial capital. Conflict centered around the terms of access to the market at a time when market-oriented production was on the increase. Found in the crafts and agriculture, such conflicts were most common in manufacturing outworking.

One version developed in the boom years of the late 1830s, as the first mechanized spinning mills were built, creating a demand for more handloom weavers than were immediately available in the labor market. Manufacturers tried to recruit one anothers' outworkers, sending agents to the lower Rhine textile villages, to hand out free drinks to the weavers and offer them ever-larger advances on their work. The weavers found themselves in a favorable labor market, something quite atypical for the *Vormärz* lower classes. They utilized the situation to work more slowly on each job or to take orders from several different manufacturers at once, doing the work in the order of the size of the advance. Some enterprising outworkers even took the raw material from one manufacturer and then turned around and sold it to another. There was a whole group of small manufacturers in the Krefeld silk industry whose stock consisted entirely of such stolen goods.[2]

It would have been "economically rational" to raise wages, but while the manufacturers were quick to cite the law of supply and demand when it was in their interest to do so, they were reluctant to follow its dictates when it worked against them. Rather, they turned to one of the more obscure aspects of Rhenish law, reviving the "manufacturing tribunals" [Fabrikgerichte]. Like other aspects of the Rhenish legal system, this was just a translation into German of a Napoleonic creation, the "conseil des prud'hommes," which governed French labor relations throughout most of the nineteenth century.[3]

[2] HSTAD RD Nr. 2181 ff. 122–26, 340–48; Nr. 2182 ff. 121–33; Nr. 2175 ff. 185–87; Nr. 2171 ff. 151–54.

[3] These courts are little discussed in the literature. There is a brief mention of them in Ringel, *Bergische Wirtschaft*, pp. 90–91, and a more detailed account in Peter Schöttler, "Die rheinischen Fabrikgerichte im Vormärz und in der Revolution von 1848/49. Zwischenergebnisse einer sozialgeschichtlichen Untersuchung," *Zeitschrift für neuere Rechtsgeschichte* 7 (1985): 160–80, an article regrettably filled with dubious judgments and errors of fact. Originally founded under the French, the courts, had all died out by the 1820s, except the ones in Aachen and Cologne, which led a shadow existence, and were revived in Krefeld in 1833, in Mönchengladbach in 1835, and in the Wuppertal and Bergisches Land over the next ten years. See Jeffry M. Diefendorf, *Busi-*

The tribunals were a form of industrial mediation, designed to avoid the expense and delay of the civil courts, using lay judges empowered to resolve disputes and enforce their decisions by imposing small fines and handing out jail sentences of up to three days. They were also an odious example of class justice. Half the lay judges were manufacturers; the other half were their foremen, or the small minority of outworking masters assessed for taxes at an unusually high rate. These criteria for membership ensured that the court would not have "in its midst judges who would not do the institution honor," that is, find in favor of the workers.[4]

Both manufacturers and outworkers were eligible to bring suit, and, in theory, weavers could complain to the tribunal about fines levied against them by a manufacturer for ostensibly poor-quality work, or about being paid for less cloth than they had actually woven. However, not only was the composition of the tribunal's personnel stacked against the outworkers, the proceedings themselves worked against them. Weavers needed to take a day off from work to appear in court, while the manufacturers could send a clerk or other representative, ask for delays, and spin out the proceedings if they not were going in their favor, until the outworkers gave up in disgust. Small wonder that the weavers of Waldniel, asked in 1840 if they wanted their village included in the jurisdiction of the court in Mönchengladbach, replied they regarded it as a bad idea, "since the manufacturing tribunals usually decide in favor of the manufacturers."[5]

It is not hard to understand why the manufacturers would have preferred to send their workers to jail rather than pay them higher wages, but the manufacturing tribunals included a carrot for the outworking master craftsmen as well as a stick. The masters themselves could use the courts to bring suit, not just against their employers, where they would not have much chance of success, but against their journeymen and apprentices. Between one-third and nine-tenths of the cases coming before the different tribunals pitted masters against their helpers, typically, concerning apprentices and journeymen who broke their contracts and left master weavers to work for manufacturers on their own account.[6]

---

nessmen and Politics in the Rhineland, 1789–1834 (Princeton: Princeton University Press, 1980), pp. 310–13; HSTAD RD Nr. 2178 ff. 1–71; Nr. 2181 ff. 3–7; Nr. 2194 ff. 1–84; Nr. 2175 ff. 1–87; Nr. 2171 ff. 1–47; Nr. 2152 ff. 1–3; Nr. 2186 ff. 36–37.

[4] HSTAD RD Nr. 2171 ff. 138–42.

[5] HSTAD RD Nr. 2181 ff. 275–88. The Mönchengladbach court, stung by the weavers' charges, sent in to the Düsseldorf district authorities a précis of decisions involving Waldniel weavers that their court had handed down between 1836 and 1839 (ibid.), which, showing the delaying tactics of accused manufacturers and their aggressiveness in pursuing outworkers with whom they had disputes, unintentionally proved the weavers' point.

[6] Report of the tribunal in Lennep for the year 1846–1847, HSTAD RD Nr. 2189; HSTAD RD Nr. 2182 ff. 176–83; HSTAD RD Nr. 2178 ff. 188–91. Schöttler, "Die rheinischen Fabrikgerichte," pp. 170–75, argues that the tribunal was an institution that provided strong protection for

Obviously, the master weavers had an interest in prohibiting this action, as it meant more competition for them, bringing down wages. Manufacturers, however, also had an interest in the masters' cause, since hiring away journeymen was how new, competing manufacturers set themselves up in business. In calling for the creation of these tribunals, and in yearly reports on their activities, businessmen described social relations in manufacturing as characterized by disorder and violation of contract: Apprentices and journeymen left their masters without permission; masters turned in their cloth to the manufacturers late or not at all; the latter attempted to steal one another's outworkers. The upshot was moral decay and widespread poverty, with incompletely trained weavers setting up for themselves, marrying and founding families at too young an age, or taking large advances from the manufacturers and spending them in the taverns or on superfluous consumer goods. They would end up dependent on poor relief.

Courts would provide a remedy by ensuring the "exact fulfillment of apprenticeship contracts so especially important for moral and occupational education . . . prompt delivery by weavers of work they have undertaken, order in the spinning and dyeing works . . . ," and prohibition of the public auction of consumer goods or of manufacturers' offering large advances to weavers. By themselves, the courts were just part of the answer; Elberfeld businessmen denounced "occupational freedom in completely unlimited fashion" and called for "a kind of guild system, based on reasonable and up to date principles. . . ." Contrary to their reputation as advocates of unlimited laissez-faire, Rhenish textile manufacturers were among the most important proponents of the reinstitution of the guilds, or even of their creation where they had not existed before, as part of a broader plan to preserve their power in the market against the nominally independent small producers they employed.[7]

By the mid-1840s, some two thousand to three thousand cases were moving through the tribunals of the Düsseldorf District each year, and the outworkers were having difficulty finding an effective reply to the manufacturers' offensive. The only instance of organized resistance came in Kettwig, near Essen, in the summer of 1843, when the town's weavers organized a collective slowdown, weaving only in the mornings, and spending the afternoons meeting in the taverns. They would emerge from them occasionally to smash the windows of local woolens manufacturers, who were trying to cut their wages at a time when bread prices were very high. Rather more typical was an impotent expression of frustration, such as that of the weaver August Fichthan, who got

---

workers against the manufacturers, conveniently ignoring his own figures, which show that most cases won by employees, and most cases brought overall, concerned masters versus journeymen and apprentices, not masters against manufacturers.

[7] HSTAD RD Nr. 2181 ff. 122–26; Nr. 2178 ff. 188–91; similarly, Nr. 2181 ff. 172–79; and Nr. 2171 ff. 255–57. On the practice of hiring away apprentices, see Hae-Bon Chung, "Das Krefelder Seidengewerbe," pp. 160–61.

into a violent argument in 1844 with the cotton manufacturer Kaspar van der Baeck, president of the Elberfeld tribunal, over proper payment for woven cloth. Eighty weavers waiting to have their cloth measured for payment heard Fichthan get angrier and angrier, finally shouting, "Damn it, I'm no slave!" He was promptly brought before the manufacturing tribunal and sentenced to a day in jail. Even before the commercial crisis of 1847 brought mass layoffs and large wage reductions, the manufacturers seem to have had a fair amount of success in imposing labor discipline on the outworkers.[8]

Similar conflicts between merchants and outworking master artisans and between masters and their journeymen and apprentices also developed in those trades that worked for a more local market. They were organizationally less one-sided than in textile outworking, since both masters and journeymen, at least in the larger cities, possessed organizational resources that most outworkers were lacking. Cooperative sales halls were one possible way for masters to strike back at merchants. The trades' association [Gewerbeverein] in Mainz, which sponsored the first such institution in the Rhineland, announced its intention of intervening in the city council elections to fight the influence of the "wholesalers, the aristocracy of money." Cologne's first municipal elections in 1846 would be held under similar auspices. Following the real estate crash that year, outraged master masons and carpenters protested the various forms of credit trickery practiced by the "capitalists"—the first use of this word in Cologne for political purposes—who had financed their construction projects and then foreclosed on them.[9]

Conflicts in this economic sector sometimes involved guild survivals. While the guilds had been abolished, guild sentiment still lingered, and in some towns artisan corporations maintained a shadow existence as voluntary mutual benefit societies or religious brotherhoods. Nowhere was this more common than in Trier, where the masters of every single craft possessed such a group and were constantly pressing the authorities to prohibit outworking, to prevent peddlers and outside craftsmen from selling their wares in the city, or to refuse to allow anyone who wanted to set himself up in business. The spokesman for the master butchers, Johann Blasius, would be a prominent democratic activist in 1848–1849.[10]

Similar circumstances prevailed among the journeymen. In larger cities

[8] Schöttler, "Die rheinischen Fabrikgerichte," p. 173; cf. also *RhBA* 2/1, Nr. 120; HSTAD RD Pr. Nr. 790 ff. 86–115. The events in Kettwig are mentioned by Dieter Dowe, in his *Aktion und Organisation. Arbeiterbewegung, sozialistische Bewegung und kommunistische Bewegung in der preußischen Rheinprovinz 1820–1852* (Hannover: Verlag für Literatur und Zeitgeschehen, 1970), p. 35, but described, somewhat misleadingly, as a strike.

[9] *KnZ*, 8 July 1841; Ayçoberry, *Cologne*, pp. 158–64.

[10] StdT Tb 33/179; and ZSTAM Rep. 77 Tit. 505 Nr. 5 Vol. IV ff. 192–96; on the survival of guild sentiment in Cologne, cf. Ayçoberry, *Cologne*, p. 89; in Koblenz, LAK 441 Nr. 1329 pp. 473–79.

each craft had its inn, where newly arrived journeymen could stay while looking for work. Both masters and the authorities complained that such inns
housed illicit successors to the old regime journeymen's brotherhoods, which
organized boycotts of masters paying low wages or treating their men badly,
and encouraged the celebration of Blue Monday and other forms of alcoholic
recreation involving less work for the same pay.[11]

Market conflicts were also fought out in villages, most frequently over use
of the common lands. The French revolutionary regime had not abolished such
precapitalist agricultural tenures as usage rights to the commons, the related
right to pasture animals on other people's private property at certain times of
the year, or compulsory collective cultivation. These tenures continued to exist in the Rhineland during the first half of the nineteenth century, involving a
dense thicket of old regime customs, often varying from locality to locality,
different and contradictory laws and decrees of the revolutionary and Napoleonic authorities, and bewildered and tentative attempts of the three German
governments to deal with the situation.[12]

Division of the commons, occurring on the grain-growing plains of the
lower Rhine, created difficulties for small peasants and day laborers, who
lacked land to pasture their animals and grow potatoes for their families. Paradoxically, preservation of the commons and rights to common pasturage on
private lands also hurt the rural lower classes of this area. Wool was very much
in demand, thanks to the growth of the textile industry, so enterprising individuals began using traditional rights to pasture on the commons or on other
people's land, previously exercised for a few sheep per family, with herds of
several hundred. In effect, they were exploiting precapitalist agricultural tenures for the distinctly capitalist textile industry, and the poor who lacked the
capital to purchase such large herds found all the grass for their farm animals
stripped bare. Attempts by the authorities to limit or regulate this practice led
to a literally twilight world of illegal, nocturnal pasturage.[13]

Winegrowing, as the most commercialized of all forms of Rhenish agriculture, was also the scene of the most conflicts over agricultural markets, pitting
large vineyard owners or wine merchants against small vintners, as each group
sought to maintain its position in the face of declining wine prices. The most

[11] Ayçoberry, *Cologne*, pp. 192–94; Wittgenstein, "Entstehung der sozialen Frage," p. 169;
Sperber, *Popular Catholicism*, pp. 12–13.

[12] Wilhelm Engels, *Ablösungen und Gemeinheitsteilungen in der Rheinprovinz. Ein Beitrag
zur Geschichte der Bauernbefreiung* (Bonn: Röhrscheid, 1957), is very disappointing in this regard. There is useful material on commons and rights of common pasturage in LAK 403, Nr.
9451; cf. also Heukeshofen, "Die wirtschaftliche Entwicklung des Jülicher Landes," pp. 51–55;
Hoffmann, *Rheinhessische Volkskunde*, pp. 52–53; Konrad Regula, "Die Allmenden der Pfalz in
Geschichte und Gegenwart" (Staatswiss. Diss., Würzburg, 1927), pp. 41–63.

[13] This problem was especially prevalent in Neuss County, situated on the left bank of the Rhine
near Cologne and the Aachen industrial area. See HSTAD RD Nr. 2238. Cf. also HSTAD RA
Nr. 234 ff. 18–19.

spectacular and explosive conflict concerned charges of wine fraud. Small vintners of the Nahe and Ahr Valleys accused wine merchants of adding sugar and chemicals to their wines; when consumers drank them, they would turn blue and suffer insomnia, severe head- and stomachaches, or temporary paralysis. The charges may well have been true, but fraud was really not the issue. Adulteration is as old a practice as winegrowing, and a veritable industry of wine adulteration had existed in Kreuznach and Bingen since the mid-eighteenth century, although the fruit brandy added there to the weak and sour Nahe Valley vintages made them stronger and sweeter, that is, probably more and not less marketable. Cynics also noted that the vintners were not innocent victims of conniving merchants but were perfectly capable of adulterating wines on their own.[14]

What was actually at stake appeared in the publicization of the fraud charges. The wine merchants were accused of ruining the reputation of the Ahr Valley wines by their adulteration, thus driving down the price and forcing the vintners to "sell to the manufacturers [of adulterated wine] at ridiculously low prices . . . who in this way have the entire trade of the Ahr Valley in their hands. . . ." Charges of fraud were a way of speaking about the relations of the small vintners to the wine merchants who provided them with credit and to whom they were then forced to sell their grapes at unfavorable prices. Once again, the real issue, with vintners, as with handloom weavers or master masons, was the dependence of nominally independent small producers on mercantile capitalists for access to the market.[15]

FISCAL CONFLICTS WITH THE STATE

No one likes to pay taxes and the economic problems of the *Vormärz* did nothing to increase popular fiscal enthusiasm. Collecting government revenue was especially problematic in the three Rhenish provinces, since it raised in the most direct, tangible, and universally felt way their relationship to their respective core states. Many Rhinelanders shared the suspicion that their relatively well-off region was being taxed exorbitantly, to pay for the expenses of the poorer, trans-Rhenan provinces. In Rhine-Hessen, the peasants said, "The cow is fed by us, and it's milked on the other side [of the Rhine]." On hearing the news of the annexation of his native city by the Prussian monar-

---

[14] LAK 441 Nr. 11377; Nr. 1306 pp. 33–44; Nr. 1310 pp. 17–23; Nr. 1311 pp. 83–94; *KnZ*, 23 Oct. 1844 (Beilage).

[15] Besides the sources cited in the previous note, see *KnZ*, 4 Sept. 1844 (Beilage), 29 Sept. 1844 (Beilage), 3–4 Oct. 1844, and 6 Oct. 1844 (Beilage). The man who brought the vintners' complaints to public attention was the Cologne rentier Franz Raveaux, leader of the *Vormärz* democrats there, and the city's representative to the Frankfurt National Assembly in 1848–1849. On his activities before the revolution, see Chapter Three.

chy, one Cologne banker issued the oft-repeated bon mot, "Well, we have married into a poor family."[16]

Interprovincial fiscal inequity was hotly debated in newspapers and pamphlet literature before 1848—at least as much as the censorship allowed. All participants agreed, and contemporary scholars have followed on this point, that Prussia's Rhenish subjects paid a disproportionate share of taxes. Defenders of the monarchy's policy asserted that this was only right, since the Rhinelanders were wealthier, while opponents pointed to the exemption of knights' estates [Rittergüter] from the property tax. Most owners of such estates were East Elbian Junker noblemen, and the taxes they did not pay had to be made up by commoners, especially in Prussia's westernmost province, where such estates were a rarity.[17]

Even the most ardent defenders of the Munich government had to admit that in the 1820s the Bavarian state had ruthlessly exploited its Rhenish possession to pay off the debts it had contracted during the Napoleonic era as part of its futile attempt to climb into the ranks of the European Great Powers. After the near-revolution of 1832 in the Palatinate, tax policy had changed, giving the Rhenish Bavarians a better deal, especially as the system of feudal tenures had different fiscal implications than in Prussia. Since the state was the largest feudal landlord in trans-Rhenan Bavaria, peasants there paid it large sums in feudal dues. Counting these as taxes made the per capita burden to the east of the Rhine higher than in the Palatinate, whose inhabitants, thanks to the Rhenish Institutions, were free of such fedual relics.[18]

Whether levied equitably or inequitably, taxes had to be paid, and they were, the Prussian authorities noting with a certain pride that even in economically bad years, direct taxes came in precisely according to plan. Although paid in full, taxes were also paid grudgingly, since in 1844, a relatively prosperous year, over 74,000 late notices were issued by tax collectors in the Düsseldorf District, which had some 900,000 inhabitants. Plans to abolish the fine charged for these notices threatened to plunge tax collectors, who received no regular salary but a percentage of fines and administrative fees, into total poverty.[19]

Two indirect taxes imposed by the Prussian state, in a highly inequitable and selective way, met with widespread opposition and hostility. One was the tax on must, wine fermenting in barrels. Levied by volume, it was first im-

---

[16] Döhn, "Eisenbahnpolitik," pp. 21–22; Ayçoberry, *Cologne*, p. 67.

[17] Faber, *Die Rheinlande*, pp. 239–44.

[18] The discussion in Faber, *Die Rheinlande*, pp. 244–47, is not as good as the corresponding section on Prussian tax policy. The archival volumes BHSTAM MInn Nr. 45374 and LAS H1 Nr. 501 contain copies of the contending pamphlets and interesting computations. See also Weidmann, "Wirtschaftliche Probleme," pp. 34–36. The situation in Rhine-Hessen was apparently similar to that in the Palatinate. Cf. Döhn, "Eisenbahnpolitik," pp. 11–13.

[19] HSTAD RD Pr. Nr. 1476 ff. 291, 356; Pr. Nr. 1477 f. 124.

posed in the mid-1820s, at the highpoint of prosperity for Prussia's Rhenish vintners; the collapse of wine prices following the second half of the 1820s made its weight unbearable. Although Berlin would remit the tax in an especially bad year, the Ministry of Finance stubbornly refused to consider abolishing it, even when the local authorities cautiously suggested it might be for the best. Prussia's bureaucrats, accustomed to drinking only the finest of vintages, thought the vintners' tax burden was tolerable, because they estimated wine prices at twice what winegrowers actually received for ordinary-quality wine.[20]

Opposition to the tax mounted in the vineyards along the Rhine, Moselle, Saar, Ahr, and Nahe throughout the 1830s and 1840s. Vintners met in the taverns or private houses to consume some of their otherwise unsalable product, and talk about the days of French rule, when taxes were low and wine prices high, comparing them unfavorably with the diametrically opposed current circumstances. In 1837, at the very nadir of wine prices, the vintners in Reil, on the Moselle, took action, gathering together and driving out of town a bailiff, who had come to perform a forced sale to collect back taxes.[21]

No more popular than the must tax was the meat and flour octroi [Schlacht-und Mahlsteuer], imposed in the larger walled cities of the Prussian monarchy in place of the graduated poll tax collected elsewhere. While the latter was at least vaguely progressive, the former, taxing basic necessities that weighed most heavily on the budgets of the poor, was a deeply regressive tax. The workers' loss was the Prussian treasury's gain, since the octroi produced far more revenue for it than did the poll tax. During the 1830s, the octroi in Aachen brought in some 60,000 taler yearly, while in Elberfeld, also a manufacturing town with about the same population, but no wall and no octroi, the poll tax produced just 23,000 taler. Rising food prices following the mid-1820s made things hard enough for the Rhenish lower classes; a tax so visibly adding to their burdens was correspondingly hated.[22]

Smuggling on a wide scale also arose from the combination of high food prices, hard times for the lower classes, and attempts to raise state revenues.

---

[20] On the must tax, see Meyer, "Entwicklung des Moselweinbaues," sec. II/4/b/2; LAK 442 Nr. 3441. Official estimates of wine prices in the mid-1830s, at 6 taler per Eimer (LAK 403 Nr. 179 pp. 233–34) contrast with 2–3 taler per Eimer paid to Saar Valley vintners at that time (Steuer-Controller Saarburg to RT, 4 Feb. 1844, LAK 442 Nr. 2298) and with average wholesale prices for Moselle wines in 1835–1839 in Koblenz of 10.4 taler per Oxhoft of three Eimer (see Chapter One, note 11). More generally, on official skepticism about the winegrower's plight, see *RhBA* 1, Nr. 69.

[21] RT to MInn, 31 May and 6 June 1837; LR Kr. Bernkastel to RT, 29 July and 5 Dec. 1837, LAK 442 Nr. 3441.

[22] Nießner, *Aachen*, p. 32; Karl Breuer, "Ursachen und Verlauf der Revolution von 1848/1849 im Moseltal und seinen Randgebieten," (Diss. phil., Bonn, 1921), p. 67; Richard Noack, "1848/49 in der Saargegend," p. 38; ZSTAM Rep. 77 Tit. 505 Nr. 2 Vol. 1 ff. 4–6; LAK 441 Nr. 1309 pp. 163–69.

Both the Prussian Rhine Province and the Bavarian Palatinate were border provinces, abutting states that did not belong to the all-German customs union. For the inhabitants of the border districts, smuggling was an almost irresistible temptation. Smugglers specialized in coffee, in heavy demand by weavers, who sat at their looms twelve to fourteen hours a day, and highly lucrative because of the 53 percent import tariff levied on it by the customs union.[23]

The Prussian authorities took energetic measures to close this gap in state finances. A special border police commissariat was created in the Düsseldorf District, which carried out some 23,000 night raids yearly in villages near the Dutch border. Hundreds of suspected smugglers were placed under police surveillance. Local notables were recruited into an Anti-Smuggling Society, which attempted to find construction work for smugglers and, more important, apprentice their children to silk weavers, so that they might learn an honest trade and break with the illegal ways of the older generation.

Official reports were full of optimism, but a little reading between the lines tells a different story. The twenty-three thousand raids produced just twelve arrests; the notables of Breyell, unofficial capital of the smuggling district, had earned their fortunes in the trade of illegal importing; and the handloom weavers, given the work they did, were the smugglers' best customers. All the campaign accomplished was to spread hostility toward the authorities; the day of reckoning with them would come in 1848.[24]

A state attempting to extract wealth from a society where a large proportion of the population was living in poverty, and standards of living for the majority were in decline was certain to experience difficulties in doing so. The manifestly inequitable way in which revenue was raised, sparing inhabitants of the older, trans-Rhenan provinces at the expense of the Rhinelanders and sparing nobles and the bourgeoisie at the expense of outworkers, vintners, and the urban poor only aggravated the situation, sharpening the social tensions of fiscality. Before 1848, censorship made taxes at most a subject reserved for debate by the educated population. But popular hostility toward fiscality was present in inchoate form and would instantly emerge once the constraints of the police state were cast aside.

The Market and the State

Under the protection of the Rhenish Institutions, market forces could determine wages, prices, and capital investment without hindrance from guilds or feudal tenures. The three core states endorsed and actively supported this pre-

[23] Wittgenstein, "Entstehung der sozialen Frage," p. 140.

[24] On smuggling in the Düsseldorf District, see HSTAD RD Pr. Nr. 735; Pr. Nr. 1462 ff. 308–09, 332–33; Pr. Nr. 1463 ff. 27–28; Nr. 8806 ff. 51–54. Elsewhere in the Rhineland, cf. Heuckeshofen, "Die wirtschaftliche Entwicklung des Jülicher Landes," pp. 159–60; LAS J1 Nr. 263 ff. 155–60.

dominance of the capitalist market. Accepting the reign of the market, however, did not mean abandoning the idea that the state should play a leading role in determining the pace and direction of economic development. Rather, the three states' authorities sought to accomplish this goal by working through the institution of the market. The upshot was what might be called an unfree market economy, in which everyone competed in the unrestrained market, but some, thanks to government assistance, competed on more favorable terms.

Of course, the free market economy is itself an economists' fiction. Through tax and tariff policies, subsidies, and legal codes, the state always influences economic affairs. However, in the *Vormärz* Rhineland, where there were no precapitalist restraints on the market, three state bureaucracies determined to guide the market, and no effective parliamentary representation of social or economic interests to guide, direct, or even restrain the bureaucracies, the combination of state action and market forces was particularly potent. Conflicts over access to the market immediately involved the state, whenever, as was so often the case, the core states' policies limited or determined that access. Conversely, state actions could affect market access, even when they were not intended to, with a powerful effect in a society susceptible to the unchecked prevalence of market forces. Conflicts involving the state and the market were among the most bitter in the *Vormärz* and existed throughout the economy, in trade and transport, manufacturing, agriculture, and services.

Water and Steam, Taxes and Tolls

Transportation was a major arena of state action. By building particular railroad lines, the state could influence economic development in an era when commerce was both expanding and moving in new directions. Railroad construction became one of the main political issues in Rhine-Hessen during the 1840s, the debate centering on the future of Mainz commerce, so badly hurt by the abolition of the staple in 1831.

Rail transport magnified Mainz's difficulties, as railroads going north from Mainz's upstream competitor, Mannheim, and from Frankfurt to Mainz's right bank competitor, Biebrich, cut further into the city's commerce. Seeking to promote the economic development of its trans-Rhenan provinces, the government of Hessen-Darmstadt began building rail lines to connect with this growing net on the right bank of the Rhine. Outraged Mainz and Worms businessmen saw their taxes being used by the state to subsidize their competitors, while no lines were built in their province.

A proposal in the 1830s for a left bank line from Mainz running south to Strasbourg, with connections to Paris and southern France, was quashed by the Prussians, who feared the railroad could facilitate a French invasion. The government of Hessen-Darmstadt refused to consider funding even a more modest project from Hessen to the Palatinate, since it would have competed with the authorities' plans for tracks on the right bank of the river. Although paying over a third of the state's taxes, Rhine-Hessen was receiving none of its railroad expenditures. When Mainz and Worms businessmen formed a corporation to build a left bank railroad financed purely from private funds, the state even refused at first to issue a construction permit. The government finally agreed to do so in 1845, after a nine-month delay, repeated petitions from Mainz, and acrimonious debate in the Hessian parliament.

Throughout the entire controversy, state censors allowed scarcely a word of it to appear in the province's major newspaper, the *Mainzer Zeitung*. Even an account of the victory banquet given for Mainz's parliamentary deputies after the construction permit was issued fell victim to the censor's blue pencil. It was, in any event, a premature celebration, since the newly formed corporation was promptly caught up in the subsistence crisis of 1846 and the commercial collapse of 1847–1849; construction began only after 1850.[25]

The Rhine-Hessian railroad controversy showed both the unfree market economy and the authoritarian *Vormärz* state in action. Attempting to promote economic growth, the Hessian government exacerbated the difficulties experienced by its Rhenish subjects in adapting to a free market in transportation, while simultaneously bringing to the fore issues of interprovincial equity in taxation and government expenditures, thus hampering the integration of Rhine-Hessen into the core state. Although ultimately forced to back down, in part by the Hesssian parliament, exerting all its meager constitutional powers, the authorities did their best to ensure that the railroad issue—a thoroughly nonrevolutionary, bourgeois political question—be kept as far away from public discussion as possible.

The Rhine watermen's attempts to adapt to a new market situation were also hampered by state policy. Their adversary was not one individual government, but all the riverain states represented in the Central Commission on Rhine Navigation, the body set up by the Congress of Vienna to regulate river traffic. While the boatmen could not compete with steam tugs in carrying heavy cargoes over long distances upstream, they had an advantage over the steamboat companies in carrying small loads and making trips on short notice from one harbor to another. Steamboats needed large loads contracted in advance, for a sailing to be economical, which the boatmen, with their lesser capitalization,

[25] On the controversy, see Döhn, "Eisenbahnpolitik," pp. 33–83. Since the records of the provincial government of Rhine-Hessen, along with those of the Hessen-Darmstadt Ministry of the Interior and Ministry of Justice were destroyed in the Second World War, I cannot prove it was state policy that prevented Mainz's chief newspaper from reporting on a issue crucial to the town's economic future. When one compares the detailed reporting of the *Kölnische Zeitung* on the railroad issue—16, 24 May, 15 June, 26 July, 12 Aug., 11 Sept., 1, 4, 23 Oct., 14 Dec. 1844; 13, 17 Feb., 3–4 Apr., 8 May, 19, 26 July 1845—with the brief notices on the question appearing in the *Mainzer Zeitung*—just 24 June, 17 July, 16–17, 20 Aug. 1844—it is hard to see this as having resulted from anything else but censorship.

did not. The navigation commission's policy of levying substantial river tolls, set by a boat's tonnage, not by the amount of freight actually carried, neutralized the boatmen's potential advantage, forcing them to wait in port for a cargo, rather than flitting empty to a nearby harbor where a small load was waiting to be transported. River tolls on the trip made without cargo would have eaten up their narrow profit margin.

Toll policies prevented boatmen from filling market niches and adapting to new conditions created by the steam tugs; selective enforcement of regulations by the shipping commission also worsened their lot. The rule permitting steamboats to tow several barges while boatmen were limited to just one was strictly enforced. Requirements restricting the steamboat companies were treated much more laxly: They could ignore with impunity clauses in their licensing agreements obliging them to tow boatmen as well as their own barges. The commission refused to hear complaints of riverfront property owners about damage to their property from the steamboats' wake or to receive the boatmen's petitions for redress of the inequities in the regulation of Rhine navigation. If the watermen's troubles were due primarily to the growth of steam transport, official policy played a role as well, discriminating against them, hampering their adaptation to new conditions in the authorities' search for higher revenues from river tolls.[26]

Trademarks, Foundries, and Prayer Circles

The Solingen steel wares trade faced unfavorable market conditions in the first half of the nineteenth century. These problems were in part a result of state policy; manufacturers' attempts to remedy them were circumscribed by state actions, dramatically increasing tensions among manufacturers, between manufacturers and outworkers, and between most of those involved in the trade and the Prussian government.

The area's reputation in the world market for quality work was breaking down in the first half of the nineteenth century, rendering it vulnerable to competition from British craftsmen in Sheffield. Not only could the British work better than the Germans could; they could also work more cheaply. The steel they used to manufacture knives, scissors, or files was produced in the coke-fired blast furnaces of Britain's industrialized steel manufacture, while Solingen manufacturers had to get their steel from the inefficient, charcoal-fired ovens in the states of the German tariff union. These mills were protected from foreign competition, and Solingen manufacturers cut off from cheap British steel, by steep import duties.[27]

---

[26] See esp. LAS H3 Nr. 193 ff. 7–30; also, LAK 441 Nr. 1309 pp. 13–16; Nr. 1330 pp. 147–60. The Rhine Navigation Commission, one of the earliest intergovernmental agencies in Europe, deserves its historian.

[27] Boch, *Handwerker-Sozialisten*, p. 61; Wolfgang Radtke, *Die Preussische Seehandlung*

One remedy for the situation was to raise quality. Manufacturers, supported in their efforts by the outworking smiths, grinders, and finishers, demanded a return to the old regime system of trademarks [Fabrikzeichen], stamped on each item produced, as a guarantee of a quality product. Such a scheme could only work if the trademarks could be registered and their exclusive use legally enforced. The Berlin authorities refused to go along with this plan, in spite of contrary recommendations from officials in Solingen and Düsseldorf, taking the not entirely comprehensible position that the exclusive use of a trademark was a violation of freedom of commerce.[28]

An alternative action was to reduce wage costs. Merchant manufacturers could try to bring more outworkers into the trade, thus lowering wages, but, unlike weaving, the various forms of metalworking in Solingen manufacture were highly skilled crafts, requiring a long apprenticeship. The outworkers, retaining a shadow version of their old regime guilds, kept apprenticeships carefully under control, reserving them for relatives and assaulting or even murdering anyone who tried to train outsiders.[29]

The merchants turned to paying in truck in order to cut wages. Although found throughout the manufacturing regions on the lower Rhine, truck payments were especially common in the steel wares trade. Outworkers were paid in IOUs, drawn on distant banks and due several months in the future, which they could redeem for cash only at a substantial discount; in chits, good only at a company store, where inferior wares were sold at inflated prices; or, worst of all, in seconds, which they would themselves have to sell—often back to the manufacturer or his agent, who would pay only a small fraction of the wares' value.[30]

These two programs for the manufacturers' economic survival were mutually exclusive. Lowering wages meant lower-quality products. Outworkers paid in truck had to produce more to earn the same as they would have at better pay, which meant working faster and paying less attention to finish and detail. Individual manufacturers oscillated between the two possible solutions to their problems, although the outworkers obviously preferred the attempts to raise quality. Once enough manufacturers started paying in truck, lowering wages and prices, the others were compelled by the pressure of the market to follow. The quality work option was possible only if truck payments were prohibited

---

zwischen Staat und Wirtschaft in der Frühphrase der Industrialisierung (Berlin: Colloquium, 1981), pp. 215–28.

[28] HSTAD RD Nr. 2194 ff. 4–9, 16–22; Nr. 283 ff. 1–6; Pr. Nr. 1462 f. 284.

[29] Boch, Handwerker-Sozialisten, pp. 68–69.

[30] An excellent description of truck payments is in Körner, Lebenskämpfe 1:387–89; similarly, Sigfrid Kuhn, "Der Aufstand der Kleineisenindustriearbeiter im Stadt- und Landkreis Solingen am 16. und 17. März 1848, seine Ursachen und seine Ergebnisse" (Diss. phil., Munich, 1938; partially printed, Solingen: Buchdruckerei B. Boll, 1938), pp. 1–32; HSTAD RD Nr. 2189 ff. 255–57; Nr. 2181 ff. 163, 172–79; Nr. 2194 ff. 16–22, 26–29; Nr. 2152 ff. 21–23, 32–36, 48, 53–56, 61–64; Nr. 1587 f. 107; KnZ, 4, 7 Sept. 1845.

by law, something the Berlin authorities, once again citing freedom of commerce, refused to do.[31]

Frustrated in their negotiations with the authorities, the manufacturers supporting quality work turned to confrontation, utilizing as their vehicle the Solingen manufacturing tribunal. In 1844, the merchant manufacturers Peter Knecht of Dorp and Wilhelm Jellinghaus of Solingen launched a public campaign against the members of the court, accusing them—with good reason—of wasting their time trying to improve apprentices' morality and neglecting the vital issue of the trade: the improvement of quality, to be achieved by prohibiting truck payments and imposing trademarks. The two manufacturers published articles in the area's newspapers, and even carried their agitation into the taverns. The tribunal pressed libel charges against Jellinghaus; his trial and triumphant acquittal made him a highly popular figure among the outworking craftsmen. Early in 1845, Knecht and Jellinghaus led twenty merchant manufacturers to the polling place in Solingen for the tribunal elections, where they voted out the old judges and made Jellinghaus president of the court and Knecht his deputy. The newly organized tribunal scrapped the previous emphasis on moral improvement and started a public campaign to denounce truck payments and to take other measures to improve the quality of production, including the creation of a technical school.[32]

The manufacturer Josua Hasenclever took no part in these efforts, for he had found a different solution to the trade's problems. Half a year before the dramatic tribunal elections, he opened a metalworking factory in Burgthal, outside of Solingen. There, articles of the trade were produced in industrialized fashion, by pouring molten metal into molds, rather than by craft methods of smithying, grinding, and finishing. Although smaller versions of such foundries had existed before, Hasenclever's, employing fifty-six workers, was a substantially larger establishment than had ever been seen in the Bergisches Land. It was so large that everybody in the trade wondered where he had gotten the capital to build it. Rumors, never officially confirmed, but in fact accurate, named the *Seehandlung*, the Prussian State Bank, as the source of his funds.

Hasenclever's foundry raised a storm of controversy in the metalworking district. Feelings ran so high that the authorities feared a mob would gather and destroy the factory. Throughout the Bergisches Land both outworkers and

---

[31] On the connection between low wages/truck payments and poor-quality work, and the need for state action, which Berlin refused to provide, see Boch, *Handwerker-Sozialisten*, p. 91; Kuhn, "Aufstand," pp. 31–32; HSTAD RD Nr. 2194 ff. 8–9, 16–22, 26–39. The Dorp merchant manufacturer Peter Knecht, a leading figure in the opposition to truck payments during the 1840s, had in the previous decade himself attempted to open a company store and pay his workers in truck. HSTAD RD Nr. 2194 ff. 52–65.

[32] HSTAD RD Nr. 2194 ff. 4, 8–9, 26–39, 83–84, 199–201, 213–14, 223–24, 231–32, 248–49 and passim; HSTAD RD Nr. 2175 ff. 36–38; *KnZ*, 3 May, 2–3 Oct. 1845.

merchant manufacturers accused Hasenclever of producing cheap and shoddy goods. His scissors were said to break when they were dropped on the floor, or even grasped too hard. Hasenclever's products, his critics asserted, would force down prices and wages, and ruin once and for all the reputation of the trade in the export market for quality work.

The foundry's enemies did not spare the Prussian state in their criticism, expressing their outrage about the "oppression of the smaller manufacturing establishments by a great financial institution of the state." If the government were to let the foundry continue to exist, then they demanded—supported in this by the local authorities, the district authorities in Düsseldorf, and even the Rhenish provincial governor—that it be prohibited from manufacturing articles in competition with craft production. Were this not possible, they wished to see the products of the factory stamped with the trademark "foundry goods" to distinguish them from quality craft work. The Solingen Chamber of Commerce proposed a slightly more moderate alternative, placing the special distinguishing mark on the craft products, but not on the foundry's wares.[33]

Most historians have viewed this conflict, and the violent events of 1848 that resulted from it, as a clash between the forward march of modern, factory industry (and a farseeing Prussian government, committed to the support of economic modernization), on the one hand, and a group of backward artisans, clinging desperately to their outdated techniques and remnants of the guilds, on the other. A closer examination of the situation shows that none of these assertions is correct. Hasenclever's factory was not a forerunner of industrialization; his opponents, both craftsmen and merchant manufacturerers, were motivated by market considerations; state policy had little to do with modernization or even economics.[34]

The smiths' and grinders' insistence on well-paying quality work had substantial support from the manufacturers, as the 1845 tribunal elections showed. Nor was their orientation toward expensive, quality production archaic traditionalism; it was a perfectly rational market attitude, which still

---

[33] On the factory at Burgthal and the controversy it raised, see LAK 403 Nr. 166 ff. 1–87 (partially printed in *RhBA* 1, Nr. 283); HSTAD RD Pr. Nr. 1463 f. 3; *KnZ*, 18, 25, 28 July, 13 17, Aug., 21 Aug. (Beilage) 1844. The 1845 statutes of the factory's health insurance plan have fifty-six signatures, presumably the number of workers employed there (HSTAD RD Nr. 25097).

[34] Standard interpretations of the Solingen conflict include Hamerow, *Restoration, Revolution, Reaction*, p. 103; Thomas Nipperdey, *Deutsche Geschichte 1800–1860. Bürgerwelt und starker Staat* (Munich: Beck, 1984), p. 218; Hermann-Josef Rupieper, "Die Sozialstruktur der Trägerschichten der Revolution von 1848/49 am Beispiel Sachsens," in Hartmut Kaelble et al., *Probleme der Modernisierung in Deutschland* (Opladen: Westdeutscher Verlag, 1978), pp. 80–109, esp. pp. 99–100; Manfred Gailus, "Soziale Protestbewegungen in Deutschland 1847–1849," in *Sozialer Protest*, pp. 76–106, esp. p. 94; or the textbook version in Peter N. Stearns, *1848: The Revolutionary Tide in Europe* (New York: W. W. Norton, 1974), p. 143. Boch, *Handwerker-Sozialisten*, pp. 89–91, offers an opposing interpretation, which I follow and expand upon here.

characterizes products of the Solingen industry today, as anyone who has shopped for wedding presents can testify. Hasenclever's foundry was not the industrial wave of the future, since the post-1850 industrialization of Solingen manufactures centered on the mechanization of the process of smithying steel knives and scissors and had nothing to do with the founding of cast-iron wares. The foundry is better understood as a mechanized version of the program of producing cheap and shoddy goods, its brittle cast-iron products probably breaking when dropped, as Hasenclever's enemies claimed. Rather than being a technological pioneer, Hasenclever seems to have been engaged in a process common to Third World manufacturers today: producing cut-rate imitations of more expensive work designed to fool consumers into thinking they were getting quality items at discount prices.[35]

Nor were the Prussian state's motives the modernizing ones attributed to it by historians. The *Seehandlung* had a long record of subsidizing industrial enterprises, but all of its projects, except Hasenclever's foundry, were located in East Elbian Prussia. The exceptional use of government money at the western end of the monarchy came from Hasenclever's use of personal connections, acquired through his religious activities. The manufacturer was one of the adherents of the Awakening. In 1827, he met the Prussian crown prince, who shared his evangelical viewpoint, and the two were united in prayer and friendship. When the prince ascended the throne as Friedrich Wilhelm IV in 1840, he gave the state bank direct orders to provide his good friend with anything he wanted, conditions that the pious manufacturer was quick to exploit. The founding capital of the Burgthal factory was 13,000 taler, of which Hasenclever and his partner put up 8,000 and the *Seehandlung* 5,000, but the 50,000 taler cost of building the factory and furnishing it with machines was paid entirely by the state bank.[36]

The *Seehandlung*'s investment was a form of state intervention in an ongoing dispute between merchant manufacturers and outworkers and among merchant manufacturers over the future of the Solingen steel wares trade. To be sure, the state's action was not the result of a conscious industrial policy—unless royal participation in prayer meetings counts as such—but it was just one in a series of measures, along with establishing a prohibitive tariff on imported steel and refusing to register trademarks or prohibit payment in truck, through which Berlin came out in favor of cheap, shoddy production against expensive, quality work. In doing so, the Prussian authorities helped create a pattern of social tensions that would determine the political dynamics of the region during the revolutionary years.

---

[35] On the industrialization of Solingen manufactures after 1850, see Boch, *Handwerker-Sozialisten*, pp. 94–95, 114.

[36] Wolfgang Radtke, *Die Preussische Seehandlung*, pp. 215–28, 370; *Josua Hasenclever aus Remscheid-Ehringhausen. Erinnerungen und Briefe*, ed. Adolf Hasenclever (Halle/Saale: Karras, Kröber & Nietschmann, 1922), pp. 62–68, 71–96; Quandt, "Eduard Colsmann," passim.

Hard Times for the Educated Classes

Since state service made up a large portion of the labor market for university-educated men, it was inevitable that government policies would have a decisive effect on the economic condition of the intelligentsia. The 1830s and 1840s have been regarded, with good reason, as a period when there was a "surplus of educated men" in central Europe, an early phase of a long-term tendency that the sociologist Hartmut Titze has called the "cyclical overproduction of university-trained professionals [Akademiker]" in Germany. While there were substantial university enrollment increases during the 1820s and 1830s, employment in the German state bureaucracies did not expand to match the number of new graduates. Instead, senior state service positions were held constant or cut back, the German states shunning new expenditures that might call for higher taxes and corresponding increases in the power of parliamentary bodies. The unemployed intellectual was an increasingly common figure in *Vormärz* Germany: the unpaid assistant in the judicial or executive bureaucracy [Referendar, Assessor, Accessist], working uncompensated for over a decade in the hope that a tenured civil servant would die and he might get his position; or the journalist and pamphleteer, scratching out a meager living with his frequently censored pen.[37]

The Rhineland was no exception to this, but the peculiar relationship of the Rhenish provinces to the core states affected intellectuals' perceptions of their job market. Educated Rhinelanders were convinced that they were victims of discrimination in state service, government jobs in the west of Germany going to outsiders from the trans-Rhenan provinces. Confessional tensions were mixed into this situation, Rhenish Catholics sure that the Protestant Prussian state was refusing to give them positions in the governnment and Palatine Protestants having similar suspicions about Bavaria.[38]

Statistical studies of provincial state service personnel suggest that these suspicions, if not totally without foundation, were somewhat exaggerated. More important than discrimination against particular groups was the refusal of the German governments to hire anyone, or at least its hiring of far fewer applicants than were willing and eager to take government posts. Even the

---

[37] See the two articles of Leonore O'Boyle, "The Democratic Left in Germany, 1848," *Journal of Modern History* 33 (1961): 374–83; and "The Problem of an Excess of Educated Men in Western Europe 1800–1850," ibid. 42 (1970): 472–95. O'Boyle's pioneering works suffer from a tendency to take at face value the attacks on this group by contemporary conservatives. John Gillis, *The Prussian Bureaucracy in Crisis, 1840–1860* (Stanford: Stanford University Press, 1971), pp. 37–66 and passim; Hartmut Titze, "Die zyklische Überproduktion von Akademikern im 19. u. 20. Jahrhundert," *Geschichte und Gesellschaft* 10 (1984): 92–121; an excellent synthesis of the literature in Wehler, *Deutsche Gesellschaftsgeschichte* 2:210–38, 305–09.

[38] On perceptions of discrimination, see Keinemann, *Das Kölner Ereignis* 1:34–35; LAK 442 Nr. 3926 p. 73; LAK 403 Nr. 18518 pp. 257–59; Weidmann, "Wirtschaftliche Probleme," pp. 31–33; LAS J1 Nr. 215 (alt) ff. 516–21; *MZ* 1 July 1847; Kolb, *Lebenserinnerungen*, p. 95.

most impartial and scrupulous hiring system—and actual practices were far from this ideal—could not have pacified all the rejected job applicants.[39]

One might expect those who could not obtain work with the government to try a career in the private sector, but state policies interfered here as well. In the realm of Rhenish law, freedom of occupation was guaranteed for all trades—except lawyers. The governments of Hessen-Darmstadt and Bavaria introduced into their Rhenish provinces the system prevailing in their core states, which made private attorneys state servants. A small number of law graduates were appointed, with lifetime tenure, to posts at each court; all others could not practice law but had to wait, unpaid, for a position to become open. In Prussia, any university law graduate who had served as an unpaid judicial apprentice [Gerichtsassessor] and passed the state exams could appear in court in criminal cases, as an *Advokat*. Court appearances in the far more lucrative civil suits, as an *Advokat-Anwalt*, were restricted to a few attorneys chosen at the whim of the authorities.[40]

Aspiring lawyers could not look to careers elsewhere in Germany, since the Napoleonic Code, in which they had been trained, was not the basis for the legal system outside of the Rhineland. Prussian proposals to introduce the law code of 1795 into its Rhenish province and abolish the French legal system were a sword of Damocles suspended over the legal profession of the Rhineland throughout the entire *Vormärz*. It is no surprise to find that lawyers were at the head of the movement to defend the use of the Napoleonic Code in the Rhineland and to expand its use to all provinces of the German states.[41]

Journalists also faced state-built barriers to their careers. Newspapers could be founded only with a government concession, which was often withheld for political reasons, but also because the authorities simply felt there was no "need" for another newspaper. All these restrictive measures led to the growth of an "intellectual proletariat," as contemporaries said, although the group possessed as many characteristics of marginal peddlers or small traders as it did of wage laborers. Some worked as hole-and-corner legal advisors

[39] The Prussians seem to have had a better record in regard to integrating Rhinelanders into state service than that of the Bavarians, at least after 1830. Cf. Gillis, *Prussian Bureaucracy*, pp. 35–36; Wehler, *Deutsche Gesellschaftsgeschichte* 2:320; similarly, at a lower level of the administration, LAK 442 Nr. 3926 pp. 77–87, against Haan, "Die bayerische Personalpolitik," passim. On the other hand, the only native Rhinelander to become governor of his province before 1850 was the Palatine Franz Alwens, in 1846. Werner Schindler, "Franz Alwens, Regierungspräsident der Pfalz von 1846–1849," *MHVP* 78 (1980): 415–26.

[40] Wehler, *Deutsche Gesellschaftsgeschichte*, 2:229–30; Heinz-Günther Böse, "Ludwig Simon von Trier (1819–1872). Leben und Anschauungen eines rheinischen Achtundvierzigers" (Diss. phil., Mainz, 1951), p. 6.

[41] *Lebenserinnerungen . . . von Alexander Pagenstecher* 2:75; LAK 403 Nr. 6576 pp. 67–73; ZSTAM Rep. 77 Tit. 343A Nr. 24 ff. 19–22; Dirk Blasius, *Bürgerliche Gesellschaft und Kriminalität. Zur Sozialgeschichte Preußens im Vormärz* (Göttingen: Vandenhoeck & Ruprecht, 1976), p. 126; *KnZ*, 16, 20 Jan. 1840, 9, 11, 14, 16, 21, 29–30 July, 3 Aug. 1841.

[Winkelconsulenten], without the right to practice law or go before a court, specializing in offering advice about dealing with the authorities to those who could not afford a lawyer. Others were notaries' or attorneys' clerks, who thought they could do a better job than their employers—and probably could have. Still others were law graduates, unable to practice; aspirants to government jobs shut out of permanent positions by hiring freezes, working for local authorities in temporary positions; or free-lance journalists who would have preferred a regular editorial or reporting job with a newspaper, if there had been one to employ them. The conditions under which such men (and a few women) lived, made them prime candidates for the post of revolutionary activist, but one must wonder if their difficulties were caused primarily by an oversupply of educated men, or an oversupply of government regulations restricting their ability to make a living.[42]

Prussian Trees and German Oaks: Conflicts over
Use of the Forest

The Rhineland, or to be more precise, the hilly up-country on either side of the river, was one of the most heavily forested areas in central Europe. Some 30 percent of the land area of the Prussian Rhine Province was forest in 1815, against 14 percent in the state as a whole. The 39 percent of Palatine agricultural land in forest at the end of the nineteenth century was the highest figure in all of Germany. Except on the lower Rhine, where forests were smallest in extent, over 80 percent of the woodland was the property either of the state or of rural and urban municipalities. Since the latter forests could be used only under state supervision, the Bavarian and Prussian governments controlled the use of the bulk of the forest land in the most heavily wooded parts of the Rhineland. The policies pursued by the forest authorities, in the context of increasing demand for wood and rising wood prices, brought them into conflict with the upland peasantry. It was the bitterest and most widespread of all conflicts resulting from the interaction between the state and the market in the Vormärz Rhineland.[43]

---

[42] Just a few illustrations of the Vormärz living conditions of this class include LAK 403 Nr. 3806 pp. 11–24, 73–84 and passim; LAK 403 Nr. 2307; "Rheinhessische Justizgebrechen," Der Demokrat [Mainz], 23 July 1848; "Zunftzwang und freie Advokatur," ibid., 13 Aug. 1848 (two evocative descriptions of the miseries of law graduates unable to practice); LAS J1 Nr. 205 ff. 417–30; LAS J1 Nr. 215 (alt) ff. 170–75, 516–21.

[43] Extent of forests: RhG 3:32–33; Müller, "Grundlagen der pfälzischen Landwirtschaft," p. 14. Lying almost entirely in the Rhine Valley, Rhine-Hessen had virtually no forest and imported almost all its wood. Döhn, "Eisenbahnpolitik," pp. 1–2; Hoffmann, Rheinhessische Volkskunde, p. 195. Property relations: Tabellen und amtliche Nachrichten 4:16; LAK 403 Nr. 8558 pp. 9–16, 21–29, 239–50; memorandum, dated Speyer, 9 July 1832, on Palatine forests, BHSTAM MInn Nr. 43887. On state control of the use of village forest, see LAK 403 Nr. 9455 pp. 85–90

Market conditions helped create this conflict. Demand for wood was rising in the first half of the nineteenth century. A growing population needed more firewood and construction timber. The expansion of the output of tanneries and ironworks, two major industrial wood consumers, also increased demand for forest products, especially as Rhenish blast furnaces were entirely charcoal fired before 1850. Although the German customs union as a whole was a net wood importer before mid-century, much of the wood cut in those Rhenish forests within reach of navigable rivers was exported. In face of this demand, supply was threatened, many towns and villages having sold their forests or cut them down to pay off debts contracted during the French revolutionary and Napoleonic wars.[44]

Forest officials took vigorous action to deal with the situation. They built roads into previously impassable areas and expanded cutting, doubling the yearly output of some state forests between the 1820s and 1840s. At the same time, they reforested thousands of acres of wasteland, introducing new species, nondeciduous trees, such as pine and especially spruce, which grew more rapidly than did the native oak and beech. Extra cutting and reforestation were complementary rather than contradictory policies, since nondeciduous trees grow poorly in the shade of others. Bavarian and Prussian foresters followed contemporary forest management theories by cutting down all the oak and beech in an area (the so-called *Lichtschlag*) and planting in their place spruce and pine, a policy known as the "artificial rejuvenation" [künstliche Verjüngung] of the forest. Forestry statistics have been preserved only very incompletely in the archives, but the remaining material shows that five to eight times as many deciduous as nondeciduous trees were cut down, while three to five times more spruce and pine seedlings and saplings than oak and beech were planted.[45]

Having thus secured and increased wood supply, foresters then sought, with substantial success, to turn the wood into a regular supply of cash for the state. Income from forests and other state domains made up about one-quarter of the Bavarian state income during the *Vormärz*, and about one-eighth the revenues of the Prussian state, money that was not under the control of any parliamentary body. One way foresters ensured the regularity of such revenue was to sign long-term contracts with the owners of ironworks, offering these large-

---

(the account in *RhG* 3:218–20 is somewhat garbled); and the previously cited memo on the Palatine forests.

[44] Rubner, *Forstgeschichte*, pp. 117–18; HSTAD RA Pr. Nr. 475 ff. 292–93; HSTAD RA Pr. Nr. 472 f. 143; LAK 403 Nr. 9455 pp. 79–84; LAK 403 Nr. 8558 pp. 9–18, 197–206, 251–56; LAK 442 Nr. 10595 pp. 327–29; LAK 441 Nr. 6042–43; memo on Palatine forests, BHSTAM MInn Nr. 43887.

[45] On forest policy, and general German trends, see Rubner, *Forstgeschichte*, pp. 119–28, 153–54. Figures (admittedly very incomplete) on cuttings and plantings can be found in HSTAD RD Pr. Nr. 1470 ff. 10, 111–12, 192, 256–57; HSTAD RA Pr. Nr. 471 f. 144, RA Pr. Nr. 475 ff. 279–80; LAK 441 Nr. 6054 ff. 590–603.

scale wood consumers up to one-third of forest output at discount prices. Fiscal measures fit nicely into a policy of encouraging industry, since cheap wood helped German ironmasters compete with British iron and steel exports.[46]

While the state profited from this system, it was of dubious benefit to industry. In effect, the authorities were subsidizing the technologically obsolete process of forging pig iron from ore using charcoal, thus discouraging the introduction of coal-fired blast furnaces. State forest policy also stirred up substantial resentment among other wood consumers, whether commercial or subsistence users, who saw no reason why the ironmasters should receive subsidized wood from the authorities while they did not. Even more infuriating was the ironmasters' habit of using the cheap wood the state provided in their forges, and then selling off wood cut on their own property for all the market would bear.[47]

The main victims of this combination of market conditions and state policy were the upland peasants. If they needed to buy wood, they were forced to compete at auctions with tanners, exporters, or ironmasters wanting more than their fixed-price quotas, all of whom had substantially more money than the impoverished farmers. Furthermore, auctions of wood from state-owned forests were regularly held in the spring (woodcutting, hauling, and stacking being wintertime activities), when the peasants had no cash available, rather than in the fall, when they did.[48]

The upland peasants, and the Rhenish lower classes in general, rarely entered the market for wood in any event, relying on their traditional rights [Berechtigungen] to gather branches and fallen wood [Raff- und Leseholz] in state and village forests, or to use these forests to pasture their cattle and feed their pigs. As heath and underbrush were planted in nondeciduous trees, opportunities for pasture declined; as oaks were cut down and replaced with spruce, the pigs had nothing to eat. And as the foresters strove to increase wood sales to provide more money for the treasury, they cast an ever more skeptical eye on peasants' traditional rights, demanding written evidence of their existence (a policy begun by the French revolutionary and Napoleonic authorities) and redefining the amount and size of wood that could be gathered.[49]

---

[46] State revenues from Wehler, *Deutsche Gesellschaftsgeschichte* 2:375–76; on contracts with ironworks, see HSTAD RD Pr. Nr. 1740 ff. 9, 100; LAK 442 Nr. 10596 pp. 55–62, 87–90; LAK 441 Nr. 6051–54, esp. Nr. 6051 pp. 91–130 and Nr. 6054 pp. 155–57.

[47] LAK 403 Nr. 9446 pp. 5–25; LAK 441 Nr. 6050 pp. 123–26, 149–63, 193–97, 201–207; Nr. 6054 p. 349; memo of vintner and wine dealer Sebastian Breuning of Zeltingen, 12 July 1840, LAK 442 Nr. 3441.

[48] LAK 403 Nr. 9446 pp. 5–25; LAK 442 Nr. 10595 pp. 41–43, 434–41; Nr. 10596 pp. 195–97, 199–206; 1832 report on Palatine forests in BHSTAM MInn Nr. 43887.

[49] LAK 403 Nr. 9446 pp. 41–47, 97–100; LAK 441 Nr. 10919 pp. 294–310; RP to MInn, 20 Dec. 1835, BHSTAM MInn Nr. 43888; LAS J1 Nr. 205 f. 478. These examples contradict the contention of B. K. Hasel, "Forstverwaltung und Jagd in der Revolution von 1848 und 1849,"

Throughout the 1820s, 1830s, and 1840s, foresters, on the one hand, and mountain peasants and the rural lower classes, on the other, waged a cold war in the woods. Villagers resisted government forest management policies, refusing to plant the "Prussian tree," as peasants of the Eifel and Hunsrück called the spruce, and fighting to keep their heath, underbrush, and "low forest" [Niederwald]—oak woods cut every fifteen to twenty years, with the bark sold to tanneries—from being replanted with nondeciduous trees. Forestry officials at first tried to "educate" the stubborn peasants, but quickly turned to commands and threats, when they proved unwilling to learn.[50]

Above all, villagers resisted the state by engaging in "wood theft," insisting on exercising their traditional rights to use the forest, not only to obtain wood for subsistence, but also to cash in themselves on rising wood prices, by selling "stolen" wood to exporters, or reducing it to charcoal to sell to ironworks. The number convicted of this crime mounted steadily. It was 37,500 in the Palatinate in 1821–1822, almost 100,000 in 1829–1830, and 141,000 in 1840–1841, rising to a dizzying 185,000 in 1846–1847—this in a province with some 600,000 inhabitants! While the crime rate for wood theft in the Prussian Rhine Province was just one-tenth of what it was in the Palatinate, the difference probably reflected a lesser ability to catch offenders rather than fewer instances of the crime.[51]

Both the forest administration and the criminal justice system proved incapable of mastering the situation. Fines were no deterrent, since many of the thieves had no money to pay them. Jail sentences were even less effective. For the poor, a few weeks in a warmly heated prison, with regular meals, was not without its attractions in the middle of the winter; the prisons soon had no room for all the wood thieves. Setting them to work in the forest repairing the damage they had done seemed like a good idea, only there were so many "criminals" in relation to the supervisory personnel, that such a sentence merely offered them new opportunities to repeat their crimes. Recidivism tri-

ZGO NF 86 (1977): 297–313, that peasants invented complaints of stricter forest policies' impinging on their largely mythical rights.

[50] HSTAD RA Pr. Nr. 477 f.143; LAK 403 Nr. 8558 pp. 197–206; LAK 403 Nr. 9455 pp. 79–90; LAS J1 Nr. 249 (alt) ff. 221–24; Heinz Monz, "Der Waldprozeß der Mark Thalfang als Grundlage für Karl Marx' Kritik an den Debatten um das Holzdiebstahlgesetz," *JhwL* 4 (1977): 395–418.

[51] Bavarian crime statistics in *1832–1982. Hambacher Fest. Freiheit und Einheit. Deutschland und Europa*, ed. Joachim Kermann and Cornelia Foerster (Neustadt a.d.W.: D. Meininger, 1982), pp. 97–99; Prussian crime statistics in Dirk Blasius, *Bürgerliche Gesellschaft und Kriminalität. Zur Sozialgeschichte Preußens im Vormärz* (Göttingen: Vandenhoeck & Ruprecht, 1976), p. 146. A Prussian forester's report shows that for 9,759 instances of wood theft committed in Kreuznach County during the years 1823–1830, there were only 370 arrests. LAK 403 Nr. 9446 p. 6. Examples of the commercial use of traditional wood-gathering rights (a situation with some similarities to the commercial exploitation of sheep-pasturing rights) in RT to MInn, 23 Sept. 1849 (draft), LAK 442 Nr. 4567; LAK 442 Nr. 10595 pp. 41–43; LAK 441 Nr. 10919 pp. 372–83; LAK 441 Nr. 1315 pp. 1–7; reports on wood theft in StdT Tb 15/716.

umphed, so that in Trier and vicinity "one month peasant" [Monatsbauer], became a common phrase. It referred to farmers who, after five convictions for wood theft, received a month in jail.[52]

The situation in the forest near Kleve got so out of hand in 1840, that the army was called in to protect the woods. More commonly, though, the foresters were on their own, and they took out their frustrations over the flouting of their authority on those thieves they could catch. These were usually women and children, whom foresters would beat and then tie up and leave in the forest. The forester Finne, stationed in Trier, who had a reputation for being especially brutal, was shot in June 1845 by two young peasants he caught in the Himmeroth forest, carrying off straw for their farm animals. They were charged with assault, and brought before the Trier Assizes. Their defense attorney, the young lawyer Ludwig Simon—in 1848–1849 a leader of the Trier democrats and the city's deputy to the Frankfurt National Assembly—turned the proceedings into an indictment of the cruelty and inhumanity of the forest personnel. The jury acquitted the defendants to the jubilation of the large crowd of spectators.[53]

Rather like the conflicts in the Solingen steel wares trade, the forest struggle has been portrayed by historians—following, in their accounts, the view of contemporary forestry officials—as a conflict between modernity and tradition. Scientific, enlightened foresters tried to avoid erosion, deforestation, and ecological disaster, while ignorant, backward peasants opposed them, stubbornly insisting on chopping down trees and clearing land for pasture without any understanding of the environmental consequences of their actions. This interpretation is a dubious one, since forestry officials were attempting to introduce a foreign species and make it dominant in a new environment, creating a forest monoculture dominated by nondeciduous trees, designed solely for maximum wood production. In doing so, they were following an ecologically dubious course, since their massive cutting of oaks and beeches and their clearing of the underbrush removed the leaves that were the source of natural fertilizer for the forest.[54]

---

[52] LAK 403 Nr. 9446 pp. 5–25; proposals for ever stricter laws on wood theft, with supporting material, in BHSTAM MInn Nr. 44404; Hans Ziegler, "Das Gefängniswesen in der Pfalz (1800–1862)," *MHVP* 61 (163): 87–144, esp. p. 127; Hermann Stahl, *Die Revolution von 1848/49 an der Mittelmosel* (Bernkastel: Buchdruckerei der Bernkasteler Zeitung, n.d. [1923]), p. 8.

[53] HSTAD RD Pr. Nr. 1470 f. 109; Ziegler, "Gefängniswesen," p. 125; *KnZ*, 22 Dec. 1845, 27 Dec. 1845 (Beilage), 4 Jan. 1846, 6 Jan. 1846 (Beilage). The Trier case, which caused a stir throughout the entire Prussian Rhine Province, rather tells against Dirk Blasius' argument that the Rhenish bourgeoisie clung to the jury system since that way they could issue stricter sentences against wood thieves. Dirk Blasius, "Der Kampf um die Geschworenengerichte im Vormärz," in *Sozialgeschichte Heute Festschrift für Hans Rosenberg zum 70. Geburtstag*, ed. Hans-Ulrich Wehler (Göttingen: Vandenhoeck & Ruprecht, 1974), pp. 148–61; and id., *Bürgerliche Gesellschaft und Kriminalität*, pp. 122–23.

[54] The standard view in Rubner, *Forstgeschichte*, p. 153, and, following him, Nipperdey,

The peasants' insistence on a mixed-use forest with varied vegetation may well have been environmentally sounder, even if the foresters' contention that the peasants engaged in overcutting was true. By 1900, one school of German forestry had caught up with the ignorant peasants of a half-century earlier, denouncing all-spruce forests and calling for a better-balanced combination of deciduous and nondeciduous trees in forest plantings.[55]

Rhenish forest conflict has also obtained a certain canonical status in the history of Marxism, since Karl Marx himself years later saw it as the initial impulse for the development of his social theory. However, the interpretation he provided—a struggle of peasants clinging to subsistence agriculture and precapitalist property rights against the incursion of the capitalist market economy—fits the actual circumstances of *Vormärz* Rhenish society poorly. Peasants were not just stealing wood for subsistence, but for sale in the market to exporters, tanners, ironmasters, and coopers or for use in their own highly commercial winegrowing. Nor was the question of property rights in the forest quite so clear, as a good deal of the conflict concerned the government's attempts to limit the villages' right to dispose freely of the forest property they owned.[56]

The wood market and the resulting conflict over forest use are best understood as particularly blatant examples of the practice of the unfree market economy. State forest policy, stemming from a mixture of fiscality and a misdirected drive to encourage industry, produced more government revenue, profits for the ironmasters, damage to the environment, and economic disadvantages for all other consumers of wood. It particularly threatened the hardpressed upland peasantry's access to the market by reducing grazing land for their animals, and denying them the chance to cut and sell wood. Like the other examples discussed in this section, state intervention in the economy sharpened preexisting market conflicts or helped create new ones. Both kinds

---

Deutsche Geschichte, p. 157; or *RhG* 3:218–20. For opinions of contemporary foresters, cf. HSTAD RA Pr. Nr. 472 f. 143; LAK 403 Nr. 9455 pp. 79–84; memorandum on Palatine forests cited in notes 45 and 49 above; RP to MInn, 20 Dec. 1833, BHSTAM MInn Nr. 43888. An excellent criticism of the standard interpretation (including extensive bibliographical references) and a contrary account, similar to the one provided here, in Joachim Radkau, ''Holzverknappung und Krisenbewußtsein im 18. Jahrhundert,'' *Geschichte und Gesellschaft* 9 (1983): 513–43, esp. p. 517. Contemporary documents, showing that massive plantings of nondeciduous trees after cutting down all the beeches and oaks were not always successful, support this criticism. See forest inspection reports in HSTAD RA Nr. 3578–79 and LAK 442 Nr. 909 ff. 154–60.

[55] Advocates of nondeciduous forests continued to have their spokesmen, and the issue has remained a controversial one in twentieth-century German forestry. Rubner, *Forstgeschichte*, p. 156.

[56] On Marx and wood theft, see Chapter One, note 13. The article by Heinz Monz, ''Der Waldprozeß der Mark Thalfang,'' situates the theory nicely in Marx's personal history, pointing out that his father Heinrich had defended in court a group of peasants striving to maintain collective forest use rights against the Prussian forest authorities.

of conflicts, when politicized, would play a major role in the revolutionary dynamics of 1848–1849.

CONFLICTS OVER RELIGION

Religion shaped social conflict in the *Vormärz* Rhineland no less than did the market. Religious conflicts could be interconfessional in nature, pitting Catholics against Protestants or Christians against Jews. Intraconfessional differences, usually, if not always, involving opposition between adherents of rationalism and neoorthodoxy, were also a major source of conflict. As with market conflicts, state intervention in religious quarrels sharpened existing tensions and also created new ones.

Calvinist Heretics and Papist Idolators

In this period, a pronounced Protestant-Catholic antagonism was a part of everyday life. Ordinary members of each Christian confession thought those of the other at best alien, at worst Calvinist heretics or Papist idolators. These feelings might go along beneath the surface for years, only to be brought out by some spectacular action. Religiously mixed marriages were a constant sticking point, with Protestants accusing Catholics of "intolerance" and "proselytization"—that is, demanding a promise of Catholic upbringing for the children. In a sense, these charges were unfair, since priests regularly consigned to hell any of their flock who even wanted to marry a Protestant, no matter in what religion the children were to be raised. The Corpus Christi procession was a regular source of trouble, most noticeably in Essen in 1845, when a riot broke out after the (false) rumor spread that the Protestants were trying to steal one of the Catholics' sacred flags.[57]

On the middle and upper Rhine, where confessionally mixed villages were common, this hostility became institutionalized. Intemperate quarrels over school and church buildings, or the cemetery, whose physical premises were often shared by Protestants and Catholics, were an accepted fact of life. Increasingly, the villages were split into two feuding "parties," based on the

---

[57] Körner, *Lebenskämpfe* 1:18–21; Schurz, *Lebesnerinnerungen*, p. 51; *Josua Hasenclever . . . Erinnerungen und Briefe*, p. 30; ZSTAM 2.2.1. Nr. 15139 ff. 58–62; Keinemann, *Das Kölner Ereignis* 1:26–71 (various causes and background of intolerant feelings); LAK 403 Nr. 10755 pp. 85–92; ZSTAM Rep. 77 Tit. 505 Nr. 5 Vol. IV ff. 40–46; Noack, "Saargegend," p. 29 (mixed marriages); LAK 403 Nr. 2523 pp. 165–78; LAK 441 Nr. 1363 pp. 129–36; HSTAD RD Pr. Nr. 791 ff. 94–100, 106–17, 141–44 (Corpus Christi disputes in Essen and elsewhere); LAK 403 Nr. 2523 pp. 665–68; ZSTAM Rep. 77 Tit. 505 Nr. 2 Vol. 2 ff. 174–76 (other disputes, sparked by deathbed conversions).

two confessions and reflected in the elections to the village council, public festivities, and even the taverns visited.[58]

Contrasts between Christians and Jews were certainly also present, and outside of such large cities as Cologne, Düsseldorf, or Mainz, Jews tended to be socially isolated from their Christian neighbors. Yet, in comparison to other parts of Germany, acts of anti-Semitic violence were a rarity in the *Vormärz* Rhineland. There were several smaller incidents but only one series of major anti-Semitic riots, occurring in the summer of 1834 in rural areas and small towns on the left bank of the river to the north of Cologne, sparked by charges of usury and rumors that a "Christian girl had been mishandled by a Jew." As unpleasant and substantial as these events were—the government had to send in troops to restore order—they found no sequel before 1848. They were far outnumbered by acts of violence stemming from inter- and intraconfessional conflict among Christians, who seem to have been too busy being hostile to each other to have had a lot of enmity left over for Jews.[59]

Riot and Uproar in the Church

Intraconfessional tensions were often played out to a limited audience, with little public participation, as adherents of rationalism and those of neoorthodoxy maneuvered for positions in cathedral chapters, on consistories, in theological seminaries, or on university theological faculties. Isaak Rust, the neoorthodox senior councillor [erster geistlicher Rat] of the Speyer Consistory from 1833 to 1846, fortified his position in his battle against Palatine rationalism by offering key pastors his daughters' hands in marriage. Such tactics were impossible for Catholic theologians, but a more celibate version might be seen in the banquet militant Koblenz Catholics prepared for the visiting trier bishop Wihelm Arnoldi in 1844. Arnoldi, not a very forceful leader of his diocese, given to balancing between the two religious tendencies, wanted to know where the Catholic rationalists were, especially their leading figure in Koblenz, the pastor Karl Joseph Holzer. Informed they had not been invited, he denounced the banquet as a "factional demonstration," and walked out the

---

[58] Hoffmann, *Rheinhessische Volkskunde*, pp. 105–07; *MZ*, 23 June 1848; LAK 441 Nr. 1322 pp. 75–83; BHSTAM MInn ff. 47–54; LAS J1 Nr. 202 I (alt) ff. 384–87, 390–93; LAS J1 Nr. 205 ff. 454–55; Major Klemens Scheidtel (Mutterstadt) to Armee Corps-Commando (Speyer), 24 Aug., 12 Sept. 1849; petition of Catholics of Oppau to Major General Prince Thurn und Taxis, 21 July, 1849, both in BHSTAM KA Nr. B771.

[59] Examples of Jewish social isolation before 1848, seen by contrast in 1848, LAK 441 Nr. 1329 pp. 515–32; LAS J1 Nr. 200 ff. 101–05. On the 1834 anti-Semitic riots, see ZSTAM Rep. 77 Tit. 505 Nr. 2 Vol. 1 ff. 252–55; Eleonore Sterling, *Judenhaß. Die Anfänge des politischen Antisemitismus in Deutschland (1815–1850)* (Frankfurt: Europäische Verlagsanstalt, 1969), pp. 158, 172. For other incidents, cf. Uhrig, "Worms," p. 15; HSTAD RD Pr. Nr. 790 ff. 207–08. Anti-Semitic riots were much more common in *Vormärz* Baden. Wirtz, *"Widersetzlichkeit, Excesse, Crawalle, Tumulte und Skandale,"* pp. 60–87, 130–45, 232–38.

door. The assembled pious laity and clergy continued their festive meal without its guest of honor, omitting the planned toast to him, but carefully including one to the Pope.[60]

However, there were times when ordinary, lower-class parishioners would mix into these controversies in a less subtle way. If a popular pastor was transferred, they might occupy the church and refuse to let him go, or physically assault his successor. At least among Catholics, these events were usually tied up with the conflict between rationalism and neoorthodoxy, as was the case with the peasants of Kelberg (Adenau County, in the Eifel) in 1832. Their temporary pastor, Heimer, an advocate of "obscuranticism and the introduction and encouragement of processions and other previously abolished practices pleasing to the mob," was passed over for the permanent position in spite of his parishioners' pleas to the bishop. The new, unwanted parish priest compounded lay hostility to him by appearing to celebrate his first mass in a frock coat, the symbol of Catholic clerical rationalism, rather than a cassock. The women of the village assaulted him, one even attempting to brain him with the incense beaker, driving him amidst "screaming, cursing and stamping" into the sacristy. The neoorthodox pastor Stroth in Gey (Düren County, not far from Aachen) met a similar fate when he was severely beaten by a group of his parishioners after getting into a quarrel with them about seating arrangements on Pentecost Sunday in 1838. The leader of the violent laity was the farmer Mathias Braun, brother of the rationalist Catholic theologian Johann Wilhelm Braun, professor in Bonn and thorn in the eye of the neoorthodox.[61]

The prevalence of the presbyterial system for choosing Protestant pastors on the lower Rhine provided another sort of opportunity for popular intervention in intraconfessional quarrels. Disputes over the election of a new pastor could be vociferous but were usually confined to that small minority of the wealthiest members of the congregation eligible to vote. In the Bergisches Land, however, the turbulent and self-assured skilled metalworkers refused to be shut out of church governance. Rather like the lower classes of eighteenth-century England, who were ineligible to vote for Parliament but played a large part in the elections nonetheless, they took part in tavern caucusing for potential pastors and demonstrated in the streets in favor of one or the other candidate. On polling day, they crowded the church, cheering for their favorite,

[60] Scherer, "Zur pfälzischen Kirchengeschichte," pp. 146–50; LAK 441 Nr. 3055 pp. 79–82. In general, on this sort of maneuvering, see the two articles of Scherer, "Zur pfälzischen Kirchengeschichte" and "Zur Geschichte kirchlicher Parteien," and Weber's fine study, *Aufklärung und Orthodoxie*, passim.

[61] Reports on the events in Kelberg, July 1832, in LAK 441 Nr. 6792. Similar, if not always such violent incidents, LAK 403 Nr. 18081 pp. 2–5; and HSTAD RD Nr. 236 ff. 149–50. Events in Gey, LAK 403 Nr. 2523 pp. 95–100. Other popular attacks on neoorthodox or defense of rationalist clergy, ibid., pp. 39–49, 79–82, 123–28.

physically attacking his opponents if he lost, marching in riotous fashion to his home if he won, and demanding payment for their support.[62]

It is not entirely clear if religious differences lay behind these disputes. The authorities denied it, blaming the troubles on personal and local rivalries, condemning quarreling notables for getting the masses incited. Doctrinal controversies did lead to conflicts in the nearby Wuppertal, when the region's strict Calvinists refused to accept the Prussian government's proposed liturgy. A particularly militant wing, led by the Elberfeld bankers Carl and Daniel von der Heydt, was so incensed by the religious authorities' actions that it seceded from the state church. Denouncing the Calvinists who stayed in it as "a cowardly band of traitors" and as "bondsmen of the state," the secessionists formed an independent, sectarian congregation, which renounced infant baptism, and sponsored its own translation of the Bible.[63]

These religious hostilities, however, had no political repercussions. The great Elberfeld Calvinist preacher Gottfried Daniel Krummacher explained that in spite of his opposition to royal authority on religious matters, in worldly affairs he was "His Majesty's most subordinate subject." For all their denunciation of government religious policy, the Wuppertal separatists would be politically the most extreme conservatives and Prussian royal loyalists in the entire Rhineland during the 1848 revolution. In Germany, Calvinist doctrine was in no way a school of democracy, whatever the validity of claims in this regard made by historians of English-speaking countries. But the presbyterial system of church governance associated with Calvinism did serve as a school of riot and disorder, a useful preparation for the turbulent events of 1848–1849, if not a function generally associated with such a strictly disciplined faith.

The sources on intraconfessional conflicts among Jews are not as detailed as those for Christians. Some scattered evidence does suggest that the clashes between adherents of a Reformed Judaism and those of a Jewish religious orthodoxy during the *Vormärz* were not limited to rabbinical disputation or to a narrow circle of intellectuals but included heated public controversy and the single most vehement episode of criticism of a differing point of view. In 1844, the pious Jews of Immendorf (on the right bank of the Rhine, opposite Koblenz) murdered their schoolteacher, Tobias Jacob, a fatally overenthusiastic advocate of religious reform.[64]

---

[62] *Josua Hasenclever . . . Erinnerungen*, pp. 26–27; HSTAD RD Nr. 279 ff. 104–98; HSTAD RD Pr. Nr. 1465 f 260, Nr. 1466 ff. 146–48; ZSTAM Rep. 77 Tit. 505 Nr. 3 Vol. 3 ff. 23–24 (a riot at elections to the presbytery).

[63] Wickelhaus, "Einheit und Freiheit," passim; Wegner, "Elberfeld in den vierziger Jahren," pp. 10–11; Herberts, *Kirche und Handel*, p. 98. Hostile freethinkers implied Carl von der Heydt only discovered his piety after impotence caused by a venereal disease contracted in his youth prevented him from doing any more sinning. Körner, *Lebenskämpfe*, 2:26–27.

[64] LAK 441 Nr. 3035 pp. 73–74. For a more peaceful, but still heated controversy in Mainz, cf. *KnZ*, 18 May 1845.

Religious Conflict and the State

Since the governments of the German states were closely identified with the confession of the ruling princely house, interconfessional conflicts invariably involved relations between church and state. And since these relations were very close, at times painfully so, intraconfessional conflict inevitably brought confrontations between church and state in its wake. This multiple interaction can be seen in the two great religious controversies of the *Vormärz* Rhineland, the Cologne troubles [Kölner Wirren] and the struggle between rationalists and revivalists among Palatine Protestants.

In November 1837 the Prussian government arrested the archbishop of Cologne, Clemens August von Droste-Vischering, for his refusal to endorse the agreement of his predecessor with the Prussian government, sanctioning religiously mixed marriages without requiring a promise of Catholic upbringing for the children. This move was quickly known and discussed everywhere in the province, even in the remotest villages. The Catholic majority of the province's population reacted to the arrest with great hostility. There were riots in various towns over the next several years, and eventually even the stiff-necked, authoritarian Prussian bureaucracy was forced to back down. Negotiations with the Vatican produced a face-saving compromise. Clemens August did not return to his see, but his newly named coadjutor and eventual successor, Johannes von Geissel, was, if more diplomatic, every bit as firm on the mixed-marriage question and church-state relations in general as his predecessor.[65]

The Cologne troubles may seem like a classic confrontation between church and state—what could be a greater interference of the state in church affairs than arresting an archbishop?—but on closer examination, all the other forms of religious conflict were also involved. Clemens August was an enthusiastic supporter of the neoorthodox in his archdiocese, and their rationalist, Hermesian opponents, including a large majority of the canons of the Cologne cathedral chapter, openly endorsed the government's action in arresting him. But by identifying themselves with this violent, illegal measure of the authorities, they allowed the neoorthodox, who were themselves not averse to using connections with the state if it could serve their purposes, to paint them as lackeys of the Protestant government, and traitors to the Catholic cause.[66]

The Cologne troubles were also perceived as an interconfessional conflict, as Protestants oppressing Catholics. When the reserves were mobilized early in 1839, fifteen months after the archbishop's arrest, with no settlement of the

[65] On the event, and its public ramifications, see Keinemann, *Kölner Ereignis*, passim; the diplomatic negotiations ending the affair are discussed by Rudolf Lill, *Die Beilegung der Kölner Wirren 1840–1842* (Düsseldorf: Droste, 1962).

[66] The relationship of the Cologne troubles to internal tensions with the Catholic church is well explained by Weber, *Aufklärung und Orthodoxie*, pp. 79–87.

affair in sight, a group of reservists recalled to Neuss, thirty miles north of Cologne, mutinied, shouting, "The reserves will not march, not against Belgium! There are our brothers, and good Catholics. Down with the Calvinists!" The lower classes of the town joined in the calls, and street disturbances continued all day until suppressed by a contingent of cavalry. The Prussian government's arrest of the archbishop both intensified preexisting tensions between the Christian confessions and was seen to exemplify them.[67]

A similar bundle of tensions appears in the decades-long religious controversy among Palatine Protestants. The central figure on one side was the Speyer consistorial councilor, Isaak Rust. Following a conversion experience in the late 1820s brought on by reading the works of Martin Luther, Rust had renounced the Hegelian rationalism he had previously professed and become an advocate of revivalism. As a church official, Rust placed the University of Heidelberg, with its rationalist Protestant theological faculty, off limits to Palatine theology students and insisted that future pastors attend the University of Erlangen, where they might imbibe the pure milk of neoorthodox Lutheranism. He attempted to revoke the rationalist catechism of the Palatine Union Church, and some of his subordinates were heard denying that such a union of Lutherans and Calvinists was in any way legitimate. Only those clergy who accepted his theological opinions had any expectation of being named to well-paying parishes.

Rust's main opponent was the pastor of Ingenheim, Friedrich Theodor Frantz, who edited a theological monthly entitled *The Dawn of a New Age* [Die Morgenröthe], with the equally enlightened motto "Light, Freedom, Love and Unity in Faith." If this were not enough to show the rationalist sentiments of Frantz and his supporters, he compounded the issue in 1845, by denying in the pages of his magazine the divinity of Jesus, on the good Protestant grounds that there was no reference to it in the Bible. Rust had him suspended from his post for heresy, causing an enormous public uproar.

This theological dispute also contained elements of church-state conflict. Rust and his supporters had been sent to Speyer in 1832, following a purge of the consistory by the Bavarian government, which blamed its members for the enthusiastic support shown by many rationalist Protestant pastors for the near-revolution in the Palatinate that year. Rust's presence was a constant reminder that the Palatine Union Church was ultimtely subordinate to the Protestant Superior Consistory in Munich, staffed by neoorthodox Lutherans. Frantz's supporters combined their rationalism with advocacy of a presbyterial selection of pastors and of the independence of Palatine Protestantism from the conservative Lutherans of trans-Rhenan Bavaria.

Just as in the Cologne troubles, only with all the signs reversed, the Palatine

---

[67] Keinemann, *Kölner Ereignis* 1:184–85; cf., on similar events in Kleve, the following year, ibid. 1:192–98.

rationalists were able to brand their neoorthodox opponents as tools of a Roman Catholic Bavarian government. The mystical-romantic Ludwig I and his conservative prime minster, Carl Abel, supported Rust. They also insisted that Protestant militiamen kneel during the Corpus Christi processions, prohibited the Gustav Adolphus Association, designed to aid small Protestant congregations in predominantly Catholic regions, and even helped to found Catholic monasteries in the Palatinate, where they had not existed since the French Revolution.[68]

Palatine Protestant rationalists promptly launched a campaign to keep the monasteries out of their province, untroubled by their inconsistency in advocating an end to state and consistorial interference with the freedom of religion in the matter of Pastor Franz while denying the same religious freedom to their Roman Catholic fellow provincials. In a similar way, members of the circle of neoorthodox Roman Catholic Munich intellectuals around the Koblenz native Joseph Görres were leading advocates of the arrested archbishop of Cologne. Their pamphlets in his favor were prohibited by the Prussian authorities but nonetheless widely read in the Rhineland. They were celebrated then, and by Catholic historians today, as pioneering ventures in the demand for freedom of religion. Curiously enough, Görres and his friends showed no concern about state policies in Bavaria that limited Protestants' freedom of religion; in fact, they were leading advocates of these policies. Perception of conflicts between church and state as struggles between the Christian confessions was not limited to the peasantry or the urban lower classes, but common among intellectuals and the bourgeoisie as well, testimony to the importance of Protestant-Catholic dualism, and foreshadowing its major role in shaping events during the revolution.[69]

Church, State, and Schoolteachers

A different form of religious conflict involving the role of the state stemmed from the struggles of schoolteachers for social recognition and professional autonomy. Elementary school teaching was not one of the learned professions. The aspiring teacher attended neither secondary school nor a university, but a "teachers' seminary," where the main emphasis of course work was placed on religious songs and Bible stories. Pedagogical theory or instruction in any subject matter beyond what would be needed in the elementary school classroom was banished from the seminary as useless knowledge, just leading teachers to be discontented with their lot.[70]

[68] Scherer, "Zur pfälzischen Kirchengeschichte," passim; Brinkhoff, Kirche der Pfalz, pp. 69–101; Blessing, Staat und Kirche, pp. 107–109; Kolb, Lebenserinnerungen, pp. 94–95.

[69] On Görres and his circle, see the short treatment, with extensive references to the literature, in Handbuch der Bayerischen Geschichte 4/1:195–204. The campaigns of the Palatine Protestant rationalists during the 1840s and their political implications are discussed in Chapter Three.

[70] In general, on conditions of schoolteachers in the first half of the nineteenth century, see

Teachers had quite a bit to be discontented about. They were not state servants and so had neither a fixed salary nor the right to a pension upon retirement. Instead, they were paid by the communities in which they worked, so their income varied greatly from place to place: respectably lower middle class in large cities, often beneath that of a day laborer in impoverished rural areas. Occasional government subsidies to the poorest villages did little to bring salaries up to a decent level. Plans of the Prussian government to meet a teacher shortage in the Rhine Province reveal the low esteem in which the ''profession'' was held: Rather than raise salaries to attract people into teaching, the authorities proposed to revive a practice from the days of Frederick the Great and assign retired NCOs to the schoolhouses.[71]

Probably the most difficult aspect of a teacher's life was his subordination to the clergy. The parish priest or Protestant pastor was local school inspector, ex officio member of the local school board (and usually its dominant figure), and the teacher's supervisor in the latter's capacity as choirmaster, church organist, and sexton. All the Catholic clergy, whatever their theological opinions, were convinced that teachers owed them ''total obedience,'' not just at work, but outside it as well. Priests expected teachers to shun taverns, subscribe to Catholic religious newspapers and magazines, and avoid any interest in progressive pedagogy or in joint work with Protestant schoolmasters. In raising these demands, they could count on the full support of the state authorities, even the Prussian ones who had arrested Cologne's archbishop.[72]

Protestant clerical rationalists were usually more willing to make concessions to teachers' demands for autonomy, but their neoorthodox counterparts were every bit as domineering as Catholic priests. Johann Georg Wagner, director of the Protestant teachers' seminary in Kaiserslautern, and one of Isaak Rust's sons-in-law, told the students that in all his actions he was inspired and driven by the Holy Ghost. Among other measures, the Holy Ghost prompted him to prohibit aspiring teachers from reading any newspapers except Protestant missionary monthlies.[73]

Under these circumstances, it is hardly surprising that anticlericalism spread widely among schoolteachers, leading them into conflict with both church and

---

Anthony J. Lavopa, *Prussian Schoolteachers: Profession and Office, 1763–1848* (Chapel Hill: University of North Carolina Press, 1980); Blessing, *Staat und Kirche*, pp. 63–75; Werner Weidmann, ''Schulbidlung und Lehrerstand in der Pfalz um die Mitte des 19. Jahrhunderts und die 1848/49er Revolution,'' *JbGStLK* 22/23 (1984/85): 269–98.

[71] Besides the sources cited in the previous footnote, see LAK 403 Nr. 10702 pp. 121–71; and *KnZ* 24 Aug. 1844 (Beilage).

[72] HSTAD RD Pr. Nr. 1466 ff. 1–19; LAK 403 Nr. 10605 pp. 93–101, 127–97; LAK 442 Nr. 3927 pp. 1–35; *KnZ*, 30 July 1842 (Beilage), 27 Aug. 1846; *NSZ* 27 Apr., 2 May 1848; similarly, Körner, *Lebenskämpfe*, 1:246–48.

[73] Weidmann, ''Schulbildung und Lehrerstand,'' p. 274; *NSZ*, 2 Apr., 23–24 Apr., 7 May 1848 (Beilage). The vociferously anticlerical *Neue Speyerer Zeitung* frequently opened its pages to attacks by teachers on both Protestant and Catholic clergy. For similar Protestant neoorthodox attitudes in the Wuppertal, cf. *KnZ*, 14 Aug. 1847.

state. Schoolmaster Theodor Wilhelm Imans in Xanten (Geldern County, on the lower Rhine) got into hot water for asserting that the veneration of the Virgin was an invention of monks; the teacher Ziegler in Maikammer (Landau County, in the forward Palatinate) found himself in similar trouble for denying the literal existence of Biblical miracles. Collective action taken by teachers to improve their lot invariably involved a confrontation with the clergy. In 1842, schoolteachers in the Koblenz District of the Prussian Rhine Province, where salaries were particularly dismal, began organizing, illegally, to demand better pay. The activist teacher Weigand from Vallendar went around during the summer vacation seeking out those teachers "who lived in strife with their pastors" to join the effort. Threats by the clerical school inspectors brought the movement to an end.[74]

The logical next step for the teachers was left-wing politics, and the ranks of democratic activists would be swollen by discontented schoolmasters. The most prominent of them was Anton Gladbach of Odenthal (Mülheim County, on the right bank of the Rhine across from Cologne), who was dismissed from teaching in 1847 for his insubordinate attitude toward the parish priest and village mayor. He went to work for the eccentric left-wing noblewoman the Countess Hatzfeld, whose other employees included the future socialist leader Ferdinand Lassalle. During the revolution, Gladbach sat on the extreme left of the Prussian National Assembly in Berlin as the deputy representing Mülheim County. The leader of the left in Eupen (near Aachen, today part of Belgium) during the revolution was the schoolteacher Theoder Hegner, an enthusiast for the progressive pedagogy of Friedrich Diesterweg, who had narrowly escaped dismissal in the 1840s for quarreling with the school inspector and refusing to take the schoolchildren to mass three times weekly at the "mountain chapel" outside the city. Gladbach and Hegner were just two of a small army of teachers whose frustration with their lot made them leftist activists and who helped give democratic politics a strongly rationalist and anticlerical coloring.[75]

MUSICAL CATS AND BROKEN WINDOWS: SYMBOLIC FORMS OF *VORMÄRZ* SOCIAL CONFLICT

Like most Europeans and North Americans in the first half of the nineteenth century, Germans engaged in charivaris, the symbolic public chastisement of individuals who had violated collective moral codes. The central European

---

[74] LAK 403 Nr. 10605 pp. 127–297; LAK 441 Nr. 8119 pp. 30–36 and passim; *NSZ*, 24 May 1848 (Beilage). Religious rationalism and anticlericalism seem to have been prevalent among Jewish schoolteachers as well. Cf. note 67, above, and *NSZ*, 6 July 1848 (Beilage).

[75] Dörte Gernert, *Die Revolution von 1848/49 im Rheinisch-Bergischen (Landkreis Mülheim am Rhein)* (Remscheid: Kierdorf, 1984), pp. 105–11; Theodor Jeuckens, "Die 48er Bewegung in Eupen unter Theoder Hegners Einfluß," *Zeitschrift des Aachener Geschichtsvereins* 64/65 (1951/52): 5–71.

version was known as "cat music" [Katzenmusik], from the high-pitched screaming accompanying the usually nocturnal action. Its standard victims had engaged in sexually dishonorable behavior: prostitutes and the brothels in which they worked, a young woman who had not kept her virginity, or even worse, had lost it with an already married man, a wife cheating on her husband, or a couple whose first child arrived several months before it should have. The participants in the cat music sometimes supplanted their screaming by placing bits of straw in front of the offender's house, or smearing it with manure. More drastically, they might physically assault the victim, sometimes in brutal and violent fashion, or smash the windows of his or her house and even break in and destroy the furniture. For all the open public disorder caused by such affairs, the local authorities rarely intervened, tacitly sanctioning the actions and the moral code they upheld.[76]

This whole procedure has a very nasty ring to it, patriarchal oppression of women never far beneath the surface of the cat music. However, even during the *Vormärz*, the crowd extended its list of dishonorable targets beyond the group of helpless females who had transgressed sexual norms, turning the cat music into a confrontation with the authorities rather than a scene of tacit cooperation with them. Merchants speculating in grain during periods of dearth were targets for window breaking, as were rationalist Catholic priests, who dishonored Catholicism by being too close to Protestants. The most remarkable example of such a symbolic assault on a priest took place in Cologne, about a year after the arrest of the archbishop.

During the Octave of St. Ursula, Pastor Johann Beckers of St. Ursula's parish church, a militantly neoorthodox priest, known for his strong anti-Prussian sentiments, preached a sermon comparing the saint, a native daughter of Cologne who had been martyred for her faith by the heathen Romans along with forty thousand other virgins, to Archbishop Clemens August, martyred for his faith by the Prussians. After hearing his denunciation of "traitors" in Catholic ranks, some of the large crowd rushed out of the church to the house of Dean Filz of the Cathedral Chapter, a leading Hermesian and open enemy of the arrested archbishop. Shouting, "Filz must hang, hurrah!", they

---

[76] In general, on charivaris, cf. Edward Shorter, *The Making of the Modern Family* (New York: Basic Books, 1975), pp. 218–27. In Germany, such events have usually been studied by folklorists. Cf., for instance, Martin Scharfe, "Zum Rügebrauch," *Hessische Blätter für Volkskunde* 61 (1970): 45–68; or, more historically oriented, Carola Lipp, "Katzenmusiken, Krawalle und 'Weiberrevolution': Frauen im politischen Protest der Revolutionsjahre," in *Schimpfende Weiber und patriotische Jungfrauen. Frauen im Vormärz und in der Revolution 1848/49*, ed. Carola Lipp (Moos and Baden-Baden: Elster, 1980), pp. 112–30. Examples of Rhenish cat music, with revealing accounts of official inaction, can be found in HSTAD RD Pr. Nr. 794 f. 251; HSTAD RD Nr. 236 ff. 149–50; HSTAD RK Nr. 62 f. 43 (here, the police did intervene); HSTAD RK Nr. 63 ff. 39–44, 112–37; LAK 403 Nr. 10605 pp. 1–126; LAK 441 Nr. 1310 pp. 113–16. All these accounts support Shorter's contention that German charivaris were unusually violent and ill natured.

smashed windows and doors, and as the terrified dean fled out the rear of his house, they broke in and were busy destroying furniture when troops arrived. The soldiers dispersed the crowd and arrested thirty-five of them, mostly youthful journeymen artisans, with a sprinkling of master craftsmen and day laborers.[77]

For all the physical violence in this, and other such events, the main thrust of the movement remained symbolic, to mark the victim of the action as a traitor, a violator of moral codes, a dishonorable person deserving of public shame. As long as the rioters and the authorities agreed, at least tacitly, that the victim deserved this rebuke, the cat music and its violent extensions tended to uphold the existing social order and the values underlying it. The people's notions of dishonorable behavior did not always coincide with those of the authorities or the upper classes. In these cases, the cat music could become a vehicle for social conflict, one that could be easily politicized, as it would be in the course of the revolution.

THE PRESERVATION OF PUBLIC ORDER DURING THE *VORMÄRZ*

Any consideration of riot and disorder leads naturally to the question of how they could be suppressed, how public order could be preserved. In the *Vormärz* Rhineland this was no easy task, basically because there was no one to do the job. The day-to-day preservation of public order was the responsibility of the gendarmerie, the paramilitary state police. Their ranks were ludicrously thin, with only 76 gendarmes stationed in the Düsseldorf District of the Prussian Rhine Province in 1848, one for every 14,000 inhabitants of this densely populated, urbanized, industrialized area. Nor was this handful of policemen always available for riot work, since much of their time was taken up with such legal duties as guarding the sessions of the Assizes or transporting prisoners to and from court. The Palatinate was somewhat more heavily policed, this largely rural but thickly populated province possessing 188 gendarmes in 1849, or one for every 3,200 inhabitants, still not a very impressive figure.[78]

To be sure, the larger cities possessed their own municipal police forces, but these were of dubious value. A chorus of complaints trailed them through the *Vormärz*, condemning the men as drunken, senile, or cowardly and their officers as disorganized, lazy, and incompetent. Even if the municipal police

---

[77] ZSTAM 2.2.1 Nr. 15125 ff. 5–46; HSTAD RK Nr. 62 ff. 15–24; Friedrich Keinemann, "Die Unruhen bei Feier des Ursulafestes 1838 in Köln," *AHVN* 174 (1972): 138–47. Similar disturbances directed against grain speculators in Koblenz, 1847, LAK 441 Nr. 3035 pp. 143–48; against rationalist clergy, HSTAD RD Nr. 236 ff. 149–50.

[78] Hauptmann der 8. Gendarmerie Brigade (Düsseldorf) to RD, 22 May 1848, HSTAD RD Nr. 89; Gendarmerie Hauptmann Sturz (Speyer) to König. Corps Commando der Pfalz (Speyer), 25 June 1849 (copy), BHSTAM MInn Nr. 45532.

had been younger, soberer, smarter, and more energetic and courageous, they could not have done much to counteract a serious breach of public order since there were so few of them, generally one for every three or four thousand town dwellers.[79]

The authorities could have called for volunteers, handing out weapons to reliable—that usually meant propertied—citizens in the event of major disturbances. On occasion, such civic guards were formed, most dramatically in Aachen during the mass rioting of the workers there in 1830. In general, though, the authorities were reluctant to put weapons into the hands of the Rhenish citizenry. The civic guard of Aachen remained virtually alone in the Prussian Rhine Province before 1848. While trans-Rhenan Bavaria possessed, in the militia [Landwehr], a kind of standing urban civic guard, the authorities never introduced it into the Palatinate, ostensibly because the French administrative system there made no legal distinction between town and country, in fact, because the Bavarian government did not trust its Rhenish subjects.[80]

When disturbances did occur, the main response of the authorities was a symbolic one. A high-ranking official—judge, mayor, county commissioner, even sometimes district governor—would "betake himself to the scene" [sich an Ort und Stelle begeben], as the action was invariably described, and show himself to the unruly crowd, express his concern, the personification of the monarch's care for his subjects, explain the situation to them, and appeal to them to disperse peacefully and go home. In a remarkable display of social deference, the crowd often did just that.[81]

This willingness to defer to the authorities was not always present, or the crowd was sometimes too big and too noisy to hear the officials' pleas for calm. The authorities could and occasionally did try to use police or gendarmes to disperse the rioters by force, which might work, but more often risked a humiliating defeat of the undermanned forces of order. In the end, there was nothing to do but call for troops. Since none of the German states

---

[79] HSTAD RK Nr. 62 ff. 84–85, Nr. 63 ff. 100–02 LAK 403 Nr. 122 pp. 65–73, 97–152; Alf Lüdtke, *"Gemeinwohl," Polizei und "Festungspraxis." Staatliche Gewaltsamkeit und innere Verwaltung in Preußen, 1815–1850* (Göttingen: Vandenhoeck & Ruprecht, 1982), pp. 149–59, 358–59. Lüdtke's imaginative study is by far the best work on the preservation of public order in nineteenth century Germany.

[80] Lüdtke, *"Gemeinwohl," Polizei und "Festungspraxis,"* p. 290; BHSTAM MInn Nr. 30676, 44615; LAS H1 Nr. 1752. Unlike its Prussian counterpart, which was a self-administered division of the army reserve, the Bavarian militia was designed primarily for the preservation of internal order.

[81] Cf. Lüdtke, *"Gemeinwohl," "Polizei und Festungspraxis,"* p. 285; examples of officials going to the scene include RT to MInn, 31 May and 6 June 1837, LAK 442 Nr. 3441; HSTAD RD Nr. 214 f. 96; LAK 403 Nr. 2523 pp. 13–36, 39–48, 95–100, 123–28, 57–63, 131–50, 165–78, 171–206, 233–39, 665–68; LAK 403 Nr. 18081 pp. 153–56 (personal intervention of the Düsseldorf District Governor); ZSTAM 2.2.1. Nr. 15215 ff. 5–6 (ditto Cologne District Governor), 58–62.

was at war during the *Vormärz*, internal police work was the only occasion for their armies to fire a shot, or use their bayonets or rifle butts in anger. This use of the armed forces ranged from the massive pacification campaign carried out when one-half the entire Bavarian army was stationed in the Palatinate following the near-revolution of 1832, to confrontations with smugglers or wood thieves, to suppression of smaller riots and street disturbances—what would have been police work, had there been any police capable of doing it.

Calling out the army to quell disorder had the potential to increase it. The troops garrisoned in the three Rhenish provinces got along poorly with the locals. In part, religious and cultural differences between the soldiers of the trans-Rhenan provinces and the Rhinelanders led to hostility. Economic problems also arose, as the poorly paid soldiers worked at various trades during their off-duty time, driving down wages in urban labor markets. The single most important factor, however, seems to have been that traditional cause of tensions in civilian-military relations, namely, women. Brawls between soldiers and civilians over differences of opinion about female company, occurring in bars, at dances, or at fairs, were a constant feature of life in garrison towns.[82]

In and of themselves, these brawls were relatively minor, if one-sided, events—the soldiers involved in them being given to using, in most unsportsmanlike fashion, their sabers, which they were required to carry, even when off duty. When the military was called out to preserve public order, the soldiers seem to have regarded this activity as a continuation of their private quarrels, and taken the occasion to attack civilians in a particularly brutal and unconstrained fashion. The events occurring around the parish fair of Big St. Martin's Church in Cologne in 1846 went from a minor incident to a major cause célèbre and important precursor of the revolution because the Prussian army units called on to quiet an unruly crowd, after the outnumbered police were unable to do so, went totally wild, pursuing innocent bystanders for blocks, clubbing and bayoneting everyone they could catch. Several weeks previously, a number of the soldiers had been involved in a large-scale brawl, stemming from a quarrel with civilians over women, at the parish fair of Little

---

[82] Examples of brawls, or more serious disturbances arising from military-civilian quarrels, include HSTAD RD Pr. Nr. 790 ff. 214–22, 232–41; HSTAD RA Nr. 234 ff. 6–17; HSTAD RK Nr. 62 ff. 26, 29–31; 39–40, 131–32; LAK 403 Nr. 2523 pp. 703–707; LAK 403 Nr. 18081 pp. 7–10; LAK 442 Nr. 6545 pp. 1–90; LAK 441 Nr. 3055 pp. 109–11; LAK 441 Nr. 17289 ff. 1–4; Oberbürgermeister Koblenz to RKO, 26 June 1839, 25 July 1842; Gouvernment von Koblenz und Ehrenbreitstein to RKO, 2 Mar. 1846, all in LAK 441 Nr. 17274; ZSTAM Rep. 77 Tit. 505 Nr. 2 Vol. 1 ff. 116–17, 272; *KnZ*, 15, 28 Sept. 1841, 9 June 1846, 7 Jan. 1847; Lüdtke, *"Gemeinwohl," Polizei und "Festungspraxis,"* pp. 297–98; Hubert Freilinger, " 'Die Hambacher' Beteiligte und Sympathisanten der Beinahe-Revolution von 1832," *Zeitschrift für bayerische landesgeschichte* 41 (1978): 701–37, esp. pp. 730–32. On economic causes of civilian-military tensions, see Oberbürgermeister Aachen to RA, 15 Feb. 1849 (plus attached), Stadtarchiv Aachen OB Reg. 125/15; HSTAD RD Nr. 8804 ff. 6–10.

St. Martin's Church. Police were unable to stop the brawl, and eventually the commanding general of the Cologne fortress had to come out and personally order the soldiers back to barracks, but not before one of them shouted, "We carried a coffin away from last year's parish fair; we'll do it again this year." They would have the opportunity to do so, with their officers' approval, six weeks later.[83]

Any disturbance of public order in the *Vormärz* Rhineland put the authorities in an extremely awkward situation. The ordinary forces of repression were usually inadequate and if an appeal to deference failed to calm the situation, then there remained only the choice between acquiesence and escalation. In a society riven by social and confessional conflict, where popular acceptance of the legitimacy of the rule of the existing states was at best partial and at worst nonexistent, this lack of a reliable means of repression implied a constant potential for serious political trouble. Whether this potential would be realized, whether all the sources of social conflict could be welded together to overthrow the existing regimes, or whether they would just produce numerous but isolated incidents, depended on the ability of politically conscious actors to mobilize and channel existing popular discontent.

[83] HSTAD RK Nr. 63 ff. 12–14, 17–22, 32. On the riots at the Big St. Martin's parish fair, see Chapter Three. Lüdtke's discussion of the use of soldiers to preserve public order, in *"Gemeinwohl," Polizei und "Festungspraxis,"* pp. 238–322, neglects this element of private vendetta.

Popular Politics during the *Vormärz*

Even Prussia, the most authoritarian of the three core states to which the Rhineland belonged, allowed a certain degree of political organization and expression of political dissent. The limits of political life varied from time to time, and from government to government, but in general they can be described by three sets of restrictions. Political organization might be tolerated, provided it was informal in nature and local in scope; political agitation was sometimes allowed, provided it was addressed to a limited and upper-class audience; political dissent was permitted, provided it was moderate in form and expressed with the consent of the authorities.

Within these constraints, political tendencies, even nascent forms of radical politics, could appear. However, no matter how left wing the content of any political tendency was, as long as it remained within the boundaries of officially permitted political expression, it would never be a mass movement, which meant that it could never be effective as political radicalism. At different times during the *Vormärz*, political life would break through the offical limitations surrounding it and become, however briefly, and to however limited an extent, a mass politics. Repression invariably followed these incidents, but not before they revealed the depth of social and political tensions, mobilized segments of the population for political action, and provided a cadre of potential future activists with training in mass political leadership.

FORMS OF *VORMÄRZ* POLITICAL ORGANIZATION

Informal Organization: The Circle

Since political associations were prohibited, and the authorities looked with disfavor on organized election campaigns, the politically like-minded gathered in loosely knit conversation circles. These circles might be based on a social club, such as "Harmony" [Eintracht] in Kaiserslautern, founded by newspaper editor Nikolaus Schmitt. The club's members included many young clerks of the city, who would support Schmitt in 1848–1849, when he sat on the extreme left of the Frankfurt National Assembly as Kaiserslautern's deputy and led the republican element in Palatine politics. Germans are well known for their love of formal organization, but even they need no statutes to eat and drink together. During the 1840s, the Cologne rentier Franz Raveaux, already recognized as leader of the city's democrats, would join his friends each afternoon, at Romberg's coffeehouse. Waking up from their heavy midday dinner, they would also discuss political issues or take up a collection for the exiled left-wing writer Karl Heinzen.[1]

These circles might be formed by a group of younger men gathered around a mentor, like Schmitt's circle in Kaiserslautern. In a similar way, a group of Trier Gymnasium alumni, including the future radical leader Ludwig Simon, formed a "young German circle" [jung deutsches Kränzchen], meeting regularly with their former principal, Wyttenbach, who in his youth had been one of the German Jacobins. On the other hand, no older figure was involved in the group of procommunist Prussian artillery officers who met while serving in the fortress of Wesel, on the lower Rhine, and several years later in Cologne, as civilians, after their political views had made it impossible for them to serve in the armed forces.[2]

All the above are examples of informal gatherings of leftists, but the circle as an organizational form was not limited to them. The members of the Elberfeld social club "Frugality" [Genügsamkeit] formed the basis for the center-right, constitutional monarchist association in the city during the revolution. In Koblenz, militant, anti-Prussian, neoorthodox Catholic clergy and laity met in various informal settings during the *Vormärz*, finally forming a Rosary Brotherhood, which provided an organizational backbone for their activities and a starting point for Catholic politics there in 1848.[3]

One basis for membership in these informal groups, contemporaries often noted, was family relations. An angry East Elbian Protestant described neoorthodox Rhenish Catholics as "all related, or related by marriage, creditor and debtor, patron and client." Just the same could be said of the Protestant Palatine rationalists, both clergy and laity, who supported the embattled Pastor Franz.[4]

The importance of family ties for these informal groupings provided a po-

---

[1] LAS J1 Nr. 205 ff. 287–89; LAK 403 Nr. 2545 pp. 99–100. For similar examples in Elberfeld and Worms, see Körner, *Lebenskämpfe* 1:257–58; LAS H1 Nr. 595 ff. 12–14.

[2] Böse, "Ludwig Simon," pp. 12–13; Wilhelm Schulte, "Fritz Anneke geb. 1818 Dortmund-gest. 1872 Chicago. Ein Leben für die Freiheit in Deutschland und in den USA," *Beiträge zur Geschichte Dortmunds und der Grafschaft Mark* 57 (1960): 7–100, esp. pp. 11–13; Walter Kühn, *Der junge Hermann Becker. Ein Quellenbeitrag zur Geschichte der Arbeiterbewegung in Rheinpreußen* (Dortmund: Max Thomas, 1934), pp. 34–45.

[3] Eberhard Illner, *Bürgerliche Organisierung in Elberfeld 1775–1850* (Nuestadt a.d. Aisch: Ph.C.W. Schmidt, 1982), p. 156; Weber, *Aufklärung und Orthodoxie*, pp. 28–29, 103–12. (Ibid., pp. 28–58, has interesting general remarks on the circle and *Vormärz* religious life.) A similar circle of militant Catholics also existed in Cologne. ZSTAM Rep. 77 Tit. 505 Nr. 2 Vol. 2 ff. 228–29.

[4] ZSTAM Rep. 77 Tit. 864 Nr. 7 Bd. I ff. 53–64; Scherer, "Zur pfälzischen Kirchengeschichte," pp. 150–53.

litical role for women, at a time when they otherwise had few opportunities for political activity. As the communist Prussian artillery officers were forced, one by one, to leave the military, they remained in contact with one another largely through the journalist Mathilde Franziska Gieseler. She married one of them, the lieutenant Fritz Anneke, and created a communist salon in their house in Cologne. Particularly in the southern Rhineland, the children of German Jacobin activists of the 1790s often married one another and continued their parents' political radicalism, a tradition carried on by the Jacobins' daughters, as well as by their sons.[5]

As vehicles for political activity, rather than just political discussion, circles had their limitations. They tended to be local creations and were not very effective at expanding into areas where they did not previously exist. Only occasionally did like-minded circles in different towns or cities become linked up, and connections across provincial boundaries, even within the Rhineland, were unknown. Membership, usually limited to self-selected insiders, worked against this, as it did against the circles' becoming mass organizations, even if the authorities had permitted them to. Circles could become politically effective only if their members were active in other, ostensibly nonpolitical organizations.

Gymnasts and Sharpshooters

Paramilitary organizations were well suited to *Vormärz* political activism, and the martial habits cultivated in such associations would strongly influence the political style of the democrats during the 1848 revolution and help shape their vision of an armed citizenry. German gymnastics of the first half of the nineteenth century had a noticeably military air, characterized by close order drill and unison movement, not the later floor exercises or apparatus work. Gymnastics developed in a martial context, as a movement of opposition to Napoleonic rule in Germany, before and during the Wars of Liberation in 1813–1815. Ideologically, the early gymnastics movement was a very mixed affair, combining populist, even democratic, sentiment with hostility to the egalitarian ideals of the French Revolution and glorification of the Prussian monarchy, nationalist enthusiasm with xenophobia and anti-Semitism. In any event, it seemed altogether too active and threatening to the Austrian chancellor Metternich and other architects of the Restoration, who suppressed the movement and prohibited the gymnastics societies.[6]

---

[5] Schulte, "Fritz Anneke," pp. 16–24. The issue of the continuity of the revolutionary movement in the Rhineland between 1793 and 1848 is a controversial one, but Helmut Haasis, in *Morgenröte der Republik. Die linksrheinischen deutschen Demokraten 1789–1849* (Frankfurt, West Berlin, Vienna: Ullstein, 1984) pp. 205–35, provides a whole series of left-wing family histories.

[6] On the development of organized gymnastics in Germany, see the excellent study of Dieter

Such groups reemerged in the 1840s, but the movement had undergone considerable changes in the intervening decades. In contrast to the 1810s and 1820s, when the associations were found primarily in Prussia's eastern provinces and Mecklenburg, the later groups existed primarily in southwest Germany: Baden, Württemberg, and the Rhine-Main region, from Darmstadt through Frankfurt and Hanau to Mainz. Membership in the gymnastic societies encompassed different social groups. The formerly dominant secondary school and university students now took a back seat to craftsmen and clerks, as well as a growing number of older members, local notables who did not themselves do the actual gymnastics—and hence were known as "jawbone gymnasts" [Maulturner]—but supported the ideals of the movement. The south German gymnasts of the 1840s were much more explicitly left wing than their predecessors, openly democratic and republican, socially egalitarian, rejecting both hostility to France and anti-Semitism. During their workouts, and especially afterwards, drinking in the taverns, or at their banquets and festivals, the gymnasts openly espoused their revolutionary ideas.

In the mid-1840s, the gymnastics movement found its way west across the Rhine. An association in Mainz had avoided the prohibitions of the 1820s, but led a shadow existence until 1842, when it was revived and grew until it counted 243 members in 1847. A second group in Rhine-Hessen was founded in Worms in 1845, and in six smaller towns over the two following years. The gymnasts of Rhine-Hessen were strongly left wing. At their 1847 festival in Bingen, they passed a resolution praising the radical Badenese parliamentary deputy Gustav von Struve as a "man of the deed, fighting unceasingly for Germany's liberation from tyranny and servitude," expressed their support for the victorious radical side in the Swiss Civil War, and called out pereats to Prince Metternich and the king of Prussia.[7]

From this point, it was a short step to revolutionary activity and 46 of the 243 individuals on the June 1847 membership list of the Mainz gymnastics society were members of the democratic club there a year later. During the revolution, the Mainz gymnasts helped spread their movement throughout the province of Rhine-Hessen, all the while cooperating closely with the democrats. The gymnasts of the province would play a leading role in the insurrection of May–June 1849.[8]

Düding, *Organisierter Gesellschaftlicher Nationalismus in Deutschland (1808–1847)* (Munich: Oldenbourg, 1984). The paranoid fear shown by the Prussian authorities to anything connected with it, even secondary school physical education classes, is documented in LAK 403 Nr. 7056 pp. 63–64, 69.

[7] On gymnastics in Rhine-Hessen, see Harald Braun, *Geschichte des Turnens in Rheinhessen. Band 1: 1811 bis 1850*, 3 vols. (Alzey: Verlag der Rheinhessischen Druckwerstätte Alzey, 1986–), 1:24–48; for a report on the Bingen festival, see BAF Fn 7 Anhang 4 Gagern ff. 36–39, 45–48.

[8] The membership list of the gymnastics society is in BAF Fn 7 Anhang 4 Gagern ff. 57–59;

The mid-1840s also saw the founding of a number of gymnastics societies in the Palatinate: Frankenthal, Kaiserslautern, Kirchheimbolanden, Neustadt a.d.W., and Speyer in 1846, Zweibrücken in 1847. A whole series of future democratic activists were founding members, among them the Speyer notary Martin Reichard, in 1848, Speyer's representative to the Frankfurt National Assembly, where he sat on the extreme left, and in May–June 1849, head of the provisional revolutionary government of the Palatinate. Rank-and-file gymnasts were also democratic activists. About a third of the organized Kaiserslautern gymnasts in 1846 belonged to the "People's Association" [Volksverein] there two years later, suggestive of the large role Palatine gymnastic societies would play in the revolutionary events.[9]

Gymnastics societies were also founded in the Prussian Rhine Province in the mid-1840s, primarily in the more urbanized areas of the lower Rhine. The largest group was in Elberfeld, with some 250 members by the middle of 1847. It was also the most conservative. Just a few months before the Mainz gymnasts were calling for the king of Prussia to perish, their Elberfeld counterparts were listening to a speaker at a banquet in the neighboring city of Barmen tell them to have "[c]onfidence in our king, the free-thinking protector of all that is beautiful and noble." Although "freethinking" [freisinnig] was a highly implausible way to describe the political ideals of mystical, medievally minded Friedrich Wilhelm IV, its use suggested the political orientation of the gymnasts in 1848–1849. Not only did they oppose revolutionary movements in the Wuppertal; they also provided leadership for that branch of the national German gymnastics movement (the so-called "Elberfeld tendency") that opposed left-wing political activity.[10]

While other gymnastics societies in Aachen, Rheydt, and Barmen shared the conservative outlook of their Elberfeld comrades, there was a left-wing minority among the lower Rhine gymnasts. The anticlerical schoolteacher Theoder Hegener was active in the Eupen gymnastics association and encouraged a more radical orientation there. A number of local leftists were involved with the Cologne gymnastics society, but when that group could look up from its constant quarrels over internal organization, most of which seem to have had little to do with politics, it supported neither conservative nor democratic ideas.[11]

---

the membership list of the democratic club, a printed pamphlet, "Namens-Verzeichniß der Mitglieder des Demokratischen Vereins in Mainz. Im August 1848," is in the Stadtbibliothek Mainz.

[9] On the Palatine gymnastics societies, see LAS H3 Nr. 158 passim; the Kaiserslautern membership list, ibid., f. 13. Membership list of the people's association there, LAS J1 Nr. 244 ff. 42–45. The presence of Jewish names on the membership lists of gymnastics societies in the southern Rhineland is a further proof that the movement had abandoned its earlier anti-Semitism.

[10] LAK 403 Nr. 7056 pp. 412–13; Illner, *Bürgerliche Organisierung in Elberfeld*, pp. 109–14.

[11] HSTAD RA Pr. Nr. 697 ff. 11–14; RD Pr. Nr. 859 ff. 24–25, 44–48, 71–72; LAK 403 Nr. 7056 pp. 477–79; Marcel Seypel, "Die Demokratische Gesellschaft in Köln während der Revolution von 1848/49," (Diss. phil., Cologne, 1988) pp. 236–45.

The leading advocate of gymnastic radicalism on the lower Rhine was the free-lance languages teacher Caspar Immandt of Krefeld. The very epitome of an underemployed *Vormärz* intellectual, Immandt had turned to teaching gymnastics as a way of supplementing his income, and brought his politics with him to work. He and his followers eliminated balloting on new members of the Krefeld gymnastics society in 1847, changing the group from a private club to an open democratic organization. That same year, Immandt extended his operations to Düsseldorf, taking over the gymastics society there and putting it on a radical course. He also founded a monthly gymnastics magazine, the *Rheinische Turnhalle* [The Rhenish Gymnasium], which reported on gymnastics festivals, called for an extension of gymnastics to the "poorer classes" through the creation of free municipal gymnasiums, and suggested joining a gymnastics society could help artisans in their fight against capitalism. Immandt went on to be a prominent democratic activist in 1848–1849, along with his brother Peter, who played a similar role among the gymnasts and democrats of Trier.[12]

For all Caspar Immandt's efforts, most lower Rhine gymnasts remained politically more conservative, both during the *Vormärz* and in the years of the revolution. This is in strong contrast to the situation on the middle and upper Rhine, where gymnastics societies were a bulwark of the left, often of the extreme left. It is not the only occasion we will have to observe this difference between a politically more conservative northern part of the Rhineland and a more left-wing south.

Sharpshooting had quite different antecedents from those of gymnastics, sharpshooting societies originating in medieval religious brotherhoods cum municipal or village militias. It was a far more widespread pastime than gymnastics in the first half of the nineteenth century, especially prevalent in rural areas where possession of firearms was fairly common. Members of sharpshooters' associations in larger cities tended to be more affluent, as they had to pay for rifles, ammunition, and the sharpshooters' elaborate uniform.[13]

Vormärz sharpshooters were thus generally less interested in politics than gymnasts, and when they were, tended more toward the conservative side. There were occasional exceptions, the most important being in Düsseldorf, where a reorganization of the sharpshooters' society in 1846 brought it under the control of a circle of leftists, led by the merchant Lorenz Cantador. The leftists greatly expanded the yearly sharpshooters' festival and gave it a dis-

[12] On Caspar Immandt, see Gottfried Buschbell, "Joh. Anton Caspar Immandt. Begründer des ersten Krefelder Turnvereins, Deutschkatholik und Revolutionär von 1848," *Die Heimat* 19 (1940): 39–52; copies of his magazine, which contain information about his activities in Krefeld and Düsseldorf, can be found in LAK 403 Nr. 7056 pp. 320–447; cf. also HSTAD RD Pr. Nr. 859 ff. 26–27. On Hegener and the Eupen gymnasts, see HSTAD RA Pr. Nr. 697 ff. 5–6.

[13] On sharpshooting, see Sperber, *Popular Catholicism*, pp. 33–35; LAS H3 Nr. 171, esp. f. 117.

tinctly oppositional and nationalist flavor, to the point where the authorities threatened to prohibit it in 1847, if politics were not kept out. Cantador would go on to use his position as president of the sharpshooters' society to have himself elected commander of the Düsseldorf civic guard during the revolution, and would lead the guard into confrontation with the Prussian authorities during the tax boycott crisis of November 1848.[14]

Carnival: The Politics of Fools

The months between New Year and Lent, especially the week before Ash Wednesday, are carnival time in the Rhineland. This "season of fools" [die Narrenzeit], is celebrated with costume balls, comic skits, public masquerades, elaborate parades on the Monday before Ash Wednesday, and a most un-German atmosphere of chaos and disorder. Since the disorder could go beyond harmless fun—in Cologne, for instance, crowds would mock and insult Prussian soldiers—the first Rhenish carnival societies, founded during the 1820s and 1830s by notables of the larger cities, organized elaborate parades to direct popular street celebrations into more orderly channels. A high admission fee to the private "sessions" of the societies, at which members performed satirical skits, reserved these for an elite audience.[15]

Prussian officials, most prominently King Friedrich Wilhelm III, initially regarded carnival with enormous mistrust, their feelings fed by a fear of any sort of disorder, Protestant hostility toward having fun, or a generalized mistrust of the Rhinelanders. Some never overcame this attitude and continued to harass celebrants throughout the Vormärz, but a majority, like their counterparts in Rhine-Hessen and the Palatinate, soon came to appreciate the work done by the carnival societies in preserving public order. Even the commanding general of the Cologne fortress put on the fool's cap and joined in the festivities, as clear a sign of their political harmlessness as one could wish.[16]

At the same time the gymnastics societies were being revived, a new spirit began to appear in the celebration of carnival. A group of dissidents seceded from the Cologne carnival society in 1842, declaring that "the republican carnival constitution" was the only one "under which true foolishness could

[14] Sperber, Popular Catholicism, pp. 34–35; Lenger, Zwischen Kleinbürgertum und Proletariat, p. 154; KnZ, 30 July 1845, 27 July 1846, 15 July 1847; HSTAD RD Pr Nr. 811 ff. 48–51, 94–100; other examples of the left-wing public activities of Cantador and his circle include HSTAD RD Pr. Nr. 790 f. 158, Pr. Nr. 810 ff. 18–20 and the festivals of the carnival society, discussed in the next section. The sharpshooters of Kleve were also dominated by leftists. Cf. ZSTAM Rep. 77 Tit. 505 Nr. 3. Vol. 3 ff. 109–24.

[15] Ayçoberry, Cologne, p. 76; Friedrich Schütz, "Das Verhältniß der Behörden zur Mainzer Fastnacht im Vormärz (1838–1846)," JbwL 6 (1980): 291–318; LAK 403 Nr. 2616 pp. 21–33; Becker, Pfälzer Volkskunde, pp. 297–301; Hoffmann, Rheinhessische Volkskunde, pp. 240–42.

[16] Besides the sources cited above, see LAK 403 Nr. 2616 pp. 45, 87–120 and passim; Nr. 7061 pp. 313–14; ZSTAM 2.2.1. Nr. 15274–76.

flourish,'' accusing the notables of disenfranchising Cologne's citizens and aiming at the enthronement of a "carnival king" who would hold his opponents in check with a "standing army of fools." The dissidents, quickly known as the "democrats," opposed to their rivals, "the aristocrats," included a number of prominent members of the Cologne Democratic Society in 1848–1849: the attorney Friedrich Borchardt, who would sit on the extreme left of the Prussian National Assembly during the revolution, the rentier Carl Cramer, editor of the society's newspaper, and the merchant Carl Wachter, member of the association's executive committee.[17]

A reunion of the two groups in 1844 was merely the prelude to a further split, when the new leader of the "democrats," rentier Franz Raveaux, ran for a seat on the carnival society's executive committee. His platform called for more explicit political satire in the festivities and lower entrance fees for the private "sessions" of the carnival society, allowing for a greater public participation in them. Defeated in the elections, the democrats formed their own society, under Raveaux's energetic leadership, which soon counted over a thousand members. Sometimes the political satire in Raveaux's group extended to making fun of the king himself, but strict police surveillance usually kept the targets more modest: the portrayal of a drunken ex-N.C.O. as a schoolmaster, for instance, or the persecution of schoolteachers by neoorthodox Protestant clergy. Forced into a more aggressive stance by Raveaux's competition, the original carnival society included more politics in its own ceremonies, such as the float in its 1844 parade showing the "wagon of progress," which was drawn by three snails and "checked [in its movement] from the start."[18]

Just as Raveaux and his followers were mounting their challenge to the notables in the Cologne carnival society, its Mainz counterpart was being taken over by future democrats, including the society's president in 1843–1844, the attorney Franz Zitz, later Mainz's extreme leftist deputy to the Frankfurt National Assembly; Ludwig Kalisch, editor of the carnival magazine *Narhalla*, who would edit the democratic club's newsweekly in 1848; and future democratic activist Philipp Wittmann, who became one of the carnival society's two permanent secretaries in 1845. The new leadership brought politics into the festivities, attacking czarist influence on the neighboring

[17] *KnZ*, 6 Jan. 1842, 12 Jan. 1842 (Beilage), 14 Jan. 1842 (Beilage), 25 Jan. 1842, 8 Mar. 1842 (Beilage), 7 Mar. 1843 (Beilage); ZSTAM 2.2.1. Nr. 15274 f. 31; ZSTAM Rep. 77 Tit. 505 Nr. 2 Vol. 2 ff. 224–27.

[18] Most accounts of the split in the Cologne carnival society (Ayçoberry, *Cologne*, pp. 210–11; Seypel, "Die Demokratische Gesellschaft in Köln," pp. 38–39) attribute it exclusively to Raveaux—as the less than modest activist wanted it known—ignoring the initiatives of 1842–1843 before he became involved. On the Cologne carnival in the years 1844–1847, cf. LAK 403 Nr. 7061 pp. 115–22, 241, 301–302, 307–11, 315–25; *KnZ*, 25 Feb. 1844 (Beilage), 30 Jan. 1847, 3 Feb. 1847 (Beilage).

Duchy of Hessen-Nassau in the 1845 carnival parade, taking on both the Prussians and Austrians (whose troops were stationed in the Mainz fortress) at a session of the society the following year, and producing an anticlerical skit as well, a reference to the plans of the Hessian government to abolish civil marriage, one of the cherished Rhenish Institutions.[19]

Perhaps the most aggressively controversial of the Rhenish carnival societies was in Düsseldorf, led from the mid-1840s onward by future democrats, including the sharpshooters' leader, Lorenz Cantador, and the city's left-wing deputy to the Frankfurt National Assembly, the attorney Hugo Wesendonck. The society's members were constantly offending the authorities. In 1844, they applauded a satirical diatribe mocking the Prussian king's love for feudal society and shouted down the playing of the Prussian royal anthem, *"Heil Dir im Siegekranz,"* during a session of the society. They then commissioned the painter Wilhelm Kleinenbroich to produce a mural, which showed, among other things, a knout outweighing a law book entitled "Liberty, Equality, Foolishness" on the scales of justice. Three years later, they offered forty honorary memberships to prominent radicals as well as to a minor official recently transferred from Düsseldorf to Siegburg, seat of the Provincial Insane Asylum. That final satirical act was the last straw for the Ministry of the Interior, which ordered the society dissolved.[20]

Senior Prussian officials were never known for having a sense of humor, and one could well argue that their humorlessness led them to a false reaction. For all their satire, the carnival societies helped preserve public order; even Raveaux's group boasted of its activities in this respect. The satire itself was not necessarily a political danger, since it was confined to a time of the year when forbidden things were allowed because they were forbidden at any other time. As a few more astute bureacrats understood, the political opposition these societies expressed, the appeal to memories of the French Revolution, even the republicanism which sometimes came to the surface was specific to the "world turned upside down" [die verkehrte Welt] of the "realm of fools" [das Narrenreich], valid there precisely because it was invalid in ordinary reality.[21]

---

[19] Schütz, "Mainzer Fastnacht," pp. 295–301. For similar developments in Trier, see Emil Zenz, *Andreas Tont Karnevalist und Revolutionär* (Trier: K.G. Heuschreck 1848 e.v., 1979), passim; in Bonn, Kühn, *Der junge Hermann Becker*, p. 18; LAK 403 Nr. 7061 pp. 115–22. The earliest example of the use of carnival for political satire occurred in Speyer in 1837, when a float satirized the neoorthodox clergy sent by Munich to run the Protestant consistory in the Palatinate. LAS H1 Nr. 1110.

[20] A detailed dossier on the society, HSTAD RD Pr. Nr. 810. On the leftist politics of Kleinenbroich, and other members of the Düsseldorf school of artists, see Hanna Gagel, "Die Düsseldorfer Malerschule in der politischen Situation des Vormärz und 1848," in *Die Düsseldorfer Malerschule*, ed. Wend von Kalnein (Mainz: Philipp von Zabern, 1979), pp. 68–87.

[21] On bureaucrats' awareness of the character of carnival, cf. HSTAD RD Pr. Nr. 810 f. 82; or

But as political tensions increased in the 1840s, the carnival world began to seem closer to the everyday one. When word got out that the officials were trying to censor the politically oppositional comic skits in the Düsseldorf carnival society, one of its members stood up in the session of January 31, 1844, tore off his fool's cap and shouted, ''I speak to you not as a fool, but as a solemn man who will not tolerate such treatment and calls on you to do the same!'' The audience broke out in applause and tumultuous cries of approval; the police official engaging in political surveillance of the session fled, fearing for his life. The scene was a precursor to the events of 1848–1849, when the world was turned upside down and politics previously confined to the realm of fools became a part of sober reality.[22]

Artisans' Societies: Secret and Otherwise

The only overtly revolutionary groups in *Vormärz* German society were not in Germany: They were the secret societies formed by journeymen artisans and émigré intellectuals living in Paris, Brussels, or London. These organizations have pride of place in the history of the German labor movement, and, indeed, of world revolution, since one of them, the League of the Outcast, later the League of the Just, came under the influence of two such intellectual émigrés, Karl Marx and Friedrich Engels, who helped transform it into the Communist League, for which they wrote their celebrated manifesto. In spite of these future implications, it is far from clear whether such organizations constituted abroad had much influence on events in Germany during the *Vormärz*, or even in the years of revolution.[23]

The émigrés did succeed in forming secret cells in the Rhine-Main region, but their organization was penetrated by the police, who arrested some thirty conspirators, mostly artisans, in Mainz at the beginning of the 1840s. About half were subsequently released and the others just charged with a lesser crime, concealing knowledge of a revolutionary conspiracy, probably because the authorities feared bringing felony charges before a jury. Even so, the trial was a fiasco for the prosecution. A number of informers changed their stories on the witness stand, and the defense attorneys successfully portrayed their clients as meeting together not for subversive purposes but for laudable, patriotic ones: to discuss the improvement of commercial relations between the

---

LAK 403 Nr. 7061 pp. 315–25. Raveaux's carnival society emphasized its role in preserving order during the festivals in its public statement, published in *KnZ*, 30 Jan. 1847 (Beilage).

[22] HSTAD RD Pr. Nr. 810 ff. 22–27.

[23] On these organizations, see Wolfgang Schieder, *Anfänge der deutschen Arbeiterbewegung. Die Auslandsvereine im Jahrzehnt nach der Julirevolution* (Stuttgart: Klett-Cotta, 1963). The history of the Communist League is outlined in great detail in *Der Bund der Kommunisten. Dokumenten und Materialien*, ed. Institutes for Marxism-Leninism, Moscow and East Berlin, 3 vols. (East Berlin: Dietz, 1970–1984).

different German states or the defense of the Rhineland against French attack. All the accused were acquitted by the judges of the Mainz police court.[24]

The verdict notwithstanding, it does seem that a secret, revolutionary society existed in Mainz at the beginning of the 1840s and that some of the people associated with it were also revolutionary activists at the end of the decade. One direct connection is certain, the ex-army officer and professional revolutionary Germain Metternich, son of the Mainz Jacobin Matthias Metternich. He fled to Switzerland rather than stand trial and would only return in 1848, when he would play a most active role in the democratic club. Two of the defense lawyers, Friedrich Müller and Philipp Wittmann, were also 1848 democrats, as were probably several of the defendants.[25]

These connections rather suggest that, at least in Mainz, informal ties existed during the *Vormärz* between local democrats and a revolutionary conspiracy organized in exile. The Mainz democrats do not seem to have gained much from these connections. Their open work in legal organizations, like the gymnastics society, of which Germain Metternich was an active member, or the carnival society, where Wittmann was a permanent secretary, probably contributed a good deal more to spreading the popularity of their cause than engaging in secret meetings ever could have. While secret societies of journeymen artisans may have excited the fears of the authorities and the interest of the political police they do not seem to have been a politically significant force.

Nor, apparently, was this the case with legal artisans' associations, mutual benefit societies. Whether as religious brotherhoods or in more secular form, they were extraordinarily common during the *Vormärz*, some six hundred of them existing in the Düsseldorf District of the Prussian Rhine Province in the 1840s. Given the great importance of artisans during the 1848 revolution and the important role their mutual benefit societies played in the emergence of German trade unionism later in the century, one might expect such groups to have been hotbeds of radicalism, but there is virtually no evidence linking them to any form of left-wing politics before or during the revolution. In fact, they were particularly prevalent in lower Rhine manufacturing towns, such as Barmen—where one hundred of these groups existed in 1837—Duisburg,

[24] Ibid., pp. 27–28, 144; *KnZ*, 13 Mar., 24 May, 17 Sept., 1841; 15, 19–20, 22–25, 28–30 Nov., 1, 3 Dec. 1842.

[25] Names of defendants and their lawyers are scattered through the articles cited above; their 1848 affiliations on the basis of the membership list of the Mainz Democratic club (see note 8) and the slate of democratic electors for the Frankfurt National Assembly in Mainz (a copy in Kölnisches Stadtmuseum, Graphische Sammlung RM 1939/112/42). Identification of the rank-and-file activists is uncertain because the newspaper accounts give neither their first names nor their professions. The only biography of Germain Metternich, Richard Falck, *Germain Metternich. Ein deutscher Freiheitskämpfer* (Mainz: Verlagsbuchhandlung Krichtel, 1954) is very unsatisfactory, but cf. p. 51.

Mülheim a.d. Ruhr, and Rheydt, whose lower classes were unusually supportive of conservative politics during the revolution.[26]

ARENAS OF AGITATION

Whether linked informally in conversation circles, members of formally organized but ostensibly nonpolitical associations, or simply acting on their own, *Vormärz* political activists needed both to find an audience and to express their views to it in spite of censorship and government restrictions. Radicals, whose message was least likely to be tolerated by the authorities and was aimed at the widest possible audience, found the situation most difficult. There were various possibilities for political agitation, but in the end all of them ran up against the problem of repression: Effective agitation would be suppressed, and tolerated agitation was permitted precisely because it was ineffective.

Petitions

In and of themselves, petitions were hardly radical or even dissenting documents; a written request for the personal favor of a paternal ruler was entirely compatible with both theory and practice of absolute monarchy. Collective petitions, directed toward political ends, on the other hand, were expressly prohibited by the Hessian and Bavarian constitutions. Naturally, the same was true in absolutist Prussia, where the authorities took such petitions as almost a personal insult. The Cologne and Düsseldorf attorneys and notaries who signed a petition protesting the banning of the radical *Rheinische Zeitung* in 1843 were called up on orders of the Ministry of Justice and informed that the king was personally displeased at their activities and hoped they would have ''more mature views'' in the future. When the estate owner R. Valdenaire of Roscheid (in the Saarland) turned in a petition, signed by 160 peasants, to the crown prince in 1836, protesting the destruction of viticulture by the must tax, he was indicted for slandering the state.[27]

Under these circumstances, *Vormärz* petition drives could be adventurous affairs, sometimes involving clandestine gathering of signatures. Probably the most active in this respect were the Palatine liberals, who were constantly sending petitions to Munich, protesting the appointment of neoorthodox offi-

---

[26] On these groups see Sperber, *Popular Catholicism*, pp. 31–32; Lenger, *Zwischen Kleinbürgertum und Proletariat*, pp. 188–91; Ute Frevert, *Krankheit als politisches Problem 1770–1880* (Göttingen: Vandenhoeck & Ruprecht, 1984), pp. 302–26. Surveys of these organizations in HSTAD RD Nr. 13060; see also RD to MInn, 6 Nov. 1845 (draft), HSTAD RD Nr. 25097. The one possible connection between mutual benefit societies and political radicalism may be found in Trier. Cf. Chapter 2, note 10; and Chapter Six, notes 26–27. More detailed local research may well establish other examples.

[27] Büttner, *Parlamentarismus in Hessen*, p. 37; Obenaus, *Parlamentarismus in Preußen*, pp. 279–80; *KnZ*, 11, 14 May 1843.

cials to head the Protestant church in the Palatinate and the transfer of liberal civil servants who opposed them, calling for amnesty for political prisoners, opposing laws limiting the hours taverns might be opened, and denouncing plans to found monasteries in the province. These petition drives were both widespread, frequently drawing signatures from across the province, and popular, as notables passed lists around in taverns for signatures, or even went with them from door to door.[28]

Such activities were much less tolerated in Rhenish Prussia, and throughout most of the *Vormärz* the few petitions signed there tended to be more localized and signed by smaller, usually more elite groups. It was only in 1845, at the opening of the Provincial Diet that the first provincewide petition drive was mounted, calling for such liberal demands as freedom of the press, a constitution, and an all-Prussian legislature. These petitions also found a wider audience. The one from Cologne was placed in five different public places for signature, and a substantial meeting of no less than 170 men gathered in Trier to formulate the petition. The meeting was broken up by the police, but that did not stop the originators from obtaining five hundred signatures for the petition, and for a second one, protesting the suppression of the first.[29]

Probably the single largest *Vormärz* petition drive, and the only one to cross provincial boundaries, started in Rhine-Hessen in 1846. The government proposed to introduce a new civil code for all of Hessen-Darmstadt, including Rhine-Hessen, which would, among other things, have abolished civil marriage, one of the Rhenish Institutions. Over two thousand inhabitants of Mainz—about one adult male in five—signed the petition against the proposed code, as did thousands elsewhere in the province. Addresses of support came from Neustadt a.d.W., Dürkheim, Deidesheim, Frankenthal, and Grünstadt in the Palatinate, and Aachen and Burtscheid in the Prussian Rhine Province. Mass meetings were held in Mainz and Alzey, denouncing the legislation.[30]

The success of this petition drive also showed its limitations. The grand duke refused to receive the petitions, pointing out, quite rightly, their unconstitutional nature; a "Citizens Association to Defend the Rhenish Institutions," created in Mainz to coordinate the action, was immediately dissolved by the authorities. Petitioning was always an activity on the border of legality;

[28] BHSTAM MInn Nr. 45605 ff. 8–9, 24, Nr. 43715 ff. 26–29, 56–59, 71–73, 75–77, 121–24, 175; RP to MInn, 12 Mar. 1847, BHSTAM Nr. 43902; LAS H1 Nr. 1090 ff. 10–15.

[29] Ayçoberry, *Cologne*, p. 209; *KnZ*, 6–7, 11 Feb. 1845; Obenaus, *Parlamentarismus in Preußen*, p. 585; Peter Ness, "Der Trierer Versammlungs- und Petitionsstreit von 1845," *Neues triersches Jahrbuch* (1967): 39–45. Similar meetings in Düsseldorf, Elberfeld, and Krefeld were tolerated by the local authorities. HSTAD RD Nr. 8811 ff. 1–4; HSTAD Pr Nr. 791 ff. 3–42.

[30] *KnZ*, 1, 4, 14, 20 Nov., 1, 19 Dec. 1846; *MZ*, 23, 25, 27–29 Oct., 15, 20, 27, 29, Nov., 9–10 Dec. 1846; LAS H1 Nr. 1090 ff. 83–85; *Deutscher Liberalismus im Vormärz. Heinrich von Gagern Briefe und Reden 1815–1848*, ed. Paul Wentzcke and Wolfgang Klötzer (Göttingen, West Berlin, and Frankfurt: Musterschmidt, 1959), Nrs. 206–19; Schütz, "Der Vormärz in Mainz," p. 98; Büttner, *Parlamentarismus in Hessen*, pp. 219–20.

taking further steps would quickly go beyond it and bring down the weight of repression on those who tried them.

Petitioning was a tactic that supporters of the government could also use, sometimes more successfully than could the opposition. When Palatine liberals gathered signatures of the notables in 1846 on a petition to the Bavarian parliament against the king's plans to finance the creation of monasteries in the province, Catholic activists responded with a mass petition of their own in favor of the monks. The liberals considered and rejected the idea of a competing mass petition drive, realizing they could never match the Catholics signature for signature: The authorities favored and supported the Catholic petitions, allowing signatures to be collected for them openly, while the liberals would have had to circulate theirs in secret.[31]

Business as Politics; Politics as Business

The political potential inherent in business institutions, such as Chambers of Commerce, and business issues, such as free trade versus protectionism, have often been studied by historians, usually with a focus on their importance for a moderate liberalism given to tempering its opposition to government policies with attempts to come to terms with the authorities. Mid-nineteenth-century radicalism, often closely connected to anticapitalism, would hardly seem to have been at home in the business world. Yet *Vormärz* radicals could sometimes find opportunities for agitation in business questions, exploiting the inequities of the unfree market economy for political purposes. Franz Raveaux of Cologne and Franz Ludwig Zitz of Mainz, during the revolution their respective cities' deputies to the Frankfurt National Assembly, both began their careers as democratic leaders with this sort of agitation.

After fighting with the Belgian revolutionaries in 1830, and the Spanish liberals later in the decade, Raveaux returned to his native Cologne in 1839. He made a fortune in the mid-1840s real estate boom, leaving him free to neglect his nominal business as a cigar dealer and attend to his real interest, turning himself into a tribune of the people, representing their interests against the state and capital. One basis of his efforts was the carnival society, where the main thrust of his activities was against the Prussian state, but another was in matters of business, with Cologne capitalism as his chief target. He joined the "trades association" [Gewerbeverein] and helped transform that moribund body into an organization active in supporting the interests of small businessmen, retailers, and freight forwarders, against the bankers and wholesale merchants who dominated the Chamber of Commerce. Raveaux's public agitation in favor of the Ahr Valley vintners in 1844, denouncing the winegrowers' dependence on mercantile capital, was a sideswipe at the Cologne wholesal-

---

[31] August Culmann to G. F. Kolb, 12 Mar. 1846, BAF FN 9 G. F. Kolb.

ers, so important in the wine trade, and also one of the very few examples of *Vormärz* political activity among the rural population.[32]

Franz Zitz's *Vormärz* career was strikingly similar. The Mainz attorney was, like Raveaux, president of the local carnival society and he also attempted to enlist political support by throwing himself into business issues, taking up the question of the left bank railroad from Mainz to Ludwigshafen. The granting of a construction permit by the grand-ducal authorities had not brought the railroad question to an end. In the wake of the 1847 financial crisis, the value of the railroad's shares plummeted on the Frankfurt stock exchange; Frankfurt and Mannheim stockholders called for the liquidation of the company. Rhine-Hessians immediately suspected that these shareholders had just invested in the project in order to sabotage it, since their cities were served by the competing right bank railroad lines.

Zitz made himself spokesman for the provincial demand that construction be continued regardless of financial difficulties and directed the preparations for the crucial stockholders' meeting of May 26, 1847. He enlisted the prominent liberal estate owner Heinrich von Gagern, during the revolution a bitter enemy of Zitz and the Mainz democrats, but beforehand united in common effort. Zitz also brought to the meeting several hundred nonstockholders, recruited from the lower classes of Mainz. Acting on Zitz's orders, they shouted down the proposals of the Frankfurt and Mannheim stockholders, prevented a secret ballot on resolutions concerning the liquidation of the company and the composition of the board of directors, and physically intimidated the trans-Rhenans present into supporting the Rhine-Hessian proposals. The atmosphere was more like that of a Jacobin club than that of a business gathering; the stockholders' meeting, although the very last venue one might expect for it, had become a practice ground for revolutionary activity.[33]

The controversies in the Solingen steel wares trade showed an even more direct relationship between discrimination, or perceived discrimination, in the market and political alignments. The pious manufacturer Josua Hasenclever, who took the state's help in building his foundry, repaid the Prussian government by being one of the few commoner deputies in the Rhenish Provincial Diet to vote against the liberal demands for a free press and a constitution. His antagonists, the merchant manufacturers Peter Knecht and Wilhelm Jellinghaus, were both adherents of the *Vormärz* political opposition. Jellinghaus

---

[32] On Raveaux's biography, see the entry "Franz Raveaux," in *Allgemeine Deutsche Biographie* 27:465–70; and Seypel, "Die Demokratische Gesellschaft in Köln," pp. 37–45. For a good commentary on his activities, see Ayçoberry, *Cologne*, pp. 210–11.

[33] On Zitz and his career, see K. G. Bockenheimer, *Mainz in den Jahren 1848 und 1849* (Mainz: Mainzer Verlagsanstalt und Druckerei, 1906), pp. 12–14; and the entry for his wife, Kathinka, in *Allgemeine Deutsche Biographie* 45:373–79. For his role in the railroad campaign, see *Deutscher Liberalismus im Vormärz*, Nr. 246; *MZ*, 23, 28, 30 May 1847, 26 June 1847 (Beilage).

would go on to become president of the Solingen Democratic Club during the revolution, his popularity gained in fighting for small producers against the state and mercantile capital rebounding politically in favor of the left.[34]

Eating, Drinking, and Dissenting—in Moderation and in Excess

Probably the most common form of political activity during the *Vormärz* was the banquet, often accompanied by other forms of festivity. At these events, the line between tolerated and prohibited dissent could be seen with great clarity. A good example of the limits of the permissible was the tour of the director of the division of Rhenish law in the Prussian Ministry of Justice, Karl Friedrich Ruppenthal, through the Prussian Rhine Province in the summer of 1841, ostensibly undertaken to inspect the province's judicial system.

A native Rhinelander, Ruppenthal was, his high post in the Prussian bureaucracy notwithstanding, also one of the leading advocates of Rhenish law. In every major town where he stopped, from Kleve to Saarbrücken, he was guest of honor at a festive banquet, attended by members of the legal profession and the notables. At each of these banquets, toasts were offered to and speeches made on the preservation of Rhenish law in the Rhineland and its extension throughout Germany.

The climax of his trip came in Cologne—the Rhineland's largest city and the seat of the court of appeals for those parts of the Prussian Rhine Province governed by Rhenish law—on July 14, 1841. The date was no coincidence, and the two hundred notables assembled in a restaurant of the right bank suburb Deutz heard Ruppenthal himself deliver a eulogy of the French Revolution, pointing out its destructive character, even calling it a "great catastrophe," yet praising it for the "new boons [neue Wohltaten]" it had brought, pointedly comparing Cologne's condition in 1841 with fifty years previously. Ruppenthal praised the Napoleonic Code, concluding, "On the Rhine, people fear nothing so much as losing what they have; elsewhere, people fear nothing so much as the preservation of the old."

The whole series of banquets was an open challenge to the policies of the Prussian monarchy, which had striven since the 1820s to eliminate the French legal system in the Rhineland with its basic principle of equality before the law, and to preserve and reinforce old regime distinctions between nobility and commoners, town dwellers and country folk. A speaker at the banquet in Elberfeld (no doubt a conservative, pious Protestant) understood the political undertones of Ruppenthal's activities and struck the only sour note in his otherwise triumphal tour, offering a toast to the king, calling on the monarch to

---

[34] On Hasenclever's uniquely conservative role in *Vormärz* politics, see Koselleck, *Preußen zwischen Reform und Revolution*, pp. 613–14; *RhBA* 1, Nr. 245, 333.

"rebuke presumption with mild dignity." For all the sentiments expressed at them, the banquets took place with official sanction, since Ruppenthal was a senior state official, and the provincial authorities—not just judges or states' attorneys, but the provincial governor, district governors, and even the fortress commandants in Cologne and Koblenz—attended, made speeches, and offered toasts. The praise of the French Revolution was not expressed in earshot of any Rhenish sans-culottes: Attendance at the banquets was limited and strictly upper class.[35]

Such political banquets were particularly common at the end of a legislative session. When the Rhenish deputies to the Hessian and Bavarian parliaments returned home, they would be feted by their constituents, as would deputies to the Prussian Provincial Estates. Like Ruppenthal's banquets, these events treaded the line between support and opposition. Government officials were present; speeches and toasts praised cooperation between monarch and legislature.[36]

It was possible, however, for things to get out of hand. When the electors of Osthofen in Rhine-Hessen sponsored a banquet for their deputy in 1842, the liberal estate owner Heinrich von Gagern offered a toast expressing regret that monarch and legislature had not cooperated well. The Hessian county commissioner present treated the remark as an attack on government policy, which it was, albeit very mildly formulated, got up, and stomped out.[37]

The most notorious case of this kind occurred in Düsseldorf in 1843. After the Rhenish Provincial Diet had refused to give its consent to a government proposal to abolish the Rhenish code of criminal law, Cologne and Düsseldorf liberals organized a "festival of fraternization." One thousand men from Cologne, seen off at the harbor by a huge crowd, traveled thirty miles downstream on two chartered steamboats to Düsseldorf, seat of the Provincial Diet. They arrived shooting off fireworks, were met by a flag-waving marching band, and proceeded through the city in a torchlight parade, while the men of Düsseldorf lined the streets cheering, and the women waved handkerchiefs from windows and balconies. A delegation brought an address of thanks to the marshall (presiding officer) of the Diet.[38]

[35] *KnZ*, 7, 9, 11, 14, 16, 21, 29 July, 3 Aug. 1841; RK to MInn, 31 July 1841, ZSTAM Rep. 77 Tit. 505 Nr. 2 Vol. 2; ZSTAM Rep. 77 Tit. 505 Nr. 5 Vol. IV ff. 178–79; *RhBA* 1, Nr. 85. On Ruppenthal and his career, see Faber, *Die Rheinlande*, pp. 147–49.

[36] A good study of such festivals in the Palatinate is Cornelia Foerster, " 'Hoch lebe die Verfassung'? Die pfälzischen Abgeordnetenfeste im Vormärz," in *Öffentliche Festkultur. Politische Feste in Deutschland von der Aufklärung bis zum Ersten Weltkrieg* (Reinbek: Rowohlt, 1988), pp. 132–46. Cf. also *KnZ*, 16, 20 Jan. 1841 (Mainz); 4 Mar. 1843 (Remscheid); HSTAD RD Nr. 131 f. 5 (Elberfeld); *MZ*, 26 Oct. 1843 (Zweibrücken); Obenaus, *Parlamentarismus in Preußen*, p. 604.

[37] *Deutscher Liberalismus im Vormärz*, Nrs. 144–47. Gagern was involved in another such controversial banquet several years later in Worms, this time celebrating him as a liberal oppositional deputy. *KnZ*, 16 July 1847.

[38] *KnZ*, 24 June 1843 (Beilage); *RhBA* 1, Nr. 240.

The content of the demonstration was the same as that of the banquets for Ruppenthal two years previously, and the notables were careful to include in the festivities cheers for the king of Prussia—which were, admittedly, less enthusiastically sounded by the crowd than those for the Diet. But by organizing a large street demonstration with a mass audience, they had gone beyond the limits of tolerated dissent. The banquet for the deputies to the Diet, which followed in Düsseldorf two weeks later, although held in private, was equally an episode of transgression.

There were five hundred guests at the tables, most from Düsseldorf itself, but others from all the major cities of the province, as well as a large crowd in the gallery. The toast to the king was put off for an inappropriately long time and, when finally offered, met with a weak response, while a countertoast, "to the brave men of the Diet," was greeted with a thunderous roar of approval. An official attempt to defend the king was shouted down by the gallery, leading all the state officials and the conservative deputies to walk out, and the meeting broke up in wild cheers and shouts.[39]

Once again, the limits of dissent had been violated, this time by the open expression of anti-Prussian, perhaps even anti-monarchical sentiment. Small wonder that the Interior Ministry prohibited all further public festivities for the returning deputies and ordered local officials to attend any private ones and dissolve them at once should they get out of hand. In 1847, an attempt to hold a similar banquet for the Rhenish deputies to the Prussian United Diet was instantly prohibited, the authorities clearly having learned from their mistake four years previously.[40]

Banquets, like the other forms of political organization and agitation considered here, had their limitations. Above all, they were urban events and institutions. The rural population, which certainly had social and political grievances enough, remained almost untouched by efforts at *Vormärz* mass politics. To a lesser extent, this was the case with the urban lower classes as well. They were, to be sure, audiences for the satire of the carnival societies, and sometimes even participants in overtly political events, such as the Cologne-Düsseldorf fraternization festival of 1843. Except perhaps for some journeymen artisans who joined gymnastics societies, however, the only organizations they belonged to were seemingly nonpolitical, even nonprotopolitical mutual benefit societies. *Vormärz* politics was a politics of the notables—a bit less so in large cities than in small towns or the countryside, in the southern than in the northern Rhineland, in the years 1830–1832 and 1843–

[39] *Lebenserinnerungen von . . . Alexander Pagenstecher*, 3:26–27; *KnZ*, 8 July 1843 (Beilage) (clearly censored); HSTAD RD Pr Nr. 811 ff. 19–23; ZSTAM Rep. 77 Tit. 874D Nr. 1 ff. 37–41. Cf. Obenaus, *Parlamentarismus in Preußen*, pp. 602–603.

[40] HSTAD RD Pr. Nr. 8 ff. 9, 26, 48–100; LAK 403 Nr. 6580 pp. 56–98. A prohibition, for similar reasons, of a planned banquet for the Palatine deputies to the Bavarian Parliament in 1837, in LAS H1 Nr. 1090 ff. 52–60; and LAS H1 Nr. 1017 passim.

1847 than in those between, but overall mass participation in it was decidedly limited.

PATTERNS OF POLITICAL LIFE, 1830–1848

In the decade and a half before the 1848 revolution the salient political issues, the extent of popular political participation, and the severity of governmental repression all varied considerably. Putting aside for the moment regional differences, the years 1830–1848 can be divided into three periods. In the first, during 1830–1832, the impact of the revolutions of 1830 was felt strongly in at least some parts of the Rhineland, and democratic and republican ideas were openly expressed. There followed a long decade of reaction, political repression, and the creation of an officially sponsored conservatism, from 1833 to 1842. This was also a time when the political expression of Protestant-Catholic dualism was at its peak. The decade of reaction was succeeded by a period of renewed political turbulence, 1843–1847, in which, however, new political issues—communism and radicalized religion—came to the fore. By the middle of the 1840s, all the political tendencies found in the 1848–1849 revolution and most of their leaders were already present.

Rehearsal for Revolution, 1830–1832

A series of mediocre harvests from 1828 to 1832 brought food prices up and created a tense mood in the Rhenish population, noticeably sharpened by the news of revolution in neighboring France and Belgium. In August 1830, crowds ran through the streets of Cologne, shouting, "Vivat, long live Napoleon!" and "Abolish the excise!" The inhabitants of Elberfeld also tumultuously praised Napoleon, while calling out, "We don't want high [elementary] school fees. . . . They should not pay us in truck. . . . The mayor should bring down the price of bread." Threatening placards were posted throughout the countryside, demanding lower taxes and the resignation of hated officials; forest riots in the Saarland could be suppressed only by sending troops. The most violent events occurred in Aachen and Eupen, where textile outworkers destroyed machines, demanded higher wages, and demolished the houses of unpopular manufacturers.

There, as elsewhere on the lower Rhine, the disorder was strictly limited to the lower classes. "Only the mob can be blamed" for the disturbances, the Cologne district governor noted, while "the solid citizenry [die Bürgerschaft] has proved to have the best sentiments for the preservation of peace and order." In the larger towns, where the police, as usual, were helpless against the disturbances, and most of the troops were away on maneuvers, property owners formed civic guards, which quickly restored order, with the consent and cooperation of the authorities.[41]

The bourgeoisie of the upper and middle Rhine, far from fearing the events of 1830, seized the occasion to press for drastic changes in government, revealing a north-south contrast in the political behavior of the Rhenish upper classes, which would strongly mark the political landscape during the *Vormärz* and revolution. At first, the upper Rhine notables confined their actions to the permissible limits of dissent, electing deputies to the Bavarian and Hessian parliaments who supported the efforts of the opposition there to obtain liberal reforms. The monarchs and their ministers, however, showed no inclination to follow such policies; instead, they moved in an increasingly reactionary direction.[42]

Oppositional journalists transferred their newspapers from Munich to the west bank of the Rhine, where the Rhenish Institutions, in particular the prospect of a jury trial for press offenses, offered them greater protection from government suppression. Under their leadership, the vaguely leftist opinions of the Palatine notables, already apparent in the campaign for the Protestant Union of 1817, and in associations for the support of the Greek and Polish revolutionaries in 1826 and 1830, respectively, took on clearer and more militant contours. They sponsored a series of festive banquets for returning deputies in 1831, and then founded a political society, the Press and Fatherland Association, which soon counted some five thousand members in the Palatinate, neighboring Rhine-Hessen, and elsewhere in southwestern Germany. High grain and wood prices combined with low ones for the Palatine cash crops, wine and tobacco, in part a result of Bavarian trade policies, which taxed heavily goods imported into the Palatinate but provided no duty-free export markets for its products, created a mood of lower-class discontent, which complemented the bourgeois political agitation.

The situation came to a head in the spring of 1832, as the Bavarian authorities could no longer control either an increasingly prorepublican political agitation or popular disorders, in the form of forest and bread riots. The tumultuous planting of "trees of liberty" in dozens of localities combined the two forms of oppposition. In April, a group of Neustadt notables—many of whom, such as the mayor and banker Ludwig Dacqué, the merchant and rentier

---

[41] ZSTAM Rep. 77 Tit. 505 Nr. 2 Vol. 1 ff. 4–52; Heinrich Volkmann, "Wirtschaftlicher Strukturwandel und sozialer Konflikt in der Frühindustrialisierung. Eine Fallstudie zum Aachener Aufruhr von 1830," in *Soziologie und sozialgeschichtliche Aspekte und Probleme* (Opladen: Westdeutscher Verlag, 1973), pp. 550–65; Michael Müller, "Die preußische Rheinprovinz unter dem Einfluß von Julirevolution und Hambacher Fest 1830–1834," *JbwL* 6 (1980): 272–90. In general, on events of the years 1830–1832 in Germany, see Heinrich Volkmann, "Protestträger und Protestformen in den Unruhen 1830–1832," in *Sozialer Protest*, pp. 56–75.

[42] Büttner, *Parlamentarismus in Hessen*, pp. 174–83; *Handbuch der Bayerischen Geschichte* 4/1:149–57.

Johann Philipp Abresch, and the merchant and estate owner Iganz Rassiga, would be active democrats in 1848–1849—called for a giant political banquet to be held on Pentecost Sunday at a ruined castle in the nearby village of Hambach.

Some thirty thousand people came to this "National Festival of the Germans in Hambach," on May 27, 1832, among them a contingent of women, whose participation had been especially requested by the organizers, a group of peasants behind a black flag with the inscription "the vintners must mourn," a number of émigré Polish insurgents, and four hundred inhabitants of Mainz, led by the wine dealer Georg Strecker, a democratic activist in 1848–1849, and the ubiquitous revolutionary Germain Metternich. They all marched from the railroad station in Neustadt a.d.W. to the castle, a steep hour-and-a-half uphill climb, as anyone who has followed in their footsteps knows, surrounded by a whirl of flags and cocardes in the black-red-gold German national colors and a sprinkling of Phrygian caps. The many speeches given at the ruins, ranging in tone from moderate to Jacobin, from invitations for the Rhinelanders to reunite with France to a Francophobia reminiscent of 1814, left a confused impression—on that small part of the crowd close enough to the speakers' rostrum to hear what was being said.

The organizers, perhaps a little surprised at their own success, were unclear what to do next. While they temporized, the authorities acted, sending 8,500 troops, half the entire Bavarian army, to pacify the unruly province, imposing a strict press censorship, and arresting the leaders of the movement. They were acquitted in a sensational trial before the Landau assizes in 1833—the first but hardly the last time Rhenish jurors would confound the authorities' repressive plans—but renewed indictments on lesser charges, which could be tried without juries, forced them to flee, fall silent, or spend several years in jail. When thousands of Neustadters decided, spontaneously and in unorganized fashion, to have a picnic in Hambach on Pentecost Sunday, 1833, the troops drove them off the hillside with rifle butts and bayonets, killing one civilian and injuring countless more, bringing the near-revolutionary episode to an end.[43]

It left behind a group of activists across the entire province who would continue to associate over the following years: raising money for the political

---

[43] The literature on the Hambach Festival is enormous, but most of it has been superseded by several newer works: two essays of Hubert Freilinger, "Die 'Hambacher'. Beteiligte und Sympathisante der Beinahe-Revolution von 1832," *Zeitschrift für bayerische Landesgeschichte* 41 (1978): 701–37; and "Die vorletzte Weisheit des Volkes. Der politsiche Aktionismus der Hambacher Bewegung und seine Grenzen," in *Hambach 1832*, pp. 31–59; the study of Wolfgang Schieder, "Der rheinpfälzische Liberalismus von 1832 als Protestbewegung," in *Vom Staat des Ancien Regime zum modernen Parteienstaat. Festschrift Theodor Schieder* (Munich: Beck, 1978), pp. 169–95; and especially the work of Schieder's student Cornelia Foerster, *Der Preß- und Vaterlandsverein von 1832/33. Sozialstruktur und Organistionsformen der bürgerlichen Bewegung in der Zeit des Hambacher Festes* (Trier: Verlag Trierer Historische Forschungen, 1982); and the model exhibition catalog she coedited, *Hambacher Fest 1832–1982*.

refugees, trying to elect oppositional parliamentary deputies and planning further banquets and festivals for them or for liberal bureaucrats, organizing petitions against Protestant neoorthodox church officials or the planned founding of monasteries, joining with the supporters of the beleaguered rationalist Pastor Frantz. They were to be found, as the provincial governor noted in 1846, "wherever a political or religious movement among the people, or a demonstration of any kind against the government comes to the fore." In 1848–1849, many of the veterans of a near-revolution would have a shot at a real one.[44]

Repression and Different Conflicts, 1833–1842

The Bavarian government's policies were just part of a broader wave of repression throughout the German states following 1833, as monarchs intimidated, stonewalled, or bypassed oppositional parliaments, tightened still further restrictions on the press and the right of association, dismissed overly liberal officials from state service, created a secret political police, and made the German Confederation even more authoritarian and reactionary than it had been before. Near the beginning of the 1840s, the authorities went beyond repression and began to sponsor certain political tendencies, hoping to use for their own ends popular sentiments expressed ten years previously.[45]

In the second half of the 1830s, political conflict was almost entirely dominated by confessional dualism, these years seeing the Cologne troubles in Rhenish Prussia and the great kneeling controversy in Bavaria. To some extent, religious conflict was a continuation of political struggles by other means, as Palatine liberals, for example, unable to agitate openly as they had at the beginning of the decade, fell back on the struggle against the kneeling militia or the neoorthodox Protestants imposed on their church by a Catholic monarch. However, religion could also create divisions crossing previously existing political boundaries, as happened in the Cologne troubles. The leading public advocates of the imprisoned archbishop and bitter enemies of the Prussian authorities were the Catholic nobility of the northern Rhineland, a group who had previously been quite friendly to a government attempting to restore some of their feudal privileges abolished by the Rhenish Institutions. A number of Protestant liberals were not very enthusiastic about criticizing the Prussian government's actions in the affair, in part because they found it too

---

[44] Citation, LAS H1 Nr. 595 ff. 12–14. Examples of the further activity of ex-Hambach activists include LAS H1 Nr. 1017 ff. 1–60; Nr. 1090 ff. 52–55, 69; BHSTAM MInn Nr. 44354 ff. 25, 53–56, 120–23; Nr. 44358 ff. 3–4; Nr. 45605 ff. 1–6; Nr. 43715 ff. 189–91 and passim; Scherer, "Zur pfälzischen Kirchengeschichte," pp. 150–51 and passim.

[45] On the repression, cf. Büttner, *Parlamentarismus in Hessen*, pp. 174–94; Müller, "Die preußische Rheinprovinz," pp. 281–84; *Handbuch der Bayerischen Geschichte* 4/1:175–86; Wolfram Siemann, *"Deutschlands Ruhe, Sicherheit und Ordnung." Die Anfänge der politischen Polizei 1806–1866* (Tübingen: Max Niemeyer, 1985), pp. 87–106, 190–95, 211–20; Kolb, *Lebenserinnerungen*, pp. 94–95.

difficult to support the Catholic Church in anything, even when their own principles suggested they should have, in part because of the dubious allies the church had in its confrontation with the state.[46]

A second, and quite different, feature of this period was the further development and official sponsorship of a conservative German nationalism, first seen at the time of the Wars of Liberation against Napoleon in 1813–1815. Unlike the leftist nationalism of the Hambach Festival, which included a prounouced hostility toward the thirty-nine existing German states and the German Confedaration in which they were tied together, the conservative nationalists praised the existing governmental institutions as the basis of a politically conservative nation. This sentiment received a strong impetus from the Rhine crisis of 1840, when vague threats of a French invasion produced a tumultuous response. Nicolas Becker's poem on the "German Rhine," first performed in the Cologne theater, was set to music in over two hundred different tunes and sung in impromptu and organized festivities throughout western Germany. The Prussian authorities supported and encouraged these demonstrations, since they presented their state in its existing, authoritarian form, as the bulwark of Germany against a radical France. Becker's song was known as the "Colonaise," suggesting a conservative German patriotic anthem, in contrast to the Marseillaise, a revolutionary French one.[47]

This wave of conservative nationalism peaked at the first construction festival of the Cologne cathedral in 1842. Conceived as a sign of reconciliation between church and state following the resolution of the Cologne troubles, it was also a nationalist, conservative counterfestival to the radical one at Hambach a decade earlier. The Cologne cathedral, unfinished since the Middle Ages, was to be seen as a symbol of an unfinished German national unity, whose construction would be carried out by the existing authoritarian states, rather than involving their reform or destruction, as left-wing nationalists wished. The presence at the festival of the new king of Prussia, Friedrich Wilhelm IV, fresh from rebuking any plans for liberal reform in conjunction with his coming to the throne, Archduke Johann of Austria, one of the heroes of the conservative Tyrolean uprising against Napoleon, and Austrian chan-

[46] Scherer, "Zur pfälzischen Kirchengeschichte," p. 148; *RhG*, 2:527–31; Keinemann, *Das Kölner Ereignis* 1:224–43. Heinrich von Gagern's correspondence on the Cologne troubles provides an instructive account of the hesitations of a Protestant liberal who understood that his liberal principles meant supporting the Catholic Church in its struggle with the state. *Deutscher Liberalismus im Vormärz*, Nrs. 78–80, 82–85.

[47] On Rhenish response to the Rhine crisis, cf. Ayçoberry, *Cologne*, p. 206; Faber, *Die Rheinlande*, pp. 379–405; Keinemann, *Das Kölner Ereignis*, 1:281–92; *RhBA* 1, Nrs. 64, 66–68, 70. A good general account of the political ramifications of the crisis is Manfred Püschner, "Die Rheinkrise von 1840/41 und die antifeudale Oppositionsbewegung," in *Bourgeoisie und bürgerliche Umwälzung in Deutschland 1789–1871*, ed. Helmut Bleiber (East Berlin: Akademie-Verlag, 1977), pp. 101–34.

cellor Metternich, architect of the Restoration, underscored its political intent.[48]

Public opposition to this view only surfaced in the Palatinate, suggested by several small incidents in and around Neustadt a.d.W. A drunken master tailor was arrested in November 1840 for saying in a tavern that the German princes were guilty of inciting the French to war, since they wished to replace the "citizens' throne" [Bürgerthron] of France with a legitimist regime, and that "[t]hese gentlemen by the grace of God are all thieves [Spitzbuben] and rotten bums [schlecte Lumpen]." His views were shared by his social superiors, as became clear at another incident two days later. Two Jewish traveling salesmen, staying in the Four Seasons Hotel in Bad Dürkheim, the watering hole of the "bourgeois aristocracy" of the Palatinate, were playing the role of ardent German patriots, demonstrating their desire to defend the Rhineland against a French invasion. To their astonishment, the locals vehemently disagreed with them, in doing so, "expressing themselves about the person of His Majesty, King Ludwig of Bavaria, in a most indecent and crude way." The salesmen denounced them to the mayor the next day, who casually dismissed their allegations as exaggerated. Even some Palatine peasants expressed their skepticism about conservative patriotism in 1840. Fifteen young men from the vintners' village of Mußbach marched in June 1840 to the parish fair in Neustadt a.d.W. behind a tricolor French flag, remained there the whole day without anybody's taking offense, and would no doubt have returned home uneventfully, had not the Neustadt police commissioner seen their banner. On being arrested, they calmly asserted they did not know that "people were prohibited from using a false flag at this amusement."[49]

This skeptical attitude about the war scare and its politically conservative implications was apparently shared by all classes of Palatine society, or at least all of them living in the viticultural areas at the foot of the Haardt Mountains. It was very different from the patriotic war fever dominant on the lower Rhine, and is once again suggestive of a north-south dualism in Rhenish political behavior. The Palatines' political attitude owed a good deal to the memory of the emancipatory side of the French Revolution and its embodiment in Rhenish Law. The hostility towards the existing German states which opposed these institutions and friendship towards a French government supporting them did not stem from a desire to be reannexed to France but from the wish to create a national German state embodying the emancipatory ideals of the French Revolution.

---

[48] Norbert Trippen, "Das Kölner Dombaufest 1842 und die Ansichten Friedrich Wilhelms IV. von Preußen bei der Wiederaufnahme der Arbeiten am Kölner Dom," *AHVN* 182 (1979): 99–115.

[49] LAS H1 Nr. 1090 ff. 26–27, 33, 36–39, 42–48.

New Life in Politics, 1842–1845

One way to see the development of a new political spirit in the 1840s is to consider the books prohibited by Prussian censorship. Between the mid-1830s and 1842, most of the banned books were religious polemics, held back from the market because the authorities feared they might incite confessional hatred. Such polemics did not disappear after January 1, 1843, and officials did their best to prevent such works as *Peter, Prince of the Apostles and Vicar of Christ* from reaching the public, but, increasingly, new kinds of works began appearing on the forbidden lists, with such titles as *The Fate of a Proletarian. A Book for the People*, or *The Prussian Bureaucracy*, or *Forwards! People's Pocket Book for 1845*, by the famous Leipzig radical (and native son of Cologne), Robert Blum. The hostile official attention paid to such books is suggestive both of the creation of more clearly delineated political tendencies and the parallel coming to the fore of new political issues, trends beginning in the Prussian Rhine Province, and spreading throughout the Rhineland in the five years before the outbreak of revolution.[50]

Perhaps the first, and certainly the most celebrated, example of open radicalism in the Rhineland, clearly differentiated from a more moderate liberal opposition, was the brief and stormy appearance of the *Rheinische Zeitung* [the Rhineland News] in Cologne, in 1842–1843. Following the institution of new, somewhat milder censorship regulations, and the settlement of the Cologne troubles in a way favorable to the church, the Prussian authorities granted a concession for a new daily in Cologne, which they thought would be a counterweight to the pro-Catholic attitudes of the city's and the province's leading newspaper, the *Kölnische Zeitung*. (The liberal, nonclerical editorial policy for which that paper would later be known was not adopted until 1845.) The founding stockholders for the *Rheinische Zeitung* included many of the town's leading businessmen, so the authorities scarcely feared anything might go amiss.

However, they were quickly disabused of that notion when the new paper was staffed by a circle of young intellectuals, whose editorial policy featured a heavy dose of philosophical Hegelian radicalism, as much a surprise to Rhenish newspaper readers as it was to the state censors. The resulting product was not particularly successful, since the atheism of the Hegelian left offended Catholic sentiments, and the philosophical abstraction and lack of hard news left the less clerically minded indifferent. In October 1842 the publishers turned to a new editor in chief, the unemployed doctor of philosophy, Karl Marx. Unlike many of his late twentieth century admirers, Marx never mixed

[50] Cf. HSTAD RD Pr. Nr. 692 ff. 1–16 (a list, from early March 1848 of all books prohibited under the censorship decree of 23 Jan. 1843), with censorship records from the years 1835–1842, HSTAD RD Pr. Nr. 677–79; HSTAD RA Pr. Nr. 529; or LAK 442 Nr. 3753 pp. 27–29. Also see *Lebenserinnerungen . . . von Alexander Pagenstecher* 3:23–24.

philosophy in with politics. Under his direction, the newspaper played down theological speculation, while covering business and political news in detail. Editorials denounced bureaucratic authoritarianism; high taxes on the Moselle vintners, leading to the area's impoverishment (the newspaper's Bernkastel correspondent would lead the democrats there in 1848–1849); and the lack of a constitution, legislature, or freedom of the press. Readership rose, along with the censor's blood pressure, and the paper's concession was withdrawn as of April 1843. Marx left Cologne and several months later went into exile in Paris.[51]

The successful aspect of the radicalism of the *Rheinische Zeitung* lay not so much in its new ideas, since Hegelianism never found much support in the Rhineland, as in the vigor with which its editors defied the censor and openly raised political demands. Immediately following on the newspaper's suppression, the Prussian authorities faced another political controversy with a similar import. They laid before the Rhenish Provincial Diet a proposal for a new criminal code, which would be valid throughout the monarchy and so replace Rhenish law. The proposal would have limited the number of crimes eligible for jury trials; it introduced the penalty of "derogation from the nobility," with the implication that being turned from a nobleman to a commoner was a decline in status, contravening the idea of equality before the law. By creating crimes whose punishment was removal from church office, it offended Catholic opinion, implying yet another attempt by the Protestant state to intervene in church affairs, right after the Cologne troubles had been settled. Finally, and perhaps most seriously, the new code would have introduced corporal punishment for certain offenses, meaning that Rhinelanders would, in the future, be beaten by Prussian officials from the East Elbian provinces.[52]

The proposal had something to offend everyone, and it was opposed by radicals and moderates, by enemies of Prussian rule, but also by its friends, by Hegelian intellectuals who had worked for the *Rheinische Zeitung*, and by pious Catholics who had rejoiced at the suppression of the godless newspaper. The threat of corporal punishment made the new criminal code a popular issue and the authorities regretfully noted that it was not just lawyers, intellectuals,

---

[51] Still the best sources for the stormy history of the *Rheinische Zeitung* are found in *RhBA* 1, Nrs. 49 to 248, esp. Nrs. 174–221. Wilhelm Klutentreter, *Die Rheinische Zeitung von 1842/43 in der politischen und geistigen Bewegung des Vormärz*, 2 vols. (Dortmund: Ruhfus, 1966–1967), adds little. Among the many commentaries on the newspaper, the most useful are Ayçoberry, *Cologne*, pp. 202–04; and Seypel, "Die Demokratische Gesellschaft in Köln," pp. 33–37. The account in Hammen, *The Red '48ers*, pp. 44–63, is unnecessarily hostile. Helmut Asmus, "Die 'Rheinische Zeitung' und die Genesis des rheinpreußischen Bourgeoisliberalismus," in *Bourgeoisie und bürgerliche Umwälzung*, pp. 135–68, is interesting, but his thesis that the newspaper represented the first appearance of a new Rhenish liberalism, linked to the industrial bourgeoisie, is unconvincing.

[52] Faber, *Die Rheinlande*, pp. 175–76; Blasius, *Bürgerliche Gesellschaft und Kriminalität*, pp. 115–26.

or the upper classes who were interested in the proposed criminal code, but
the common people as well. Their daily experiences with the state in the form
of customs agents, foresters, or tax collectors made the specter of physical
chastisement seem very real. Perhaps spurred on by a nervous mood following
the bad harvest of 1842, which brought very high food prices the following
spring, the issue was the center of tavern conversation throughout the province. The Diet's rejection of the proposed code was greeted with public jubilation, both spontaneous and, as in the Cologne-Düsseldorf fraternization festival and subsequent banquet for the deputies, well organized.[53]

DEMOCRATS AND COMMUNISTS

Although the controversy surrounding the *Rheinische Zeitung* suggested there
were different political tendencies developing in Rhenish Prussia, the struggle
over the penal code, which immediately followed it, united all of them in
opposition to the government. Two developments in 1844–1845 would bring
differences among political groups into sharper relief. One of them was the
growth of a communist or socialist (contemporaries used the two terms inter-
changeably) movement in the Rhineland. It is difficult to avoid seeing the
impact of this event on contemporaries in terms of the European labor movement of the later nineteenth and twentieth centuries, especially given the for-
mative role in it of two Rhenish communists, Karl Marx and Friedrich Engels.

However, just as mid-nineteenth-century social structure cannot be understood in the terms used for the latter part of the century, social movements of
the 1840s ought not to be confused with those of the 1890s, even if the youthful participants in the former, like Engels, became the respected veterans of
the latter. Rhenish communists of the mid-1840s were of and on the left, generally emerging from and acting within *Vormärz* democratic circles. They
were by no means necessarily on the extreme left, and if individual communists were, it was not because of their social doctrine, which tended to moderate rather than radicalize their political ideas. Nor was early communism a
workers' movement. Its protagonists, like other *Vormärz* political activists,
were from the middle and upper classes. There is no evidence that Rhenish
communists made any special effort to gain proletarian support; if anything,
others on the left did much more in this respect.

Communists and the Social Question

The Prussian government gave the Rhenish communists their first chance to
propagate their ideas openly in 1844, when the Berlin authorities sponsored

[53] LAK 403 Nr. 6576 pp. 67–73; ZSTAM Rep. 77 Tit. 874D Nr. 1. ff. 6–7; Rep. 77 Tit. 343A
Nr. 23 ff. 4–5, 17–20; Rep. 77 Tit. 343A Nr. 24 ff. 19–22; *RhBA* 1, Nrs. 230, 243, 249.

the creation of an "Association for the Welfare of the Working Classes." The group was to seek solutions to the problem of pauperization more basic than simple charity, but not threatening to the existing political order. Inhabitants of the provinces were invited to found their own societies, which might affiliate with the central association in Berlin. With this invitation, the government set in motion events that it could not control.[54]

Indeed, the whole program was destroyed by what happened in Cologne. A series of meetings held there between November 1844 and April 1845 for the purpose of founding an affiliated society, drew large crowds, at times as many as a thousand participants, and proceeded in turbulent fashion, with sharp disagreements surfacing about the name of the proposed group, its organizational structure, and its potential membership. The political tendencies that had been united the previous year in rejecting the government's proposed criminal code broke apart, and after acrimonious debate, leftist forces outvoted moderates on several occasions, leading them to leave the organization. Denouncing the influence of "theories of socialism and communism," on the association that had emerged, the authorities prohibited the group and discouraged the formation of other, affiliated societies, even politically innocuous ones.[55]

A number of communists were among the proponents of a radical course for the association, including the social theorist Moses Hess, the charity physician Andreas Gottschalk, who would be the first president of the Cologne Workers' Association in 1848, the physician Karl D'Ester, and the law graduate Heinrich Bürgers. The latter two were both close associates of Karl Marx. However, they were part of a broader front with other, noncommunist leftists, such as Franz Raveaux, once more playing his role of tribune of the people, the future democratic journalist Carl Cramer, or the small chemical manufacturer Karl Hospelt, in 1848–1849 a member of the executive committee of the Cologne Democratic Society. Nor was it the proposal of specifically communist goals, which caused such a controversy at the founding meetings. To be sure, the radicals' draft statutes talked of creating institutions that would enable the "propertyless worker . . . to endure the struggle of competition with

---

[54] The general history of the association, Jürgen Reulecke, *Sozialer Frieden durch soziale Reform* (Wuppertal: Peter Hammer, 1983), is mostly concerned with ideology and has little to say about organization, political controversies, or conditions in the provinces. For what follows, the main sources are printed in *RhBA* 1, Nrs. 286, 288–91, 294–97, 300–301, 303, 306–307, 356; a useful, detailed discussion can be found in Schneider, "Bürgerliche Vereinsbestrebungen," pp. 23–44; cf. also Dowe, *Aktion und Organisation*, pp. 69–78.

[55] While future 1848 moderate liberals, such as the banker Ludolf Camphausen led the moderate forces in the debate on the organization, as the literature stresses, secondary sources have nothing to say about the role of future Catholic-clerical politicians in this debate. They did not play a prominent role, and at most five of the seventy-nine signatories of the final, radical statutes (LAK 403 Nr. 166 pp. 324–25) can be identified as signatories of the Catholic electoral program of 1848 (*RhBA* 2/2:50–51), suggesting, although not proving, that most members of strict Catholic circles supported the moderates on this issue.

the power of capital,'' but this was to be accomplished by founding savings banks, soup kitchens, consumers' cooperatives, employment offices, and trade schools. Such institutions were in no sense communistic or radical; political moderates and even the Prussian authorities had themselves created similar ones over the previous several decades. Compared with the mutual benefit societies counting tens of thousands of members and the experiments with cooperative sales halls in which ordinary artisans were engaged at the time, the leftist proposals look pretty tame.

Radical ideas about the nature of group membership were much more controversial. Moderates wanted yearly membership dues of one taler, and a self-coopting executive committee at the head of the association, both of which would have kept the group in the hands of the notables. The radicals proposed instead yearly dues of a modest five silbergroschen, which would have permitted small proprietors and even more frugal members of the lower classes to join. They also wanted the executive committee elected by a monthly general meeting of all the group's members. Both suggestions looked toward the creation of a mass organization, perhaps not so different from Raveaux's carnival society, but much more overtly political.

The question of the proposed group's name started a particularly bitter argument. The radicals wished to drop the official designation ''Association for the Welfare of the Working Classes,'' and rename the association ''Mutual Aid and Educational Society'' [Gegenseitiger Hülfs- und Bildungsverein], thus implying a change from a group of notables, who would, in paternalist fashion, do something for the working classes, to an association whose members would act for themselves. Heinrich Bürgers defended this intent in a debate by stating that ''the association must be based on the principle of mutuality since the other institutions of the Rhine Province are based on the principle of equality before the law.'' This equality before the law, embodied in the Rhenish Institutions was, as, nineteenth-century liberalism saw it, perfectly compatible with a leading role in public life for substantial property owners. Bürgers was reinterpreting the Rhenish Institutions, expanding the idea of equality to include equal participation of all social classes in public life, a firmly democratic but once again not explicitly communist idea. This statement, by a future member of the Communist League, was typical for the stance of the Cologne communists, who took part in the debate over the association with and as democrats, rather than as an independent communist group, separate from other leftists.[56]

In the nearby Wuppertal, the Berlin government's appeal also produced a controversy in which the communists played a role. The main point at issue was religion, the freethinking bourgeoisie of Elberfeld, Barmen, and the surrounding towns wishing to create trade schools for factory children and young

<hr />

[56] Bürger's statement, *RhBA* 1, Nr. 288.

artisans and workers, while the pious Protestants of the region wanted to form Bible study groups and catechism classes. This conflict was a reprise of an earlier one over alcoholism, in which the pious had wanted to combat excess working-class consumption of strong spirits by forming abstinence societies, while the freethinkers had helped found beer halls to provide the workers with a cheap, family-oriented, mildly alcoholic alternative to spirits.

The meeting on the proposed new organization, held in the Elberfeld city hall, led to a ferocious debate, which became so frenzied that sand and mortar were knocked loose from the ceiling and rained down on the participants. The freethinkers were victorious, and the devout walked out to form a separate "Society for Christian Popular Education." In suburban Hardenberg, on the other hand, the neoorthodox kept control of the association.[57]

Led by the young Friedrich Engels, the handful of Elberfeld communists had been part of the freethinking coalition. Engels and Moses Hess from Cologne followed up on this victory by sponsoring public meetings in February–March 1845, held in some of the better restaurants in Elberfeld. Often known as the first communist meetings in Germany, they were rather more like public debates. The communists made proposals for the abolition of private property; then, others, including the theatrical director Roderich Benedix, a moderate liberal in 1848, and an official of the Düsseldorf District government, Karl Otto, later a Catholic-clerical political activist, disputed with them, maintaining that private property was part of human nature. The occasions became a minor sensation, attracting up to two hundred, mostly bourgeois spectators. As Engels noted, in one of his first letters to Marx, all social classes were represented, with the exception of the proletariat. The fear that workers might show up in the future and transform a harmless entertainment into a danger for social order led the authorities to prohibit any further meetings after three had been held.[58]

It helps to understand their fears if one realizes that agitation among the Wuppertal working class had been occurring in the preceding months, albeit not carried out by communists. Following the Elberfeld freethinkers' victory in the fight over creating a branch society for the welfare of the working classes, Calvinist ministers had vociferously denounced their efforts, preaching fire-and-brimstone sermons about the uselessness of material improvement without spiritual progress, condemning the immoral dissipation of the godless rich. The rationalist Superior Procurator von Kösteritz feared that such denunciations of the bourgeoisie in front of the handloom weavers who belonged to the Calvinist congregations would help spread communism. Further investi-

---

[57] HSTAD RD Nr. 1587 ff. 23–25, 73–74; Quandt, "Eduard Colsmann," passim; Schneider, "Bürgerliche Vereinsbestrebungen," pp. 28–30; Körner, *Lebenskämpfe* 1:386–87, 399–400; Wegener, "Elberfeld," pp. 24–25.

[58] These meetings have been discussed many times. Dowe, *Aktion und Organisation*, pp. 81–86, provides an account incorporating the literature and most of the unpublished sources.

gation, however, revealed that the sermons had not attacked all the rich, just those who did not go to church, and had taken on sinful amusements of the poor, such as sharpshooters' festivals, as well.[59]

An even more serious threat to social order was posed by one Henseler, a defrocked Catholic priest in Barmen, who had gotten married and was earning a meager living as a teacher of foreign languages. In January 1845 he held meetings for master silk weavers, calling on them to form an association that would negotiate better arrangements among masters, journeymen, and manufacturers. In particular, he incited the weavers to demand that they receive pay for setting up the patterns on Jacquard looms, a complex process that could take up to three weeks, during which the workers were uncompensated. Henseler announced his intention of carrying the agitation from Barmen to weavers throughout the Wuppertal, creating a united association for them.[60]

In the light of these events, the Elberfeld communists can be seen as part of the freethinking Wuppertal bourgeoisie, opposed to the region's devout bankers, merchants, and manufacturers, condemning the exploitation of their workers the latter carried on behind a veil of piety. Yet the Wuppertal rationalists were also uneasily aware that the Calvinist or revivalist proclivities of the majority of the region's upper class gave them a direct connection to the workers that the freethinkers lacked. One might have expected the communists to have attempted to break through this barrier and carry their ideas directly to the proletariat. They did not, remaining with a bourgeois audience and, at least partially, within the bounds of tolerated *Vormärz* political dissent. It was the noncommunist democrat Henseler who attempted to reach beyond the bourgeoisie, agitating around the real social grievances of the Wuppertal manufacturing outworkers. Henseler's continuing efforts in 1848–1849, as editor of the democratic newspaper in Barmen, to win the city's workers away from conservative piety would make him known to the authorities as a "most dangerous man."[61]

Communists and the State: The Trier'sche Zeitung

Most *Vormärz* Rhenish collectivists were "true socialists." Following a left-Hegelian philosophical radicalism, they saw capitalism as a social order whose exploitation and oppression stunted human potential, and imagined a

---

[59] Oberprokurator Kösteritz (Elberfeld) to RD, 3 Mar. 1845; and OB Elberfeld to LR Kr. Elberfeld, 12 Mar. 1845, both in HSTAD RD Nr. 8811. The Düsseldorf authorities took the threat of religiously motivated communism with great seriousness, and all official correspondence on it was conducted in secrecy.

[60] LR Kr. Elberfeld to RD, 29 Jan. 1845; BM Barmen to LR Kr. Elberfeld, 31 Jan. 1845; LR Kr. Elberfeld to RD, 25 Mar. 1845, all in HSTAD RD Nr. 8811. This important source was not used by Dowe.

[61] ZSTAM Rep. 77 Tit. 505 Nr. 3 Vol. 4 ff. 174–77. On bourgeois freethinkers' feelings of contempt for the pious manufacturers, but also of isolation from the Wuppertal workers, cf. Körner, *Lebenskämpfe* 1:385–403.

communist society that would allow that potential to be expressed in full. Such a society was to be brought about peacefully, by convincing all social groups of the benefits of a new order of things. Somewhat inconsistently, the true socialists continuously denounced the bourgeoisie they were trying to win over for communism, and not just for their economic and social ideas, but for their political ones as well. According to Karl Grün, one of the most influential of the Rhenish true socialists, the liberal demand for constitutional government in Prussia was just "an egoistical wish of the possessing classes."[62]

Many democrats, who were themselves no friends of capitalism and the bourgeoisie, nonetheless sharply criticized this attitude, sensibly pointing out it would not do to denounce the aspirations of liberalism while authoritarian government and a semifeudal ruling class still dominated the Prussian state. They were joined by Marx and Engels, who broke with most of their fellow communists on this issue. Indeed, the true socialists are largely remembered today as the targets of a particularly vituperative section of the *Communist Manifesto*, where their attacks on the bourgeoisie were condemned for giving aid and comfort to Prussian absolutism, and their writings described as "foul and enervating."[63]

Because of a curious legal technicality, a true socialist newspaper, the *Trier'sche Zeitung*, came to be the only openly radical oppositional journal in the entire Rhineland between the suppression of the *Rhineische Zeitung* in 1843 and the outbreak of revolution five years later. The chief—in fact, virtually the only—newspaper in the southwestern part of the Prussian Rhine Province, the *Trier'sche Zeitung* had followed an increasingly oppositional political course since the loosening of censorship restrictions in 1841. When Karl Grün was hired as a correspondent in 1844 and Joseph Weydemeyer, one of the communist ex-artillery officers, was hired as assistant editor in 1845–1846, the paper's editorial policy became ever more socialist.[64]

The newspaper's first clash with the censors occurred in 1842, and in the following years it became increasingly aggressive, openly flouting the authorities and attacking seemingly every political and social institution within the Prussian monarchy. Although formally subject to prior censorship, the editors announced their intention of combating it. They found ways to get prohibited

---

[62] Surprisingly, there is no detailed study of the true socialists, but cf. Faber, *Die Rheinlande*, pp. 335–38; Obenaus, *Parlamentarismus in Preußen*, pp. 639–40; Dowe, *Aktion und Organisation*, pp. 59–69.

[63] Wehler, *Deutsche Gesellschaftsgeschichte* 2:683–84; Obenaus, *Parlamentarismus in Preußen*, p. 641; Dowe, *Aktion und Organisation*, pp. 93–111. The account of Marx and Engels's break with the true socialists in Hammen, *The Red '48ers*, pp. 122–30, 180, completely ignores the contemporary political debate and is therefore very misleading.

[64] A broad general account of the newspaper is provided by Dieter Dowe, "Die erste sozialistische Tageszeitung in Deutschland. Der Weg der 'Trierschen Zeitung' vom Liberalismus über den 'wahren Sozialismus' zum Anarchismus (1840–1851)," *Archiv für Sozialgeschichte* 12 (1972): 55–107. On newspapers and their readership in the Trier District, see the survey of 1842 in LAK 442 Nr. 3378.

ideas past the censors, who often had difficulty understanding the true socialist jargon. The editors would constantly repeat prohibited articles until the fatigued censor let them go by. If they were still refused, they would appeal every unfavorable censor's decision to the censorship court in Berlin. When all else failed, the editors would engage in the prohibited practice of printing blank spaces where a censored article should have appeared. The newspaper was too much for the Trier District government, which ran through seven different censors in five years, one of whom died of a stroke, no doubt in part brought on by the exasperation he faced trying to keep the *Trier'sche Zeitung* in line.[65]

In view of what happened to the *Rheinische Zeitung* in 1843, one might expect the radical Trier newspaper to have shared its fate, and in fact the Interior Ministry threatened to withdraw its concession as early as August 1843, a good half-year before the journal began developing a socialist editorial policy. To the authorities' grave embarrassment, it turned out to be impossible to withdraw the newspaper's concession because it had none. Its first publisher, Privy Councillor von Hetzrodt, the very epitome of a well-connected insider, who had held important positions in the old regime, in the French government, and then under the Prussians had simply begun publishing in 1814 when the French authorities had fled. The Prussian government had tolerated the newspaper and allowed it to pass on to his heirs on his death in the early 1830s. This toleration, the government's legal experts in Koblenz and Berlin ruled, was as good as a concession to publish—actually, even better, since, never having been explicitly extended, it could not be revoked.[66]

Clashes with the censor were for the *Trier'sche Zeitung* literally an everyday affair, and two lists have survived in the archives of 307 separate incidents of censorship, in July–October 1846 and all of 1847. The reasons the censor exercised his blue pencil are described in Table 3.1. Explicitly communistic ideas made up only a small portion of the offending material, far outweighed by attacks on the government and authorities, stock themes for noncommunist radicals. The *Trier'sche Zeitung* was censored far more often than were other oppositional newspapers, such as the moderate liberal *Kölnische Zeitung* or the Catholic-clerical *Rhein und Moselzeitung* in Koblenz, but it was censored mostly for its radical-oppositional ideas, not for its specifically socialist ones.[67]

---

[65] LAK 403 Nr. 3805 pp. 189–92, 219–22, 255–62, 377–81, and passim; LAK 441 Nr. 6480 pp. 61, 177–80, and passim; ZSTAM Rep. 77 Tit. 991 Nr. 3 Bd. 1 ff. 85–91; Bd. 2 ff. 278–99.

[66] ZSTAM Rep. 77 Tit. 991 Nr. 3 Bd. 1 ff. 163–69; LAK 403 Nr. 3805 pp. 31–57, 129–33, 235–36. The speculation sometimes advanced that the government voluntarily refrained from suppressing the newspaper to put pressure on the liberal-oppositional *Kölnische Zeitung* (Obenaus, *Parlamentarismus in Preußen*, p. 640) is false.

[67] The dossiers of these more moderately oppositional newspapers, LAK 403 Nrs. 3807 and 18158, show only one or two incidents of censorship.

TABLE 3.1

Reasons for Censoring the *Trier'sche Zeitung*

Reasons for Censorship	Instances	%
Advocating communism, inciting the poor against the rich	46	15
Anticlericalism, advocating immorality	30	10
Attacks on Prussian state and its laws	57	19
Attacks on bureaucracy and individual officials	46	15
Attacks on censorship	32	10
Attacks on the army	17	6
Attacks on monarchy	12	4
Attacks on other German states	24	8
Attacks on foreign countries, German nationalism	27	9
Other	16	5
Total	307	101

Sources: Compiled from LAK 403 Nr. 3085 pp. 399–404, 407–408, 419; and ZSTAM Rep. 77 Tit. 991 Nr. 3 Bd. 2 ff. 304–18.

Socialism had little appeal for the newspaper's readers. In 1840, when censorship was still strict and the newspaper had no political tone at all, its press run was about 500–600. Adopting an increasingly oppositional editorial policy almost doubled subscriptions, bringing them up to some 1,080 by 1844, but they declined to 920 in 1845 and only 850 in 1847, at least suggesting that readers were either bored or offended by true socialism. The Catholic clergy was particularly hostile, priests in Trier preaching against the newspaper and Bishop Arnoldi firing off letters to the Berlin authorities denouncing its articles and at least implying that it should be suppressed.[68]

While other oppositional newspapers in the southern Rhineland, such as the *Mainzer Zeitung* and the *Neue Speyerer Zeitung*, made their hostility to Catholic neoorthodoxy clear even through the censorship, the *Trier'sche Zeitung* was careful to avoid offending Catholic sentiments. Its attacks on religion in general, and neoorthodoxy in particular, were confined to Protestants. Perhaps it was the newspaper's communist ideas that so offended the bishop, although Jacob Marx, professor at the Trier theological seminary, and often the bishop's right-hand man in political questions, wrote a pamphlet in 1847 praising the Catholic communism of the sixteenth-century Paraguay Jesuits. Most likely, the clergy could not tolerate the atheistic, Hegelian language of true socialism.[69]

[68] Press run figures, LAK 403 Nr. 3805 pp. 255–62, 494–506; LAK 442 Nr. 3378 pp. 65–103; the clergy's condemnations, *RhBA* 1, Nr. 300; *RhBA* 2/1, Nrs. 153, 189. Most of the decline in the newspaper's press run came from a decline of subscribers outside of Trier, which might have resulted from the bishop's ordering the diocesan clergy to cancel their subscriptions.

[69] LAK 403 Nr. 3805 pp. 173–84; Zenz, *Geschichte der Stadt Trier* 1:93. As will be seen

These first open appearances of communism in Trier, Elberfeld, and Cologne suggest something of its political limitations. It was not a popular doctrine, its adherents being largely confined to small circles of bourgeois intellectuals and army officers. Nor was it especially dangerous or radical. The authorities did try to suppress it, but mostly for what it had in common with other radical tendencies. The unique aspects of communist doctrine were, at best, a dubious addition to the left-wing opposition, a state of affairs that would continue even after the outbreak of revolution.

THE GERMAN-CATHOLICS AND RADICAL RELIGION

Overshadowing communism in the interest of both the educated public and the common people was a great controversy over religion, beginning in 1844 and continuing through the outbreak of the revolution. The occasion for it was the extraordinary religious pilgrimage to the Holy Shroud of Trier the diocesan authorities sponsored that year. In a six-month period, over half a million pilgrims made the trip to Trier to venerate the precious relic. Not only was the pilgrimage a giant public manifestation of Roman Catholic neoorthodoxy, it was also a right-wing political event, called by the episcopal leadership after consultation with Prince Metternich and carried out with the full consent and close cooperation of the Prussian authorities and with the prominent participation of the very conservative Catholic nobility of Westphalia.[70]

The rationalist response was not long in coming, sparked by a dissident Catholic priest in Silesia, Johannes Ronge, who issued an open letter to the bishop of Trier, condemning the pilgrimage as an example of worship of idols, superstition, and obscuranticism. Quickly excommunicated, Ronge responded by organizing a schismatic church, the German-Catholics. The new religion fulfilled demands raised by the militant rationalists in the Catholic Church, abolishing the ecclesiastical hierarchy, clerical celibacy, confession, veneration of saints, indulgences, pilgrimages, and processions, and introducing a vernacular church service and the election of pastors by their congregations. By 1848, there were sixty thousand schismatics who increasingly understood themselves as pioneers of a new, rationalist Christianity that would unite the once hostile confessions, overcoming Protestant-Catholic dualism.[71]

---

below, Karl Marx in his political activities during the revolution, took great care to avoid offending Rhenish Catholics.

[70] Wolfgang Schieder, "Kirche und Revolution. Sozialgeschichtliche Aspekte der Trierer Wallfahrt von 1844," *Archiv für Sozialgeschichte* 14 (1974): 419–54. Rudolf Lill's reply, "Kirche und Revolution. Zu den Anfängen der katholischen Bewegung im Jahrzehnt vor 1848," ibid. 18 (1978): 565–75, does point out a number of errors of fact, without, however, casting doubt on Schieder's main points.

[71] On the German Catholics, the most general history is Friedrich Wilhelm Graf, *Die Politisierung des religiösen Bewußtseins* (Stuttgart-Bad Cannstatt: Frommannholzboog, 1978), which is very sympathetic but not entirely satisfactory. Alexander Stollenwerk, *Der Deutschkatholizismus*

Many political radicals enthusiastically supported the new religion, the most famous being the Leipzig journalist and Cologne native Robert Blum. Leftists, such as the Krefeld gymnast Caspar Immandt and the militantly anticlerical Elberfeld teacher of draftsmanship Hermann Körner, not only joined the sect but became leaders of their respective congregations. The German-Catholics were most active on the upper Rhine, where their adherents included the Neustadt merchant Ignaz Rassiga, one of the organizers of the Hambach festival and a revolutionary activist in 1848–1849, and his fellow Neustädter, watchmaker Johann Valentin Weber, another future revolutionary activist, the first Palatine communist. The Rhenish schismatics were most successful in Rhine-Hessen, having created seven different congregations there before 1848, also with prominent leftists as members. One such was Johann Mohr, a Mainz judge pensioned off for his participation in the Hambach festival, who would be a democratic leader during the revolution from his retirement seat in the village of Oberingelheim.[72]

Public manifestations of the schismatics in the southern Rhineland produced extraordinary crowds. Fifteen thousand people came to Worms to see Johannes Ronge celebrate a German-Catholic mass in October 1845, including some four thousand from neighboring areas in the Palatinate. All the available wagons in Neustadt a.d.W. were rented for the occasion. One-third of Neustadt's inhabitants joined the funeral procession of a German-Catholic on July 14, 1845, the coffin carried by fifteen distinguished citizens, followed by fifty maidens clad in mourning.[73]

Both Worms and Neustadt a.d.W. were predominantly Protestant towns, and most of the crowds cheering Ronge, the "Luther of the nineteenth century," as he liked to call himself, were themselves Protestants. Protestants openly favored the new religion, congregations in Kreuznach, Saarbrücken, Krefeld, Elberfeld, and Duisburg volunteering use of their churches or schools for the Catholic schismatics' worship. Some Palatine Protestants petitioned the Bavarian parliament in favor of the German-Catholics; others distributed anti-Catholic literature, ostensibly in favor of the new religion. In Neustadt a.d.W., crowds parodied the Holy Shroud of Trier; in Edenkoben, they broke the windows on the house of the Roman Catholic parish priest.[74]

---

in der preußischen Rheinprovinz (Mainz: Gesellschaft für mittelrheinische Kirchengeschichte, 1971), is a good regional study; Friedrich Wilhelm Kantzenbach, "Zur Geschichte des Deutschkatholizismus in Bayern und in der Pfalz im Vormärz," *BPfK* 39 (1972): 5–15, a poor one. Körner, *Lebenskämpfe* 1:281–378, reminiscences of an active lay participant who saw the sect's strengths and weaknesses in retrospect, is probably the best account.

[72] Buschbell, "Johann Anton Caspar Immandt," pp. 43–47; Körner's memoirs as cited in the previous note; LAS H1 Nr. 617 f. 29; Nr. 595 ff. 7–8; *MZ*, 19 June 1845, 14 Apr. 1847; Schütz, "Vormärz in Mainz," pp. 84–85.

[73] LAS H1 Nr. 617 ff. 35, 42–43; *MZ*, 30 Oct. 1845.

[74] LAS H1 Nr. 617 ff. 4, 13–14, 85; LAK 403 Nr. 10755 pp. 51–58, 75–80, 101–105, 149–56, 169–75, 303–26.

Most Roman Catholics who converted to German-Catholicism were living in a religiously mixed marriage, and tired of hearing from priests how they were going to hell for it, yet evidently unable to take the step of becoming Protestants. They found joining the new religion, quasi-Protestant in its ritual but still nominally Catholic, a tolerable compromise. Infant baptisms seem to have been especially prominent in early German-Catholic church services, not surprising in view of the role the sect played in resolving the sticking point of offspring among religiously mixed couples.[75]

The vast majority of Roman Catholics vehemently rejected the schism, seeing it as a Protestant-sponsored plot to destroy their religion. Crowds of thousands disrupted German-Catholic services in the Wuppertal, Krefeld, and the Hunsrück village of Hottenbach. The elderly Catholic pastor Aloys Licht of Leiwen, on the Moselle, a veteran clerical rationalist who went over to the new religion, was held captive by his own parishioners and had to be rescued in a nighttime operation by Elberfeld German-Catholics with the assistance of the Trier masonic lodge.[76]

Although the founders of German-Catholicism thought their religion would overcome Catholic-Protestant dualism, in practice it ended up affirming and promoting it. If Protestants in both the northern and southern Rhineland patronized the schism, they were different Protestants in each area, and the political implications of their patronage were equally varied. Both the Prussian government and the neoorthodox clergy of the lower Rhine coquetted with the schismatics, seeing their church as a step for Roman Catholics on their way to Protestantism. When the rationalist doctrine and the left-wing political connections of the new religion became clear, the previously favorable attitude gave way to hostility. But this belated opposition came too late to gain the approval of Roman Catholics, who never lost the feeling that the whole movement had been secretly sponsored by the Protestants. Even at the end of 1849, the bishop of Trier retained the anger he felt at the Prussian government five years previously for not having suppressed the movement and the many attacks it had directed against him.[77]

Bavarian and Hessian authorities, unlike their Prussian counterparts, opposed the movement from the very first, prohibiting public German-Catholic

[75] LAS H1 Nr. 617 ff. 15–18, 29; LAK 403 Nr. 10755 pp. 15–17, 75–80, 85–92, 183–85, 231–41, 277–87, 369–71; Körner, *Lebenskämpfe* 1:330. Similarly, Stollenwerk, *Deutsch-Katholizismus*, p. 94. Of course, adherents, like the watchmaker Johann Weber of Neustadt a.d.W., could be radicals who were also living in a religiously mixed marriage.

[76] LAK 403 Nr. 10755 pp. 51–58, 389–90; HSTAD RD Pr. Nr. 1466 ff. 185–86; Körner, *Lebenskämpfe* 1:317–24; Stollenwerck, *Deutschkatholizismus*, pp. 126–27.

[77] LAK 403 Nr. 10755 pp. 75–80, 85–92, 135–41, 505–08; Körner, *Lebenskämpfe* 1:335–39, 352–57; LAK 442 Nr. 6659 pp. 47–48; Stollenwerck, *Deutschkatholizismus*, pp. 22–41. The correspondence of the Protestant liberal Heinrich von Gagern, with and about his brother Max, a convert to Catholicism, contains interesting material on attitudes toward the German-Catholics. *Deutscher Liberalismus im Vormärz*, Nrs. 179, 193–94.

services or even the founding of congregations and keeping the adherents of schism under police surveillance. The neoorthodox minority of upper Rhine Protestants denounced the schismatics as godless subversives hiding behind Luther's memory. Protestant supporters of German-Catholicism in the Palatinate and Rhine-Hessen were rationalists who made the new religion another one of their political causes, along with Pastor Frantz in the Palatinate and the preservation of civil marriage in Rhine-Hessen. The frenzied welcome given Johannes Ronge in Worms by an enormous but largely Protestant crowd showed that supporting the schismatics was an effective means of mass political mobilization, but one that guaranteed that neoorthodox Roman Catholics, not a very likely group for radical sympathies in any event, would be sworn enemies of the left in the forthcoming period of political turmoil.[78]

POLITICAL ALIGNMENTS ON THE EVE OF REVOLUTION, 1845–1847

All the political and ideological tendencies of 1848–1849 had been apparent three years previously. But there remained a brief breathing spell before the actual outbreak of revolution, in which the different tendencies jockeyed for position, interacting with the authorities and with one another.

The St. Martin's Parish Fair Riots in Cologne, 1846

These riots, a major cause célèbre, arose from utterly trivial antecedents, namely, the explosion of firecrackers, which was how the inhabitants of the parish of Big St. Martin, south of the Cologne cathedral, celebrated their yearly parish fair. During the reign of Friedrich Wilhelm III, the fair, which occurred at the beginning of August, had approximately coincided with the king's birthday. Since the birthday was an officially sponsored day of festivity, the police turned the other way when firecrackers were set off or rifles fired in the air, acts formally prohibited within the city limits. When Friedrich Wilhelm IV ascended the throne in 1840, not only did he disappoint Cologne's liberal notables by refusing to sponsor political reforms his authoritarian father had opposed; he disrupted the festive harmony of St. Martin's parishioners by having being born in October. The police dusted off the rule book and began to intervene at the parish fair each year, charging through the dark and narrow streets of the neighborhood, little changed since the Middle Ages, trying to arrest the mostly teenaged gunpowdered rulebreakers. The crowd openly resented the interference with their fun and would gather together and forcibly liberate the arrested youths from the police.

---

[78] BHSTAM MInn Nr. 44358 ff. 3–4; LAS H1 Nr. 617 ff. 23–27, 82–83; Nr. 585 ff. 3–4, 12–14; *MZ*, 15 Aug., 5 Oct. 1845; Kantzenbach, "Deutsch-Katholizismus in Bayern," passim; Bonkhoff, *Kirche der Pfalz*, pp. 106–08; Hofmann, *Rheinhessische Volkskunde*, p. 109.

Events went on this way for years, until in 1846 the Cologne police commissioner, smarting from a rebuke issued him by the district government for not showing enough energy in combatting disorder, requisitioned troops for the evening of August 4. Just bivouacked en masse on the Alter Markt (the Old Marketplace), the main square in the neighborhood, the soldiers completely disrupted the festivities. When provoked by taunts and perhaps some thrown stones from the frustrated celebrants, they went completely out of control, charging the crowd, beating with their rifle butts and stabbing with their bayonets anyone they encountered. The soldiers broke into private homes, assaulting the inhabitants and smashing the furniture; they pursued people on the street as far as the Cathedral Square.

In and of itself, what these events revealed—that the police could not preserve public order, that Prussian officials carried following the rules a little too far, that Rhinelanders and soldiers from East Elbian Prussia did not get along very well—had been frequently shown before, if perhaps on not quite so large a scale and not in the heart of the provincial metropolis. What occurred the following day, however, was something quite new. An outraged crowd of thousands gathered at city hall, and after prolonged negotiations among its leaders, the mayor, the district governor, and the commandant of the fortress, it was agreed that the soldiers would be withdrawn to their barracks and order in the city preserved by an unarmed civic guard. The guard's leaders included liberal and democratic notables, among them, naturally, Franz Raveaux. The agreement was approved that evening by the provincial governor and the commander of the Prussian Eighth Army Corps, who had hurried to the scene from Koblenz. This sensible action, which restored order in the city, was later violently condemned by the king personally and his entire Council of Ministers, as a surrender to subversion and a blot on the honor of the army.

The funeral procession of a rioter bayoneted to death by soldiers was held on August 6, escorted by the civic guard and attended by a great crowd of spectators. There were two speakers at the grave: Pastor Kerp of St. Albans, in 1838 a passionate adherent of the arrested archbishop and enemy of the authorities, who eight years later said nothing to stir up the crowd, and the communist physician Karl D'Ester, who gave a speech violently attacking the government.[79]

This was not the first time civic guards had been formed in the Prussian Rhine Province, but on the previous occasion, during the disturbances in 1830, they had been created, with the authorities' approval to protect the bour-

[79] Material on the riot, its precursors and aftermath, and a detailed collection of press clippings, can be found in HSTAD RK Nr. 62 ff. 4–6, 48–68, 71–73, 70, 84–85, 115; Nr. 63 ff. 12–14, 17–22, 32, 53–102; LAK 403 Nr. 18081 pp. 11–30, 37–40, 263–528; ZSTAM Rep. 77 Tit. 505 Nr. 2 Vol. 3 passim, in very condensed form in *RhBA* 2/1, Nr. 36. Among the more helpful commentaries on this event are Ayçoberry, *Cologne*, pp. 211–12; and Seypel, "Die Demokratische Gesellschaft in Köln," pp. 52–54.

geoisie from the crowd in the absence of the army. This time, the guard was created to protect the bourgeoisie and the crowd from the army, with the forced consent of the authorities—who were promptly disowned by their superiors for their action, in effect told they should have prolonged and exacerbated the bloodshed. Add to this constellation of forces the haranguing of the crowd by an open radical, and the contours of a revolutionary situation become apparent.

The Prussian Municipal Elections of 1846

The immediate political relevance of the riots, however, was that they occurred in the midst of Cologne's first election campaign, the Prussian authorities having finally agreed after thirty years of rule to allow municipal elections in their Rhenish province. These elections were far from democratic, since a stiff property franchise meant that only a small fraction of the adult males were eligible—in Cologne about a fifth. The eligible voters were grouped into three classes by the amount of taxes paid. The top third elected as many city councilmen as the bottom, even though they were only one-fourth as numerous.

Public meetings were held to discuss the elections, their very existence a novelty. At these meetings conflicts became apparent between "the people" and the "aristocracy of money," as they had at the founding meetings of the branch association for the welfare of the working classes in 1844. Spearheaded by demands for cheap municipal credit for small independent businessmen, measures to improve the condition of the workers, and more money for poor relief, a left-wing coalition of democrats and communists won a number of seats in the third class. Their victorious candidates included the heroes of the events following the riots, Raveaux and D'Ester.[80]

A similar conflict pitting future democrats as self-proclaimed representatives of the people against the "moneybags" occurred in the 1846 municipal elections in Saarbrücken as well, but this was an atypical political alignment. Far more common, found in Aachen, Düsseldorf, Krefeld, Koblenz, Kreuznach, Trier, and many smaller cities and towns, were elections fought out on confessional lines between Protestants and Catholics. Given the relationship between confession and social class, the former were typically victorious in the first class (representatives of the very wealthiest) and the latter in the third, with the second hotly fought over. An interesting exception was in Trier, where expressly Catholic candidates obtained only half the seats in the third class of voters, the predominantly Protestant liberals, with the help of the communists of the *Trier'sche Zeitung*, taking the rest.[81]

[80] Seypel, "Die Demokratische Gesellschaft in Köln," pp. 48–54; Dowe, *Aktion und Organisation*, pp. 115–21.

[81] ZSTAM Rep. 77 Tit. 343A Nr. 24 ff. 77–84; LAK 441 Nr. 1321 pp. 131–43; Nr. 1322 pp. 75–83; *KnZ*, 25 July 1846 (Beilage), 27 July, 25 Aug., 2, 10, 15, 22 Oct. 1846; Noack, "1848/

There were few Catholics living in the largely Protestant Wuppertal wealthy enough to be eligible to vote, and the city council elections in Barmen and Elberfeld pitted the freethinkers, calling themselves "the party of the people," against the neoorthodox, whom they dubbed "the aristocrats." Religion and social structure did coincide to an extent, as rationalist candidates were victorious in the third class, while the candidates of the very wealthy and very religious merchants, bankers, and manufacturers dominated the first two. Of course, election results there, as elsewhere in Rhenish Prussia, revealed nothing about the political opinions of the workers, since the poorest 80 percent of the adult male population were ineligible to vote.[82]

The elections did suggest the existence of four increasingly fixed political tendencies: a neoorthodox Protestant conservatism, a mostly Protestant but freethinking liberalism, a specifically Roman Catholic party, largely composed of the neoorthodox, but also including more moderately rationalist Catholics, and a left, containing only vaguely differentiated democrats and communists. The authorities were sure to support the first group and oppose the last, but their relations with the middle two were not entirely fixed, possibilities varying between alliance and hostility. The franchise for the municipal elections, with its stiff property qualification and division of the eligible voters into three groups by income, was a product of cooperation between liberal deputies in the Provincial Diet and Prussian officials. Both groups wished to exclude the lower and middle classes from the ballot, perceiving them as probable supporters of the democrats and the Catholic party. Liberal demands for a constitution and parliamentary government, however, found no support in Berlin, so these tentative efforts toward political cooperation with the authorities remained just that.[83]

Roman Catholic interests also pressed for political cooperation with the Prussian state in the wake of the 1844 Trier pilgrimage. Catholic activists in Cologne, so determined in their opposition to the government after the arrest of the archbishop in 1837, were conspicuous by their absence in the events following the St. Martin's parish fair riots. Indeed, the *Rhein- und Moselzeitung* in Koblenz, the one newspaper in the Prussian Rhineland with a pro-Catholic editorial policy, actually took the government's side in the riots, blaming them on communist philanthropists who had spoiled the lower classes by giving them chocolate, tobacco, and schnapps as charity, making them unruly and ruining their willingness to work.[84]

---

49 in der Saargegend," pp. 41–42; Zenz, *Geschichte der Stadt Trier* 1:72; Nießner, *Aachen*, p. 35.

[82] *KnZ*, 12 June 1846; Herberts, *Kirche und Handel*, pp. 118–19; Köllmann, *Stadt Barmen*, pp. 223–24.

[83] Obenaus, *Anfänge des Parlamentarismus*, pp. 617–48, is a good account, although I think the democrats and socialists were less sharply differentiated than Obenaus describes them as being.

[84] Article cited in *KnZ*, 8 Aug. 1846. On this newspaper, see Friedrich Mönckmeyer, *Die*

This was a twisted explanation of events, but it fit into a political strategy of putting Catholicism forward as an enemy of communism. Catholics hoped to use their anticommunism to convince the government to issue a concession to start a newspaper with a Catholic editorial policy, something the Prussian authorities had previously refused to do. (The *Rhein- und Moselzeitung* had been a Protestant, governmental journal until a reader boycott sponsored by a circle of Koblenz Catholic militants cost the publisher so much money that he changed editors.) In 1846 rumors flew about the founding of an officially sponsored conservative but Catholic daily in the Prussian Rhineland. Proposals for independent Catholic newspapers in Trier, Krefeld, and Cologne stressed they would be anticommunist and counterrevolutionary.

Most Rhenish Catholics, however, would not support a newspaper under the control of the Protestant, Prussian state, no matter how sensitive the authorities promised to be toward Catholic sentiment. The Prussian authorities, for their part, were unprepared to offer a concession to an independent Catholic newspaper, no matter how politically conservative it claimed to be. Just as had been the case with the moderate liberals, attempts of Rhenish Catholics to cooperate with the government foundered on Berlin's refusal to make any concessions. Both Catholics and liberals were forced to remain in opposition until revolutionary events in 1848 changed both the government and the political situation.[85]

Anticlericalism and Political Opposition in the Southern Rhineland

In contrast to the tangled web of political alignments and overlapping issues prevalent in the Prussian Rhine Province in the years before the 1848 revolution, the political situation in Rhine-Hessen and the Palatinate was much simpler. There, the main political issues were religious ones; the political opposition consisted of religious rationalists—mostly Protestants, but including some Catholics and Jews as well—while the neoorthodox were aligned with the authorities.

This link between religious rationalism and political opposition was most direct in the Palatinate, where the main demands of the opposition in the years 1845–1847 were the reinstatement of the suspended rationalist Pastor Frantz, the liberation of the Palatine Union Church from the neoorthodox Superior

---

Rhein- und Moselzeitung: ein Beitrag zur Entstehungsgeschichte der katholischen Presse und des politischen Katholizismus in den Rheinlanden (Bonn: Marcus und Weber, 1912).

[85] *RhBA* 2/1, Nrs. 31, 312; Michael Klöcker, *Theodor Brüggemann (1796–1866)* (Ratingen and Kastellaun: Aloys Henn, 1975), pp. 174–79; LAK 403 Nr. 3085 pp. 255–62; Nr. 7171 pp. 67–70; LAK 442 Nr. 6140 pp. 457–65. Church newspapers, ostensibly nonpolitical, but often dealing circumspectly with political affairs, provided a partial substitute for the lack of a major Catholic newspaper. Rudolf Pesch, *Die kirchlich-politische Presse der Katholiken in der Rheinprovinz vor 1848* (Mainz: Grünewald, 1966).

Consistory in Munich, and the prohibition of the founding of monasteries in the province. A meeting in Edenkoben, on November 10, 1846 (Luther's birthday), with prominent participation of ex-activists of the Hambach Festival, issued a declaration about the Union Church, which was printed up and distributed through the province in an edition of ten thousand. Copies were placed in taverns or brought around door to door for signature. Protestant revivalists countered with their own meeting the following year in Frankenstein, in the western Palatinate, drawing up an opposing declaration, which was also circulated and received several thousand signatures. In a similar way, Roman Catholic petitions in support of the Franciscans were distributed and signed en masse.[86]

The main political issue in Rhine-Hessen before the revolution was the defense of the Rhenish Institutions against the government's proposed all-Hessian civil code. Unlike the religious controversies in the Palatinate, this might not seem like a divisive question, since the previous campaign in defense of the Rhenish Institutions, the movement in the Prussian Rhine Province against the proposed criminal code of 1843, had united Catholics and Protestants, rationalists and neoorthodox, moderates and radicals. In Rhine-Hessen, however, the main issue raised by opponents of the code, reiterated in petitions and mass meetings, was that the new legal system would abolish civil marriage, thus opening the door to religious bigotry and intolerance, proselytization and excesses of clerical power. These were all code words for Protestant opposition to Catholicism and especially rationalist opposition to religious neoorthodoxy. Even though the bishop of Mainz also opposed the new criminal code, which did abolish civil marriage but still allowed divorce, the Rhine-Hessian campaign in favor of the Rhenish Institutions had a strong anticlerical favor.[87]

When the proposal was put through the Hessian Parliament late in 1846, the women and girls of the Mainz bourgeoisie responded by coming to the 1847 New Year's Ball in the Casino, the exclusive social club, dressed in mourning. That same day, the plebians of the city showed their disapproval by bringing a cat music to the provincial governor. The actions were a rebuke to the authorities but also to the strict Catholic element in Mainz, which had dominated the 1846 city council elections.[88]

Also in contrast to Rhenish Prussia, the political opposition in the southern Rhineland showed few signs of splitting into moderate and radical elements before 1848. Differences between liberals and democrats in Mainz do seem to have surfaced in conjunction with a banquet held in honor of the Rhine-Hes-

[86] Bonkhoff, *Kirche der Pfalz*, pp. 102–106; Scherer, *Zur pfälzischen Kirchengeschichte*, pp. 157–59; LAS H1 Nr. 969 passim; RP Alwens to Gesammt-Staats-Ministerium, 20 Aug. 1849, BHSTAM MInn Nr. 45533 (an interesting postrevolutionary retrospective view).

[87] On the campaign, see sources cited in note 30.

[88] Schütz, "Vormärz in Mainz," p. 98; *KnZ*, 12, 23 Sept. 1846.

sian parliamentary deputies in the summer of 1847, but even this one occasion could not be found in the Palatinate. Although future radicals and moderates were both certainly active there during the *Vormärz*, before the outbreak of revolution they remained united in their opposition to the Bavarian government and religious neoorthodoxy. Political differences already apparent on the lower Rhine in 1844 would only emerge slowly in the Palatinate in the course of the revolution.[89]

The Popularity of Popular Politics

In comparing the tensions of *Vormärz* society discussed in the previous chapter with the forms of popular politics explored in this one, certain areas of overlap emerge but so do wide regions of lack of contact. Problems specific to rural society were the area where social tensions and popular politics diverged most greatly. Political activists in general, and leftists in particular, certainly thought about the problems of the peasantry. The condition of viticulture, admittedly not just a peasant problem, but one shared by wine merchants and large vineyard owners, was frequently discussed. Conflict over forest use was also an occasional political issue, albeit not one as pressing for those who thought about politics as it was to the peasants.

But the political debate on these issues rarely addressed the peasants themselves. Political organization simply did not exist in the Rhenish countryside before 1848: Banquets, politicized festivity, most petition drives, carnival and gymnastics societies, and informal political circles were all urban affairs. There was, in addition, a conceptual failure of political activists, who, with interesting exceptions, such as Franz Raveaux, could not see the rural population as a political subject. Forest conflict, to take a burning issue to the peasants, was discussed as a problem of criminality, as proof of rustic misery, or as an example of failed governmental policy, but not as a means to mobilize the countryfolk.

The social problems of the urban lower classes and manufacturing outworkers received more attention from bourgeois or intellectual political activists. On certain occasions, such as the founding of the Cologne affiliate of the Association for the Welfare of the Working Classes, or the controversy over the iron wares foundry in Burgthal near Solingen, they even addressed the lower classes themselves about them. Although they were becoming more common in the late 1840s, such events remained relatively infrequent. When they did occur, they brought official repression in their wake. Even without it, a certain distance remained between bourgeois activists and members of the lower classes. The temptation for the former to act on behalf of the latter, instead of

---

[89] Circumspect, and clearly censored accounts of differences between Mainz radicals and moderates in *MZ*, 2, 5, 20, 22 Aug. 1847.

agitating among them was stong and even the communists made no special efforts to gain proletarian followers.

There was a much greater connection between self-consciously political actions and social tensions in two areas: conflicts with the state and conflicts between and among religious confessions. Taxes and relations between the bureaucracy or the army and the civilian population, between representatives of the trans-Rhenan core states and the Rhinelanders, between Protestants and Catholics, or between rationalists and the neoorthodox were issues that were emphasized by political activists, from moderate liberals, through strict Catholics, to democrats and communists, and that found a substantial resonance in the population. There may have been divergent class viewpoints—the bourgeoisie more concerned about the struggle over the proposed Prussian criminal code of 1843 about the preservation of jury trials, the people more concerned about being beaten by East Elbian bureaucrats—but there were also common interests and points of action.

Given the differences in the existence of political or protopolitical organizations between town and country, these, like all other issues, were most likely to be politicized, to be channeled into a movement behind an organized leadership, in an urban setting. Besides this familiar rural-urban dichotomy, another one existed, separating the northern Rhineland from its southern part. In the Palatinate and Rhine-Hessen, questions of religion and relations of the trans-Rhenan provinces to the core state dominated political life on the eve of the revolution so that the potential for mass political mobilization by leftist activists was much greater than in the Prussian Rhineland. The existence of constitutions and a regular political life in these two southern provinces gave activists regular practice in politics; the bourgeoisie of the region were less fearful of stirring up the masses, as the example of the events of 1832 showed. No less than the differences between city and country, those between north and south would mark the events of the revolutionary years soon to come.

PART TWO

An Incomplete Revolution

"The King of Bavaria is a thief, a robber, and the state officials are his accomplices."

—Isaak Herold, innkeeper of Bobenheim, overheard by a gendarme in a Worms tavern, December 13, 1848.

CHAPTER FOUR

From Crisis to Revolution, September 1845–May 1848

PRELUDE IN CRISIS, 1845–1847

From its overuse in the currency of historical expression, the concept of crisis has suffered an inflationary loss of value, but it still seems appropriate to the second half of the 1840s. Between the disastrous harvests of 1845 and 1846, which produced near-famine conditions in much of Europe, the "commercial crisis"—today we would call it a severe recession—of 1847–1849, and the growing political tensions across the continent, whose first violent manifestation was the Swiss Civil War of 1847, the entire stucture of socioeconomic and political order appeared in question. The Rhineland, as much as any other German or European region, experienced this crisis, prelude to the revolutionary events of 1848–1849.

From Famine to Unemployment

Given that the harvest was always closely monitored by the authorities, the news of the outbreak of the potato blight in the fall of 1845 came as no surprise. Nor was it cause for alarm, officials and the upper classes agreeing that the situation could be met by a combination of education, laissez-faire, and private initiative. True, the potato harvest had been disastrous, but university scientists and practical agronomists sought ways to save the remaining crop from the blight. Putting potatoes in a pit lined with coal tar and pouring sulfuric acid out of a lead pipe over them would cure the blight, they asserted, and storing them in a mixture of horse dung, ashes, and broken glass would preserve healthy potatoes from it. Potatoes were the food of the poor, but the grain harvest had been a rich one, so private charity or the actions of municipal governments in opening soup kitchens and distributing cheap bread and potatoes to the workers would ensure that while some belt tightening might be necessary, there would be no disaster.[1]

Complementing these plans was a trust in the beneficial results of the free market. To be sure, the Prussian government imposed an embargo on potato exports outside the German customs union in the fall of 1845, followed by the Bavarians the following winter, but this was in response to French, Belgium,

---

[1] RA to MInn, 8 Sept. 1845, LR Kr. Düren to RA, 8 Nov. 1845, LR Kr. Malmedy to RA, 13 Jan. 1846, HSTAD RA Nr. 1775; LAK 403 Nr. 2398 pp. 71–84, 87–93, 139–43, 207–10, 351–63, 431–38; LAS H1 Nr. 1396 ff. 5–48; *KnZ*, 23 Aug., 5, 24 Sept., 3 Oct., 3 Nov. 1845.

and Dutch embargoes. Proposals to extend the embargo to other foodstuffs, or even to abolish the tariff on imported grain and flour were turned down; price controls or distribution of stores from military magazines, trusted remedies of the mercantilist eighteenth century, were rejected out of hand. Even the Munich authorities, who had fought the famine of 1817 by such measures as banning Jews from the marketplace, supported laissez-faire. And, just as the doctrines of Adam Smith would have it, the invisible hand seemed to be working its magic: Prices fell in late 1845 and early 1846, topping out at levels seen in 1843 after the bad harvest of the previous year. The future could be met with a cautious optimism.[2]

A closer look at the situation shows regional variations, the results of long-term economic developments, which contained within them the seeds of coming difficulties. The large peasants of the grain-growing upper and lower Rhine plains did well from the rising prices, and could provide both employment and private charity to the day laborer lower classes of the area. But this affluence was purchased by massive grain exports to France and the Low Countries, substantially higher than in previous years, drawing down available stocks of foodstuffs. For impoverished up-country peasants, already living on the margin of subsistence, the failure of the potato crop was a disaster, since they lacked both the means to earn money to purchase alternative food supplies and an affluent rural population that could help support the poor. In urban areas, purchasing power was even more the key to the economic situation: If trade was good, the workers could get by, even with higher prices; poor business conditions, and increasing unemployment, even with lower grain prices, would be catastrophic.[3]

The unusually hot and dry summer of 1846 mitigated somewhat the effects of the potato blight but produced the worst grain crop in living memory, the rye harvest just 20 to 30 percent of normal. Between this meager crop and ever-growing exports, discontent and prices climbed throughout the fall. As the latter peaked in the winter and spring of 1847 at twice their 1844 levels, open panic spread throughout the Rhineland. Even wealthy farmers, who usually marketed a large surplus, had to buy food for their families; spot shortages appeared in various markets; supplies were held back, illegally, by local officials.[4]

---

[2] Besides the sources cited above, see LAK 403 Nr. 2398 pp. 19–21; Nr. 17951 pp. 73–76, 477–78; MInn to RP, 2 Sept. 1846, and to the king, 25 Sept. 1846, BHSTAM MInn Nr. 46240; "Vortrag die Theurung und den Mangel des Getreides betr.," 2 Oct. [1846], BHSTAM MInn Nr. 46253. Monthly wholesale and retail (black bread) market prices for Aachen (HSTAD RA Nrs. 12758–59) and retail (also black bread) prices for Elberfeld (Barmen/Elberfeld Chamber of Commerce to RD, 10 Oct. 1855, HSTAD RD Nr. 2261) show a peaking and falling off in late 1845 or early 1846.

[3] Besides the sources cited in the two previous notes, see HSTAD RD Pr Nr. 1330 ff. 53, 58–59, 147–48, 259–60; Aachen/Burtscheid Chamber of Commerce to RA, 5 Sept. 1845, LR Kr. Heinsberg to RA, 6 Sept. 1845, 27 Mar. 1846; LAK 403 Nr. 2398 pp. 255–65, 557–75.

[4] Harvest and conditions in fall 1846: HSTAD RD Pr. Nr. 1331 ff. 4–42; reports of the county

In the uplands, near-Irish conditions of famine obtained. Two-thirds of the inhabitants of Sistig (Schleiden County) were beggars, bursting into houses and government offices to demand food, but the remaining one-third had nothing to give them, possessing just enough for their families. Nearby in Allendorf, the schoolteacher reported that almost half the households had literally nothing to eat. While the adults remained in bed all day, children came to school "but sit as though dead, unmoving, with tears in their eyes." With nothing to lose, peasants swarmed out of the hills into the river valleys, begging—or demanding—bread.[5]

The voluntarism and local initiative that had seemed so successful as late as the spring of 1846 no longer sufficed to master the situation. The Prussian, Bavarian, and Hessian authorities, showed that, unlike their English counterparts in Ireland, they were unwilling to apply free market dogma to the point of mass starvation. Starting in late fall 1846 and continuing through until the next harvest, they employed their respective governments' wealth and authority to combat famine. Consumption taxes and import duties were abolished for the duration of the crisis, while restrictions on sales outside the marketplace and a 25 percent duty on grain exported outside the customs union helped keep food in the country. Government grain purchases in Russia and North America brought imports up the Rhine equal to exports down it. The Prussian government released flour from its military magazines for civilian consumption. These measures checked the famine, and the good harvest of 1847 brought it to an end, food prices falling to modest levels by the end of that year.[6]

Rather to the surprise of the authorities, the population remained passive throughout the period of rising prices. Just a few smaller subsistence riots occurred, mostly at the beginning of the harvest failures in 1845 and 1846. The largest was in Aachen, when the bakers refused to give their regular cus-

---

commissioners in HSTAD RA Nr. 1776; HSTAD RA Pr. Nr. 682 ff. 31–52; LAK 403 Nr. 17952 pp. 161–220, 315–20, 409–15, 427–32; reports of the Palatine authorities, Aug.–Sept. 1846 and a note from Mainz, 15 Sept. 1846, in BHSTAM MInn Nr. 46240. On crisis conditions in spring 1847, see the reports of the county and municipal authorities in HSTAD RD Nr. 2261; HSTAD RA Nr. 1776–77; LAK 403 Nr. 17945 pp. 93–99; LAK 403 Nr. 2399 pp. 441–45; LAK 403 Nr. 17955 pp. 33–34, 303–306; RP to MInn, 8 Apr. 1847, BHSTAM MInn Nr. 46240; *RhBA* 2/1, Nr. 129.

[5] BM Sistig to LA Kr. Schleiden, 15 Feb. 1847; and J. Stollenwerk (Allendorf) to RA, 17 Mar. 1847; more generally, LA Kr. Schleiden to RA, 2 May 1847, all in HSTAD RA Nr. 1777. Similarly, LAK 441 Nr. 1322 pp. 119–30; Nr. 1326 pp. 45–59; Police Commissioner Homburg to LK Homburg, 14 Aug. 1846, RP to MInn, 27 Jan. 1847, BHSTAM MInn Nr. 46240.

[6] LAK 403 Nr. 17952 pp. 515–21, 613–16; Nr. 17953 pp. 99, 107, 273, 305, 355–56; Nr. 17954 pp. 487–502; Nr. 2399 pp. 244–53, 447–49; Nr. 17955 pp. 29–35, 303–306; Nr. 17956 pp. 159–66; OPK to RD, 23 Mar. 1847, HSTAD RD Nr. 2261; "Nachweis über die Verwendung des dem Regierungs-Bezirk Aachen im Jahre 1847 überwiesenen Brod Materials," 28 Sept. 1847 (draft), HSTAD RA Nr. 1778; MInn to RP, 24 Oct. 1846 (draft), and MInn to King, 14 Apr. 1847, BHSTAM MInn Nr. 46240. The documents strongly suggest that the Prussian government did considerably more for its Rhenish subjects (who admittedly may have needed it more) than did its Bavarian counterpart.

tomers the traditional free Easter bread in 1846. Thousands of rioters marched through the streets, displaying loaves, shouting, "Poschweck!" (the name of the bread), cursing the bakers, and smashing bakery windows, until dispersed by troops. The district government ordered the bakers to provide the bread, carefully avoiding any appearance of interfering in the free market by arguing that the bakers had violated an implicit contract with their customers.[7]

The Aachen rioters were far from showing rational market logic. Their protest was laden with symbolic and religious elements (Easter being when all good Catholics take communion), proving that the inhabitants of the economically most advanced factory town in the Rhineland could display the culturally most archaic behavior. The disturbances, or lack of them, also suggest that the subsistence crisis in itself did not have a direct political effect; its significance for the coming revolutionary period lay in the further strain it placed on the already difficult position of the region's lower classes.

The return to reasonably priced bread and potatoes by late 1847 did not mean an end to the economic effects of the two successive bad harvests. Especially in its second year, the subsistence crisis had gone beyond the ability of private charity to cope, and municipal and village governments had been forced to raise substantial sums, either by tax surcharges or taking on additional debt. Debt was in fact the most palpable result of the near-famine. Grain purchased by the government overseas or distributed from army stores was not handed out free of charge, but advanced as a loan, to be paid back by local government and, ultimately, by the consumers of the emergency aid. Contemporaries often noted the heavy weight of this debt on workers, peasants, and artisans, even those enjoying a certain modest affluence before the bad harvests.[8]

It was this combination of high food prices and debts contracted because of them that led into the second phase of the economic crisis. As consumers spent ever-greater portions of their income on foodstuffs, their ability to purchase manufactured goods or the services of artisans declined. The additional debt required, just to buy food, proved too much for the primitively organized German credit market, already overstrained by the financial demands of railroad

---

[7] HSTAD RA Pr. Nr. 686 ff. 1–17, *KnZ*, 15 Apr. 1846; for other disturbances, cf. *KnZ*, 25 Sept. 1845 (Wesel), 20 July 1846 (Mainz); LAK 441 Nr. 3055 pp. 143–48 (Koblenz). In general, on food riots in Germany during the near-famine, see Manfred Gailus, "Soziale Protestbewegungen in Deutschland 1847–49," in *Sozialer Protest*, pp. 76–106, esp. pp. 76–85.

[8] Surveys of emergency aid measures show that by 1847 local government funds substantially outweighed private charity: RD to OPK, 6 May 1847, HSTAD RD Nr. 1586; LAK 403 Nr. 17954 pp. 175–95; Nr. 2399 pp. 97–133. On the burden of debt, see HSTAD RD Nr. 1586 f. 11; reports on debt repayment, especially RA to OPK, 11 Jan. 1848, HSTAD RA Nr. 1779; LAK 403 Nr. 17597 passim; LAK 441 Nr. 1326 pp. 133–51, 179–84; Nr. 1329 pp. 321–29; Nr. 1330 pp. 323–29; Nr. 3056 pp. 137–40; RP to MInn, 21 July 1847, BHSTAM MInn Nr. 46238; memo of R. P. Alwens on events of 1848–1849, BHSTAM MInn Nr. 45533; "Der Bericht des Regierungspräsidenten von Zenetti," pp. 146, 167.

construction. The upshot was a severe business contraction, beginning in 1847, aggravating the final and most critical phase of the food shortages. Unemployment among workers and artisans soared in cities and manufacturing districts; businessmen proved ever less capable of meeting their obligations, from the three "most solid, most frugal and most active" merchants of the wine town Cochem on the Moselle, who went bankrupt in August 1847, to the Schaafhausen banking house in Cologne, the largest in the Rhineland, which failed in March 1848. While reports of dramatic political events filled the front pages of the *Neue Speyerer Zeitung* in 1848, the reader who turned to the end of the newspaper could see the daily notices of bankruptcies and forced liquidations throughout the Palatinate. In spite of several temporary and partial improvements in business conditions, a general recovery took place only in the second half of 1849.[9]

The social and political effects of the economic crisis of 1845–1849 might best be compared to a boxer's combination of blows. Already weakened by a decades-long decline in popular standards of living, Rhenish society was hit first by consecutive bad harvests, combined with massive foodstuff exports, followed by a substantial accumulation of debt. It was then decked by a commercial crisis, with widespread bankruptcy and unemployment. This final blow was the political knockout, giving the impetus for mass disturbances in early 1848. Since it went unresolved throughout that year, it also created a background of economic discontent, which leftists could utilize to mobilize large segments of the population. Like a boxer's knockout punch, bringing his opponent to the canvas because he was weakened by a series of body blows, the commercial crisis had such a strong political effect because it followed a long period of mass impoverishment and then two years of near-famine.

Crises of Government

The year 1847 also saw a number of governmental crises in central Europe, three of which had a pronounced effect on future politics in the Rhineland. The most dramatic was in Prussia. Needing a large loan to build strategic railways, the king and his ministers were forced to summon a representative assembly to Berlin by the law of 1820 requiring the consent of such a body for any new state debt. They called a "United Diet," composed of members of

---

[9] In general, on the nature and extent of the economic crisis, see Jürgen Bergmann, "Ökonomische Voraussetzungen der Revolution von 1848. Zur Krise von 1845 bis 1848 in Deutschland," in *200 Jahre amerikanische Revolution und moderne Revolutionsforschung*, ed. Hans-Ulrich Welhler (Göttingen: Vandenhoeck & Ruprecht, 1976), pp. 254–87. For its effects in the Rhineland, see LAK 403 Nr. 166 pp. 517–625; LAK 403 Nr. 9569 passim; LAK 441 Nr. 1329 pp. 37–51 and passim; Nr. 1330–31 passim; LAS J1 Nr. 205 ff. 417–30; Gerd-Ekkehard Lorenz, "Das Revolutionsjahr 1848/49 in Wuppertal. (Ein Beitrag zur Stadtgeschichte Elberfelds und Barmens im 19. Jahrhundert)" (Diss. phil., Marburg, 1962), pp. 155, 184–88; Nießner, *Aachen*, p. 94; Lenger, *Zwischen Kleinbürgertum und Proletariat*, pp. 151–53; *RhBA* 2/1, Nr. 375.

all the Provincial Diets. Contemporaries could hardly miss the parallel to the calling of the Estates General in 1789, and the sessions of its Prussian counterpart were hardly less confrontational. Led by Rhenish liberals, a majority of the deputies demanded that in return for granting the government's request, the Diet meet regularly and receive the authority to approve taxes. The king and his ministers had no intention of agreeing to such steps on the road to a constitutional government, and adjourned the Diet. With the events of 1843 in mind, the authorities worked hard to prevent banquets, festivities, and other demonstrations for the Rhenish deputies as they returned home. In the main successful, they were nonetheless unable to prevent a mass parade for Krefeld's representative, Hermann Beckerath, led by the gymnastics society, or a reception for the estate owner Franz Aldenhoven in Zons, where the band played the Marseillaise.[10]

The governmental crisis in Bavaria, as befits that state's role in central Europe, had more the character of a comic opera. The elderly monarch, Ludwig I, had become totally enamored of the Spanish dancer Lola Montez. Not content with making her his mistress, he awarded her the title Countess Landsfeld, dismissed all the Bavarian government ministers, and replaced them with new ones on her request. The first action surely would have been accepted, and the second might have been grudgingly tolerated, but the third raised grave doubts about the mental soundness of the head of state.[11]

The brief Swiss Civil War of 1847 had no direct effect on the Rhineland itself, but it did suggest forthcoming violent events. Although it may be hard to believe today, early nineteenth century Switzerland was one of the most turbulent countries in Europe. Deeply affected by the events of 1830, political and social struggles there had never really ceased, and almost two decades of insurgencies, putsches, and lesser disturbances climaxed in the summer of 1847, when the Catholic and conservative cantons attempted to secede from the Swiss Confederation and were defeated in open warfare by the forces of the Protestant and radical ones.

All these events, especially when set in the context of an economic crisis, suggested politically stormy weather ahead, and as has often been noted, the 1848 revolution was one of the least surprising in history. Yet if the signs were unambiguously set on drastic political change, they were far from clear about what that change would be. Oppositional elements in the Palatinate, for instance, could only see the Lola Montez affair as proof of the corruption and decadence of Bavarian monarchism. Yet the intrigues of the royal mistress, who, as historian Jacques Droz has suggested, "probably confused liberalism with libertinism," resulted in the dismissal of the conservative ministry and

---

[10] On the politics of the calling of the Diet, see the excellent account in Obenaus, *Parlamentarismus in Preußen*, pp. 649–716. For demonstrations, and the authorities' response, see sources cited in Chapter Three, note 40; and *RhBA* 2/1, Nrs. 135, 143, 149.

[11] *Handbuch der bayerischen Geschichte* 4/1:210–14.

its replacement with a liberal one, more sympathetic to the religious and political demands of the Palatine opposition.[12]

The confrontation between king and United Diet in Prussia had even more problematic political implications. On the left, the true socialists denounced the whole campaign as bourgeois egoism, the *Trier'sche Zeitung* refusing to print any news of the proceedings of the United Diet. Democrats and more militant liberals called for a boycott of the representative body, composed as it was of the members of the Provincial Diets, elected by a grotesquely archaic system of estates. The strict Catholics of the Rhineland were displeased with the United Diet, and the possible future of Prussia as a constitutional monarchy, since they feared being constantly outvoted in a predominantly Protestant state. Only the moderate liberals had enthusiastically supported participation in the representative body, hoping to reach a compromise agreement with the crown. Their strategy was foiled by the obstinacy of the king and his ministers, and they were forced into a more oppositional position.[13]

The Swiss Civil War certainly suggested Rhenish analogies, only the analogies differed dramatically, depending on who was doing the interpreting. The leftist gymnasts of Rhine-Hessen praised the victorious radicals and declared the Catholic-conservative cantons had been the tools of Prince Metternich and the reactionary Prussian government, who hoped to end Switzerland's status as a refuge for persecuted German radicals. Quite a different interpretation came from Wilhelm Emmanual von Ketteler, Catholic nobleman and future bishop of Mainz, who compared the struggle of the Catholic cantons against the Protestant ones with the struggle of the Catholics of western Germany against the Protestant Prussian government.[14]

All these examples suggest something of the mood of the politically interested minority of Rhinelanders at the beginning of 1848. No one could doubt that society and the economy were in crisis, or that the existing governments would, in the long run, be unable to maintain their position. But just what would come afterwards was unclear, what should come afterwards, disputed, and how it would come to pass, unclear and disputed at the same time.

THE PROVINCES IN REVOLUTION

The barricade fighting in Paris at the end of February 1848, the flight of the Orléans monarch Louis-Philippe, and the proclamation of the republic in France opened the floodgates for revolution throughout the European continent. March 1848 saw the revolutionary wave wash across Germany, sweeping away the authoritarian *Vormärz* regimes. In some capital cities, such as Berlin, Vienna, and Munich, this required insurrectionary street fighting;

---

[12] Ibid.; Jacques Droz, *Les révolutions allemandes de 1848*, p. 123.

[13] Obenaus, *Parlamentarismus in Preußen*, pp. 632–33, 640, 668–94.

[14] BAF FN 7 Anhang 4 Gagern ff. 36–69; Schulte, *Volk und Staat*, pp. 104–05.

rulers of smaller, weaker states, such as the grand duke of Hessen-Darmstadt, often gave in to the opposition without risking a trial of strength on the barricades. While the obsessed king of Bavaria was forced to abdicate in favor of his son, elsewhere the March revolution, as contemporaries said, "stopped at the feet of the thrones." The revolution did bring into office new government ministers. These liberal "March ministries" were largely composed of leaders of the moderate *Vormärz* opposition and proceeded to carry out its demands, introducing freedom of speech, press, association, and assembly and taking steps in the direction of parliamentary government.

The pendant to reform of the individual states was the movement toward national unity. At the end of March, a provisional assembly, the so-called preparliament, whose members were mostly *Vormärz* oppositional activists, met in Frankfurt, and issued an appeal for elections to an all-German National Assembly, which would write a constitution for a united German state, to replace the German Confederation. The individual German governments, now led by March ministers, themselves friends and associates of the delegates to the preparliament, accepted and endorsed this appeal, setting elections for the beginning of May.[15]

These events in the German and European capital cities provided the framework for political developments in the provinces. Although varying slightly in timing, events in the three Rhenish territories all followed a similar course. The Parisian February revolution led to a more energetic and steadily growing reprise of the campaigns of the *Vormärz* opposition. The news of the triumph of the revolution in the individual states touched off spontaneous celebrations and created a mood of seeming harmony, quickly destroyed when the lower classes seized on this news to further their own ends. Finally, the calling of elections for the Frankfurt National Assembly crystallized the different tendencies into more sharply defined political parties and also provoked a series of armed confrontations. At the end of this process, in June 1848, Rhenish democrats were confronted with a crisis of their movement.

The News from Paris

The universality of republicanism today has dulled our sensibilities to the sensation made by the report of the proclamation of the republic in Paris. It had last happened in 1792, with consequences known to all. In the Rhineland, where the First French Republic and Napoleonic Empire were still living memories in 1848, it was an event whose significance was felt by everyone, from the richest Cologne banker to the poorest Eifel or Westrich peasant. In Moselle villages, where usually no one but the parish priest looked at a news-

---

[15] In general, on events in central Europe in March–April 1848, see Veit Valentin, *Geschichte der deutschen Revolution von 1848–49*, 2 vols. (Berlin: Ullstein, 1930–1931), 1:338–568.

paper, the vintners gathered in the evenings to have someone read out loud to them the latest events. Shaken out of their usual apolitical attitude, they wondered "whether for us, as well, things can and must be changed." Joyful crowds gathered in the streets of Düsseldorf, debating the revolution, shouting loudly, and gesticulating; similar street scenes could be seen in the Wuppertal, albeit with the discussions proceeding more quietly and sedately. In Cologne, customers in taverns and coffee shops called for the Marseillaise and shouted down anyone who tried to get the band to play *"Heil Dir im Siegekranz."*

Jubilation was mixed with anxiety: The previous proclamation of the republic had meant war and a French invasion of Germany. While bellicosity toward France was in 1848, as it had been in 1840, one way that right-wing viewpoints could be expressed, even some leftists had trepidations about the foreign policy of the new republic. Fear of war was widespread, reaching well into the ranks of those who otherwise never thought about politics.[16]

For the organized opposition, the Parisian revolution was a reason to redouble its efforts toward political change; the first weeks of March 1848 saw a wave of mass meetings, street demonstrations, and political petitions the length and breadth of the Rhineland. The movement in the southern part of the region was particularly militant and well organized. Petitions from the entire province of Rhine-Hessen to Darmstadt were forcefully seconded by mass meetings held in Mainz during the week of February 28–March 5. Led by *Vormärz* activist (and since 1847, one of Mainz's deputies to the Hessian parliament) Franz Zitz, these meetings climaxed in an appeal for a mass march on the grand duchy's capital to force a change in government. The grand duke capitulated to the leftist demands, dismissing his reactionary prime minister, Carl Wilhelm Du Thil, and appointing the liberal leader Heinrich von Gagern in his place. The march was then called off, but news of this arrived in Bingen too late. No less than 1,500 men from the northernmost city of the province responded to the appeal, arriving by boat in Mainz on March 7, just in time to join in the celebration of a new regime.[17]

Much the same was the case in the Palatinate, although the movement there was centrally organized from the very beginning. After an appeal from the Palatine deputies to the Bavarian parliament and preparatory meetings in towns and cities through the province, a mass meeting was held in Neustadt a.d.W. on March 12, 1848, the first of many held there in the course of the

---

[16] Körner, *Lebenskämpfe* 1:408–10, 423–25; Sepyel, "Die Demokratische Gesellschaft in Köln," p. 58; Konrad Repgen, *Märzbewegung und Maiwahlen des Revolutionsjahres 1848 im Rheinland* (Bonn: Ludwig Röhrscheid, 1955), pp. 13–14; LAK 442 Nr. 3388 pp. 74–81; similarly, HSTAD RD Pr. Nr. 793 f. 92; ZSTAM Rep. 77 Tit. 343A Nr. 72 Vol. I ff. 16–17, 25–26.

[17] Uhrig, "Worms," pp. 32–33; Buckler, "Die politischen und religiösen Kämpfe," pp. 14–15; K. G. Bockenheimer, *Mainz*, pp. 6–7; *MZ*, 5, 8 Mar. 1848; *KnZ*, 3 Mar. 1848. On the contrast between Rhine-Hessen and Rhenish Prussia in early March, see ZSTAM Rep. 77 Tit. 343A Nr. 72 Vol. I ff. 182–83.

revolution. The planning meeting for this event, held in Neustadt three days earlier, had proceeded stormily, with some speakers advocating a republic, the first public reference to this form of government in the Rhineland during the revolution. Thousands of participants turned up on the twelfth, too many for any indoor venue, and a speaker's stand was hastily improvised outside city hall. Above it flew the black-red-gold flag, displayed for the first time since the Hambach Festival of 1832. The crowd was lively, and when one speaker addressed them as "Gentlemen," they shouted back at him, "Citizens!"

Besides the usual demands for civil liberties, parliamentary government, and national unity, speakers called for, and the spectators endorsed, additional demands for democratic suffrage and local self-government, including local control over forest lands—an issue also raised in the preparatory meetings elsewhere in the province. Continunity with *Vormärz* issues and movements was apparent in the calls for amnesty for political crimes, including those committed at the time of the Hambach Festival, the reinstatement of Pastor Frantz, the liberation of the Palatine Union Church from the Munich Superior Consistory, and the prohibition of monasteries in the province. These religious demands were underscored by the holding of the first public German-Catholic church services in Neustadt directly before the meeting. The meeting chose a seventy-six-man delegation, led by Speyer notary Martin Reichard, to bring its demands to the king in Munich. Arriving at the train station, the delegates were met by a cheering crowd, shouting, "Up the Palatines!" and discovered that the Bavarian government, like its Hessian counterpart, was now in the hands of a liberal March ministry.[18]

Generally, the agitation in the Prussian Rhine Province was less dynamic and the demands raised less extreme than in the southern Rhineland. Petitions were more likely to be sent to the king by city councils than by mass meetings; their content stopped short of demanding drastic reforms, calling primarily for the recall of the adjourned United Diet. This moderation had little effect, since the Berlin authorities refused to budge, the king finally agreeing to summon the body back into session, but only at the end of April.[19]

Even in the Prussian Rhineland, centers of incipient radicalism existed, particularly in the southern part of the province. Mass meetings in Trier on March 12–13 led to a march through the city streets, the participants wearing black-

[18] *NSZ*, 8, 12, 15, 17, 19, 23–24 Mar., 1 Apr. 1848; *KnZ*, 14 Mar. 1848; Scherer, "Zur Geschichte kirchlicher Parteien," p. 231; Helmut Renner, "Die pfälzische Bewegung in den Jahren 1848/49 und ihre Voraussetzungen" (Diss. phil., Marburg, 1955), pp. 73–79.

[19] Repgen, *Märzbewegung und Maiwahlen*, pp. 55–78. Repgen's work has, with good reason, obtained the status of a classic, but as critics have noted, it tends to exaggerate the conservatism of the Rhenish population and downplay instances of radicalism. Cf. Horst Lademacher in *RhG* 2:850; Seypel, "Die Demokratische Gesellschaft in Köln," pp. 72–73; Lenger, *Zwischen Kleinbürgertum und Proletariat*, p. 154.

red-gold cocardes, singing the Marseillaise, and calling out cheers for the republic. Smaller cities in the south were similarly miltant. The young men of the mountain town of Bitburg paraded through the streets behind the German tricolor, after which a mass meeting was held and all the inhabitants signed a petition to the king. At the carnival festivities in Bernkastel, the Marseillaise was sung and the county commissioner noted "the electrifying effects of the words liberty, equality, republic." The petition drawn up there by Johann Peter Coblenz, former correspondent of the *Rheinische Zeitung*, bitterly denounced the must tax, which had reduced the Moselle Valley in twenty years from "the heights of unparalleled affluence to the depths of a universal impoverishment."[20]

Events proceeded similarly in the city of Düsseldorf, on the lower Rhine, where mass meetings, led by prominent members of the carnival and sharpshooters' societies, were held throughout the first half of March. Here, as in all the other instances described above, the movement, although militant, was unanimous. There was no open opposition to it, and participation extended from bourgeois notables to impoverished craftsmen or peasants. In two other lower Rhine cities, however, social tensions and political differences arose at the very beginning of the revolution.[21]

The biggest confrontation occurred, appropriately enough, in the largest city. As the provincial metropolis, Cologne had to take the lead, and the city's liberals arranged for a mass meeting on March 3 and a simultaneous city council session, both of which would draw up strongly worded petitions to the king. Liberal activists were not the only ones at work; many democrats turned out for the mass meeting, which had some seven hundred participants, and arranged for more sharply worded addresses than the liberals might have preferred. The news of the revolution in France had set the city's communist circle in motion, and its members held secret, conspiratorial gatherings with selected artisans in late February.

What they had in mind became apparent on the afternoon of March 3, as a crowd of some five thousand appeared before city hall, led by three communists: the municipal charity physician Andreas Gottschalk, and two former army officers, August Willich and Friedrich Anneke. They read out the "demands of the people," including such radical democratic points as abolition of the standing army and arming of the people, the vaguely antibureaucratic "legislation and administration by the people," and a call for universal manhood suffrage. Demands for "protection of labor," a minimum standard of living for all, and free public education suggested a socially oriented, if hardly expressly communist, radicalism. When a delegation sent to propose these

[20] Repgen, *Märzbewegung*, pp. 67–69, 73–75; Zenz, *Geschichte der Stadt Trier* 1:126; Breuer, "1848/49 im Moseltal," p. 91–93; LAK 442 Nr. 3388 pp. 64–66, 74–81.

[21] On Düsseldorf, see Lenger, *Zwischen Kleinbürgertum und Proletariat*, pp. 153–54; HSTAD RD Pr. Nr. 793 ff. 33–38.

demands to the city council received no satisfaction, the crowd pressed into the council chamber and forced the city fathers to flee, one jumping out a window and breaking his leg. Troops dispersed the crowd and arrested the communist leaders.[22]

There were similar, if more chaotic, disturbances in Elberfeld a week later. The neoorthodox Protestants of the Wuppertal supported the king, and even a very mild petition requesting a recall of the United Diet passed the Elberfeld city council by just one vote. Some of the freethinking activists who had opposed the neoorthodox in the 1846 city council elections called a mass meeting for March 8, which was to raise more militant demands for civil liberties and national unification.

Two thousand people appeared, and speeches calling for national unity and freedom were well received, but the first speaker to discuss other demands was interrupted by a group of workers who stood up and shouted, "What do we care about freedom of the press [Pressefreiheit]? Freedom to stuff our faces [Fressefreiheit] is what we want." Although this incident has been endlessly cited by historians as proof of the lower classes' lack of interest in politics and exclusive concern with material conditions, such an interpretation seems exaggerated. The workers supported unity and freedom, applauding the first speeches calling for them, but they also expected freedom to mean something for them, for the material difficulties into which they had been plunged by the economic crisis, for the social conflicts that they fought out during the *Vormärz*. If political activists did not grasp this, then the lower classes would take matters into their own hands.[23]

As the first half of March wore on, the Prussian authorities in the Rhineland became increasingly worried. The pace of petitioning was picking up, its tone becoming more determined. Ever-larger crowds were in the streets. The urban and manufacturing lower classes seemed angrier: Spurred on by unemployment, they were ready to take violent action. While some provincial officials thought they could tough it out, others implored Berlin to make concessions while there was still time.[24]

No such intentions were apparent in the capital. Instead, press censorship was tightened and troops were made ready to march to the western border, in

[22] Basic documents in *RhBA* 2/1, Nrs. 275–77; accounts of this celebrated incident include Ayçoberry, *Cologne*, pp. 228–31; Dowe, *Aktion und Organisation*, pp. 133–36; Seypel, "Die Demokratische Gesellschaft in Köln," pp. 58–62; Repgen, *Märzbewegung*, pp. 16–23; Gerhard Becker, *Marx und Engels in Köln 1848–1849: Zur Geschichte des Kölner Arbeitervereins* (East Berlin: Rütten & Loening, 1963), pp. 16–22.

[23] All accounts stem from Körner, *Lebenskämpfe* 1:417–18; the official report (HSTAD RD Pr. Nr. 793 ff. 104–12) is similar, if less dramatic. The background is ably discussed in Lorenz, "1848/49 im Wuppertal," p. 131, while Repgen's version, *Märzbewegung*, p. 53, is based on a misreading of Körner.

[24] *RhBA* 2/1, Nr. 319; HSTAD RA Pr. Nr. 527 f. 230; LAK 403 Nr. 2550 pp. 81–83, 101–109, 249–63; ZSTAM Rep. 77 Tit. 343A Nr. 72 Vol. II ff. 165–77.

part to preserve order in the Rhine Province, in part to prepare for war with France—an eventuality that ultraconservative circles in Berlin saw as the ideal resolution of the political crisis. The news of revolution in Vienna and the flight of Prince Metternich led some high Prussian officials to propose concessions to the movement, but reactionaries at court succeeded in blocking their initiatives right down to the end. Only after barricades were built and street fighting between the army and the inhabitants of the capital took place on March 18–19, did Prussia's leaders, last of all the German states, concede to some of the revolutionary demands.[25]

The Joy of Freedom

If the news of the Parisian uprising was met in the Rhineland with a mixture of excitement and fear, the reports of the appointments of the March ministries, that is, of the initial victory of the revolution in Germany, were greeted with open jubilation and massive public celebrations. The very first was in Mainz, on March 8, 1848, Ash Wednesday, which, in light of the concessions announced by the grand-ducal government in Darmstadt, was transformed into a day of festivity. Early in the morning all the church bells rang. Thousands gathered in the cathedral and sang Luther's "*Ein' feste Burg*," followed by a high mass with Te Deum, and a sermon by the bishop, praising the new era of freedom. The spectators included not only members of both Christian confessions, but many of Mainz's Jews as well. That evening, the city's houses were illuminated, and a torchlight parade marched through the city. The marchers cheered the commandants of the Austrian and Prussian troops garrisoned in the fortress, and the parade climaxed at the Gutenbergplatz, where the black-red-gold flag of the gymnastics society was raised, and deputy Zitz spoke from the balcony of the theater to an enormous crowd.[26]

A little venture into the semiotics of these festivities may suggest some of the meaning that freedom had for the inhabitants of Mainz. Freedom implied a state of unity, with citizens no longer divided along religious lines, singing a Protestant hymn before hearing a Catholic mass, while members of both Christian confessions and Jews looked on. In a similar way, the cheers for the generals during the parade showed that officials and citizens, soldiers and civilians were no longer divided. The church services themselves consecrated the new state of freedom, and the festive parade took posssession of the space of the city for it, a possession reaffirmed by the planting of the German tricolor, the "flag of freedom," in a central square. Illumination, placing candles in one's windows, was a standard procedure for festivity; by doing so

---

[25] LAK 442 Nr. 6480 pp. 255–56; Konrad Canis, "Der preussische Militarismus in der Revolution 1848" (Diss. phil., Rostock, 1965), pp. 28–34; Veit Valentin, *Geschichte der deutschen Revolution von 1848–49*, 2 vols. (Berlin: Ullstein, 1930–1931), 1:413–60.

[26] *MZ*, 10 Mar. 1848; *KnZ*, 11 Mar. 1848.

spontaneously, Mainz's citizens endorsed from their homes the celebration of freedom.[27]

These events, including a demonstration of the union of the citizenry, a religious celebration, a parade through the locality, and the raising of the black-red-gold flag, usually followed by speeches about freedom, occurred time and again throughout the Rhineland during March and April of 1848. In Rhenish Prussia, the religious celebration was often merged with a memorial service for the victims of the barricade fighting in Berlin. Increasingly, the parades involved the armed citizenry, as civic guards were formed, the Rhinelanders thus demonstrating their willingness to bear arms for freedom.[28]

Sometimes, as happened in the town of Jülich and the village of Kuchenheim, the ceremonies consciously recalled a past revolution, the German flag being raised on the same spot where the tree of liberty had been planted during the 1790s. More commonly, though, the celebration of the new realm of freedom was also a reaffirmation of the existing order of government at the local level. Mayors and county commissioners placed themselves at the head of the parade, and ordered the previously forbidden German tricolor raised over public buildings. Prussian district governors attended the funeral services in honor of the deceased barricade fighters, accompanied by their senior officials. Their Bavarian counterparts hastily began growing beards, unshaven chins having been, ever since the Hambach Festival in 1832, a symbol of support for freedom.[29]

The memorial services held in honor of the victims of the Berlin barricade fighting were usually more calls for law and order than celebrations of revolutionary martyrdom. Canon Smets of the Aachen cathedral praised the soldiers killed in the street fighting for following orders even unto death, and memorialized the fallen insurgents on the other side of the barricades, whose bodies had created a bridge between king and people. The parish priest in Kuchenheim used the occasion to call for "the preservation of order and the putting aside of every passion opposed to Christianity." The Protestant superintendent and pastor in Lennep struck a similar tone, using such a memorial

[27] On the practice of political festivity in nineteenth-century Germany, see Dieter Düding, "Das deutsche Nationalfest von 1814. Matrix der deutschen Nationalfeste im 19. Jahrhundert," in *Öffentliche Festkultur*, pp. 67–88.

[28] For this, and the following paragraphs, see *KnZ*, 10, 21–25, 28, 30 Mar., 31 Mar. (Beilage), 1 Apr. (Beilage) 5 Apr. 1848 (Beilage); *NSZ* 1 Apr. 1848; LAK 442 Nr. 3388 pp. 83–85, 95–96, 104–106, 115; LAK 441 Nr. 1329 pp. 495–503, 515–32; HSTAD RD Pr. Nr. 793 ff. 24–42, 262–63; Pr. Nr. 794 ff. 29–31; Seypel, "Die Demokratische Gesellschaft in Köln," pp. 72–73; Repgen, *Märzbewegung*, pp. 86–87; Peter Fischer, *Das politische Leben im Kreis Jülich 1848–1918*, Part 1 (Jülich: Jos. Forscher, n.d. [c. 1923]), p. 13; Nießner, *Aachen*, pp. 75–77, 84; Herberts, *Alles ist Kirche und Handel*, pp. 99–101; Uhrig, "Worms," p. 32; Noack, "Saargegend," pp. 50–51; Stahl, *1848/49 an der Mittelmosel*, p. 6.

[29] Besides sources cited in the previous note, see Becker, *Pfälzer Volkskunde*, p. 76; cf. Körner, *Lebenskämpfe* 1:413.

to remind the faithful of the "duty and necessity for loyalty to and support of the king and fatherland."[30]

Even the military participated, fortress commandants ordering their troops to join the parades in honor of freedom, and to place the tricolor cocardes on their caps. No less than the senior civil administrators, the generals were present at the memorial services in honor of the victims of the barricade fighting— which, given the praise showered on the king's soldiers during them, was only appropriate. Events in Mainz show the rapidity of the military's turnabout: On March 6, 1848, the Austrian fortress commandant had forbidden the wearing of the black-red-gold cocarde; two days later, he and his Prussian deputy were cheered by members of the torchlight parade on their way to plant the tricolor flag in the center of the city; on March 25, Prussian and Austrian troops raised that very same tricolor over the fortress.[31]

The authorities thus raced to embrace the new order of freedom, using its celebration to reaffirm their continued rule. Everyone had become an adherent of freedom, except for some Protestants on the lower Rhine who reasserted their ties to the monarchy so closely linked to their religion. Villagers in Schaan raised the Prussian flag, instead of the tricolor, and sang "*Heil dir im Siegekranz*," rather than the nationalist "What is the German's fatherland?" The neoorthodox Protestant pastors of the Wuppertal all refused to hold a memorial service for the victims of the barricade fighting. Instead, the service was held in the church of the small Roman Catholic minority there, which was crowded with freethinkers of all confessions, including the schismatic German-Catholics, celebrating the victory of the revolution.[32]

A few hints of a more revolutionary mood could sometimes be perceived. The parade in Düsseldorf, led by the president of the sharpshooters' society and future democratic activist Lorenz Cantador, brought cheers to the district governor and the liberal Prince Friedrich of Prussia, but issued jeers and whistles at the houses of the fortress commandant, the county commissioner—also censor of Düsseldorf's newspaper—and a nobleman who had referred to a citizen wearing the tricolor cocarde as a "*Schweinehund*." Members of the newly founded civic guard of Cochem, a wine town in the mid-Moselle Valley, marched up into the surrounding hills to the castle, which was the hereditary seat of the Metternich family, took down the family emblems of the "oppressor of German freedom," and paraded them around Cochem in triumph

[30] Nießner, *Aachen*, p. 84; *KnZ*, 5 Apr. 1848 (Beilage); HSTAD RD Pr Nr. 793 ff. 24–42; other, similar examples in *RhBA* 2/1, Nr. 374. The Protestant rationalist clergy in the Palatinate struck a different, more revolutionary tone, cf. *NSZ*, 1 Apr. 1848.

[31] On events in Mainz, *KnZ*, 10–11, 28 Mar. 1848. Other examples of military participation in the festivities of freedom include HSTAD RD Pr. Nr. 793 f. 183; Nießner, *Aachen*, p. 85; Fischer, *Kreis Jülich*, p. 15; *KnZ*, 1 Apr. 1848 (Beilage).

[32] HSTAD RD Pr. Nr. 793 ff. 262–63; similarly in Rheydt and Duisburg, ibid., ff. 264–48, 265–66, 272. On events in Elberfeld, see Herberts, *Alles is Kirche und Handel*, pp. 99–101.

before burning them. In Mainz itself, a second celebration of freedom on March 20 took a painful turn for the authorities when democratic leader Franz Zitz appeared more frequently and met with greater public recognition than did the heir to the grand-ducal throne. The most openly radical of these celebrations took place in Palatine Kaiserslautern, where the parade came to a stop in front of the house of editor Nikolaus Schmitt, who gave a speech calling for the creation of the republic.[33]

A different kind of radicalism was on view in Trier. The memorial services for the victims of the Berlin barricade fighting, held there on March 29, were designed to stress unity and reconciliation. High civilian and military officials were present, including the fortress commandant and the acting district governor, as were the city councilmen and the armed citizenry. The Christian confessions were also to be reconciled, both Protestant and Catholic church services to be held, with a parade of the participants and spectators between the two churches. All went well at the Protestant services, but Matthias Eberhard, director of the theological seminary, who preached the sermon in the Catholic memorials, violently condemned Prussians and Protestants for their oppression of Rhenish Catholics, including such remarks as "The noose is torn asunder and we are free."[34]

Now Düsseldorf, Cochem, Mainz, Kaiserslautern, and Trier would all be important radical centers during the revolution (Trier including, in addition to the numerous and active democrats, an unusually left-wing group of devout Catholics), but the intimations of this found in their celebrations of freedom must be set against a far larger number of celebrations that centered on the preservation of order and reaffirmation of the power of the local authorities. To find the revolutionary aspects of events in the provinces in the spring of 1848, it is necessary to leave the planned festivities and consider the spontaneous acts of the lower classes.

THE MASSES IN MOTION

Rhenish peasants, artisans, and workers responded enthusiastically to the proclamation of freedom, albeit in ways that were both strange and disturbing to the upper classes, the educated, the authorities—and sometimes to modern historians. For the lower classes, freedom meant above all the right to resolve, in uninhibited fashion, the social tensions they had experienced during the decades of the *Vormärz*, which had been sharpened by the economic crisis since 1845. Criticism that had previously been grumbled in the taverns was

[33] *KnZ*, 22–23 Mar., 1848; HSTAD RD Pr. Nr. 793 ff 143–44; LAK 441 Nr. 1329 pp. 515–32; LAS J1 Nr. 105 ff. 201–12.

[34] Zenz, *Geschichte der Stadt Trier* 1:128; Breuer, "Revolution von 1848/49 im Moseltal," p. 104; LAK 442 Nr. 6659 ff. 1–2; ZSTAM Rep. 77 Tit. 505 Nr. 5 Vol. V f. 18.

now openly shouted at public meetings; anger formerly held within check was now physically expressed.

"Raging Peasants"

Those were the words used by one official to describe a band of three hundred to four hundred men who entered the royal forest Neupfalz in the Hunsrück, felled countless trees, marched on the home of the chief forester, burned it to the ground, forced the forester to flee for his life, drove off the small army detachment on the scene, and took its officers hostage. The conflicts in this particular forest were extreme, because government policies of providing cheap wood for ironmasters and peasant claims of traditional rights to wood-cutting had clashed particularly strongly during the *Vormärz*. They were hardly atypical; everywhere in the Rhenish up-country, from March through May of 1848, similar scenes were to be observed.[35]

The peasants of St. Goar County were said to "rob day and night, to their hearts' content, the most beautiful trees"; in the village of Ulmen in the Eifel, said the forester there, "[The inhabitants] obey neither law nor the authorities, their first word is liberty, equality." Forest disturbances raged unchecked in the Eifel woods to the north of Trier; the peasants of Sitzenrath were reported to have announced at the end of March 1848 that they were "now the rulers; they [would] go into the forest and cut wood and no longer search around [on the ground] for it." The same situation obtained in the Bergisches Land on the lower Rhine, where the peasants of Dhünnwald planted a black-red-gold tri-color on the tallest oak of the forest and declared it free. Foresters were "mocked and threatened"; illegally felled wood was openly carted off.[36]

The disturbances spread out of the up-country into the valley and plains. Rhine Valley and Moselle Valley vintners raided the woods, seeking stakes for their vines. Peasants in Jülich County on the lower Rhine declared that a "free republic" existed and began parceling out the land in the royal forest of Hambach. In neighboring Neuss County, whole villages organized wood theft from the royal forest, proceeds from the sales of the stolen trees being used to procure tricolor German flags.[37]

Limitations on woodcutting were not the only issue on which the peasants

[35] LAK 441 Nr. 10919 pp. 39–41 (a very important dossier on the forests during the revolution).

[36] Ibid., pp. 249, 261–62; LAK 442 Nr. 909 ff. 37–38 (another key dossier); Dr. Hahn, "Noch ein vierter Brief von Vincenz von Zuccalmaglio aus dem Jahre 1848," *Monatshefte des Bergischen Geschichtsvereins* 20 (1913): 91–93; *KnZ*, 15 May 1848 (Beilage); similarly, in the Palatinate, LAS H1 Nr. 1103.

[37] LAK 441 Nr. 10919 pp. 137–39; LAK 442 Nr. 3423 ff. 37–40; Fischer, *Kreis Jülich*, p. 18; HSTAD RD Nr. 8806 ff. 181–88; cf. also HSTAD RD Pr. Nr. 794 ff. 59–60, 157, HSTAD RA Pr. Nr. 2226 ff. 178–80. Similarly in the Palatinate (LAS H3 Nr. 154b ff. 214–15) and, apparently, Rhine-Hessen (Bockenheimer, *Mainz*, p. 97).

took action. Following another major *Vormärz* forest issue, they physically attacked the cultivation of nondeciduous trees. Early in April, the residents of Schmitthoff, near Aachen, marched into the village forest, led by their mayor, preceded by a flag, and destroyed the nondeciduous saplings, the ash heap used as fertilizer for them, and the forestry planting tools. The peasants concluded by cutting down several groves of these trees. They may have been unusually elaborate in their actions, but pines and spruces were frequent objects of attack in the forests of the Eifel and Hunsrück.[38]

The peasants gave the authorities no rest. They combed the forests in bands of ten to fourteen, intimidating foresters or gendarmes trying to stop them from cutting wood. Whole villages threw themselves on officials trying to confiscate illegally felled trees; in one memorable case six hundred peasants from several villages in St. Goar County combined in a nocturnal offensive against soldiers and foresters trying to cart off such expropriated wood.[39]

The peasantry and small-town lower classes refused to recognize the legitimacy of the judicial system for forest crimes. A menacing crowd surrounded the justice of the peace in Rockenhausen, in the northwestern Palatinate, and forced him to declare he would suspend all trials for forest offenses. A group of defendants in forest cases brought before the police court of Rheinberg, on the lower Rhine, refused to be sentenced, declaring that "they allow the poor nothing any more, so disturbance comes into the land." Riotous defendants disrupted forest court proceedings in Mülheim a. Rhein, opposite Cologne, in Sobernheim, in the Hunsrück, and in Hermeskeil, north of Trier. Peasants came down out of the forested hills into Trier and, joining forces with that city's lower classes, demonstrated menacingly in front of the jail, forcing the authorities to release the "one month peasants" serving terms for repeated wood theft.[40]

Both the Prussian and Bavarian governments issued amnesties for convicted forest criminals, which mostly had the effect of convincing the peasants that it was now legal to deal with the forests as they wished. Eventually mobile troop columns suppressed the worst of the disorders, and by May–June 1848, the authorities could note that things were somewhat calmer, but wood theft was never totally ended. Massive incursions into the forest occurred from time

[38] HSTAD RA Pr. Nr. 2226 f. 175; similarly, LAK 441 Nr. 10919 pp. 79–82; LAK 442 Nr. 909 ff. 154–60; Nr. 3423 ff. 37–40.

[39] LAK 441 Nr. 10919 pp. 63–64, 71–73, 113–16, 137–39, 175–79, 201–04; LAK 442 Nr. 909 ff. 100–01, 111–12. 197–98; Gendarmerie Station Elmstein to Gendarmerie Commando Speyer, 10 May 1849 (copy), BHSTAM MInn Nr. 45531; LAS H3 Nr. 154b ff. 214–15.

[40] LAS J1 Nr. 249 (alt) ff. 207–210; HSTAD RD Pr. Nr. 793 f. 206; Gernert, *1848/49 im Rheinisch-Bergischen*, p. 74; LAK 441 Nr. 10919 pp. 19–22; LAK 442 Nr. 909 ff. 129–30; Breuer, "1848/49 im Moseltal," p. 74. The violent expulsion by the crowd of the justice of the peace in Andernach, hated for his strict sentencing policies, was probably also related to forest struggles. LAK 441 Nr. 3056 pp. 99–104.

to time in the rest of 1848 and 1849, sometimes requiring renewed use of troops to be contained.[41]

Another source of disorder in the countryside, this perhaps particularly prevalent on the plains of the lower Rhine, was the use of village common land. Small peasants and day laborers protested the unequal division of the commons, which left them unable to keep cows or even goats, and denounced the practice of renting out the village commons in one or several large blocks. They demanded that it either be parceled out in equal amounts to all families or rented to them at a nominal fee, giving force to their demands by breaking into meetings of the village council, and threatening to kill the councilmen. Poor peasants destroyed the ditches, used on the lower Rhine, as hedges were elsewhere, to separate former commons parceled out or rented in a large block. In Wevelinghoven (Grevenbroich County), the ditches so destroyed were from a divison that had taken place in 1820(!), showing that the rural lower classes had a long memory.[42]

A closely related source of rural disturbance was resistance to fiscality. There were some scattered refusals to pay taxes, but more common, and better organized, were village boycotts of the administrative guidelines for local government. Village councils refused to submit their budgets for official approval and demanded the village treasuries back from the tax collectors who administered them. Peasant crowds insisted that the pay of schoolteachers be reduced—in one Eifel village the inhabitants drove out the teacher by force—or that fines for violating compulsory school attendance laws be remitted and the laws themselves rescinded. Everywhere, rustics called for lowering expenses by abolishing such positions as county forester or field and forest watchman.[43]

These actions ought to be seen against the backdrop of the subsistence crisis

---

[41] LAK 441 Nr. 10919 pp. 67–70, 223–25, 233–34, 299–310, 321–24; Circular of Ministerium des Königlichen Hauses, Zweite Abteilung, 31 Mar. 1848, LAK 441 Nr. 23868; LAK 442 Nr. 909 ff. 197–98, 201–03, 218–19, 227; HSTAD RD Pr. Nr. 794 f. 136; memorandum of ex-RP Alwens on events of 1848/49, BHSTAM MInn Nr. 45533; LAS H3 Nr. 154b ff. 26–27; Otto Fleischmann, *Geschichte des Pfälzischen Aufstandes im Jahre 1849* (Kaiserslautern: Emil Thieme, 1899), p. 79.

[42] HSTAD RD Pr. Nr. 794 ff. 81, 86, 119, 147, 183; HSTAD RD Nr. 8806 ff. 81–85, 122–26, 153, 158, 175; HSTAD RA Pr. Nr. 2226 ff. 39–40, 183–84; LR Kr. Jülich to RA, 11 Apr. 1848, HSTAD RA Nr. 170. Similarly, in the up-country, LAK 442 Nr. 3388 pp. 138–39. Disturbances along these lines in Nettenheim (Neuss County) took on an anti-Semitic character, when a Jew cast the decisive vote in favor of renting out the commons in a block to the highest bidder during a hotly contested village council meeting. HSTAD RD Nr. 8806 ff. 44, 71

[43] BM Adenau to RKO, 30 Apr. 1848, LAK 441 Nr. 6792; LAK 441 Nr. 3056 pp. 125–28, 137–40; LAK 403 Nr. 3388 ff. 92–93, 103–104, 156–58; LAK 442 Nr. 909 ff. 37–38, 143–45, 183, 191–92; LAK 442 Nr. 2376 passim; LR Kr. Saarburg to Oberregierungsrat Birk (Trier), 13 Apr. 1848, LAK 442 Nr. 6547; HSTAD RA Nr. 222 ff. 45–46, 54–55, 86–87, 182; HSTAD RD Pr. Nr. 794 f. 53; HSTAD RD Nr. 8806 ff. 181–89; LR Kr. Jülich to RA, 11 Apr. 1848, HSTAD RA Nr. 170; *RhBA* 2/2, Nrs. 9, 16, 30; *NSZ*, 15 Mar. 1848.

of 1845–1847, which had severely strained the resources of both villages and villagers. At a time when every penny counted, it was intolerable to insist on collecting fines for violating the wishes of a schoolteacher, a person the authorities themselves did not take seriously. Similarly ridiculous to the peasants was requiring villages to raise taxes instead of selling off forest property in order to pay off the debts they contracted to buy grain. The only appropriate response, now that freedom had been declared, was to boycott the whole budget process.

Often these demands were accompanied by actions against local officials. The victims of these demonstrations, as the Aachen District government noted, were "those who exercised their duties in an especially conscientious way," that is, who vigorously enforced the authorities' unpopular policies about use of the forests, the commons, or the village budget. Whether in the form of a relatively peaceful demand or combined with death threats, smashing of windows, and bodily assault, the peasants forced the resignation of, or drove out of the village, forest and field watchmen, foresters, police, village mayors and councilmen, and low-level state administrators.[44]

These actions were not entirely unwelcome to the county or district authorities, who sometimes retrospectively sanctioned them when the official in question was excessively brutal, dishonest, or administratively inept, but not otherwise dismissable because of civil service regulations. Such cases, however, were rather more the exception, as the authorities themselves noted, and even there other circumstances played a role. One administrator was dismissed on the demand of many village councils in Bitburg County for embezzling public money, but what made everyone so angry was that the money he stole was intended to repay the debts the villages had contracted buying government-supplied grain during the famine years. While peasant hostility toward local officials showed a tendency toward the personalization of politics, this did not mean that rustic politics could be reduced to questions of personalities.[45]

Urban Troubles

The urban and small-town lower classes also had their particular notions of the realm of the freedom, stemming from *Vormärz* social conflicts and the

[44] Quotation, *RhBA* 2/2, Nr. 16. Besides the instances cited in notes 35–43, see BM Kaiserersch to Oberprocurator Koblenz, 12 May 1848 (copy), LAK 441 Nr. 12929; LAK 441 Nr. 3056 pp. 86–97, 151–52; LAK 442 Nr. 3388 ff. 106–108, 116–17, 137–39, 145–48, 157–59; LAK 442 Nr. 909 ff. 16–17, 29–30, 100–101; HSTAD RD Nr. 8806 f. 75; HSTAD RA Nr. 222 ff. 3, 13, 19; Gernert, *1848 im Rheinisch-Bergischen*, pp. 72–73; LAS H3 Nr. 154b ff. 77–78; *NSZ*, 17 Sept. 1848 (Beilage).

[45] HSTAD RD Nr. 8806 ff. 81–85; LAK 441 Nr. 3056 pp. 86–92; LAK 442 Nr. 909 ff. 62–70. Konrad Repgen's contention that these rural revolts resulted from discontent with individual officials, jealousy, and greed (*Märzbewegung*, p. 55) does not correspond to what is found in a detailed study of the sources.

economic crisis of the preceding years. Taxes were one thing on their minds. On hearing the news of the victory of the barricade fighters in Berlin, the lower classes of Aachen attacked the house of the mayor, accusing him, among other things, of refusing to oppose the octroi. In Trier, the crowd went one step further, and forced the officials at the city gates to stop levying the tax; its collection was not resumed until May.[46]

The largest tax revolt occurred in the smuggling district on the Dutch border. Once again, the proclamation of freedom brought hidden social tensions to the surface, the smugglers announcing their intention of driving out all the customs agents and border police. Every time the latter showed themselves on the streets, they were met with jeers and surrounded by hostile crowds threatening to cut their throats. Eventually, all forty-seven of them barricaded themselves in the customs house in Kaldenkirchen, rifles pointing out windows, waiting for an attack. This meant that the smugglers could bring in their illegal imports unhindered, and in broad daylight.

Members of the antismuggling society were induced to make "voluntary" contributions to the smugglers. The latter showed their appreciation for their best customers, the weavers, by forcing the manufacturer Cornely in Breyell, who had a reputation for cutting wages and levying fines, to contribute 1,500 taler to the poor fund. The notables of Breyell, the smugglers' capital, showed not the slightest inclination to form a civic guard or cooperate with the authorities in any way to restore order. The officials were finally forced to transfer several particularly strict customs officials as a pacifying gesture. Troops were brought in, but they made no effort to collect customs duties and the entire northwestern border district was open to free trade in the spring of 1848.[47]

Another issue that stirred up the urban masses was bread and potato prices. There were, curiously, more episodes of popular price-fixing in the spring of 1848, when foodstuff prices were low, than during the famine years 1845–1847. One action was carried out in April 1848 by women workers employed in spinning mills in Lennep, in the Bergisches Land, the female industrial proletariat proving more unruly than its male counterpart. The urban crowd clearly had not forgotten the dearth of the near past: Rioters demolished the house of a grain speculator in Trier, and accusations of speculation had been an additional reason for demanding the resignation of Aachen's mayor.[48]

The largest and most violent disturbances in the spring of 1848 were created

[46] Nießner, *Aachen*, pp. 53–54; *RhBA* 2/2, Nr. 51; LAK 403 Nr. 6583 ff. 26–27. Similarly in Saarbrücken, LAK 442 Nr. 3388 ff. 99–101.

[47] HSTAD RD Nr. 8806 ff. 1–5, 10, 15–19, 25–34, 51–54, 66–69. The smugglers were organized and were represented by a "hole-and-corner legal advisor" in their negotiations with the authorities.

[48] *KnZ*, 15 Apr. 1848; HSTAD RD Pr. Nr. 794 ff. 61–62, 99–100, 102–04, 158–59; HSTAD RD Nr. 8806 ff. 108–09; Nießner, *Aachen*, pp. 53–54; *RhBA* 2/2, Nr. 13. Such actions are neglected by Gailus, "Soziale Protestbewegungen," pp. 87–97, a result of his overly schematic typology.

by clashes with the military. Both the Prussian and Bavarian governments had sent additional troops to the Rhine to defend against a possible attack by the republican French government and to preserve internal order in their Rhenish possessions. The Second French Republic, unlike its predecessor, proclaimed its intention of conducting a peaceful foreign policy, and German units stationed on the border quickly discovered that the French officer corps was more interested in marching on Paris and overthrowing the republic than in attempting to regain the Rhine frontier.[49]

The troop units could easily have been disbanded, or Prussia's sent to the other end of the monarchy, where there existed a genuine danger of invasion by forces of the czar. Instead, they were kept on the Rhine, ostensibly to meet the threat of an incursion by thousands of unemployed German workers returning from France to loot and pillage under communist leadership, and to preserve internal order. This threat existed only in the overheated imagination of German diplomats, and if the troops sometimes could preserve internal order, more often they disrupted it.[50]

The reservists and militiamen from the East Elbian provinces recalled to active service deeply resented being torn away from their homes to defend the distant Rhineland while their Rhenish counterparts were not called up for duty. They did not blame the government for this state of affairs, but the Rhinelanders, acting toward them with contempt and hostility. The East Elbian troops marched into Rhenish cities behind the black-white flag, assaulted civilians in the streets, tore the black-red-gold cocardes off their hats, and insulted, grabbed, and sometimes carried off their wives or other female companions.

These actions, reminiscent of the brutal and arrogant behavior of soldiers during the *Vormärz*—if anything, worse, since military discipline was visibly weakened—openly contravened to the urban lower classes the existence of a new realm of freedom, so proudly celebrated just days previously. The situation was worst in Mainz, since the city's fortress was not under the control of the government of Hessen-Darmstadt. Rather, it was a fortress of the German Confederation, governed by an Austrian commandant and his Prussian deputy, garrisoned by Austrian and Prussian troops. Although not formally dissolved until June 1848, when the Frankfurt National Assembly created a pro-

---

[49] Kriegsminister to Generalquartiermeister Stab, 24 Mar. 1848; Hauptmann v. Varicourt (Homburg) to Generalquartiermeister Stab (Munich), 5 Apr. 1848, BHSTAM KA Nr. B735; ZSTAM Rep. 77 Tit. 343A Nr. 72 Vol. I ff. 93–94; Canis, ''Der preußische Militarismus,'' pp. 33–34; Jörg Calliess, *Militär in der Krise: die bayerische Armee in der Revolution von 1848/49* (Boppard: Boldt, 1976), pp. 118–19.

[50] On threats of an invasion of communist workers, a sort of 1848 ''Great Fear'' of the German ruling class, see Generalmajor von Lesuire (Karlsruhe) to Kriegsministerium, 27 Mar. 1848, and Colonel Joseph von Xylander (Frankfurt) to King of Bavaria, 27 Mar. 1848, BHSTAM KA Nr. B735.

visional German Central Power, the German Confederation had for all practical purposes ceased to exist by April of that year, after the March ministries recognized the authority of the Frankfurt pre-Parliament to call for elections to a German National Assembly. Since the fortress government retained ultimate veto power over municipal affairs, Mainz had become the confederate fortress of a nonexistent confederation, ruled in its name by foreign military authorities and garrisoned by East Elbian and Czech troops—a situation of anarchy and lawlessness persisting throughout the entire revolution.[51]

Between late March and early May of 1848, there were clashes between Prussian troops and the people in Aachen, Düsseldorf, Eupen, Mainz, and Trier. The Aachen riots, in mid-April, saw the crowd drive the civic guard from the streets and force the authorities to transfer several particularly hated army units to Eupen (where they promptly became involved in more rioting) before order was restored. These disturbances in the Rhineland's leading industrial city involved few industrial workers. Just 23 of the 151 people arrested were factory or textile workers, members of the group making up over half the city's labor force. Artisans and day laborers, with 49 and 26 arrestees, respectively, seem to have been the chief participants. As usual, the professional designations do not indicate whether the arrested craftsmen were masters or journeymen, but since 83 of the 151 arrestees were over thirty years of age, there may well have been a fair number of masters among them.[52]

Aachen had experienced serious rioting in 1830, during the previous wave of revolution in Europe. Those riots had centered on conflicts between manufacturers and workers, with almost half of those arrested coming from the industrial work force. None of this was the case in 1848. Hostility toward the Prussian state was the main cause of disturbances, and the city's artisans and day laborers provided the bulk of the street fighters. Aachen's industrial labor force remained politically passive, as it would throughout the revolution.[53]

Outraged Outworkers and Angry Artisans

Unlike the factory proletariat, outworkers and artisans engaged in highly visible economic actions during the spring of 1848. None impressed contemporaries more than the riots of the Solingen area metalworkers. While most movements awaited the news of the victory of revolution in the capital city,

[51] HSTAD RD Nr. 8804 f. 15; HSTAD RA Pr. Nr. 226 ff. 187–88; LAK 403 Nr. 6583 ff. 12–17; *KnZ*, 17, 19–20 Apr., 9 May 1848; *RhBA* 2/2, Nr. 39; Bockenheimer, *Mainz*, pp. 23–30, 74–75; Buckler, "Die politischen und religiösen Kämpfe," pp. 25–27.

[52] List of those arrested from HSTAD RA Pr. Nr. 660 ff. 119–27; cf. also Nießner, *Aachen*, pp. 59–60.

[53] On the 1830 rioting, see Volkmann, "Die Aachener Aufruhr," esp. p. 555. The clashes between troops and populace in Düsseldorf, Mainz, and Trier, were politically more organized and will be discussed below.

the Solingen craftsmen acted a few days before the Berlin barricade fighting became known in the Rhineland. Gathering together in Solingen from their scattered villages on March 16, 1848, they marched to several smaller foundries in the vicinity and destroyed them, and then returned to Solingen, intending to attack the houses of manufacturers who paid in truck. Dissuaded by the manufacturer Peter Knecht, the metalworkers marched out once more, this time to the controversial foundry of Josua Hasenclever. Cheering Knecht and calling out, "We're not allowed to make counterfeit Thaler; the king should not make counterfeit goods!" they attacked and completely destroyed the factory in the predawn hours of March 17.[54]

The Solingen riots were not, as so many interpretations have it, mindless machine breaking by artisans terrified of capitalist-industrial modernity. They reflected the *Vormärz* controversies over the future of steel wares manufacturing, the rioters taking the side of the adherents of expensive quality production as against those who stood for cheap work, attacking Hasenclever's foundry while denouncing government support for it and praising one of the leaders of the anti–truck payment campaign. The manufacturers understood this and, in what was universally seen as a major concession, posted signs on their businesses the day after the riots announcing that they would no longer pay in truck. If the rioters had been interested only in attacking machines rather than the whole complex of elements of cheap production, such a move would not have had the conciliatory effect this one did.

Even more reminiscent of the *Vormärz* controversies was the attitude of the area's notables. The property-owning members of the Solingen and Remscheid sharpshooters' societies refused to interfere with the rampaging workers and in fact made little secret of their sympathies for the rioters' cause; the county commissioners in Lennep and Solingen quietly observed the destruction of the foundries without calling for troops. Hasenclever's partner remained convinced until his dying day that competing manufacturers had put the workers up to storming the foundry.[55]

Many merchant manufacturers did have a common interest with the outworkers in opposing cheap, low-quality production, but suspicions of a conspiracy and of rabble-rousing miss what was novel about the situation in 1848. In contrast to the *Vormärz*, when merchant manufacturers led the campaign against the production of cheap, shoddy wares, at the outbreak of the revolution the initiative passed out of their hands into those of the outworkers themselves. Looking back in the fall of 1849 on the events of the revolutionary period, the members of the Solingen city council would see the March riots as

[54] On the riots, see HSTAD RD Pr. Nr. 793 ff. 131–33, 137–39, 165, 197–98, 210, 237–38; *KnZ*, 19 Mar. 1848 (Zweite Ausgabe), 21 Mar. 1848; Kuhn, "Aufstand der Kleineisenindustriearbeiter," pp. 68–101; Wilhelm Helf, *Die Revolutionsjahre 1848/49 im ländlichen Bereich der alten Landkreise Solingen und Lennep* (Opladen: Heggen, 1968), p. 75.

[55] Radtke, *Die preußische Seehandlung*, pp. 227–28.

a turning point in the political atmosphere of the Bergisches Land, as events that brought to the "consciousness [of the lower class] a feeling of its physical and moral influence on property and on the sentiments of the owners of property."[56]

Much the same as in the steel wares industry was occurring among the Rhine watermen in the spring of 1848. The towmen of Cologne and Mainz demonstrated menacingly, demanding the right to continue towing upstream ships passing through the city limits. The villagers of Weißenthurm, north of Koblenz, who earned their living leading tow-horses, gathered on an island in the Rhine outside their village and let loose salvos of rifle fire on steamboats as they came by. Mainz dock laborers and shippers showed a similarly energetic side when they crossed the Rhine on April 5, 1848, and destroyed several miles of the Frankfurt-Biebrich railroad, bringing the rails back to Mainz in triumph.[57]

The boatmen were less violent and more organized, calling a congress of all their number to Cologne for April 14. The 250 participants issued demands that included the abolition of all river tolls and bridge passage fees, an end to state subsidies and profit guarantees for steam navigation, and a separation of mercantile and navigation interests by a prohibition of steamboat corporations. They asked for, and received, the mediation of the Frankfurt pre-Parliament; the commissioners included, putting himself forward as always, Cologne's Franz Raveaux. The commissioners eventually worked out a compromise agreement by which the steamboat companies agreed to lower their fees for tugging wooden boats, making steam towing affordable to the boatmen, and to pay an indemnity to the towmen, compensating them for technological unemployment.[58]

Just as in Solingen, one can see the small producers' hostility, not so much toward mechanized competition as toward a state-subsidized capitalism. It was a popular cause among the Rhinelanders, and the boatmen's petition containing their demands received thousands of signatures when circulated in Cologne. The Mainz railroad riots show another parallel to events in Solingen. In both cases there existed an economic controversy that pitted all classes of society against the state—the government-subsidized foundry in Solingen, the state's refusal to allow a left bank railroad in Rhine-Hessen and its subsidization of competing right bank lines. During the *Vormärz*, the notables had led the opposition to the state, looking for support from the lower classes, using the peaceful means of petition and assembly; in the spring of 1848, the lower classes took the initiative into their own hands, violently, rather to the embarrassment of the notables. Even if these riots were not explicitly political, they

[56] HSTAD RD Nr. 8809 ff. 95–122.

[57] *RhBA* 2/2, Nrs. 8, 19, 30; *MZ*, 7 Apr. 1848; Bockenheimer, *Mainz*, pp. 34–35.

[58] *KnZ*, 4 Apr. 1848 (Beilage), 18 Apr. 1848 (Beilage); *MZ*, 25 Apr. 1848; Ayçoberry, *Cologne*, pp. 234–35; memo of Ober-Inspector der Rheinschiffahrt, 14 July 1848, LAS H3 Nr. 193.

announced the beginning of a new role for the masses as the subject and no longer just the object of politics.[59]

Vormärz social tensions in lower Rhine textile manufacturing had pitted outworking weavers directly against manufacturers, with the state playing a much smaller role than in other branches of the economy; the events of the spring of 1848 took a correspondingly different path. Except for parts of the cotton-weaving district around Mönchengladbach and the Aachen area woolens manufacture, all the textile regions experienced disturbances. Weavers joined together, sometimes spontaneously, as happened in Krefeld during the celebrations of the revolutionary events in Berlin, sometimes, as in Elberfeld, following a public meeting, and marched on the houses of manufacturers, shouting slogans—in Werden, "liberty, equality"—smashing windows, invading and destroying furniture. These actions were not machine breaking, since there were no machines to break, nor were they plundering. All accounts agree that the manufacturers' personal property was destroyed, not stolen. Rather, they were a kind of cat music, a public labeling of the entrepreneurs as dishonorable, for failing to pay a decent wage, for fining weavers unjustly, or for harassing them through the manufacturing tribunals. One such victim was Elberfeld tribunal president Kaspar van der Baeck. On March 18, 1848, a crowd of thousands of weavers paid him back for his *Vormärz* persecution of their colleague August Fichthan by demolishing his house.[60]

The Düsseldorf District government sent its expert on social and economic affairs around the textile districts to mediate between manufacturers and outworkers. Somewhat reluctantly, sometimes only after the weavers surrounded them, issuing threats to their personal safety, the manufacturers agreed to negotiate. They introduced the so-called Krefeld scale, agreeing to pay all outworkers the wages earned by the weavers of the leading silk-manufacturing town. They also allowed weavers to work for more than one manufacturer, offering to finance the weavers' purchase of looms in areas where the manufacturers owned them. Their most important concession was the agreement to submit disputes about wages, fines, and contractual obligations to binding arbitration.

The arbitration boards—the one in Barmen was known, appropriately enough, as the Council of Honor [Ehrenrath]—were made up of representatives of the manufacturers and an equal number of weavers, elected by the newly created weavers guild [Innung]. The creation of such guilds had been advocated by the manufacturers during the *Vormärz*, but with the intent of helping master weavers keep their journeymen and apprentices in line, rather

[59] On the popularity of the watermen's demands, cf. Gothein, *Geschichtliche Entwicklung der Rheinschiffahrt*, pp. 261–67; LAK 441 Nr. 1330 pp. 147–60.

[60] On disturbances in the weaving districts, see HSTAD RD Pr. Nr. 793 ff. 191, 222–29; Pr. Nr. 794 ff. 1–2, 33–37; HSTAD RD Nr. 8806 ff. 12, 48–49, 57–60; HSTAD RA Pr. Nr. 527 ff. 254–55, 263; *KnZ*, 25 Apr. 1848.

than providing a means for the masters to negotiate with the manufacturers. Similarly, the arbitration boards were modeled on the *Vormärz* manufacturing tribunals, with the crucial difference that the outworkers were equally represented on them. The outcome of the negotiations was the resolution of *Vormärz* social tensions on the basis of *Vormärz* social institutions, revised in favor of the workers, the revolutionary situation changing, at least temporarily, the social balance of power.[61]

Small-scale craftsmen and urban day laborers were as active as outworkers in the spring of 1848, if generally in a more peaceful way. In the course of street demonstrations, at public meetings of members of the different crafts and at the first gatherings of workers' associations (which, in spite of their name, contained many master craftsmen as members), they advocated a policy of social restrictionism, of reserving jobs and sales opportunities for locals. At the communist-led demonstrations in Cologne on March 3, the participants called for the expulsion of "outsiders," who were taking their jobs away from them. Elberfeld master shoemakers proposed that all outsiders practicing their craft be barred from moving to the city. Trier coopers demanded that all barrels sold in that center of the wine trade be manufactured by master craftsmen living within the city walls. The quarry workers of Obermendig (Mayen County) refused to let anyone from Niedermendig work in the quarries, driving them off and burning down the shacks in which they lived while on the job.

Artisans often saw the state as both the cause of their problems and a potential solution to them. Aachen rioters demanded the resignation of the mayor, since he had given a contract for furniture in city hall to "outsiders" rather than to the unemployed cabinetmakers of the city. Their counterparts in Trier prevented a public auction of the furniture of the departing district governor, since this would harm their chances of selling any furniture they made. Elberfeld bookbinders, who earned additional money selling books, demanded that schoolteachers be prohibited from improving their incomes in the same way. In a number of garrison towns, local tailors, shoemakers, and construction craftsmen demanded that they receive all army contracts.[62]

Another, more divisive kind of demand looked toward a limitation of job opportunities within the urban artisanate itself. Independent master tailors in Elberfeld and Düsseldorf called for the prohibition of outworking, as did Cologne journeymen tailors employed in craft workshops. Such demands would

---

[61] Besides the sources cited in the previous note, see Ayçoberry, *Cologne*, p. 234; Herberts, *Alles ist Kirche und Handel*, pp. 62–66; Lorenz, "1848/49 im Wuppertal," pp. 169–70; Hae Bon Chung, "Das Krefelder Seidengewerbe," pp. 162–63; *RhBA* 2/2, Nr. 4; *KnZ*, 30 Mar., 1 Apr. 1848; HSTAD RD Pr. Nr. 794 ff. 3–6, 87–88; HSTAD RD Pr. Nr. 795 ff. 139–40.

[62] Ayçoberry, *Cologne*, pp. 230, 234–35; *Vbl*, 19 May 1848; Nießner, *Aachen*, pp. 53–54; Lenger, *Zwischen Kleinbürgertum und Proletariat*, p. 172; Lorenz, "1848/49 im Wuppertal," p. 157; LAK 441 Nr. 1330 pp. 89–96, 147–60; *RhBA* 2/2, Nr. 42.

have meant unemployment for both masters and journeymen dependent on outworking merchants. Sometimes, although less frequently than one might at first suspect, masters and journeymen squared off against one another: the former demanding limitations on the number of journeymen who could go into business for themselves, the latter calling for better wages and shorter hours.[63]

This whole palette of demands reflected both the long-term tendency toward an "overfilling" of the crafts and the short-term rise in unemployment brought about by the commercial crisis. The largely spontaneous response of crafts-men and laborers to this situation was to call for ways to cut down the number of people eligible for a limited number of jobs, rather than expanding, via economic growth, the number of jobs available. Such a preference for social restrictionism reflected memories of the guild system and the less than happy experience with several decades of laissez-faire and occupational freedom in the Rhineland. In the spring of 1848, it was unclear whom the main targets of this restrictionist impulse would be: other urban craftsmen, peasants earning extra money practicing simple crafts, merchants employing outworkers, or the state. The ultimate direction of the politicization of craftsmen's demands would depend on the choice of the main target.

The Prepolitics of Mass Actions

Virtually all historians have asserted that these popular disturbances of the spring of 1848 were apolitical. It is certainly true that the lower classes rarely articulated explicit ideas about the creation of a German national state, the granting or revising of a constitution, the election of a parliament—or any other issue. If, however, one does not hold spontaneous popular actions to the same standards of clarity and exactitude expected of a political platform writ-ten by members of the educated classes, but considers instead the forms of these actions and the symbolism associated with them, then it is possible to gain some idea of the attitudes of the lower classes toward state and society and suggest implications of them for the more explicitly political events of the coming phases of the revolution.

A good place to start is with the distinction between common and individ-ualized actions. The latter certainly existed in the spring of 1848, and were perhaps how class conflict was most openly expressed. Day laborers extorted money from large farmers and estate owners on the lower Rhine plains by threat of violence. Poor women in Trier approached their rich sisters on the street and told them that their jewelry would soon be changing hands. Anti-Semitic riots, not terribly frequent in the Rhineland in comparison to other parts of Germany, but nonetheless occurring, usually took the form of extort-

---

[63] Lenger, *Zwischen Kleinbürgertum und Proletariat*, pp. 172–73; Ayçoberry, *Cologne*, pp. 234–36; Lorenz, "1848/49 im Wuppertal," pp. 157–64; *Vbl* 19, 24 May 1848.

ing money from Jews. Such disturbances were most severe in Bingen, at the northern end of Rhine-Hessen, where they lasted for several weeks and eventually had to be suppresed by troops.[64]

In contrast to these, the riots and demonstrations discussed in the sections above were carried out collectively. The participants marched behind a drummer and a flag bearer, even if the latter carried nothing more than pieces of an old sack fastened to a stick, the standard of the Solingen metalworkers. By marching together behind a flag—in the countryside, often led by the village mayor and council members—the participants were proclaiming the legitimacy and collective nature of their actions, carried out in the name of the village or the craft. As the spring of 1848 wore on, the black-red-gold German flag was ever more commonly flown at the head of the demonstrations; indeed, its public raising provided the occasion for them. The lower classes thus justified the resolution of their grievances by the political changes taking place in the capital cities. An example, toward the end of the period of spring disorders, shows this connection in a highly developed form. On May 1, 1848, the day of the elections to the Frankfurt National Assembly, the inhabitants of Lutzerath, in the Eifel, marched into the forest and cut down seven nondeciduous trees. They brought them back to the village and planted the German flag on the three largest of them, shouting, "Long live freedom."[65]

Another symbolic action characteristic of the disturbances were the assaults committed during them on the Prussian eagle, the insignia of state. In Wenlo, on the lower Rhine, the magistrate was forced to resign; the eagle was then taken from his office, followed by a "two-hour anarchy." The eagle was taken from the office of the tax collector in Bernkastel, on the Mosel; in nearby Cochem, it was smeared with manure; in the Eifel village Antweiler, torn from the village hall; in Blankenrath, taken from the village hall, repainted black, red, and gold, and placed on top of a cut-down spruce tree. The officials in Trier took the eagle from the district government office to prevent its destruction by the crowd, which had to be content with smashing the bust of the king in the marketplace while soldiers of the thirtieth infantry regiment (native Rhinelanders) looked on, joking and smoking their pipes. The villagers of Lingerhahn, in the Hunsrück, proclaimed the republic and their secession from Prussia, refusing to keep the civil registers any longer. Led by a man

[64] HSTAD RD Pr. Nr. 793 ff. 267–68; Pr. Nr. 794 ff. 53, 65–66, 87–88, 107–09; HSTAD RA Nr. 222 ff. 32–35; LAK 442 Nr. 3388 ff. 104–06; LR Kr. Merzig to RP v. Auerswald, 27 Mar. 1848, LAK 442 Nr. 6457; LAK 441 Nr. 1330 pp. 115–20; *RhBA* 2/2, Nr. 42; LAS H3 Nr. 154b f. 60; *MZ*, 16 Mar., 26 Apr. 1848. Some or most of the inhabitants of Schweich, Merzig, and Linnich, on the other hand, showed their solidarity with their Jewish neighbors and rebuffed efforts to start anti-Semitic riots or suppressed them after they had begun. LAK 442 Nr. 3388 ff. 89–92, 154–55; HSTAD RA Nr. 222 ff. 22–31.

[65] Forester in Lutzerath to County Forester Cochem, 3 May 1848, LAK 441 Nr. 12929; a similar interpretation in Gernert, *1848/49 im Rheinisch-Bergischen*, p. 73.

dressed as Napoleon, they marched to the nearby town of Langenfeld, smashed the Prussian eagles on public buildings, and attempted to attack the authorities, but were driven out by the townspeople. One did not even have to be Prussian to destroy the insignia of the Prussian state, the inhabitants of Bingen in Rhine-Hessen tearing the eagle from the posts marking the border with the Prussian Rhine Province.[66]

Every single incident of this kind took place in largely Roman Catholic areas, the inhabitants accompanying their attacks on unloved local officials, tax collectors, or foresters, their felling of trees, and similar actions by the removal of the sign of the authority of the Protestant, Prussian state. The insurgency of the Catholic villagers of Lingerhahn had been preceded, a few days previously, by their parish priest telling them, in a state of considerable intoxication, that a "war of religion" was in preparation in the Rhineland; the goal of their march was the Protestant town of Langenfeld.[67]

The Protestant lower classes of the Prussian Rhine Province were also riotous in the spring of 1848, pressing their demands for a resolution of social grievances dating from the *Vormärz*. Most of them showed their support for the new reign of freedom and the prospect of a united Germany. They did not, however, accompany these actions with demonstrations against the symbols of the Prussian state, but instead used these symbols to legitimize their grievances. Solingen area metalworkers came to Elberfeld the night of March 20, 1848, armed with clubs, to see their comrades who had been arrested for their role in the machine breaking—and, it was feared, forcibly liberate them from jail. They were diverted into the taverns, where they made toasts to the king of Prussia's future role as emperor of Germany. Rioters in the predominantly Protestant lower Rhine textile town of Rheydt broke out the black-white flag; the sight of this flag flying from the house of an unloved manufacturer was enough to prevent them from attacking it.[68]

Religious tensions in and of themselves provided occasion for only a relatively small number of riots in the spring of 1848. Protestants drove a Franciscan monk out of Frankenthal and the Catholic parish priest out of Bad Dürkheim, while Catholics attacked the house of the Protestant pastor in Erkelenz, on the lower Rhine. A few unloved priests were threatened with assault, as were opponents of well-liked clergymen; some brawls took place between

[66] HSTAD RD Pr. Nr. 794 f. 63; LAK 403 Nr. 2550 pp. 363–64; Beigeordneter Baum (Cochem) to LR Kr. Cochem, 5 May 1848, LAK 441 Nr. 12929; BM Antweiler to RKO, 8 May 1848, LAK 441 Nr. 6792; LAK 441 Nr. 1329 pp. 613–19; Böse, "Ludwig Simon," p. 25; *RhBA* 2/2, Nr. 42; LAK 441 Nr. 1329 pp. 545–63; Nr. 3056 pp. 15–17, 61–63, 86–92, 99–104. Other examples of similar or related actions: HSTAD RD Nr. 8806 ff. 81–85; HSTAD RA Nr. 222 ff. 39–40; LAK 403 Nr. 17332 pp. 14–17; LAK 442 Nr. 3388 ff. 116–17; 157–58; LAK 442 Nr. 909 ff. 16–17; 19–21, 154–60; LAK 442 Nr. 7853 pp. 91–93; *KnZ*, 22 Mar. 1848.

[67] LAK 441 Nr. 3056 pp. 27–28.

[68] *KnZ*, 20 Mar. 1848; HSTAD RD Pr. Nr. 793 ff. 246–48; similarly, LAK 441 Nr. 3056 pp. 61–63.

Protestants and Catholics in religiously mixed villages. But it was confessional allegiance that provided the link between social grievances and attitudes toward the Prussian state, Catholics expressing the former in conjunction with hostility toward the latter, Protestants, with loyalty towards it. The confessional alignments of popular disturbances in March and April of 1848 were a preview of the election results that would follow in May.[69]

The reader may have noted how frequently examples from the Prussian Rhine Province have appeared in the previous discussion. It is impossible to give as detailed an account of disorders in Rhine-Hessen, since the relevant records were destroyed during the Second World War, but historians who looked at them before 1939 found many instances of disturbances similar to those occurring further north. In the Palatinate, on the other hand, both contemporaries and later historians denied that there was any significant violence in the spring of 1848, praising the Palatines' abhorrence of the unsanctioned use of force and strong belief in the peaceful legal process.[70]

While violent actions in the Palatinate may have been fewer than in Rhenish Prussia, and certainly never obtained the scale of the peasant uprisings of the spring of 1848 across the Rhine in Baden, it is not entirely clear whether this reflected a more peaceful population or more intimidated forces of order. The peasants of the up-country to the west of Neustadt a.d.W. so terrified the gendarmes stationed there in April 1848 that the paramilitary police allowed them to have free reign of the forests and were still afraid to talk of the matter a year later. Elsewhere, countryfolk simply refused to appear when called before the forest court, and there was no one who dared to compel them. The hated *Regierungsdirektor* Luft in Speyer, a radical activist in 1832 who had gone over to the authorities and even received a medal from the czar, did not wait for the crowd to drive him out of town, but fled before it had a chance to do so. Similarly, while no town and village mayors or councilmen in the Palatinate were driven from their positions in the spring of 1848, there was a province-wide wave of "voluntary" resignations from local office. Although the revolutionary events of the spring of 1848 may have proceeded more peacefully in the Palatinate than elsewhere in the Rhineland, they were no less revolutionary.[71]

[69] Religious riots: *NSZ*, 28 Mar. 1848; memo of ex-RP Alwens on events in the Palatinate, 1848/49, BHSTAM MInn Nr. 45533; HSTAD RA Pr. Nr. 527 f. 262; HSTAD RD Pr. Nr. 794 ff. 15–16, 21–22, 58, 91; HSTAD RD Nr. 8806 ff. 162–65; LAK 442 Nr. 3388 ff. 150–51; LAK 442 Nr. 909 ff. 29–30, 97, 121. Konrad Repgen denies that any significant sentiment for secession from Prussia existed among Rhenish Catholics in the spring of 1848, on the basis of the fact that almost no political programs called for it (*Märzbewegung*, pp. 47–55), ignoring or downplaying the many symbolic, anti-Prussian gestures.

[70] Bockenheimer, *Mainz*, p. 97; Katz-Siebert *Radikalismus in Hessen*, p. 17; Renner, "Die pfälzische Bewegung," p. 75; Kurt Baumann, "Volkserhebung und Konspiration in der pfälzischen Bewegung von 1848/49," *MHVP* 68 (1970): 292–317, esp. pp. 298–99; *Anklag-Akte*, pt. 1, pp. 1–2.

[71] Gendarmerie Station Elmstein to Gendarmerie Company Command (Speyer), 10 May 1849

CIVIC GUARDS AND THE RESTORATION OF ORDER

In the spring of 1847, as the subsistence crisis reached its peak, the Prussian authorities became increasingly concerned about the preservation of public order. Following directives of the Interior Ministry, the Rhenish provincial governor called the five district governors to a conference in Koblenz. The assembled senior officials decided to edge away from the policy of keeping weapons out of the hands of civilians, and to allow the creation of armed security watches if police could not keep order and soldiers were unavailable. This decision was taken in complete secrecy, and instructions about it were passed on to mayors and county commissioners orally, to avoid any possibility of its becoming known.[72]

Consequently, with the victory of the revolution in Berlin and the beginnings of disturbances in the provinces, the March 24, 1848, circular of the provincial governor authorizing the creation of civic guards found the authorities fully prepared and in some cases already in action. Most such armed corps were formed under official aegis for the purpose of upholding order and protecting property. In some localities, it was formally asserted that only property owners or those possessing the municipal franchise were eligible to join. Elsewhere these qualifications were hidden behind the phrase "reliable inhabitants," but almost everywhere it was made clear that the lower classes were unwelcome, since it was to put down their riotous actions that the guards were created.[73]

The guards were not perfectly suited to this purpose. In rural areas, where ownership of firearms was widespread, it proved more difficult to exclude the lower classes, and the civic guard could become a vehicle for enforcing their demands rather than repressing them. More important, property-owning peasants were often the leaders of riotous actions, and under their influence, the

---

(copy), BHSTAM MInn Nr. 45531; LAS J1 Nr. 267 ff. 157–66; report of ex-RP Alwens on events of 1848/49, BHSTAM MInn Nr. 45533; *NSZ*, 11, 15, 23, 30 Mar., 1–3, 27 Apr. 1848; LAS H3 Nr. 154b f. 14; 1st Infantry Brigade (Billigheim) to Corps Command (Speyer), 18 Aug. 1849, BHSTAM MInn Nr. B771; Hans Ziegler, "Landau in der Vormärzzeit und im Jahre des pfälzischen Aufstandes 1849," *MHVP* 61 (1963): 201–24, esp. p. 210.

[72] LAK 442 Nr. 6163 pp. 9–11.

[73] On the formation of the civic guards, the eligibility to join them, and their role in restoring order, see LAK 403 Nr. 2275 pp. 255–56, 259–60, 267, 363–65; HSTAD RD Pr. Nr. 793 ff. 152–53, 230, 235–36, 261, 267–68, 273; HSTAD RD Pr. Nr. 794 ff. 1–2, 7–8, 20–22, 24–25, 29–31, 40–41, 58, 167–68, 99–101, 110–11, 144; HSTAD RD Nr. 8806 ff. 72–74, 162–63; HSTAD RA Nr. 222 ff. 8–9; BM Stolberg to LR Kr. Aachen, 6 Mar. 1848; Kreis Sekretär Heinsberg to RA, 28 Mar. 1848; LR Kr. Aachen to RA, 8 Apr. 1848; LR Kr. Heinsberg to RA, 21 July 1848, all in HSTAD RA Nr. 170; LAK 442 Nr. 3388 ff. 86–87, 94–95, 104–08; RP v. Auerswald to LR Kr. Saarbrücken, 17, 21 Mar. 1848; excerpt of Trier city council minutes, 20 Mar. 1848; LR Kr. St. Wendel to Oberregierungsrat Birk (Trier), 4 Apr. 1848, all in LAK 442 Nr. 6547; Decision of Koblenz City Council, 19 Mar. 1848, LAK 441 Nr. 7960; LAK 441 Nr. 3056 pp. 86–97; *RhBA* 2/1, Nr. 334; Körner, *Lebenskämpfe* 1:421.

villagers refused to form guards or, if they did, to allow foresters or other officials to join them.[74]

Similar problems could occur in the city. Called out to stop workers from forcing the sale of potatoes at a below-market price in April 1848, the civic guard of Elberfeld took over the price-fixing itself. Urban guards faced additional difficulties. They were unequipped to handle really masssive rioting, which occurred in Trier and Aachen. Occasionally, leftists could penetrate the guard leadership: They gained control of a few companies of the Cologne civic guard and came to dominate the entire organization in Düsseldorf, electing as its commandant the *Vormärz* radical activist and president of the sharpshooters' society Lorenz Cantador.[75]

Yet these remained isolated episodes. The civic guards usually elected state officials and politically moderate citizens as their officers; they acted incisively to help preserve order, taking the pressure off the incompetent police and the overworked army. The quick and decisive action of the authorities of the Prussian Rhine Province in arming the propertied citizenry, turning over to them no less than forty thousand rifles from military magazines—many, admittedly, archaic flintlocks dating from the Napoleonic wars—had helped restore order after several weeks of near chaos.[76]

Some historians have seen the guards, in retrospect, as a largely ceremonial force, a comic-opera militia given over to self-important display. To be sure, the guardsmen did parade around, and they did have a prominent role in the ceremonies of raising the black-red-gold flag and others later in the revolution, but it would be a serious mistake to see their chief function as having been playing soldier. The civic guards of the Prussian Rhine Province were a vehicle for cooperation between the authorities and the property-owning citizens for the suppression of lower-class disorders and for defense against political radicalism—and a largely successful one at that.[77]

The formation of civic guards in the southern Rhineland occurred quite differently, with equally different political implications. Armed corps appeared in larger cities of the Palatinate in March–April 1848, without either the consent or the encouragement of the Bavarian authorities. The Munich government chose to legalize them retrospectively and even provide them with a few, usually antiquated, weapons from the military magazines, but the authorities'

[74] HSTAD RD Nr. 8806 f. 153; HSTAD RA Nr. 222 ff. 32–35, 39–40; HSTAD RA Pr. Nr. 2226 ff. 178–80; LAK 442 Nr. 3388 ff. 138–39; LAK 442 Nr. 909 ff. 19–21.

[75] HSTAD RD Pr. Nr. 794 ff. 61–62; Lenger, *Zwischen Kleinbürgertum und Proletariat*, p. 154; Seypel, "Die Demokratische Gesellschaft in Köln," pp. 261–72; sources cited in notes 52–53 and 105. For a rebuff of leftist elements, supported by unemployed Moselle watermen, to gain control of the civic guard of Saarburg, see LR Kr. Saarburg to Oberregierungsrat Birk (Trier), 13 Apr. 1848, LAK 442 Nr. 6547.

[76] Number of rifles handed out according to LAK 403 Nr. 17987 pp. 93–96, 103–04, 556–61.

[77] Cf. Stadelmann, *Social and Political History*, pp. 76–77; Fischer, *Kreis Jülich*, p. 15; Meisenburg, "Stadt Essen," pp. 211–12; more discreetly in Nipperdey, *Deutsche Geschichte*, p. 601.

attempts to regulate the guards, bring them under official control, or appoint officers for them were firmly and decisively rebuffed throughout the entire revolution.[78]

The desire for the preservation of order, so decisive for the formation of these groups in Rhenish Prussia, was not entirely lacking in the Palatinate. Riots of the lower classes in Speyer, the news in April 1848 of a republican uprising across the Rhine in Baden, and fears of armed bands crossing the river to plunder provided the incentive for the formation of some units. More often, though, the primary motive seems to have been mistrust of the Bavarian government and the wish to create an armed force independent of it.[79]

Nor were the elected officers of the Palatine guards quite so moderate as those in Prussia. The 483-man-strong civic guard of the provincial capital, Speyer, elected the republican notary Martin Reichard as its commander; similarly, leftist individuals were chosen officers of the guards in smaller towns, such as Rockenhausen and Lauterecken, and the guards of these towns quickly became vehicles for radical politics. The different political implications of arming the citizenry were not the result of a different social composition of the civic guards—the membership list of the Speyer civic guard records no day laborers or watermen and few construction craftsmen as members—but rather a consequence of the more radical attitudes of the property-owning classes of the southern as compared to the northern Rhineland.[80]

The story in Rhine-Hessen was much the same. At least in the larger cities, the civic guards were formed by city councils or by popular initiative. From the very start, the civic guard of Mainz, which encompassed four thousand men by April 1848, was a controversial entity, since all armed forces in the city were supposed to be under the command of the fortress authorities, but the city council insisted on retaining control over the guard and the one thousand rifles it had received from the Hessian arsenal in Darmstadt. However, the guard quickly slipped out of control of the municipality, the guardsmen electing democratic activist Franz Zitz as their commander in chief, refusing to act when called out to protect steamships from attack by towmen, and arresting drunken and disorderly soldiers against the express orders of the fortress commandant. The civic guard of Mainz was engaged not in protecting property from the lower classes but in protecting the citizenry from Prussian soldiers, a state of affairs that would soon lead to armed confrontation.[81]

[78] The key dossier on the guards and official attitudes towards them is BHSTAM MInn Nr. 30676.

[79] LAS J1 Nr. 263 ff. 155–56; LAS J1 Nr. 264 ff. 794–97; LAS J1 Nr 269 ff. 133–34; *NSZ*, 11 Mar. 1848; MInn to King, 29 Apr. 1848, and RP to MInn, 19 June 1848, BHSTAM MInn Nr. 30676.

[80] LAS J1 Nr. 252 (alt) II ff. 832–37; LAS J1 Nr. 215 (alt) ff. 51–60, 170–74; LAS J1 Nr. 249 (alt) f. 91.

[81] Bockenheimer, *Mainz*, pp. 37–44; Uhrig, "Worms," p. 34; *KnZ*, 17 May 1848 (Außerordentliche Beilage); *MZ*, 16 May 1848.

An Unexpected Democracy: The Elections of May 1848

By April 1848 the initial phase of revolution in Germany had come to an end. The authoritarian *Vormärz* regimes had been replaced by the liberal March ministries; the German Confederation was to be superseded by a National Assembly elected under universal manhood suffrage. Simultaneously, the Prussian government scheduled equally democratic elections for a Prussian National Assembly to write a constitution for the monarchy.

The revolution had not been unlimited. It had left intact the thirty-seven individual German states and their usually monarchical form of government as well as leaving in office the leading civilian and military officials who ruled in the name of the monarch. A majority of the pre-Parliament had voted down a radical proposal that it declare itself sovereign; a republican uprising in Baden following this decision was easily suppressed. The elections to the National Assembly were administered by the individual states. Almost all of them rejected the pre-Parliament's call for direct elections and replaced them with an administratively more cumbersome but politically more conservative indirect procedure, the Bavarians even going so far as to exclude non–property owners from the franchise.[82]

Organized political activity increasingly centered on these elections, but they had a different meaning for contemporaries than would elections in the twentieth century or even in 1849. Rather than being a contest between different political parties for voter approval, the elections of the spring of 1848 were primarily ceremonies of unanimity. Just as the celebrations of freedom had expressed the unity of all citizens, contemporaries felt elections should do the same. In order to do this, the results had to be decided upon in advance.

In many cities, towns, and villages, local election committees were formed, which would call a "preelection" [Vorwahl], an open public meeting at which political questions would be discussed, and the electors to be chosen agreed upon. The results of these meetings were considered binding on all participants, thus creating the desired unity of the inhabitants. The provincial governor of the Palatinate recalled talking to one man who told him, " 'I would have voted for other people [that is, electors] had I not felt myself bound [sich unterworfen] by the decisions of the pre-election held in the Corn Hall.' "[83]

Even in large cities with clearly defined, differing political groups, the wish for unanimity was strong. Among the signatories of the "constitutional monarchist" (characteristic 1848 term for moderate liberal) program of the Central

---

[82] Valentin, *Geschichte der deutschen Revolution* 1:461–568.

[83] RP to MInn, 6 Aug. 1848, BHSTAM MInn Nr. 47267; similarly, *KnZ*, 21 Apr. 1848 (Beilage); HSTAD RD Pr. Nr. 794 ff. 129–31; LAK 441 Nr. 4922 pp. 27–28; *RhBA* 2/2, Nr. 63; *NSZ*, 26 Apr. 1848; Fischer, *Kreis Jülich*, pp. 24–25; Noack, "Saargegend," pp. 56–64; Stahl, *1848/ 49 an der Mittelmosel*, p. 9.

Election Committee for the Cologne District of April 1848 were a number of both democrats and adherents of political Catholicism, who withdrew their signatures, with considerable reluctance, only after it became clear that existing differences of opinion were too great to be reconciled. Although in Koblenz a liberal and a Catholic-clerical election committee confronted each other from the very start of the campaign, the existence of two such separate and competing groups had not been intended but resulted from the unexpected outcome of meetings designed to demonstrate unity.[84]

As these examples suggest, the desire for unanimity did not mean that there were no competing political tendencies. Rather, the election campaign would center around the question of which political tendency could successfully portray itself as the bearer of that unanimity appropriate to the realm of freedom. The answers to this question would be very different in the northern and southern parts of the Rhineland, revealing once again substantial differences in political culture.

Victory of the Left in the Southern Rhineland

Events in the Palatinate demonstrated the importance for the left of prior political experience. On March 27, 1848, a mass meeting in Neustadt a.d.W. called for the creation of a provincewide "People's Association" [Volksverein]. Two weeks later, on April 9, delegates from twenty-five different cities and towns, mostly from the forward Palatinate, but a few from the Westrich as well, met in Kaiserslautern to found this organization, which would dominate politics in the province throughout the revolution. Many of the delegates, as far as their previous political affiliation can be traced, had been active in the campaigns of the mid-1840s for Pastor Frantz (who was chosen a member of the association's first provincial executive committee) and against the founding of monasteries; a number of the older ones, such as Ignaz Rassiga or Philipp Hepp of Neustadt, had been involved in radical politics since the days of the Hambach Festival.[85]

The People's Association had little opposition. It was the only organized political group in the Palatinate, a projected Catholic conservative organization apparently never getting off the ground. Some neoorthodox Protestant clergy and a somewhat larger number of Catholic priests preached preelection sermons denouncing Jacobin revolutionaries and proclaiming that religion was in danger. Since Catholics were a minority in the Palatinate and religious ra-

---

[84] Seypel, "Die Demokratische Gesellschaft in Köln," pp 90–95; Repgen, *Märzbewegung*, pp. 187–89; *RhBA* 2/2, Nr. 31.

[85] Pamphlet, "Protokoll über die Berathung und Beschlüsse der am 9. April 1848 zu Kaiserslautern in dem Fruchthallesalle stattgefundenem Versammlung . . . zum Zweck der Grüundung eines Volksoder Vaterlands-Vereins," a copy of which is in the Landesbibliothek der Pfalz, Speyer, sig. Hv 5901.

tionalism was widespread in both Christian confessions, the influence of the more conservative clergy could not prevail against preelection meetings, such as the one in Speyer described above, and sermons preached in support of the People's Association by rationalist Protestant pastors.[86]

The leadership of the People's Association included both open republicans and more moderate elements, but the debate at the preelection meeting of all the electors chosen in the Palatinate, held once more in Kaiserslautern, showed the strong position of the radicals. Martin Reichard of Speyer spoke in favor of the republic; Nikolaus Schmitt of Kaiserslautern, chairman of the People's Association, announced that he regarded the republic as the ideal form of government, but since it was, at the moment, unattainable for all of Germany, he would accept a monarchy with democratic institutions. When Professor Lau of Speyer, however, spoke in a "moderate" way (that is, endorsed monarchy as a good thing) he was shouted down by the spectators.[87]

All the candidates to the Frankfurt National Assembly endorsed by the People's Association were elected, including Friedrich Schüler, an activist of the Hambach Festival, who had been living in exile since 1833. If Schüler's election shows a continuity with past struggles, the fact that all the Palatine deputies sat on the left or the extreme left in the National Assembly demonstrates the extent to which the Palatine democracy was able to use the celebration of unanimity for its own purposes.[88]

The elections in Rhine-Hessen also resulted in a radical victory. As in the Palatinate, the democrats created a provincewide association, but in Rhine-Hessen, the political initiative proceeded in a more decentralized fashion. A citizens' committee, founded by a mass meeting in Mainz early in March 1848, called on villagers and townspeople throughout the province to follow its example. The appeal was well received, and in the countryside, village committees joined together to form cantonal committees, one of which, the cantonal committee of Wöllstein, suggested that all committees from the province meet in Wörrstadt, southwest of Mainz, on April 12, 1848.[89]

Like the Palatine People's Association, the citizens' committees of Rhine-Hessen contained both radical and moderate (constitutional monarchist) elements, but the radicals dominated the Wörrstadt meeting. The political platform they put through, containing the demand for direct elections to the Frankfurt National Assembly, to be carried out against the wishes of the new, liberal Hessian government (which, like most governments of the German

---

[86] LAS J1 Nr. 264 ff. 543–48; *NSZ*, 29–30 Apr., 4 May 1848, 12 May 1848 (Beilage); Scherer, "Zur Geschichte kirchlicher Parteien," pp. 239–41.

[87] LAS J1 Nr. 105 ff. 201–12.

[88] On the candidates elected, see Renner, "Pfälzische Bewegung," pp. 88–89; BHSTAM MInn Nr. 30064.

[89] Bockenheimer, *Mainz*, pp. 15–17; Uhrig, "Worms," pp. 32–33; BAF ZSg 8/55 ff. 16, 93, 169–70, 122–23.

states, preferred the indirect procedure), led to a split in the organizations. Moderate members first denounced the controversial decision, and then resigned from the committees, proposing their own slate of candidates for Frankfurt. The openly republican Rhine-Hessian radicals proved the stronger party at the ballot box, the leftist slate of electors in Mainz gaining about three-and-a-half times as many votes as its constitutional opponent and electing democratic leader Franz Zitz as the city's deputy to Frankfurt.[90]

The elections in the two more rural constituencies were closer, but the leftists were victorious there as well. The electors for the southernmost constituency gathered in Worms, and their deliberations took place in the presence of a large crowd, which made known its approval when they chose the veteran radical and German-Catholic Johann Mohr of Oberingelheim as deputy. This public participation in the selection of the deputies, which also occurred in similar fashion in Mainz, shows that the democrats of Rhine-Hessen had not given up their claim to the direct expression of the popular will, even if they had resigned themselves to participating in indirect elections.[91]

Religion and Politics in Rhenish Prussia

The creation of provincewide political organizations in the Palatinate and Rhine-Hessen reflected decades of experience with parliamentary elections, something quite lacking in the Prussian Rhine Province, with the result that no similar organization appeared there. The Prussian Rhine Province was much bigger and more populous than Rhine-Hessen or the Palatinate, but even district political committees (one Prussian district being about the size of one of the other two provinces) existed largely on paper, no meetings of representatives from different localities ever taking place. The elections to the Frankfurt National Assembly and the simultaneous elections to the Prussian National Assembly in Berlin occurred in a much more locally restricted environment.

If political life was more localized in Rhenish Prussia than in the southern Rhineland, it was also more complicated, political programs being published by constitutional monarchist, Catholic-clerical, and democratic groups. All these programs were alike in calling for civil liberties, national unity, a broad franchise, and social reforms. There were differences in emphasis, of course. While the other programs called unspecifically for freedom of religion, the Catholic-clerical one made detailed proposals in this regard; democratic election programs contained precise proposals for social reforms, while constitutional monarchist ones just endorsed unspecified measures to help the working class. Yet what remains and was most apparent to contemporaries was their

[90] Buckler, "Die politischen und religiösen Kämpfe," pp. 41, 43; Bockeheimer, *Mainz*, pp. 63–64; Uhrig, "Worms," p. 46; Katz-Seibert, *Radikalismus in Hessen*, p. 18; *MZ*, 12 May 1848.
[91] Uhrig, "Worms," p. 49; *NSZ*, 19 May 1848.

similarity. Artisans in both Trier and Düsseldorf endorsed the constitutional monarchist election program under the impression that they were supporting the democratic one.[92]

The only clearly exceptional political program was one issued by the Cologne Workers' Association, which called on people not to vote. Founded by the hero of the demonstrations of March 3, 1848, the charity physician Andreas Gottschalk, on his release from jail after the change of government in Berlin, the association held a series of turbulent public meetings and quickly grew to a nominal membership in the thousands. Observers expected it to provide the key to a decisive victory of the left in the elections, and it apparently endorsed a slate of electors, but Gottschalk convinced the members instead to issue an appeal calling for a boycott of any indirect elections.[93]

Without functional political organizations or electoral experience, and with a number of confusingly similar political programs, elections in Rhenish Prussia, that is, the expression of popular attitudes toward the state, were primarily dependent on local influence. As suggested by the disturbances of March–April 1848, this meant that political alignments correlated with confessional allegiances and that the clergy would be the most important group in determining the outcome of the political process.[94]

It was primarily the clergy who called and dominated the preelection meetings, usually held right after church services, and who were chosen as electors in overwhelming numbers—not entirely surprisingly, since elections were often held in the church and precinct and parish boundaries coincided. Political rhetoric at the local level—as distinct from the programs drawn up by notables in Cologne or Koblenz—displayed pronounced confessional antagonisms. The parish priest in Mansbach, near Aachen, told his parishioners that "true liberty and equality" had been destroyed by the Reformation, and regretted that the colors of the old regime Prince-Archbishopric of Cologne were lacking in the new tricolor flag. Members of the *Vormärz* Rosary Brotherhood in Koblenz conducted an active election campaign, going from door to door in the city and out into the surrounding countryside, telling the peasants that free elections meant choosing the parish priest as elector and informing everyone

---

[92] The programs are reprinted in *RhBA* 2/2, Nrs. 17, 22–23, 29, 32, 34–35, 46; for a detailed analysis of them, see Repgen, *Märzbewegung*, pp. 155–97. For the confusion of them, see Lenger, *Zwischen Kleinbürgertum und Proletariat*, p. 155; *Vbl*, 26 Apr. 1848; similarly, Seypel, "Die Demokratische Gesellschaft in Köln," pp. 101–06, 111; Wegner, "Elberfeld," pp. 110–11.

[93] The Cologne Workers' Association and its first leader have often been studied. Cf., for example, Dowe, *Aktion und Organisation*, pp. 145–51; Gerhard Becker, *Karl Marx und Friedrich Engels in Köln*, pp. 26–51; or, in English, Hammen, *The Red '48ers*, pp. 218–19. The boycott appeal is reprinted in *RhBA* 2/2, Nr. 65. Opinions of outside observers about the importance of the association, *Vbl*, 28 Apr. 1848; *MZ*, 28 Apr. 1848.

[94] In general on the elections and the dominant role played in them by confessional allegiances, see Repgen, *Märzbewegung*, pp. 207–308.

that Protestants had caused the potato blight and subsequent famine. Everywhere, Catholics were told to vote only for coreligionists, preferably those who went to church as often as possible.[95]

The election campaign proceeded similarly in predominantly Protestant areas, though here confessional and monarchist loyalties were closely connected. Elections included a profession of loyalty to the king of Prussia, and electors voted for high officials, or, in one case, for the Prussian deputy commandant of the fortress in Mainz. In confessionally mixed regions, the two confessions squared off at election time, Catholics charging election fraud or gerrymandering. Protestant villagers from Hochhausen marched through Catholic Neukirchen (both in Grevenbroich County on the lower Rhine) on election day singing the Prussian royal anthem. Two weeks later, the day the electors chose a deputy, Catholics from Neukirchen responded, marching through Hochhausen shouting, "Long live the Catholics, the Calvinists shall be made kaputt."[96]

The elections in Cologne showed in dramatic fashion the strength of confessional allegiances in the provincial metropolis. The left and extreme left had dominated both the streets and the public meetings there since March 1848, and observers expected an easy triumph for the democrats, with most opposition to them coming from the constitutional monarchists. They did not count on divine intervention, which occurred when St. Ursula's parish church was mysteriously illuminated at night just after Easter and the saint herself appeared at the altar, holding a sword and surrounded by a swarm of maidens. The parish priest decided this was a sign of imminent danger to the city and called for a procession to avert it. Every day for the following week—the week before the elections—thousands marched with crosses and flags from St. Ursula's to the image of the Virgin in the Schnurgasse. This calling on Cologne's very own martyr reaffirmed the city's pre-1789 role as Catholic metropolis, suggesting a confessionally oriented unity of its citizens. Ten percent of the electors chosen in the city were priests, and the city sent Archbishop von Geissel to Berlin as its representative. The clerical victory was incomplete, the other Berlin deputy being the constitutional monarchist banker Ludolf Camphausen, and the Frankfurt deputy being democratic leader Franz Raveaux, but no one had expected any Catholic-clerical candidates to be successful in the largest city in the province.[97]

[95] Repgen, *Märzbewegung*, pp. 214–19, 229, 237, 277–79, and passim; *RhBA* 2/2, Nrs. 67–69, 75, 78; LAK 403 Nr. 9726 pp. 255–61; HSTAD RD Pr. Nr. 794 f. 146; HSTAD RD Nr. 8806 f. 142; HSTAD RA Pr. Nr. 2226 ff. 197, 199, 212–13; *KnZ*, 29 Apr. 1848 (Zweite Beilage).

[96] Repgen, *Märzbewegung*, pp. 268–69; LAK 403 Nr. 9726 pp. 269–74; 281–88; LAK 441 Nr. 1330 pp. 115–20; HSTAD RD Nr. 8806 ff. 162–65; *KnZ*, 20 May 1848 (Beilage); Noack, "Saargegend," pp. 66–67, 72.

[97] On the Cologne elections, see Repgen, *Märzbewegung*, pp. 245–51, Ayçoberry, *Cologne*, pp. 237–41; Seypel, "Die Demokratische Gesellschaft in Köln," pp. 100–17; on St. Ursula's

This confessional orientation of politics was, if anything, especially pronounced in manufacturing regions, elections in both Krefeld and Mönchengladbach being fought out along confessional lines and resulting in a victory for the Roman Catholic majority. Religious viewpoints were most pronounced in the leading manufacturing towns, Aachen and the twin cities Barmen-Elberfeld. In both urban centers, the initial public meetings on political questions were called by committees whose members included a small minority of democrats but most of whom were respectable and politically moderate bourgeois. The religious orientation of the activists, however—Protestants and freethinkers in Aachen, Protestant rationalists in the Wuppertal—was totally at odds with the dominant milieu. The Elberfeld committee was even so uncautious as to make fun of revivalists while debating a slate of electors. Both groups were promptly denounced in church by neoorthodox clergy as enemies of religion and as godless subversives planning red revolution, an accusation seconded in public meetings, in taverns, and on the streets by lay religious activists. The pious working classes of both industrial regions voted for religion on election day, swamping the candidates of the moderate left.[98]

Both these examples suggest that while Protestant and Catholic electoral initiatives may have been aimed at each other, confessionally oriented activists of both Christian confessions also directed their fire at the democrats. The pastor of Mansbach's praise for the "true liberty and equality" found in the Catholic church was an oblique attack on the ordinarily accepted meaning of those words, stemming from the French Revolution. Similarly, a Cologne Catholic layman writing to justify the clergy's electoral activity, noted that had the priests remained politically passive, it would have meant "everywhere conceding the field to the democratic party." In and around the university town of Bonn, the clergy moved "heaven and earth" to oppose the candidacy of the democratic professor of art history, Gottfried Kinkel. They told women in the confessional to inform their husbands that "Kinkel wants to abolish the Catholic religion. He wishes freedom for every sect [Kultus] and separation of church and state." Neoorthodox Protestants were not left behind in antidemocratic polemics, the officiating pastor in an Elberfeld suburb describing "liberty, equality, fraternity" in an April 1848 sermon as the "battle cry . . .

role in the Cologne election campaigns, *NSZ*, 15 May 1848 (Beilage). Of course, had the Workers' Association not called for a boycott of the election, then even divine intervention might not have defeated the left.

[98] On Krefeld and Mönchengladbach, see HSTAD RD Pr. Nr. 794 ff. 133–34; *RhBA* 2/2, Nr. 74; Otto Röttges, *Die politischen Wahlen in den linksrheinischen Kreisen des Regierungsbezirks Düsseldorf 1848–1867* (Kempen: n.p., 1964), pp. 71–72; for Aachen, see Repgen, *Märzbewegung*, pp. 112–13, 279–85 (exaggerates the radicalism of the opponents of the Catholic party); *RhBA* 2/2, Nrs. 5, 16; LAK 403 Nr. 7045 pp. 149–62; HSTAD RA Pr. Nr. 701 ff. 11–12; for the Wuppertal, see Lorenz, "1848/49 im Wuppertal," pp. 210–20; Wegner, "Elberfeld," pp. 110–11, 125–26; *Lebenserinnerungen . . . Alexander Pagenstecher* 2:42–44; *RhBA* 2/2, Nr. 70.

of those who have turned away from the hearth of holiness to light the torch of murder and arson.''[99]

Under these circumstances, democrats in Rhenish Prussia faced an extraordinarily difficult task. Their stronghold on the lower Rhine was the city of Düsseldorf, whose population was unusually familiar with organized politics, since the city had been the seat of the Provincial Diet during the *Vormärz*, and home to dramatic political demonstrations during the 1840s. The circle of Düsseldorf democrats had been especially active in spreading mass propaganda before the revolution through the carnival and sharpshooters' societies. The leftists went right into action the day they received news of the Berlin barricade fighting, electing sharpshooters' chairman Lorenz Cantador commander of the civic guard, and holding an active and energetic election campaign with daily political meetings. Predominantly Protestant constitutional monarchists and Catholic-clerical elements united against them, with the support of the authorities, but election day showed that the only firm supporters of the constitutional monarchy were soldiers of the Düsseldorf garrison, who voted as their officers commanded. The elections themselves were marked by fighting between soldiers and civilians, the latter resenting the soldiers' disruption of political unanimity, and the democrats were victorious both in the streets and at the polls.[100]

A number of smaller towns were also democratic strongholds. In the Eifel county town of Adenau, a group of notables, led by a merchant, a master tanner, and an innkeeper, held a whole series of public meetings, mixing celebrations of freedom seen everywhere in the Rhineland with agitation centering on *Vormärz* social tensions. They demanded lower taxes, the resignation of the mayor, and the abolition of the office of county forester, while condemning bureaucratic red tape. A violent, nocturnal cat music drove the county commissioner out of town.

The democratic activists reached out into the nearby countryside, encouraging villagers to tear down the Prussian eagle from public buildings. A mass cat music the evening before the election threatened anyone unwilling to vote for the democrats. Election day featured a shouting match at the polls between the parish priest and the leader of the ''people's party.'' All the latter's electors were chosen in Adenau, and they convinced enough rural electors to send the ''people's president'' (that is, the presiding officer of the popular meetings),

---

[99] *KnZ*, 29 Apr. 1848 (Zweite Beilage) (this reference is cited in Repgen, *Märzbewegung*, pp. 214–15, without, however, mentioning either the antidemocratic or the anti-Protestant nature of the priest's speech); *RhBA* 2/2, Nr. 97; Repgen, *Märzbewegung*, pp. 253–54; Kersken, *Bonn in den Revolutionsjahren*, p. 147 n.118; Köllmann, *Stadt Barmen*, p. 235; similarly, Röttges, *Die politischen Wahlen*, pp. 69–70; *KnZ*, 14 Apr. 1848 (Erste Beilage).

[100] Correcting and amplifying Repgen, *Mäzbewegung*, pp. 297–300, is Lenger, *Zwischen Kleinbürgertum und Proletariat*, pp. 153–62. On the election day riots, see *RhBA* 2/2, Nr. 73; HSTAD RD Nr. 200 pp. 2–3, 312–15, 367–71.

the merchant Johann Nicolas Baur, to Berlin as the county's representative. There, he sat on the left of the Prussian National Assembly, periodically returning to Adenau in moments of crisis to stir up his constituents against the government.[101]

The democrats did best in the southwestern end of the province, the Saar and Moselle valleys. Saarbrücken, where, rather as in Düsseldorf, *Vormärz* activists were quick to exploit the new political situation, was the only predominantly Protestant city in the Prussian Rhine Province controlled by the democrats. The constituencies Saarbrücken-Saarlouis and Merzig-Saarburg both sent militant leftists to sit in Frankfurt. Democratic electors were chosen in the wine towns Cochem and Bernkastel, but they were outvoted by rural electors, whose selection reflected clerical influence and who voted in more moderate deputies.[102]

Above all, the democrats were strong in the Moselle metropolis of Trier. The authority of the Prussian state there had completely vanished. No taxes were collected; the state insignia had been taken down from public buildings; part of the garrison was on the verge of mutiny. The election campaign was correspondingly tumultuous, the democrats demanding in mass meetings, attended by thousands, the secession of the Rhineland from Prussia. Moderates (who elsewhere might have been considered leftists), the military and civilian authorities, and the clergy and neoorthodox Catholic activists united against the democrats behind a constitutional monarchist program. People spoke of them as the "Prussians," calling the democrats the "Germans."

After the democrats' leader, the young attorney Ludwig Simon, publicly burned the constitutional monarchist program and the democrats' newly founded newspaper issued threats against the clergy, the Catholic-clericals realized they had, in trying to uphold order, identified themselves too closely with the Prussian state. On the eve of the elections, they withdrew from the constitutionalist alliance and promoted the candidacy of seminary professor Eberhard, known for his anti-Prussian sermon in honor of the victims of the Berlin barricade fighting. The move came too late, and virtually all the electors chosen were democrats, who duly sent Simon to Frankfurt, where he sat on the extreme left.[103]

These and a few other victories of the left suggested what the democrats

[101] BM Adenau to RKO, 30 Apr. 1848; BM Antweiler to RKO, 22 April and 8 May 1848; Kreis-Deputierte (Adenau) to RKO, 23 May 1848; Lieut. V. Wobeser (Adenau) to Commander of 2nd Batallion (Andernach), 2 May, 1848, all in LAK 441 Nr. 6792; LAK 403 Nr. 2275 pp. 353–55. Repgen's assertion (*Märzbewgung*, p. 55) that no county commissioners were driven out of office is thus not quite correct.

[102] Noack, "1848/49 in der Saargegend," pp. 58–64, 86; Repgen, *Märzbewegung*, pp. 270–73; LAK 441 Nr. 1330 pp. 45–56.

[103] Breuer, "1848/49 im Moseltal," pp. 96–121; Böse, "Ludwig Simon," pp. 22–40; "Die Geistlichkeit und das Volk zu Trier," *Vbl*, 23 Apr. 1848; LAK 403 Nr. 6583 pp. 19–21.

would have to do to be successful in the Prussian Rhine Province: organize and agitate broadly and aggressively, mobilize politically both social conflicts and hostility toward the state, and either neutralize or take over for their own purposes issues of confessional allegiance and interconfessional conflict. Since most democrats had not done this, they suffered a serious political defeat in the most populous part of the Rhineland, the twenty-eight deputies of the center and right sent by the voters of the Prussian Rhine Province to the Frankfurt National Assembly outweighing both the five leftist deputies they elected and the thirteen leftists sent from Rhine-Hessen and the Palatinate together.

CRISIS OF THE LEFT, MAY–JUNE, 1848

Shortly after the Rhenish democrats were defeated at the polls, they suffered a defeat in the streets. Clashes between Prussian troops and the people in Mainz and Trier badly disrupted the democrats' position in these two most revolutionary cities of western Germany. In both places, the old authorities had been rendered powerless by the events of March 1848. While in Trier, increasingly, anarchy reigned, in Mainz, a new revolutionary authority was created: the citizens' committee, which took its seat in city hall, meeting in permanent session. A representative of the committee always accompanied the mayor at any public appearance he made. While the committee collapsed at the end of April 1848, after its politically moderate members resigned, the civic guard it created remained in place and under leftist control.[104]

The radical regimes in Mainz and Trier collapsed in the same way in May 1848. Fighting broke out during the elections in Trier between citizens and Prussian soldiers—East Elbians brought in to replace the native Rhinelanders, who had shown too much sympathy for the revolution—continuing and escalating the following day. The civic guard refused to restore order, some guardsmen even wanting to join the civilians fighting the soldiers. Barricades were built and someone raised the red flag from the tower of St. Gangolph's church.

While leading leftists, such as true socialist Carl Grün, in 1848–1849 editor of the *Trier'sche Zeitung*, tried to calm the masses, lower-level leaders, such as the cigar manufacturer Andreas Tont, the first "prince" of Trier's carnival society, or the innkeeper Theodor Gassen, "an exalted republican," urged the crowd on and helped in building barricades. The soldiers were driven back to their barracks, which the crowd attempted to storm. The troops withdrew to the citadel and the commander of the Prussian Eighth Army Corps, the appropriately named general Roth von Schreckenstein, in Trier to inspect the garrison, threatened to bombard the city with the fortress's artillery if the insurgency were not immediately ended. It was, and order was restored, the civic

[104] Bockenheimer, *Mainz*, pp. 18, 60–62.

guard dissolved, the Prussian eagle returned to public buildings, taxes collected once more—and leading democrats arrested, even if they had opposed the insurrection and attempted to calm the crowd.[105]

These events were repeated, almost identically, two and a half weeks later in Mainz. Tavern brawls between Prussian soldiers and Mainz radicals occurred on May 19, 1848 and were repeated the following evening. The subsequent day saw large-scale confrontations in the street between soldiers on the one hand and the civic guard, members of the gymnastics society, and citizens on the other. Shots were exchanged; four soldiers and five guardsmen were killed. The soldiers were forced off the streets and the crowd prepared to storm the barracks. Prussian deputy fortress commandant, General von Hüser, besieged in the citadel, announced that if the disturbances did not cease immediately, he would turn his artillery on the city, and fired several warning shots to make his point clear. Once again, the threat of a bombardment brought the riots to an end, the civic guard was disbanded, and democratic newspapers temporarily placed under military censorship.[106]

By the beginning of June 1848, the democratic movement in the Rhineland had reached a point of frustration. The revolutionary struggles of March 1848 in the capital cities and the widespread disorders in the provinces suggested mass discontent with the existing order and wide potential support for the democrats. Just a few months later, all the hopes of the left seemed to have dissolved: the cautious attitude of the new, moderately liberal governments was insufficient for the radicals; the new regimes' use of the authorities and especially the military of their *Vormärz* predecessors seemed to threaten even what modest victories had been won in March 1848. Karl Marx, returning to Cologne from exile in Paris to bring out a continuation of the radical newspaper he had edited in 1842, expressed the feeling that the revolution was in danger in the lead article of the very first issue of the *Neue Rheinische Zeitung*. He explained that the paper was coming out a month ahead of schedule, because of the ''renewed, arrogant appearance of reaction.''[107]

Nothing the democrats did had been able to counter this trend. Their peaceful participation in indirect elections to the Frankfurt National Assembly had resulted in a conservative majority in both the Rhineland and all of Germany. Bonn democrat Gottfried Kinkel wrote dispiritedly, ''The five fingers of despotism, clergy, nobility, moneybags, soldiers, officials, have triumphed and will dominate the parliaments.'' Armed struggles, whether planned uprisings to push the revolution further to the left, as tried in Baden, or the chaotic

[105] On the ''days of the barricades'' in Trier, see Breuer, ''1848/49 im Moseltal,'' pp. 120–34; LAK 403 Nr. 6583 pp. 12–17, 26–36; *RhBA* 2/2, Nr. 64; *Vbl*, 31 Aug.–7 Sept. 1848; Zenz, *Andreas Tont*, passim.
[106] Bockenheimer, *Mainz*, pp. 66–72; Buckler, ''Die politischen und religiösen Kämpfe,'' pp. 48–51; *KnZ*, 24 May 1848 (Beilage), 25 May 1848 (Beilage); *Vbl*, 26 May 1848.
[107] *RhBA* 2/2, Nr. 120.

clashes between soldiers and the people in Mainz or Trier, had merely made matters worse.[108]

A completely new political strategy was needed, one outlined by the Mainz democrat Johann Baptist Müller-Melchiors, in a speech given toward the end of June 1848. Both the democrats and their opponents, he noted[109]

> so great the number of their present adherents may be, are unimportant and weak when compared with the enormous mass of the people, who, at the present time, be it from laziness or indifference, be it from lack of political insight, have not inclined to any party. Whichever party succeeds in attracting the people, succeeds in impressing on the people the conviction that for the protection of its rights, its freedoms, it must pledge allegiance to that party's flag, such a party will have won a victory, solved its problem, and will harvest the rich fruits of its efforts.

The further story of the revolution would be the attempts of the democrats to gain popular support and organize it for their cause.

[108] Kinkel, cited in Kersken, *Bonn in den Revolutionsjahren*, p. 56.
[109] *Der Demokrat*, 2 July 1848.

CHAPTER FIVE

The Organization of a Democratic Movement

EVEN as Müller-Melchiors spoke, Rhenish democrats were acting as he suggested, albeit in loosely coordinated and sporadic fashion. They carried out their agitation in town and country, through the press and street demonstrations, in mass meetings and in individual tavern conversations, striving to gain popular support by presenting their vision of a just social and political order. As they gained adherents, they enrolled them in democratic political clubs, aiming to create an effective agency for political action, whether of a peaceful or a violent nature. The work of the democrats began in the late spring and early summer of 1848 and continued throughout the following year. They achieved varying degrees of success, but everywhere they recruited a larger and better-organized group of adherents than had existed at the outbreak of the revolution.

ORGANIZED DEMOCRACY: THE POLITICAL CLUB

The characteristic form of democratic organization was the political club, usually going under the name "Democratic Club" or "People's Association." Such clubs first arose in the spring of 1848, when members of ad hoc committees created to direct the elections to the Frankfurt National Assembly saw the need for better-organized and -financed and formally constituted political organizations, complete with statutes and membership dues. The founding of the Palatine People's Associations was the earliest and most effective transition from ad hoc committee to permanent association. Left-wing activists founded the political clubs in Barmen and Elberfeld at about the same time, but in the more conservative environment of the Wuppertal, they achieved just a mediocre showing in the May 1848 elections. A variant form of development, seen in Cologne, Mainz, and Trier, occurred when unitary election committees split apart, as irreconcilable differences between leftists and constitutional monarchists became apparent in the course of writing a political platform and nominating candidates. This breakdown of civic unity quickly impelled the democrats to create their own, more permanent political organization.[1]

---

[1] Illner, *Bürgerliche Organisierung*, pp. 150–55; Seypel, "Die Demokratische Gesellschaft in Köln," p. 116; Buckler, "Die politischen und religiösen Kämpfe," p. 48; *Vbl*, 7 June 1848.

Over the following year, democratic clubs spread outwards from the larger cities where they were first formed. Table 5.1 summarizes this process of the expansion of the democrats' political organization.[2] Over three-fourths of all the democratic clubs existing in the Rhineland during the revolution were founded after the summer of 1848, two-thirds of them, in winter 1848–1849 and spring 1849. The existence of such an ever-expanding political network is the key to understanding the continuation of a revolutionary movement, even after the initial popular disorders of spring 1848 had been suppressed and more moderate or outright conservative forces had dominated the new governments of the individual German states and the elections to the Frankfurt National Assembly.

The location of the clubs reveals once more a sharp north-south distinction in political culture. Although the Prussian Rhine Province had three times the

TABLE 5.1
Democratic Clubs in the Rhineland, 1848–1849

	Number of Democratic Clubs Existing in:		
Region	Aug. 1848	Nov. 1848	May 1849
Prussian Rhine Province	29	51	91
Rhine-Hessen	37	62	120
Palatinate	24[a]	40	173

Sources: See note 2, this chapter.
[a] April 1848.

[2] For the Prussian Rhine Province: LAK 403 Nr. 7045 pp. 3–73, 77–104, 107–43, 149–62; HSTAD RD Nr. 200 passim; HSTAD RD Pr. Nr. 819 ff. 31–38; HSTAD RD Pr. Nr. 816 ff. 155–56; HSTAD RD Nr. 8808 ff. 1–10; HSTAD RD Nr. 8806 ff. 178–82; HSTAD RD Pr. Nr. 796 ff. 24–25, 28; HSTAD RD Pr. Nr. 823 ff. 8–9; HSTAD RD Pr. Nr. 827 ff. 15–17; HSTAD RA Pr. Nr. 2226 ff. 264–65; HSTAD RA Nr. 222 f. 105; HSTAD RA Pr. Nr. 2229 ff. 124, 152–54; LAK 403 Nr. 7172 pp. 33–36; LAK 441 Nr. 1330 pp. 269–73, 521–29, 531–38, 565–71; LAK 442 Nr. 6497 pp. 205–21, 311–18; ZSTAM Rep. 77 Tit. 1095 Nr. 1 ff. 19–20, 29; LAS J1 Nr. 246 ff. 3–18; NRhZ, 4 June, 13 Sept., 23 Dec. 1848, 7 Jan. 1849 (Zweite Ausgabe), 20 Jan. 1849; Vbl, 7, 28 June, 9 July, 20 Sept. 1848; ZAVK, 13 July 1848; FBA, 17 Apr., 13 May 1849; Gerhard Becker, "Der Kongreß der Arbeitervereine der Rheinprovinz und Westfalen am 6. Mai 1849," Beiträge zur Geschichte der deutschen Arbeiterbewegung 10 (1968): 373–83; Dowe, Aktion und Organisation, p. 182; Lenger, Zwischen Kleinbürgertum und Proletariat, pp. 159, 199–200; Illner, Bürgerliche Organisierung, pp. 150–52, 171–73, 200; Meisenburg, "Essen in den Revolutionsjahren," pp. 242, 259–60; Seypel, "Die Demokratische Gesellschaft in Köln," p. 116 and passim; Kersken, Stadt und Universität Bonn, p. 56; Gernert, 1848/49 im Rheinisch-Bergischen, pp. 122–23; Benedikt Schneider, Die Verfassungskämpfe der Jahre 1848/49 unter Berücksichtigung der Ereignisse im Siegkreise (Honnef: Siebengebirgsbuchhandlung, 1929), p. 18; Stahl, 1848/49 an der Mittelmosel, p. 16; Noack, "Saargegend," pp. 91–92. For Rhine-Hessen: BAF DB 54 Nr. 74 ff. 22–23; Braun, Geschichte des Turnens in Rheinhessen 1:174–85; MZ, 12 May 1849 (Erste Ausgabe). For the Palatinate: "Protokoll über . . . Gründung eines Volks- oder Vaterlands-Vereins"; NSZ, 10 Nov. 1848, 17 Apr. 1849.

population of the Palatinate and Rhine-Hessen combined, it had less than one-third as many democratic clubs as did its two southern neighbors, a difference in extent most apparent in the countryside. About 140 of the 173 Palatine associations were in rural areas, 60 of them in the two western upland counties Homburg und Zweibrücken. A democratic club existed in all the county towns in the Palatinate, in every one of the thirty-one cantonal seats, and in about every fifth village. The network of clubs was even denser in Rhine-Hessen, with one in each of the nine county or cantonal towns and in 111 of 175 villages. Small wonder that Mainz democratic leader Ludwig Bamberger could proclaim at a New Year's rally in 1849, "Our entire province is one single democratic club."[3]

Only thirty-one of the ninety-one clubs in the Prussian Rhine Province were located in rural areas. Sixty-four, or two-thirds of the entire total, were found in the urbanized, densely populated Düsseldorf and Cologne districts. In particular, they were most prevalent in the area on the right bank of the Rhine from Düsseldorf south to Königswinter, across the river from Bonn. The three counties of Solingen, Mülheim a. Rhein and Sieg accounted for twenty-seven of the clubs, or about 30 percent of all those existing in the entire province. This was also the only region in the Prussian Rhineland where the democratic movement ever really firmly set foot in the countryside, nineteen of the thirty-one rural democratic clubs existing in these three counties.[4]

Temporal and spatial dimensions taken together provide a good measure of the difference between the Prussian Rhine Province and its southern neighbors. It was precisely in the fall of 1848 and the winter and spring of 1849 that urban activists organized rural clubs on a large scale, an activism seen throughout Rhine-Hessen and in the Palatinate, but just in a few scattered parts of the Prussian Rhineland. To some extent, clubs in smaller urban centers attracted rural democrats; radicals in Cochem and Bernkastel made a real effort to encompass the vintners by holding meetings of their clubs in different parts of their respective counties. These measures to stir up and organize the peasantry were not without success, as would be seen in November 1848, but they were no replacement for the founding of village clubs, when it came to the creation of a lasting political movement.[5]

---

[3] Cited in *MZ*, 4 Jan. 1849. The location (as distinct from the number) of the political clubs in the Palatinate is from Michael Wettengel, "Das liberale und demokratische Vereinswesen in der Pfalz während der Revolution 1848/49," *JhGStLK* 22/23 (1984/85): 73–90, esp. pp. 86–88, corrected for errors, with the addition of further clubs mentioned in LAS J1 Nr. 195 ff. 47–48, 100–14; LAS J1 Nr. 200 f. 281; LAS J1 Nr. 218 ff. 113–14; LAS J1 Nr. 133 f. 16; LAS J1 Nr. 263 ff. 80–81, 108–17, 290–91; LAS J1 Nr. 215 (alt) ff. 169–71; LAS J1 Nr. 228 (alt) ff. 659, 686; LAS J1 Nr. 243 (alt) ff. 30–35, 80–81; LAS J1 Nr. 249 (alt) ff. 13–15.

[4] Of the remaining twelve rural clubs, eight were either in the Cologne suburbs or in the countryside between Cologne and Bonn, that is, on the other side of the Rhine from the rural strongholds of the democrats.

[5] Stahl, *1848/49 an der Mittelmosel*, p. 16 (his mention of a democratic club in the up-country [Hochwald] is not confirmed by any other source); LAK 403 Nr. 7045 pp. 97–104.

Another way to see the difference between the Prussian Rhineland and the two southern provinces is to compare the size of the network of democratic clubs with those of competing political organizations. Expressly conservative or counterrevolutionary groups were rare in the Rhineland; the main alternatives to the democrats were the constitutional monarchists and the Roman Catholic Pius Associations. Although everywhere outnumbered by the organized left, the latter groups were much stronger in the Prussian province.

No constitutional monarchist associations at all were founded in the Palatinate during the revolution. Moderate liberals who wished to be politically active had to join one of the local branches of the People's Association, usually leaving again after unpleasant experiences at the hands of the democrats. Pius Associations were the only organized opposition to the Palatine democrats, but not a truly effective one, since by the spring of 1849 there were only some twenty local Catholic groups in existence.[6]

The constitutional monarchists did slightly better in Rhine-Hessen: The two liberal clubs in Mainz and Worms founded in the summer of 1848 were followed by three more in the fall of that year, and another nine in the winter and spring of 1849. Although the Catholic movement began in Rhine-Hessen, with the first Pius Association founded by a circle of neoorthodox Mainz Catholics in March 1848, there were only twelve such groups created in the province over the course of the revolution. Once again, the democrats substantially outnumbered any competitors.[7]

In the Prussian Rhineland, on the other hand, constitutional monarchism was a substantial force, with twenty-seven clubs from the Rhine Province represented at the Rhenish-Westphalian congress of constitutional monarchist associations in July 1848. While about equal to the number of democratic clubs existing then, the constitutional monarchists could not match the expansion of democratic organizations over the next six to eight months. Only forty-six Rhenish clubs were represented at the January 1849 congress of the constitutionalist groups (some of which were about to secede and affiliate with the democrats), rather less than the sixty or seventy democratic clubs existing at the time. Although I have been unable to find any systematic listing of Pius Associations in the Prussian Rhineland, there seem to have been a substantial number, somewhere between twenty and forty, in existence by the spring of 1849.[8]

[6] On Palatine constitutional monarchism, see LAS J1 Nr. 104 ff. 16–21, 49, 51; LAS J1 Nr. 203 ff. 364–66; LAS J1 Nr. 245 ff. 263–67; LAS J1 Nr. 267 ff. 157–66; for the Pius Associations, see Hans Ziegler, *Die Jahre der Reaktion in der Pfalz (1849–1853)* (Speyer: Verlag der Pfälzischen Gesellschaft zur Förderung der Wissenschaften, 1985), p. 251; and LAS J1 Nr. 203 ff. 385–92.

[7] Wettengel, *1848/49 im Rhein-Main-Raum*, pp. 364–65, 421–23, 636–37, 642.

[8] On constitutionalist associations, see ZSTAM Rep. 77 Tit. 1095 Nr. 1 ff. 3–4; and *KnZ*, 6

As the revolution continued, all political groups made efforts to expand the number of their local affiliates. Overall, it was the democrats who were most successful at this, but their margin of superiority was smallest in the Prussian Rhine Province, where, in contrast to the Palatinate or Rhine-Hessen, they always faced substantial organized competition.

Broader Vistas: Regional and National Associations

The organization of individual democratic clubs occurred in conjunction with attempts to create regional federations of these groups and to build a national democratic organization. The first step in this direction was the all-German congress of democratic clubs, which met in Frankfurt on June 14–17, 1848. The congress elected a provisional central committee, whose seat was to be in Berlin, and created seventeen district committees [Kreisausschüsse] to serve as intermediaries between the local clubs and the central office and to act as centers for the coordination of local agitation. A resolution also called on democrats to strengthen their political position by entering into alliances with workers' associations and gymnastics societies.[9]

The democrats of Rhine-Hessen carried out these decisions with the most enthusiasm and with the greatest success. The province-wide meeting of the cantonal citizens' committees in April 1848, which had been dominated by the left, was already a provincial democratic congress in embryo; a second such meeting held in Wörrstadt on June 6, 1848, called on the local and cantonal committees to transform themselves into democratic clubs and send delegates to the national congress in Frankfurt. Under these circumstances, the formation of a district committee by a congress of delegates from thirty-eight different democratic clubs (including one from the Prussian border town Kreuznach), gymnastics societies, and workers' associations, once again in Wörrstadt, on August 13, 1848, was more the formalization of an already existing political network than the creation of a new one.[10]

The Rhine-Hessian democrats held several provincial congresses; the last, in May 1849, was attended by delegates from 100 of the 120 affiliated clubs. The provincial directory, composed of Mainz democratic leaders, coordinated an energetic agitation, sending speakers out into the countryside to found new

---

Jan. 1849. The number of Pius Associations in the province is an impression based on widely scattered sources.

[9] Botzenhart, *Deutscher Parlamentarismus*, pp. 338–42; Joachim Paschen, *Demokratische Vereine und preußischer Staat. Entwicklung und Unterdrückung der demokratischen Bewegung während der Revolution von 1848/49* (Munich and Vienna: R. Oldenbourg, 1977), pp. 53–63; Gerhard Becker, "Das Protokoll des ersten Demokratenkongresses von Juni 1848," *Jahrbuch für Geschichte* 8 (1973): 379–405.

[10] Uhrig, "Worms," p. 50; Katz-Seibert, *Radikalismus in Hessen*, p. 25; Botzenhart, *Deutscher Parlamentarismus*, pp. 343–44; *MZ*, 18 Aug. 1848; *NRhZ*, 10 June 1848; BAF DB 54 Nr. 74 ff. 2–26.

clubs, preside over mass rallies, and oppose organizing efforts of the constitutional monarchists and the Pius Associations. Mainz leaders kept regular office hours, so small-town and village democrats could come and get their advice about political organizing, relations with the state authorities, and relations with village and municipal government. In the spring of 1849, the Rhine-Hessian democrats were preparing to create a provincial mediation service, which would settle legal disputes between democrats more quickly and efficaciously than would going to court. If anything, the provincial organization was too successful, Mainz leaders informing the affiliated clubs that it was physically impossible for them to accept all the invitations they received to speak.[11]

Delegates from several democratic clubs and workers' associations in Rhenish Prussia also attended the Frankfurt congress and, like their counterparts in Rhine-Hessen, followed its recommendations to create a district committee. Still reeling from their electoral defeat, and lacking the experience in political agitation of their Rhine-Hessian counterparts, the democrats of the Prussian Rhineland had less success in their efforts. A founding congress called to Cologne by the Cologne Democratic Society and Cologne Workers' Association, was attended by representatives of just fourteen clubs, perhaps half of those already in existence, plus two from the neighboring province of Westphalia, on August 13–14, 1848.[12]

The district committee's subsequent history was marked by less than auspicious beginnings: The office of corrresponding secretary went unfilled after September 24; correspondence between the Berlin central office and the provincial clubs sat around for weeks at a time until members of the Cologne Democratic Society could get to it. The provincial directory, formed by Cologne democratic leaders, including Karl Marx, met once between the fall of 1848 and a session of April 1849, called by Marx and his followers for the purpose of dissolving the association and seceding to form their own. Far from encouraging the formation of new clubs, the provincial directory had no idea of their existence, and when Marx was seeking out clubs that would support his planned secession, he was forced to place notices in the newspapers, asking for their addresses.[13]

The Palatine People's Associations sent no representatives to the Frankfurt Democratic Congress and in general seem to have lapsed into a state of organizational lethargy following the victories of their candidates in the elections to the Frankfurt National Assembly. Over the summer, it slowly became clear to Palatine activists that their provincewide association, a model of organization in April 1848, would no longer suffice for the political tasks of this new

---

[11] *MZ*, 29 Aug., 9, 13, 19–20 Sept., 13, 24 Oct., 1848, 1 Feb., 1, 28 Apr., 12 May 1849 (Erste Ausgabe); *Der Demokrat*, 8 Feb., 29 Apr. 1849.

[12] Dowe, *Aktion und Organisation*, pp. 166–75, 181–86.

[13] Kühn, *Der junge Hermann Becker*, pp. 162–64.

phase of the revolution, especially organization and agitation in the country-side. At a meeting in Neustadt a.d.W. on October 8, 1848, the provincial committee drafted new statutes, creating a tiered system of associations, from the local through the cantonal to the county and, finally, to the provincial level.[14]

The revised statutes encouraged the creation of new local groups, making the activists in the cantonal towns responsible for organization of the nearby rural areas, and giving the larger groups in the county seats the function of supervising the associations in their respective counties. Once, when the Neustadt People's Association became paralyzed by vehement internal dis-agreements between moderates and radicals, this supervision worked in re-verse, the rural clubs organizing the cantonal association themselves. To fa-cilitate the process of organization, the provincial committee created a weekly newsletter, the *Volksvereinsblatt*, which eventually appeared in a press run of five thousand copies.[15]

The reorganization proved eminently successful, since the number of affil-iated associations climbed from 40 in November 1848 to 173 by April 1849. Suggestions for petition campaigns and organization drives could be passed up to the provincial committee from local groups, and finished addresses back down, ready to be circulated for signatures—to be sure, a familiar practice in the Palatinate, but one that could now be carried out on an unprecedented scale. The new structure of the People's Association proved equally effective for electoral politics: the association called on local groups to nominate can-didates to the Bavarian legislature in November 1848, selected a slate from the broad list of nominees they submitted, and completely dominated the elec-tions in early December, all its candidates being chosen by wide margins.[16]

As the German revolution entered a critical phase in the fall of 1848, with major political confrontations occurring in Frankfurt, Vienna, and Berlin, democrats looked to create a better, more effective national organization than the provisional structure set up by the Frankfurt congress in June. Two sepa-

[14] Wettengel, ''Vereinswesen in der Pfalz,'' p. 76; *NSZ*, 6 July, 1848, 20 Aug. 1848 (Beilage), 12 Oct. 1848 (Beilage); LAS J1 Nr. 244 ff. 342–44. It is something of a mystery why the Palatine People's Associations had so little to do with the Frankfurt Democratic Congress. Wettengel con-tends that the republican ideas espoused there were tco radical for the Palatines, but as will be seen in the section on agitation below, Palatine activists were busy sponsoring equally radical activities at the time.

[15] On the workings of this new organizational system, see LAS J1 Nr. 244. ff. 15–16, 157–61, 169, 180–85, 195–96, 211–12, 218; LAS J1 Nr. 200 f. 281 and LAS J1 Nr. 249 (alt) f. 336. For events in Canton Neustadt, see LAS J1 Nr. 244 (alt) ff. 641, 659, 684, 686. On the *Volksvereins-blatt*, see LAS J1 Nr. 244 f. 175; regrettably, the newsletter does not seem to have been preserved. Similar club newsletters appeared in Cologne, Elberfeld, and Mainz, but on a smaller and more local scale.

[16] Petition drives: LAS J1 Nr. 244 ff. 190, 319–20; elections, ibid. ff. 182–85, 204, 340; RP to MInn, 18 Dec. 1848, BHSTAM MInn Nr. 46129; *NSZ*, 2, 9 Dec., 1848.

rate attempts to found such a national organization were made in November 1848, neither entirely successful. One stemmed from the provisional central committee appointed by the first democratic congress, which called a second nationwide congress to Berlin in November 1848. This congress, largely an affair of the extreme left, became bogged down in acrimonious political debate and was unable to create an effective political organization.[17]

In some ways more promising was the group created by most of the deputies of the center-left and extreme left of the Frankfurt Parliament shortly after the Berlin congress, the "Central Association for the Preservation of the Victories of March [1848]." Its name was too long, even for Germans, so it was commonly known as the "Central March Association." At its highpoint, 950 clubs with half a million members are said to have been affiliated. Although Cologne's deputy to Frankfurt, Franz Raveaux, was deeply involved in founding the group, and a member of its executive committee, it found little favor among Rhenish democrats. They usually rejected it as too moderate, unlikely to take decisive action when necessary—a justified fear, as the association's activities in May 1849 would show—and refused to affiliate. Just one of the democratic clubs of Rhine-Hessen joined, and only five from the Prussian Rhine Province did, all politically moderate groups, members of a left-wing breakaway from the federation of constitutional monarchist associations.[18]

After a number of individual People's Associations in the Palatinate joined the Central March Association, the provincial central committee decided the Palatine groups should affiliate en bloc. They did, making up about one-eighth of the affiliated societies in Germany, even though the Palatinate had only 1.5 percent of Germany's population. The reasons for this affiliation are not entirely clear, although controversies within individual People's Associations seem to have played a role. Radicals in Zweibrücken and Kirchheimbolanden used affiliation of their respective groups with the national one as a weapon in a power struggle with moderates, reversing at the local level the general regional pattern, which saw only moderate groups affiliating with the national association.[19]

To sum up, an effective provincial democratic association, a widespread network of democratic clubs, and a dominant position for the democrats vis-à-vis political rivals went closely together. An active provincial directory

[17] Botzenhart, *Deutscher Parlamentarismus*, pp. 360–66; and esp. the detailed account in Paschen, *Demokratische Vereine*, pp. 96–112, although the latter's attempt to reverse the prevalent opinion and pronounce the congress a success, is unconvincing.

[18] Botzenhart, *Deutscher Parlamentarismus*, pp. 398–406; Illner, *Bürgerliche Organisierung*, pp. 171–73; *MZ*, 29 Nov. 1848; *Der Demokrat*, 3 Dec. 1848; *NRhZ*, 17 Mar. 1849; LAS J1 Nr. 246 ff. 3–18 (list of affiliated societies, a condensed version printed in Botzenhart, *Deutscher Parlamentarismus*, pp. 402–03).

[19] LAS J1 Nr. 244 f. 167; LAS J1 Nr. 267 ff. 157–66; *NSZ*, 15 Mar. 1849 (Beilage); Wettengel, "Vereinswesen in der Pfalz," p. 77.

greatly helped facilitate political agitation in small towns and rural areas, where a majority of Rhinelanders lived. In this respect, the political experiences of the *Vormärz* proved decisive. Provincewide parliamentary election campaigns or petition drives in Rhine-Hessen and the Palatinate and, further back, the near-revolutionary events of 1832 had created a cadre of activists who could agitate in a broader arena, once it became legally possible. Such activists were present only in a few scattered locations in the Prussian Rhineland, and it took time and effort to bring them together, in the end with much less effect.

All Rhenish democrats saw themselves as part of a broader political movement, and took part in attempts to create a national organization. None of them was entirely successful, being unable to overcome political and regional differences. The democrats were not alone in this respect, the constitutional monarchists having similar problems in creating a national movement. Such difficulties were a reflection of the still-primitive state of communications and transport and the substantial regional differences in political experience. These worked against the creation of an effective organization that could bring together groups across wide geographical distances and no less broad cultural ones.[20]

One Democratic Movement? Moderates and Radicals

The democratic movement in the Rhineland was by no means politically homogeneous, and factional differences appeared within it, sometimes mounting to the levels of serious antagonisms. Controversies among Cologne leftists in the spring of 1849, for instance, had reached the point that outsiders felt the radicals of the provincial metropolis were more interested in defaming one another than in fighting the movements' enemies. Such vehement internecine hostility was atypical. Democrats representing differing political positions usually worked well together—perhaps in part because poor communications prevented them from knowing how different the ideas of fellow democrats outside the immediate vicinity might be. Nor should the importance of different tendencies for the practical work of the movement be overstated. Factional differences never reached the countryside, where most democratic clubs were located. Even in politically more sophisticated urban areas, where activists were capable of articulating different political positions, the prevailing attitude of the general population often led to the domination of one tendency in political work for purely pragmatic reasons. Leftist activists in the conservative, neoorthodox, Prussian loyalist Wuppertal, whatever their actual opinions may

---

[20] On constitutional monarchist organizing efforts, see Hartwig Gebhardt, *Revolution und liberale Bewegung. Die nationale Organisation der konstitutionellen Partei in Deutschland 1848/49* (Hamburg: Schünemann Universitätsverlag, 1974).

have been, were forced to appear in public as more moderate than their counterparts in such centers of popular radicalism as Mainz or Trier.[21]

Frictions arose and had a significant impact on political life when two separate left-wing groups existed in a single locality, something usually occurring in a more radical environment. The best-known examples are Cologne, with its Workers' Association and Democratic Society, and Düsseldorf, where the Democratic Club, originally called the Association for a Democratic Monarchy, and the openly republican People's Club were simultaneously present on the left. In both these cities, the two groups went through periods of close cooperation and greater distance to one another, never quite reaching the stage of open conflict, but never losing their separate identities either. Mergers were consistently voted down, in Düsseldorf on four separate occasions.[22]

Internal conflicts within the democratic movement were most prevalent and also at their nastiest in the Palatinate, precisely because of the establishment there of a provincewide political organization at the very beginning of the revolution. At one time or another, all sorts of democrats, republicans, democratic monarchists, communists, and even constitutional monarchists—in the Palatinate, mostly the Bavarian state officials—were members of the People's Associations. Of all the political groups, only the strict Catholics organized outside the People's Association umbrella. Some of the local branches, those in Grünstadt and Bergzabern, for instance, were dominated by the extreme left from the beginning of the revolution. In many other towns the groups are better described as left leaning but politically heterogeneous.[23]

Local radicals were discontented with this and they organized, mostly in the spring and summer of 1848 but occasionally later, separate democratic clubs alongside the People's Associations. Such groups existed in Frankenthal, Bad Dürkheim, Edenkoben, Landau, Kirchheimbolanden, Zweibrücken, Kaiserslautern, and Neustadt a.d.W. The idea of a separate organization did not prove terribly successful, and gradually the militant leftists dissolved their clubs and led their followers back into the People's Associations. They established themselves as a left-wing caucus within the associations, holding a provincial meeting in March 1849, and making plans to found their own newspaper.[24]

[21] On controversies among Cologne democrats, see Dowe, *Aktion und Organisation*, pp. 216–17.

[22] Seypel, "Die Demokratische Gesellschaft in Köln," pp. 295–97, 332–36; Lenger, *Zwischen Kleinbürgertum und Proletariat*, pp. 162–70; *RhBA* 2/2, Nr. 289; HSTAD RD Nr. 200 pp. 117–21.

[23] The best study of political tendencies within the Palatine People's Associations is the essay of Wettengel, "Das liberale und demokratische Vereinswesen," which, however, is based on a narrow range of sources and so is occasionally inaccurate and also incomplete.

[24] *NSZ*, 2, 6 July, 23 Aug., 12 Oct. 1848 (Beilage); 15 Mar. 1849 (Beilage); LAS J1 Nr. 218 ff. 121–26; LAS J1 Nr. 203 ff. 11–18, 167–74; LAS J1 Nr. 205 ff. 417–30; LAS J1 Nr. 267 ff. 157–66; LAS J1 Nr. 245 ff. 263–67; LAS J1 Nr. 247 ff. 46–55; LAS J1 Nr. 228 (alt) ff. 638–726; LAS J1 Nr. 235 f. 805; *Anklag-Akte*, pt. 2, pp. 75–77 (original in LAS J1 Nr. 247 ff. 6–7).

In most towns, the radicals were successful in pushing the local People's Association to the left, but in two of the largest their actions resulted in bitter struggles. The situation was most complicated in Kaiserslautern, where there were three separate factions within the People's Association: the democrats, known as the "Sunday Circle," the state officials and others of constitutional monarchist sentiments calling themselves the "Citizens' Club," and between them a third, centrist group, the "People's Club." The leftists were best organized, sitting together at meetings, cheering their speakers, and booing others. They voted as a bloc, all raising their hands simultaneously on the signal from the young radical Philip Schmidt, secretary to Nikolaus Schmitt, Kaiserslautern's deputy to the Frankfurt National Assembly, and leader of the Palatine republicans. The moderates were unable to match this organization and, in addition, wanted nothing to do with Bavarian state officials, so the leftist faction, although a minority, was able to dominate the town's People's Association. The Kaiserslautern radicals, however, were careful to preserve the organization's unity: When they passed an overly militant decision in November 1848 and the other groups threatened to walk out, they agreed to rescind it.[25]

Similar factional conflicts took place in Neustadt a.d.W., although the political positions represented were swung over far to the left. As the postrevolutionary provincial governor Johann Baptist von Zenetti noted, while in most German cities the struggle during the revolution was between "conservatives and republicans," in Neustadt it was "between republicans and the declared adherents of universal anarchy." Leaders of the extreme left formed a democratic club, which held its weekly meetings jointly with the Workers' Educational Association, the Workers' Choral Society, the Gymnastics Society, and the Vintners' Association. This last group was the only example of a left-wing peasant's organization in the Rhineland during the revolution, in contrast to the many such groups for the urban lower classes.

Early in 1849, the radicals joined the People's Association en masse. Their participation in the new election of its executive committee at the beginning of February split the group apart, the two factions expelling each other, each declaring itself the legitimate People's Association. Negotiations to reestablish unity only led to the two groups' trading recriminations about who was responsible for the split. The upshot was to re-create the previous situation of two separate leftist organizations, one moderate and one radical, only both now calling themselves People's Associations, with some 500 members between them. To tell them apart, they were known by their meeting places, the moderates forming the People's Association of Köhler's coffeehouse and the radicals the People's Association of Bub's Wineshop.[26]

[25] LAS J1 Nr. 105 ff. 201–12; LAS J1 Nr. 245 ff. 263–67, 383–84, 387–89, 397–98; LAS J1 Nr. 247 ff. 41–44, 46–55.

[26] The whole story, depressingly familiar to anyone who has been involved in left-wing politics,

Even when openly split apart, the two groups, by retaining a common name, preserved the fiction of organizational unity. This desire for unity, pronounced among rank-and-file democrats, in spite of their leaders' differences, helped maintain common democratic organizations and preserve the ability to take joint action, even when deep factional differences appeared. In the end, the Rhenish democrats remained one political movement containing different tendencies, rather than dividing into several opposing groups.

Membership

The existence of almost four hundred democratic clubs in the Rhineland is suggestive of the extent of the democratic movement, but much more could be learned about it by identifying the clubs' membership. This has proven to be quite difficult. The few and sparse sources rarely give an idea of how many people joined democratic clubs, much less provide the material for a detailed breakdown of the social or confessional composition of their membership. For what follows, I can only warn the reader that the evidence is fragmentary, the conclusions it warrants drawing at best tentative.

The scattered figures on club membership point, once again, toward a north-south difference. Clubs in the Palatinate, Rhine-Hessen, and the Moselle Valley in the Prussian Rhine Province generally had larger memberships and encompassed a greater proportion of the population than those further north. The 700 members of the Zweibrücken Peoples' Association, made up about three-eighths of the adult male population of the city, while the 348 organized democrats in Cochem were over half the adult males of this Moselle Valley wine town. Figures for rural clubs are harder to come by; the 150 adherents of the Peoples' Association in Bellheim, a large village in the southeastern Palatinate, were between one-fifth and one-fourth of the adult male villagers.[27]

The two largest clubs in the southern Rhineland were in Trier and Mainz. Both counted at their founding in May–June 1848 400–600 members, increasing to 1,300–1,500 in the fall of 1848, about one-fourth of the adult men in Trier. The Mainz democrats claimed 2,000 adherents in May 1849, one adult male in five. Figures on membership at several different times are unusual, so there is no way of knowing if the considerable growth in the number of organized democrats in these two cities was typical.[28]

---

can be followed from the documents in LAS J1 Nr. 228 (alt) ff. 638–726. Cf. also ibid. ff. 61, 254–58; *Anklag-Akte*, pt. 2, pp. 74–77.

[27] Membership figures are from the sources cited in note 2 unless otherwise specified. I have assumed that adult males were about one-fourth the entire population. On the question of female membership (which existed but was almost certainly quite uncommon) see the section on women in the revolution in Chapter Six.

[28] On membership in the Mainz democratic club, see "Namens-Verzeichniß der Mitglieder . . ." (Aug., 1848); BAF DB 54 Nr. 74 f. 2 (Nov. 1848); *Der Demokrat*, 6 May 1849 (May 1849).

Equally hard to come by are broader membership figures. The only ones I have been able to find, and they are hardly exact, give the total membership of all the local groups affiliated with the Palatine People's Association in April 1849 as somewhere betweeen 15,000 and 18,000. With a total population of some 600,000, this would mean that between 10 and 12 percent of the adult males of the entire province were politically organized leftists, by the standards of the time (and those of today, for that matter) an impressive total.[29]

There were far fewer organized democrats, both absolutely and proportionately, in the northern Rhineland. The 600 members of the Cologne Democratic Society were less than 3 percent of the adult male population of the Rhenish metropolis with its 88,000 inhabitants, while the 300–600 in the Elberfeld Political Club were between 3 and 6 percent of the adult males of that pious, conservative manufacturing town. The Wuppertal leftists were well organized when compared with their counterparts in the Rhineland's leading industrial city, the People's Association only enrolling between 10 and 150 of Aachen's 48,000 inhabitants. Lower Rhine democrats were only slightly better represented in smaller market towns, the 170 organized leftists in Neuss and the 50 in Xanten making up about 7.5 and 6.5 percent of the respective adult male populations.

Where the democratic clubs of the northern Rhineland were most thickly clustered, their members were also most numerous. The 600 Bonn democrats were a seventh of the university town's adult males; the 500 members of the Workers' Association of Mülheim a. Rhein (the Mülheim Workers' Association acted as a democratic club and was affiliated with the provincial democratic association) were a third of the Cologne suburb's adult male inhabitants. Democrats were most numerous in their lower Rhine stronghold Düsseldorf, the city's two leftist groups having together between 2,000 and 3,000 members out of the 6,000 civilian male adults living there.

These figures are fragmentary enough, and make no distinction between members who were active in club life, those who just paid dues regularly and attended meetings, and those who paid and attended irregularly or not at all. Such evidence is rich indeed, however, when compared with material on the social composition of the democratic clubs, since I have more or less complete figures on only 2 of the 390 that existed in the Rhineland (see Table 5.2). The percentages are quite similar for both cities, making it possible that the results might be applicable to other urban areas in the southern Rhineland. A surprisingly large number of merchants, estate owners, and professionals were members, the bourgeoisie overrepresented in the membership in comparison to their position in the population. Also heavily overrepresented were innkeepers, bakers, and brewers, three overlapping occupations, whose members had

[29] *NSZ*, 17 Apr. 1849; Ferdinand Fenner von Fenneberg, *Zur Geschichte der rheinpfälzischen Revolution und des badischen Aufstandes* (Zurich: E. Kierling, 1849), p. 29.

TABLE 5.2
Social Composition of Mainz and Kaiserslautern Democratic Clubs

Occupation	Kaiserslautern		Mainz	
	N	%	N	%
Merchant, manufacturer, rentier	42	12.3⎱	139	22.5
Clerk, foreman	23	6.7⎰		
Professional	14	4.1	48	7.8
State official (including teachers)	9	2.6	22	3.6
Innkeeper, baker, brewer	34	9.9	56	9.1
Construction crafts	27	7.9	39	6.3
Mass crafts[a]	20	5.8⎱	114	18.5
Other crafts	85	24.9⎰		
Waterman, laborer	5	1.5	18	2.9
Other	1	0.3	5	0.8
Unknown	82	24.0	176	28.5
Total	342	100.0	617	100.0

Sources: For Kaiserslautern, LAS J1 Nr. 244 ff. 42–45, 291–96; for Mainz, recalculated from figures in Herbert Pauly, ''Zur sozialen Zusammensetzung politischer Institutionen und Vereiine der Stadt Mainz im Revolutionsjahr 1848,'' *AfhGA* 34 (1976): 45–81.

[a] Shoemaker, tailor, cabinetmaker (cabinetmaker counted in Mainz with construction crafts).

a distinct business interest in encouraging political meetings. The very lowest classes—laborers, watermen, construction workers, members of the poorest, mass crafts—on the other hand, were underorganized by the democrats in comparison to their numbers in society.[30]

The large number of unknown occupation means a complete analysis requires some guesswork, but the most plausible explanation is that these members were journeymen artisans without their own household, either those traveling through, or single and underage locals, still living with relatives. If this was the case, then a large majority of the organized democrats in Mainz and Kaiserslautern were craftsmen: masters and journeymen, married with their own household and single without it, outsiders and natives. Professional designations rarely distinguish between master and journeyman, so it is impossible to know how many of the artisans belonged to either of the two groups.[31]

---

[30] Contemporary observers noticed the lack of the lowest classes in the organized democratic movement of these two cities. LAS J1 Nr. 245 ff. 287–89; Bamberger, ''Erlebnisse,'' pp. 73–74.

[31] Next to the names of several of those with unknown occupation in the Kaiserslautern membership lists, one finds the remark ''moved away,'' reinforcing the notion that they were journeymen artisans. Pauly, unable to find any of the names of the unknown in the Mainz address book, rejected, for no good reason, the most plausible explanation, that they were journeymen, not heads of households. Some historians have assumed that any artisan lacking the professional

It would be worthwhile seeing whether there were any social differences between radical and moderate democrats. Separate membership lists for the Kaiserslautern People's Club and the Sunday Circle as well as for the Köhler's People's Association in Neustadt have survived, and they provide some idea of the differing social groups from which moderates and militants drew their support (see Table 5.3). The bourgeoisie was clearly disproportionately over-represented among the membership of the moderate groups, while journeymen artisans—following the reasoning above, identifying names on the member-ship list without occupational designation as journeymen—were the largest group of supporters of the extreme left. Although the membership lists of the Neustadt radicals have not been preserved, we have a clue to the social com-position of their supporters from the issue that caused the moderates and rad-icals to split apart. The moderates insisted that only men who were permanent residents of Neustadt a.d.W. be admitted as voting members of the local Peo-ple's Association, a demand the radicals rejected, and one that stood in the

TABLE 5.3
Moderate and Radical Democrats

Social Group	Kaisers-lautern Moderates		Kaisers-lautern Radicals		Neustadt a.d.W. Moderates	
	N	%	N	%	N	%
Merchant, manufacturer,						
rentier, estate owner	32	15.5	10	7.4	60	31.3
Professional	12	5.8	2	1.5	6	3.3
Clerk	13	6.3	6	4.4	4	2.1
Official	6	2.9	—	—	3	1.6
Teacher	3	1.4	—	—	1	0.5
Innkeeper, baker,						
brewer, miller	21	10.1	13	9.6	26	13.5
Mass crafts	13	6.3	7	5.2	19	9.9
Construction crafts	17	8.2	10	7.4	14	7.3
Other crafts	58	28.0	27	20.0	45	23.4
Laborer	4	1.9	1	0.7	9	4.7
Farmer	3	1.4	1	0.7	2	1.0
Other, unknown	25	12.1	58	43.0	3	1.6
Total	207	99.9	135	99.9	192	100.2

Source: LAS J1 Nr. 244 ff. 42–45, 296–96; LAS J1 Nr. 228 (alt) f. 640.

designation "master" was a journeyman, a presupposition decisively refuted by Lenger, *Zwischen Kleinbürgertum und Proletariat*, pp. 157–58, 293 n.54.

way of any successful conclusion of the unity negotiations. From this controversy one might surmise that many of the radicals' followers were not municipal citizens: that they were underage male relatives of Neustadt burghers, nonresident journeymen, or laborers and small masters, unable to meet the stiff registration fee required for municipal citizenship.[32]

All this suggests that where conflicts between moderates and radicals on the left came to the surface, extremists were likely to be poorer and younger than moderates. Before turning such differences into either class or generational struggles, it should be noted that both wings of the democratic movement had a broad social base in common. Resident artisans, whether masters or settled (probably married) journeymen, brewers, and innkeepers accounted for between 40 and 50 percent of the organized supporters of radicals and moderates alike, forming a core of small producers at the heart of the democratic movement.[33]

Having arrived at some tentative conclusions, I now need to introduce three caveats. To start with the top of the social scale, although the bourgeoisie may have been overrepresented among members of the democratic clubs, it was far more overrepresented among the democrats' political opponents. Of the five hundred members of Mainz's constitutional monarchist citizens' association, for instance, 62.8 percent were businessmen, rentiers, and professionals.[34]

Secondly, it is unclear whether the figures on the social composition of upper Rhine democratic clubs can be applied to those on the lower Rhine. No membership lists have been preserved to provide definitive evidence, and remarks of the officials, that the democrats' supporters were from the "mob" or the "lower classes," are not very helpful, but there are some indications suggesting that things were different further north. If nothing else, the lower Rhine social structure included a far greater proportion of manufacturing outworkers, day laborers, and factory workers than in the southern Rhineland. Weavers do not seem to have been organized democrats very often, since, of all the centers of textile outworking, democratic clubs only existed in the two silk-weaving cities, Mülheim a. Rhein and Krefeld. The smiths and grinders of the Bergisches Land, admittedly more affluent than the outworking weavers, were very much involved in democratic politics. Solingen County had at

---

[32] On the dispute in Neustadt, see LAS J1 Nr. 228 (alt) ff. 690–99. A similar dispute seems to have separated radicals and moderates in Zweibrücken: *NSZ*, 15 Mar. 1849 (Beilage). Of the eighteen Neustadt journeymen artisans interrogated in 1850 about their role in the revolutionary Palatine gymnasts' congress of April 1849 (remember that the Neustadt gymnasts were supporters of the city's extreme left), twelve were sons, nephews, or younger brothers of master craftsmen of the city. LAS J1 Nr. 105 ff. 152–59. On a similar extreme leftist role for youthful gymnasts in internecine controversies of the Trier democrats, see *Vbl*, 16, 19 Sept. 1848.

[33] Similar conclusions in Lenger, *Zwischen Kleinbürgertum und Proletariat*, pp. 162–66.

[34] Pauly, "Vereine der Stadt Mainz," p. 74.

least ten democratic clubs, all observers agreeing that the metalworkers made up the bulk of the membership in at least seven of them.[35]

In some factory towns, such as Aachen or Mülheim a.d. Ruhr, democratic clubs were very small and overshadowed by more conservative organizations. Larger democratic groups did exist in the industrialized textile centers of Mönchengladbach, Lennep, Kettwig, Werden, and Eupen, and in three of Aachen's metallurgical suburbs. These cities had large contingents of outworkers as well as factory proletarians, and, in any event, there is no solid evidence about which inhabitants were card-carrying democrats. Some descriptions of the membership of the democratic clubs of the largest lower Rhine cities, Cologne, Düsseldorf, and Barmen-Elberfeld, suggest a dominance of freethinking bourgeois and small proprietors, as in Mainz, but others mention the presence of outworkers, impoverished master artisans of the mass crafts, journeymen, and day laborers. Without any lists, it is simply impossible to say whether the latter were a more important element in these democratic clubs than they were on the upper Rhine.

The third, and most important, point to remember is that three-fourths of the clubs were located in villages, not in cities or towns. Although perhaps fifteen of these villages were centers of rural outworking or suburbs of large cities, most inhabitants of the vast majority of them earned their living in agriculture. Once again, membership lists to provide definitive proof are lacking, but it seems likely that there were more peasants among members of Rhenish democratic clubs than representatives of any other social group. Peasants were, of course, the largest social group in mid-nineteenth-century Rhineland. Judging by the number of rural political clubs, I would say that the peasantry was substantially underrepresented in the ranks of the organized democrats of the Prussian Rhine Province, but in Rhine-Hessen and the Palatinate, peasants were present in the democratic movement in proportion to their numbers in society. The recruitment of the peasantry by the democrats and the size of the organized democratic movement—the two being closely related, since most people were peasants—has been underestimated by most historians, fixed on the idea of the mid-century revolution as an urban phenomenon.[36]

Statistical information on the democratic leadership is more frequently available than material on the rank-and-file members, and with greater variation as well, so I can present three samples of leadership personnel at different levels of the movement. The topmost level, also the narrowest group, is the executive committee of a democratic club; Table 5.4 gives a breakdown of the social composition of executive committee membership in Mainz, the Saar-

---

[35] This discussion of the membership of lower Rhine democratic clubs is based on the sources cited in note 2.

[36] An admirable exception to the usual point of view in Wettengel, *1848/49 im Rhein-Main Raum*, pp. 286–305.

TABLE 5.4
Democratic Leaders—Executive Committee Members

Occupation	Mainz		Ottweiler		Palatinate (29 Towns)	
	N	%	N	%	N	%
Merchant, manufacturer, rentier ⎫	6	20	2	29	107	29.7
Clerk, foreman ⎭			—	—	19	5.3
Professional	9	30	1	14	40	11.1
State official (including teachers)	3	10	—	—	28	7.8
Innkeeper, baker, brewer, miller	—	—	3	43	60	16.7
Construction crafts	—	—	—	—	7	1.9
Mass crafts[a] ⎫	6	20	—	—	5	1.4
Other crafts ⎭			—	—	54	15.0
Laborer, factory worker	—	—	—	—	7	1.9
Farmer	—	—	1	14	17	4.7
Other, unknown	6	20	—	—	16	4.4
Total	30	100	7	100	360	99.9

Sources: Pauly, ''Vereine der Stadt Mainz,'' p. 74; LAK 442 Nr. 6497 pp. 311–18 (Ottweiler); LAS J1 Nr. 113/2. (These last are members of the cantonal committees created by the revolutionary Palatine government in May 1849, composed of members of the executive committees of the People's Associations in the cantonal towns and the officers of the towns' civic guards, usually dominated by leftists.)

[a] Tailor, shoemaker, cabinetmaker.

land town Ottweiler, and twenty-nine cantonal towns in the Palatinate. Democratic nominees for the position of elector in the indirect elections represented a broader sample of leadership figures; the examples in Table 5.5 are taken from three democratic strongholds, Mainz, Düsseldorf, and Trier. The last and broadest level is that of militant or activist, individuals who spoke up at meetings of democratic clubs, or who were noted as troublemakers by the police. Table 5.6 gives statistics on such activists in two major lower Rhine cities, Cologne and Elberfeld, as well as from six villages in Landau and Germersheim Counties in the southeastern Palatinate. In comparison to the membership figures, the bourgeoisie, tavernkeepers, and, in the countryside, schoolteachers were much more strongly represented among the leadership; artisans, peasants, and the lower classes, much less represented.

All these results suggest that participation in the democratic movement should be considered as several, overlapping forms of activity, each dominated by different social groups. The top leadership, which made policy, sitting on the executive committees and giving the chief orations in the clubs of large cities, was heavily bourgeois, including university-trained professionals and, especially in the southern Rhineland, merchants, estate owners, and ren-

TABLE 5.5
Democratic Leaders—Electors

Occupation	Düsseldorf		Trier		Mainz	
	N	%	N	%	N	%
Merchant, manufacturer,						
rentier, retailer	15	18.3	14	22.6	39	26.7
Clerk, foreman	—	—	2	3.2	3	2.1
Professional, official	22	26.8	15	24.2	24	16.4
Innkeeper, baker,						
brewer, miller	20	24.4	15	24.2	20	13.7
Artisan	17	20.7	16	25.8	48	32.9
Farmer	8	9.8	—	—	1	0.7
Laborer	—	—	—	—	2	1.4
Other, unknown	—	—	—	—	9	6.2
Total	82	100.0	62	100.0	146	100.1

Sources: Lenger, Zwischen Kleinbürgertum und Proletariat, p. 165 (Düsseldorf); Kölnisches Stadtmuseum, Graphische Sammlung RM 1939/112/42 (Mainz); Vbl, 24 Jan. 1849 (Trier).

tiers as well. More petit bourgeois figures, such as innkeepers, and better-off master craftsmen were also represented at this level. Below them was a group that might be called, misappropriating a phrase from the Leninist vocabulary, the movement's transmission belt: people who did not themselves set policy but connected the leading figures with the ordinary members. The single most important occupation for this group was the tavernkeepers, astonishingly over-represented in democratic slates of electors, when compared with their po-sition in the labor force. A similar role was played in the countryside by schoolteachers, along with the innkeepers, the leading propagandists for rural democracy.

Proceeding to the level of ordinary, dues-paying members, one finds, in the cities, artisans, apparently both masters and journeymen, seemingly from the more affluent crafts. Where, as was the case on the upper Rhine, rural clubs existed in large numbers, peasants were probably also a significant group of ordinary members. The extent to which day laborers, factory workers, manu-facturing outworkers, and members of the impoverished mass crafts were club members is not entirely clear, although it was perhaps more common on the lower than on the upper Rhine. When members of such groups did participate in the democratic movement, and, as will be seen in later chapters, they did, they were more likely to do so in individual events, mass demonstrations or uprisings, than in any permanent, organized form.[37]

[37] This typology owes a good deal to the suggestions in Lenger, Zwischen Kleinbürgertum und Proletariat, pp. 168–70.

TABLE 5.6
Democratic Leaders—Activists

Occupation	Cologne		Elberfeld		Palatinate (6 Villages)	
	N	%	N	%	N	%
Merchant, manufacturer, rentier	11	22	23	28.3	8	7.4
Clerk, foreman	2	4	1	1.2	4	3.7
Professional	20	40 ⎫			6	5.6
State official	—	— ⎬	21	25.9	11	10.3ᵃ
Teacher	—	— ⎭			13	12.1
Innkeeper, brewer, baker, miller	1	2	2	2.4	19	17.8
Crafts	5	10	10	12.3	16	15.0
Laborer, factory worker	2	4	4	4.9	4	3.7
Soldier	9	18	—	—	5	4.7
Farmer	—	—	—	—	21	19.6
Unknown	—	—	20	24.7	—	—
Total	50	100	81	99.7	107	99.9

Sources: Sepyel, ''Die Demokratische Gesellschaft in Köln,'' p. 187 (Cologne); Illner, *Bürgerliche Organisierung*, p. 200 (Elberfeld); LAS J1 Nr. 263 ff. 49–51, and LAS J1 Nr. 202 I (alt) ff. 276, 328–29 (Palatinate).

ᵃ This total is somewhat inflated, since it includes members of the village councils, usually village notables, and not state servants.

The confessional composition of the democratic clubs is even more elusive than their social composition, since lists or police reports occasionally give individuals' occupations, but never their religion. Clubs' locations might provide a clue to this. Of the Palatine People's Associations, 41 percent were located in towns or villages whose population was over 75 percent Protestant; 25 percent were in communities that were between 51 and 75 percent Protestant, and only 27 percent were in predominantly Catholic communities. However, 45 percent of all towns and villages in the Palatinate were over 75 percent Protestant; 23 percent were 51–75 percent Protestant, and 31 percent had Catholic majorities. The confessional distribution of the People's Associations thus closely conformed to that of the Palatine population as a whole, suggesting that Palatine democrats were able to overcome confessional barriers and organize adherents of both Christian confessions.[38]

However, in a predominantly Catholic village, the leftists could have been members of the Protestant minority—and sources suggest this was sometimes the case. Furthermore, membership in the only organized opposition to the

[38] Location of clubs according to sources cited in note 3; confessional composition of all communities according to figures (from 1857) in *Verzeichniß . . . nebst . . . einer Gemeindestatistik der Pfalz*, pt. 2, pp. 2–51.

People's Associations in the Palatinate, the Pius Associations, was by definition restricted to Roman Catholics. Just as the bourgeoisie was overrepresented in the membership of democratic clubs in comparison to its proportion of the total population but underrepresented in comparison to its membership in constitutional monarchist associations, it might be reasonable to say that Palatine Roman Catholics were organized by democrats roughly in proportion to their share of the population but underrepresented in comparison to their position among the democrats' opponents.[39]

A similar situation with all the confessional signs reversed existed in the Prussian Rhine Province, whose population was about three-quarters Roman Catholic. Table 5.7 compares the location of the province's democratic clubs with that of the forty-six Rhenish constitutional monarchist associations represented at the Rhenish-Westphalian congress in January 1848. The confessional distribution of places with democratic clubs corresponded roughly to that of all communities in the province, while the constitutional monarchist associations were clearly overrepresented in predominantly Protestant areas. It is also likely that in some of the mostly Roman Catholic communities, the constitutional monarchists were members of the Protestant minority. In both the Palatinate and the Prussian Rhine Province, members of the same confession as that of the royal house were noticeably more likely to support the politically more conservative position and somewhat less likely to support the democratic one than members of the other Christian confession.[40]

TABLE 5.7
Location of Democratic and Constitutional Monarchist Associations in the Prussian Rhine Province

Confessional Composition of the Community	Democratic Clubs		Constitutional Monarchist Associations	
	N	%	N	%
Over 75% Protestant	16	18	16	35
51–75% Protestant	3	3	6	13
Plurality Protestant			2	4
51–75% Roman Catholic	5	6	6	13
Over 75% Roman Catholic	67	74	16	35
Total	91	101	46	100

Sources: For location of democratic clubs, see note 2, this chapter; constitutional monarchist associations according to KnZ, 6 Jan. 1849; confessional statistics according to Tabellen und amtliche Nachrichten 1.

[39] LAS J1 Nr. 202 I (alt) ff. 134–36; Renner, "Die pfälzische Bewegung," pp. 88–89, 113.
[40] For heavy Protestant overrepresentation in the constitutional monarchist association of pre-

Jews, of course, had no religious affiliation with any monarch, and one must wonder about their political allegiances. To find out, one cannot use the same procedure as with the Christian confessions, since Jews were nowhere a majority and were a plurality in only one or two villages. Jews however, usually did have distinctive names, and on that basis it is possible to estimate their political participation. Looking for typically Jewish names would miss those Jews, such as the Düsseldorf radical and future socialist leader Ferdinand Lassalle, whose names were indistinguishable from those of Christians. On the other hand, Rhenish Protestants, in view of their Calvinist heritage, frequently had Old Testament given names, so it is possible that the two sources of error—Jews with Christian-sounding names, Protestants with Jewish-sounding names—might cancel each other out.

I have tried to use as varied a group of lists as possible, considering the proportion of Jewish signatories on a Prussian loyalist, constitutional monarchist petition from Düsseldorf in December 1848, the proportion of Jews in the membership of the Mainz Democratic Club, and also the proportion of Jews in its adversary, the constitutional monarchist Citizens' Association. The sources for the Palatinate are richest, and I have considered the proportion of Jews among the members of the moderate and radical factions in the Kaiserslautern People's Association, among the leadership of the People's Associations of the cantonal towns, and among the democratic activists in two southeastern Palatine villages, Herxheim and Rülzheim, both of which had a substantial Jewish population.[41]

The results (see Table 5.8) show that Jews were involved in expressions of all political views in roughly the same proportions as they were found in the population. The one major exception was in Mainz, where Jews were heavily overrepresented in the left wing of the city's politics, but just as overrepresented on its right wing. Nothing in the results supports the common view that Jews had a special affinity for the left; if anything, the figures from Rülzheim and Herxheim suggest that Jews living in the countryside (as most did) had a visible disinclination for it. The idea that Jews were leftists is probably a result of prejudices from the Nazi era (nowadays applied with all the moral signs reversed), confusion of German Jews with those from the czarist empire, and, perhaps most of all, taking a few spectacular examples for the typical case. Jewish intellectuals, such as the Cologne radicals Karl Marx and Andreas Gottschalk (albeit both baptized) or the Mainz democratic journalists Ludwig Bamberger and Ludwig Kalisch, stood out both to contemporaries and to later historians, but there is no reason to think they were representative of the mer-

---

dominantly Catholic Krefeld, see Wolfgang Schwentker, *Konservative Vereine und Revolution in Preussen 1848/49* (Düsseldorf: Droste, 1988), p. 171.

[41] The reader may note that the last entry in this table comes from the same source used in Tables 5.4–5.6 to analyze the democratic leadership in six southeastern Palatine villages. However, the other four villages involved—Herxheimerweiher, Bellheim, Offenbach, and Rheinzabern—had no Jewish inhabitants.

TABLE 5.8
Political Affiliations of Rhenish Jews

Group under Consideration	Size of Group (N)	Locality	Percent Jews in Group	Percent Jews in Locality
Signatories to loyalist petition	1,123	Düsseldorf	1.7	1.8 (in 1849)
Members of Democratic Club	617	Mainz	12.0	6.5 (in 1861)
Members of Citizens' Association	505	Mainz	14.5	6.5 (in 1861)
Members of People's Association (moderates)	207	Kaiserslautern	3.4	2.0 (in 1852)
Members of People's Association (radicals)	135	Kaiserslautern	1.5	2.0 (in 1852)
Members of People's Association executive committee	360	Palatinate (29 cantonal towns)	4.2	4.2 (in 1857)
Democratic activists	61	Rülzheim, Herzheim	3.3	9.2 (in 1857)

Sources: Confessional statistics: *Tabellen und amtliche Nachrichten*, vol. 1; *Beiträge zur Statistik des Grossherzogtums Hessen* 3 (1864): 24–25, 244–51. *Verzeichniβ . . . nebst . . . einer Gemeindestatistik der Pfalz*, pt. 2. pp. 2–51. Lists: ZSTAM Rep. 77 Tit. 505 Nr. 3 adhib. 2 (Düsseldorf); "Namens-Verzeichniβ . . . des Demokratischen Vereins," and "Namens-Verzeichniβ der Mitglieder des Mainzer Bürgervereins (Aufgestellt am 27. Juli 1848)" (like the preceding, pamphlet in the Stadtbibliothek Mainz); LAS J1 Nr. 244 ff. 42–45 (Kaiserslautern moderates); LAS J1 Nr. 244 ff. 291–96 (Kaiserslautern radicals); LAS J1 Nr. 113/2 (Palatine cantonal towns); LAS J1 Nr. 263 ff. 49–50; LAS J1 Nr. 202 I (alt) ff. 276, 328–29 (Herxheim and Rülzheim).

chants, currency dealers, cattle traders, peddlers, and petty moneylenders who made up the vast majority of Rhenish Jewry.[42]

Available information does not suffice to say whether social class was more important than confession in determining membership in democratic clubs or vice versa; all one can say is that both played a significant role. The information does suggest that club membership was not the only form of participation in the democratic movement. Rather, it was one aspect of a broader spectrum of left-wing activities, which need to be considered if the movement is to be fully understood. A study of organization leads to one of agitation.

[42] Jakob Toury, one of the few historians to investigate the question systematically, has suggested that most Jews in mid-nineteenth-century Germany were politically conservative (*Die politischen Orientierungen*, p. 98), which may be going too far in the other direction, but is certainly closer to the truth than the idea that they were mostly radicals.

AGITATION

Democratic activists addressed widely varied audiences—rural and urban, bourgeois and plebian, large crowds and single individuals. They addressed these groups in very different settings: at club meetings, in taverns, at markets and fairs, from the platform at mass meetings with thousands of spectators, or in the streets during both planned and spontaneous demonstrations. Unlike their *Vormärz* precursors, whose agitation, if permitted at all, was restricted to individual events or to a limited audience, the 1848 democrats were able to engage in a sustained mass agitation, employing for it a wide variety of techniques.

Club Life

Political clubs are often perceived as miniparliaments, with regular sessions devoted to practical organizational issues, to debate among members over theoretical and political questions, or to the taking of decisions on forms of political action. This familiar picture fits, in part, Rhenish democratic clubs at mid-century, especially those located in larger cities. At the theoretical end of the spectrum, there was the August 1848 debate in the Elberfeld Political Club about the best way to solve the "social question." On a more practical note, members of both democratic associations in Düsseldorf discussed at length, and over several meetings, whether they should take part in the celebration of national unity to be held on August 6, 1848. Theoretical questions played a role in the discussion, since the festivities were to honor the imperial regent elected by the Frankfurt National Assembly, Archduke Johann of Austria, and many democrats, while fervent supporters of national unity, had their doubts about princes as symbols of it. On a still more prosaic note, the July 1, 1848, meeting of the Trier Democratic Club began with an announcement that the club's treasury had been exhausted buying benches for the members to sit on, so those who were behind in their dues were requested to pay up. The meeting continued with a discussion of the planned mass rally in the nearby village of Schweich.[43]

This view of the clubs is, at best, incomplete. While there may have been many debates, it seems that relatively few members participated in them. Spontaneous comments from the floor were rare, democratic leaders in both Mainz and Trier regretting that the same few people were always speaking up and calling on others to become involved. It is not entirely clear if such mass participation was really always desired; on one occasion, Trier democratic

---

[43] Illner, *Bürgerliche Organisierung*, p. 160; HSTAD RD Nr. 200 pp. 177–89; *Volksblatt*, 7 July 1848. In general, on club organization, statutes, and dues, see Paschen, *Demokratische Vereine*, pp. 40–44, whose findings are also valid for the Rhineland.

leaders informed a member who wanted to give a speech on reaction that he could only do so after the topics on the agenda—and presumably the members as well—had been exhausted. Additionally, while some of the debates reflected strong differences of opinion within the associations, even if they were expressed only by a few speakers, others seem to have been staged by the leadership. An example of such a staged debate might be the one in the Mainz Democratic Club in November 1848 about whether the creation of national unity, the proclamation of the republic, or the solution of the social question should have political priority. All the speakers agreed, if with slightly different nuances, that the three causes should be valued equally.[44]

Such practices suggest that the main purpose of club meetings was not the determination of the opinion of a majority of the membership and the formation of policy based on it, but the education and enlightenment—a hostile expression would be the propagandizing—of members by their leaders. This goal was even more pronounced at the meetings of rural clubs, since only a few residents of a village, typically, the innkeeper, schoolteacher, and rationalist Protestant pastor, might be both sympathetic to the democrats and comfortable with abstract political ideas and, more generally, the culture of the written word. The farmer Carl Müller of Schoeneberg, in the northwestern Palatinate, described the meetings of the People's Association in his village as follows: "In them [the meetings] the newspapers written for the people were read out loud and baker Jacob as well as Jacob Früher explained to us the meanings of the foreign words which occurred in the articles."[45]

Sessions of more urban democratic clubs, such as those of Düsseldorf or Saarbrücken, also included public newspaper reading. A related practice, encountered in the clubs of larger cities, was the weekly political survey, in which one member would talk of significant events that had occurred across the continent. These talks, the single most common kind of speech given at meetings of the Cologne Democratic Society, may not have involved a direct reading of newspaper articles, but were almost certainly a summary of them.[46]

Club meetings are best understood as a form of political agitation, carried out by a largely bourgeois leadership, familiar with written culture and effec-

[44] *MZ*, 7 Sept., 29 Oct., 4 Nov. 1848; *Vbl*, 16, 22 July 1848; *Der Demokrat*, 12 Nov. 1848. Actual meeting minutes of democratic clubs have, as far as I know, not been preserved. This discussion is based on four main sources: police reports on Düsseldorf club meetings in HSTAD RD Nr. 200; accounts of meetings of the Mainz democratic club in *MZ* and *Der Demokrat*; and reports on the meetings of the Trier Democratic Club in *Vbl*.

[45] LAS J1 Nr. 242 ff. 133–34; similarly, ibid. ff. 186–88; LAS J1 Nr. 195 ff. 497–98; LAS J1 Nr. 235 ff. 151–52; LAS J1 Nr. 215 (alt) ff. 51–60, 505–506; LAS J1 Nr. 243 (alt) ff. 50–55; LAS J1 Nr. 202 I (alt) f. 100; LAK 403 Nr. 6583 ff. 139–42.

[46] HSTAD RD Nr. 200 pp. 175–76, 181–83; LAK 403 Nr. 9632 pp. 18–21; LAK 442 Nr. 6497 p. 169; Seypel, "Die Demokratische Gesellschaft in Köln," p. 169; *Vbl*, 7, 16, 19, 26 July, and esp. 9 Aug. 1848. The statutes of the democratic club in Saarbrücken forbade public reading of newspapers, thus proving it was done.

tive forms of public speaking, among a predominantly plebian, less formally educated rank and file. A strong element of social deference was thus present within the democratic movement. Ordinary members came to meetings primarily to be informed about public affairs by bourgeois speakers and not necessarily to express their own opinions. Loud, repeated demands for the weekly survey at a meeting of the Trier democrats caused the chair to table another agenda item before it had been fully discussed. A not entirely sober day laborer burst onto the tribune at a meeting of the democratic club in the lower Rhine border town of Emmerich and demanded, to the great amusement of the spectators, that the leaders let a worker speak. When it became clear that he was not just drunk, but also serious about speaking, he was shouted off the stage. The following evening, a group of similarly intoxicated harbor workers advanced on him, shouting, "Long live liberty and the republic," forcing him to flee.[47]

An Unbridled Press

The introduction of freedom of the press in March 1848 revealed a long-pent-up demand for news, with newspapers founded as quickly as publishers could manage. Of the seventy dailies and weeklies appearing in 1848 in the three districts of Aachen, Düsseldorf, and Koblenz, thirty-four, or almost half, had started publishing that very year, following the abolition of censorship. Newspapers that had previously suffered under the *Vormärz* censor now could appear unfettered. The Rhineland's largest daily, the *Kölnische Zeitung*, dropped the Prussian eagle from its masthead, as of April 1, 1848, one of the more civilized indignities this bird had to suffer. Such changes were also noticeable in even the most obscure of local presses, such as the *Weekly Sheet for Erkelenz County and Vicinity*, which began printing political news once it was free to do so.[48]

Leftist newspapers predated the revolution in the southern Rhineland, the abolition of censorship allowing them to express their views without need for circumlocution. The major Palatine newspaper, the *Neue Speyerer Zeitung*, was owned and edited by Georg Friedrich Kolb, a veteran activist from the days of the Hambach Festival. In 1848, Kolb was elected mayor of Speyer, and deputy for the Bergzabern constituency in the Frankfurt National Assembly, where he sat on the left. To cap off his year, he was chosen by the voters

---

[47] *Vbl*, 9 Aug. 1848; HSTAD RD Nr. 8806 ff. 178–82.

[48] Figures compiled from LAK 403 Nr. 7153 pp. 141–51, 155–73, 177–85; this volume gives a good picture of the press of the Prussian Rhine Province in the revolutionary period. In general, on the German press during the mid-century revolution, the introductory essay to Martin Henkel and Rolf Taubert, *Die deutsche Presse 1848–1850. Eine Bibliographie* (Munich: Saur, 1978), pp. 9–44, is quirky and stimulating, if not always convincing. Cf. also Siemann, *Die deutsche Revolution von 1848/49*, pp. 114–24.

as one of the Palatine deputies to the Bavarian parliament. Following his personal views, Kolb's editorial policy was on the more moderate side of the democratic movement, steering clear of republicanism, and denouncing communists. Militant Speyer radicals became annoyed and started their own, much smaller newspaper, as competition to his, but even Kolb's mild views so angered the Munich authorities that they took steps to suppress his newspaper after the end of the revolution.[49]

The chief newspaper in the provincial capital of Rhine-Hessen, the *Mainzer Zeitung*, was also under left-wing influence before the revolution. Its publisher, Theodor von Zabern, was one of the members of the democratic slate of electors for the elections to Frankfurt National Assembly in May 1848. With the outbreak of the revolution, and an end to the Hessian censorship, probably the strictest in the entire Rhineland, he increased the size of the paper, added extensive political coverage, and adopted an openly republican and increasingly radical editorial policy. All the editors of the paper during the revolution, Ludwig Bamberger, Karl Bölsche, and J. Friedrich Schütz, were leading democratic activists.[50]

The *Trier'sche Zeitung*, since the outbreak of the revolution edited by true socialist Karl Grün, gave the democrats a major, if somewhat erratic, voice in the Moselle and Saar valleys, but it was little read elsewhere in the Prussian Rhineland, so the left there was lacking a flagship newspaper of the sort which existed in Speyer and Mainz. Scarcely was freedom of the press granted, when voices in Cologne called for a revival of the radical paper of five years previously, the *Rheinische Zeitung*. At first, the true socialists Moses Hess and Andreas Gottschalk attempted togather a staff and financing, but they were quickly outmaneuvered by the previous newspaper's last editor, Karl Marx, returning to Cologne from Parisian exile. Gottschalk had to be content with the presidency of the Workers' Association, but he felt cheated by Marx's action and became his sworn enemy.[51]

Appearing at the beginning of June 1848, the *Neue Rheinische Zeitung* [New Rhineland News] was named by the Frankfurt Democratic Congress one

[49] On Kolb's life, see his memoirs, *Lebenserinnerungen eines liberalen Demokraten*. Material on offical anger toward his newspaper and its suppression in BHSTAM MInn Nr. 45279; and Ziegler, *Die Jahre der Reaktion*, pp. 193–215. Kolb's correspondence in BAF FN 9 Nachlaß Kolb contains just a few items from the revolutionary period.

[50] On the *Mainzer Zeitung*, see Bockenheimer, *Mainz*, pp. 99–101.

[51] On the *Trier'sche Zeitung* during the revolution, see Dowe, "Die erste sozialistische Tageszeitung," pp. 91–100. On the founding of the *Neue Rheinische Zeitung*, Dowe, *Aktion und Organisation*, pp. 142–44; Becker, *Marx und Engels in Köln*, pp. 23–24. All the many works on Marx and Engels contain accounts of their newspaper; two particularly useful discussions of its political views, written from very different ideological viewpoints, are Hammen, *The Red '48ers*, and Joachim Strey and Gerhard Winkler, *Marx und Engels 1848/49. Die Politik und Taktik der 'Neuen Rheinischen Zeitung' während der bürgerlich-demokratischen Revolution in Deutschland* (East Berlin: Dietz, 1972).

of the three newspapers in which the reports of the democratic central committee would appear, thus justifying the slogan printed on the masthead, "Organ of the Democratic Movement" [Organ der Demokratie]. The press run reached the eminently respectable figure of five thousand, although the newspaper was never out of financial difficulties. Its circulation was not limited to the provincial metropolis; the paper was found in the most obscure corners of the Prussian Rhine Province. It was read out loud at meetings of the democratic club in Münstermaifeld and posted for the public to read by radicals in the Eifel town of Adenau. Articles from it were reprinted in the *County Intelligencers* of Wittlich and Bitburg, and were discussed, a correspondent claimed, in the taverns of the metalworking town Velbert, a "democratic oasis in the black-white [that is, Prussian loyalist] ocean of the Bergisches Land."[52]

Marx's editorial policy placed his journal on the far left, although it was not any more radical than the *Mainzer Zeitung*. What was extreme about the *Neue Rheinische Zeitung* was its language, the zeal and vehemence with which it went after the democrats' enemies, the imagination and energy of its invective. The Cologne police commissioner, in requesting Marx's expulsion from Prussia, described him as someone who "allows himself each and every libel of our constitution, our king and our highest state officials in his ever more widely read newspaper." The polemical brilliance which gained the newspaper so many readers simultaneously limited its appeal, since Marx did not restrict his nastiness to universally recognized enemies of the democratic movement, but turned it on fellow leftists, whom he regarded as too moderate or politically incorrect. A Düsseldorf democrat noted of this habit, "Even men of decisively radical sentiment accuse the newspaper of perfidiousness."[53]

All these flagship newspapers, and most other democratic journals as well, were replete with foreign words and literary allusions, written in a style immediately accessible only to someone with at least a secondary school education. A few attempts were made to supplement them with more easily understandable, popular newspapers. One such was the *Volksblatt* [People's Sheet] in Trier, appearing for the first time on April 23, 1848. The mottos on its masthead were a concise political program: "May each labor, but may labor receive its due," and "Everything with the people, by the people and for the people." The editor's statement of principles explained that the revolution had allowed workers and artisans to participate in politics, and while their interests and demands were voiced at mass meetings, not all could attend and even those who did might like to think more intensively about the issues raised there—hence the newspaper, whose articles would be written in a nonlearned style, as befitted a journal designed for the people, not "the men of money

---

[52] LAK 403 Nr. 6583 ff. 139–42; LR Kr. Adenau to RKO, 18 Dec. 1848, LAK 441 Nr. 4120; LAK 442 Nr. 3379 pp. 45–47, 115–16; *NRhZ*, 17, 27 Jan. 1849.

[53] LAK 403 Nr. 7172 pp. 5–6; Lenger, *Zwischen Kleinbürgertum und Proletariat*, p. 164. For more on the *Neue Rheinische Zeitung*, see the section on Marx's politics in Chapter Seven.

and commands.'' The *Volksblatt* would offer short and easily understandable accounts of political events and report in detail on the conditions of workers (understood in the broader sense of the small-producer lower classes, including master craftsmen) of Trier, the Rhineland, and Europe. It did just that, and in spite of (or because of?) its editor's deep involvement in factional struggles in the Trier Democratic Club, the 360 copies it sold in the city of Trier at the beginning of 1849 made it the most widely read newspaper there, outpacing the 290 sold by the far more intellectually written *Trier'sche Zeitung*, although the latter had a large circulation outside the city of Trier, which the *Volksblatt* did not.[54]

A parallel project further north was the *Neue Kölnische Zeitung für Bürger Bauern und Soldaten* [New Cologne News for Townfolk, Countrypeople and Soldiers], which began publishing in September 1848. Officially it was edited by the communist ex-army officer Friedrich Anneke, but the real editor was his wife, Mathilde Franziska, who had earned her living as a free-lance journalist following her divorce from her first husband. Much like the *Volksblatt* in format, the *Neue Kölnische Zeitung* adopted a still simpler and rather more didactic tone. Unlike the popular and the intellectual left-wing newspapers in Trier, which were politically at odds with each other, the two in Cologne cooperated closely. Marx praised the popular agitation of the Annekes' paper, especially its attempts to gain support for the democrats among the soldiers of the Cologne garrison. When Marx was expelled from Prussia in May 1849 and the *Neue Rheinische Zeitung* prohibited, he designated the *Neue Kölnische Zeitung* its official successor.[55]

Two such popular newspapers existed in the Palatinate. The more significant of them, the *Messenger for Town and Country* [Der Bote für Stadt und Land], in Kaiserslautern, had been edited since 1838 by law graduate Nikolaus Schmitt, a decade later the city's deputy to the Frankfurt National Assembly. Lacking any substantial local competition and sold aggressively door to door, it had already built up a substantial following when the abolition of censorship allowed it to express openly its editor's republican ideas. The other newspaper, *The Trumpet of Speyer* [Die Trompete von Speyer], begun in March 1849, was much slighter. Its most interesting feature was a regular comic dialogue conducted in Palatine dialect between two Speyer proletarians, Jokel and Hannsel, or their wives, Kredel and Lene, in which they attacked the police, forest laws, the octroi, corruption in the municipal government, and the Catholic clergy.[56]

[54] LAK 442 Nr. 3379 pp. 111–13. A complete run of the *Volksblatt* is available in the municipal library of Trier.

[55] On the *Neue Kölnische Zeitung*, see LAK 403 Nr. 7153 pp. 211–23; and the brief comments in Henkel and Taubert, *Die deutsche Presse*, pp. 31–33. The January–June 1849 issues are available at the municipal and university library in Cologne. For the relationship of the newspaper to Marx's, see *NRhZ*, 18 Oct. 1848; Dowe, *Aktion und Organisation*, p. 230.

[56] A brief account of the Kaiserslautern newspaper is provided by Harold Jaeger, ''Politische

Whatever the varying literary merits, political orientation, or popular appeal of these newspapers, they were all written by members of the educated middle class. There was, as far as I know, only one revolutionary newspaper not just for the people, but by one of them as well, the *Persecutor of Evil* [Verfolger der Bosheit], owned, published, edited, and mostly written by the master baker Mathias Wessel of Cologne. The author was an activist in the Cologne Workers' Association, a self-proclaimed communist and red republican, but his version of radicalism, as the very title of his paper indicates, was strongly marked by a moralizing and personalizing perspective. He persecuted evil, as he put it, in the pages of his newspaper, filling them with exposés of corrupt lower officials, greedy landlords, oppressive capitalists, or priests who thought only of themselves and refused to provide charity for the poor. Although similar accounts were occasionally found in the *Neue Kölnische Zeitung* and the various organs of the Workers' Association, no other Cologne democrat showed such a persistent and detailed interest in the everday problems and oppressions of the lower classes in the city and surrounding countryside.[57]

Wessel was particularly concerned with rural agitation, hawking his paper from door to door and in taverns of nearby villages. (It was, in part, also a business venture to supplement the earnings of his apparently not too profitable small bakery.) With a number of rustic correspondents ready to report on the latest vexations of life among the countryfolk, Wessel was the only Cologne leftist who knew about and was concerned with the forest struggles of the peasantry. He defended incisively their right to gather wood, and commented bitterly on the Prussian government's policies of massive plantings of nondeciduous trees.[58]

There are other aspects of his ideas that are rather less admirable. He was a vehement anti-Semite, seeing Jews as self-interested, money-grubbing capitalists, hinting that the people would one day take a terrible revenge on them. It would be unfair to describe Wessel as a proto-Nazi, however, since he was a great admirer ("one of the apostles") of the Jewish leader of the Cologne Workers' Association, Andreas Gottschalk. He also published an article denouncing the charge that Jews ritually murdered Christian babies.[59]

Lyrik im revolutionären 'Bote für Stadt und Land' aus Kaiserslautern,'' *JhGStLK* 22/23 (1984/85): 161–88; on its influence and circulation, see LAS J1 Nr. 105 ff. 215–19; LAS J1 Nr. 244 ff. 180–81. A complete run of the Speyer sheet is in LAS J1 Nr. 252 II/1–2 (alt).

[57] On this little-known newspaper, see LAK 403 Nr. 7153 pp. 211–13; the municipal and university library in Cologne has an incomplete set (missing the second half of 1849). Wessel's personal involvement in the Workers' Association and its factional politics can be traced through *FBA*, 14 Sept., 12 Nov., 7 Dec. 1848; *FA*, 17 June 1849.

[58] Every single issue of *VdB* contained material on social and political struggles in the countryside; for Wessel's sale of it, see 3 Mar., 30 June 1849; his criticism of state forest policies, 31 Mar. 1849.

[59] *VdB*, 12, 19 May, 2, 9 June 1849, 5 Jan., 2 Feb. 1850. The charge of ritual murder was no

Wessel's main bête noire was the "damned priests" [die Pfaffen], whom he excoriated at every conceivable opportunity, usually for denying alms to the poor, or denouncing democrats from the pulpit—two activities the master baker saw as part of the same counterrevolutionary attitude. Most priests, he thought, had betrayed the true, communist ideas of Jesus Christ, except for an occasional pastor whom Wessel praised for visiting the sick and making generous charitable contributions. One is reminded by all this of polemics and popular attitudes from the age of the Reformation, but contemporary controversies also showed through, Wessel denouncing neoorthodox Catholic hostility toward Protestants and praising Count Spiegel, Cologne's early nineteenth century rationalist archbishop.[60]

In his newspaper one can see all the issues of the revolution, but through a distorting mirror as it were, lacking the precision, analysis, and intellectual rationalizations of the rest of the left-wing press and its educated editors. Perhaps it might be more appropriate to say that the rest of the press was the distorting mirror, that the voice of the Persecutor of Evil—Wessel referred to himself, personally, in this way, as well as to his newspaper—for all its considerable idiosyncracies, is the closest we can come to what the democratic sympathizers among the Rhenish lower classes themselves thought.

With regard to the press, much the same north-south contrast appears as in other aspects of revolutionary politics. Although the press runs of individual newspapers were usually under the modest figure of two thousand, the Palatine press was totally dominated by the democrats. The one conservative, Bavarian-loyalist newspaper, published, significantly, not in any of the larger cities, but in the little town of Annweiler, was able to appear only irregularly, because of both lack of readership and physical intimidation of its publisher. Insofar as the Bavarian government had any support at all in the press, it came from the Speyer diocesan newsletter, *The Christian Pilgrim* [Der Christliche Pilger].[61]

The more moderate elements in Rhine-Hessen were somewhat better represented in the press. Constitutional monarchist journals in both Worms and

---

medieval remnant, but had been raised in the anti-Semitic riots of 1834 in the rural areas to the north of Cologne and justified in a pamphlet written by the prominent neoorthodox Catholic pastor Joseph Anton Binterim of Bilk, near Düsseldorf (which he later repudiated). Sterling, "Emanzipation der Juden im Rheinland," p. 302.

[60] *VdB*, 17, 24 (includes an attack on Protestant clergy), 31 Mar., 14 Apr., 12 May, 2 June 1849; 19 Jan., 2 Feb. 1850, and passim. As one descends the social scale of Cologne's left-wing newspapers, anticlericalism increases—carefully avoided in the *Neue Rheinische Zeitung*, occasionally mentioned in the *Neue Kölnische Zeitung*, omnipresent in the *Verfolger der Bosheit*—suggesting that anticlerical attitudes were not just the product of intellectual Hegelianism, but had independent roots in popular experience.

[61] Ziegler, *Jahre der Reaktion*, pp. 232–48; Kurt Hoffmann, "Sturm und Drang in der politischen Presse Bayerns 1848–1850," *Zeitschrift für bayerische Landesgeschichte* 3 (1930): 205–65, esp. pp. 256–59.

Mainz competed with the democratic newspapers in those cities, although unsuccessfully, the moderates' flagship newspaper, the *Rheinische Zeitung*, in Mainz, ceasing publication a half-year after it began. The strongest opposition to the democrats came from neoorthodox Catholics, the editor of the religious weekly *Der Katholik*, Franz Sausen, starting a daily newspaper, the *Mainzer Journal*, in June 1848. Its readership spread beyond the provincial boundaries, its denunciations of the democrats read and appreciated by Palatine Catholics, lacking any daily of their own.[62]

The democrats of Rhenish Prussia did not do badly with the press, the authorities counting during the revolution thirty-five daily and weekly newspapers in the districts of Düsseldorf, Cologne, Aachen, and Trier whose editorial policies were sympathetic to the left. Nine of the twelve newspapers in the Trier District were as prodemocratic. The five thousand copies coming off the presses of the *Neue Rheinische Zeitung* six times a week were probably as much as any three other Rhenish democratic newspapers put together. However, these thirty-five democratic newspapers competed with fifty-nine apolitical, conservative, constitutional monarchist, and Catholic-clerical journals, including the constitutional monarchist *Kölnische Zeitung*, whose press run of seventeen thousand made it the largest newspaper in the Rhineland and one of the most significant in all of Germany.[63]

What such statistics tend to hide is the way all democratic newspapers, from Karl Marx's to Mathias Wessel's (and probably those of other political tendencies as well), had their greatest political effect: when read jointly in public—at a club meeting, in a tavern, on the street—and often orally, with explanations, emendations, and perhaps changes of emphasis. In a society where, in spite of widespread literacy, the written word was still unfamiliar in the everyday life of the rural population and the urban lower classes, democratic newspapers could be most successful as instruments of agitation when they were part of a collective enterprise. The slogan on the masthead of the *Neue Rheinische Zeitung*, "Organ of the Democratic Movement," was true in more ways than one.

Verbal Agitation: Retail and Wholesale

The democrats gathered in taverns, wineshops, and coffeehouses, not just for formal club meetings but also to talk among themselves and to propagandize

[62] Bockenheimer, *Mainz*, pp. 106–109; Uhrig, "Worms," pp. 44–47; Anton Diehl, *Zur Geschichte der Katholischen Bewgung im 19. Jahrhundert. Das "Mainzer Journal" im Jahre 1848* (Mainz: Kirchheim & Co., 1911); on the latter's readership in the Palatinate, see LAS J1 Nr. 179 ff. 512–42; LAS J1 Nr. 105 ff. 30–31; Anon. to MInn, 20 July 1849, BHSTAM MInn Nr. 45533.

[63] LAK 403 Nr. 7153 pp. 155–73, 177–85, 189–290, 211–13; LAK 442 Nr. 3379 passim; Ayçoberry, *Cologne*, p. 243. The reports from the Koblenz District do not give the political orientation of the newspapers there, but probably just one or two were democratic, so the left-wing press of the Prussian Rhineland was even more outnumbered than these figures indicate.

others. If one visited the Republic taverns [Wirtshaus zur Republik] in Grün-stadt or Neustadt a.d.W., one could count on meeting the respective towns' radical activists discussing politics. Rural democrats seeking political advice would turn up to join the discussions. The "Sunday circle" [Sonntags-kränzchen] of Kaiserslautern radical democrats met in a tavern, which be-came known, ironically, as "St. Paul's Church," after the meeting place of the Frankfurt National Assembly. Cologne democrats regularly gathered at the former Café Royal, renamed in March 1848 Stollwerck's German Coffee House.[64]

Where no club existed, tavern meetings could serve as a partial substitute. In Gerresheim, an up-country village on the east bank of the Rhine, the former schoolteacher, dismissed for his "improper conduct" [wegen unordentlichen Lebens], made the rounds of the taverns, accompanied by the son of the radi-cal physician Joseph Neunzig, who attended meetings of the left-wing clubs in nearby Düsseldorf. Together, they read out loud, "in the spirit of democ-racy and the so-called red republic," slanderous poems directed at the king of Prussia and sold brochures and pamphlets designed "to call forth insurrection-ary sentiments among the inhabitants of the countryside, people endowed with little intelligence." In a similar way, no democratic club was ever formed in Bergheim County, west of Cologne, but "the . . . [local] republicans are mostly people who enjoy hanging out in ordinary taverns, and, even though in other respects occupying the higher ranks of society, they are not afraid to drink hard spirits with day laborers and attempt to win their favor."[65]

Although certainly an effective and enjoyable form of political agitation, such tavern meetings could only reach a few people at a time; democrats needed other means to address a larger audience. They turned to forms devel-oped in the *Vormärz*, expanding them and opening them up to fit the new mass politics. The first political campaign of the Cologne Democratic Society fol-lowing the May 1848 elections was a petition drive, conducted neither in se-cret nor just among a small group of notables, as was usually done before 1848. Instead, the democrats placed tables on street corners and incited pas-sersby to sign, collecting 8,300 signatures in one day. Political banquets, with as many as two thousand participants, were held in February and March 1849 to mark the anniversaries of the revolution.[66]

The most important *Vormärz* precedent, however, was the Hambach Festi-val, the mass political rally, begun with a march and culminating in open-air

[64] LAS J1 Nr. 235 ff. 17–21; LAS J1 Nr. 229 I (alt) ff. 199–201; LAS J1 Nr. 245 ff. 263–67; Seypel, "Die Demokratische Gesellschaft in Köln," pp. 129–31; similarly, in Wesel, HSTAD RD Nr. 8806 ff. 263–66.

[65] HSTAD RD Pr. Nr. 795 ff. 181–82; LAK 403 Nr. 9671 pp. 41–42; similarly, LAK 403 Nr. 7045 pp. 115–22; LAK 403 Nr. 17332 ff. 325–36; HSTAD RD Pr. Nr. 812 f. 2; LAS J1 Nr. 215 (alt) ff. 505–06.

[66] On the Cologne petition drive, *RhBA* 2/2, Nrs. 84–85; Seypel, "Die Demokratische Gesell-schaft in Köln," pp. 250–51. The anniversary banquets will be discussed in Chapter Seven.

speeches before thousands of spectators from both town and country. Appropriately enough, the first of these was held at another ruined castle near Neustadt a.d.W. on May 28, 1848, the sixteenth anniversary of the original event. This was followed by mass rallies on the weekend of Pentecost Sunday (June 10–12, 1848) in towns and villages along the Haardt mountains, from Neustadt a.d.W. south to Edenkoben and Gleisweiler. Sponsored by a Neustadt festival committee, whose members were active in the People's Association, the meetings featured deputies from the left wing of the Frankfurt National Assembly. Their speeches, like many of those given at the Hambach Festival anniversary meeting, called in scarcely veiled language for a German republic. The practice was picked up by the democrats of Rhine-Hessen, who held mass meetings all along the Rhine Valley throughout the year: Hahnheim, Worms, and Oberingelheim in the summer, Oberolm, Gaulsheim, and Niederolm in September and October, Großwintersheim, Oppenheim, and Bingen, the following March and April. Attendance at these meetings, as the sponsoring democrats and the authorities engaged in police surveillance agreed, was in the neighborhood of five thousand to seven thousand.[67]

Such mass meetings were fewer in number in the Prussian Rhine Province and generally started somewhat later than further south. The first was organized by the Trier Democratic Club and held in the vintners' village of Schweich on July 2, 1848. A convoy of fifty small boats, all flying the black-red-gold flag, moved up the Moselle, accompanied on the banks by a marching column with band and chorus. The Trier democrats were greeted in the village by its civic guard and a "great crowd of countrypeople." A rally, with speeches by the visiters from Trier, followed. Democrats in the small towns of the mid-Moselle Valley were even more energetic. A mass meeting sponsored by the club in Bernkastel on the "Paulsberg," a high plateau overlooking the river between Lieser and Wehlen, on October 8, 1848, drew ten to fifteen thousand participants according to the organizers; one held outside of Cochem at the end of November was also very large. Koblenz democrats organized a rally in the town of Münstermaifeld on the day after Christmas, with a claimed six thousand participants from the Rhine and Moselle valleys and the Eifel up-country.[68]

Düsseldorf radicals began preparation for such a mass meeting in August 1848 and finally carried it out a month later, September 10, 1848. The city's democrats marched over the Rhine bridge to a meadow outside the town of Neuss, where they were joined by some five thousand (so the authorities esti-

[67] Renner, "Pfälzische Bewegung," pp. 99–100; NSZ 10, 14 June, 1848; MZ, 11 July, 10 Aug., 13, 20 Sept., 24 Oct. 1848, 20 Mar., 12 Apr. 1849; BAF DB 54 Nr. 74 ff. 44–45; NRhZ, 31 Mar. 1849.

[68] Vbl, 9 July 1848; KnZ, 6 July 1848; Breuer, "1848/49 im Moseltale," pp. 187–88; Stahl, 1848/49 an der Mittelmosel, pp. 17–18; Gendarme Breisser (Cochen) to LR Kr. Cochem, 24 Nov. 1848, LAK 441 Nr. 12929; NKZ, 5 Jan. 1849.

mated) from Neuss, and Krefeld, along with peasants from many lower Rhine villages. In October, the Düsseldorf democrats did an about-face and marched east, eight hundred strong, to hold a similar if smaller rally in the up-country village of Gerresheim. The best known of all these events occurred on September 17, 1848, on the Fühlingen Heath, north of Cologne, in the village of Worringen, where some eight thousand spectators from town and country heard the leaders of Cologne's extreme left, including Friedrich Engels, call for the "social and democratic republic," speaking to the crowd from a platform dominated by a gigantic red flag.[69]

The flag was not just a colorful touch, but crucial to the political significance of the meeting. A crowd of thousands could not follow open-air speeches closely when no means of voice amplification existed, so in contrast to tavern conversations, club meetings, or smaller rallies, the exact content of the speech itself was less important to the meaning of these large events than the nonverbal symbols displayed at them. Black-red-gold and red flags were everywhere, while Prussian, Bavarian, or Hessian insignia were never to be seen. Groups marched to the events in a body: The laborers employed in Düsseldorf municipal public works projects crossed the Rhine and marched into the hills behind a red flag; the gymnasts paraded in ordered ranks to begin the rallies in Rhine-Hessen. Symbols of purity and renewal were common. Maidens clad in white, with oak wreaths in their hair, welcomed Mainz democratic leader Franz Zitz to the rally in Oberolm. In Gerresheim, a Prussian flag and a placard with the date 1847 were placed in a dead poplar on the village square; on the flourishing tree next to it stood a red flag and the year 1848.

The mass rally itself was as much the message as the symbols displayed in it. It was an extraordinary event, overcoming rivalries between villages and between town and country. Contingents from many villages came together for the meetings; townspeople marched into the countryside and fraternized with the peasantry. All accounts stress the festive atmosphere, the participation of women and children, the presence of vendors selling food and drink. Sometimes dances were held after the meeting, just as at a parish fair or sharpshooters' festival. This is not to suggest that the participants saw the events as just another festival, an opportunity for a walk in the country or for some apolitical fun. Both the speeches, however poorly heard, and the symbolism of the events distinguished them from other festivals. At most parish fairs one did not see contingents of workers marching behind red flags, or hear speakers ask spectators if they favored a German republic—expecting the crowd to roar its

[69] For Düsseldorf: HSTAD RD Nr. 200 pp. 195–96, 203–04, 216–21; HSTAD RD Pr. Nr. 812 ff. 27–30, 34–40. On the rally in Worringen, see *RhBA* 2/2, Nr. 250; Becker, *Marx und Engels in Köln*, pp. 125–27; Seypel, "Die Demokratische Gesellschaft in Köln," pp. 315–16; Ayçoberry, *Cologne*, p. 245; Hammen, *The Red '48ers*, pp. 301–03. Apparently unaware of the many precedents, these authors (except for Boberach's editorial comment in *RhBA* 2/2:417 n.1) tend to exaggerate the originality of the Worringen mass meeting.

assent, as it invariably did. The mass meetings were indeed festivities, and that was doubtless a large part of their attraction, but they were also politicized festivities in which the fun was mixed with something rather more serious.

Cat Musics in the Service of the Revolution

The attacks on foresters, local officials, and manufacturers in the spring of 1848 had a cat music–like side to them, combining nocturnal noise, verbal threats, and breaking of windows, but only occasional physical violence toward the victims. Although much more frequent and widespread than similar instances in the *Vormärz*, these riotous events of the early phase of the revolution were similarly spontaneous and locally oriented. A popular disorder in Cologne at the end of June 1848 suggested that the revolution might introduce political dimension to them.

A meeting called by anonymous handbills to discuss the grievances of the Rhine watermen attracted thousands of participants, but proceeded turbulently and chaotically, finally dissolving in disorder. The participants poured into the streets, two hundred to three hundred of them, "singing hateful songs, screaming and whistling," proceeding to the house of the banker Ludolf Camphausen and throwing stones at the windows until driven off by the civic guard. The crowd returned the following afternoon and evening, once more throwing stones, battling with the guard, and even attempting to build barricades.[70]

Camphausen was a leader of the *Vormärz* liberal opposition, a prominent member of the board of directors of the Cologne Steam Navigation Company, former president of the Chamber of Commerce, and, as of a few days before the disturbance, former prime minister of Prussia. Appointed by the king in April 1848, his efforts to lead a moderately liberal ministry collapsed between the opposition of reactionary court circles and pressure of the leftists in the Prussian National Assembly and in the streets of Berlin. The cat music brought against him could have referred both to his dishonorable economic role in the steamship company and also to his political activity and the unexpectedly conservative actions of the government he led.[71]

While the charivari had been largely a spontaneous event, and several members of the Cologne Democratic Society had tried to calm the crowd at the preceding meeting, the target of the demonstrators showed the possibilities for the ritual's further politicization. From the summer of 1848 onwards, there

[70] HSTAD RK Nr. 63 ff. 202–210; *RhBA* 2/2, Nr. 176; *KnZ*, 30 June 1848 (Beilage); Seypel, "Die Demokratische Gesellschaft in Köln," pp. 208–10.

[71] On Camphausen's role in politics, see Jürgen Hofmann, *Das Ministerium Camphausen-Hansemann. Zur Politik der preußischen Bourgeoisie in der Revolution 1848/49* (East Berlin: Akademie, 1981).

developed a symbiotic relationship between such spontaneous popular disturbances and organized democratic agitation. As they absorbed the democrats' message, members of the crowd added enemies of the left to their expanding list of powerful but dishonorable figures. Typically occurring towards the end of an organized demonstration, mass meeting, or club session, cat musics were hurled against government officials who took repressive measures against democrats, officers of civic guards who insisted the armed corps of the citizenry be used for the preservation of order rather than revolutionary action, conservatives or constitutional monarchists who denounced leftists, clergymen who preached sermons against them, or politically moderate parliamentary deputies. Along with the usual broken glass, off-key music, and derisive screams of street urchins, these charivaris would include the yelling of political slogans as well, as did the one in Cologne in October 1848, where the participants shouted at the house of a moderate parliamentarian and at the editorial offices of the constitutional monarchist *Kölnische Zeitung*, ''Down with the traitors to the people!''[72]

Increasingly, democrats endorsed such actions. Part of the nature of a cat music was its spontaneity, and leftist attempts to turn it into an organized activity tended to spoil its point. The Neuss democratic club arranged a rehearsal for a cat music, in November 1848, complete with ''dogs, cats, watering cans, kettles, flutes,'' but the charivari itself never came off. A contrast to this failed cat music was the more successful and more typical one in Emmerich, occurring at the same time. A crowd gathered to break the windows of the town's moderate deputy to the Prussian National Assembly, and authorities saw two prominent local democrats placing themselves at the head of the demonstration.[73]

Paradoxically, the growing numbers of such spontaneous demonstrations were a sign of the democrats' success at political organization, proof that their message was reaching the masses, who were taking the democrats' enemies as their own. Other political groups engaging in such popular agitation—usually not the constitutional monarchists, but religiously oriented monarchical loyalists—could sometimes also gain the crowd's imagination, producing

[72] *NRhZ*, 19 Oct. 1848 (quotation); *NRhZ*, 18 Nov. 1848 (Außerordentliche Beilage); LAK 441 Nr. 3056 pp. 205–10; *KnZ*, 22 Sept. 1848; HSTAD RD Nr. 8806 ff. 221–24 (deputies); HSTAD RD Pr. Nr. 812 ff. 19–20; LAS H1 Nr. 1974 ff. 5–15; LAS J1 Nr. 215 (alt) ff. 51–60; *MZ*, 31 Aug. 1848 (authorities); *RhBA* 2/2, Nr. 349; LAS J1 Nr. 205 ff. 663–88; HSTAD RK Nr. 63 f. 211 (civic guard officers); LAS J1 Nr. 179 ff. 512–42; *NRhZ*, 2 Feb. 1849; HSTAD RD Nr. 217b ff. 1–8 (moderates denouncing democrats); Weber, *Aufklärung und Orthodoxie*, p. 156; BAF FN 7 Anhang 4 Gagern ff. 85–88; RP to Army Corps Command (Speyer), 18 Sept. 1849; *NSZ*, 7 July, 1 Nov. 1848 (Beilage) (clergy).

[73] HSTAD RD Pr. Nr. 795 ff. 155–56; HSTAD RD Nr. 8806 ff. 221–22. The disapproval of cat musics expressed in *Der Demokrat*, 10 Sept. 1848, was quite atypical.

charivaris aimed at leftists. Such conservative cat musics, however, were few and far between. The democrats' agitation, far more substantial than the efforts of their political rivals, enabled the left to dominate ever more the meeting halls, the streets, and the popular imagination as the revolution continued through the fall of 1848 and the winter of 1848–1849.[74]

[74] A conservative cat music inspired by the Palatine Pius Associations is described in *NSZ*, 4, 10 Jan., 9 Apr. 1849; and LAS J1 Nr. 264 ff. 543–58; another, inspired by the Prussian loyalist "Society for King and Fatherland," is described in *NRhZ*, 3 Feb. 1849.

CHAPTER SIX

The Democrats and Their Supporters

THE MASS public that the democrats addressed was not a blank slate on which leftists could simply impose their ideas. Even if sometimes politically unsophisticated, the Rhenish common people had strong ideas about their long-standing social grievances, which they had vociferously expressed in March–April 1848. Democratic agitation and organization involved an interaction with social groups newly in motion, freed by the revolution to assert themselves and confront their enemies, both real and imagined. Relations between the democrats and one such group—urban workers and artisans—have frequently been studied by historians. However, as was suggested in the previous chapter, the democrats' mass base was not limited to urban areas or the working class, and leftists' interactions with other groups, in particular, with peasants, soldiers, and women, while less studied, were no less significant.

DEMOCRATS AND LABOR: WORKERS AND WORKERS'
ASSOCIATIONS

It has become an historian's commonplace to talk of the 1848 revolution as the occasion for the birth of the German labor movement. This is certainly true, and one can trace the origins of the future Social Democratic party and trade union movement back to activists and organizations present during the mid-century revolution. Historians pursuing this line of inquiry sometimes forget that the first Social Democrats did not begin their political careers as Social Democrats, or that the issues, supporters, and place of the labor movement in the political universe was different at its birth than later on in its life. In 1848–1849, the labor movement was not at the heart of the left; class consciousness and political radicalism were very far from going hand in hand.

A Prototype? The Cologne Workers' Association

Searches for the origin of the German labor movement often begin with the Cologne Workers' Association. At first glance, this seems like a reasonable idea, since the group's claimed membership of eight thousand in the summer of 1848 made it the largest of its kind in Germany. Moreover, the association came under Marxist influence, Karl Marx himself serving as its interim president during the fall of 1848. The association's first leader, however, was not

Marx but a rival of his, the municipal charity physician and true socialist Andreas Gottschalk. It was Gottschalk who called the founding meeting of the association in mid-April 1848 and was its dominant figure until his arrest at the beginning of July. His period of ascendancy reveals a good deal both about the difficulties of using true socialism as a guide to political action and also about the peculiar nature of the workers' movement during the mid-century revolution.[1]

The organization's executive body consisted of a president (Gottschalk, of course), secretary, and treasurer and a committee made up of representatives from forty-nine different trades, mostly artisanal ones. Public sessions of the committee were held twice weekly, with many ordinary members in attendance; the monthly general assemblies attracted crowds of thousands. It was easy to become a member: One signed a list, kept by Gottschalk, and received a card. Dues were expressly rejected; the organization would finance itself from voluntary contributions and the sale of its newspaper, the *Cologne Workers' Association News* [Zeitung des Arbeitervereins zu Köln].[2]

Since most members did not attend the committee meetings, and when membership reached the thousands, they could not have fit into the meeting hall, even if they had wanted to, the newspaper became the central element of the organization. It published the minutes of the committee and general meetings and the resolutions and addresses adopted at them, and publicized the complaints and demands of the individual trades. Above all, it exposed the oppression of the workers of the city and the injustices committed against them. The newspaper denounced capitalists who refused to give contracts to master artisans but, instead, hired journeymen directly to work for them; it condemned "the arrogant behavior . . . of the small bourgeois of the shoe-making trade," that is, the masters who had refused to let journeymen participate in the meeting called to formulate the grievances of their craft. Its other targets included the military bakeries, which took sales from private bakers, sugar refinery owners who paid their workers low wages for long hours in good times and laid them off in bad, and priests who refused to give charity to the hungry poor.[3]

---

[1] The Cologne Workers' Association has been intensively studied. Besides the sources cited in Chapter Four, note 93, see Hans Stein, *Der Kölner Arbeiterverein (1848–1849). Ein Beitrag zur Frühgeschichte des rheinischen Sozialismus* (Cologne: Gilsbach & Co, 1921), a pioneering work, now somewhat dated but still worth reading, and Karl Stommel, "Der Armenarzt Dr. Andreas Gotschalk, der erste Kölner Arbeiterführer 1848," *AHVN* 166 (1964): 55–105. P. H. Noyes, *Organization and Revolution: Working-Class Associations in the German Revolution of 1848–1849* (Princeton: Princeton University Press, 1966), is superficial and adds little to the discussion.

[2] Dowe, *Aktion und Organisation*, pp. 145–49; Becker, *Karl Marx und Friedrich Engels in Köln*, pp. 26–32.

[3] On the importance of the newspaper, cf. Gottschalk's remarks in *ZAVK*, 4 June 1848; demands mentioned, with many others, can be found in issues from 23 April to 4 June. Cf. Ayçoberry, *Cologne*, pp. 235–37.

The association's membership list has not been preserved, so its exact social composition is unknown and, unless new sources turn up, unknowable. The demands suggest a membership drawn from many different elements of Cologne's lower class, an interpretation supported by the city's police commissioner, who reported that the members were "[m]aster craftsmen in lesser numbers, mainly [vorzugsweise] journeymen artisans and other workers or day laborers." Although not a whole lot to go on, it does tend to imply that while there may have been some overlap between the supporters of the Workers' Association and of the city's Democratic Society, the former were apparently poorer and more proletarian.[4]

Given the heterogeneous character of its membership, how could the Workers' Association have a common goal for its actions? Many of the rank-and-file members saw such a goal arising from social restrictionism, that is, from limitations on the market for labor or small-commodity production. Corporate traditions influenced the demands of the individual trades and were especially apparent in the composition of the association's committee from the members of different crafts, reminiscent of municipal institutions in old regime Cologne, constituted by guild representatives. Gottschalk, however, would have none of this, firmly denouncing guilds and particularist demands of the individual trades, announcing at the committee session of May 18, "The purpose of the Workers' Association and its goal is the triumph [Sieg], the rule [Herrschaft] of the working classes."[5]

Gottschalk apparently thought this could be accomplished without political action, since the Workers' Association never seemed to do anything. It denounced vehemently the practices of capitalists, but took no steps to change them, unlike the outworkers in neighboring areas of the Wuppertal, the Bergisches Land, or the textile districts of the lower Rhine, who, at the time, were busy intimidating manufacturers and negotiating better arrangements with them. Nor did the Cologne Association engage in other activities typical of the early labor movement, such as forming a mutual benefits fund. The association's forays into politics were equally verbal rather than active. It did demand that the municipal and Prussian authorities abolish the octroi and create public works for the unemployed, but it is difficult to see these demands as

---

[4] Quote cited in Dowe, *Aktion und Organisation*, p. 146. Some master craftsmen, unhappy with the Workers' Association, left it, and, with the help of activists from the Democratic Society founded an "Association of Workers and Employers" [Verein für Arbeiter und Arbeitgeber], which fell apart after a few months' existence. Seypel, "Die Demokratische Gesellschaft in Köln," pp. 230–36.

[5] *ZAVK*, 21 May 1848 (Extrabeilage). Cf. his statements in the committee meetings of 21 Apr. (ibid., 30 Apr. 1848) and 11 May (ibid., 21 May 1848), the denunciation of the guild revival efforts in the Bonn Workers' Association (ibid., 6 July 1848), or the article "Der Commis und der Geselle," ibid., 14 May 1848.

anything other than rhetorical, since the group never engaged in a campaign for them, and Gottschalk expressly discouraged it from doing so.[6]

This combination of verbal militancy and practical inactivity was even more apparent and, to contemporaries, even less comprehensible in the Workers' Association's position on major political issues. In late April 1848, the group denounced "the seductive appeals of certain election committees," condemning the democrats as well as the more conservative groups. At first the Association's committee proposed nominating its own candidates; then, on Gottschalk's request, it denounced the indirect elections as a fraud dominated by the bourgeoisie and called for a boycott of them.[7]

Even more outrageous was the behavior of the association, once more on Gottschalk's prompting, during the campaign against the recall of the prince of Prussia. Prince Wilhelm, the king's brother and heir to the throne, was known as one of the leading reactionaries at court. His suggestion that the army use its artillery on the insurrectionary crowd in Berlin had earned him the sobriquet "the Grapeshot Prince," and following the victory of the barricade fighters he had fled to London. In May 1848, the liberal Prussian government, at the time led by the Cologne banker Ludolf Camphausen, recalled the prince from exile. Public opinion in the Rhineland was strongly opposed to this move, and democrats throughout the province saw the situation as an opportunity to recover from their defeat in the recent elections. They condemned the recall as evidence of growing reaction and counterrevolution and mounted mass petition drives against it. The Cologne democrats were particularly energetic, collecting some eight thousand signatures, but not only did Gottschalk refuse to participate—he publicly expressed his personal sympathies for the prince and insisted the whole campaign was a false move.[8]

To compound the confusion, he began calling a few weeks later for a German republic, and not just any republic, but a "workers' republic." Attending the Frankfurt Democratic Congress in mid-June, he returned a protagonist of unity on the left, and began campaigning for a merger of the Workers' Association and the Democratic Society. Throughout all these twists and turns he retained the loyalty and admiration, frequently and noisily expressed, of the members of the Workers' Association while provoking an ever-growing hos-

---

[6] *ZAVK*, 21 May 1848 (Extrabeilage), with Gottschalk's opposition to a campaign against the octroi. The "Democratic Brotherhood Workers' Association," founded July 1848 in the Cologne suburb of Frechen (a center of popular radicalism), included a mutual benefits fund. ZSTAM Rep. 77 Tit. 1095 Nr. 1 f. 29.

[7] On the Workers' Association's actions during the elections, see Dowe, *Aktion und Organisation*, pp. 149–51; Becker, *Marx und Engels in Köln*, pp. 49–51; quote from *ZAVK*, 23 Apr. 1848.

[8] *RhBA* 2/2, Nrs. 84–87, 89, 96; LAK 403 Nr. 6583 pp. 40–41; HSTAD RA Pr. Nr. 2226 f. 227; HSTAD RD Pr. Nr. 794 f. 170; *NRhZ*, 2 June 1848; Stahl, *1848/49 an der Mittelmosel*, p. 13; Breuer, "1848/49 im Moseltale," p. 163; Dowe, *Aktion und Organisation*, pp. 151–53; Seypel, "Die Demokratische Gesellschaft in Köln," pp. 250–51.

tility among Cologne's democrats. The latter began spreading the rumor that Gottschalk had been "bought off and bribed by the government and the bourgeoisie to mislead the workers with pretty sounding words until the reaction was able to regain its strength."[9]

Gottschalk's actions certainly seemed to justify such an accusation. To use twentieth-century terminology, he acted like an ultraleftist, spurning any cooperation with the democrats, boycotting parliamentary elections and refusing to recognize the parliaments that resulted from them, and calling for a workers' republic when the demand for an ordinary republic was enough to send chills down the spines of the bourgeoisie. He differed from latter day ultraleftists in one key respect: Gottschalk never called for insurrection or violent action of any sort. Quite the opposite, he used his position in the Workers' Association to denounce barricade building, street fighting, demonstrations, cat musics, or any kind of organized or unorganized political militancy. In all smaller matters and the two main ones arising in Cologne during his leadership of the Workers' Association—the May 1848 elections and the petition against the recall of the prince of Prussia—his was a voice calling for political passivity.[10]

In doing this, Gottschalk was neither an agent provocateur nor a political muddlehead, but a true socialist trying to carry out the doctrine he espoused in the middle of a revolution. The organization's newspaper, which took up its "entire strength," would, by reporting instances of oppression and exploitation, bring the workers to a sense of their common fate. In the language of his enemy Marx, it would raise their class consciousness. At the same time—and this was characteristic of the views of the true socialists—by printing these reports, the newspaper would act as a "moral improvement institute for the bad conscience of your [the workers'] oppressors." Gottschalk figured that the bourgeoisie would feel trapped by the anarchy of a capitalist economy in crisis, with thousands willing to work but unable to find employment, the high taxes needed to pay for an army, and the resurgence of reaction. Always a friend of order and opponent of anarchy, the bourgeoisie would voluntarily associate itself with the workers' cause, bringing peacefully and without struggle the social and political order true socialists felt would enable humanity to reach its fullest potential.[11]

[9] Becker, *Marx und Engels in Köln*, pp. 65–78; Dowe, *Aktion und Organisation*, pp. 152–53, 166–75; Seypel, "Die Demokratische Gesellschaft in Köln," pp. 295–97. Quote from *ZAVK*, 4 June 1848, where a speaker in a committee meeting of the Workers' Association attributes it to "the reactionary party," but it can only have been the democrats who would have said such a thing.

[10] Cf. how Becker, *Marx und Engels in Köln*, pp. 32–34, writing from a Marxist-Leninist viewpoint, has difficulty deciding whether Gottschalk was an ultraleftist or a reformist.

[11] Gottschalk expounded his political strategy in speeches at the committee meetings of 18 and 29 May and the general assembly of 4 June 1848, *ZAVK* 7 May, 4, 11 June 1848. Cf. also the reiteration of his strategy in the light of the Parisian June Days, *ZAVK*, 6 July 1848.

The Workers' Association under Gottschalk's leadership surely did raise the class consciousness of the Cologne workers, making the city's artisans, factory proletariat, and waterfront laborers more aware of their exploitation by the bourgeoisie. But the class consciousness it created led the workers away from rather than toward political action, condemning all political groups, the democrats as well as the Prussian authorities, as representatives of a system of exploitation. Gottschalk's call for passivity as the highest form of revolutionary activism was well received by Cologne's lower classes. They had been schooled to passivity, to living from charity, by decades of un- and underemployment due to the decline of the port and lack of demand for the products of the city's artisanal trades.[12]

Gottschalk's attitude towards the Rhenish bourgeoisie was equally peculiar, although firmly in the tradition of the true socialists, who believed that public berating of capitalists was the way to convince them of the moral superiority of a socialist society. When Gottschalk told the Workers' Association that the bourgeoisie would support the demand for a workers' republic, out of fear of anarchy and love for order, he was getting mixed up in his own metaphors, confusing the socialist indictment of the anarchy of capitalist productive relations with the feelings the spontaneous demands and street actions of his own followers—acting against his advice—were creating among the city's upper classes. If Cologne's bourgeoisie feared anarchy, it would call for the police and the army, not the workers' republic. Gottschalk himself became the victim of these fears when the authorities cracked down on the Workers' Association early in July 1848 and arrested its president for inciting the revolutionary overthrow of the Prussian monarchy.[13]

There existed another current of opinion in the leadership of the Workers' Association during Gottschalk's ascendancy, represented by friends and associates of Karl Marx: two close allies, the veteran revolutionary Karl Schapper and the watchmaker Joseph Moll, both pre-1848 activists in the exile Communist League, and, a bit more distanced, the ex-artillery officer Fritz Anneke. Given Gottschalk's enormous popularity, they were unable to oppose him openly, but they could and did suggest an alternative policy. They proposed the creation of affiliated societies, "several smaller associations or clubs," whose members would meet to discuss curent affairs, and for "instruction" [Belehrungen]. Gottschalk was not against this plan, but not interested in it either; he regarded the newspaper as the key to communication

---

[12] The radical democrat Hermann Becker noted in his memoirs that he refused to join the Workers' Association because "Gottschalk promised the people, if they would make the republic for him, then he would know how to take care of them," and that the workers understood socialism as help "from so-called philanthropic means. . . ." Quoted in Kuhn, *Der junge Hermann Becker*, pp. 106–110.

[13] On Gottschalk's arrest, see Dowe, *Aktion und Organisation*, pp. 175–77.

between the leadership and the members and never attended a session of the these smaller groups once they had been formed.[14]

Marx's associates were proposing, in effect, to transform the Workers' Association from a true socialist league for liberation of the proletariat and universal human improvement into a workers' educational society. Following Gottschalk's arrest, they were able to carry out their plans. The twice weekly committee meetings were taken up by lectures on Marxist-style political economy, along with a regular overview of political events, copied from the practice of the democratic clubs. The association's newspaper no longer printed the demands of the individual crafts and only rarely noted instances of oppression of the workers, but instead concentrated on reporting political news, taken in simplified form from the pages of the *Neue Rheinische Zeitung*.[15]

The newspaper continued to provide, as it had under Gottschalk, abbreviated minutes of committee meetings. Since the association's leadership also controlled the content of the newspaper, these cannot be taken as verbatim accounts, but precisely because they were edited by the group's leaders, they can be seen as examples of their preferred styles of leadership. Gottschalk encouraged different opinions, and possibly even arranged beforehand to have followers voice them, prompting the group to turn to him as the final arbiter. The Marxists preferred a more didactic style, with discussion serving primarily to illustrate a politically correct point of view, which the lecturer or discussion leader expounded.[16]

Organizational changes embodied the new didactic format. The association's September general assembly voted to introduce monthly dues for members and to have the committee elected by the general assembly and not by the representatives of the different crafts. At the February 1849 general assembly, the reorganization was completed with the approval of new statutes, increasing the number of affiliated societies to nine, outfitting each with a popular library and lecture series and requiring every member to enroll in one of these groups, where the regular monthly dues would be collected. The first para-

[14] *ZAVK*, 21 May, 27 July 1848. On the opposition to Gottschalk in the Workers' Association, see Becker, *Marx und Engels in Köln*, pp. 44–47; Dowe, *Aktion und Organisation*, pp. 151–53.

[15] On political and organizational changes in the association, see Dowe, *Aktion und Organisation*, pp. 177–81, 199–205, 212–21; Becker, *Marx und Engels in Köln*, pp. 112–14, 224–33; a shrewd commentary in Ayçoberry, *Cologne*, pp. 244, 249–50.

[16] Becker, *Marx und Engels in Köln*, p. 50 n.185, notes that the published minutes cannot be regarded as verbatim accounts of meetings, since they were edited by Gottschalk, but fails to add that the subsequent leadership could do the same. For examples of different leadership styles, cf. the committee sessions of 1, 15, 18 May 1848 (*ZAVK*, 7, 21 May 1848) with those of 13, 17, 24 July, 24, 28 Aug., 11 Sept., 30 Nov. 1848 (ibid., 20, 30 July, 31 Aug., 3, 21 Sept. 1848; *FBA*, 7 Dec. 1848). A nasty and amusing account of the Marxist leadership style by a supporter of Gottschalk can be found in *FA*, 18 Jan. 1849.

graph of the new statutes described the goals of the Workers' Association in terms very different from those of a year before:[17]

> The Workers' Association in Cologne has as its goal the political, social, and scientific education of its members, to be achieved through purchase of books, newspapers, pamphlets, and through scholarly lectures and discussions. The Association will, in addition, in so far as it can [so viel in seinen Kräften steht], attempt to protect its members from oppression and support them in case of need.

This subordination of resistance to oppression to education reflected a change in the political function of the Workers' Association. Under Gottschalk, it had been a locus of independent political action, as often as not directed against the democrats. Led by Marx and his friends, the association acted as part of the democratic movement, mobilizing its members to support the campaigns of the Cologne Democratic Society and helping to push them in a more militant direction. It was a policy that followed from Marx and Engels's *Vormärz* criticisms of the true socialists, which they had outlined in the *Communist Manifesto*: In Germany, feudalism and absolutism—that is, the Prussian state and the East Elbian landed aristocracy—would have to be overthrown before the proletariat could take on the bourgeoisie. Paradoxically, the Marxist approach involved lowering the workers' class consciousness to make them active and effective revolutionaries.

This was a much more demanding political concept than the one Gottschalk had espoused, requiring verbal moderation and political activism rather than verbal militancy and political passivity. Not surprisingly, it had less appeal, dues-paying membership in the Workers' Asssociation running only somewhere between 250 and 700 from the fall of 1848 to the spring of 1849. This was a far cry from the 5,000–8,000 in the period of Gottschalk's leadership, but membership had a very different meaning in the two periods of the association's history.[18]

---

[17] On the reorganization, only carried out after a struggle with Gottschalk's supporters, see sources cited in 15. The statutes are printed in *FBA*, 22 Feb. 1849.

[18] Previous studies have never offered even approximate membership figures for this period, but argued in vague terms over whether and why membership fell off after Gottschalk's arrest (a good summary of the debate in Ayçoberry, *Cologne*, p. 244). I can give three estimates. (1) The association's income for September (*FBA*, 29 Oct. 1848) less the entrance fees to the September general assembly (*ZAVK*, 7 Sept. 1848) divided by the monthly dues gives a figure of 707 members. The assumption that the difference between income and entrance fees was membership dues is exaggerated but gives a maximum estimate. (2) Total membership dues collected at October committee meetings (*ZAVK*, 12, 15, 19, 22 Oct. 1848; *FBA*, 26, 29 Oct. 1848) divided by the monthly amount gives a figure of 261 members. This is an undercount, since not all committee meetings were reported in the newspaper and some members may have paid dues at the October general assembly. (3) Membership in five of the nine affiliated societies created in February 1849 (the other four seem never to have gotten off the ground), was given as 464 (*FBA*, 11 Mar. 1849). The figure of 2,000 members sometimes mentioned for the winter of 1849 is based on the com-

Under Gottschalk, membership just involved signing a list, an act requiring no more involvement than did signing a petition. The 8,000 residents of Cologne who joined the Workers' Association were about as many as the 8,300 who signed the petition against the recall of the prince of Prussia. Other activities of the association, requiring greater involvement, had a correspondingly smaller participation. Early in June 1848, the Cologne district governor reported that 2,000 were present at the general assemblies of the group; by July, about 1,400–1,500 copies of the weekly newspaper were being sold. Substantially fewer attended the twice-weekly committee sessions, a police report in June 1848 giving 250 participants. Not all those who attended were members, since complaints were raised that nonmembers would show up and take the best seats, leaving cardholders and even the committee members themselves sitting in the back.[19]

In other words, even in Gottschalk's heyday, the number of even marginally active members—as distinct from signatures on a list the charity physician carried around with him—was probably between one-fifth and one-tenth the maximum number of advocates claimed by the Workers' Association and uncritically accepted by historians. If so, then it is likely that the association's importance has been exaggerated in retrospect, a suspicion reinforced by a look at similar groups elsewhere in the Rhineland.

An Alternative: Workers' Associations in the Southern Rhineland

A Workers' Association, to be more precise, a Workers' Educational Association [Bildungsverein für Arbeiter] was created in Mainz at the end of March 1848, several weeks before any such action in Cologne. The founders were members of the Communist League, acting with the personal encouragement of Marx and Engels. For the first months of its existence the Mainz association called itself the Provisional Central Committee of the German Workers. But the communist leadership of the organization, along with the entire Mainz section of the Communist League, collapsed within a few weeks, and the group came under the influence of prominent Mainz democrats. A disgruntled member described to Marx in a letter of mid-April 1848 how the inhabitants of Mainz were all "south German black-red-gold jackasses," and no one

mittee's decision to print 2,000 membership cards (*FBA*, 4 Mar. 1849), a far cry from any actual membership.

[19] HSTAD RA Pr. Nr. 701 f. 4; *ZAVK*, 6 July, 6 Aug. 1848; *RhBA* 2/2, Nr. 140. The figure of 60–120 members in the Workers' Association mentioned by the authorities in October 1848 (*RhBA* 2/2, Nr. 290), probably referred to the number who attended the regular committee sessions, one-half to one-fourth what it had been under Gottschalk.

dared admit he was a communist. His letter contained a heavily sarcastic account of the Workers' Association there:[20]

The Workers'-Bourgeois Association counts 300 members and Wallau [a member of the Communist League] is President, but the whole thing is a joke, just like an ABC-school. The workers learn reading, writing and arithmetic and Kalisch [Ludwig Kalisch, editor of the leftist weekly *Der Demokrat*] gives a one hour lesson weekly where these oxen learn how to speak in public!

Had this member gone to a few more meetings, he would no doubt have been even more incensed to find the workers taking singing lessons, but might also have noticed Mainz democrats giving lectures on political economy, delivering weekly summaries of important political events, and directing discussions on these topics. Only a few of these have been preserved, but they seem to have been directed towards encouraging the workers to participate in a broader democratic movement. Editor J. Friedrich Schütz of the *Mainzer Zeitung*, for instance, told a meeting of the association on June 21, 1848, that its members should fight the bourgeoisie but the latter were not to be confused with employers and businessmen [die gewerbetreibende Klasse], who were suffering from the economic crisis as much as the workers were: "It is only the rule of the aristocracy of money which we must fight; but not incite hostility or hatred among the different elements of the democratic party."[21]

The Mainz democratic leadership formed a sort of interlocking directorate, the same names turning up on the editorial board of the leftist daily, the *Mainzer Zeitung*, on the executive committees of the Democratic Club and the staff of its newsletter, *Der Demokrat*, and on the executive committees of the Workers' Association and the Gymnastics Society. The two latter groups seem to have been especially close, both meeting in the same tavern. It was probably following the example of the Gymnastics Society that the Workers' Association turned to overtly revolutionary activity in the spring of 1849, commis-

[20] Quotation from *Bund der Kommunisten* 1, Nr. 236. Cf. also Nrs. 242, 246, 251. It is likely that the group was formally reorganized by its noncommunist leadership, since the association celebrated the first anniversary of its founding on 20 Apr. 1849 (*Der Demokrat*, 25 Apr. 1849). The available sources on the Mainz Workers' Association are explored in detail in Eckhart G. Franz, "Die hessischen Arbeitervereine im Rahmen der politischen Arbeiterbewegung der Jahre 1848–1850," *AfhGA*, n.s., 33 (1975): 167–272; and Hanno Broo, "Die Anfänge der vereinsmäßig organisierten Arbieter(bildungs)bewegung in Mainz (1848–1853/54)," *Mainzer Geschichtsblätter* 3 (1986): 61–85. There may exist additional material in the Mainz municipal archives, but I was denied access to them.

[21] *MZ*, 25 June 1848; other meetings of the association are discussed ibid., 19 Apr., 1 Aug. 1848; *Der Demokrat*, 21 May, 23 July, 17 Sept. 1848, 25 Apr. 1849. Even less is known about the membership of the Mainz Workers' Association than about its Cologne counterpart, a police report of October 1848 describing it as consisting of master, journeymen, and apprentice artisans (BAF DB 54 Nr. 74 f. 7). Cf. Broo, "Arbeiter(bildungs)bewegung in Mainz," pp. 81–83.

sioning a Mainz merchant who had previously been an NCO in the French Foreign Legion to lead the group's members in close order drill.[22]

The drillmaster counted six hundred men under his command, making the Mainz Workers' Association as large as its Cologne counterpart. It encompassed a much larger percentage of the population, since Mainz had less than half Cologne's inhabitants. The group was well integrated into the democratic movement, ready to act for it in revolutionary fashion. In other words, it was everything Marx tried to make the Cologne Workers' Association, but with much less success. In terms of social and economic structure, Mainz was a city very much like Cologne, both towns large but declining river ports with many craft workshops, some outworking manufactures, and little industry. As in Cologne, there were spontaneous demands from the Mainz lower classes in the spring of 1848 for the restoration of guilds, and actions of the watermen against steamships and railroad lines. Mainz even had its own potential Andreas Gottschalk, in the person of the merchant Heinrich Straedel, an eccentric member of a distinguished local family, who issued a widely read leaflet in March 1848, calling for the return of the staple to the city's port and the abolition of railroads and steamships in Hessen, in the name of "civilization" and "progress."[23]

Unlike their Cologne counterparts, the Mainz democrats acted swiftly and incisively to intervene in these spontaneous workers' movements, channeling them into a cross-class coalition of small producers and redirecting proletarian hostility against the "aristocracy of money" and the state. The lower classes of Mainz were more revolutionary than those of Cologne precisely because they were less class conscious, because their social grievances were channeled into the demand for a German republic. In some ways, "south German black-red-gold jackasses" seem to have been more appropriate for the 1848–1849 revolution than class-conscious proletarians.

A Workers' Association very similar to the one in Mainz existed in the Palatinate, in Neustadt a.d.W. It was actually two groups, a Workers' Choral Society, and a Workers' Educational Association, the latter claiming six hundred members. Like their Mainz counterpart, the associations sponsored lectures on politics and political economy as well as more recreational activities. Scanty information suggests that the members were mostly artisans (perhaps predominantly journeymen); the leadership was closely cross-connected with that of the radical wing of the city's People's Association and its Gymnastics Society. It was also, like much Palatine radicalism, tied to the German Catholics. Association president, master watchmaker Johann Valentin Weber, was the leading lay member of the sect in Neustadt. He was assisted in his activities

---

[22] Broo, "Arbeiter(bildungs)bewegung in Mainz," p. 74; BAF ZSg 8/55 f. 112; BAF Fn 7 Anhang 4 Gagern f. 27; LAS J1 Nr. 110 ff. 45–46.

[23] Bockenheimer, *Mainz*, pp. 34–35; BAF ZSg 8/55 f. 78; *Der Demokrat*, 16 Apr. 1848.

by the city's German Catholic preacher, the former Protestant pastor Heinrich Loose.[24]

The leaders of the Neustadt association called themselves communists, and were referred to as such by their contemporaries. Their communism, unlike Marx's version, was centered around the creation of workers' productive associations, and the corresponding notion of a unity of all small producers against financial capital and outworking merchants. Weber himself became involved with Marx and the Communist League, but only in exile after the suppression of the revolution.[25]

Events in Trier took a still different path. The Workers' Association there may well have been the only one in Germany that had to inform journeymen artisans that they were eligible for membership. This was due to the strength of corporate sentiment among the city's master craftsmen. Their mutual benefit societies, which had been calling for a restoration of the guilds for the previous decade, founded the Trier Workers' Association in April 1848.[26]

Such corporate sympathies did not imply, as historians have often asserted, sympathy for political reaction. The association's members, the authorities noted, were strongly sympathetic to the democrats, and the group's first president and leading figure was the architect and construction engineer Karl Weyrich, a prominent democratic activist. Under Weyrich's guidance, the association stood on the extreme left. It sent a delegation to the Frankfurt Democratic Congress, and endorsed its demand for a German republic, which the delegate of Trier's Democratic Club, the true socialist Karl Grün, refused to do. Like the Mainz and Neustadt democrats, Weyrich attempted to redirect the artisans' hostility towards politically more propitious targets. He denounced high taxes and the exploitative practices of wholesalers as the causes of the workers' misery and called for the creation of producers' sales cooperatives. Along with other democrats, Weyrich remained an active presence in the association through January 1849, and the organization's 600 members (the authorities' count; the group itself claimed 1,200), continued to stand on the left, supporting such radical actions as the November 1848 tax boycott.[27]

---

[24] Bernd Schwarzwälder, "Frühe 'Arbeiterbewegung' in Neustadt an der Haardt," *MHVP*, 81 (1983): 371–404; *NSZ*, 4 May 1848 (Beilage); LAS J1 Nr. 228 (alt) ff. 61, 254–56; LAS J1 Nr. 229 I (alt) ff. 1–2, 119–20; *Anklag-Akte*, pt. 2 pp. 75–77 (original in LAS J1 Nr. 247 ff. 6–7).

[25] Besides the sources cited above, see *NSZ*, 15 Apr. 1849 (Beilage); and Schwarzwälder, "Die Ursachen der Reichsverfassungskampagne," pp. 245–50.

[26] A brief, as will be seen, not entirely accurate history of the Trier Workers' Association in Dowe, *Aktion und Organisation*, pp. 160–63; the invitation to journeymen printed in *Vbl*, 19 May 1848.

[27] *Vbl*, 7 June, 2 July (Extrabeilage), 16 July, 11 Oct., 14 Nov., 1 Dec. 1848; 24 Jan. 1849; LAK 403 Nr. 7045 pp. 123–43 (more briefly in *RhBA* 2/2, Nr. 289). On the relationship between artisans' corporate sympathies and their political allegiances in 1848/49, see Lenger, *Zwischen Kleinbürgertum und Proletariat*, pp. 184–87, and his *Sozialgeschichte der deutschen Handwerker*, pp. 84–87.

Even then, a political change was under way, an odd counterpart to those simultaneously taking place in Cologne. The association was reconstituted as the ''United Trades Committees'' in October 1848. New statutes adopted then imposed dues on members for the first time, leading to a large decline in membership as the poorer master artisans dropped out. Weyrich was reelected president, but his leadership was increasingly criticized for inactivity, for giving political speeches that did nothing to help craftsmen. Instead, his critics proposed practical policies of social exclusionism, such as petitioning the city council and the diocesan general vicariat to contract out construction only to local craftsmen. Elections to the organization's commmittee in December 1848 went against the democrats, and Weyrich was forced to resign his position.[28]

While such practical policies led to nothing, the group receiving the runaround from both the municipal and diocesan authorities, they were seized upon by supporters of other political tendencies. Replacing Weyrich as the dominant figure in the association was the merchant J. B. Ney, a member of the executive committee of the Trier Pius Association. Discussion of political themes he suggested—such as the excessive number of Protestants occupying state offices in the Prussian Rhineland—were approved by the members, and in the spring of 1849 the association devoted its energies to a joint project with the Pius Association: the creation of a trade school in which journeymen artisans would learn to be more moral and religious and obey their masters. Since the poorer masters, who could not afford dues, and presumably also employed no journeymen, had left the association, the Catholic political leadership's focus on the journeymen as target for the social restrictionist demands of the masters found support among the remaining members, enabling the Catholic politicians to dominate a much smaller group.[29]

What the workers' associations in Cologne, Mainz, Neustadt, and Trier all had in common was their function as a vehicle for the politicization of the spontaneous demands of the urban lower classes, stemming from tensions in *Vormärz* society and so dramatically expressed in the spring of 1848. These demands and the hostilities expressed in them could, however, be politicized in very different ways, as the respective histories of the different groups suggest. The organizations were largest and most effective precisely when they served as a means of mobilizing the lower classes of Rhenish society—impoverished master craftsmen, journeymen, day laborers—into a multiclass democratic coalition aimed at financial-mercantile capital and the state. When they became instruments of class conflict, whether in the peculiar way this occurred

[28] LAK 403 Nr. 7045 pp. 325–31; *Vbl*, 13 Aug., 18 Oct., 1 Nov., 15 Dec. 1848, 30 Jan., 9 Mar. 1849.

[29] *Vbl*, 30 Nov., 3, 27 Dec. 1848; 19 Jan., 7, 25 Feb., 20, 27 Mar., 4, 12 Apr., 8 May 1849. The main weakness of Dowe's account of the Trier Workers' Asssociation is his neglect of the contention among adherents of different political tendencies for control of the group.

under Gottschalk in Cologne or, more explicitly, in the alliance between better-off masters and Catholic activists in Trier, they were less helpful for the democrats, and do not seem to have done much for the economic interests of their members either.

A Different Alternative: Workers' Asssociations in the Manufacturing Districts

In the wake of the disturbances of March–April 1848, outworkers in the lower Rhine manufacturing districts began forming organizations in order to negotiate a reordering of economic life with the now intimidated merchant manufacturers. These organizations, the weavers' guilds in the Wuppertal and Krefeld and the brotherhood of swordsmiths in Solingen, did not call themselves "workers' associations"; nor were they formed, as were the groups in Cologne or the southern Rhineland, under left-wing auspices. Instead, it was the constitutional monarchist merchant Peter Knecht who organized the swordsmiths, and neoorthodox Protestant Prussian loyalists who encouraged the Wuppertal weavers to press their economic demands, rather than considering the political questions raised by the moderately leftist Political Club.[30]

This idea of leading the outworkers in a politically conservative direction by encouraging them to engage in a form of collective bargaining had one major flaw: The manufacturers refused to keep their side of the bargain. Under pressure to cut costs in view of the continuing commercial crisis, individual entrepreneurs reneged on the agreements of spring 1848, lowering outworkers' wages, thus forcing their competitors to follow suit or lose sales. From the summer of 1848 through the spring of 1849, the outworkers sounded a steady chorus of complaints about this, sometimes reinforcing their point by riotous public gatherings.[31]

Since the manufacturers were closely associated with the constitutional monarchists and the conservative Prussian loyalists, this situation offered the democrats a chance to gain influence over the outworkers' organizations. The Workers' Association of the silk-weaving center Mülheim a. Rhein—note the difference in name from earlier groups—was firmly under democratic control from its founding in July 1848. Krefeld democrats, led by the revolutionary gymnast and German-Catholic Caspar Immandt, gained influence and support in the weavers' guild in the summer of 1848, and led many of its members into a workers' educational association, which launched a campaign to bring the Krefeld pay scale to all the silk weavers in the entire Prussian Rhine Prov-

[30] Rolf Schaberg, "Die Geschichte der Solinger Arbeiterbewegung von ihren Anfängen bis zum Ausbruch des 1. Weltkrieges" (Diss. phil., Graz, 1958), pp. 30–31; Lorenz, "1848/49 im Wuppertal," pp. 167–70; 212–13; Herberts, Alles ist Kirche und Handel, pp. 62–64.

[31] Herberts, Alles ist Kirche und Handel, p. 65; HSTAD RD Pr. Nr. 794 ff. 193–94; HSTAD RD Pr. Nr. 795 ff. 3–4, 6–7, 137–45; HSTAD RD Nr. 8805 ff. 1–3; ZAVK, 18 June 1848.

ince. About that time, the Solingen democratic club was reorganized, "placing the unsolved social question at the head of its [political] stance." The Solingen democrats organized branch clubs in the metalworkers' villages, some of which called themselves workers' associations; they reported on the proceedings of the smiths' brotherhoods in the newly founded democratic newspaper, the *Bergisches Organ.*[32]

The left found the going hardest among the textile workers of the Wuppertal and neighboring Lennep County, where the powerful influence of neoorthodox Protestantism kept the lower classes tied to the Prussian royal house and made it extraordinarily difficult for the democrats to mobilize economic discontent toward political ends. From the summer of 1848 through the spring of 1849, democrats contended with constitutional monarchists and loyalist conservatives for control of the Industrial Central Association of the Wuppertal, formed in November 1848 by the merger of the weavers' guilds of several different cities. Similar political conflicts took place in the Lennep Workers' Association, which was founded in August 1848, and was one of the few such groups to include in its ranks workers in mechanized spinning mills. Although the evidence is scanty, it would seem the democrats made headway—aided perhaps by the growing interest of the Elberfeld weavers in producers' cooperatives. The Industrial Central Association, which renamed itself a "Workers' Association" in March 1849, steered a more leftist course, culminating in its participation in the Elberfeld uprising of May 1849.[33]

The emphasis these groups placed on industrial relations, makes them most similar to trade unions and the usual picture of the nineteenth-century labor movement, although their members were not propertyless proletarians but nominally independent master craftsmen. They were, however, the last to call themselves workers' associations, a circumstance showing that the name "workers' association" referred as much to a group's political program as to its membership. It described an organization of the lower classes, whether

---

[32] Gernert, *1848/49 im Rheinisch-Bergischen*, pp. 122–23; Dowe, *Aktion und Organisation*, pp. 182–83; HSTAD RD Pr. Nr. 795 ff. 108–109, 141–45; HSTAD RD Nr. 8806 ff. 214–19; HSTAD RD Nr. 8808 ff. 1–10; HSTAD RD Nr. 8809 ff. 126–39; Schaberg, "Die Solinger Arbeiterbewegung," pp. 46–47; *NRhZ*, 28 Dec. 1848 (Uerdingen).

[33] The sources on the workers' movement in the Wuppertal are few, the secondary accounts undetailed and sometimes contradictory, but see Lorenz, "1848/49 im Wuppertal," p. 170; Illner, *Bürgerliche Organisierung*, pp. 148–49; Wittgenstein, "Entstehung der sozialen Frage," pp. 161–62; *Lebenserinnerungen . . . Alexander Pagenstecher* 3:43–46; Körner, *Lebenskämpfe* 2:37–38, 102–04; *Die Allgemeine Deutsche Arbeiterverbrüderung 1848–1850. Dokumente des Zentralkomitees für die deutschen Arbeiter in Leipzig*, ed. Horst Schlechte (Weimar: Hermann Böhlaus Nachfolger, 1979), Nrs. 95–97. On the workers' movement in Lennep County, see Wolfgang Hoth, "Der Beginn der Arbeiterbewegung in Remscheid. Der Lenneper Arbeiterverein von 1848 bis 1850," *ZBGV* 87 (1974/76): 110–15. Rolf Taubert, *Autonomie und Integration. Das Arbeiter-Blatt Lennep* (Munich: Dokumentia, 1977), performs a useful service by providing a facsimilie reprint of the surviving issue of the association's newspaper (pp. 177–214), but his anarchist interpretation of the group's history is, as Hoth shows, at best eccentric.

outworkers, impoverished master artisans, journeymen, day laborers, or, most rarely, factory workers, which was part of the democratic movement.

At least as far as the Rhineland is concerned, these organizations' role in the 1848 revolution should not be overrated: They were much less common than democratic clubs; their membership was usually smaller; and more "workers"—in the broad sense of the urban lower classes—participated in organized political activity via the democratic clubs than via the workers' associations. Class conflict and political leftism was not linked in the workers' associations as they were to be in the late nineteenth century social democratic movement or in Marxist theory. Groups that stressed class conflict were less effective on the left than those that mobilized the workers to participate in a cross-class democratic movement, and many of the former were hardly on the left at all.

INTO THE COUNTRYSIDE

For all the difficulties involved in organizing the urban lower classes, the democrats were operating on familiar terrain. *Vormärz* radicals had considered the problems of urban society in their discussion circles and carried on their political or protopolitical campaigns mostly in urban areas. A short walk from even one of the largest Rhenish cities would take an activist out into the countryside, but the country was as culturally distant as it was physically close. Urban radicals were strangers, and unless they received an invitation from a sympathizer on the land—schoolteacher, innkeeper, or a figure such as the estate owner Kemmerich in Worringen, "an rare exception among the rich . . . who, true to his convictions has joined the democrats"—they faced at best an uncertain response. Even leaving aside a hostile welcome from the local authorities or the clergy, the peasants themselves might refuse to let the leftists speak, or drive them out of the village. The rural world was alien and threatening to urban activists; it required a strong effort of will to enter into it.[34]

Feelings of trepidation about approaching the peasantry, and perceptible relief at receiving a favorable welcome from the strange denizens of the countryside, are apparent in a report made by a member of the Cologne Workers' Association on an agitation trip south of the city. He told the committee, "Everywhere, underneath the coarse exterior of the countryfolk, there was a heart unspoiled by the egoism of our time, receptive to the principles of justice, humanity and equity. . . ." If the members of the Workers' Association, re-

[34] Seypel, "Die Demokratische Gesellschaft in Köln," p. 370; *KnZ*, 14 Jan. 1849; *FA*, 28 Jan. 1849. All these examples are drawn from the Cologne area; a few similar instances, elsewhere in the Rhineland, would include LAS J1 Nr. 252 (alt) ff. 89–90, 154–58; LAS J1 Nr. 244 ff. 195–96; *Die Trompete von Speyer*, 24 Apr. 1849; *Vbl*, 28 June 1848; *MZ*, 19 Aug. 1848.

garded even by other democrats as radical wild men, saw the peasants in this way, one can only wonder what more fastidious leftists might have felt.[35]

Even with friendly feelings on both sides, there still existed a problem of communication, the peasants having trouble with the abstract language of the urban or better-educated revolutionaries. The mayor of Bliesdahlen in the southwestern Palatinate, trying to ascertain the content of a public speech given by a schoolteacher suspected of leftist sympathies, finally had to give up in disgust. The witnesses all contradicted each other, and "simply did not know, as countryfolk usually do not, how to repeat, with certainty or exactitude, what the accused had said."[36]

Talking to the Peasantry

Whether conversing in the taverns, holding large mass meetings, or engaging in "traveling sermons in the surrounding villages every Sunday," as Speyer leftists did, democrats faced the challenge of expressing their ideas in ways that would gain support from the rural population. They had their best successes when they dealt with material problems closely connected to rural life. For most of the Rhineland, this meant, more than anything else, the right to use the forests.[37]

Between November 1848 and April 1849, Zweibrücken democrats agitated in the surrounding countryside, ultimately organizing thirty-seven village branches of the People's Association in their county, by far the most in the entire Rhineland. No sooner were founding meetings held, then the villagers marched in groups into the nearby state forests, mocking and threatening the foresters who tried to prevent them from appropriating royal property. The democrats claimed they merely told the peasants that the left was planning to introduce a proposal in the Bavarian legislature to reform the current law on collective rights of forest use, explicitly noting the existing law should be obeyed until the new legislation could be passed. The peasants, however, seemed to have heard that because of the revolution, the old laws were invalid: The forest now belonged to the "citizens" who could take from it what they wanted.[38]

Perhaps it was a rural-urban misunderstanding. What were the peasants of Gersheim and Reinheim to think when a Zweibrücken activist told them on New Year's Day 1849 that they should form a People's Association so that

---

[35] *FBA*, 10 Dec. 1848; similarly, *NKZ*, 19 Jan. 1849.

[36] LAS J1 Nr. 195 f. 173.

[37] Quotation, LAS J1 Nr. 252 (alt) ff. 154–58.

[38] LAS H3 Nr. 154b ff. 200–201, 219–21; LAS H1 Nr. 1972 ff. 67–72; *NSZ*, 13 Jan. 1849. In general on the rural organizing campaign of the Zweibrücken democrats, see the depositions of the village mayors in LAS J1 Nr. 195 and LAS J1 Nr. 277 (alt).

they would no longer be "dominated by the forest officials"? The Zwei-brücken democrats announced at the founding meeting of a People's Association in the village of Ommersheim that their actions were designed to preserve the laws, but the meeting itself proceeded in turbulent fashion, the remarkable sight of city democrats speaking from an open-air tribune outweighing the moderate content of their speeches. Village activists were more direct or less cautious than their urban counterparts, schoolteacher Orschied in Hengstbach, a leading figure in the People's Association there, telling the peasants they could gather as much brush in the forest as they wanted.[39]

Whatever the actual circumstances may have been, the campaign showed the centrality of the forest question to rural agitation. Democrats in many different parts of the Rhineland exploited this issue. Village democrats in Palatine Neuhembach drew up an elaborate proposal for the reorganization of the entire Bavarian forest administration, which they circulated among the People's Associations. As early as the elections to the Frankfurt and Berlin National Assemblies, the democrats of Sieg and Mülheim counties, on the right bank of the Rhine opposite Cologne, had brought up the forest issue. The Mülheim County Democratic Association drew up a list of the collective forest use rights each village possessed, to help them in their struggle with the authorities over this question. These actions help explain how this area became the rural stronghold of the democrats in the Prussian Rhine Province.[40]

Another issue useful to the democrats in their rural agitation was village self-government, the villagers' right to choose their own officials and administer their own affairs, in particular to dispose of communal property, without any interference from the state authorities. In its essentials, this was a disguised version of the demand for the right to use the forests, since village property was, to a great extent, woodland, and a main reason the authorities wanted to keep control over village officials was precisely because they were responsible for administering the communal forest. Electors in three upland villages of Trier County made the connection explicit in March 1849 when they called for a democratic law on local government to end a situation "when it seems like the forest belongs to the officials or the state and not the community." Trier democrats sent the petition on to the Berlin parliament, where Cologne communist Karl D'Ester, sitting for Mayen County, had been a prominent advocate of just such a law.[41]

Village self-government was a popular cause in the countryside, and the peasants petitioned the Frankfurt National Assembly for it on their own behalf, without needing any organized political group to suggest it to them. Demo-

[39] LAS J1 Nr. 195 ff. 18–21, 24; LAS J1 Nr. 277 (alt) ff. 244–45.

[40] LAS J1 Nr. 244 ff. 319–20; *KnZ*, 25 Apr. 1848; *NRhZ*, 19 Oct. 1848 (Beilage); similarly, LAK 403 Nr. 6583 ff. 77–78; Jeuckens, "Die 48er Bewegung in Eupen," p. 38.

[41] *Vbl*, 6 Mar. 1849; similarly, LAS J1 Nr. 195 ff. 18–21, 100–01; Kersken, *Bonn in den Revolutionsjahren*, p. 78; *RhBA* 2/2, Nr. 218, esp. p. 367 n.1

cratic endorsement of the demand was a happy coincidence of principle and practicality in revolutionary politics. In the spring of 1848, the peasants had often demonstrated against or driven out unloved local officials, and the underlying tensions, usually centering on state forest policy, had by no means died out several months or a year later. By encouraging peasants to continue these sorts of actions, and by publicizing and supporting their demands, the democrats worked to retain or revive the insubordinate spirit of the outbreak of the revolution, but also to politicize it, directing it against the existing states, not just their local representatives.[42]

A final issue, popular everywhere, but put forth especially frequently in rural areas, was the burden of fiscality. In their rural agitation, democrats constantly reiterated demands for lower taxes, diminished government expenditures, and lesser fees for notaries, lawyers, and court clerks. Moselle Valley leftists, some of whom, such as Bernkastel activist Peter Josef Coblenz, had been pressing this issue since the *Vormärz*, stormed away at the must tax, denouncing it as the cause of the region's misery. This tax was a main theme of the great mass meeting held in October 1848 on the heights overlooking the river. After speakers denounced it, and a petition against it circulated among the ten thousand to twelve thousand spectators, Trier true socialist Karl Grün told the crowd that the social question was the most important issue in the revolution but in the Moselle Valley this question could be resolved only by abolition of the hated tax.[43]

All these themes of rural agitation leave the impression that talking to the peasantry meant stressing practical, concrete, easily grasped material issues. Thinking along these lines, Karl Schapper told the August 1848 congress of democratic clubs from the Prussian Rhine Province: "Let us speak to the peasants about material interests! Ideas are not attractive to someone who has no bread to eat or who is bent over by debt."[44]

This was certainly not wrong, but by itself incomplete. The peasants knew very well about their material interests, and had fought for them in the spring of 1848. The question for the democrats was whether these localized, particular material interests could be connected to the broader, more general demands of their movement. What the democrats needed was expressed in rustic fashion by some inhabitants of the magistracy of Hambach in Jülich County

---

[42] Besides the sources cited in the two previous notes, see Gernert, *1848/49 im Rheinisch-Bergischen*, p. 121; *NRhZ*, 17, 23 Dec. 1848, 20 Jan. 1849; LAK 403 Nr. 7045 pp. 101–04; *RhBA* 2/2, Nr. 221; Stahl, *1848/49 an der Mittelmosel*, pp. 13, 15; BM Tries to LR Kr. Cochem, 8 Nov. 1848, LAK 441 Nr. 12929; ZSTAM Rep. 77 Tit. 1095 Nr.1 ff. 19–20; *MZ*, 29 Aug. 1848; *VdB*, 21 Apr. 1849.

[43] Breuer, "1848/49 im Moseltal," pp. 188–89; Stahl, *1848/49 an der Mittelmosel*, p. 18; BM Tries to LR Kr. Cochem, 3 Nov. 1848, LAK 441 Nr. 12929; LAK 442 Nr. 6506 ff. 30–31; LAK 403 Nr. 7045 pp. 101–104; ZSTAM Rep. 77 Tit. 1095 Nr. 1 ff. 19–20; LAS J1 Nr. 178 ff. 213–14; LAS J1 Nr. 267 ff. 157–60; LAS J1 Nr. 195 ff. 18–24.

[44] Cited in Dowe, *Aktion und Organisation*, p. 183 n.450.

on the lower Rhine (not to be confused with the Palatine village of Hambach, site of the 1832 Hambach Festival). At the outbreak of the revolution, the villagers had set out to divide the royal forest there among themselves and drive from office any local officials who opposed them. In May 1848, they even sent a representative to Cologne, to get the advice of Andreas Gottschalk, the leader of the Workers' Association of the Rhenish metropolis, then at the height of his fame. One village councillor opposed the peasants' plans, asking what the "men of the people" in Berlin and Frankfurt would think of such a petty, self-seeking attitude. He was told "that precisely the same aristocratic tendency and usurpations of the bureaucratic rule of state officials [exist] in miniature in Selgersdorf as on a large scale in Frankfurt and Berlin. They must [both] be fought and in the firm German way rejected out of hand."[45]

The magistracy of Hambach was one of the most left-wing areas in the countryside of the lower Rhine plain, and the peasants of Selgersdorf were unusually sophisticated in seeing the connection between struggles at the village level and those at the national level. More commonly, democratic agitation was directed at making the connection for them, and leftists did this in two ways. First, and most obviously, they pointed out the larger political context of the peasants' grievances. Taxes were high because of the expenses for the luxurious courts of thirty-four different German princes, a problem that would not exist in a unified national state, preferably one with a republican constitution. The bureaucracy could impose its will on the villagers because government and administration were not controlled by the people, a state of affairs that would be remedied by the introduction of a democratic form of government.[46]

This connection between the democrats' political program and the peasants' grievances remained abstract and purely verbal. In most places, it was all the democrats could accomplish. Their influence in the countryside was greatest where they could go further: not just identifying the peasants' complaints with a leftist political program, but making the democratic movement part of village life, merging the democratic clubs with forms of peasant sociability, linking political agitation with village festivals, and encompassing the entire rural population—women, children, and adolescents, as well as adult men. The left was most successful at this in Rhine-Hessen, where the network of democratic clubs in the countryside was at its thickest.

The village of Oberolm was such a stronghold of the left that it abolished its democratic club and constituted itself a "democratic community," with political activities funded by the village treasury. The inhabitants celebrated the first anniversary of the February 1848 proclamation of the republic in

---

[45] Fischer, *Kreis Jülich*, pp. 18–19; *ZAVK*, 11 June 1848 (Extra Beilage); HSTAD RA Nr. 222 ff. 92–93. The rustics contacted Gottschalk via a cousin of one of them, a Cologne cabinetmaker active in the Workers' Association.

[46] All the examples of rural agitation cited in notes 38–43 contain these connections.

France with a torchlight parade, led by the village musicians and drummer. Planned fireworks and a gymnastics exhibition had to be called off because of bad weather, but the whole village was illuminated. Signs and banners were hung, and the evening ended in the tavern with speeches and music. Entire families attended, parents carrying small children in their arms.[47]

Gymnastics societies were formed in at least fifty villages of Rhine-Hessen during the revolution. Their members, largely unmarried young men, were responsible for the festive aspects of the mass rural rallies at which Mainz democratic leaders spoke. They provided a guard of honor for the village maidens, clad in white with oak wreaths in their hair, who greeted the radical visitors, presenting them with flowers; they led the parade with drum corps and marching band; they decorated the speakers' platform with wreaths and garlands, hung the red flags from windows and the church tower, put out the pictures of the Badenese revolutionary republicans, Struve and Hecker, and, with the help of the innkeepers, arranged the dancing that concluded the day.[48]

Such actions combined revolutionary politics with a traditional folkloric role. In the Rhineland throughout much of the nineteenth century, the unmarried young men of the village were responsible for the organization of rustic festivities, such as parish fairs and sharpshooters' festivals. The same group of villagers joined the gymnastics society and organized the democratic mass meetings, the upshot a successful synthesis of leftist politics with familar forms of rural festivity and village social role playing.[49]

Who was responsible for this combination of urban politics and rural folkways? Innkeepers certainly played a role, handily mixing business and politics. Perhaps most important were those outposts of urban society in the countryside, schoolteachers and rationalist Protestant pastors. The new pastor in the Rhine-Hessian village of Gimbsheim formed a gymnastics society in the spring of 1848, quickly counting sixty gymnasts and forty "friends," who made no secret of their republican sympathies. Members of the group marched through the village led by their drummer, stopping at night to bring cat musics to their political enemies. Schoolmaster Wisserbach in Budenheim joined the

---

[47] *MZ*, 1 Mar. 1849. For similar festivities in Mülheim County, organized, however, by urban democrats, and not by the villagers themselves, see Gernert, *1848/49 im Rheinisch-Bergischen*, pp. 156–57.

[48] On the gymnastic societies, see Braun, *Geschichte des Turnens in Rheinhessen* 1:47–63; "Mittelrheinischer demokratischer Turnbezirks-Verband" (pamphlet in the Mainz municipal library). My account of the ceremonies is based above all on the detailed police report in BAF DB 54 Nr. 74 ff. 44–45; similar, if sketchier, accounts in *MZ*, 11 July, 29 Aug., 13, 20 Sept., 24 Oct. 1848.

[49] On village bachelors, Hoffmann, *Rheinhessische Volkskunde*, p. 179; Becker, *Pfälzer Volkskunde*, pp. 332–37. The classic account of the interaction of folkloric customs and revolutionary politics in the mid-nineteenth-century countryside is Maurice Agulhon, *The Republic in the Village: The People of the Var from the French Revolution to the Second Republic*, trans. Janet Lloyd (New York: Cambridge University Press, 1982).

democratic club in the nearby cantonal town of Wöllstein and organized a choral society in the village, whose members subscribed to the radical *Mainzer Zeitung* and refused to join in the funeral services for the deceased grand duke.[50]

Another significant group was the progressive and freethinking bourgeoisie of the cantonal towns, in close contact with the rural population in densely populated Rhine-Hessen, where the peasants lived in large, nucleated villages. Mainz justice Johann Mohr, forcibly pensioned off for his leftist views after the Hambach Festival, retired to an estate in Oberingelheim. During the revolution he sat for Worms in the Frankfurt National Assembly and played a major role in the democratic movement of northern Rhine-Hessen—although he was always careful to stay in the background, as the authorities discovered to their dismay, when they tried to indict him. His personal servant, one Samuel Weidmann, organized a democratic children's club, led the youngsters in cheers for Hecker and Struve, and marched out with them into the countryside, where they joined the village children in bringing cat musics to the Hessian loyalist pastor of Großwintersheim.[51]

These events suggest some of the reasons why the democratic movement was most successful in rural areas of Rhine-Hessen and, more generally, in the southern Rhineland: prevalence and popular acceptance of religious rationalism and free thought, close contact between town and country, and the leading example of a leftist bourgeoisie. With all these preconditions in place, a synthesis between forms of rural culture and a political movement originating in urban society was most easily accomplished. When added to elements existing elsewhere—prepolitical rural discontent, democratic efforts to link localized peasant grievances with broader political themes—the result was a democratic movement firmly anchored in the countryside and thus a formidable political force.

SOLDIERS AND DEMOCRATS

The conflicts between crowds of civilians celebrating the realm of freedom and undisciplined soldiers professing their monarchist loyalties did not end with the dramatic confrontations of May 1848 in Mainz and Trier. Rather, they persistently reoccurred throughout the following year, in the form of both small tavern brawls and veritable pitched battles between soldiers and civilians, as were fought in Düsseldorf in August, where one soldier was killed, or in Cologne in September, when the fighting led to a major revolutionary episode. Common soldiers' indiscipline, however, was not always directed

[50] Braun, *Geschichte des Turnens in Rhein-Hessen* 1:61–62; BAF FN 7 Anhang 4 Gagern ff. 109–10.

[51] BAF FN 7 Anhang 4 Gagern ff. 85–88; BAF ZSg 8/55 ff. 169–70; Uhrig, "Worms," pp. 47–49; *Verhandlungen*, pp. 98–99.

against civilians, but could be turned against their superiors, as the lower ranks complained of bad food, low pay, or long terms of service, gathered together, and marched through the streets, denouncing their officers and shouting out cheers for the republic or for the Badenese revolutionaries Hecker and Struve.[52]

As civilian-military conflicts continued, they began to appear politically more problematic to the democrats. They had not hesitated to articulate the visceral hostility frequently expressed by the urban lower classes against the soldiers from the trans-Rhenan provinces, as a means of gaining popular support. However, in doing so they were forfeiting any chance of recruiting soldiers into the democratic movement. The soldiers' demonstrations against their officers suggested this might be possible; the armed clashes occurring after March 1848, from the republican uprising in Baden that April through the street fighting in Vienna in October, made the desirability of armed support all too clear. Consequently, about the same time the democrats began their rural agitation, they began a similar effort among the soldiers, both campaigns involving an attempt to expand the democrats' base of support by gaining previously untouched social groups.

The best organized effort was made in Cologne, led by the communist ex-army officers, Friedrich Anneke and Friedrich von Beust. They were seconded by a number of other officers of the Cologne garrison, mostly native Rhinelanders or ethnic Poles, who already felt like aliens in an officer corps dominated by East Elbian aristocrats, even before they expressed their democratic sentiments in the spring of 1848 and were driven out of the army for them. Military agitation was harder than other kinds; any soldier identified as having been at a democratic meeting would be arrested. Consequently, gatherings took place in darkened taverns, sometimes beginning with cries of "corporals out," to eliminate the NCOs, thought to be spying for the officers. The democrats called for higher wages and better food and housing for the common soldiers, to be financed by cutting officers' salaries. They also advocated

[52] General mood of indiscipline: Kühn, *Der junge Hermann Becker*, pp. 221–22; Callies, *Militär in der Krise*, pp. 125–36. Conflicts between soldiers and civilians: Kühn, *Der junge Hermann Becker*, pp. 199–201; *RhBA* 2/2, Nrs. 219, 244; HSTAD RA Pr. Nr. 621 ff. 78, 109, 153, 166, 178; HSTAD RA Pr. Nr. 2226 ff. 268, 271, 282–83, 286–87, 294; HSTAD RD Pr. Nr. 795 ff. 44–52; HSTAD RD Nr. 8804 ff. 59–60; HSTAD RD Nr. 8806 ff. 265–66; LAK 441 Nr. 3057 pp. 193–94, 201–04; *NRhZ*, 14 Oct., 28 Dec. 1848, 24 Jan., 25 Feb. 1849; *NKZ*, 29 Mar. 1849; *KnZ*, 1 Dec. 1848 (Außerordentliche Beilage), 3, 5 Dec. 1848, 8 Apr. 1849; ZSTAM Rep. 77 Tit. 505 Nr. 5 Vol. VI ff. 7–8; Bockenheimer, *Mainz*, pp. 114–17; Buckler, "Mainz während der Revolutionsjahre," p. 61; *MZ*, 3 Mar. 1849; LAS H1 Nr. 1112. Conflicts between soldiers and their officers, or among soldiers: Kühn, *Der junge Hermann Becker*, pp. 219–21, 227, 232–33; Tageszettel, 1, 5 June 1848, 10 Apr. 1849, HSTAD RA Pr. Nr. 621; HSTAD RA Pr. Nr. 2226 ff. 252–53, 282–83, 286–87; LAK 403 Nr. 6583 pp. 85–86; *NRhZ*, 17 Dec. 1848 (Zweite Ausgabe), 6 Feb., 12 Apr. 1849; *KnZ*, 28 Nov. 1848; Buckler, "Mainz während der Revolutionsjahre," p. 63; Callies, *Militär in der Krise*, pp. 137–38.

shorter times of service and a less harsh military discipline. A separate campaign was launched among the NCOs, apparently centering on the artillery, since reports mentioned explosives specialists and bombardiers as targets of left-wing activity. Radicals demanded that officers no longer be chosen by examination but be elected by the soldiers, bringing democratic principles to the army while offering new career prospects to technically trained corporals. These formal meetings were supplemented by tavern conversations, well lubricated with alcohol, and the distribution of copies of the *Neue Kölnische Zeitung*, edited by Anneke's wife, Mathilda Franziska, and specializing in publicizing soldiers' grievances. Similar, if less systematically organized, activities were carried out by democrats in Wesel, Düsseldorf, Aachen, Trier, and Mainz; soldiers began showing up at mass meetings and rallies, at sessions of the democratic clubs, and at taverns frequented by leftists.[53]

This situation began to worry the officer corps. While individual military activists could be arrested and unreliable detachments transferred or even dissolved, something more seemed to be needed. Officers began their own barracks-room political indoctrination, a major telling troops in the Düsseldorf garrison at roll call:

> Soldiers, I have heard that some of you ran along to Gerresheim [where the Düsseldorf democrats had held a mass meeting]. You no doubt heard what nonsense they said there. Don't anyone go to [such events again] for they [the participants] are all criminal scum and bloodhounds [Lumpengesindel und Bluthunde]. To be sure, they are not the same as those in Frankfurt who wish to be everything, but they want to do it here and try and talk you into it.[54]

In his barracks language, the major was making a political point. He denounced the democrats, differentiating them from the moderates of the Frankfurt National Assembly, whom he also attacked, for attempting to place themselves and the national interest they claimed to represent over that of the Prussian monarchy.

Royalist loyalism almost always figured in street brawls between soldiers and civilians, the former waving the black and white Prussian or the blue and white Bavarian colors, cheering the king, while the latter flew black-red-gold

---

[53] For Cologne, see Seypel, "Die Demokratische Gesellschaft in Köln," pp. 211–17; Kühn, *Der junge Hermann Becker*, pp. 219–25; *RhBA* 2/2, Nrs. 146, 278; *ZAVK*, 6 Aug. 1848. Elsewhere, LAK 403 Nr. 6583 pp. 85–86; HSTAD RA Pr. Nr. 621 f. 169; HSTAD RA Pr. Nr, 2226 f. 330; HSTAD RD Nr. 8804 f. 26; HSTAD RD Nr. 8806 ff. 265–66; HSTAD RD Pr. Nr. 812 ff. 44–45; HSTAD RD Nr. 200 pp. 216–25, 244–50; *NRhZ*, 15 Apr. 1849 (Zweite Ausgabe); *MZ*, 3 Nov. 1848; Buckler, "Mainz während der Revolutionsjahre," p. 63.

[54] HSTAD RD Nr. 200 pp. 226–28. For other measures, see Kühn, *Der junge Hermann Becker*, pp. 225–28, 232–33; *RhBA* 2/2, Nrs. 273, 278, 306; Fischer, *Kreis Jülich*, pp. 58–59. Similarly in the Bavarian army, where the officers admitted quite openly that since they could not preserve discipline, they would attempt to turn the soldiers' hatred on the democrats: Calliess, *Militär in der Krise*, p. 136.

or red flags, calling for the republic. Democrats claimed that officers or NCOs put the soldiers up to it, getting them drunk, inciting them with royalist phrases, and even being present at the scene of street brawls, circumspectly choreographing the action. The military denied this, but the one time they were so incautious as to allow an independent civilian judicial investigation, following an incident in Speyer on July 17, 1848, its results confirmed the democrats' charges.[55]

A lieutenant had invited common soldiers into a tavern, to tell them it was disgraceful that a picture of the Badenese radical republican Friedrich Hecker was hanging in a bookstore window, next to that of the king of Bavaria and that it had to come down. The same evening, soldiers gathered in front of the bookstore, cheering the king and getting into a brawl with gymnasts and other civilians cheering Hecker. Witnesses saw officers encouraging the soldiers to fight and, afterwards, praising them for their defense of the honor of king and army.

The Speyer incident shows the officers countering the democrats not by restoring military discipline but by subverting it in their own fashion. They were also engaged in political agitation, exploiting the soldiers' grievances, blaming them on the left. It worked in Speyer, because the soldiers involved were natives of trans-Rhenan Old Bavaria, desirous of returning to their base in Würzburg, blaming Hecker and his admirers in Speyer for their being so far from home.[56]

Soldiers were thus exposed to two politically opposing forms of political agitation, both aimed at their material grievances. What decided their political loyalties, though, were not the grievances themselves but the soldiers' regional origins. The Bavarian troops sent across the Rhine to the Palatinate in March 1848, who had distinguished themselves by getting into a major riot with native Palatine soldiers and leftist civilians in the fortress city of Landau at the beginning of July 1848, were withdrawn the following month. As the Landau incident suggests, the native Palatine regiments remaining in Bavaria's western province were thoroughly unreliable; they would desert en masse during the uprising of May 1849. The army of Rhine-Hessen was not a serious fighting force, even for political police work. As early as September 1848, the Hessian authorities were asking for and receiving Prussian troops to restore order in portions of their Rhenish province.[57]

At a crucial moment, the Prussian army could act militarily in the entire Rhineland, so the loyalty of the Prussian soldiers was the decisive question for

---

[55] *NSZ*, 4 Aug. 1848; *ZAVK*, 24 Aug. 1848; LAK 403 Nr. 6583 pp. 54–55, 63.

[56] The dossier on the affair is LAS H1 Nr. 1112. See esp. ff. 8–9, 12–14, 17–18, 22–23, 27–31, 67–68. A brief account in Calliess, *Militär in der Krise*, pp. 138–39.

[57] Calliess, *Militär in der Krise*, pp. 137–38; Major von Varicourt (Speyer) to General Quartier Meister Stab, 9 Aug. 1848, BHSTAM KA Nr. B735; BAF DB 54 Nr. 50 f. 9; cf. BAF DB 54 Nr. 74 f. 50; and *MZ*, 22 Oct. 1848.

the fate of the revolution. The agitation of the democrats was not without effect among the regiments raised from inhabitants of the Prussian Rhine Province. By the fall of 1848, certainly by the spring of 1849, these troops were regarded by their officers as politically unreliable, likely to mutiny if called upon to suppress an insurrection in their homeland. Since the officers were able to smash any efforts at clandestine democratic organization among the soldiers, however, this disaffection remained purely passive.

The East Elbian troops, on the other hand, especially the Thirty-Fourth Infantry Regiment from Pomerania and East and West Prussia, including many Polish-speaking soldiers, and the Twenty-Seventh from Prussian Saxony and the Old Mark, responded postively to the "agitation" of their officers, and remained firmly loyal to their king. They marched behind the black and white Prussian flag, fought it out in the taverns and the streets with civilians in Cologne, Aachen, Trier, Mainz, or Düsseldorf, and, if ordered to, used their weapons against them. Unable to rely on the native-born Rhinelanders in its ranks, the Prussian army was stretched thin in crisis situations, in November 1848 or May 1849, but, in the end, was able to hold down not just the Prussian possessions but the entire region.[58]

SPECTATORS OR PARTICIPANTS? WOMEN IN REVOLUTIONARY POLITICS

Even within the limited realm of public political participation during the *Vormärz*, women's place was especially restricted. When two steamboat loads full of Cologne's citizens set out for Düsseldorf in 1843, to praise the Provincial Diet's rejection of the government's proposed abolition of Rhenish law, a newspaper report noted that the trip was no pleasure cruise, since "no women or maidens beautified the ships; just men filled [the boats], crowded thickly, head upon head." On reaching Düsseldorf, Cologne's men marched through its streets, the sidewalks similarly lined with men, while women waved their handkerchiefs from windows and balconies. Public space and political opinions were male perogatives; women were spectators, restricted to the private sphere.[59]

Both spectators and participants in this event were probably disproportionately bourgeois, but the lower classes, whose everyday lives required women to appear regularly in public, nonetheless had similar ideas about women's

---

[58] Loyalty of different units is discussed in the sources cited in notes 53–55. On the Thirty-Fourth Infantry Regiment, cf. the account of how they got into a brawl with other soldiers upon being called "watered-down Polacks" [Wasserpolacken], *KnZ*, 4 Jan. 1849 (Beilage). For obvious reasons, most historians have not wanted to mention that some of the king of Prussia's most energetic supporters in the Rhineland during the 1848 revolution were ethnic Poles (although possibly Polish-speaking Protestants, East Prussian Masurians).

[59] Report of the event in *KnZ*, 24 June 1843 (Beilage).

place in society. When in 1832, a crowd of women and girls drove the new, rationalist priest out of his parish in Kelberg, the villagers expressed "the crazy idea, that their crime, since committed by women, was not punishable." The idea, as it turns out, was not so crazy: most of the participants in the disturbance, teenage girls, were severely beaten by their fathers. The judicial authorities accepted this private, patriarchal chastisement as appropriate punishment for the female sex, just bringing up a few of the rioters on minor charges and handing down light sentences.[60]

Although the revolutionary victories of March 1848 completely transformed the nature of participation in public life, at first glance it might seem that here, as so often the case in historical events, the changes had passed women by. I know of no instance during the revolution where women were speakers at club sessions; no women are known to have been officers of political clubs; and available club membership lists show no female names. Until May–June 1848, women were barred from even being present at mass meetings or sessions of the clubs. No woman was ever indicted for political crimes in the many trials held during and after the revolution (a handful in Aachen and Elberfeld were accused of the explicitly apolitical offense of plundering), officials regarding female political activists as ludicrous, unsexed, and pitiable, rather than threatening.[61]

There were democrats who shared these sentiments. Baker Mathias Wessel wanted all schoolmistresses fired, since they sought to turn their pupils into "lace dolls" unfit for proletarian women's true destiny, family life. The crusty persecutor of evil can easily be seen as spokesman for popular prejudice, but better-educated and more bourgeois leftists might second him in polished form. Rudolf Bamberger, brother of the Mainz democratic leader, and an activist in his own right, described the position of women in the United States, a country that he, like many Rhenish democrats, saw as a model for Germany's future:[62]

> The female sex is distinguished by the purity of its morals and lives very withdrawn; the avoidance of improper expressions in conversation with women is carried even further than in England. Women, even of the most exalted position in society, devote

[60] BM Kelberg to LR Kr. Adenau, 23 July 1832; Staatsprokurator Deuster (Kelberg) to Oberprokurator von Offen (Koblenz), 30 June 1832, both in LAK 441 Nr. 6792.

[61] Women barred: *Vbl*, 23 Apr. 1848; Seypel, "Die Demokratische Gesellschaft in Köln," pp. 123–24. Women and the law: HSTAD RA Pr. Nr. 660 ff. 119–26; Lorenz, "1848/49 im Wuppertal," p. 307; *Anklag-Akte*, pt. 2, p. 102. (Women activists just earned "mockery . . . the usual reward of persons of the female sex who leave the sphere allotted to them by nature and custom.")

[62] "Die Demokraten der nordamerikanischen Union," pt. 2, *Der Demokrat*, 17 Dec. 1848; Wessel, in *VdB*, 23 June 1849. Similar sentiments in "Ueber Gemeindeverfassung," pt. 4; and "Die Emanzipation der Frauen und ihre nothwendigen Folgen," both in *Der Demokrat*, 28 Jan., 1 Mar. 1849.

themselves entirely to house and home; men are always busy with their occupational activities. Marriages are usually happy.

Such views, however, did not represent a majority opinion. While almost never challenging the idea that women's lives should center around home and family, or that women should act as political spectators, not participants, leftists gradually came to advocate and support an expanded female public political role. In doing so, their actions corresponded to the greater self-expectations that women had developed as a result of the revolutionary events.[63]

Starting in the summer of 1848, democrats began admitting women to club sessions, reserving special front row seats for them in Mainz. Tickets for these seats were handed out free of charge before the sessions, and soon women were standing in line to obtain them. The rural mass meetings of the summer and fall of 1848 enjoyed a substantial female participation, as did at least some of the celebrations of the first anniversary of the revolution in February and March 1849. Half the participants in Cologne were women. Admittedly, organizers of this celebration waived the entrance fee for women, which does, however, show their interest in encouraging female participation.[64]

There was no inherent reason for women to be present at club sessions, revolutionary anniversaries, or mass meetings, and some still did occur without them, but there was one public festivity typical of the revolution unthinkable without female participation, indeed, requiring it by its very nature. This was the flag consecration ceremony for civic guards or gymnastics societies, at which the married women and maidens, clad in white, handed over the flag they had sewn to the men who were to use it as their banner. Such ceremonies were a public representation of idealized gender relations, the flag consecrated by women dressed in the symbol of purity, turned over to armed, uniformed men who would swear to protect them.

---

[63] In subsequent material, I am following the lead of Tübingen folklorist Carola Lipp, whose work on women's role in 1848 is by far the best on the topic. See, in particular, the collection of essays of hers and her students, *Schimpfende Weiber und patriotische Jungfrauen*, and her two excellent articles, "Bräute, Mütter, Gefährtinnen—Frauen und politische öffentlichkeit in der Revolution 1848," in *Grenzgängerinnen. Revolutionäre Frauen im 18. und 19. Jahrhundert*, ed. Helga Grubitzsch, Hannelore Cyrus, and Elke Haarbusch (Düsseldorf: Schwann, 1986), pp. 71–92, and (with Sabine Kienitz and Beate Binder), "Frauen bei Brotkrawallen, Straßentumulten und Katzenmusiken—Zum politischen Verhalten von Frauen 1847 und in der Revolution 1848/49," in *Transformationen der Arbeiterkultur*, ed. Peter Assion (Marburg: Jonas, 1987), pp. 49–60. Her suggestions, taken from research on conditions in the kingdom of Württemberg, are fully confirmed by my work on the Rhineland.

[64] *MZ*, 31 July, 10 Aug., 29 Oct. 1848, 27 Feb., 1 Mar., 12 Apr. 1849; *Vbl*, 21 July 1848, 27 Feb. 1849; *NSZ*, 14 June 1848; *KnZ*, 15 June 1848, 21 Mar. 1849; HSTAD RD Pr. Nr. 812 f. 12; Seypel, "Die Demokratische Gesellschaft in Köln," pp. 123–24; Ayçoberry, *Cologne*, p. 250; Gernert, *1848/49 im Rheinisch-Bergischen*, pp. 156–5; Illner, *Bürgerliche Organisierung*, pp. 159–60. The Mainz Citizens' Association, in contrast, refused to let women attend its sessions. Buckler, "Mainz während der Revolutionsjahre," pp. 47–48.

The democrats used these ceremonies to link public and private life, identifying political goals with an idealized family life. At its consecration ceremony, the civic guard of Neustadt a.d.W. sang of how the "people had arisen from disgrace and shame," and taken its "rights with a strong hand." Thanks to that, citizens might now carry weapons, which they would use to protect their "own hearth," their women and children, and the fatherland. This equation of freedom, citizenship, nationalism, bearing arms, and protecting women and children, was crucial to the revolution, and helps explain the anger male Rhinelanders felt when Prussian soldiers molested their women, and the political significance of the brawls and street fighting that arose from such incidents.[65]

Consecration ceremonies were the only ones at which women spoke publicly, a white-clad maiden telling the Mainz gymnasts that beneath the banner the women had consecrated for them, they were to gather as "true German men . . . who, inspired to freedom, justice and unity, will dare to do the highest and holiest deeds. . . ." In the democratic world they would create, ran the commentary of the *Mainzer Zeitung* on the ceremony, "woman will find the full recognition of her worth, of her participation in life. Ruling in the family, she will bring the influence of her feelings to bear on the outer world, on political strivings."[66]

Women became a necessary audience, before which democratic men could display their masculinity, their rhetorical skills and martial virtues. Women also acted as a representation of the goals of the revolutionary movement, a society in which domesticity might be assured. The revolution allowed women to leave the window seats and balconies, to come down to the meeting halls and speakers' tribunes, without, however, stepping out of their role as political spectators. The female private sphere was endowed with public purpose, as the democratic married women and maidens of Trier announced: "Away with servitude, begone slavery! It must be a free man who may take pride in possessing our hand, for the free man is a king of this earth and only such kings may be our spouses."[67]

Women's role as political audience was not limited to carefully planned ceremonies but was expressed spontaneously in the streets. When the police arrested a Bernkastel democratic leader, the women of the town gathered and demanded that the men free him by force. Similarly, in the street fighting between the crowd and the civic guard of Mainz and the Prussian troops of the fortress in May 1848, the women at first encouraged the inhabitants of Mainz

---

[65] Gendarmerie Brigadier Baerde (Neustadt) to Gendarmerie Commando der Pfalz (Speyer), 16 July 1848, BHSTAM MInn Nr. 30676.

[66] *MZ*, 17 Aug. 1848. Similar festivities: *NSZ*, 27 Nov. 1848 (Beilage); *MZ*, 29 Aug. 1848. A detailed discussion of the symbolism of such ceremonies in Lipp, "Bräute, Mütter, Gefährtinnen."

[67] *Vbl*, 18 June 1848.

to attack the Prussians, supporting their efforts with stones and bricks thrown from windows. Then, when the Prussians threatened to bombard the city, they rushed out into the streets and dragged their men home.[68]

For all the public nature of these activities, they involved a reaffirmation of the primacy of the private sphere, of home and family, in women's social condition. The two prominent femninists among the Rhenish democrats, the energetic Mathilde Franziska Anneke, editor of the *Neue Kölnische Zeitung*, and Kathinka Zitz, estranged wife of Mainz democratic leader Franz Zitz, active as a journalist for the Mainz Democratic Club's newsletter, *Der Demokrat*, shared these sentiments. Both denounced women who smoked cigars and wore men's clothing, such as the notorious novelist George Sand, and insisted that women's emancipation did not mean equality with men. Rather, it would create a realm of family life determined by love and mutual affection, not by male tyranny (and, of course, men who were not tyrants at home could only be found in the ranks of free, democratic citizens), the demands of social convention, or material necessity—something Mathilda Anneke knew about from personal experience, since her loveless first marriage had been arranged to pay her father's debts.[69]

The idea of feminism as the abolition of separate spheres, as women's equal right to participation in public life, a doctrine already well articulated in mid-nineteenth-century North America, was rarely to be found in the Rhineland at that time. One male democrat supported female suffrage as appropriate to women's domestic role, suggesting that preventing women from voting was as unjust as prohibiting them from "cooking, sewing, knitting, darning, dancing and playing." Endorsing a proposal to allow property-owning widows to vote for the newly created Rhine-Hessian provincial parliament, he admitted that universal female suffrage was not at the moment on the political agenda. However, if one looked at the history of Jewish emancipation—during the Middle Ages locked up in ghettos, Jews were now deputies to the National Assembly, or elected mayor of Worms—then one never knew what the future might hold in store for women.[70]

---

[68] *NRhZ*, 28 July 1848; *Vbl*, 26 May 1848.

[69] The best account of Mathilde Anneke's life remains Wilhelm Schulte's biography of her husband, "Fritz Anneke, ein Leben für die Freiheit." Maria Wagner, *Mathilde Franziska Anneke in Selbstzeugnissen und Dokumenten* (Frankfurt a.M.: Fischer Taschenbuch, 1980), is primarily useful for its documentation, largely on Anneke's feminist activities as an émigrée in the United States. For Kathinka Zitz, see the article on her in *Allgemeine Deutsche Biographie* 45:373–79; and the essay of Stanley Zucker, "Female Political Opposition in pre-1848 Germany. The Role of Kathinka Zitz-Halein," in *German Women in the Nineteenth Century: A Social History*, ed. John C. Fout (New York and London: Holmes & Meier, 1984), pp. 133–50. Anneke's and Zitz's views on women's emancipation can be found in "Für Frauen," *NKZ*, 15 Mar. 1849; and "Ueber Frauenemanzipation," *MZ*, 20–22 Apr. 1849.

[70] Johann Sponagel, "Die Emanzipation der Frauen und ihre nothwendigen Folgerungen," *Der Demokrat*, 11 Feb. 1849.

When the Cologne fortress authorities prohibited the *Neue Kölnische Zeitung* in September 1848, and ordered the arrest of one of its ostensible editors, Friedrich von Beust (the other, Friedrich Anneke, was already in jail), Mathilde Anneke announced to the subscribers that she, a woman, would step into the male places of her husband and his friend and edit a replacement, the *Women's Newspaper* [Die Frauen-Zeitung]: "Content yourselves with it, as long as it lasts . . . [afterwards] I will retire with it from the public arena, to which necessity has called me, and return to the quiet domestic sphere, for then, with much greater strength, will return: the *Neue Kölnische Zeitung.*" Since, as everyone knew, Mathilde Anneke was the real editor of the *Neue Kölnische Zeitung*, she was, in this announcement, playing with the concept of separate spheres, using it to mock the military authorities who had prohibited male citizens from exercising their rights to a free press.[71]

The one popular initiative to break out of the realm of domestic life came from the market-wives of Bretzenheim, a truck farmers' village near Mainz. They founded a "reading circle" [Lesekränzchen], gathering regularly to hear one of their number read aloud the democratic *Mainzer Zeitung*. Compared with editing a newspaper or demanding the right to vote, this may seem like a modest measure, but the implication contained in this gathering, that ordinary women—peasant women at that—had a legitimate interest in public affairs, was the one example of the revolutionary ideal of citizenship, of popular participation in public life, extended to the female sex.[72]

The democrats' revolutionary ideas were certainly not directed toward the overthrow of patriarchal authority. If anything, their basic socioeconomic and political ideals—a society made up of small-producing households, each led by an adult male, a citizenry of armed men, protecting their rights and their women—looked toward a reformulation and reestablishment of patriarchy in society. Social and political relations were to be drastically transformed, so that gender relations might remain the same.

Yet these attitudes about women were hardly limited to democrats. All political tendencies shared a common patriarchal point of view—as did the women of the time. Within this commonly accepted opinion, democrats offered women the greatest space for public political participation precisely by linking the separate spheres of domestic, female contentedness and public, male politics. Compared with future attitudes, it was a very modest step toward women's participation in public life, but it was the first example of its kind in Central Europe.

---

[71] Advertisement in the *KnZ*, 28 Sept. 1848 (Beilage). Several conservative women promptly turned the argument on Mathilde Anneke, telling her if she wished to act in public, she should do the feminine thing and open a child care center, rather than engaging in revolutionary agitation. Ibid., 29 Sept. 1848 (Erste Beilage).

[72] *MZ*, 20 Mar. 1849.

CHAPTER SEVEN

The Democratic Movement in State and Society

THE Rhenish democrats of 1848–1849 aspired to a drastic reshaping of the institutions of state and society; this chapter will be devoted to exploring these goals of the democratic movement and the means by which its adherents hoped to bring them about. In doing this, I will pay less attention to the details of printed political programs or to considerations of intellectual consistency and more to the popular expression of political ideas and to the interaction of the democrats' demands with the positions of other political groups and the actions of the state authorities and the clergy. Although democrats differed among themselves substantially over both means and ends—differences that will be discussed below—their aspirations nonetheless possessed some common characteristics. If any one document sums them up, it might be this description of the standard speech at meetings of the democratic club of Emmerich, given by the town's mayor:

> Reproach of the previous measures of the government, oppression of the poorer class, insufficient taxation of the well-to-do, censure of state officials, the city council and the mayor, all of which leading up to the assurance that things must necessarily change and would change if only everyone would show the good will they [the audience] had. Therefore they should join together ever more tightly and it would not be long until the aristocracy was vanquished, etc.

The mayor's hostile pocket summary points out several key features of democratic ideology: an attack on state authority and those who exercised it, along with an airing of social grievances, tied in, via the burdens of fiscality, with the hostility towards the state. These circumstances called for radical, if unspecified, changes in state and society. A clue to the direction of these changes is in the last line of the quote, with its talk of vanquishing the aristocracy, a piece of political rhetoric taken from the great French Revolution. The evening following one such speech, a number of those who had heard it marched through the streets shouting, "Long live the republic," suggesting it was the Jacobin version of that tradition to which they had been exposed.[1]

[1] HSTAD RD Nr. 8806 ff. 178–82.

DEMOCRATS AND THE STATE

The democrats themselves regarded the assertion of "popular sovereignty" [Volkssouveränität] or of the "rule of the people" [Volksherrschaft] as the essential feature of their movement. Constitutional and lawmaking power was to be the exclusive prerogative of an assembly chosen by the direct vote of all adult males. The Cologne democrats' election program of April 1848 began with an invocation of popular sovereignty, as did the founding session, one month later, of the Mainz Democratic Club. The principle made frequent appearances in speeches at mass rallies and club meetings, in the lead articles of democratic newspapers, and at toasts given during revolutionary banquets.[2]

Such popular sovereignty was to be expressed in all aspects of government, beginning with the commune, that is, the rural or urban municipality. Democrats wished to see village and city councils chosen by universal manhood suffrage, and meeting in public sessions, thus open to the people's scrutiny. The council's power to elect a municipal executive and to administer communal property was to be unhindered by state authority. Demands for this were an important aspect of left-wing political programs, a frequent source of petition drives and political campaigns.[3]

Like most theoretical aspects of the politics of Rhenish democrats, this one had a practical application. Local authorities, with their communal police power, could make life difficult for the democrats. In Rhine-Hessen and the Palatinate, where many village and small-town mayors were sympathetic to the left, indeed, even local leaders of it, they could help turn their municipalities into strongholds of the movement.[4]

In large cities and manufacturing regions, where mass unemployment re-

[2] In general, on the importance of popular sovereignty for German democrats in 1848–1849, see Paschen, *Demokratische Vereine*, pp. 39, 63; Wolfram Siemann, *Die deutsche Revolution von 1848/49* (Frankfurt a.M.: Suhrkamp, 1985), p. 100. Expressions of this among Rhenish democrats: Seypel, "Die Demokratische Gesellschaft in Köln," pp. 101–06; Körner, *Lebenskämpfe* 2:38–39; Illner, *Bürgerliche Organisierung*, pp. 159–60; Stahl, *1848/49 an der Mittelmosel*, p. 16; *NRhZ*, 12 Nov. 1848 (lead article); *NKZ*, 2 Mar. 1849; *ZAVK*, 21 May 1848; *MZ*, 17 Apr. 11, 17 May, 13, 29 Aug., 1 Oct., 29 Nov. 1848; *Der Demokrat*, 14 May, 25 June, 2, 9 July, 8 Oct., 10 Dec. 1848, 18 Mar. 1849; *Vbl*, 26 Apr., 9 July 1848, 20–21 Mar. 1849; *NSZ*, 19 May, 14 June, 3, 13 July, 16 Aug. 1848; *RhBA* 2/2, Nrs. 77, 121; LAS J1 Nr. 240 ff. 8–9; BM Tries to LR Kr. Cochem, 3 Nov. 1848, LAK 441 Nr. 12929.

[3] Seypel, "Die Demokratische Gesellschaft in Köln," pp. 135–37 (best study of the topic); HSTAD RD Pr. Nr. 794 ff. 171–72; *Vbl*, 25 June 1848; *MZ*, 15 Aug. 1848, 7 Apr. 1849; *Der Demokrat*, 30 Apr. 1848, 7, 14 Jan., 1849; LAS J1 Nr. 244 ff. 8–9; see also Chapter Six, notes 41–42.

[4] *MZ*, 8, 19 Aug. 1848, 19 Jan., 1 Feb., 1, 9, 14, 16, 20 Mar., 7 Apr. 1849; BAF FN 7 Anhang 4 Gagern ff. 71–96; *NSZ*, 29 Oct. 1848 (Beilage), 4, 10 Jan., 4 Mar., 9 Apr., 12 May 1849; ex-RP Alwens to Gesammt-Staats-Ministerium, 20 Aug. 1849, BHSTAM MInn Nr. 45533; LAS J1 Nr. 249 (alt) f. 327.

mained a serious problem throughout the revolution, the municipality was the main source of public works projects. Democrats never tired of demanding that these projects be maintained and expanded. Such agitation was the chief way that leftists reached unskilled laborers, who were well represented among the unemployed but rarely to be found in democratic clubs or even workers' associations. The political importance of such efforts can be seen in Düsseldorf, where the workers of the municipal public works projects became supporters of the left, carrying the red flag in demonstrations, and mounting the barricades in May 1849, while the waterfront laborers, under the influence of the bridgekeeper Stephan Kuhl, ostensibly a leftist, but actually a secret agent of the district governor, remained politically passive.[5]

Popular sovereignty also applied to the armed forces. The call for a reduction in standing armies and their replacement by a popular militia, the "arming of the people," was a staple of political programs in the spring of 1848, advocated by constitutional monarchists, Catholic-clericals, and democrats alike. It was the democrats, though, who took the right to bear arms seriously, demanding that the civic guard replace the military of garrison towns in its tasks of occupying the city walls and gates and patrolling the streets. Democrats saw the civic guards not as a property owners' security force under the control of the authorities, but as a self-governing citizens' army, which could defend popular sovereignty against state authorities unwilling to recognize it. This was easily translated into practice in many towns of the southern Rhineland, where such armed corps were under the control of the left from the outbreak of the revolution; elsewhere, democrats encouraged their supporters to join the guards, and campaigned to have new officers elected who would view the forces in such a light. The democrats' enemies regarded these activities as preparation for a potential insurrection, but one man's insurrection was another's defense of popular sovereignty.[6]

---

[5] On public works projects, and democratic agitation concerning them, see Seypel, "Die Demokratische Gesellschaft in Köln," pp. 135–37; Lorenz, "1848/49 im Wuppertal," pp. 150–53, 184–88; Nießner, Aachen, pp. 94, 97; RhBA 2/2, Nrs. 39, 62, 73, 79; LAK 441 Nr. 1330 pp. 147–60, 447–58; NRhZ, 1 Aug. 1848. For the situation in Düsseldorf, Lenger, Zwischen Kleinbürgertum und Proletariat, pp. 163, 203; ZSTAM Rep. 77 Tit. 505 Nr. 3 Vol. 4ff. 248–53; HSTAD RD Nr. 200 pp. 119–21, 216–21, 263–65, 275, 281–90, 323–27, 341–47, 360–62, 365–66. District Governor von Spiegel kept Kuhl's role so secret that following Spiegel's death, Kuhl was dismissed from his government post as bridgekeeper for his left-wing activities during the revolution. A fair-minded reading of the transcript of his administrative hearing (HSTAD RD Nr. 199–200), however, supports Kuhl's contention that he was a secret agent, although he probably acted from mercenary, and not, as he claimed, Prussian loyalist motives.

[6] Kühn, Der junge Hermann Becker, pp. 186, 188–89, 236–37; Seypel, "Die Demokratische Gesellschaft in Köln," pp. 264–70, 308–310; HSTAD RD Nr. 200 pp. 169–72; HSTAD RD Pr. Nr. 812 ff. 34–39; Körner, Lebenskämpfe 1:425–26; LAK 441 Nr. 1330 pp. 345–59; HSTAD RD Nr. 8809 ff. 8–12; NRhZ, 1 June 1848; Vbl, 13, 18, 20 Aug. 1848; Uhrig, "Worms," pp. 58–59, 80–81; LAS H3 Nr. 154b f. 192; LAS J1 Nr. 215 (alt) ff. 51–60, 509; LAS J1 Nr. 267 ff. 133–

Rhenish democrats advocated the rule of the people within the individual German states, supporting the claims to power and authority of the Prussian National Assembly in Berlin against the assertions of monarchical authority, demanding, in vain, the calling of constituent assemblies in both Bavaria and Hessen-Darmstadt. Popular sovereignty was above all to be expressed at the national level, Rhenish democrats accepting the notion, first formulated in 1789 and reiterated throughout the nineteenth century, that the sovereign people constituted itself as a nation. When leftists talked about national politics, they spent most of their time denouncing in no uncertain terms the parliament that claimed to embody popular sovereignty, the Frankfurt National Assembly. They did so because, in their eyes, the assembly refused to act in sovereign fashion, electing an imperial regent not responsible to it, and refusing in critical circumstances to assert its authority over the individual German states. The moderate to conservative majority of the Frankfurt deputies, the democrats asserted, were ''not doing their duty'' or, more bluntly, were ''traitors to the people'' [Volksverräther], renouncing their vocation as representatives of the sovereign will of the nation. Democrats wavered between demanding that the deputies of the left walk out of such a self-degrading assembly and demanding that they continue to work within it, as the only existing institution of national unity, however wretched it was—a vacillation shared by the leftist deputies themselves.[7]

The feebleness of the Frankfurt parliament was just one further proof to the democrats that the revolutionary changes of March 1848 had not brought about the rule of the people. Power still lay in the hands of the princes, the military, and state officials, whom the democrats denounced as oppressors and thieves in an extraordinary array of colorful and violent invective. At the New Year's festivities of the Mainz Democratic Club, Ludwig Bamberger attacked ''the tyranny of state officials, their endless red tape [Schlendrian], the pernicious poison in the German states.'' Julius Wulff, Düsseldorf democrat and associate of Karl Marx, told a meeting of the People's Club that the March revolution of 1848 had left ''state officials and other thieves [Gesindel] still in charge''; the founding prospectus of the Worms democratic newspaper spoke of the ''venality and corruptibility of a degenerate caste of officials.'' A democrat in the southern Palatine village of Oberotterbach told a tax collector who

---

34; LAS J1 Nr. 243 (alt) ff. 74–78; LAS J1 Nr. 205 ff. 317–21; sources cited in Chapter Four, notes 79–81.

[7] HSTAD RD Nr. 8804 ff. 16–17, 29–34; HSTAD RD Pr. Nr. 812 ff. 44–45; BM Tries to LR Kr. Cochem, 3 Nov. 1848, LAK 441 Nr. 12929; *Vbl* 13 Aug., 27 Sept. 1848; HSTAD RD Nr. 200 pp. 181–83, 205–07, 229; *NRhZ*, 1 June, 12 Nov. 1848, 26 Jan. 1849; *NKZ*, 4 Apr. 1849; Gernert, *1848/49 im Rheinisch-Bergischen*, p. 109; *KnZ*, 23 June 1848; *MZ*, 29 Aug., 6 Sept., 11 Oct. 1848; *Der Demokrat*, 18 Mar. 1849; Katz-Seibert, *Radikalismus in Hessen*, pp. 47–48; *NSZ*, 1, 14, 30 June, 3, 13–14 July, 8, 15 Aug. (Beilage), 1 Oct. (Beilage) 1848, 7, 12 Jan. 1849; LAS J1 Nr. 244 ff. 8–9; RP to MInn, 11 Oct. 1848, BHSTAM MInn Nr. 46129; Strey and Winkler, *Marx und Engels 1848/49*, pp. 28–37.

had been opposing the leftists that he was a thief, like the princes and most officials, all of whom belonged in hell. Democrats called for the abolition of the "standing army of soldiers and officials"—a popular phrase, frequently reiterated. They made it clear that the Germans, like "all free peoples, should not allow the violence of state officials and the power of the police to arbitrarily restrict their political movements." To that end, democratic clubs would form a "standing army of freedom against any attack or usurpation of forces hostile to the people."[8]

The Cochem democratic leader Hugo Keiffenheimer neatly connected bureaucratic oppression, the burdens of taxation, the failures of constitutional monarchist politics, and the advocacy of popular sovereignty in a speech given in the marketplace of the Moselle village of Tries. He told the vintners:[9]

> [T]he princes and high state officials squander the large quantities of money raised in taxes; the king alone needs 2 million yearly from which 10,000 families could live. The taxes are unjustly assessed, the people too oppressed and things must be better; the laws must come from the people. The military, which costs 30 million, is unnecessary and consists mostly of idle strollers. The Frankfurt National Assembly is not doing its duty.

This hostility was expressed explicitly against the soldiers, officials, and princes of the three core states to which the Rhenish provinces belonged. A campaign of Rhine-Hessian democrats for the calling of a Hessian constituent assembly ended in an orgy of conflict between inhabitants of the core state and its Rhenish province when a mass march on Darmstadt by Rhine-Hessians in July 1848 to press this demand was broken up by inhabitants of the capital city. Wearing cornflowers as a sign of "true-blue" loyalty to the royal house, and fearing for the future of the grand-ducal court and their livelihoods, they assaulted the Rhenish demonstrators and drove them out of town.[10]

In this spirit of provincial hostility, the democrats of Rhine-Hessen launched a massive campaign to boycott the paper money issued by the Darmstadt government. To be sure, they had good economic reasons, since the notes' value was not guaranteed by the Hessian treasury and Frankfurt bankers would only accept them at a deep discount. Mainz democrats, however, chose to see the issuance of the notes as part of a broader policy of "impoverishment of a province . . . through bad government measures and oppressions of many

[8] Quotations: *MZ*, 8 Aug. 1848, 4 Jan., 12 Apr. 1849; *Der Demokrat*, 9 July 1848; HSTAD RD Pr. Nr. 812 ff. 44–45; BAF ZSg 8/55 f. 74; LAS J1 Nr. 178 ff. 213–14. Similarly: *MZ*, 31 July, 1848, 20 Feb. 1849; *Vbl*, 16 July 1848; Noack, "1848/49 in der Saargegend," pp. 127–28; *NRhZ*, 9 Aug. 1848, 19 Jan. 1849; *VdB*, 17 Feb., 7 Apr. 1849, and passim; LAS J1 Nr. 267 ff. 157–66; ZSTAM Rep. 77 CCXLV Nr. 4 ff. 88–89; *RhBA* 2/2, Nrs. 279, 336; LAK 442 Nr. 6388 pp. 201–202; LAK 442 Nr. 6506 ff. 30–31; LAS J1 Nr. 205 ff. 680–82.

[9] BM Tries to LR Kr. Cochem, 3 Nov. 1848, LAK 441 Nr. 12929.

[10] *Der Demokrat*, 30 July, 6 Aug. 1848; *MZ*, 11, 31 July 1848.

different kinds . . . ,'' including the stationing of Prussian troops at the request of Darmstadt and the Provisional German Central Government and the drafting of the young men of Rhine-Hessen into the prince's army.[11]

Such sentiments were stronger in the Palatinate. Even the *Neue Speyerer Zeitung*, the most moderate of the major democratic newspapers in the Rhineland, mocked official fears that Bavaria's uniqueness would be destroyed by French-style centralization in a unified German state. The journal acerbicly pointed out that most of the monarchy's subjects, Franconians, Swabians, and Palatines, were not Bavarians, and that Bavaria had only maintained its independent existence over the previous century by opposing German nationalism and kowtowing to French interests. If the moderate democrats spoke that way, radical Palatines were a good deal more forthright. A radical from the northeastern town Grünstadt told peasants in the vicinity that "our province [Land] has been milked and exploited by the king long enough." Democrats in the northwestern town of Lauterecken menaced a tax collector who had dared to hang out a Bavarian flag on the day of the elections to the Frankfurt National Assembly; in the southeastern village of Rheinzabern, they threatened the gendarme for months about the lion, the Bavarian insignia, he wore on his cap.[12]

Palatine leftists took their anti-Bavarian attitudes with them into the broader democratic movement. After affiliating with the Central March Association, the provincial committee of the Palatine People's Associations refused to recognize the Munich March Association's claim to be the leading branch of the group in the Bavarian kingdom. The Palatines had affiliated with the national left-wing organization to escape Bavarian rule, not to submit to it.[13]

These hostilities pale before the ones expressed in the Prussian Rhine Province. As Friedrich Engels told the provincial democratic congress, "The character trait of the Rhineland is hatred of Prussianism, especially the Prussianism of the state officials [Beamten- und Stockpreußentum]; this sentiment will, hopefully, continue." It did, the democratic club in Xanten celebrating the first anniversary of the March 1848 revolution in a room graced with a poster showing the Prussian eagle on the gallows. Democratic mass rallies were not complete without at least one speaker attacking Prussia, such as the Düsseldorf laborer who bore the red flag in the parade to the nearby village of Gerresheim and then spoke at the meeting, "cursing the Prussian [royal] house and officials in the crudest way." At the same end of the political spectrum, although the opposite end of the literary one, was Karl Marx in the *Neue Rheinische*

---

[11] *MZ*, 3 Mar. 1849; *Der Demokrat*, 25 Mar. 1849.

[12] *NSZ*, 11 June 1848; LAS J1 Nr. 235 ff. 134–36; LAS J1 Nr. 263 f. 220. Similarly, LAS J1 Nr. 195 ff. 18–21; LAS J1 Nr. 264 ff. 44–66; Police Commissioner Neustadt to LK Neustadt, 25 Apr. 1849, BHSTAM MInn Nr. 45531. As will be seen in Chapters Ten and Eleven, the Palatine uprising of May–June 1849 was accompanied by an orgy of destruction of symbols of Bavarian sovereignty.

[13] LAS J1 Nr. 244 f. 151.

Zeitung, whose sarcastic and intellectualized attacks on the Prussian state, its monarch, officials, soldiers, laws, and institutions, drove the authorities to a fury and led some NCOs to break into his house and threaten to let their soldiers loose on him.[14]

Democrats in the Prussian Rhine Province and in those cities in Rhine-Hessen with a Prussian garrison, constantly played on popular opposition to the rule of the monarchy and its civilian and military officials, with the result that the crowd, at least in predominantly Catholic areas not well disposed to Prussian rule to begin with, was constantly alert to this topic. The behavior of soldiers and officers, waving the black-white flag and making such statements as "We're no Germans, we're Prussians," only added fuel to the fire. Members of the crowd responded with traditional epithets, such as "stinking Prussians," "Prussian bums in rags" [Lumpenpreußen], and "hungry Prussians"—the last two implicitly pointing out the poverty of the core provinces of the monarchy and the higher taxes paid by the more affluent Rhinelanders to support them. The crowd had a new insult in 1848–1849, a two-line bit of doggerel, whose mass shouting preceded brawls with soldiers and moments of insurrection. The verse had several different variants, one of which went, "Liberty, equality republic/If we were just rid of the Prussians." Democratic ideals simultaneously expressed confessional and regional hostilities.[15]

THE STATE AND THE DEMOCRATS

The democrats' emnity toward the three core states reflected decades of accumulated grievances against authoritarian rule, but the attitudes of the provincial representatives of the liberal March ministries did little to placate the hostility of the left and much to inflame it. The new German governments largely retained their former senior provincial administrators. While the Prussian district governors in Aachen and Cologne were replaced in March 1848 with moderate liberals (both the new men were, additionally, nominal, if not especially devout, Roman Catholics), the district governors of Düsseldorf and Koblenz, as well as the provincial governor, all remained at their posts. The liberal Trier district governor Rudolf von Auerswald was appointed to the in-

---

[14] Quotations: *RhBA* 2/2, Nrs. 215, 279; similarly, ibid., Nr. 250; *KnZ*, 6 July, 27 Aug. 1848; HSTAD RD Pr. Nr. 812 ff. 44–45; *ZAVK*, 13, 30 July 1848; *FBA*, 26 Oct. 1848; *NKZ*, 1 Mar. 1849; *NRhZ*, 12 Sept., 17 Nov., 15–16, 20 Dec. 1848, 19 Jan., 17–18 Mar. (Zweite Ausgabe), 1 Apr. 1849, and passim; LAK 403 Nr. 6583 pp. 76–84; attacks on the bureaucracy, sources cited in note 9. On the authorities' attitude toward Marx, see LAK 403 Nr. 7152 pp. 5–6; and Kühn, *Der junge Hermann Becker*, pp. 229–32.

[15] For confrontations between Prussian soldiers and civilians, see sources cited in Chapter Six, note 52; examples of curses and epithets, *KnZ*, 20 Aug. 1848; Kühn, *Der junge Hermann Becker*, pp. 201, 205; HSTAD RD Pr. Nr. 812 ff. 19–20, 34–39; ZSTAM Rep. 77 Tit. 505 Nr. 3 Vol. 4 ff. 248–53; LAK 403 Nr. 6583 p. 56; Fischer, *Kreis Jülich*, p. 18. In German, the verse ran "Freiheit, Gleichheit Republik [or sometimes, Hoch lebe die Republik]/Wären wir nur die Preußen quitt."

terior ministry, but this liberalization of the Prussian monarchy was not re-flected in the Rhineland: Auerswald's eventual successor in Trier, the district councillor Karl Friedrich Sebaldt, was known as a brutal and authoritarian bureaucrat.[16]

A number of the leading military commands in the Prussian Rhine Province were also reshuffled. Most important was the transfer in April 1848 of the commandant of the Cologne fortress, Lieutenant General Karl Wilhelm von Safft, who had striven, largely successfully, to avoid clashes between troops and civilians and had recognized the importance and authority of the new civic guard. A formal successor to Safft was never named, and the deputy fortress commandant, Colonel Karl Engels, an energetic individual and eminently po-litical officer, emerged as the strong man of the forces of repression in the Rhenish metropolis.[17]

The March ministries in Bavaria and Hessen-Darmstadt acted similarly. The Palatine provincial governor Franz Alwens, known even in the *Vormärz* as a moderate liberal, retained his office. The provincial government of Rhine-Hessen was reorganized, ostensibly to make it more responsive to the citizenry of that province, but the appointment of a new provincial governor in August 1848 hardly confirmed these motives. Reichard Karl Friedrich Freiherr von Dalwigk, had, as *Vormärz* county commissioner in Worms, developed such a reputation for repression and authoritarianism that even constitutional monar-chists found it impossible to support him, to say nothing of the democrats. He did eventually leave his post, but only because he was appointed prime min-ister, leading Hessen-Darmstadt into an era of reaction and counterrevolu-tion.[18]

Unlike high-ranking army officers, or members of the "camarilla" at the Prussian royal court, who conspired against the liberal government from the moment of its appointment, the leading state officials in the three Rhenish provinces were loyal supporters of the March ministries. They conscientiously carried out the formerly oppositional doctrine of constitutional monarchism, now that it was official state policy, but they did so in their accustomed, *Vor-märz* authoritarian manner, this political style weighing heavily on the activi-ties of the new governments' supporters and opponents.[19]

---

[16] Information about changes in the leading personnel of the administration of the Prussian Rhine Province is conveniently summarized in documents and editorial notes of *RhBA* 2/1:700–01; *RhBA* 2/2:14 n.3, 31–32, 87–88. I am aware of no politically motivated changes in the next level of Prussian administrators, the county commissioners.

[17] Seypel, "Die Demokratische Gesellschaft in Köln," p. 256; *RhBA* 2/2, Nrs. 166, 176, and p. 440 n.4, are just a few documents giving a good example of Colonel Engels's prominent role in political repression.

[18] Schindler, "Franz Alwens"; Uhrig, "Worms," pp. 67–68, "Reichard Karl Friedrich Frei-herr von Dalwigk," *Allgemeine Deutsche Biographie* (Nachtrag) 47:612–15.

[19] On bureaucratic opposition to the new liberal regimes, cf. Valentin, *Geschichte der deutschen Revolution* 2:231–33; Siemann, *Die deutsche Revolution von 1848/49*, pp. 79–80.

The primary concern of the state authorities during the elections of May 1848 was the selection of supporters of constitutional monarchist doctrines. When constitutional monarchist political clubs, usually known as "citizens' associations" [Bürgervereine], were organized, officials joined in substantial numbers. It may have been a rhetorical exaggeration when a Düsseldorf democrat described his city's constitutional monarchist association as consisting of "25 officers, 3 princes, 3 or 4 clergymen, 6 to 8 gendarmes, 20 tax collectors . . . the others bourgeois." Such groups were, however, often known as "state officials' clubs" [Beamtenvereine], and the 10 percent of the membership of the Worms or Mainz civic associations consisting of army officers and civilian state officials, usually senior ones, suggests that the formerly oppositional movement had now obtained a strongly official character.[20]

Democrats, on the other hand, were treated in ways more reminiscent of *Vormärz* authoritarianism. The authorities disciplined any state official or soldier who joined a democratic club and placed the clubs' meetings under surveillance by uniformed police or secret informants. Indeed, the only real issue open to debate was whether organized democracy could be a tolerated enemy of the state, or whether it should be prohibited outright.[21]

The issue was joined early in the revolution, one example being the response to an address of Düsseldorf democrats issued at the end of May 1848 to the Berlin National Assembly, calling on it to hold fast to the "rights and freedoms of the people," even if they were incompatible with the "monarchical principle." The district authorities promptly denounced the "criminal tendency" of the address, and demanded that the judiciary prosecute its authors. Asked for his advice, the city's mayor replied that a more effective way to fight such criminal behavior would be for the authorities to support the constitutional monarchist citizens' association currently being formed in Düsseldorf.[22]

The first response might be described as a maximalist official position: Democracy, that is, the rule of the people, was incompatible with monarchy, even in its constitutional form. All democrats were, at least implicitly, republicans, and a republican form of government in Germany could come into

---

[20] On official attitudes to the elections, cf. *RhBA* 2/2, Nrs. 16, 24, 38, 42–43, 45, 52, 64, 81; and sources cited in Chapter Four, notes 100, 103; for Düsseldorf, Mainz, and Worms, see *RhBA* 2/2, Nr. 215; Pauly, "Vereine der Stadt Mainz," pp. 77–78; Uhrig, "Worms," pp. 53–57. Similarly in Cologne, Koblenz, Bonn, Schleiden, Trier, and Saarbrücken, Seypel, "Die Demokratische Gesellschaft in Köln," pp. 220–26; LAK 403 Nr. 7045 pp. 77–96, 115–22, 149–62; *Vbl*, 25 Mar. 1849; LAK 403 Nr. 9671 pp. 489–93; elsewhere in Germany, Gebhardt, *Revolution und liberale Bewegung*, p. 165.

[21] *RhBA* 2/2, Nrs. 194, 209; HSTAD RD Nr. 200 pp. 117–21, 200–02, 208–11, 365–66; HSTAD RD Pr Nr. 795 ff. 195–210; LAK 403 Nr. 9632 pp. 18–21; LAK 403 Nr. 17332 ff. 140–46, 325–26; *NKZ*, 15 Apr. 1849; *Der Demokrat*, 13 Aug. 1848; LAS J1 Nr. 104 ff. 44–56; *NSZ*, 8 Aug. 1848.

[22] HSTAD RD Nr. 8804 ff. 16–20.

existence only by the violent overthrow of the existing system of constitutional monarchy. Advocating democracy was thus illegal, and even if democrats proclaimed that they would strive to obtain their ends exclusively in peaceful, legal, parliamentary fashion, they were dissembling, such a declaration merely "the usual trick of indirect provocation."[23]

Officials taking this view believed that democratic clubs, newspapers, and political agitation all should be prohibited; expediency was the sole ground for their toleration. Any speech in favor of the republic and against the monarchy rendered the orator liable to arrest; flying the red flag, or even wearing red ribbons, was to be prohibited as symbolic advocacy of a democratic republic. Mass meetings of the democrats, by their very nature, contributed to disorder and created circumstances harmful to the constitution; they were therefore not to be held. Democratic clubs were liable to closure; their leaders, to arrest.[24]

In principle, the government in Munich was the leading exponent of the hard line, in August 1848 issuing a prohibition of democratic clubs in Bavaria. At least in the Palatinate, Bavarian practice was by no means so harsh. Some democratic clubs were investigated, and their leaders were briefly arrested. None was ever prohibited, and the provincial authorities exempted the many branches of the People's Associations from the decree.[25]

Prussia presents the opposite picture, most officials believing democratic groups were not a priori illegal, but those who did vigorous in their persecution of the left. One of their favorite targets was the Cologne Workers' Association, all of whose presidents fell afoul of the law. Andreas Gottschalk was arrested in July 1848. A warrant was issued in September for his successor, the watchmaker Joseph Moll, which Moll evaded by fleeing the country. The next two presidents of the group, Karl Marx and, following him, Marx's political associate, the veteran revolutionary Karl Schapper, were both expelled from Prussia in the spring of 1849. Although legal reasons were always proffered, it is hard to avoid the impression that many Cologne authorities, including the police commissioner and the acting fortress commandant, thought the group, in view of both its organization of the lower classes and the openly republican views it espoused, had no right to exist.

Gottschalk's arrest was a particularly blatant act of repression, given his strict adherence to nonviolence and the use of his considerable influence on the workers toward this end. None of this was a secret to the authorities, and

[23] Quotation, LAK 403 Nr. 6583 pp. 74–75.

[24] For examples of this point of view, see LAK 442 Nr. 7853 pp. 91–113; HSTAD RD Pr. Nr. 812 ff. 46–58, 175–76; BAF FN 7 Gagern Anhang 4 ff. 85–88; and *MZ*, 1 Aug. 1848; MInn to King, 5 Aug. 1848, BHSTAM MInn Nr. 46129; LAS H3 Nr. 154b ff. 88–89; *RhBA* 2/2, Nrs. 166, 172, 176; Dowe, *Aktion und Organisation*, p. 176.

[25] For the Bavarian state policy, see Botzenhart, *Deutscher Parlamentarismus*, p. 348; on its execution in the Palatinate, cf. MInn to King, 5 Aug. 1848, BHSTAM MInn Nr. 46129; LAS H3 Nr. 154b ff. 88–89; LAS J1 Nr. 203 ff. 223–46; BAF DB Nr. 54 ff. 17–18.

the only reliable piece of evidence they had against Gottschalk was his having addressed a General Assembly of the Workers' Association with the words "Citizens, republicans." Confronted with this accusation in his interrogation by the police commissioner, Gottschalk replied, "I was, so it seems, under the pleasant illusion that freedom of the press, or at least freedom of speech exists," to which the official fired back, "The misuse of these [rights] can not be permitted and you have created a threatening state of excitement [Aufregung] in this city."[26]

The bureaucratic moderates shared their hard line counterparts' opinion about the incompatibility of democracy and constitutional monarchy, but saw no legal means to prohibit the left out of hand, as long as its adherents avoided violence or its advocacy in their political activities. This opinion does not mean that the moderates were ready to tolerate indefinitely an organized democracy. As the patient Düsseldorf district governor von Spiegel explained, "Quiet will only return when it is possible to issue a general prohibition of all the [democratic clubs] in a legal way." In other words, legislation was needed restricting freedom of press, association, and speech to monarchists, a proposal neatly blending constitutionalist practice with absolutist spirit.[27]

In the summer of 1848, drafts of laws to that end circulated in Berlin ministries and in the offices of the Provisional German Central Power in Frankfurt. They were never presented for legislative action, the Prussian government reluctantly concluding they would have no chance of passing the Prussian National Assembly. The government of Hessen-Darmstadt was fully convinced of the need for a legislative prohibition of the democratic movement but doubted that it possessed the authority to carry it out, in view of the massive popular support enjoyed by the left, especially in Rhine-Hessen. Consequently, it looked to the Provisional German Central Power to issue a nationwide prohibition and, if necessary, provide the troops to back it up. The Frankfurt authorities, who had their own plans to suppress the democrats, were unwilling to act arbitrarily and doubted they could get such legislation through the German National Assembly, so there the matter rested.[28]

Lacking the desired universal legal weapon, officials were forced to act on an ad hoc basis, indicting democratic activists for slandering state officials,

[26] "Die beiden Verhöre des Herrn Dr. Gottschalk," *ZAVK*, 20 July 1848. On the authorities' arrest of Gottschalk, primarily to weaken Cologne's radicals, rather than for anything he specifically did or said, see Kühn, *Der junge Hermann Becker*, p. 188; HSTAD RA Pr. Nr. 701 ff. 2–4; *RhBA* 2/2, Nrs. 166, 172, 176, 194.

[27] Quotation, HSTAD RD Pr. Nr. 753 ff. 173–74; for similar views, see HSTAD RD Pr. Nr. 812 ff. 3, 46–60; HSTAD RD Nr. 200 pp. 263–65; LAK 442 Nr. 7853 pp. 104–06; *RhBA* 2/2, Nr. 355; BAF DB 54 Nr. 74 ff. 13–14.

[28] Paschen, *Demokratische Vereine*, pp. 84–90; Botzenhart, *Deutscher Parlamentarismus*, p. 345; Von Closen (Bavarian representative in Frankfurt) to king, 30 June 1848, BHSTAM MInn Nr. 46129; BAF DB 54 Nr. 74 ff. 2–50; Siemann, *"Deutschlands Ruhe Ordnung und Sicherheit,"* pp. 223–41; *RhBA* 2/2, Nr. 262.

sedition, inciting to overthrow the existing government, or actually trying to overthrow it whenever the judicial authorities felt such legal action was warranted. These attempts ran into an unexpected roadblock, the jury trials required for felony offenses under Rhenish law. The large majority of political trials during the revolution resulted in embarrassment to the authorities, since the jurors stubbornly refused to convict the defendants. Gottschalk and the other leaders of the Cologne Workers' Association were acquitted in December 1848 after a six-month-long criminal investigation. His rival Marx was acquitted twice on trials for press offenses, as was editor Steinberg of the *Volksblatt* in Trier. The state procurator in Kaiserslautern won several convictions of the town's democrats by bringing them before nonjury tribunals, but the convictions were reversed on appeal, the provincial high court holding the cases should have come before a jury. To the authorities' total astonishment, the Aachen rioters of April 1848 were all acquitted at their trial a year later. The trial of the participants in the May 1848 "time of the barricades" in Trier was first transferred to Cologne rather than being brought before local jurors, and then the accused were pardoned rather than the government's chancing another legal defeat. Even after the suppression of the revolution, the authorities could do little better: All the Rhine-Hessian insurgents of May 1849 were acquitted, as were most of those in the Wuppertal and the Palatinate. Newspapers published detailed trial transcripts, allowing the public to follow the trials while they were in progress. The courts were full of spectators, sympathizing with the defendants. When the jurors' verdict was announced, jubilation and mass demonstrations would follow, the trials ending in a public humiliation of the authorities, undermining public respect for law and order.[29]

These results are as astonishing in retrospect as they were to contemporaries, since the pool of potential jurors was drawn from the ranks of adult males paying the highest taxes. Their political sympathies especially in the northern Rhineland, were certainly closer to the constitutional monarchists than to the democrats. Unlike the authorities, or the former leaders of the liberal opposition, who joined or supported the March ministries, the bourgeoisie chosen for jury duty had not abandoned the region's traditional respect for civil liberties. Their support for Rhenish law and the rights embodied in it created a breathing space for the democrats, so that the authorities' attempts to use the courts to crush the left, while costing the imprisoned activists much personal suffering and taking up the time, money and efforts of the democratic movement, were never completely successful.

[29] Dowe, *Aktion und Organisation*, pp. 212–13, 229; LAK 403 Nr. 9632 pp. 22–40; LAS H1 Nr. 1974 ff. 5–6; *NSZ*, 15 Aug. 1848 (Beilage), 16 Mar. 1849; HSTAD RA Pr. Nr. 660 f. 128; Breuer, "1848/49 im Moseltal," pp. 133–34; LAK 403 Nr. 6583 pp. 66–74, 118–20; *Verhandlungen*, pt. 2, pp. 527–29; LAS J1 Nr. 308 f. 1; LAK 403 Nr. 2253 pp. 398–405.

DEMOCRATS AND REPUBLICANISM

The clash between the authorities' attitudes toward the democrats and the democrats' toward the state authorities did produce a vicious cycle of hostile speeches and demonstrations, arrests and prosecutions, trials and acquittals, still angrier and more hostile speeches and demonstrations. At the end of the cycle was a growing identification of democracy with republicanism. This had not been the case at the beginning of the revolution, when most democratic activists, if in principle republicans, had admitted that their ideal state was not on the practical political agenda in Germany. Only a small minority, most influential in Mainz, insisted on a republic. Some leftists even proclaimed themselves monarchists, such as the Düsseldorf democrats who called the political club they founded in April 1848 the Association for the Democratic Monarchy.[30]

Over the subsequent year, the influence of republicanism increased steadily. By the fall of 1848, the Düsseldorf club, while never formally changing its name, was commonly known as the Democratic Association, the change in nomenclature reflecting the fact that there, as elsewhere, principled adherents of monarchism had broken with the left. They had not been thrown out: Democrats never excluded monarchists from their movement, and, characteristically, democratic clubs never called themselves republican. Some leftists continued to talk of a political future for royalty in Germany, but their advocacy of a "monarchy on the broadest democratic basis" was entirely for pragmatic reasons—they believed republicanism was still too unpopular, or the forces opposing it too powerful, for it to be politically successful.[31]

As a regional and national democratic movement developed, organized itself, and showed increasing political strength, while the authorities of the existing monarchies multiplied their efforts to repress it, the feelings of restraint began to drop away, and Rhenish leftists became ever more open about their republicanism. In popular political agitation, advocacy of a republic was closely tied to attacks on the state bureaucracy, the army, and the burdens of taxation. The German princes and their decadent courtiers, democrats claimed, swilled champagne paid for by heavy taxation of the common people. The tyranny of bureaucracy and military was exercised in the name of the

---

[30] See sources cited in note 31; and LAS J1 Nr. 105 ff. 201–12.

[31] In general, on democratic monarchists, see the excellent account in Seypel, "Die Demokratische Gesellschaft in Köln," pp. 153–57; and Scherer, "Zur Geschichte kirchlicher Parteien," pp. 240–42; on Düsseldorf, see Repgen, *Märzbewegung*, p. 298; *RhBA* 2/2, Nr. 289; HSTAD RD Nr. 200 pp. 184–89, 197–99, 205–09. Quote from the meeting of the democrats of Mülheim County in *NRhZ*, 19 Oct. 1848 (Beilage); other examples of pragmatically motivated support for a democratic monarchy, HSTAD RD Nr. 200 p. 229; *RhBA* 2/2, Nr. 289 (Political Club in Elberfeld); Jeuckens, "Die '48er Bewegung in Eupen," p. 33; Breuer, "1848/49 im Moseltal," pp. 187–88; *Vbl*, 1 Oct. 1848; *MZ*, 29 Aug. 1848; LAS J1 Nr. 263 ff. 218–19.

princes. And as if the existing thirty-four German princes, each with his court, army, and bureaucracy, were not enough, the Frankfurt National Assembly, by electing an imperial regent and planning to replace him with a permanent emperor, had created a thirty-fifth, the very last thing the country needed.[32]

This line of argument was exemplified by the oft-repeated comparison between Germany and the United States. In the latter, the democrats asserted, even the slaves were better off than German workers, which was only to be expected from a country that had low taxes, no state bureaucracy, and an elected chief executive who lived in republican simplicity and drew a salary to match. This was how a witness reported Bergzabern radical Valentin Borscht's speech to the vinters of Oberotterbach in favor of the republic:[33]

He described America as a model. He maintained this country was the happiest on earth, because people there will have nothing to do with all these state officials; they just have a president with a salary of 20,000 Thaler. But citizens, he said, think that Germany, this small realm compared to America, must support 34 princes with a civil list of far more than 100 million Gulden, and how we citizens must pay this monstrous sum with our blood and sweat.

Important in linking popular grievances with support for the republic, such speeches were complemented by a brief and easily visible symbol of republicanism, the red flag. Unlike France during the 1848 revolution, or central Europe later in the nineteenth century, in mid-nineteenth-century Germany, the red flag was the symbol of the democratic republic, and not of socialism; the flag was flown in conjunction with the black-red-gold tricolor, not in opposition to it. From June 1848 onward, the red flag, or its condensed version, the red ribbon worn in a buttonhole, became steadily more common. Mainz democrats wore the insignia of the city's democratic club on a red ribbon; members of the radical Ninth Company of the Cologne civic guard wore such a ribbon when they refused to present arms to the constitutional monarchist guard commandant, District Governor von Wittgenstein, during a review in

---

[32] On the increase in open republicanism in the summer and fall of 1848, see HSTAD RD Pr. Nr. 812 ff. 27–30; LAK 403 Nr. 7045 pp. 43–73, 77–96; report of MInn to king, 12 Oct. 1848, BHSTAM MInn Nr. 46129; Armee Corps Commando in der Pfalz (Speyer) to Gesammt Staats Ministerium, 1 Oct. 1849, BHSTAM MInn Nr. 45533; LAS J1 Nr. 247 ff. 37–38; BAF DB 54 Nr. 74 ff. 47–48; Schurz, *Lebenserinnerungen*, p. 156. On the ideology of popular republicanism, cf. HSTAD RD Pr. Nr. 812 ff. 34–39; HSTAD RD Pr. Nr. 827 ff. 15–17; HSTAD RD Nr. 200 pp. 226–28, 231–34; HSTAD RA Pr. Nr. 2229 ff. 255–56, 304–306; ZSTAM Rep. 77 Tit. 1094 Nr. 1 ff. 19–20; "Täuschung," *ZAVK*, 13 Aug. 1848; *FBA*, 2, 9 Nov. 1848, 8 Apr. 1849; *RhBA* 2/2, Nr. 279; *MZ*, 31 July, 1848; *Der Demokrat*, 3 Sept. 1848; *NSZ*, 4 Apr. 1849; LAS J1 Nr. 172 ff. 421–22; LAS J1 Nr. 180 ff. 609–12; LAS J1 Nr. 263 ff. 221–22, 461–66; LAS J1 Nr. 202 I (alt) f. 100; LAS H3 Nr. 154b f. 192.

[33] LAS J1 Nr. 178 ff. 213–14; similarly, HSTAD RD Nr. 200 pp. 231–34; HSTAD RA Pr. Nr. 2229 ff. 253–54; *FBA*, 22 Apr. 1849; *NRhZ*, 7, 19 Jan. 1849; *RhBA* 2/2, Nr. 279; *Der Demokrat*, 17 Dec. 1848; LAS J1 Nr. 242 ff. 55–57; LAS J1 Nr. 245 ff. 280–81.

June 1848. Married women and maidens consecrated red flags as standards of the gymnastics societies of the southern Rhineland; red flags were present at political mass meetings, and the banquets celebrating the first anniversary of the February and March revolutions took place in halls graced with large red flags, their presence indicating the extent to which the vague and manifold aspirations for freedom felt in the spring of 1848 had been crystallized, under the pressure of official attempts at repression, into the demand for the republic.[34]

A DEMOCRATIC FOREIGN POLICY

Rhenish democrats carried their nationalism and antimonarchical sentiments over into their considerations on foreign affairs. This enabled them to combine nationalism and internationalism, to link their struggles with those of the Italians, Hungarians, and especially the Poles, the cause of the Polish nation having been a popular one in the Rhineland since 1830. These were not esoteric issues but a constituent part of popular political agitation: No mass meeting lacked a speech on international affairs; no weekly political overview at a club session was without a discussion of events in Venezia, Galicia, or the Hungarian plain. Schoolteachers reading left-wing newspapers out loud brought news of these struggles even to isolated villages.[35]

Just as the Rhenish democrats supported the national cause of the Poles or Hungarians, they had a great enemy abroad, the absolutist Russian Empire. Democrats never tired of pointing out the dangers posed to Germany by the armies of the czar, poised on the frontiers. There could be no compromise

[34] On the meaning of the red flag to contemporaries, see LAS H1 Nr. 154a ff. 88–89; *RhBA* 2/2, Nr. 176; *MZ*, 2–3 Nov. 1848; Kühn, *Der junge Hermann Becker*, p. 59. On the use of the red flag, see ibid.; *MZ*, 24 Oct. 1848, 27 Feb. 1849; BAF DB 54 Nr. 74 ff. 43–44; *RhBA* 2/2, Nrs. 166, 176, 250, 279; HSTAD RD Pr. Nr. 812 ff. 34–39; Kühn, *Der junge Hermann Becker*, pp. 206, 233; Seypel, "Die Demokratische Gesellschaft in Köln," pp. 267–70.

[35] Strey and Winkler, *Marx und Engels 1848/49*, pp. 175–89, 227–44; Hammen, *The Red '48ers*, pp. 272–81; Gernert, *1848/49 im Rheinisch-Bergischen*, p. 153; Nießner, *Aachen*, pp. 88–89; Kersken, *Bonn in den Revolutionsjahren*, p. 131; HSTAD RD Nr. 8804 f. 28; *RhBA* 2/2, Nrs. 89, 279; *Vbl*, 7 July, 13 Aug. 1848; *NKZ*, 28 Apr. 1849 (lead article); *ZAVK*, 3 Sept. 1848; *MZ*, 17, 20 May, 31 July, 10 Aug. 1848, 27 Feb. 1849; *Der Demokrat*, 25 June, 29 Oct., 5 Nov. 1848, 6 May 1849; LAS H1 Nr. 1974 ff, 5–6; LAS J1 Nr. 263 f. 140. Most Rhenish democrats, like their counterparts across Germany, were hostile to the smaller Slavic nationalities, who supported the Habsburg monarchy against revolutionary forces. A good study of this attitude can be found in Roman Rosdolsky, "Friedrich Engels und das Problem der 'Geschichtslosen' Völker (Die Nationalitätenfrage in der Revolution von 1848/1849 im Lichte der 'Neuen Rheinischen Zeitung')," *Archiv für Sozialgeschichte* 4 (1964): 87–282. The inhabitants of Mainz had another opinion, the city's democrats calling, in the name of popular sovereignty, for a foreign policy of cooperation with the "Slavic peoples," and the crowd getting along much better with the Czech troops who made up the Austrian garrison of the Mainz fortress than with the German-speaking Prussian soldiers. *MZ*, 10 Aug. 1848; Bockenheimer, *Mainz*, p. 26; *Vbl*, 26 May 1848.

with the czarist empire; any hint of cooperation between Prussia and Russia to suppress Polish nationalism was an "attempted assassination of German freedom, an annihilation of the principle of popular sovereignty." Rather war with Russia, the left insisted, than any concessions to its demands.[36]

"The Russian knout is the last recourse of kings," Mainz democrat Philipp Wittmann proclaimed, and Rhenish democrats were quick to tar their domestic enemies with the czarist brush. Democrats described the acting county commissioner of Adenau as an "enemy of the people's rights and the people's freedom, enamored of the Russian knout"; Cologne cigar workers wrote to the *Neue Rheinische Zeitung* to complain of an oppressive manufacturer who treated them "in the Russian manner." Mainz democrat Wittmann concluded his speech, delivered in May 1849, at the time of the final crisis of the revolution, by saying that outcome of the struggle would determine whether "humanity and liberty would be victorious, or barbarism, whether Germany is to be Cossack or free."[37]

In 1848–1849, as was generally true in the nineteenth century, the cry "Go back to Russia" was flung by the left at the right rather than vice versa. At the time of the controversy over the recall of the prince of Prussia, Rhenish democrats parodied Nicholas Becker's Rhine song of 1840, which began, "They are not to have it, the free German Rhine," singing, "We don't want to have him, the Herr Grapeshot Prince/Russia should bury him, in its ice province." By taking a song originally directed against France and turning it into one directed against Russia, the democrats were making in brief a political point, which they often elaborated. A united Germany should be allied with democratic and republican France, not tyrannical, czarist Russia; Prussian troops should be guarding the eastern, not the western, border; German nationalism should be Francophile and Russophobe rather than hostile to France and favorable to the czar, as Prussian loyalists wanted it.[38]

---

[36] Quotation: *Der Demokrat*, 25 June 1848; similarly, ibid., 5 Nov. 1848; *MZ*, 24–25 Feb. 1849; *NKZ*, 10 Jan. 1849; Seypel, "Die Demokratische Gesellschaft in Köln," pp. 276–78; HSTAD RD Nr. 8804 f. 26; HSTAD RA Pr. Nr. 2229 ff. 255–56; *ZAVK*, 10 Sept. 1848; *RhBA* 2/2, Nrs. 77, 322; Strey and Winkler, *Marx und Engels 1848/49*, pp. 89–90. Historians have sometimes seen this as political paranoia, radical warmongering, or even, bizarrely, proto-Nazism, but the czar's armies really were poised on the frontiers, and he and his ministers did have plans to intervene against the central European revolution. This intervention finally took place against Hungary in the spring of 1849, but Friedrich Wilhelm IV had previously requested one in Prussia, should the democrats succeed in seizing power. Strey and Winkler, *Marx und Engels 1848/49*, p. 50; cf. Valentin, *Geschichte der deutschen Revolution* 1:546–48, 2:183, 232–33.

[37] *Der Demokrat*, 6 May 1849; sources cited in Chapter Four, note 101; *NRhZ*, 5 Mar. 1849; similarly, "Bürgerverin in Sinnersdorf," *FBA*, 15 Mar. 1849; *NRhZ*, 22 Oct. 1848; LAS J1 Nr. 202 I (alt) ff. 103–04. Wittmann was playing on Napoleon's celebrated remark that in fifty years Europe would be either Cossack or republican.

[38] The Prince of Prussia song can be found in Ulrich Otto, *Die historisch-politischen Lieder und Karikaturen des Vormärz und die Revolution 1848/49* (Cologne: Pahl-Rugenstein, 1982), p. 37. Further on the Russophobia and Francophilia of the left, versus the reversed attitudes of the

A Society and Economy on Democratic Lines

Popular sovereignty, journalist Ludwig Kalisch insisted in a speech at the founding meeting of the Mainz Democratic Club, must obtain in society as well as the state: "With political freedom, social equality shall also be won and assured." In one way or another, all Rhenish democrats would probably have assented to these assertions, but they would have understood them in very different ways. When it came to social and economic issues, democrats displayed a wide array of different views. Their ranks included supporters of laissez-faire, of a reestablishment of the guilds, of Marxian socialism, and of the most popular position, "associationism," a vision of an economy based on small producers' cooperatives. Often, several of these ideas might be held simultaneously by the same individual, social and economic alternatives being posed differently in the mid-nineteenth century than they would be fifty years later.[39]

Some leftists were outspoken proponents of a capitalist market economy. Editor Georg Friedrich Kolb of the *Neue Speyerer Zeitung* never tired of explaining the blessings of the free market and the pernicious consequences of communism in the pages of his newspaper. Like so many German advocates of the free market, Kolb also supported protective tariffs against foreign competition. Both aspects of his economic ideas corresponded to the interests of the bourgeois aristocracy of the Palatinate, the large vineyard owners of the Haardt mountains and the merchants and bankers of Neustadt a.d.W. Many of these men were active in the People's Associations, sometimes in surprisingly radical fashion.[40]

Karl Cramer, editor of the *Watchman on the Rhine* [Der Wächter am Rhein], the newsletter of the Cologne Democratic Society, was equally anti-communist and a convinced adherent of the free market, praising the lower prices to consumers that unrestrained competition would bring. However, many of his fellow leaders of the Cologne Democratic Society denounced the "power of money," attacking the large merchants, railroads, and steamship lines who squeezed small businessmen and freight forwarders. Cologne democrats called for measures to allow the latter to compete more equitably with the former, and Cramer also supported such interference with the market, even at the price of giving up the consistency of his economic ideas.[41]

These adherents of laissez-faire were joined in one aspect of their thinking

right, see HSTAD RD Nr. 8804 f. 26; *NSZ*, 27 Apr., 29 July 1848; *MZ*, 15, 21, 25 June 1848; Körner, *Lebenskämpfe* 1:423–25

[39] Speech cited in *Der Demokrat*, 14 May 1848.

[40] For Kolb's economic positions, see *NSZ*, 7 Apr., 8 Aug., 15 Dec. 1848; on the political affiliations of the Palatine bourgeoisie, cf. LAS J1 Nr. 228 II (alt) f. 640; Schwarzwälder, "Politische Bewegung in Neustadt an der Haardt," p. 135.

[41] Seypel, "Die Demokratische Gesellschaft in Köln," pp. 135–36, 146–52.

by a much wider assortment of democrats, whose economic and social ideas had been shaped by the Rhenish Institutions. They strongly supported the right to occupational freedom and opposed any guild restrictions on the practice of the crafts, vociferously denouncing the corporate schemes proposed by the master craftsmen delegates to the German Artisans' Congress, which met in Frankfurt during July 1848. In Mainz, the Democratic Club, the Workers' Association, the Trades' Association (representing craft masters) and the constitutional monarchist Citizens' Association met jointly to denounce the guild masters' "particularism," and sponsor petition drives in favor of occupational freedom. Similar petitions came into the Frankfurt National Assembly from many towns in the Palatinate. The Palatine provincial Trades' Association, whose leaders included democratic activists, was uncompromising in its support of the right to free occupational choice.[42]

Rhenish communists shared this uncompromising attitude. Both Gottschalk and, later, Marx and his followers informed the members of the Cologne Workers' Association that the guilds were hopelessly reactionary, pouring scorn on "the rusty club of the guild system," and the "bewigged compulsory guilds of the last century." The Workers' Association of Neustadt a.d.W., founded and led by the Palatine communists, Johann Weber and Heinrich Loose, made the establishment of occupational freedom throughout all of Germany one of the main points of its agitation.[43]

Leading Mainz leftists were also strongly committed to laissez-faire, Ludwig Bamberger telling the Democratic Club in a charming analogy, "Many physicians have already taken on the social question as a patient; if we took all the perscribed cures and if all the mixtures worked, we would soon be under the earth. Therefore, out the window with these mixtures, and let the fresh air in." Unlike Kolb, however, they were willing to admit the shadow side of the free market, after decades of experience with it in the Rhineland, France, England, and Ireland. Mainz democrats feared that if occupational freedom were extended to all of Germany, the result would be the impoverishment of the middle class and small business and the enslavement of journeymen artisans and laborers to "the aristocracy of money," to the "power of capital," to the "men of money," to the "bourgeoisie."[44]

The solution to this dilemma, Mainz democrats asserted, was the "Orga-

---

[42] MZ, 1 Aug. 1848; NSZ, 1 Jan. 1849 (Beilage), 12 Jan. 1849; LAS J1 Nr. 244 ff. 329–30. Similarly, in Düsseldorf, HSTAD RD Nr. 200 pp. 193–94. On the Frankfurt artisans' congress, see Hamerow, Revolution, Restoration, Reaction, pp. 144–50; Lenger, Sozialgeschichte der deutschen Handwerker, pp. 74–79.

[43] ZAVK, 6 July, 3, 6 Aug. 1848; NSZ, 4 May 1848 (Beilage), 15 Apr. 1849 (Beilage); Die Allgemeine Deutsche Arbeiterverbrüderung, Nr. 259.

[44] Bamberger's speech: MZ, 4 Nov. 1848. Similar invocations of laissez-faire, ibid., 30 Mar., 1 July 1848; Der Demokrat, 28 Jan., 7 Feb. 1849; recognition of impoverishment of masses and power of capital, MZ, 25 June, 15–16 July, 29 Oct. 1848; Der Demokrat, 16 Apr., 14 May, 2 July, 5 Nov. 1848, 25 Jan. 1849

nization of Labor,'' the magic phrase of Parisian socialist Louis Blanc, so important to the ideas of the revolution of 1848. Part of the slogan's magic was its vagueness, but it seems to have been taken as implying "association," that is, producers' cooperatives, enjoying government sponsorship through tax breaks and cheap credit from a state bank, enabling craftsmen to maintain their independence vis-à-vis merchant capitalists in a free market economy. Given that Rhenish artisans were already experimenting with cooperatives before the revolution, it is hardly surprising that the twin slogans "association" and "organization of labor" were widely propagated and accepted.[45]

Worms democrats wished to see the social question solved by the "free, powerful development of the spirit of association," which they hoped to foster by having the municipal savings bank provide loans to artisans, thus leading to the "victory of democracy." The Palatine communists energetically propagated the gospel of association; true socialist and democratic journalist Karl Grün of Trier regarded Proudhon's speech on state credit as "a world-historical deed even more important than the June struggle [of the Parisian workers]." Weavers of the Industrial Central Organization of the Wuppertal looked to "self-help" (that is, cooperatives) to "tear us from our servitude to capital." Düsseldorf democrats drew up blueprints for the creation of artisans' cooperatives, to be financed by taxation of the rich.[46]

Although Marx and his followers regarded these ideas as a petit bourgeois illusion, an ineffective palliative against the downfall of master craftsmen and small business before the growing power of industrial capital, they recognized their popularity and tried to exploit them for their own purposes. Denouncing the corporate schemes of the Frankfurt Artisan Congress, the committee of the Cologne Workers' Association declared that if the German National Assembly needed help with the social question it should call a congress of "workers, masters [Gewerbetreibenden] and industrialists represented in proportion to their numbers," which would discuss with the assembly the "organization of labor."[47]

The ideal of a society of small producers is apparent in the call for associa-

---

[45] "Doch nicht so ganz unrecht," and "Zunftwesen und Gewerbefreiheit," *Der Demokrat*, 16 Apr. 1848, 28 Jan. 1849, both explicitly combine an account of the dreadful consequences of occupational freedom, a rejection of the reestablishment of the guilds, and an advocacy of the organization of labor. Similarly, *MZ*, 3, 5 July 1848, 24–25, 27–28 Mar. 1849.

[46] BAF ZSg 8/55 f. 74; Reuter, "Johann Philipp Bandel," pp. 48–49; *NSZ*, 4 May 1848 (Beilage), 15 Apr. 1849 (Beilage); LAS J1 Nr. 263 ff. 290–91; *Vbl*, 17 Aug. 1848; *Die Allgemeine Deutsche Arbeiterverbrüderung*, Nr. 96; Lenger, *Zwischen Kleinbürgertum und Proletariat*, p. 16; similarly, LAK 442 Nr. 6506 ff. 30–31. Although Andreas Gottschalk's social and economic ideas were, at the height of his political influence, extremely vague, he (or at least his followers) also seems to have developed into a supporter of associationism. See *FA*, 12, 25 Feb. 1849.

[47] *ZAVK*, 6 Aug. 1848. Cf. the account of the committee session of 24 July 1848, devoted to explaining why the "organization of labor" was impossible in the current society: ibid., 27, 30 July 1848.

tion; it can also be seen in the democrats' criticism of the rich and their role in the economic crisis of the revolutionary years. Most explicitly developed in Mainz, this critique was apparent in outline elsewhere. When Mainz leftists denounced the upper classes, it was not for their wealth as such, but for their use of it in a way "hostile to the people." The bourgeoisie had used the revolution as a pretext to "lock their money up in chests," and "provide no occupation for industry." In the language of the twentieth century, the democrats were accusing the bourgeoisie of engaging in a capital strike for political reasons; the solution to the economic crisis lay in active investment, "great sacrifices of the rich"—it was unclear whether these sacrifices were to be voluntary or compulsory—that would maximize production and provide gainful employment for workers and artisans.[48]

What disturbed most democrats about the upper classes was their role as financial and mercantile capitalists, refusing to provide credit and market outlets to small producers, or only doing so on such exploitative terms that impoverishment and economic crisis were ensured. By today's standards, or even those of 1900, this analysis, with its contrast between small producers on the one hand, and financial and mercantile capitalists on the other, was archaic and archaicizing, blind to the future dominance of industrial production, but it was by no means inappropriate to the actual relations of production as they existed in the Rhineland at the middle of the nineteenth century. Under these circumstances, it is not surprising that it was the most common kind of left-wing economic program.

Most Rhenish democratic leaders were advocates of either laissez-faire or a mixture of laissez-faire and small producer anticapitalism, but a few advanced two quite different economic programs. One group was the Marxists, with their calls for government economic planning, nationalization of transport and large industry, and state control of credit. Such ideas were seldom found in the *Neue Rheinische Zeitung*, with its heavily bourgeois readership; rather, they were reserved for lectures on political economy at meetings of the Cologne Workers' Association—some given by Marx and Engels personally—and the quasi-clandestine distribution of the seventeen demands of the Communist party in Germany.[49]

---

[48] *MZ*, 25 Apr. 1848; "Das Elend der arbeitenden Klasse," *Der Demokrat*, 29 Oct. 1848. Similar ideas in *MZ*, 25 June 1848; "Kapital und Arbeit," *Der Demokrat*, 7 May 1848; "Demokratische Vereine oder Bürger-Vereine" (pamphlet in Mainz municipal library), comparing the self-seeking, tax-evading, coupon-clipping constitutional monarchist "moneybags" with the self-sacrificing, affluent democrats. Outside of Mainz, cf. "Dem Handwerker gewidmet," *Vbl*, 7 June 1848; *NSZ*, 12 Apr. 1849 (lead article); or *KnZ*, 24 Oct. 1848 (Erste Beilage), where Franz Raveaux denounced the Cologne "aristocracy of money" as parasitic drones in comparison to the productive "citizenry . . . artisans, merchants, manufacturers, foremen, clerks, scholars, artists."

[49] *ZAVK*, 23, 27 July, 31 Aug., 3 Sept. 1848; *FBA*, 9 Nov. 1848, 15 Feb. 1849. Martin Hundt, "Die 17 Forderungen der Kommunistischen Partei in Deutschland von März 1848," *Beiträge zur*

Although today far more familiar than rival conceptions, Marx's ideas were strange and exotic to contemporaries, and required some familiarization to reach their intended proletarian audience. Some idea of how this was done comes from a speech that one of his supporters, Julius Wulff, gave to the radical People's Club in Düsseldorf:[50]

> In Germany, we must have the red republic, then we will elect every four years a head of state, who will be neither by birth a prince, [nor] duke nor bear the title by grace of God, but a man from the people, an enemy of the rich and a friend of the poor, thus the opposite of what we have now. The man elected must then ensure that the state gets for itself so much money that the rich factory owners [Fabrikbesitzer], who now suck the workers' last drops of blood for a mockery of a wage . . . be suppressed. He must ensure that the state provides jobs, that the railroads, currently in the hands of the capitalists, become state property, then each and every one of us will be able to live and have enough to eat.

Quite the opposite of the Marxists were the democratic supporters of a revival of the guilds. This position was strongest among rank-and-file democrats, such as the many Trier master artisans, simultaneously members of the city's guilds and its Democratic Club. Another adherent of guilds and democracy was Düsseldorf's delegate to the Frankfurt Artisan Congress, the master furnituremaker Franz Hollender. Endorsing the congress's decisions, Hollender returned home to propagate them among his fellow craftsmen, while simultaneously continuing his democratic political activism.[51]

Leading democrats who supported the guilds were scarcer, the most prominent being the radical Bonn professor Gottfried Kinkel. An artisans' educational society he founded called a small Rhenish artisans' congress, meeting in June 1848, which helped prepare for the strongly guild-oriented national congress in Frankfurt the following month. Although using the language of small producer radicalism, calling for "association," cooperative sales outlets [Gewerbehallen], and cheap credit, Kinkel advanced a program of artisanal social restriction, complete with the limiting of admission to master status to those who passed examinations and the prohibition of peddling. A telling characteristic of the society he founded was its exclusion of journeymen from the right to speak or vote at meetings, a decision that won it the scathing criticism of the Cologne Workers' Association. Whatever left activists of the Rhenish metropolis felt, the measure seems to have been popular enough in Bonn, since Kinkel followed up on his artisans' society by forming the Bonn Dem-

---

Geschichte der deutschen Arbeiterbewegung 10 (1968): 203–36. On Marx's reluctance to discuss the seventeen demands in public, cf. his comments to Hermann Becker, in Kühn, *Der junge Hermann Becker*, p. 109, a source not utilized in Hundt's article.

[50] HSTAD RD Nr. 200 pp. 231–34.

[51] See sources cited in Chapter Six, notes 26–27; and Lenger, *Zwischen Kleinbürgertum und Proletariat*, pp. 178–87.

ocratic Club, which grew to six hundred members by the fall of 1848, obtaining a dominant position in the city's political life.[52]

Although Rhenish democrats had very different ideas about the economy, they were all willing to blame existing economic problems, at least in part, on the actions of the state, tapping powerful popular hostilities toward the government for their economic programs. Enemies of both the guild system and of occupational freedom, for instance, saw the existence of opposing systems as the result of state action.

All Palatine leftists, whether bourgeois free market theorists, master craftsmen, or communists, opposed the guilds. Such a remarkable unanimity of views among such different elements was, more than anything, a reflection of the enmity felt by Palatines toward the Bavarian state, of all the German governments, the one most in favor of the guild system. One can see the importance of anti-Bavarian sentiment in the decision of the Palatine provincial trades' congress, to endorse occupational freedom. It required a hot debate, in the course of which a proposal to deny to inhabitants of states without occupational freedom (that is, trans-Rhenan Bavaria) the right to settle freely in areas with occupational freedom was narrowly voted down.[53]

Gottfried Kinkel, on the other hand, denounced the sale of business licenses [Gewerbescheine], all that was required to set up for oneself under a regime of occupational freedom, as the act of an "army of state officials," who were "sucking the blood" of the workers (that is, artisans): "Every peddler, travelling musician and beggar is a sin, which a rotten administrative system throws off itself and onto the people." If peddling were prohibited, and craftsmen allowed to become masters only by examination, Kinkel asserted, the state would have less money, but its citizens would be richer. While leftists in the southern Rhineland denounced the guilds as the pernicious consequence of state policy, and demanded occupational freedom, Kinkel presented occupational freedom as the exploitative action of a reactionary government, which would not exist in a democratic "people's state."[54]

Proponents of small producer anticapitalism also had no difficulty in identifying their enemies with the state. Mainz democrats held that occupational freedom under the existing form of government just benefited "capital," while the "propertyless or those less well off are ruined." The reason was that the "old rotten system of government [had] partially abolished the privileges and monopolies of the aristocracy but strengthened those of money," a per-

[52] Kersken, *Bonn in den Revolutionsjahren*, pp. 94–101; *ZAVK*, 11, 29 June, 6 July 1848; *RhBA* 2/2, Nrs. 179, 290; *KnZ*, 5 July 1848 (Beilage).

[53] LAS J1 Nr. 244 ff. 329–30. Rhine-Hessian leftists also regarded the support for the guilds in trans-Rhenan Hessen as a similar sign of reaction in the Darmstadt government. *MZ*, 30 Mar. 1848 (lead article).

[54] Kersken, *Bonn in den Revolutionsjahren*, p. 101, taken from a pamphlet with the significant title *Handwerk! errete dich.*

fectly logical conclusion for a movement whose activists had gained political experience in opposing a state-supported railroad system that favored the merchants of Frankfurt and Mannheim at the expense of the trade of Mainz. Cologne's Franz Raveaux, also a *Vormärz* crusader for small producers against state-supported capitalism, turned in a similar blast at the parasitic "aristocracy of money," always currying favor with the government, ruthlessly exploiting its connections to gain profitable state posts and economic advantages.[55]

What democratic economic policies thus had in common was an opposition to the *Vormärz* "unfree market economy," and those who profited from it. Some leftists wished to end this system by getting the state out of market regulation altogether; Marx and his followers wanted to see the state act to abolish the market. The largest group of democrats thought that the state should use its influence in favor of small producers instead of the "bourgeoisie" or the "aristocracy of money," but all democrats agreed that the state's role was distorting the outcome of the market system.

This idea of a misappropriative role of the state in favor of particular interests also characterizes the democrats' position on taxation. Rhenish leftists were virtually unanimous in agreeing that the burden of taxation was too great, ruinously so, and could be reduced by the introduction of cheaper government, with fewer, less well paid state officials and soldiers. They also felt that taxes were unfairly apportioned, that the lower and middle classes paid too much, the bourgeoisie and aristocracy, too little. A more equitable taxation system, the abolition of indirect taxes on basic necessities, and frequently the introduction of a progressive income tax were demands stressed by democrats in political programs, club sessions, and mass meetings. Fiscal and economic demands of the democrats coincided, both based on the idea that the state was responsible for inequities in wealth and its policies were steadily increasing them. Outside of large cities and manufacturing areas, and everywhere in talking to the peasantry, these fiscal demands were the broad social and economic program of the democrats.[56]

RELIGION AND REVOLUTION

The elections of May 1848 had shown the influence of the clergy in the new mass politics, and the democrats were forced to confront it, as they tried their hand at mass organization, especially in the countryside. "Confront" is the

[55] *Der Demokrat*, 28 Jan. 1849; similarly, *MZ*, 17 July 1848; Raveaux, in *KnZ*, 24 Oct. 1848 (Erste Beilage); similarly, "Auch ein Wort an die Urwähler," ibid., 20 Jan. 1849. The career of Wilhelm Jellinghaus of Solingen—leader of *Vormärz* small producer opposition to state-supported capitalism, in 1848–1849 president of the Solingen Democratic Club—also shows this connection.

[56] See sources cited in notes 1, 8–9, 32–33, and Chapter Six, note 43.

proper verb, for the large majority of both the Protestant and Roman Catholic clergy were vehemently hostile to the left, denouncing the democrats as "ravenous wolves," adherents of "theft, murder and plunder," "the greatest enemies of the people who wish to suppress religion," or intellectual descendents of Robespierre, those who would follow the French example and "overthrow the Lord God." Anyone who read a democratic newspaper or went to a club meeting was a "Judas" who could count on going straight to hell. The priest in Bochen refused one village activist absolution for his Easter communion in 1849, unless he renounced his democratic views. Radical or democratic politics, was for these clergymen the social expression of satanic evil, or, as Archbishop von Geissel of Cologne wrote, "the realm of the living Antichrist who can turn state and church into a Mongolian desert."[57]

Some clergymen had very different ideas. Protestant pastors formed and led local groups of the Palatine People's Association, and founded openly republican gymnastics societies in Rhine-Hessen. The Catholic parish priest in Bitburg, Dean Joseph Weber, regularly attended meetings of the Eifel town's Democratic Club. The parish assistant [Kaplan] Ohaus from Bernkastel, speaking at the great democratic mass meeting in the Moselle Valley in October 1848, told the crowd that "[h]e wished for a peaceful development, reform in legal ways. However, if that did not work, he was for something which also began with the letters 'Re.' "[58]

Priests and pastors were both the democrats' most vehement enemies and some of their leading agitators. There is a twofold explanation for such great differences in political opinion. One part of the explanation is quite simple: Leftist clergy were almost always of a different confession than that of the ruling royal house. Most clerical leftists in the Palatinate were Protestants, while virtually all the Roman Catholic priests were firm upholders of the authority of the Bavarian monarchy, the militant defender of the faith. Conversely, in the Prussian Rhine Province, Protestant pastors supported their king, the royal protector of all German Protestants since the eighteenth century; Catholic priests, on the other hand, lacking this connection, were more likely to incline to the left. Rhine-Hessen is a partial exception to this rule, a

---

[57] Quotes: *MZ*, 4 Nov. 1848; *NKZ*, 7 Jan. 1849; *NRhZ*, 7 Jan. 1849 (Zweite Ausgabe); *NSZ*, 29 Apr., 7 July (Beilage) 1848, 25 Feb. 1849 (Beilage); V. Borscht (Bergzabern) to G. F. Kolb, 3 Feb. 1849, BAF FN9 G. F. Kolb; *NKZ*, 21 Apr. 1849; *RhBA* 2/2, Nr. 285. Other examples: *MZ*, 10 Dec. 1848, 18 Mar. 1849; *NSZ*, 4 May, 30 Nov., 1, 3 Dec. 1848; *NRhZ*, 19 (Beilage), 22, 27, 31 Jan., 9 Feb. 1849; *NKZ*, 30 Jan. 1849; *FBA*, 6 Nov., 10 Dec. 1848, 15 Mar. 1849; *VdB*, 2 Feb. 1850; Gernert, *1848/49 im Rheinisch-Bergischen*, pp. 99–100; Jeuckens, "Die '48er Bewegung in Eupen," p. 61; Kerskens, *Bonn in den Revolutionsjahren*, p. 128; Köllman, *Stadt Barmen*, p. 235; Kühn, *Der junge Hermann Becker*, p. 228; LAS H1 Nr. 2006 ff. 8–22; LAS J1 Nr. 106 I ff. 304–08; LAK 442 Nr. 7853 pp. 205–40.

[58] Scherer, "Zur Geschichte kirchlicher Parteien," (which underplays the radicalism of many of the Palatine Protestant clergy); LAK 442 Nr. 6659 pp. 192–97; Stahl, *1848/49 an der Mittelmosel*, p. 18; sources cited in Chapter Six, note 50.

state with a Protestant monarch, but one where right-wing court circles showed an unusually favorable attitude toward the Catholic Church, thus not attracting the same sort of hostility that the equally conservative but anti-Catholic court in Prussia produced.[59]

Interconfessional hostilities were a necessary but not sufficient condition for clerical leftism: Most Catholic priests under the Prussian monarch were not democrats; nor were most Protestant pastors under the Bavarian king. Intraconfessional tensions must be included fully to explain the situation, producing a quite different situation in the two Christian confessions. For Protestants, there was a simple correlation: Rationalists were on the left; neoorthodoxy went along with royalist loyalism.

Constitutional monarchism was so much stronger in the Prussian Rhineland than in the two southern provinces primarily because of the support it enjoyed from neoorthodox Protestants, *Vormärz* defenders of absolutism who continued their loyalty to the Prussian royal house under a new political affiliation after the revolution. A typical constitutionalist activist was the "awakened" silk manufacturer Eduard Colsmann from the Elberfeld suburb of Hardenberg. As late as March 1848, he had signed an address of loyalty to the king, denouncing liberal demands for a constitution, but by July of that year, he had been a founding member of his hometown's constitutionalist political club and its delegate to the Rhenish-Westphalian constitutional monarchist congress.[60]

Whether in the Wuppertal, or the Bergisches Land, in the old Prussian territories on the Rhine, such as Krefeld, Moers, and Kleve, or in the predominantly Protestant areas at the southern end of the Rhine Province, devout clergy and laity organized to support their constitutional monarch, although the emphasis in their activities was more on the noun than the verb. Pious Protestants were such determined supporters of the king that state officials began to complain of their excessive monarchism. The first, and for a long time the only, openly conservative and counterrevolutionary political group in the Rhineland, the Association for the True Welfare of the Citizenry [Verein für das wahre Bürgerwohl] in Elberfeld, proclaimed that its politics were based exclusively on the Bible. It was formed by a coalition of revivalists and the sectarians who had seceded from the state church in the 1840s, the latter's theological differences with the state in no way interfering with their political loyalty to it.[61]

---

[59] On the government of Hessen-Darmstadt and the Catholic Church, cf. Büttner, *Parlamentarismus in Hessen*, pp. 124–26, 193–94.

[60] Quandt, "Eduard Colsmann," pp. 147–49.

[61] Ibid.; LAK 403 Nr. 7045 pp. 25–73 (a small part printed in *RhBA* 2/2, Nr. 289); Illner, *Bürgerliche Organisierung*, pp. 156–59; Köllmann, *Stadt Barmen*, pp. 237–38; *Lebenserinnerungen . . . Alexander Pagenstecher* 3:33, 39; Körner, *Lebenskämpfe* 1:429–31; reports on the political sympathies of the clergy of the Trier District, 1849, LAK 442 Nr. 6659.

Neoorthodox clergy and laity in Rhine-Hessen and the Palatinate held similar political views, but they could accomplish less with them than could their counterparts in the Prussian province. Religious rationalism was much stronger in the south, so both neoorthodoxy and the royalism that went with it were less common. In addition, while Palatine neoorthodox Protestants may have regarded it as their religious duty to support the Roman Catholic king of Bavaria, most of their coreligionists were unwilling to show such unswerving loyalty to a monarch of an alien faith.[62]

Catholic political commitment was not limited to supporting or opposing monarchical loyalism; 1848–1849 saw the first attempt at the creation of a specifically Roman Catholic political movement, with its own political clubs, the Pius Associations, and its own political agenda, summed up in the phrase, "the independence of the church from the state." While all the same factors—north-south dualism, conflict between rationalists and neoorthodox, loyalty and hostility to the different royal houses—existed among the Roman Catholic clergy and lay Catholic activists as they did among Protestants, the presence of an independent Catholic movement produced a politically far more differentiated outcome.[63]

While the Pius Association was the only organized political alternative to the democrats in the Palatinate, and the chief competitor of the left in Rhine-Hessen, Catholic activists in the southern Rhineland never quite found the way to be an effective, political force. The many artisans and laborers who joined the Mainz Pius Association showed that the group could compete with the democrats for popular support in a way the bourgeois constitutional monarchists could not, but its leaders did not strive for an independent political position on issues outside of religion or public education. Instead, they supported the constitutional monarchists and, like them, the Hessian royal house.[64]

[62] On the political attitudes of neoorthodox Protestants in the southern Rhineland, cf. sources cited in Chapter 8, note 6, and Chapter Eleven, notes 79–80. Although not much is known about the political attitudes of rabbis, or, more generally, about the influence of religious differences on Jews' political attitudes, it would seem that the Jewish clergy shared a similar political orientation. At least, strongly rationalist rabbis seem to have been strongly left-wing; more moderately rationalist ones, more moderately to the left. Cf. Uhrig, "Worms," pp. 46–47; LAS J1 Nr. 206 ff. 1141–42; LAS J1 Nr. 244 f. 340.

[63] The standard work on the first attempts at a Catholic political movement in Germany, Franz Schnabel, *Der Zusammenschluß des politischen Katholizismus in Deutschland im Jahre 1848* (Heidelberg: Karl Winter, 1910), is now rather dated, and a modern, comprehensive work would throw new light on the events of 1848–1849. By far, the best recent discussion is in Wettengel, *1848/49 im Rhein-Main-Raum*, pp. 95–96, 403–38. Other studies include Ernst Heinen, "Pius-verein 1848/49. Ein Beitrag zu den Anfängen des politischen Katholizismus in Köln," *Jahrbuch des Kölnischen Geschichtsvereins* 57 (1986): 147–242; Jan Roes, "Hierarchie und Demokratie. Die katholischen Bischöfe Deutschlands vor der demokratischen Frage während des Revolutionsjahres 1848/49," *Nederlands Archief voor Kerkgeschiednis*, 52 (1972): 178–232; *RhG* 3:356–62.

[64] See esp. Wettengel, as cited in the previous note, and Schnabel, *Zusmanneschluß*, pp. 40–42; Bockenheimer, *Mainz*, pp. 63, 108–109, 188; Buckler, "Mainz während der Revolutions-

Their Palatine counterparts strongly opposed the left, fighting bitterly with the democrats for control of large, predominantly Catholic villages, such as Schifferstadt or Rülzheim, and becoming the main political force in the northwestern cantonal town of Landstuhl. The Palatine Pius Associations were unable to translate these struggles into a useful political program. The organization's clerically tinged Bavarian loyalism found little sympathy with the provincial governor Franz Alwens, a Protestant rationalist and moderate liberal. The rallying cry of the Catholic movement, independence of the church from the state, was not particularly attractive to Palatine Catholics, who did not want independence from the Bavarian state, but a closer connection to it and greater support from it in their struggles with Protestants and the rationalist German Catholic schismatics.[65]

Catholic politics obtained its most independent profile and greatest degree of support in the Prussian Rhine Province. Its early phases involved little formal organization. Only two Pius Associations, in Aachen and Cologne, had been founded prior to the Catholic electoral victories in May 1848. The clergy's efforts seemed to suffice then, and in the summer of 1848, when diocesan administrations launched a broad and successful petition campaign to the Frankfurt and Berlin national assemblies for the independence of the church from the state and the preservation of church-controlled public education. Clergy and lay activists, if politically organized at all, were likely to be found in constitutional monarchist citizens' associations. This situation gradually changed following the October 1848 national congress of Catholic organizations, held in Mainz and organized by the Cologne Pius Association. The congress called for the founding of local groups, which began to appear in the Prussian Rhine Province over the subsequent half-year, leading to the formalization of the Catholic political network that had existed there since the outbreak of the revolution.[66]

---

jahre,'' pp. 69–70; *Der Demokrat*, 10 Dec. 1848; *MZ*, 1 Feb., 18 Mar. 1849; *Der Bund der Kommunisten* 1, Nr. 353. It is unclear just how well the Catholic activists and the predominantly Protestant bourgeois liberals got along; differences between them may help account for the weakness of constitutional monarchism in Rhine-Hessen.

[65] Doris Koch and Roland Paul, "Die Ereignisse im Kanton Landstuhl während der Zeit des Pfälzischen Aufstandes," *JhGStLK* 22/23 (1984/85): 313–48, esp. pp. 332–33; Ziegler, *Die Jahre der Reaktion in der Pfalz*, pp. 249–53; *NSZ*, 17, 27 June, 17 Oct. 1848; 25 Feb. (Beilage), 9 Apr. 1849; LAS J1 Nr. 252 (alt) ff. 169–70; petition of Catholics of Oppau, 21 July 1849, BHSTAM KA Nr. B771; Alwens's memorandum on the events of 1848–1849 in the Palatinate, BHSTAM MInn Nr. 45533.

[66] Repgen, *Märzbewegung*, pp. 110–14; by the same author, "Klerus und Politik 1848. Die Kölner Geistlichen im politischen Leben des Revolutionsjahres—Ein Betrag zur 'Parteiengeschichte von unten,' '' in *Aus Geschichte und Landeskunde. Forschungen und Darstellungen. Franz Steinbach zum 65. Geburtstag gewidmet*, ed. Ludwig Petry (Bonn: Röhrscheid, 1960), pp. 133–65; Breuer, "1848/49 im Moseltal," p. 186; *RhBA* 2/2, Nrs. 184, 189, 208, 233, 291; *KnZ*, 26 July 1848 (Beilage); Heinen, "Der Kölner Pius Verein," pp. 233–41; Schnabel, *Zusammenschluß*, pp. 45–53. Heinen's contention that the Cologne Pius Association was founded on

While religious neoorthodoxy and hostility to the democrats usually translated into royalist loyalism for the Catholic movement in the southern Rhineland, quite different political alignments existed in the Prussian Rhine Province. Most priests and lay activists were hostile to the democrats and would probably have designated themselves constitutional monarchists, but only a minority were supporters of the king of Prussia. Most were constitutional monarchists of the Austrian monarchy, who hoped to see the Rhine Province freed from Protestant rule and placed under a Catholic, preferably Habsburg, prince. If such a maximum program could not be obtained, then their minimum demand was for a separate constitution, legislature, and administration for the predominantly Roman Catholic western provinces of the monarchy.[67]

It seems that pro-Prussian sentiments were especially prevalent among the moderately rationalist, "Hermesian" priests. On the defensive in their struggle with the neoorthodox element in the Catholic Church ever since the mid-1830s, they had come to see the state bureaucracy as a needed ally. Hence, they would support neither the separation of the Rhineland from Prussia nor the independence of the church from the state. For both these reasons, neoorthodox Catholics took the opposite position.[68]

Hostility to the Prussian state did not imply sympathy for the democrats, and most neoorthodox clergy were anything but friends of the left. There was a minority among them, particularly prevalent in the Moselle Valley, whose hostility to Prussia and its bureaucracy was especially pronounced, combining feelings of religious oppression shared by other Rhenish Catholics and the opinion, widely held in the region, that state policies were responsible for its growing impoverishment. Some of these Catholic activists joined democratic clubs and identified with the leftist movement. Others were suspicious of the radicals' anticlericalism and republicanism, but painfully aware of the mass following the democrats had mobilized in the chief towns of the region, Trier, Cochem, and Bernkastel. Unable to oppose both the democrats and the authorities as successfully as their counterparts on the lower Rhine, they concluded, somewhat reluctantly, that Catholic interests, both religious and polit-

---

10 June 1848 ("Der Kölner Pius Verein," pp. 163–64) ignores Repgen's evidence of its previous existence, a police report on its activities dated 8 June (HSTAD RA Pr. Nr. 701 f. 2–3, cf. also f. 4), and even his own sources, which speak of a refounding or the ratification of formal organizational statutes. Although presenting much new material, Heinen's essay is conceptually inferior to the older works of Konrad Repgen and Christoph Weber.

[67] *RhBA* 2/1, Nr. 395; *RhBA*, 2/2, Nrs. 142, 152, 171, 190, 192, 281, 295; HSTAD RA Pr. Nr. 701 ff. 4, 11–12; Kühn, *Der junge Hermann Becker*, pp. 81–84.

[68] Schrörs, "Hermesianische Pfarrer," pp. 96–98, 148; Weber, *Aufklärung und Orthodoxie*, pp. 149–76 and esp. 183–89. Two politically prominent Catholic priests, the pastor Joseph Anton Hansen of Ottweiler and the parish assistant Karl van Berg of Jülich, sat on the left side of the Prussian National Assembly, and were also clerical rationalists—as a young man in the 1830s, Hansen had even been involved in the anticelibacy movement—but, as is so often the case, their prominence obscures their lack of typicality.

ical, could best be guaranteed by cooperating with the left rather than with the representatives of the Protestant state.[69]

Thanks to the existence of two investigations of the political attitudes of the clergy, carried out shortly after the suppression of the revolution, it is possible to compare systematically the leftist Catholic priests of the Trier District with the leftist Protestant pastors of the Palatinate. Although both investigations focused on the connections of the clergy with the democrats, the one from the Trier District encompassed the vast majority of the clergy, offered detailed accounts of their political views. The Palatine investigation only included about one-third of the pastors and was rather more superficial concerning their opinions, but a comparison between the two (see Tables 7.1 and 7.2) is nonetheless interesting.[70]

Even in the Trier District, the stronghold of Catholic leftism, only a small

TABLE 7.1

Political Attitudes of Catholic Clergy of the Trier District, 1848–1849

Political Attitudes	Age							
	Under 35		35–49		Over 50		Total	
	N	%	N	%	N	%	N	%
Democratic	14	28	30	20	12	8	56	16
Conservative, apolitical	19	38	96	63	104	73	219	64
Conservative, Prussian loyalist	4	8	6	4	15	11	25	7
Conservative, pro-Austrian	6	12	12	8	8	6	26	8
Unknown	7	14	8	5	3	2	18	5
Total	50	100	152	100	142	100	344	100

Sources: Reports of the local authorities in LAK 442 Nr. 6659. Reports from Saarlouis County are missing, and the county commissioner in Bernkastel just noted that all the priests in his county were anti-Prussian, a few were more democratic, and others were more conservative, without giving individual examples.

[69] Böse, "Ludwig Simon," pp. 132–37; Stahl, *1848/49 an der Mittelmosel*, pp. 15, 29; Karl Heinrich Höfele, "Die Anfänge des politischen Katholizismus in der Stadt Trier (1848–1870)," *Trierer Jahrbuch* 2 (1939): 77–112, esp. pp. 82–100; Repgen, *Märzbewegung*, pp. 275–76; BM Tries to LR Kr. Cochem, 3 Nov. 1848; Gendarme Breisser (Cochem) to LR Kr. Cochem, 24 Nov. 1848; LR Kr. Cochem to RKO, 3 Jan. 1849, all in LAK 441 Nr. 12929; LAK 442 Nr. 6425 passim. More on this tendency, especially the Trier Pius Association, the center of Moselle Valley political Catholicism, in Chapters Eight and Nine.

[70] Similar reports on the Protestant clergy of the Trier District (also in LAK 442 Nr. 6659) and the Catholic clergy of the Palatinate (LAS H1 Nr. 2017) noted, in comparison, their strong monarchist loyalism.

minority of the priests were sympathetic to the democrats, although an even smaller number were expressly loyal to the Prussian monarchy. Leftist views were most common among the youngest clergy, their prevalence falling off with age, a pattern repeated almost exactly among those priests who were pro-Austrian conservatives. Common to both groups was an overt hostility to the Protestant, Prussian state, probably stemming from a clerical education in the Trier seminary, whose faculty had been moving steadily from rationalist to neoorthodox views since the late 1830s.[71]

The relationship between age and political affiliation was precisely reversed in the Palatinate: Middle-aged and older pastors with a rationalist background, the generation of the Protestant Union of 1818 and the Hambach Festival of 1832, were sympathetic to the left. Their younger counterparts, instructed in neoorthodoxy at the University of Erlangen, as required of all aspiring Palatine clergy since the mid-1830s, were loyal to monarchical authority. The same religious tendency in both Christian confessions, the growth of neoorthodoxy since the 1830s, had produced politically opposite results.

Democrats, Clergy and Schoolteachers

Democrats had difficulty formulating a political program that would enable them both to gain the support of potentially sympathetic clergy and to counter the reproaches of hostile ones. With numerous variations, two main positions on religion emerged on the left, neither proving politically entirely satisfactory. Advocates of one position wished to exclude religion from public life, relegating it to an apolitical private sphere; adherents of the other attempted to

TABLE 7.2
Political Attitudes of Selected Protestant Clergy in the Palatinate, 1848–1849

Political Attitudes	Age						Total	
	Under 35		35–49		Over 50			
	N	%	N	%	N	%	N	%
Bavarian loyalists	10	63	6	17	4	17	20	27
Leftist sympathies	6	37	28	82	19	83	53	73
Total	16	100	34	99	23	100	73	100

Sources: LAS H1 Nr. 2006 ff. 8–22, 34–37. The ages of the leftist pastors are not given in the document; I have taken them from Georg Biundo, *Die evangelischen Geistlichen der Pfalz seit der Reformation* (Neustadt a.d. Aisch: Degener & Co., 1968).

[71] On the Trier seminary, Weber, *Aufklärung und Orthodoxie*, p. 135; LAK 403 Nr. 4069 pp. 317–60; LAK 442 Nr. 6425 pp. 3–34.

engage with organized religion, to take part in its internal disputes, and to seek to reshape religious institutions toward democratic ends.

The first point of view implied the separation of church and state, as well as complete freedom in the exercise of religion, including institutional autonomy for the churches. The Mainz democrats explained, "Jesuits, Ligurians, Redemptorists, we will allow them happily in our state, we will let the dead hand [that is, religious institutions] acquire as much property as it can, but we give them nothing save what the faithful bring them. If they are victorious in the free struggle of opinion, then that is proof that their teachings correspond to the spirit of the times. If not, they will be defeated."[72]

Democrats, this view asserted, were in no way hostile to religion, and regarded it as a private matter inappropriate for the public, political realm. Any attacks they launched were not against religion as such, but against its use— or misuse—for reactionary political ends. The left here was proposing an implicit quid pro quo: If the democrats would refrain from anticlericalism, the clergy should stay out of politics. Editor F. Christian Steinberg of the popular democratic newspaper in Trier claimed his subscribers maintained that religion did not belong in a paper discussed in taverns and also that "the Herr pastor has no business writing for newspapers. Instead, he should tend to his parish duties for which he is paid, visit the sick all the more diligently, etc., and politics will be taken care of by others."[73]

Of course, many of the clergy were not willing to enter into such an agreement, providing a good argument for adherents of the second viewpoint, who saw clerical participation in politics as inevitable, and strove to remodel religious institutions to ensure they would be favorable to the left. This approach was most fruitful in dealing with Protestantism in Rhine-Hessen and the Palatinate, where rationalism was strong and the democrats had many lay and clerical sympathizers. Such individuals met in the summer of 1848 to demand the election of provincial synods for the purpose of liberating the respective Rhenish Union churches from the governing consistories in the core states and reestablishing their institutional structure on the basis of democratically elected clerical and lay representatives. The Palatine activists threatened that if the Munich consistory refused to authorize such a synod, they would appeal to all parishes to elect delegates without official approval, the resulting meeting to place itself under the protection of the Frankfurt National Assembly.[74]

[72] MZ, 13 Dec. 1848 (lead article).

[73] Vbl, 10, 12–13, Sept. 1848 (whether these were his readers' or Steinberg's own ideas is beside the point); similarly, ibid., 2, 14 July 1848; MZ, 14 Dec. 1848; "Staat, Kirche und Schule;" and "Die Demokratie und die Religion," both in Der Demokrat, 20 Aug., 1 Oct. 1848; FBA, 6 Nov. 1848.

[74] MZ, 22 Aug. 1848; NSZ, 28 July 1848; Scherer, "Zur Geschichte kirchlicher Parteien," pp. 233–37. Munich gave in and called the synod, but the idea of a provincial congress's defying

Applying the same strategy to the Catholic Church was far more problematic in view of the smaller numbers and lesser influence of clerical rationalists within it and the more conservative political sentiments of most rationalists in the Prussian Rhine Province. Leftist demands for the restructuring of the church, including calls on the Frankfurt National Assembly to prohibit the Jesuits and related religious orders, to require that priests be elected by their parishes, and even to abolish clerical celibacy, appeared not as a democratic movement within the church, but a hostile, outside attack on it. Interestingly, such a radical anti-clericalism was not correlated with other manifestations of political radicalism. Cologne communists, such as Marx and Karl D'Ester, scrupulously avoided espousing anticlerical ideas, and even opposed their being raised by other democrats; with some exceptions, this was true of the radical Mainz democrats as well. Moderates, such as G. F. Kolb of Speyer and Hermann Körner of Elberfeld, on the other hand, positively foamed at the mouth on such topics as the Jesuits, monasteries, and the clerical hierarchy.[75]

Hostility to the institutions of the Catholic Church was most prevalent in the Palatinate, shared by moderate and radical democrats alike. It continued throughout the entire revolution, from the first mass meeting in Neustadt a.d.W. in March 1848, which demanded abolition of the monasteries, through the frequent cat musics brought against priests, to the revolutionary provisional government of May–June 1849, whose reign was marked by arrests of many priests and numerous anticlerical incidents. Leading Palatine democrats joined the sectarian German-Catholics, perceiving their religious affiliation, with its declared hostility to Christian neoorthodoxy in general, and particularly its expression in the Roman Catholic Church, as a necessary part of their democratic politics. Two of the Palatine deputies to the National Assembly, Martin Reichard of Speyer and Nikolaus Schmitt of Kaiserslautern, were both German Catholics, returning from Frankfurt to their respective hometowns to preside over founding ceremonies of schismatic congregations. The leaders of the radical wing of the Neustadt a.d.W. democrats and the city's Workers' Association, the watchmaker Johann Weber and the preacher Heinrich Loose, were also members of the sect, as were moderate democrats, including the merchant Iganz Rassiga, a veteran of the Hambach Festival. Under Rassiga's

---

Bavarian authority and placing itself under the Frankfurt National Assembly would recur in distinctly secular terms during the final crisis of the revolution in May 1849.

[75] On the Mainz democrats, see notes 72–73. For Marx and D'Ester's attitudes, see note 114; and *KnZ*, 14 Apr. 1848 (Erste Beilage). Kolb constantly reiterated his anticlericalism in his newspaper; a few particularly good examples include *NSZ*, 8, 23, 30 Apr., 27 June, 28 July, 17 Oct., 1 Nov. 1848 (Beilage). On Körner, a prominent lay German Catholic, his memoirs, *Lebenskämpfe* 1:246–48, 281–378, 300–308, 2:124–36 and passim; and ZSTAM Rep. 77 Tit. 1096 Nr. 1 Bd. 1 ff. 29–30. Other examples of these attitudes: Böse, "Ludwig Simon," pp. 142–44; *FA*, 25 Jan. 1849; *Die Trompete von Speyer* (passim), LAS J1 Nr. 252 II/1–2 (alt).

guidance, Neustadt prepared a hero's welcome for the sect's founder, Johannes Ronge, when he visited in August 1848, complete with a welcome by the civic guard, the notables, and a crowd of thousands. Ronge did not disappoint them, preaching a revolutionary sermon, calling for "one great church [recognizing] solely the rule of the spirit and . . . of eternal law, annihilating the domination of the moneybag and of tyranny."[76]

Prominent democratic activists in smaller Palatine towns were also German-Catholics. Merchant Kart Behlen of Frankenthal was constantly "in the villages attacking the [Roman] Catholics and the clergy." The leaders of the democrats in Rockenhausen were the German-Catholic innkeeper Moritz Bolza and the mayor Heinrich Brill, a Protestant rationalist who allowed the German Catholics to hold their services in the Protestant church. Together, they arranged to found a branch of the People's Association and a German-Catholic congregation on the same day. The town's Roman Catholics, already angered by the civic guard's refusal to provide an honor guard to the bishop of Speyer on his pastoral visit, were incensed when they found out that it would oppose their plans to lynch the sectarian preacher coming from Worms to Rockenhausen for the founding services. They resigned from the guard en masse and countered the preacher's visit by holding a procession to a nearby village to consecrate its new cemetery, the two events thus nicely illustrating a major political alignment in the Palatinate during the revolution: radicalism and religious rationalism versus religious (especially Roman Catholic) neoorthodoxy.[77]

All these measures, one Kaiserslautern democrat announced, had "eliminated ultramontanism in the Palatinate, or at least rendered it harmless." That was surely a dubious judgement. The democrats' campaign against the Catholic Church was seen by contemporaries, with good reason, as political hypocrisy, as a bigoted abandonment of the left's libertarian principles when it came to the Jesuits. Franz Joseph Buß, leader of the Pius Associations in Baden, noted incisively that the radicals "wanted to set everything and everyone free . . . except the Catholic Church."[78]

From a pragmatic standpoint, the democrats' indiscriminate anticlericalism was equally harmful, giving credence to Catholic claims that the real political issue, more important than any other, was defense of religion. Democratic

[76] On German Catholicism in Neustadt a.d.W., Speyer, and Kaiserslautern, see *NSZ*, 24 Aug. 1848, 9 Jan. (Beilage), 9 Mar. 1849; LAS J1 Nr. 105 ff. 201–12; LAS J1 Nr. 252 II (alt) ff. 140–45; and *Die Trompete von Speyer*, 31 Mär., 4 Apr. 1849, LAS J1 Nr. 252 II/1–2 (alt).

[77] LAS J1 Nr. 218 ff. 41–51; LAS J1 Nr. 249 (alt) ff. 79–80, 91, 327; *NSZ*, 31 Jan. 1849. In other small towns, LAS J1 Nr. 203 ff. 11–18; LAS J1 Nr. 242 ff. 137–39, 186–88. To complete the picture of religious strife, the neoorthodox Protestants of Rockenhausen opposed letting the German Catholics use their church for services.

[78] Quotes: *MZ*, 2 Feb. 1849; Wettengel, *1848/49 im Rhein-Main-Raum*, p. 46. Examples of democratic embarrassment or defensiveness at Catholic charges of political hypocrisy, *Vbl*, 5 Apr. 1849; Böse, "Ludwig Simon," p. 137; *MZ*, 13–14 Dec. 1848.

agitators frequently arrived in a village to find that the parish priest or a local official had told the peasants the leftists were coming to take their religion away from them, to force them to become Protestants or German Catholics, or to found a sectarian congregation. If allowed at all to speak, the democrats had to preface their remarks by insisting they had nothing against religion.[79]

If such an intolerant anticlericalism was so prominent among the democrats, it was not simply a result of anti-Catholic bigotry, but also reflected a social conflict, already apparent during the *Vormärz*, which reappeared in more vehement form following the outbreak of the revolution. Hardly was freedom of speech, assembly, and association proclaimed, when teachers throughout the entire Rhineland began holding meetings demanding a reform of public education. Three of their demands were the creation of an interconfessional public school system, the dispensation of teachers from giving religious education, which was to be provided by the clergy, and, as an absolute minimum, the secularization of school inspection and administration.[80]

Reactions of the Protestant clergy toward these demands were mixed, neoorthodox pastors opposing them, rationalists approving. Catholic priests, as one might expect from *Vormärz* attitudes, were unanimous and vehement in their opposition, claiming the teachers' proposals stemmed from "basically Protestant viewpoints" and were the result of "the spirit of license and perniciously understood freedom . . . which refuses to recognize any authority." Such "pernicious wishes" would lead to the reintroduction of "ancient heathenism" and destroy religion. The clergy launched massive petition drives to the Frankfurt and Berlin assemblies as well as to the Munich parliament—highly successful in the Prussian Rhine Province, noticeably less so in the Palatinate—calling for the preservation of both confessionally segregated public education and clerical control over it.[81]

This issue revealed a major difference in political principle between democrats and the Catholic clergy and lay activists over the relationship between

---

[79] *MZ*, 19 Aug. 1848; *ZAVK*, 17 Sept. 1848; Kersken, *Bonn in den Revolutionsjahren*, p. 78; LAS J1 Nr. 148 ff. 47–48; *NSZ*, 5 Nov. 1848 (Beilage); 25 Feb. 1849 (Beilage); LAS J1 Nr. 202 I (alt) ff. 390–93.

[80] *KnZ*, 7 (Zweite Beilage), 9, 15 May (Zweite Beilage), 17 July 1848 (Beilage); LAS J1 Nr. 244 ff. 28–37; *MZ*, 17 Jan. 1849; Breuer, "1848/49 im Moseltal," pp. 143–44; Schwärzwälder, "Ursachen der Reichsverfassungskampagne," pp. 100–101; *RhBA* 2/2, Nr. 207.

[81] Attitudes of the Protestant clergy: *MZ*, 22 Aug. 1848; Schwarzwälder, "Politische Bewegung in Neustadt an der Haardt," p. 104; *RhBA* 2/2, Nr. 249. For the Catholic clergy, see Repgen, "Klerus und Politik," passim; Schrörs, "Hermesianische Pfarrer," pp. 96, 149–50; *RhBA* 2/2, Nrs. 189, 195, 200, 212; *NSZ*, 11 May, 17, 21, 24 June, 2 (Beilage), 9 July 1848. The German bishops, meeting in Würzburg in November 1848, issued a declaration accepting interconfessional public education provided that religious instruction be under church control and the church be able to found private, parochial schools (*RhG* 3:360). This declaration, however, corresponded in no way to the actions of the parish clergy or of Catholic political activists, who regarded even secular school inspection in the context of confessionally separate public school systems as leading to the downfall of religion.

church and state. The expressions "independence of the church from the state" and "separation of church and state" were used indiscriminately by both groups, but in principle they had different meanings. Catholics took them to mean an end to government control over the Catholic Church, without abolishing its character as an established religion, its financing out of tax money, and its control over the public school system; democrats took them to mean the disestablishment of all religions and, in particular, the creation of a secular, interconfessional public school system, with church participation restricted to control over religious instruction. These substantial differences over the position of the schools had the practical political effect of collapsing the differences between the two attitudes of the democrats on church-state relations. What the democrats saw as separation of church and state, Catholic-clericals perceived as an attack on the institution of the church, as a blow against their freedom of religion, and as a violation of the principle of the independence of the church from the state.[82]

Practical political considerations could also reinforce the democrats' anticlericalism. The schoolteachers were strongly inclined toward the left—no less than 228 of the 1,500 schoolteachers in the Palatinate would be indicted, dismissed, transferred, or placed under police surveillance for their revolutionary activities in 1848–1849. Teachers were leading democratic activists in rural areas, making it impossible for leftist leaders—even if they had been so inclined—to abandon the teachers' demands to avoid a confrontation with the clergy.[83]

While in the more devout northern Rhineland, democrats tended to soft-pedal their advocacy of the separation of church and school, in the more strongly rationalist southern part of the region, they were considerably more aggressive. Mainz democrats campaigned vigorously to reintroduce the interconfessional public school system in their city, founded under the French revolutionary regime, and abolished as a politically repressive measure following the Hambach Festival in 1832. Democrats packed the galleries at the decisive city council meeting, shouting at the Catholic-clerical councilmen opposed to the measure, "Windischgrätz" (the name of the counterrevolutionary Austrian general) or "hang them." Mainz democratic leaders rebuked their fol-

---

[82] On the theoretical difference between the two slogans, but their indiscriminate use in both senses—an excellent example of the amorphous character of political discourse in mid-nineteenth-century Germany—see the illuminating explication of Repgen, *Märzbewegung*, pp. 162–64. For examples of different attitudes of democrats and Catholics about the public schools, see Karl Heinrich Hoefele, "Die Anfänge des politischen Katholizismus in der Stadt Trier," *Trierer Jahrbuch* 2 (1939): 77–112, esp. p. 86; Stahl, *1848/49 an der Mittelmosel*, p. 15; *RhBA* 2/2:308 n.3, 343 n.7; *Vbl*, 29 June, 2 July, 1, 4, 8 Aug. 1848; *MZ*, 24–25, 29–31 Aug., 5, 13 Dec. 1848, 4 Jan., 12 Apr. 1849; *Der Demokrat*, 20 Aug., 31 Dec. 1848; *NSZ*, 14 July 1848 (lead article); Gernert, *1848/49 im Rheinisch-Bergischen*, pp. 87–88, 94–96, 109.

[83] LAS H1 Nr. 2016 f. 62; Schwarzwälder, "Die Ursachen der Reichsverfassungskampagne," pp. 107–08. Similarly in Rhine-Hessen, BAF FN7 Anhang 4 Gagern ff. 109–10.

lowers for their excessive zeal but not for their basic opinions, typical of the radicals of the area.[84]

Combining democratic and clerical attitudes, it would appear that the relationship between leftists and Protestant clerical rationalists (as well as the handful of rationalist Catholic priests sympathetic to the left) worked out relatively smoothly. Cooperation between the left and the neoorthodox Catholic clergy and lay activists of the Prussian Rhineland, on the other hand, was possible only insofar as the two groups could agree to concentrate their action on their common enemy, the Prussian state, and overlook the many differences in their political goals. It was a limited alliance, one that could and did quickly turn into a hostile competition for the same mass audience, the Catholic lower classes, each political group seeking to exploit the masses' hatred of the Prussian state for very different ends.

THE JACOBIN HERITAGE: RHENISH DEMOCRATS AND THE
FRENCH REVOLUTION

When seeking to express their general social and political ideals, Rhenish democrats frequently had recourse to language from the great French Revolution, explicitly linking their struggles with those of the years after 1789. The manufacturer Franz Bardollo, commander of the civic guard of the very left-wing northern Palatine town of Grünstadt, told the peasants of the nearby village of Grossbrockenheim at a political rally in the summer of 1848 how to obtain "the rights they were still lacking. . . . He placed before them the image of the French Revolution, by which our forefathers were freed of all oppression and feudal burdens, and suggested to them especially that they form associations, in the democratic sense. . . ." Cruder and blunter was the assistant schoolteacher Michael Braun of Rülzheim, in the southern Palatinate, who gave a speech praising the French Revolution, saying that "just like then, prince, government and the damned priests must be overthrown, because they are sucking the people dry."[85]

While certainly having no lack of invective, both freshly manufactured in 1848 and stemming from the previous thirty years, to refer to its enemies, the left also used the old Jacobin terminology. Surprisingly often for such a bourgeois area as the Rhineland, democrats denounced their opponents as "aristocrats." Leftists referred to the state officials in Kaiserslautern and the constitutional monarchist townspeople who sympathized with them as "aristocrats," to the Second Company of the town's civic guard, where they

[84] On the campaign of the Mainz democrats, see the sources cited in note 78. Cf. also *NSZ*, 15, 24 Mar., 30 June 1848; LAS J1 Nr. 244 ff. 8–9.

[85] LAS J1 Nr. 235 ff. 17–21, 151–52; LAS J1 Nr. 264 ff. 461–66. More generally, on the French Revolution as an intellectual model for the Rhenish democrats, cf. Schurz, *Lebenserinnerungen*, pp. 156–58.

were to be found, as the "aristocrats' company," and to its commanding officer, brewer Carl von Wächter, as an "arch-aristocrat." Democrats in manufacturing districts in Solingen, Elberfeld, and Krefeld denounced the conservative or constitutional monarchist merchant manufacturers of the region who tried to intimidate the outworkers into supporting their political views as "the aristocracy."[86]

Classic revolutionary terminology was also employed to summarize the democrats' aspirations. Rhenish democrats made frequent and varied use of the motto "liberty, equality, fraternity." It graced the banner of the Cologne Democratic Society, today on display in the city's municipal-historical museum. An explication of the revolutionary slogan stood on the agenda of the Trier Democratic Club for its session of June 24, 1848, where the speaker was Gymnasium teacher Friedrich Simon, father of Trier's fire-eating deputy in the Frankfurt National Assembly. Significantly, Simon was followed on the agenda by another speaker explaining the meaning of popular sovereignty. Mainz democrats hoped that "the marvelous words liberty, equality, fraternity" would be the basis of a new democratic state, and also the spirit in which the social question could be resolved. The openly republican People's Club in Düsseldorf announced its formation with a wall poster proclaiming, "The tendency of the People's Club is directed towards the realization of social democracy, whose slogan is liberty, equality, fraternity." Even democratic monarchists made use of the motto, an editorial in the *Neue Speyer Zeitung* beginning, "No republic, but liberty, equality, fraternity."[87]

The motto found its way into the early labor movement, the first anniversary banquet of the Mainz Workers' Association including toasts to "the proletarians who have fallen on the barricades," and also to "liberty, equality, fraternity." An interesting variant of the revolutionary slogan became the motto of the Cologne Workers' Association, emblazoned on its red flag and later the title of its newspaper, "liberty, fraternity, labor."[88]

A few of the most radical democrats were more explicit about their revolutionary heritage. A good example is the banquet of the Mainz Democratic Club held in February 1849 in honor of the first anniversary of the proclama-

---

[86] Quotes: LAS J1 Nr. 245 ff. 263–67; LAS J1 Nr. 277 (alt) ff. 180–82, 184–87; *RhBA* 2/2. Nr. 215; *NKZ*, 7 Feb. 1849; prospectus for *Neue Crefelder Volksblätter*, 25 Jan. 1849, LAK 403 Nr. 7171; similarly, LAS J1 Nr. 203 ff. 167–74, 206–208; LAS J1 Nr. 205 ff. 332–33, 680–82; LAS J1 Nr. 219 ff. 1021–28; LAS J1 Nr. 242 ff. 114–17, 169–70; LAS J1 Nr. 215 (alt) ff. 129–31, 170–74; LAS J1 Nr. 249 (alt) ff. 93–94; LAS J1 Nr. 243 (alt) ff. 376–81; LAK 442 Nr. 6388 pp. 201–02; *MZ*, 18 Mar. 1849; "Ueber die Stellung und Pflicht der demokratischen Partei," *Der Demokrat*, 2 July 1848; "Aus dem Kreise Rheinbach," *KnZ*, 20 Jan. 1849 (Zweite Beilage).

[87] *Vbl*, 14, 28 June 1848; *MZ*, 16 July 1848; HSTAD RD Nr. 8804 f. 22; *NSZ*, 13 May 1848; similarly, BAF ZSg 8/55 f. 178; LAK 442 Nr. 6506 ff. 30–31.

[88] "Ein Arbeiterfest," *Der Demokrat*, 25 Apr. 1849. To translate *Freiheit, Brüderlichkeit Arbeit* into English as "Freedom, Brotherhood, Labor [or Work]" (Noyes, *Organization and Revolution*, p. 284; Hammen, *The Red '48ers*, p. 224) is extremely misleading.

tion of the republic in France. The two thousand participants gathered in the town's Corn Hall saw an illustration of republicanism. Painted in gigantic letters on the wall behind the tribune was the slogan "liberty, equality, fraternity"; on the tribune stood the black-red-gold flag, the flags of the Workers' Association and Gymnastics Society, the flags of the two great republics, France and the United States, and, towering above them all, the red flag. Pillars on the tribune were painted with the names and sayings of revolutionary heroes: Spartacus from antiquity, Gutenberg, Thomas Moore, and Martin Luther from the beginning of the modern era, Kosciuszko, Rousseau, Franklin, and Washington from the eighteenth century, as contemporaries, Robert Blum and Friedrich Hecker, and from the great French Revolution, Robespierre and St. Just.[89]

The Democratic Society and the Workers' Association in Cologne jointly sponsored a banquet to celebrate the same event, including a toast to Robespierre, St. Just, Marat, and the heroes of 1793 by a leading member of the Workers' Association and a singing of the Marseillaise by the workers' choral society. The organizers claimed two thousand to three thousand participants; twice as many are said to have shown up a month later for the banquet in honor of the first anniversary of the barricade fighting in Berlin—an event that was an open celebration of Jacobin republicanism. At the center of the tribune was a red flag, topped by the Phrygian cap; the marshalls and ushers for the festivities also wore caps of liberty and red scarves. Toasts were offered to the red republic; a new version of the Marseillaise, written by the revolutionary poet Ferdinand Freiligrath, was sung; and, as the constitutional monarchist *Kölnische Zeitung* noted ironically, "there was no lack of red caps, scarves and ribbons."[90]

Some idea of the thinking behind such symbolism comes from the speech given by the law graduate Johann Baptist Müller-Melchiors in a session of the Mainz Democratic Club devoted to debating the meaning of the phrase the "red republic." He explained that its origins lay in the Jacobins' use of the red cap of liberty and went on to express his solidarity with the ideals, if not all the actions, of the radical phase of the French Revolution:[91]

The friend of humanity may condemn the atrocities of the Jacobins; the republican must concede that it was these deeds which brought the republic to an early end and were in part responsible for the restoration of the monarchy. Yet, he who loves freedom, who sees in history more than the recounting of isolated instances, must admit that France owes to the Jacobins and their terrorism its continued existence as

[89] *MZ*, 27 Feb. 1849; Karz-Seibert, *Radikalismus in Hessen*, p. 64.

[90] *NRhZ*, 28 Feb., 21 Mar. 1849; *NKZ*, 22 Mar. 1849; *KnZ*, 21 Mar. 1849.

[91] *MZ*, 2 Nov. 1848. Cf. the feuilleton of the *NRhZ*, 19, 21–22, 26 June 1848 on the "Trial before the National Convention of Louis Capet, ex-King of France."

a state. More than that, to them belongs the honor of having placed the rule [Herrschaft] of the revolution in France on unshakable foundations, of having exterminated the old system at its roots and thus assured the victory of the ideas of the modern age.

"MODERATES" AND "EXALTEDS": TENDENCIES WITHIN THE DEMOCRATIC MOVEMENT

Since the Rhenish democrats were far more a loose coalition of local groups, with varied supporters and political interests, than a tightly led and organized political party, with a unified and binding program, they had, for all their points of agreement, substantial internal differences and different attitudes toward one another. West German historians have often talked of moderate "political" democrats and more radical "social" democrats. While criticizing this typology, scholars from the former East Germany created a similar one, distinguishing between "bourgeois" or "petit bourgeois" and "proletarian" leftists. In both versions, concern for the "social question," the advocacy of social reform or social revolution rather than an exclusive concentration on political issues, forms the basis for differentiating left from right among the democrats and, more broadly, aligning all elements in the political spectrum.[92]

While contemporaries also spoke of the "social question," and even before 1848, people were predicting the outbreak of a social rather than a political revolution, they understood it in a quite different way. Adherents of all political positions, from the extreme right to the extreme left, addressed social issues, but the similar language they used—this is a characteristic trait of political discourse in mid-nineteenth-century Germany—had very different meanings. The prospectus for the *Mainzer Journal*, the first Catholic-clerical newspaper to be founded in the Rhineland following the lifting of press censorship in March 1848, announced that the ongoing revolution was not just political but social in nature. As it had always done in the past, and was currently doing, the Catholic Church was preaching "by the deed" liberty, equality, and fraternity "to all those who are poor, sick and suffering," and the newspaper regarded it as the task of all Catholics to "support the church in its social activity." Solving the social question, in other words, meant providing charity and improving morality, a position also taken by the Pius Association of Mülheim a. Rhein, which announced in December 1848 that it would confront the "existing social grievances and evils" [die herrschenden sozialen

---

[92] See, for example, Siemann, *Die deutsche Revolution*, pp. 93–94; Nipperdey, *Deutsche Geschichte*, pp. 620–21; Paschen, *Demokratische Vereine und Preußischer Staat*, pp. 103–07; Seypel, "Die Demokratische Gesellschaft in Köln," pp. 140–83; *Illustrierte Geschichte*, pp. 93–96, 219–21. A good criticism of this approach in Peter Wende, *Radikalismus im Vormärz. Untersuchung zur politischen Theorie der frühen deutschen Demokratie* (Wiesbaden: Franz Steiner, 1977), p. 129.

Mißstände und übelstände]. While sounding quite radical, it turned out to mean encouraging couples living in sin to get married and systematically gathering charitable contributions for the poor.[93]

Moderates and conservatives raised the "social question" as a means of defusing left-wing political demands, as did the neoorthodox Prussian loyalists of the Wuppertal, when they encouraged workers to form associations in the spring of 1848 and concern themselves with the social question instead of becoming involved in the political campaigns of the (very moderately) leftist Political Club. A little ways to the west in Düseldorf, the Workers' Association founded there at the end of April 1848, dissolved within two months because of internal controversies. One faction wanted the group to consider political as well as social issues, and adopt as its motto the slogan of the Cologne Association, "liberty, fraternity, labor," while the other group insisted that discussing politics was inappropriate for an organization attempting to solve the social question, and that such a group's motto should include the words "quiet, order, legality." The leaders of the first faction were among the founders of the openly republican People's Club; those of the latter, activists in the constitutional monarchist Citizen's Association.[94]

"Social" and "political" issues were no more closely correlated among Rhenish democrats. Certainly some extreme leftists were also social revolutionaries, such as Marx and his followers, while more moderate democrats, such as the Palatine G. F. Kolb, supported a monarchy and a free market economy. However, there are just as many good counterexamples. Prominent Mainz democrats were self-proclaimed red republicans, leaders of a large and active Workers' Association, and admirers of the Jacobins, yet also strongly sympathetic to laissez-faire. Gottfried Kinkel, the major democratic proponent of a restoration of the guilds, earned thunderous applause when he addressed the Cologne Democratic Society on Germany's revolutionary future as a "social democratic republic." The extreme right wing of the democratic movement, the Democratic Constitutional Central Association of the Rhineland and Westphalia, a group formed by the secession of several clubs from the constitutional monarchist federation in January 1849, proclaimed as its three found-

---

[93] BAF ZSg 8/55 f. 92; Gernert, *1848/49 im Rheinisch-Bergischen*, p. 128. Cf. Diehl, *Das "Mainzer Journal" im Jahre 1848*, pp. 29–37; Kühn, *Der junge Hermann Becker*, pp. 74–75; predictions of a "social revolution," Wehler, *Deutsche Gesellschaftsgeschichte* 2:684. In fairness to the Catholics, it should be pointed out that they regarded improving morality as the most important but not the sole resolution of the social question, also advocating more equitable taxation, the prohibition of usury, and the restoration of the guilds.

[94] See sources cited in Chapter Six, note 30; and Lenger, *Zwischen Kleinbürgertum und Proletariat*, pp. 166, 174–76. Similarly, the first issue of the *Mainzer Journal* insisted that the real issue was not republic versus monarchy, as the Mainz democrats insisted, but the social question, which was to be resolved primarily by combating immorality and atheism. Diehl, *Das "Mainzer Journal" im Jahre 1848*, pp. 29–34.

ing points support for German national unity, a democratic but monarchist form of government for Prussia, and the "solution of the social question."[95]

Sorting out different elements on the left by their attitudes toward social issues may be a useful way to consider German politics in the second half of the nineteenth century, but it is a poor tool for understanding the democrats of 1848–1849. Contemporaries had another way of describing differences among democrats, focusing more on process, on the combination of social and political goals with the means used to achieve them. They contrasted leftists who were "exalted" or "fanatic" [exaltiert] with those who were "moderate" [gemäßigt]. The former term was applied to those democrats who were insistent, uncompromising enemies of the existing political order, oriented toward mass agitation against it and militant—if need be, violent—struggle to overturn it. Moderates were more likely to take conciliatory positions, work within the political system as it had existed since March 1848, put their primary emphasis on parliamentary activities, and not exclude a priori compromise with political tendencies to their right.[96]

Social issues entered into the distinction in a mediated fashion. "Exalted," radical democrats were given to mass political action and had to find ways to stir up the masses—often through anticapitalist economic schemes, although more commonly ones based on the slogan of the "organization of labor" rather than what would later become known as socialism. It was not the anticapitalism of these ideas that separated extremists from moderates, but their use for mass political mobilization and the insistence that their realization required the overthrow of the existing political order. The "exalted" leftists had many other issues they used for mass mobilization—denunciation of bureaucrats, taxes, the military, the royal family, and state-supported business interests. All these issues had in common a violent and vehemently expressed hostility to the existing states. Of course, moderate democrats also criticized these institutions—but they usually did so more moderately, without attempting quite the same mass broadcasts of their ideas in the vehement and violent language of their "fanatic" counterparts.[97]

The distinction between "exalteds" and moderates is not equivalent to that between democratic monarchists and republicans, since most democratic ac-

[95] On Kinkel in Cologne, see Seypel, "Die Demokratische Gesellschaft in Köln," p. 120; founding plank of the democratic constitutional association as reported in NKZ, 12 Jan. 1849.

[96] See, for example, LAS J1 Nr. 218 ff. 248–49; LAS J1 Nr. 203 ff. 206–08; LAS J1 Nr. 252 (alt) ff. 154–58; LK Kaiserslautern to RP, 2 May 1849, BHSTAM MInn Nr. 45531; HSTAD RD Nr. 8809 ff. 126–39; HSTAD RD Pr. Nr. 796 ff. 26–27, 29–30.

[97] Cf., for example, the authorities' comparison of the moderate Democratic Club with the radical People's Club in Düsseldorf, RhBA 2/2, Nr. 289. This typology owes a good deal to the work of Dieter Langewiesche, especially his essay "Republik, Konstitutionelle Monarchie und 'soziale Frage.'" For a similar typology and vigorous critique of the distinction between "social" and "political" democrats from a Marxist-Leninist viewpoint, see Strey and Winkler, *Marx and Engels 1848/49*, pp. 194–95.

tivists regarded the republic as the best possible form of government. Rather, the dividing line was between democrats who refused to accept any but a republican form of government for Germany—with all the consequences for politics that entailed—and those who would settle for a monarchy "with democratic institutions," meaning something like national unity, universal manhood suffrage, parliamentary government, and a basically symbolic role for the royal family. Metaphorically—and metaphors are important for understanding these differences, which were frequently expressed to the public in symbolic form—one might say that the "exalted" democrats were those who flew the red flag alongside the black-red-gold tricolor, and moderates, those who flew the tricolor alone.[98]

If flying the red flag expressed symbolically the difference between these two broad groups of democrats, the use of the slogan "the second revolution," articulated their differing attitudes. For the radicals, the revolution of March 1848, which had stopped at the foot of the thrones, leaving intact the existing German states, complete with their courts, bureaucracies, and armed forces, was insufficient to realize the goal of popular sovereignty, which all democrats had in common. Constrained by the authorities' willingness to arrest even advocates of a peaceful transition to a republican form of government, the most militant leftists would usually proclaim their adherence to parliamentary politics, to a process of education and enlightenment, to a struggle with "intellectual weapons," and would talk of change in terms of new elections.[99]

Sometimes, though, at political banquets, mass meetings, or club sessions they would come right out and speak of the need for a "second," republican revolution in Germany. The best-known example of this position, then and now, was the work of the poet Ferdinand Freiligrath, a contributing editor to the *Neue Rheinische Zeitung* and activist in the Düsseldorf People's Club. Elected treasurer of the group, he found its coffers bare—a familiar experience in democratic clubs, given the very modest dues they imposed—and wrote a poem whose sale would go to benefit the organization: the powerful work "The Dead unto the Living," in which the victims of the Berlin barricade fighting of March 1848 speak from their graves, condemning those still alive for their meek acceptance of the resurgence of reaction and calling on them to carry the revolution to its conclusion in the red republic.

When Freiligrath first read the poem at the August 1, 1848, session of the People's Club, the members gave him a standing ovation. Printed up as a flier, the work sold thousands of copies throughout the lower Rhine. The Ministry

---

[98] This distinction is similar to the one proposed by Nickel, *1848/49 in Augsburg und Bayerisch-Schwaben*, pp. 152–53.

[99] See, for example, *MZ*, 18, 23 July, 17 Aug., 29 Oct. 1848; *Der Demokrat*, 14 May, 2, 9 July, 1848; *NRhZ*, 5 June, 22 Oct. 1848; *NSZ*, 24 Apr., 2 July, 16 Aug. 1848; HSTAD RD Nr. 200 pp. 226–28; *Vbl*, 9 July 1848; LAK 403 Nr. 6583 pp. 74–75; Breuer, "1848/49 im Moseltal," pp. 187–88.

of Justice promptly ordered Freiligrath's indictment on charges of sedition, against the advice of the provincial judicial and administrative authorities. The latter's fears were realized when Freiligrath's trial ended in his acquittal, followed by a mass demonstration in his honor in Düsseldorf, the thousands of participants singing the Marseillaise and cheering the red republic.[100]

Freiligrath's poem was an elegant, literary expression of the self-image of the radical wing of the democratic movement. "Exalted" democrats saw themselves as carrying the work of the revolution to its final conclusion, insisting on the consequent application of democratic principles. Unlike their moderate counterparts, the "white democrats," the "gray democrats," the "pale democrats," the "halves," they were men who refused "any mediation, any half-way measures," who wanted the "realization of liberty, equality, fraternity."[101]

Clearly stung by such accusations, moderates responded by pointing out that any democratic principles at all could be realized only in a broad political coalition. By raising extreme demands and condemning all those who would not accept them, radicals were splitting the "citizenry," doing the reactionaries' work of divide and rule for them. Extremists were "self-proclaimed friends of the people, who in the truest sense of the word are enemies of the people. In their arrogant self-overestimation, they oppose with insinuation all tendencies of true patriots towards unity, in doing so acting against the first principle of all association, 'In union there is strength.' "[102]

Paradoxically, both extremists and moderates were right in their assertions. A large majority of the high state officials and many constitutional monarchists saw all democrats, no matter how conciliatory or moderate, as dangerous radicals. One Mainz democrat put it quite nicely: "Here in Germany, democrats are denounced as red republicans and their opponents do not even want a white republic." Democrats who wished to see an end to privilege were condemned for having called for "the overthrow of the universal order"; their demands for "the right to work and just taxation are denounced as communism by those who believe their interests endangered." Faced with such an outside world, all Rhenish leftists, in spite of their internal differences, were forced to remain part of one political movement.[103]

---

[100] On Freiligrath and his poem, see LAK 403 Nr. 9632 passim; *RhBA* 2/2, Nrs. 230, 236, 276. Other public calls for a second revolution: LAK 403 Nr. 9632 pp. 18–21; HSTAD RD Pr. Nr. 812 ff. 44–45; LAS J1 Nr. 105 ff. 201–12 (cf. RP to MInn, 11 Oct. 1848, BHSTAM MInn Nr. 46129); LAS H1 Nr. 1974 ff. 5–6; Strey and Winkler, *Marx und Engels 1848/49*, pp. 42–43; Katz-Seibert, *Radikalismus in Hessen*, p. 64; *Vbl*, 20–21 Mar. 1849; *Anklag-Akte*, pt. 2, p. 85.

[101] *MZ*, 2 Nov. 1848; *NKZ*, 7 Jan., 20 Apr. 1849; *FBA*, 8 Feb. 1849; *FA*, 25 Jan. 1849; similarly, *NRhZ*, 26 Jan., 17 Mar. 1849; LAS J1 Nr. 242 ff. 202–10; *Anklag-Akte*, pt. 2 pp. 75–77.

[102] Seypel, "Die Demokratische Gesellschaft in Köln," p. 332; LAS J1 Nr. 228 (alt) f. 666; similarly, *NSZ*, 12 Oct. 1848 (Beilage).

[103] *MZ*, 4 Nov. 1848.

The Revolutionary as Revolutionary:
 Karl Marx in 1848–1849

Both to contemporaries and to posterity, one Rhineland democrat seemed to be the very quintessence of a revolutionary. Yet Karl Marx's life, spanning the better part of the nineteenth century, encompassed a period when the meaning of radicalism and the nature of revolution both underwent substantial changes, in part as a consequence of Marx's own actions. At the beginning of his life, the image of radicalism was still largely dominated by the Jacobin heritage of the French Revolution; by its end the contours of twentieth-century Bolshevism and social democracy were beginning to emerge. Certainly twelve years later, on the death of his friend, interpreter, and collaborator Friedrich Engels, they had already taken shape. Looking at Marx's role in 1848–1849, it is important to keep in mind that decades-long process of transformation of the meaning of revolution—a change taking place both in radical thought and in European society—and not to judge revolutionary actions toward the beginning of his political career with conditions from the end.[104]

Marx's response to the outbreak of revolution in Germany encompassed two separate branches of activities, a sort of political double track, which he first outlined in the *Communist Manifesto* and then pursued throughout the entire year of revolution. In the *Manifesto*—not in the main section with its broad theory of history, but in the often-neglected concluding agenda for action—Marx defined the task of German communists as that of supporting the bourgeois revolution against feudalism, absolutism, and particularism, pushing it in the most radical and democratic direction possible. Simultaneously, they would have to explain to the workers that once this revolution was won, they would have to contend with the victorious bourgeoisie. From Paris, where Marx was living in March 1848, he took two courses of action, each corresponding to one branch of the two-pronged struggle. On the one hand, he prepared to return to Cologne to revive the radical newspaper he had edited in 1842–1843, the *Rheinische Zeitung*. On the other, he called on the members of the émigré Communist League to go back individually to Germany and create local workers' associations in different cities, to be linked in a national federation, led by the Workers' Association of Mainz.[105]

---

[104] The size of the Marx-Engels literature has long since passed the point of no return—in any event, most of it is concerned with the two as social, economic, or philosophical thinkers, not as historical actors—so I will renounce citing any of it. The works of Pierre Ayçoberry, Gerhard Becker, Dieter Dowe, Oskar Hammen, Marcel Seypel, and Joachim Strey and Gerhard Winkler, all have useful things to say about Marx and Engels, from quite different political standpoints. The studies of Becker, Dowe, and Hammen provide the essential biographical details, incorporating the older literature.

[105] Walter Schmidt, "Der Bund der Kommunisten und die Versuche einer Zentralisierung der deutschen Arbeitervereine in April und Mai 1848," *Zeitschrift für Geschichtswissenschaft* 9 (1961): 577–614; Dowe, *Aktion und Organisation*, pp. 142–43.

Marx's efforts at working-class organization were ill-fated. Virtually no one answered the call of the Mainz Workers' Association for a national federation, and leadership of the Mainz group itself soon passed out of the hands of members of the Communist League into those of the noncommunist Mainz democrats. In fact, the entire Mainz branch of the Communist League collapsed, some of its journeymen artisan members leaving town to look for work, others playing dominoes in a cafe when they were supposed to be engaging in revolutionary politics.[106]

The situation in Cologne might have seemed more promising for Marx's proletarian plans, since the local branch of the Communist League had more cohesion, and one of its members, Andreas Gottschalk, was president of the Cologne Workers' Association. Gottschalk, however, thought that Marx and Engels should have returned from exile not to Cologne, but to their native cities, Trier and Barmen, respectively, to campaign for the Frankfurt National Assembly, leaving him in charge of the extreme left in the Rhenish metropolis. Even if these personal rivalries had not existed, Gottschalk's true socialist ideas would have ensured a political conflict. As it was, they quickly put him at odds with Marx (to say nothing of virtually all the leading Cologne democrats), and he resigned from the Communist League but, in view of his great popularity with the lower classes, could not be dislodged from his position in the Workers' Association.[107]

These circumstances, apparent by May 1848, created a crisis for the existence of the Communist League, which seemed to have lost its purpose on return of its members from exile. Ernst Dronke, one of Marx's associates, saw the disarray of the League's local sections while on a trip to the Rhine-Main area for the combined purposes of communist organizing and fund-raising for the proposed radical Cologne newspaper. Dronke wanted to revive the League by admitting to membership radical figures, such as the rentier and city councillor Gabriel Trimborn in Koblenz or the journalist Ludwig Bamberger in Mainz. Both were democratic activists but hardly communists, and such a policy would have meant changing the Communist League back into the radical secret society from which it had emerged. Marx chose instead to deemphasize the activities of the League. There has been a long scholarly controversy over whether he dissolved it altogether, sometime in May–June 1848. The evidence is fragmentary and inconclusive, but the whole controversy is not terribly important anyway, since all participants agree that, even if still formally existing, the League was largely inactive for the following year.[108]

[106] Ibid. The documents printed in *Der Bund der Kommunisten* 1, Nrs. 236, 248, 251, paint a lively picture of the fiasco of the Mainz Communist League.

[107] On Marx and Gottschalk, see the pro-Marx account in Becker, *Marx und Engels in Köln*, pp. 23–24 and passim, and the pro-Gottschalk one in Karl Stommel, "Andreas Gottschalk," both works strongly marked by the politics of the cold war. A judicious, balanced version can be found in Dowe, *Aktion und Organisation*, pp. 142–53, 171–75, 212–17.

[108] On Dronke's trip, see *Der Bund der Kommunisten* 1, Nrs. 251, 255. The controversy over

Marx had more success in the democratic track of his actions, taking away control of the editorial board of the proposed revival of the *Rheinische Zeitung* from the Cologne true socialists and, with some difficulty, getting the money together to begin publishing the *Neue Rheinische Zeitung* at the beginning of June. He joined the Cologne Democratic Society, quickly obtaining a leading role within it. He opposed, at the end of June, Gottschalk's proposal for a merger of the Workers' Association and the Democratic Society, successfully proposing in its place a committee for joint action between the two groups.[109]

Gottschalk's arrest at the beginning of July, allowing Marx and his followers to gain control of the Workers' Association, gave Marx a second chance at the proletarian track of his strategy. Marx himself never played a major role in the Workers' Association, rarely attending its meetings, even in the fall of 1848, when he served as the organization's interim president. Historians have sometimes seen this as evidence of Marx's lack of interest in workers' affairs, but it would be fairer to point to other considerations. "Dr. Marx," as everybody referred to him, was no rabble-rousing agitator. Both he and Engels willingly admitted that all of their group, except for the native Silesian Wilhelm Wolff, lacked the "common touch." Marx's one great oration during the revolution came during his trial for press offenses, to the distinctly bourgeois audience of the jurors. Given the limits on his time and energy, Marx put his personal effort where it would do the most good, into the newspaper and the Democratic Society, while his close associates, Karl Schapper and Joseph Moll, both experienced veterans of years of artisan politics in exile, represented the Cologne communists in the leadership of the Workers' Association.[110]

As explained in the previous chapter, the Marxists saw the Workers' Association primarily as a means to mobilize Cologne's lower classes into the democratic movement. They made no attempt whatsoever to establish any connections with workers' associations in the nearby Wuppertal and Bergisches Land, completely ignoring both the spontaneous organization of the textile and metallurgical outworkers, and the attempts of the democrats on the right bank of the Rhine to work with such groups and mobilize them politically.

the "dissolution" of the Communist League is discussed with great judiciousness by Dowe, *Aktion und Organisation*, pp. 250–53, which will be the last word on the topic, unless new sources appear.

[109] Dowe, *Aktion und Organisation*, pp. 142–44, 171–75. Becker's attribution of Marx's opposition to the merger of the Workers' Association and the Democratic Society to the Leninist principle that the workers should not be subordinated to the petit bourgeoisie (*Marx und Engels in Köln*, pp. 75–76) is, as Seypel quite rightly points out ("Die Demokratische Gesellschaft in Köln," pp. 295–97), at best anachronistic. Marx, like the other Cologne democrats, was afraid that a merger would allow Gottschalk, then at the height of his popularity, to impose his peculiar political views on the entire left in the Rhenish metropolis.

[110] Noyes, *Organization and Revolution*, p. 123, provides a particularly exaggerated example of the claim that Marx wanted nothing to do with the workers. On Marx and Engels' discussion of their own abilities, or lack of them, see *Illustrierte Geschichte*, p. 158.

Writing to Marx in 1853 from exile in Philadelphia, the radical Solingen metalworker Carl Wilhelm Klein, who had joined the revived Communist League after the suppression of the revolution, noted, "Our party . . . will have to admit after the next revolution [has broken out], how important it is, *at the very least* [emphasis in original] in the interests of the [Communist] League, to have organized the workers of the industrial areas of the Rhineland and Westphalia." In other words, the communists would have to make up in the future what they had neglected in 1848–1849.[111]

In Cologne itself, this second try at resuming the proletarian track of Marx's strategy, organizing the workers independently to support the democrats, while pointing out to them the future struggle with the bourgeoisie, did not go well. Support for Gottschalk's policy of a specifically working-class politics, separate from and possibly opposed to the democrats, never entirely died out among Workers' Association activists. Gottschalk was finally brought to trial in December 1848, following six months of imprisonment, and after his triumphant acquittal, made a bid to regain control of the organization he had founded. He was unsuccessful, but his followers continued to be a disruptive element throughout the winter and spring of 1849, constantly challenging the Marxist leadership, forcing it to make tacit concessions to their views.[112]

The major and by far the most successful part of Marx's political activities from June 1848 until the final crisis of the revolution in May 1849 was devoted to the democratic track, not the proletarian one. This was particularly apparent in the editorial policy of the *Neue Rheinische Zeitung*. It was not a newspaper promoting the class struggle or workers' interests, containing little or no news of labor disputes, workers' congresses, or other efforts at proletarian organization. To be sure, Marx frequently had nasty things to say, both in public and in private, about the bourgeoisie, but denouncing the bourgeoisie was typical of most Rhenish democrats and no expression of a particularly communist sentiment.[113]

The *Neue Rheinische Zeitung* was just what its masthead proclaimed, "the organ of the democratic movement," and it expressed, in powerful, angry,

[111] *Der Bund der Kommunisten* 3, Nr. 765; cf. ibid. 1, Nr. 247; and Dowe, *Aktion und Organisation*, pp. 154–55. The only other workers' association with which the Cologne group had even the faintest contacts was the one in the textile center Krefeld. *ZAVK*, 30 July, 3 Aug. 1848.

[112] On the Cologne Workers' Association in January-May 1849, and Marx's strategies at that time, see Chapter Nine.

[113] The attitude, or lack of it, of the *Neue Rheinische Zeitung* towards the workers' movement, has often been noted. Cf., for example, Taubert, *Autonomie und Integration*, pp. 17–22; Siemann, *Die deutsche Revolution*, pp. 95–96; Noyes, *Organization and Revolution*, pp. 120–22; Hammen, *The Red '48ers*. My own reading of the newspaper confirms this view, and I find unconvincing attempts of Marxist-Leninist historians to refute it, for example, Walter Schmidt, "Die Klassenkämpfe in Frankreich 1848/49 in der 'Neuen Rheinischen Zeitung'—ein Beitrag zum Ringen der Kommunisten um die Emanzipation der deutschen Arbeiterbewegung," *Beiträge zur Geschichte der deutschen Arbeiterbewegung* 10 (1965): 263–91.

sarcastic, and vehement language, the main ideological themes of the democrats of Rhenish Prussia: the domination of the Rhinelanders by the Prussian state, the oppression, brutality, and corruption of East Elbian state officials and army officers, and their contempt and hostility toward the citizenry. Solidarity of the workers against the capitalist class was not a theme of Marx's newspaper; solidarity of the Rhinelanders against the Prussian state was. One interesting sign of this tendency was Marx's conciliatory attitude towards the Catholic Church. His was the only major left-wing newspaper in the Rhineland that avoided attacking it, hardly out of sympathy for religion, but in the hope that Catholic hostilities toward the Prussian state could be harnessed to the revolutionary cause.[114]

The paper espoused an "exalted" attitude toward political events, calling on the Frankfurt National Assembly to act as a sovereign revolutionary parliament and pouring scorn on its moderate to conservative leadership and majority for refusing to do so. It supported the Austrian and Prussian national assemblies in their struggles with royal authority, always encouraging them to act in a more decisive and radical way. The two major revolutionary struggles in Cologne, in which Marx was personally involved, the crisis of September 1848 and the tax boycott campaign of November of that year, both centered around hostility to the Prussian state and its military and bureaucratic representatives and the mobilization of the Rhenish population against them. During these crises, Marx and his followers tried to mobilize the broadest spectrum of the population for the most militant political action possible.[115]

As befitted a major left-wing newspaper, the *Neue Rheinische Zeitung* carried detailed reporting on revolutionary struggles across the European continent. One of these, the sensational Parisian workers' uprising against the republican government in June 1848, the famous June Days, provides an interesting insight into Marx's politics. Most Rhenish democrats were dismayed by the event, deploring the split in the French left it showed existed, condemning the insurgents as misled victims of czarist or French royalist conspirators, and calling for a program of renewed social reform to tie the workers to the democratic republic. The June uprising was one of the few occasions when Marx let his communist sympathies show through publicly. He openly took the side of the insurgents, printing in his newspaper the first version of

---

[114] In general, on the *Neue Rheinische Zeitung*'s attitude toward the Prussian state, cf. sources cited in Chapter Five, note 53. For some good examples of its calling for Rhenish solidarity against East Elbian Prussia and inciting Catholics against Protestants, cf. *NRhZ*, 9 Aug., 17 Nov., 9 Dec. 1848; 2 Feb., 18 Mar. 1849 (Zweite Ausgabe). Marx's political attitude toward religion is noted by Hammen, *The Red '48ers*, pp. 344–45, although he errs in describing the Protestant banker Ludolf Camphausen as a Catholic.

[115] On the September and November events, and the role of the Cologne communists in them, see Chapter Eight.

an analysis that he would elaborate after the revolution in *Class Struggles in France* and *The Eighteenth Brumaire*.[116]

Cologne democrats sharply criticized this glorification of the class struggle, and in a politically significant but little-known episode, Marx repudiated his account of the June Days. Speaking at the General Assembly of the Cologne Democratic Society on August 4, 1848, he called for the reconciliation of the interests of different classes within the revolutionary movement, since "the denial of mutual concessions and the perverted ideas [verkehrte Begriffe] of the relations between the classes has led in Paris to a bloody outcome." A revolutionary government in Germany, he went on, would have to contain representatives of different classes; the sole rule of a single class was "nonsense."[117]

Here, as in his other activities on the democratic track, Marx appears as a mid-nineteenth-century Jacobin, appealing to citizens from all social classes to make concessions to one another's interest so that they can all stand together to realize the democratic and republican ideals of popular sovereignty, requiring a struggle against the monarch and the civilian and military bureaucracy through which he exercised his authority. One might well say that Marx was a Dantonesque figure, constantly appealing in the pages of his newspaper and at meetings of the Democratic Society for an ever-greater audacity, with which the revolution might yet be saved.

The sharp language in which Marx couched his appeals and his tendency to use this language against factional rivals within the democratic movement, not just against the democrats' enemies, did not sit at all well with many Rhenish leftists. Carl Schurz, then a student and revolutionary activist in Bonn, has left an often-cited account of his meeting with Marx at the Provincial Democratic Congress in August 1848, describing how Marx treated with open contempt any of his fellow democrats who disagreed with him, denouncing them as "bourgeois, that is, as an unmistakable example of deep intellectual and moral decay." Schurz is not an entirely objective witness, since he was a protegé of the Bonn democratic leader Gottfried Kinkel, who both disagreed with Marx politically and aspired to the leadership of the provincial democratic organization in the Prussian Rhineland. Other Rhenish democrats, however, issued

[116] See *NRhZ*, 26–29 June 1848; and the commentary in Strey and Winkler, *Marx und Engels 1848/49*, pp. 55–60; attitudes of other Rhenish democrats, *MZ*, 28 June (Extrablatt), 15–16 July, 3 Aug., 2 Nov. 1848; "Betrachtungen über die Pariser Juni-Ereignisse," *Der Demokrat*, 16 July 1848; *Vbl*, 2 July 1848; *NSZ*, 12, 16 July 1848; Becker, *Marx und Engels in Köln*, pp. 79–81; Hammen, *The Red '48ers*, p. 250.

[117] The newspaper report of the speech is conveniently available in *RhBA* 2/2, Nr. 209; its context and significance are brought out by Seypel, "Die Demokratische Gesellschaft in Köln," pp. 180–81, to which I owe my account. Cf. the misleading discussion of the speech in Strey and Winkler, *Marx und Engels 1848/49*, p. 60.

similar complaints about Marx's nasty polemics, his overbearing attitude, and his tendency to see himself alone as right—as he often was.[118]

Marx was hardly the only leading democrat—to say nothing of adherents of other political tendencies—to have inflated self-esteem, and bitter polemics and condemnation of the "halves" were typical among "exalted" radicals. This attitude, however, had negative consequences for Marx's political effectiveness. He saw himself as a national political leader, whose newspaper was read throughout the country, making it an instrument of intervention in the decisive events of the revolution. As he said to the jurors at his trial for slandering state officials, "I . . . assure you, gentlemen, I would rather follow the great events of the world, analyse the course of history than spend my time dealing with local idols, with gendarmes and states' attorneys."[119]

In devoting his time, his effort, and the financial resources he could raise primarily to the newspaper, Marx neglected political organization, allowing the democratic provincial committee in Rhenish Prussia to collapse and losing touch with both existing and newly founded democratic clubs outside the provincial metropolis. He wanted to be a national political leader concerned with the struggle of the extreme left in the Prussian and Frankfurt national assemblies, not a provincial one, dealing with the local grievances of the inhabitants of Plittersdorf or Winterscheid. Yet by neglecting his provincial base, he weakened his potential influence on national politics.

In 1848–1849, Marx was politically successful largely insofar as he was a Jacobin, a proponent of building political alliances across class lines to oppose monarchical authority and the bureaucratic and military apparatus through which it was exercised. He was a self-proclaimed "red republican," but as contemporaries understood the phrase, an "exalted" democrat attempting to mobilize the masses for a militant, uncompromising, and probably violent struggle with existing political institutions. Marx the advocate of class struggle, the leader of the class-conscious proletariat, the familiar communist Marx, as known primarily from his theoretical writings, was noticeably less apparent.[120]

Marx and Engels, authors of the *Communist Manifesto* and the seventeen demands of the communist party in Germany, did not renounce their communism but found they had little success in putting it across. The ideas of class struggle, as Marx and Engels, but especially Karl Schapper, propagated them in the Cologne Workers' Association, were purely abstract and theoretical, expounded primarily in educational lectures on political economy, with few if

---

[118] Schurz, *Lebenserinnerungen*, p. 159; similarly, *Der Demokrat*, 16 July 1848; *Vbl*, 19 Apr. 1849 (lead article); letter cited in Lenger, *Zwischen Kleinbürgertum und Proletariat*, p. 164. On Marx, Schurz, and Kinkel, cf. the comments of Seypel, "Die Demokratische Gesellschaft in Köln," pp. 180–81.

[119] Quoted in Seypel, "Die Demokratische Gesellschaft in Köln," p. 177.

[120] For Marx's conception of his own red republicanism, cf. *NRhZ*, 18 July 1848 (lead article).

any connections with the actual, existing social struggles of the urban and manufacturing lower classes or with their spontaneous efforts at social and political organization. Marx and his followers talked of a struggle between the "bourgeoisie" and the "proletariat," understanding by that what we would today, largely as a result of Marx's intellectual influence: a struggle between the owners of the mechanized means of production and propertyless workers. Lower-class contemporaries and other democratic activists used these terms as well, but they had in mind a struggle between small producers and the possessors of mercantile and financial capital, the latter usually closely tied to the state—a usage corresponding much more closely to the actual social circumstances of the mid-nineteenth-century Rhineland.[121]

To use Marx's own language, because his ideological conceptions did not coincide well with the social relations of production, his attempt to use his social and economic theories to mobilize members of the Workers' Association for the political task of supporting a cross-class democratic movement was not very successful. Other democrats, in Mainz, Neustadt a.d.W., or Solingen, expounding "associationist" theories of the "organization of labor," were able to achieve more. Marx's relative political success as an "exalted" democrat and his difficulties in acting as a communist were not uncharacteristic of the democratic movement in the Rhineland, and suggest something of its relationship to state and society.

[121] Andreas Gottschalk and his followers were much more in touch with the real lives of Cologne's lower classes; their grasp on the realities of political power, however, was, in comparison to Marx's—or that of virtually any other leading democrat—much feebler. The confrontations between Marx's and Gottschalk's followers ended up reinforcing their respective leaders' political weaknesses, rather than their strengths, so that the extreme left in the Rhenish metropolis was never able to realize its full political potential.

CHAPTER EIGHT

Crisis and Conflict,
June 1848–March 1849

DURING the nine months between the meeting of the Frankfurt National Assembly and its completion of the writing of a constitution for a united German state, politics in the Rhineland, as elsewhere in provincial Germany, followed closely on events in the capital cities, Frankfurt, Berlin, and Vienna. It is not that the social, economic, political, or religious tensions found in the *Vormärz* Rhineland, and so dramatically expressed in the spring of 1848, had disappeared or had been submerged in the broader issues of national politics. Rather, as a result of the development of political organization, these tensions were expressed via political campaigns around national issues.

A FESTIVE SUMMER

The second good harvest in a row after two years of near-famine and the first signs of a recovery from the recession of 1847 helped make the summer of 1848 well suited to festivity. By electing an imperial regent to be the head of a Provisional Central Power for Germany, seemingly a concrete step on the way toward national unity, the Frankfurt Parliament had provided a cause for celebration. Brainchild of the Rhine-Hessian moderate liberal Heinrich von Gagern, this action had neatly finessed differences between democrats and constitutional monarchists over the question of popular sovereignty. The National Assembly had shown its sovereign powers by electing a regent, but at the same time had declared him the sovereign head of the Provisional Central Power, not responsible to the assembly. The individual chosen, Archduke Johann of Austria, embodied this political ambiguity. Pronouncedly populist, he had made a morganatic marriage to the daughter of an innkeeper, justifying Gagern's comment that Johann had been elected "not because he was a prince but in spite of it." Johann was also the youngest brother of Franz II of Austria, the last Holy Roman Emperor of the German Nation, and thus linked to a conservative image of German nationhood, predating the French Revolution and opposing its principles.[1]

---

[1] Valentin, *Geschichte der deutschen Revolution* 2:27–41; on the relationship of Central Power and National Assembly, Botzenhart, *Deutscher Parlamentarismus*, pp. 163–92; for the broader context of Gagern's political strategy, see Gunter Hildebrandt, "Die Liberalen um Heinrich von

Gagern liked to call this action a "daring stroke," cleverly resolving substantial political differences between democrats and liberals while reaffirming the position of the Frankfurt Assembly by establishing a central government placed over the existing German states. Whether he had actually resolved the differences or just papered them over remains debatable. Also debatable was whether Gagern's choice of an Austrian prince as imperial regent fit in well with his long-term plans to make the king of Prussia emperor of a united Germany. All these points of conflict—liberal versus democratic notions of sovereignty, a new, central German state against the existing ones, Prussia versus Austria, that is, Protestants versus Catholics—would arise in August 1848, just a few weeks after Johann arrived in Frankfurt to take up his office.

The reason was a decree, issued by the minister of war of the Provisional Central Power, naming August 6, 1848, as the day when the troops of the German states were to gather and pronounce their "fealty" to the imperial regent. Like the creation of the office of imperial regent, the decree was an act of temporization, since the troops were not asked to take an oath of loyalty to the regent, the Provisional Central Power, or the National Assembly. Nonetheless, senior officers of the armies of the different German states regarded the proclamation of fealty to an imperial regent as an act limiting the prerogatives of their royal masters, so they refused to order the celebrations of fealty, or found ways to sabotage them. The civilian population of the Rhineland, in a festive mood, was not to be held back by military disapproval, and sponsored its own celebrations in honor of the imperial regent and the national unity he represented.[2]

When actually celebrated, however, the festivals of unity turned into demonstrations of discord. The army boycotted the festivities of August 6 in Aachen, but held a separate military parade the day before, during which soldiers from the Thirty-Fourth Infantry Regiment, East Elbians and ethnic Poles, brought cheers to the King of Prussia, while troops of the Twenty-Eighth Regiment, native Rhinelanders, remained silent. Tavern brawling between soldiers in the two regiments, with Aachen's lower classes supporting their fellow provincials, occurred regularly for several weeks afterward. In Krefeld, Mönchengladbach, and Linnich (Jülich County), Protestants boycotted the celebrations, claiming the Catholics had given them a "confessional interpretation" by asserting that Archduke Johann's election meant that Prussia had ceased to exist. Protestant pastor Zilleisen in Mönchengladbach and two Protestant manufacturers of the town went further. They refused to illuminate their windows in celebration, but instead hung out of them the Prussian flag and

---

Gagern in der Phase der Vorbereitung und Konstituierung der Frankfurter Nationalversammlung," in *Bourgeoisie und bürgerliche Umwälzung in Deutschland*, pp. 267–98.

[2] On the decree and the military response, see Valentin, *Geschichte der deutschen Revolution* 2:91–92; Calliess, *Militär in der Krise*, pp. 106–08.

demanded that it be flown from the tower of city hall. The crowd smashed their windows and assaulted their houses, and the civic guard refused to intervene.[3]

In predominantly Protestant areas, hostility to the imperial regent and Prussian loyalism were more overt. A mass declaration in Elberfeld signed by workers, the unemployed, and members of the militia proclaimed their desire to remain under their king, clearly higher royalty than any "dukely Imperial Regent." The inhabitants of the little Hunsrück town of Langenlonsheim a.d. Nahe, along with peasants of the vicinity and soldiers of the Seventh Ulans stationed there, marched through the streets behind the black and white flag, singing "*Heil dir im Siegekranz.*"[4]

Protestant suspicions that Catholics were celebrating the humiliation of the Prussian state, not just the election of an imperial regent, were not entirely misplaced. In the flier on the celebration put out by the festival committee in Mönchengladbach, the words "Archduke Johann of Austria" were printed in enormous letters, far larger than any others, including "Imperial Regent" or "German unity." The common people of Eupen County understood the oath of fealty to Johann sworn by the civic guard of Eupen as making them once more Habsburg subjects, as they had been in the eighteenth century, when the area had been part of the Austrian Netherlands. The Catholic lower classes may have been politically naive, but their better-educated coreligionists agreed with them. A sensational, widely noted editorial in the Kolbenz *Rhein-und Moselzeitung*, at the time the only Catholic-clerical newspaper in the Prussian Rhine Province, proposed that Johann be elected emperor and that the Rhine Province be separated from its Protestant ruler and given to the new ruler of Germany as a crown domain in which Catholics and native Rhinelanders could run things.[5]

The festival put democrats in an awkward position, since they supported national unity, and in particular the existence of a central government above

---

[3] For events in Aachen, see HSTAD RA Pr. Nr. 621 f. 108; HSTAD RA Pr. Nr. 2226 ff. 275, 282–87; Nießner, *Aachen*, pp. 162–63. On the other cities, Fischer, *Kreis Jülich*, pp. 33–35; HSTAD RD Pr. Nr. 795 ff. 64–101; *RhBA* 2/2, Nr. 215; *NRhZ*, 13 Aug. 1848. More peaceful, although equally pro-Johann celebrations were held in Bonn, Kersken, *Bonn in den Revolutionsjahren*, p. 68, and Bernkastel, Stahl, *1848/49 an der Mittelmosel*, p. 17.

[4] Lorenz, "1848/49 im Wuppertal," p. 242; *KnZ*, 13 Aug. 1848 (Zweite Beilage). For a similar example from a Protestant village in the Saarland, see Rüdiger Moldenhauer, "Die Petitionen aus den preußischen Saarkreisen an die deutsche Nationalversammlung 1848–1849," *Zeitschrift für die Geschichte der Saargegend* 17/18 (1969/70): 38–111, esp. p. 60.

[5] HSTAD RD Pr. Nr. 795 f. 97c; HSTAD RA Pr. Nr. 2226 f. 281; lead articles of *Rhein- und Moselzeitung*, 19, 23 July 1848, in *RhBA* 2/2, Nr. 192; commentaries of *NRhZ*, 27 July 1848; and *MZ*, 17 Aug. 1848. Compare how the day to honor the imperial regent was used by the Catholic clergy of Sieg County to preach sermons declaring religion in danger and pass around petitions to the Berlin National Assembly against the separation of church and state. *KnZ*, 10 Aug. 1848 (Beilage); *RhBA* 2/2, Nr. 212.

the individual German states, but opposed the idea of a prince as head of state, especially one not responsible to the National Assembly. Some extreme leftists in Düsseldorf and Trier called for a boycott of the festivities, a position taken most consistently in the Palatinate, where August 6 went completely unnoticed. Even before the debates in the Frankfurt Assembly on the election of Archduke Johann as imperial regent had been concluded, Palatine democrats had sponsored mass rallies along the Haardt Mountains on the weekend of Pentecost, praising popular sovereignty, denouncing the idea of a prince as head of state, and calling, in scarcely veiled language, for a republic. Opposition to these efforts came from neoorthodox Protestants, who held at the same time the first provincewide revival meeting, in the Haardt village of Iggelheim.[6]

Most democrats seem to have felt there was more to be achieved by taking part in the festivities, and leading them in a leftist direction. The Rhine-Hessians adopted this position with characteristic radicalism, the civic guard of Worms holding a ceremony of fealty on August 5 rather than August 6, pledging its loyalty to the Provisional Central Power created by the sovereign National Assembly, not to the imperial regent. On the following day, the Rhine-Hessian democrats held a mass rally in Worms with thousands of participants—estimates ranged from four thousand to fourteen thousand—who heard speeches denouncing the government of Hessen-Darmstadt, the German princes and the imperial regent himself and calling for the full realization of popular sovereignty, in other words for the republic. The province's constitutional monarchists responded by demanding that such rallies be prohibited and all democratic clubs closed.[7]

Trier democrats sponsored a mass rally outside the city walls on August 6, beginning with a parade, led by the black-red-gold tricolor, the participants singing anti-Prussian songs. Six hundred militiamen participated, wearing a white cross on their caps with the insignia "with God for a united Germany," a parody of the militia's motto, stemming from its origins in the uprising against Napoleon in 1813, "with God for king and fatherland." Krefeld's silk manufacturers led the city's Protestant minority in boycotting the celebration of August 6, supported by the city council they dominated and the bourgeois officers of the civic guard. It was the city's democrats, however, led by German-Catholic gymnast Caspar Immandt, who exploited this affront to Roman Catholic sensibilities in organizing the festivity, not the Catholic clergy and lay activists who had defeated the Protestants in the elections of May 1848.

---

[6] On these Pentecost rallies in the Palatinate, see sources cited in Chapter Five, note 67; the counteractions of revivalists according to Bonkhoff, *Kirche der Pfalz*, p. 45. The debate on participation in Düsseldorf, HSTAD RD Nr. 200 pp. 181–89; in Trier, *Vbl*, 17 Aug. 1848.

[7] Uhrig, "Worms," pp. 75–76; *MZ*, 10, 13 Aug. 1848.

The day after the celebration a democratic club was formed, quickly obtaining a large membership.[8]

In predominantly Protestant Elberfeld, intraconfessional religious tensions dominated the celebration. The moderately leftist Political Club sponsored a mass meeting, at which one of their number recited a poem, "I a German/Do you know my colors?" a parody of the Prussian military song, "I am a Prussian/Do you know my colors?" The crowd carried the poet on their shoulders to the rally, held at one of the large beer halls on the hills overlooking the city, whose construction had been sponsored by the Wuppertal's religious rationalists during the temperance controversy of the early 1840s, as an answer to the neoorthodox abstinence societies. During the rally, the participants could look out from their hall, draped with the black-red-gold national colors, and see, down below in the streets of Barmen and Elberfeld, their devout political opponents hanging out black and white flags.[9]

In Düsseldorf, their stronghold on the lower Rhine, the democrats were divided about the celebration of August 6. While the festival was initiated and organized by the moderates of the Association for a Democratic Monarchy, the radical republicans of the People's Club voted to boycott the event. The course of the festivities rather suggests that the former may have had a more successful political strategy. Although the officers of the garrison refused to participate and the army took no part in the civic guard's parade in honor of the imperial regent, ordinary soldiers turned up in large numbers for the afternoon and evening festivities in the city's public gardens. As the democrats planned, citizens and soldiers "fraternized" during these celebrations, that is, drank themselves into a stupor together.

At the speeches given on the afternoon of August 6 in front of a newly erected statue of Germania, a representative of the People's Club, attacking the imperial regent and calling for a German republic, was shouted down by the spectators. The highpoint of the festivities, however, a torchlight parade that evening, proceeded quite differently. The parade was led by thirty-eight students of the Art Academy, dressed as medieval heralds, carrying the flags of the thirty-eight German princes. Proceeding from city hall, they marched to the statue of Germania on the Friedrichsplatz in the very center of the city, and laid down their flags in front of the statue, the symbol of national unity. At that moment, a thirty-ninth herald came forth, bearing the black-red-gold colors, and the enormous crowd of spectators sang Ernst Mortiz Arndt's nationalist anthem, "It Shall Be All of Germany" [Das ganze Deutschland soll es sein]. If not as militant as the city's republicans wanted it, many features of

[8] On the celebrations in Trier, see *Vbl*, 17 Aug. 1848; *KnZ*, 27 Aug. 1848; Breuer, "1848/49 im Moseltal," p. 138; for events in Krefeld, *NRhZ*, 13 Aug. 1848; *RhBA* 2/2, Nr. 215.

[9] Körner, *Lebenskämpfe* 1:413–15; Wegener, "Elberfeld," pp. 130–31. The Ronsdorf abstinence society claimed that revolutionary struggles were the result of excessive alcohol consumption: Lorenz, "1848/49 im Wuppertal," p. 243.

the Düsseldorf festivities—fraternization of soldiers and citizens against the wishes of the officer corps, symbolic subordination of all the German princes to the nation—nevertheless showed a strongly democratic and implicitly republican spirit.[10]

This interpretation is supported by the reception the inhabitants of Düsseldorf gave the king of Prussia a week later, on August 14, 1848, when he came to visit their city. Civic guard and city council voted not to honor the king, and he was met by an angry crowd, which bombarded the royal person with horse manure. Several hundred loyal Protestants from the Wuppertal, including the members of the Elberfeld city council, who had come by train to Düsseldorf to greet their monarch, were incensed by this behavior. They got even angrier when inhabitants of Düsseldorf tore the black and white cocardes from their hats. The Wuppertal Protestants responded by engaging in their own fraternization with the soldiers, drinking with them in the taverns, singing Prussian patriotic songs, and denouncing the Düsseldorf democrats. That evening, drunken soldiers assaulted a taunting crowd, whose members were blowing little whistles (a sign of insult in Europe), singing Arndt's "What Is the German's Fatherland?" and wearing red ribbons. The violence escalated rapidly; one soldier was killed, and the civic guard could restore order only with substantial difficulty.[11]

On the return home of the loyalist delegation to Elberfeld, the local democrats brought a cat music to its leader, the banker and constitutional monarchist politician August von der Heydt, which turned into a street brawl between adherents of the Prussian cause and those of the German one. The constitutional monarchists got their revenge by preparing a tumultuous welcome for the king when he visited Elberfeld on August 16. Friedrich-Wilhelm must have noted the contrast between predominantly Roman Catholic Düsseldorf and the devoutly Protestant and loyalist manufacturing towns of the Wuppertal.[12]

The opposition of Protestant to Catholic, however, only partially characterizes the political differences. Most inhabitants of Düsseldorf were nominal Catholics, but they were also democrats; the clergy had little political influence there. The festivals in honor of Johann could also lead to clashes between democrats and Catholic-clericals. The radical and anticlerical schoolteacher Anton Gladbach, elected deputy to the Berlin Assembly for Mülheim County in May 1848—one of the few democratic electoral triumphs on the lower Rhine—returned to his constituency in August and gave a speech at the festivities in honor of Johann in the town of Bergisch Gladbach.

[10] KnZ, 9 Aug. 1848; HSTAD RD Nr. 200 pp. 177–92.

[11] HSTAD RD Pr. Nr. 795 ff. 49–52; KnZ, 19–20 Aug. 1848; HSTAD RD Nr. 200 pp. 90–91, 358–60; RhBA 2/2, Nrs. 213, 231; Körner, Lebenskämpfe 2:22–24.

[12] HSTAD RD Nr. 217b ff. 3–8; HSTAD RD Pr. Nr. 795 ff. 103–109; Wegener, "Elberfeld," pp. 130–31; Lorenz, "1848/49 im Wuppertal," pp. 246–47; Körner, Lebenskämpfe 2:22–24.

Gladbach denounced his fellow Rhenish deputies, such as H. Schlink and Peter Reichensperger, both well-known Catholic activists, as reactionaries. He condemned the Frankfurt Parliament for electing an imperial regent, thus adding another prince to the burdens of the German taxpayers, attacked state officials, and attacked the burdens of paying off the tithe, whose abolition, on the right bank of the Rhine, had required compensation. It was a typically radical, implicitly republican speech. Hecklers from the audience had nothing to say about any of the issues Gladbach raised; instead, they denounced him for proposing the separation of church and school, thus endangering religion. A heated argument ensued, and the festive meeting broke up in disorder.[13]

There was little in the way of celebration in Cologne on August 6, 1848, although the inhabitants of the provincial metropolis were at least as inclined toward national unity as they were to festivity. That date was overshadowed by the much larger festival planned for the following weekend, the great construction festival of the Cologne Cathedral. Since 1848 was the six hundredth anniversary of the beginining of the cathedral's construction, the Cathedral Construction Society had already been planning a spectacular event, following the precedent of the first festival in 1842, itself a celebration of national unity from a politically conservative standpoint. The outbreak of the revolution only expanded the society's guest list to include, besides the king of Prussia, the imperial regent, and the archbishop, all of whom had been present in 1842, the ministers of the Provisional Central Power, and prominent deputies of the Frankfurt and Berlin national assemblies. Held on August 13–15, 1848, the celebration was a huge success, with virtually the entire city and some thirty thousand visitors in attendance. As with all the smaller festivals of national unity celebrated in August 1848, this one contained a distinct, divisive political point.[14]

The democrats reacted sharply against the whole event. When Archduke Johann proceeded through Mainz on his way from Frankfurt to Cologne, he met with a republican demonstration: Silent, hostile crowds filled the streets, and the whole city was decked out in red flags. Cologne's Democratic Society voted to boycott the ceremony and, in conjunction with the Workers' Association, held the first provincial democratic congress on August 13–14 instead. The constitutional monarchist newspaper in Elberfeld promptly called for the prohibition of a republican gathering in the presence of so many princes.[15]

---

[13] *KnZ*, 17 Aug. 1848 (Beilage); discussed in Gernert, *1848/49 im Rheinisch-Bergischen*, p. 109.

[14] On the festival and its background, see Leo Haupts, "Die Kölner Dombaufeste 1842–1880 zwischen kirchlicher bürgerlich-nationaler und dynastisch-höfischer Selbstdarstellung," in *Öffentliche Festkultur*, pp. 191–211; and Seypel, "Die Demokratische Gesellschaft in Köln," pp. 282–87. Unless otherwise stated, my account of events is taken from the detailed reporting in *KnZ*, 15–17 Aug. 1848.

[15] *RhBA* 2/2, Nr. 216 and p. 361 n.42; Seypel, "Die Demokratische Gesellschaft in Köln," p. 285.

Yet the Cologne radicals' hostility had something feeble about it. Even the *Neue Rheinische Zeitung*, which feared nothing and no one, treated the festival with kid gloves. Its sole comment on the ceremony while it was occurring was a complaint that the Cathedral Construction Society would not give it the schedule of events, thus making it more difficult for its readers to participate. The Workers' Association newspaper printed a lead article on the festival that expressed such a conciliatory attitude toward monarchy that a storm of protest arose at the subsequent committee meeting and the editor was forced to resign.[16]

The festival confirmed the worst fears of the Cologne left: It was wildly popular and, like its predecessor in 1842, deeply reactionary. Archduke Johann had a triumphal trip down the Rhine, greeted with jubilation in every predominantly Roman Catholic riverain town and village by all the inhabitants, led by the clergy. He received a magnificent welcome in Cologne itself on the evening of August 13: huge crowds on the docks shouting their praise, honors from the civic guard and the state and municipal officials, and a torchlight parade. The archduke reviewed the parade from the balcony of the provincial governor's office, and gave a short speech pointing out to Cologne's inhabitants that "your cathedral is the symbol of the great fatherland we are to build. In it peace, order and quiet, must be our primary concerns." Johann was on hand to greet the king of Prussia, when he arrived by steamship from Mülheim on the right bank of the river the following evening, the two princes embracing on the quay, to cries of jubilation from the crowd, followed once more by a torchlight parade. This friendly greeting in Cologne was very different from the one the king had received in Düsseldorf earlier that same day.

King and imperial regent were at the center of all the festivities, embracing at the quay in front of the crowd, reviewing parades and military marches, but never themselves participating in them. The two princes, both dressed in the uniform of Prussian generals, greeted the great parade of August 15 when it reached Cathedral Square. Following a festive high mass, celebrated by Archbishop von Geissel, the monarchs were escorted from the cathedral by a group of no less than ten bishops or their vicars-general, present for the festivities, to a giant throng pressing around the cathedral, shouting in jubilation.

Contemporaries, and following them historians, disagreed about how politically successful the appearance of Friedrich Wilhelm IV had been. Some regarded the visit as a triumph for him, while others noted coolly that the Protestant king was so popular in the largest predominantly Catholic city of his realm because he only appeared in public accompanied by the archbishop and

---

[16] *NRhZ*, 13 Aug. 1848; *ZAVK*, 13 Aug. (lead article), 20 Aug. 1848 (committee session of 14 Aug.). The *Neue Rheinische Zeitung* did eventually attack the festival two weeks later, but only in the feuilleton: *NRhZ*, 19–20, 22–23, 27, 31 Aug. 1848.

the Austrian archduke. Wherever the truth may lie—and the events in Düsseldorf and Elberfeld on August 14 and 16 rather support the second interpretation—all contemporaries were unanimous in seeing the festival as a giant success for monarchism and a rebuke to the adherents of popular sovereignty and a democratic or republican form of government. The two princes were at the center of the festivities; their cooperation symbolized German national unity. All possible competing symbols had been eliminated.[17]

Heinrich von Gagern, president of the Frankfurt National Assembly, the man who created the office of imperial regent in the first place, languished in the shadows. The torchlight parades were supposed to end where he was staying, only they were dispersed by rain and never reached him. Although so many parliamentarians came from Frankfurt to Cologne, that the National Assembly lacked a quorum and proceedings had to be adjourned, the people's representatives had a distinctly secondary role in the whole celebration. The deputies marched as a group in the great parade of August 15, but they were just one group among many, including Cologne's schoolchildren and its volunteer firemen, in sharp contrast to the central role of the princes in Cologne or of their leftist fellow deputies in the republican festivals held in Rhine-Hessen or the Palatinate. Franz Raveaux, Cologne's own deputy, suffered two bitter personal rebukes. He had hoped to put up Archduke Johann in his own house, but was foiled in that wish by Austrian diplomacy. Raveaux also proposed a toast to popular sovereignty at the concluding banquet on the afternoon of August 15 in the municipal hall, but he was allowed to speak only after all the prominent guests—princes, generals, ministers of Prussia and the Provisional Central Power—and most of the others had already gone home.[18]

All the celebrations of national unity centered around the imperial regent had revealed deep fissures within Rhenish society: hostility to the existing German monarchies in Rhine-Hessen and the Palatinate; Catholic hatred of the Prussian state and Protestant devotion to it in Mönchengladbach, Aachen, Elberfeld, Linnich, and Langenlonsheim; Catholic hostility toward Prussia exploited by the democrats in Krefeld and Düsseldorf; democrats against Catholics in Bergisch-Gladbach; Catholic and Protestant constitutional monarchists united in Cologne against the left. If such hostile feelings could turn up at a time of celebration, it is easy to see how major national crises in September and November would provoke ever sharper political confrontations in the Rhineland.

[17] For a Protestant contemporary version, see the *Elberfelder Zeitung*, reprinted in *KnZ*, 19 Aug. 1848; for a Catholic one, see the *Rhein- und Moselzeitung*, reprinted in *NSZ*, 16 Aug. 1848. Other opinions: *Lebenserinnerungen . . . Alexander Pagenstecher* 2:77; Valentin, *Geschichte der deutschen Revolution* 2:137; Kühn, *Der junge Hermann Becker*, pp. 89–90.

[18] On Raveaux's travails, Seypel, "Die Demokratische Gesellschaft in Köln," pp. 286–87; and *KnZ*, 19 Aug. 1848.

A Fall of Crisis

The September Crisis

The Schleswig-Holstein crisis of September 1848 was both the first national crisis of the German Revolution and also a crisis of German nationalism. Before 1848, the two duchies had been ruled in personal union by the king of Denmark, their inhabitants largely ethnic Germans, with a Danish minority concentrated in northern Schleswig. In March 1848, the Germans rose up against ducal rule and established a revolutionary provisional government. The Danish monarchy responded by annexing all of Schleswig-Holstein to the kingdom and sending in royal troops to back up this decision. The cause of the insurgents found tremendous sympathy in Germany, and youthful volunteers from across the country rushed north, but such irregulars were of little use against the Danish army.

The German national cause was effectively represented only when the Prussian March ministry sent troops. Following its creation in July 1848, the Provisional Central Power declared the conflict a "national war" [Reichskrieg], and troop contingents from the smaller German states joined the conflict, fighting under Prussian command but behind the black-red-gold tricolor, for the goal of liberating national territory from foreign rule (neither Germans nor Danes showed any consideration for members of the opposite nationality living in the two duchies) and integrating it into a united, national state. Yielding to diplomatic pressure exerted by Britain and, especially, the czar, both regimes concerned about control over the outlet to the Baltic, the Prussian government, agreed at the end of August 1848 to a cease-fire. Prussia took this action on its own authority, without consulting the Provisional Central Power in Frankfurt. The document it signed, the so-called Malmö armistice, left the northern part of Schleswig under Danish occupation and dismantled the revolutionary regime.[19]

Prussia seemed to have abandoned the national cause—an action broadly unpopular across the political spectrum. Democrats were especially angered because the armistice had completely bypassed the Provisional Central Power created by the National Assembly, a violation of popular sovereignty, or proof that the assembly was never serious about exercising its sovereignty in the first place. "Unity of Germany, popular sovereignty, national assembly, imperial regent. They are all renounced in this treaty. The King of Prussia, i.e. the princes by grace of God, the German Confederation, i.e. the splintering of Germany into tiny pieces, are now once more in force." This angry statement of Mainz leftists was echoed by all Rhenish democrats. The moderate *Neue Speyerer Zeitung*, described the Malmö armistice as "one of the most shame-

---

[19] A good summary of the conflict can be found in Siemann, *Die deutsche Revolution von 1848/49*, pp. 153–57.

ful tricks of treasonable diplomacy. . . . [a] product of absolutist tendencies towards separatism.'' A mass meeting in Cologne, strongly influenced by Marx and his followers, sent an address to the Frankfurt National Assembly pointing out that the Frankfurt moderates, in the name of German nationalism, had supported counterrevolution in Italy, Prague, and Prussian Poland but Denmark was the one place where ''Germany has defended the revolution against monarchical legitimism and absolutism.'' The address concluded by demanding that the assembly revoke Prussia's authority to negotiate in the name of a united Germany, ''even at the risk of a European war.''[20]

For the first time in its history, the Frankfurt Assembly responded to the democrats' addresses, nationalism causing much of the center to vote with the left in the decisive session of September 4, a narrow majority of the deputies declaring the Malmö armistice suspended. The ministers of the Provisional Central Power, interpreting this as a vote of no confidence, resigned. For almost two weeks the assembly debated its future course continuously and passionately, and mass meetings were held throughout the country, while rumors flew of a new ministry of the left, of Prussian military intervention, or of a great European war. But in the session of September 16 the assembly reversed itself, approving the armistice by the same margin of some twenty votes by which it had previously condemned it.

A mass meeting in Frankfurt the following day demanded that the deputies of the left secede from the assembly and set themselves up as a revolutionary convention. Some were ready to do so, but in the end they backed down, a decision attributed both to cowardice and to a realistic refusal to engage in a futile putsch. While the left deputies were debating, the imperial regent called for Prussian and Austrian troops from the Mainz garrison. They arrived on September 18, to find a crowd, acting against the advice of the democratic deputies, attempting to storm the assembly. There were not all that many of them, and they were easily driven off, but a familiar hostility toward the Prussian soldiers spread throughout the lower classes of Frankfurt. Without any organized leadership or well thought out plan, barricades were built, and street fighting raged for hours, in spite of attempts of the leftist deputies to arrange a peaceful settlement. Reinforcements of Hessian artillery finally decided the struggle, but not before two deputies of the extreme right, Prince Felix Lichnowsky and General Hans von Auerswald, were brutally murdered by the insurgents. This deed was immediately blamed by the right and center on the left and remained a stock item of political polemics for the rest of the revolution. Frankfurt, seat of the National Assembly, was declared in a state of seige.[21]

[20] *MZ*, 6 Sept. 1848; *NSZ*, 17 Sept. 1848; *KnZ*, 9 Sept. 1848. Similarly, *MZ*, 8–9 Sept. 1848; *NRhZ*, 12 Sept. 1848.

[21] On the background, course, and ramifications of the September crisis, see the old but excellent account of Valentin, *Geschichte der deutschen Revolution* 2:137–82. As Valentin has pointed

These revolutionary events produced ramifications in all of Germany, most dramatically in Baden, where they triggered a second, unsuccessful republican uprising. The Rhineland, physically close to the scene of the action, was also strongly affected. In the Palatinate, "the news of the armistice spread like wildfire through the province." Members of the civic guards and the People's Associations met and debated excitedly whether, as one Speyer activist put it, "the German people or its princes shall decide the fate of the fatherland." Some radicals called for a march to Frankfurt to aid the insurgents, or, as Edenkoben democrat Johann Teutsch proposed, on Speyer, to overthrow the provincial government. Cooler heads prevailed, and the Palatines contented themselves with supporting an address of the provincial committee of the People's Association, praising the province's left-wing deputies, or bringing cat musics to those who had counseled moderation.[22]

Rhine-Hessen was physically the closest part of the Rhineland to Frankfurt; Mainz, just a short train trip away. Three of the city's democratic leaders, including the ubiquitous revolutionary German Metternich, were involved in the Frankfurt street fighting or the agitation preceding it and were forced to flee the country to evade arrest. The spontaneous nature of the barricade struggles, however, and their brief duration made it impossible to arrange any organized assistance from Mainz, although it seems doubtful, in any event, that a group of armed insurgents could have evaded the troops of the fortress and crossed the Rhine to reach Frankfurt. Only one inhabitant of the upper Rhine metropolis was indicted for taking part in the uprising.[23]

There were a number of indications of support for the insurgents in different parts of the province: street demonstrations in Worms calling for the republic, and a curious incident in Alzey, where the red flag was raised over city hall. Local democrats maintained it was all a drunken prank; a lengthy investigation by the state's attorney produced nothing incriminating, and eventually all charges were dropped. Nonetheless, the democrats' own account of what happened—an all-day meeting on September 19 of the committee of Alzey's democratic club, appearance of messengers from nearby villages with the news that armed reinforcements were on the way, and the mayor's reluctance to take down the red flag from city hall—suggest a different story. Democrats in Alzey (and possibly elsewhere in Rhine-Hessen) were planning an uprising in support of the Frankfurt insurgents or perhaps a march on Frankfurt to rein-

out, Auerswald and Lichnowsky were killed while they were doing reconnaissance work for the troops fighting the uprising—an action taken on their own initiative, and an unnecessary and imprudent decision for two prominent individuals known and hated by the crowd.

[22] *NSZ*, 14 (Beilage), 20 Sept. 1848; MInn to King, 12 Oct. 1848, BHSTAM MInn Nr. 46129; LAS J1 Nr. 205 ff. 643–44, 667–89.

[23] Bockenheimer, *Mainz*, pp. 124–25, 135–36. That individual, the fifty-five-year-old master butcher Georg Ignaz Mann, was acquitted in time to participate in the uprising of May–June 1849, be arrested for it, and be acquitted once again.

force them, which was called off only on receiving news of the outcome of the street fighting. The government of Hessen-Darmstadt, admitting it lacked the ability to restore order, asked the Provisional Central Power to requisition Prussian troops. Both the Central Power and the Prussian government were willing; the soldiers occupied Alzey and Worms for four months, and, for good measure, the town of Oberingelheim, a stronghold of the democrats in the northern end of the province.[24]

The events in Frankfurt produced less of an echo in the Prussian Rhine Province, reactions rarely going beyond the sending of occasional addresses to the Frankfurt Assembly. In part this reflected the less well organized state of political life there, in part the social conditions of the industrial cities. Aachen's upper class followed the news from Frankfurt "with lively interest but without passion"; the town's factory workers were as indifferent to these struggles as they were to all political questions.[25]

This response also stemmed from a preoccupation with specifically Prussian issues. Leftists in the Berlin National Assembly had gathered support to pass a vote of no confidence in the moderately liberal Prussian ministry in mid-August and as of the outbreak of the September crisis, no successor had yet been appointed by the king. A mass meeting in Elberfeld, held to discuss the question on September 10, led to a heated debate. It was resolved in favor of a constitutional monarchist petition to the king to dissolve the assembly and send the deputies home, when Carl von der Heydt suddenly appeared with a large number of the proletarian members of the Protestant sectarian church he led, the pious workers providing the necessary majority.[26]

The only reaction to the September crisis in the Prussian Rhineland comparable to those further south occurred in Cologne, a result of the interaction of fortuitous circumstances with determined revolutionary activism of the city's communists. Prussian troops provided the spark for the incident, a dispute over a woman between civilians and soldiers of the hated Twenty-Seventh Infantry Regiment on September 11 leading to large-scale brawling, the worst in the city since the St. Martin's parish fair of 1846. The following day, the civic guard had to protect the barracks from an angry crowd.

The more moderate of Cologne's democrats used the incident to further their campaign against civic guard commandant Heinrich von Wittgenstein, a

[24] Uhrig, "Worms," p. 78; *MZ*, 25 Oct. 1848, 19 Jan. 1849; BAF DB 54 Nr. 50 f. 9.

[25] On Aachen, see HSTAD RA Pr. Nr. 2226 ff. 294, 301–302, 306–307; elsewhere, cf. ibid., f. 300; Meisen, "Essen in den Revolutionsjahren," pp. 239–40; *Vbl*, 27 Sept. 1848.

[26] HSTAD RD Pr. Nr. 795 ff. 103–104; Illner, *Bürgerliche Organisierung*, pp. 161–62; Lorenz, "1848/49 im Wuppertal," p. 250; Körner, *Lebenskämpfe* 2:26–27. (A similar petition from the Protestant manufacturing town of Odenkirchen, *KnZ*, 13 Sept. 1848 [Beilage].) Körner's memoirs, written fifteen years later, describe the meeting as having occurred during the November crisis, but it is clear, on comparing his and other accounts, that he had confused the date in his memory.

vote of no confidence in him by the guardsmen leading to his resignation. A city council meeting, held with leftists packing the galleries, voted to send a delegation to the commanding general of the Eighth Army Corps in Koblenz, asking for the removal of the soldiers of the Twenty-Seventh from the city, which the military authorities conceded. Marx and his followers, not content with such partial victories, attempted to exploit the enmity of the population against the Prussian state and the nationalist passions raised by the Malmö armistice—the two, of course, were interrelated—to push the revolutionary movement further.[27]

An open-air mass meeting on September 13, sponsored jointly by the Workers' Association and the Democratic Society (with between three hundred and ten thousand participants, according to different accounts), elected a quasi-revolutionary "committee of safety"—shades of 1793—but also split Cologne's democrats, when the moderate members refused to take their seats on it. The communists quickly followed with the mass meeting in Worringen on September 18, where the peasants were informed that the ringing of the storm bells in Cologne's churches would be the signal for them to hurry to the city and join in an insurrection. An indoor mass meeting on September 20 called on the deputies in Frankfurt to resign; those who refused would be "traitors to the people." The meeting also insisted that the Frankfurt insurgents "had served the fatherland well."

The military and civilian authorities then repeated the maneuver they had used in July at the previous highpoint of radical agitation in Cologne, namely, arresting the leading figures of the Workers' Association—this time with rather more justification than with Andreas Gottschalk. The Workers' Association responded to the arrests, on the morning of September 25, by calling a mass meeting on the Alter Markt, scene of the rioting in 1846. The meeting quickly escalated into barricade building; gun shops were plundered; Police Commissioner von Grävenitz, trying to break things up, was severely beaten. Since, as usual, the police could not preserve order, the civic guard was called out. Some of its members, particularly from the left-wing Ninth Company, joined the insurgents; the others refused to take any action against them.

The military acted cleverly, letting matters sit overnight, forcing the Cologne radicals to decide if they wanted to wage a barricade fight against the mobile artillery of the fortress (which could be turned around to face the city) all alone, the forces of order having triumphed in Frankfurt and Baden, no dramatic events taking place in the Prussian capital, Berlin, and the rest of the Prussian Rhine Province showing little political militancy. They chose, sen-

[27] In contrast to the usual image of Marx, he and his followers were noticeably quicker than the moderate Cologne democrats to exploit the political potential of nationalism. Cf. Seypel, "Die Demokratische Gesellschaft in Köln," pp. 276–78.

sibly enough, not to press the issue. The insurgents wandered off home that evening; the unmanned barricades were taken down the next day.

Acting fortress commandant Colonel Engels now played the role of the strong man of reaction. Threatening to impose martial law and create military tribunals if the civilian authorities would not go along with his plans, he forced them to agree to the proclamation of a state of siege in Cologne, abrogation of civil liberties, prohibition of the entire left-wing press, dissolution of the Democratic Society and the Workers' Association, dissolution of the civic guard and confiscation of its weapons. The district governor, Heinrich von Wittgenstein, resigned, having been disavowed by everyone in Cologne; his fellow constitutional monarchists praised the colonel and petitioned Berlin to retain the state of siege. It was finally lifted in October on direct orders of the new Prussian prime minister, General von Pfuel, who had been appointed by the king to carry out an openly reactionary policy but had proved to be unexpectedly moderate once in office.[28]

Viewed in terms of their internal dynamics, the September days in Cologne were a repetition of the confrontations of May 1848 in Mainz and Trier: a population enraged by the behavior of the Prussian soldiers and radicals who attempted to exploit civilian-military conflicts politically, only to see the situation get out of hand, escalating into a hopeless street fight against troops armed with artillery. The outcome was also the same: the disarming of the civic guard, arrest of leftist leaders, and a setback to the democratic movement. Unlike the events in May, the struggles in Cologne were directly and consciously linked by the city's radical democrats to national issues, and helped along by a series of highly organized mass meetings, both differences reflecting the evolution in political life that had taken place over the summer of 1848.

Nothing of a comparably drastic nature occurred in the southern part of the Prussian Rhineland during the September crisis, but the period saw in muted form political confrontations between democrats and Catholic-clericals over which group would most effectively exploit anti-Prussian feelings. The elections of May 1848 in Koblenz had resulted in a major Catholic political victory, accompanied by anti-Prussian and anti-Protestant demonstrations. Tensions between the city's Catholic burghers and Prussian soldiers had continued through the summer, breaking out over the question of the ceremony of fealty to the imperial regent and at a notorious incident in July, when the Koblenz civic guard had drilled publicly to the French and not the Prussian military tatoo.[29]

Franz Peter Adams, Koblenz's deputy in Frankfurt, a leading member of

---

[28] This follows the excellent and exhaustive account of Seypel, ''Die Demokratische Gesellschaft in Köln,'' pp. 303–31.

[29] See sources cited in Chapter Four, note 95; *KnZ*, 11 Aug. 1848; Kühn, *Der junge Hermann Becker*, p. 198; *RhBA* 2/2, Nr. 217; LAK 441 Nr. 1330 pp. 311–18.

the city's *Vormärz* circle of neoorthodox Catholics, sat on the right in the assembly and voted in favor of the Malmö armistice. Having long conducted a whispering campaign against him, the Koblenz democrats then spread the rumor that Adams had voted as he did because he had been bribed by the Prussian government with the promise of an ambassadorship. The day after the suppression of the Frankfurt uprising, an angry crowd smashed the windows of Adams's house, invading the house and destroying furniture, while the civic guard refused to intervene. Koblenz's democrats thus exploited the September crisis to take the issue of anti-Prussianism away from the Catholics, indeed, to brand the city's leading lay activist a turncoat and lackey of the Protestant state. They followed up on this initiative by founding the Koblenz Democratic Club, which quickly grew over the subsequent two months in membership and political influence.[30]

Events in Trier were a mirror image of those in Koblenz, the Catholic-clericals attempting to take the anti-Prussian issue away from the politically dominant democrats. After having been caught between the left and the constitutional monarchists at the elections of May 1848, Trier's Catholic clergy and lay activists had at first made no attempt to found an independent political organization. Some of them, most prominently the artist and convert from Protestantism Gustav Lasinsky, had joined the Democratic Club and attempted to use it to further Catholic interests. Lasinksy demanded that the democrats endorse church control over the public school system, and that the celebration of national unity on August 6, 1848, be centered on the person of Archduke Johann.[31]

The democrats did agree to postpone the festivities on August 6 for an hour, until the end of afternoon church services but showed no inclination to honor the imperial regent. To "avoid offense and a split [in the Democratic Club]," they passed a motion preventing discussion of religious issues at club meetings. A split in the Democratic Club, however, seems to have been what Lasinsky and the Catholic-clerical element in Trier wanted; events in September gave them their opportunity.[32]

Disgruntled at the feeble actions of the Frankfurt National Assembly during the September crisis, more impressed with the active, left-wing course of the

[30] On Adams, see Weber, *Aufklärung und Orthodoxie*, pp. 99, 148–51, 155. For the Koblenz democrats' September 1848 political initiative, see ZSTAM Rep. 77 Tit. 505 Nr. 4 Vol. III ff. 203–08; LAK 441 Nr. 1330 pp. 447–58; LAK 441 Nr. 3056 pp. 205–10; LAK 403 Nr. 7405 pp. 97–100; *KnZ*, 22, 24 Sept. 1848; *Vbl*, 20 Sept., 1 Oct. 1848.

[31] *Vbl*, 2 July, 17 Aug. 1848; cf. ibid., 1, 4, 8 Aug. 1848; Höfele, "Anfänge des politischen Katholizismus," pp. 85–86; Böse, "Ludwig Simon," pp. 132–33.

[32] *Vbl*, 14 July 1848; Böse, "Ludwig Simon," pp. 134–35. Explaining the founding of a Catholic political club in Trier to the national congress of Pius Associations in October 1848, Lasinsky noted that the Trier Democratic Club consisted "to a great extent of Catholics and, to be sure, good ones, although some lax Catholics and nihilists are among them" (cited ibid., p. 134). His actions were aimed at splitting the former off from the latter.

Prussian National Assembly in Berlin, some leaders of the Trier Democratic Club called for a rethinking of the demand for the secession of the Rhineland from Prussia, which the democrats had themselves raised in the spring of 1848. They were bitterly opposed by other Trier leftists, led by editor Steinberg of the *Volksblatt*, who insisted that the Prussian state was the main enemy of democracy in Germany and its destruction must be the democrats' political priority, even if it meant association with a monarchical Central Power. After several angry debates at September club sessions, in the course of which Steinberg was accused of being in cahoots with the ultramontanists, the former viewpoint won out. Steinberg then resigned from the committee of the Democratic Club and severed the ties of his popular newspaper to it.[33]

Precisely at that moment, the formation of the Democratic Catholic Association, later renamed Pius Association, was announced. Gustav Lasinsky described this action as a split from the democrats, brought about by their intolerant anti-Catholicism, but a look at the twenty members of the group's leading and executive committees shows that only three of them were members of the committee of the Democratic Club, and just two chosen electors in the democratic landslide in May 1848, while ten had been signatories to the constitutional monarchist election programs of the previous spring. The founding of the Catholic group is better understood as the counterpart to the actions of the Koblenz democrats, occurring at the same time: an attempt by Trier's Catholic clergy and lay activists to take over the issue of anti-Prussianism from the city's democrats, in the hope of splitting the Democratic Club and thus decisively weakening the democratic movement there.[34]

Events in Trier and Koblenz exemplify, in a somewhat atypical way, the general effect of the September crisis: a growing confrontation and polarization of political life. The last remnants of the euphoria and spirit of unity of the spring of 1848 had disappeared, replaced with increasingly bitter polemics. Democrats denounced constitutional monarchists as traitors; constitutional monarchists called for the prohibition of the democratic movement; devout Protestants and devout Catholics attacked each other, while both traded accusations with the democrats. The twin crises of November 1848 would sharpen the antagonisms in political life still further.

---

[33] *Vbl*, 10, 12–13, 15–16, 19, 22, 26 Sept. 1848. The account in Hansjürgen Schierbaum, *Die politischen Wahlen in den Eifel- und Moselkreisen des Regierungsbezirks Trier 1849–1867* (Düsseldorf: Droste, 1960), pp. 23–24, is very confused.

[34] Böse, "Ludwig Simon," pp. 134–35 (Lasinky's explanation); *Vbl*, 3 May 1848 (electors); 16 Sept. 1848 (committee of the Democratic Club); 19 Sept. 1848 (founding appeal of Democratic Catholic Association); 19 Jan. 1849 (committees of Pius Association); *RhBA* 2/2, Nr. 46 (signatories of constitutional monarchist election program); ZSTAM Rep. 77 Tit. 505 Nr. 5 Vol. V f. 42 (signatories). Schierbaum, *Wahlen in den Eifel- und Moselkreisen*, pp. 23, 26–28, uncritically accepts Lasinsky's own account.

The November Crisis

If in September all eyes had been on Frankfurt, attention shifted over the subsequent two months to the Prussian and Austrian capitals. Vienna seemed about to realize the democrats' demand for a second revolution. The departure of troops from the city to suppress the revolutionary Hungarian government on October 6, 1848, sparked an uprising, overthrowing the moderately liberal Austrian government ministry, leading the conservative deputies of the Austrian National Assembly to flee, and placing the Habsburg capital under the rule of a revolutionary committee of safety. The destruction of the feeble Austrian government was no great triumph; real state power lay with the Habsburg court, residing in Bohemian Olmütz, and especially with the imperial armies, fresh from their triumphs over revolutionary movements in Prague and in northern Italy.

Court and generals brusquely rejected proposals for mediation between them and the Viennese revolutionary regime brought by commissioners sent by the moderate majority of the Frankfurt National Assembly. A second delegation was sent by the assembly's left to the revolutionary authorities in Vienna, and one of its members, the celebrated Saxon radical (and Cologne native) Robert Blum, chose to stay in the city and fight with the insurgents when imperial troops, led by Generals Windischgrätz and Jellačić, advanced on the capital. After five days of bitter fighting at the end of October, characterized by the troops' liberal use of artillery, the city was conquered. Blum was arrested and, in spite of his parliamentary immunity—an immunity recognized by the nominal Austrian government, if not by its real military leaders—placed before a court-martial on November 8 and executed by firing squad that evening.[35]

If there was one single event in the revolution of 1848–1849 that produced a greater effect on the Rhenish population than did any other, it was the execution of Robert Blum. It showed that the authority of the Frankfurt National Assembly and the Provisional Central Power it created was nebulous, their claims to sovereignty over the individual German states, hollow. The prominent role of Slavic, especially Croatian troops in the army of General Jellačić, which conquered Vienna, stirred up nationalist passions and anti-Slavic chauvinism. All these elements had been present in the September crisis as well, but they were magnified and concentrated two months later by the focus on an individual, well known and well loved: Cologne's native son, the commissioner of the pre-Parliament who had helped the Rhine watermen in their struggle with capital, the popular and charismatic speaker at mass rallies in the Rhine-Main region and the Palatinate.

Everywhere he was mourned. Led by the civic guard, the People's Associ-

---

[35] Valentin, *Geschichte der deutschen Revolution* 2:196–226.

ation, the Workers' Association, the gymnasts and the members of the individual crafts, virtually the entire population of Speyer and vicinity marched to the cemetery on the afternoon of November 26, 1848, to hear the Frankfurt deputies G.F. Kolb and Martin Reichard give a eulogy to their fallen comrade. Similar memorial services were held in every major city of the Paltinate and many smaller towns, such as Rockenhausen, Lauterecken, and Grünstadt.[36]

The boatmen in the Mainz harbor raised the black flag of mourning for their champion; women of the city dressed in black; the municipal theater was closed; over 4,000 people crowded the meeting hall of the Democratic Club in the Frankfurter Hof to attend memorial services for him. In the Rhine-Hessian wine town of Oppenheim, the Democratic Club held a memorial service, with the room draped in black and the black-bordered portrait of the martyr placed over the tribune. Memorials were held in Mainz's trans-Rhenan suburb Kastel and across the province.[37]

The Democratic Club, its choral society, the Pius Association, the guilds, the gymnasts, and the notables of Trier—as in Speyer, a symbolic representation of the mourning of the whole city—marched in procession to the memorial services for Robert Blum. Four thousand gathered in Cologne on the Appellhofplatz and marched behind the flag of the abolished civic guard to the Minorite Church to honor their one-time fellow townsman. The left-wing villagers of Gerresheim, to the east of Düsseldorf, gathered to hear a memorial to Blum. Memorial services were held in Essen; the burghers of the town canceled all concerts for the winter season 1848–1849 as a sign of mourning.[38]

Blum personalized the fate of the revolution, making it easily understandable. "The common man," the Palatine provincial governor explained, "is basically indifferent to the parliamentary struggles between the government and the people, but is all the more open to the impressions [made by] the violent conquest of Vienna and the subsequent execution [of Blum]." Democrats launched a "six kreuzer collection," for Blum's widow and orphans. The modest sum requested was designed to gain mass participation, and it did. Literally thousands in and around Kaiserslautern made contributions after sign-up sheets were left out in taverns. The pupils of the Latin School all gave something, as did the members of the choral society of Dornmöschel, "which, to be sure, has just a few members but will gladly contribute its small share."[39]

The vast majority of the Palatines, the provincial governor admitted, even the politically moderate ones, were shocked and outraged by the events in

[36] *NSZ*, 27 Nov. (Beilage), 8 Dec. 1848; 31 Jan. 1849; MInn to King, 16 Dec. 1848, BHSTAM MInn Nr. 46129; LAS J1 Nr. 215 (alt) ff. 376–77.

[37] *MZ*, 17, 22 Nov. 1848; *Der Demokrat*, 26 Nov. 1848.

[38] *Vbl*, 24, 28 Nov. 1848; *KnZ*, 17 Nov. 1848; *NRhZ*, 20 Nov. 1848; Meisenburg, "Stadt Essen," p. 251. Similarly, in Saarlouis, LAK 442 Nr. 6388 pp. 175–79.

[39] Report of MInn as in note 36 above, LAS J1 Nr. 244 ff. 68–149; *NSZ*, 5 Dec. 1848 and Dec. 1848–Jan. 1849, passim.

Vienna. Democrats throughout the Rhineland hastened to exploit these feelings. An extra edition of the *Neue Rheinische Zeitung* announced in giant, boldface type, on a black-bordered page, "The murdering dog Windischgrätz has had the German Reichstag deputy Robert Blum shot by a military firing squad." Scarcely less angry was the moderate *Neue Speyerer Zeitung*, whose lead article of November 10 began in large and dark type: "Blum is shot! A cry of outrage goes through the National Assembly." The article continued in reference to the murders of Lichnowsky and Auerswald during the Frankfurt uprising in September, "So this is how reaction respects the 'sanctity of the deputies' it has called for!" Eulogies to Blum were occasions for radical polemics, Ludwig Bamberger denouncing those "who call us red republicans, who call the people bloodthirsty . . . [but] with cold evil . . . turned to the annihilation of a great spirit, the favorite of the nation, who with this murder have attacked the heart of the entire nation." Guilty of Blum's death were not just Windischgrätz and the Austrian reactionaries, but the constitutional monarchists, "the enemies of the people in the parliament, in the Central Power . . . ," above all, Bamberger insisted, the president of the National Assembly, Rhine-Hessian constitutional monarchist Heinrich von Gagern—an accusation the mourning crowd greeted with prolonged and stormy cries of approval.[40]

"Let us not forget the deceased but remember him, how he died, in which cause he died, and by whom he was murdered," said the commander of the civic guard and leader of the democrats of Lauterecken in his eulogy to Blum. Leftists did not forget, but bought fly sheets with his picture, placed it prominently on the "Democratic Calendar for 1849," even bought little marzipan statues of him at Christmastime. No revolutionary anniversary celebrations in February or March 1849 were complete without toasts to Blum's memory. A bust of him decorated the hall in Solingen during the anniversary celebrations; at the festivities in Trier, his portrait hung over the tribune, wrapped in a garland of helichrysum, which retain their color even after they have been dried, and so are known in German as "immortals."[41]

News of Blum's execution reached the Rhineland just as the confrontation between king and national assembly in Prussia was reaching its peak. Ever angrier at a parliament that had demanded that army officers refrain from reactionary political conspiracy, dared to strike "by the grace of God" from his title, and abolished patents of nobility, Friedrich Wilhelm IV, supported and encouraged by the reactionary court camarilla, had resolved to cut the insub-

---

[40] *NRhZ*, 14 Nov. 1848 (Zweite Ausgabe); *NSZ*, 16 Nov. 1848; *MZ*, 17–18 Nov. 1848. Similarly, Ludwig Simon's eulogy for Blum in Trier, *Vbl*, 28 Nov. 1848.

[41] LAS J1 Nr. 215 (alt) ff. 376–77 (similarly in the eulogies cited above); *Der Demokrat*, 26 Nov. 1848; *KnZ*, 6 Dec. 1848 (Beilage); *NRhZ*, 28 Feb. 1849; *MZ*, 27 Feb. 1849; HSTAD RD Pr. Nr. 796 ff. 29–30; *Vbl*, 20–21 Mar. 1849; LAS J1 Nr. 245 ff. 69–72; placard, dated 23 July 1849, prohibiting the sale of packages of tobacco containing Blum's picture in the fortress city of Landau, BHSTAM KA Nr. B771.

ordinate legislature down to size. His appointment during the September crisis of General Ernst von Pfuel as prime minster was designed to accomplish that, only the elderly officer, once in office, had belied his reactionary reputation and taken seriously the political doctrine of constitutional monarchism, striving to reach agreement between crown and legislature.

At the beginning of November, the king replaced him with the reactionary Count Brandenburg, a man more willing to carry out the royal plans. A week later, the government ordered the Prussian National Assembly adjourned for three weeks, to reconvene in the more amenable surroundings of the provincial town of Brandenburg. A right-wing minority was willing to accept this, but a majority of the deputies refused, calling the king's action illegal. The government then declared a state of siege in Berlin, sending forty thousand soldiers into the capital to create wartime conditions. Unlike the revolutionary forces in Vienna, two weeks previously, the civic guard made no attempt to fight the army, but the rump assembly, before it was dissolved by troops, proposed on November 11 and definitively declared on November 15 that the government had no right to collect taxes as long as the assembly could not meet and debate freely in the capital city.[42]

The *Neue Rheinische Zeitung* printed an extra edition, the front page beginning with the large, boldface declaration, "No more taxes!"—an appeal that appeared on the masthead every day for the following month. It then printed the assembly's declaration followed by an editorial note, "From this day on, taxes are abolished!!! Paying taxes is high treason, boycotting taxes a citizen's first duty!" In contrast to the September crisis, the Cologne radicals did not act alone, but were part of a broader movement, reaching throughout the province. At a mass meeting in Bonn on November 13, with many peasants of the vicinity in attendance, Gottfried Kinkel posed the question, "How do you boycott taxes?", replying, "You don't pay them!" to cries of jubilant affirmation from the spectators. The Workers' Association in Lennep declared itself in permanent session, as did the People's Club in Düsseldorf. "Committees of safety," "people's committees," and "citizens' committees," were formed in Cologne, Koblenz, Trier, Bernkastel, Kreuznach, Cochem, Saarlouis, and Bitburg.[43]

In and of itself, an organized campaign to boycott taxes was threat enough to the state's authority, but three additional factors—the involvement of the rural population, the potential of a tax boycott to spill over into armed con-

[42] Siemann, *Die deutsche Revolution*, pp. 170–75; Valentin, *Geschichte der deutschen Revolution* 2:225–96.

[43] *NRhZ*, 17 Nov. 1848 (Außerordentliche Beilage); Kersken, *Bonn in den Revolutionsjahren*, p. 82; Taubert, *Autonomie und Integration*, p. 193; Dowe, *Aktion und Organisation*, p. 209; Seypel, "Die Demokratische Gesellschaft in Köln," pp. 340–43; *RhBA* 2/2, Nrs. 311, 313, 319; Stahl, *1848/49 an der Mittelmosel*, p. 20; LAK 441 Nr. 3057 pp. 233–34; LAK 403 Nr. 6583 pp. 271–74; LAK 442 Nr. 6388 pp. 175–79; *NRhZ*, 21 Nov. 1848.

frontation, and the attitudes of a large portion of the Rhenish population toward events in the capital city—greatly increased the danger to the government posed by it. First, as the authorities recognized, a call not to pay taxes was a revolutionary action the peasantry could understand, an ideal means the "party of subversions" could use to "stir up the peasantry until now immune to [the radicals'] seduction." The democrats acted energetically to these ends: holding mass meetings in villages in the vicinity of Düsseldorf, passing out tax boycott fliers on the lower Rhine near Geldern, circulating petitions among villagers in Jülich County previously involved in struggles over use of the forest or the commons, agitating among the up-country peasants of Mülheim and Sieg Counties, and holding meetings in villages near the radical Eifel county town of Adenau.[44]

This rural agitation was most effective in the wine country, where the vintners had long held strong opinions about excess taxes. Pamphlets and fliers calling for the boycott were distributed in taverns of the winegrowing villages of the Rhine and Nahe valleys. Democrats in the Ahr Valley held meetings calling for a tax boycott, passed out petitions in support of the Berlin Assembly, and brought a cat music to the area's deputy for Berlin, who had voted with the minority to support the assembly's adjournment and transfer to Brandenburg. Local authorities were thoroughly intimidated; they stood by helplessly, and let the democrats call on the vintners to march on the arsenal of the militia in Andernach, arm themselves, and go on to Berlin. However, circumstances in the northernmost viticultural region were downright orderly in comparison to events in the Moselle Valley. Citizens' committees at either end of the valley, in Koblenz and Trier, as well as in the middle, in Cochem and Bernkastel, combined mass rallies, tavern agitation, and secret organization to create an insurrectionary situation among the vintners. Prussian officials had no illusions about popular loyalty to the regime or about the inhabitants' willingness to obey the authorities: The Moselle Valley, they admitted, could be held down only by armed force.[45]

The threat of insurrection hung over the entire Prussian Rhine Province throughout the second half of November 1848. Considering the appeal issued by the provincial democratic directory, signed by Marx, Schapper, and Karl Schneider II, president of the Cologne Democratic Society, it is easy to see how the tax boycott could have led to an armed uprising. The appeal noted that if the authorities tried to break the boycott by force, "any kind of resis-

[44] LAK 403 Nr. 6583 pp. 127–30; LAK 403 Nr. 17332 pp. 209–112, 225–27; *RhBA* 2/2, Nr. 314, esp. p. 529 n.6; Gernert, *1848/49 im Rheinisch-Bergischen*, pp. 134–35; LR Kr. Adenau to RKO, 4 Jan. 1849, LAK 441 Nr. 4120.

[45] On conditions in the Rhine, Ahr, and Nahe valleys, see LAK 403 Nr. 17332 pp. 209–10; LR Kr. Kreuznach to RKO, 23 Dec. 1848; LAK 441 Nr. 3057 pp. 129–31; *KnZ*, 9 Nov. 1848 (Beilage). Events in the Moselle Valley will be discussed below, but, for the authorities' view at the onset of the crisis, see LAK 403 Nr. 6583 pp. 127–30.

tance'' would be justified. To that end, it called on the Rhinelanders to organize an armed militia and to demand of all the officials whether they would
approve of the measures taken by the Berlin Assembly. Those who refused
were to be removed from their posts and replaced by a committee of safety,
preferably acting in conjunction with the city or village councils.[46]

Flashpoints of conflict were the walled cities of the province where the octroi was collected. Unlike other direct taxes, paid on a monthly, quarterly, or
yearly basis, the highly unpopular octroi was collected every single day. Since
the walled cities were also garrison towns, and soldiers could be called to
reinforce the tax collectors, any attempt to boycott the octroi meant a confrontation with the military. Democrats in Düsseldorf, Bonn, and Koblenz per-
suaded the civic guard to support the tax boycott; elsewhere, they attempted
to organize armed companies to carry it out or to enlist members of the militia
or soldiers of the Rhenish regiments to support armed resistance.[47]

In comparison to the situation in Trier in May or in Cologne in September,
the democrats' insurrectionary efforts were directed against a government
highly unpopular among their politically more moderate fellow provincials.
Thirty prominent Cologne attorneys, including many constitutional monarchists and members of the Pius Association, issued a declaration condemning
as illegal the adjournment and transfer of the assembly. The usually pious and
conservative Aacheners had, according to the district government, ''in regard
to the members of the present cabinet just one voice, disinclination, indeed
even hatred, and the resignation of the cabinet is absolutely necessary if the
flames of insurrection are not to flare up everywhere.'' While the Protestant,
up-country peasants of Simmern County were loyal to the king, in the county
seat ''many state officials and burghers'' were deeply mistrustful of the cabinet
of Count Brandenburg, fearing it was the precursor to a ''military despotism.''
Even the inhabitants of Kirchen a.d. Sieg, in Altenkirchen County on the right
bank of the Rhine, throughout the revolution a heavily conservative area, addressed the king, assuring him of their support for his actions and condemning
the tax boycott as a subversive measure, but suggesting that it might be
better if he dismissed Count Brandenburg and appointed a ''more popular
ministry.''[48]

To judge by the official reports on public opinion, and the many addresses
and petitions to the king and the assembly, coming from city councils, political clubs, and public meetings, published in the province's leading newspaper,

[46] NRhZ, 19 Nov. 1848 (Zweite Ausgabe).

[47] RhBA 2/2, Nrs. 308, 315, 320, 326, 329, 336; Seypel, ''Die Demokratische Gesellschaft in
Köln,'' pp. 343–48; Gendarme Briessen (Cochem) to LR Kr. Cochem, 24 Nov. 1848, LAK 441
Nr. 12929.

[48] Seypel, ''Die Demokratische Gesellschaft in Köln,'' p. 340; HSTAD RA Pr. Nr. 2229 f. 26;
LAK 441 Nr. 1330 pp. 565–71; KnZ, 24 Nov. 1848 (Beilage). A similar petition to that of Kir-
chem a.d. Sieg from the city council of Gummersbach, ibid., 22 Nov. 1848 (Beilage).

the *Kölnische Zeitung*, the response to the royal measure was strongly polarized along confessional lines. Villagers in the Protestant enclaves at the northern and southern ends of the province signed addresses of loyalty to their monarch. However, so did thousands of inhabitants of the predominantly Protestant manufacturing towns of the Wuppertal, inhabitants of the lower Rhine cotton town of Rheydt, and members of the Protestant minority in the silk center Krefeld. Citizens of Barmen, Duisburg, and Mülheim a.d. Ruhr not only denounced the assembly's call for a tax boycott, but even offered to pay their taxes in advance, showing devotion to their monarch far beyond the call of duty.[49]

Not all Protestants supported the king. Some eight hundred residents of Elberfeld signed a petition of the city's Political Club in support of the assembly, although in view of the reigning pro-Prussian atmosphere, the Elberfeld leftists did not dare to suggest supporting the call for a tax boycott. The mood was more militant in the city of Kreuznach, where a committee of safety was elected, and cat musics brought to the county commissioner and to other supporters of the king. The civic guard refused to intervene, and troops had to be brought in from Mainz and Koblenz to restore order. Overwhelmingly, the stronghold of the left in predominantly Protestant areas was Solingen County, where the democrats' agitation among the metalworkers was now beginning to pay off. Mass meetings in Solingen and Leichlingen, called to debate the situation, with thousands in attendance, were dominated by the democrats, the spectators shouting down "arrogant, rich master manufacturers and reactionary pietist pastors [geldstolze Fabrikherren und reaktionäre pietistische Pfaffen]" who tried to speak in favor of their royal lord and master.[50]

These were very clearly exceptions; most Protestants remained firmly loyal to the king, their addresses proclaiming their "unshakable loyalty to our constitutional king, in place [eingesetzt] by the grace of God," as the Protestants of Marienberghausen in Gummersbach County, on the right bank of the Rhine, said. The implications of this constitutionalism were most apparent in the declaration of the village council of nearby Drabenderhöhe. Councillors and inhabitants asserted that they would "hold fast to the constitutional monarchy, fast to the throne of the Hohenzollern, under whose exalted, wise and just scepter our fathers and we have felt fortunate." Since before 1848 even

[49] Petitions published in *KnZ*, 17–28 Nov. 1848. Cf. LAK 403 Nr. 6583 pp. 127–30; HSTAD RD Nr, 82 ff. 6–8. The Krefeld petition was sent by the loyalist Prussian Association, whose membership was entirely Protestant. Schwentker, *Konservative Vereine*, p. 171.

[50] Lorenz, "1848/49 im Wuppertal," pp. 253, 259; LAK 441 Nr. 3057 pp. 27–36, 55–58, 161–62; *NRhZ*, 21 Nov. 1848; on events in Solingen County, see *NRhZ*, 22 Nov. 1848; *KnZ*, 23 (Beilage), 28 Nov. 1848 (Beilage). Most of the inhabitants of predominantly Protestant Saarbrücken, who had chosen leftist deputies in May 1848, supported the assembly in November, although a proposed tax boycott was turned down after lengthy debate. Noack, "1848/49 in der Saargegend," pp. 94–95.

advocating a constitution for Prussia was illegal, the declaration had, in Orwellian fashion, turned constitutionalism into its opposite, absolutism.[51]

Even before the November crisis, Rhenish constitutional monarchism was sliding into monarchism pure and simple. Banker and religious separatist Carl von der Heydt gave a speech at an August 1848 meeting of the Elberfeld Constitutional Association praising absolute monarchy. In October 1848, the constitutional monarchists of Krefeld had founded a conservative-loyalist Prussian Association, which quickly gained well over one thousand members. The November crisis drastically revealed the failure of the moderate liberals to gain any support for their constitutional monarchist ideas among the inhabitants of the Prussian Rhine Province. Their political position could be propped up only by a decidedly nonconstitutional religious identification with the monarch.[52]

The situation was quite different, its ramifications politically more ambiguous, for the Roman Catholic population of the Prussian Rhineland. The actions of the king and Count Brandenburg served only to confirm long-held suspicions about the Prussian government, and the vast majority of addresses and petitions from Catholic cities, towns, and villages supported, more or less militantly, the assembly. However, the November crisis raised in acute form a question that had already been posed in August, during the festivities in honor of the imperial regent. Which group would exploit politically Catholic hostilities against the Protestant state: the clergy and lay notables who had dominated the elections in May 1848, or the aggressively organizing and agitating democrats?

The initial phase of the November crisis, the struggles in Vienna, found Rhenish Catholic leaders in the camp of the Habsburg emperor. The *Rhein- und Moselzeitung* in Koblenz and the *Rheinische Volkshalle* in Cologne, usually seen as representatives of a left-of-center political current among Rhenish Catholic-clericals, agreed that Robert Blum—a prominent leader of the schismatic German Catholics—had gotten what was coming to him. The newspapers praised General Windischgrätz and his troops for making Vienna a model of law and order. Writing on the eve of Count Brandenburg's appointment, they contrasted this orderly Vienna with a Prussian capital where the mob ruled the streets.[53]

This had been the position taken by the clergy and Pius Associations of the Palatinate, who had condemned and denounced the memorials to Blum. In the November 1848 elections to the Bavarian parliament, held among a Palatine population greatly stirred up by the news from Vienna and Berlin, the

[51] *KnZ*, 17 (Beilage), 25 Nov. 1848 (Erste Ausgabe and Zweite Ausgabe).

[52] Illner, *Bürgerliche Organisierung*, p. 160; Schwenkter, *Konservative Vereine*, pp. 160–61, 166, 171–72; LAK 403 Nr. 7045 pp. 43–73. Cf. *Lebenserinnerungen . . . Alexander Pagenstecher* 2:79–81.

[53] Cf. the hostile comments of *NRhZ*, 16 Nov. 1848; or "Fromme Politik," *KnZ*, 26 Nov. 1848 (Zweite Ausgabe).

Catholic-clericals had provided the only opposition to the People's Association, nominating such candidates as the cantonal physician Joseph Heine of Germersheim. A native of trans-Rhenan Bavaria, Heine had made a name for himself publicly praising feudalism and a society of estates, condemning the French Revolution for having destroyed them, and asserting that schoolteachers made too much money and dressed too well and that children needed to spend less time in school and more working in the fields.[54]

The problem with taking such a position in the Prussian Rhine Province was the simultaneous occurrence of the two crises. Most of the Rhenish deputies elected as a result of the clergy's influence in May 1848 had taken their seats on the right side of both the Frankfurt and Berlin assemblies. Increasingly fearful of the possibility of a second, republican revolution, they had joined the minority in Berlin that had voted to uphold the king's measures and the majority in Frankfurt that had condemned the tax boycott appeal of the Prussian Assembly. For their pains, they received a barrage of hostile addresses and cat musics from their constituents, frequently organized by democratic activists, using the crisis to get back at the enemies who had defeated them in May 1848.[55]

That hostility to both the left and the Protestants, typical of Catholic politics in the Prussian Rhineland since the beginning of the revolution, could no longer be maintained. Some strange, temporizing measures appeared in its place. In the absence of Archbishop von Geissel, who was attending, along with Bishop Arnoldi of Trier, the first German bishops' conference in Würzburg, throughout the entire crisis, the Cologne General Vicariat on November 20 authorized parish priests to offer a mass for the souls of the "deceased Roman Catholic members of the Blum family." On the face of it, this was an incomprehensible decision, since the one family member whose soul urgently needed prayers, namely Robert Blum, had been a schismatic and enemy of the Roman Catholic Church. The decision only makes sense as a concession to the radical mood among the Catholic population, stirred up as least as much by events in Berlin as by those in Vienna.[56]

Local Catholic political activists were unwilling to call for revolution, as the democrats did, but were unable to support the repressive measures carried out by a Protestant government. They found themselves forced to break with

---

[54] *NSZ*, 30 Nov., 1–2, 5, 9, 13, 22 Dec. 1848 (Beilage), 31 Jan. 1849. Lest it be thought that I am accepting uncritically an anticlerical distortion of the politics of Palatine Catholics, the issue of 22 Dec. contains an essay by Heine himself, stating his own ideas.

[55] On the attitudes of the Catholic-clerical deputies, see Schnabel, *Zusammenschluß des politischen Katholizismus*, pp. 96–98; *RhG* 2:522; on denunciations and cat musics, *KnZ*, 9 (Beilage), 19 (Erste Ausgabe and Zweite Ausgabe), 24 (Beilage), 25 Nov. 1848 (Beilage); *NRhZ*, 17, 18 Nov. 1848 (Außerordentliche Beilage); Schrörs, "Hermesianische Pfarrer," pp. 98–99; HSTAD RA Pr. Nr. 2229 ff. 15–16; *RhBA* 2/2:530 n.2; Röttges, *Die politischen Wahlen*, pp. 94–96. On both points, cf. *RhBA* 2/2, Nr. 349; and the address of "several citizens" to the Archbishop of Cologne, *KnZ*, 28 Nov. 1848 (Beilage).

[56] *RhBA* 2/2, Nr. 342; *KnZ*, 3, 19 Dec. 1848 (Erste Beilage).

their parliamentary leaders and join the campaigns of the left, with the intent of calming them down and leading them into more peaceful channels. Events in Aachen provide one example. The November crisis allowed the city's democrats to emerge from the total obscurity to which they had previously been condemned and hold several well-attended mass meetings denouncing the government and the deputies elected in May 1848. The Aachen proletariat, still not very politicized, but always willing to riot against Prussian soldiers, customs agents, or tax collectors, took on a threatening attitude. In response to this, the city council, dominated by members of the Pius Association, passed an address supporting the assembly, but demanding that it end the conflict with the crown as soon as possible, that is, call off the tax boycott. Following the council's instructions, the civic guard manned the city gates and took over the octroi, noting down amounts to be paid, but not actually collecting the tax on foodstuffs brought into the city.

Two days later soldiers replaced the civic guard, which retired without offering any opposition, allowing tax collection to resume. The district authorities resisted, successfully, demands from the provincial governor that the guard be dissolved, insisting that its actions had not stemmed from any revolutionary intent, or even a wish to support the National Assembly's tax boycott appeal, but from the desire to preserve order and prevent bloodshed in a critical situation. Members of the crowd agreed with this assessment, since they angrily smashed the windows of several guard officers, following their retreat from the city gates.[57]

Political Catholicism in Aachen tended toward the conservative; the clergy and Pius Association members of the Moselle Valley stood on the left wing of the Catholic movement, but they also acted in a moderating way during the crisis. The Trier Pius Association dropped its attacks on the democrats, joining them in a mass meeting on November 17, establishing a citizens' committee. The initial appeal of the committee was cautious, supporting the assembly without endorsing its call for a tax boycott. Two days later, the committee posted all over Trier a placard citing the *Neue Rheinische Zeitung*'s denunciation of taxpayers as traitors; it also issued a second, much stronger appeal, calling not just for a tax boycott but for the formation of revolutionary militias, and declaring that czarist troops were about to intervene on behalf of the king of Prussia. Before the committee took these steps in a more revolutionary direction, and presumably because of them, many, although not all, of the representatives of the Pius Association on the committee had handed in their resignations.[58]

[57] *RhBA* 2/2, Nr. 323; HSTAD RA Pr. Nr. 2226 f. 330; HSTAD RA Pr. Nr. 2229 ff. 29–30, 35–36, 46–47; Nießner, *Aachen*, pp. 187–90.

[58] *RhBA* 2/2, Nrs. 313, 322; LAK 403 Nr. 6583 p. 133, 140; *Vbl*, 8 Dec. 1848. In a similar way, the assistant parish priest Alexander Backes spoke at a mass meeting in Cochem on 22 Nov., but while the democrats who organized it were passing around sign-up sheets for a revolutionary militia, he called for exclusively peaceful measures, saying that the population should concede to

Between the revolutionary activities of the democrats and the broad disaffection of the Catholic population, it was a very open question if the Prussian government could preserve its rule in the Rhine Province. Cologne was teeming with activity. The Democratic Society under Franz Raveaux's leadership tried to revive the civic guard; the Workers' Association and Gymnastics Society formed companies of insurgents; 1,300 militiamen issued a declaration of support for the National Assembly and attempted to stop the reserves from being sent to Berlin. But the potential insurgents lacked all weapons, the five thousand rifles handed out to the civic guard having been confiscated when the guard was dissolved in September; efforts to get Rhenish soldiers in the garrison to turn their weapons against their officers were unsuccesful. Consequently, the military was able to preserve order and man the gates, preventing any attempts to boycott the octroi and bring foodstuffs into the city tax free.[59]

Acting fortress commandant Colonel Engels was convinced, however, that in view of the unreliability of the Rhenish troops only the full strength of the entire garrison prevented an outbreak; he refused to allow any soldiers to be requisitioned to preserve order elsewhere, allowing revolutionary scenes to play themselves out in two nearby cities. The crowd in Bonn responded to the tax boycott appeal by insulting and beating collectors of the octroi and tearing the Prussian eagle from public buildings. The democrats quickly called a mass meeting to establish a committee of safety, which enlisted the civic guard to enforce the tax boycott. The committee also sent a delegation to the mayor announcing that he must either support the assembly and its tax boycott or be deposed.

Bonn thus saw the entire revolutionary scenario envisioned by the democrats' provincial directory; without reinforcements from Cologne, the small garrison was powerless to intervene. The university town's constitutional monarchists sent a delegation to Cologne, personally appealing for help from the fortress authorities, who dispatched a batallion of the strongly loyalist Twenty-Seventh Regiment on November 20 to occupy Bonn's walls and collect the octroi. Bonn democrats wanted to fight. They spent the day forging bullets and manufacturing cartridges; messengers were sent across the Rhine to Sieg County, where the democrats had been agitating for several months. Following their appeals, crowds of peasants arrived and camped outside the walls, ready to help drive the soldiers out of the city. But a courier sent to the provincial directory in Cologne returned with news that the metropolis was quiet; an uprising in Bonn would have been an isolated affair, so the democrats took no further action.[60]

---

the government rather than engage in violence. Gendarme Briessen to LR Kr. Cochem, 24 Nov. 1848; and Alexander Backes to OPK, 13 Dec. 1848, both in LAK 441 Nr. 12929.

[59] Seypel, "Die Demokratische Gesellschaft in Köln," pp. 336–53.

[60] Kersken, *Bonn in den Revolutionsjahren*, pp. 81–85; Schurz, *Lebenserinnerungen*, pp. 175–78; *RhBA* 2/2, Nrs. 320, 325, 328; ZSTAM Rep. 77 Tit. 505 Nr. 2 Vol. 4 ff. 198–204.

Thirty miles downstream from Cologne, events in Düsseldorf took an even more revolutionary turn. A mass meeting, called jointly by the People's Club and the Democratic Club, proclaimed a tax boycott and an embargo on any funds in the district treasury being sent to Berlin for the use of the government of Count Brandenburg. The civic guard, since its founding under left-wing leadership, had declared itself in permanent session. Its members gathered, fully armed, on November 19 and issued a statement placing themselves at the disposition of the Berlin Assembly and supporting the tax boycott. The city council promptly voted to appropriate funds for weapons and ammunition; democrats began forging bullets and manufacturing cartridges. The constitutional monarchist association, in which the Catholic-clerical element was strongly represented, announced its support for the assembly, if not for the revolutionary actions being taken in the city.

The revolutionary situation quickly spread beyond the city walls. In the neighboring town of Ratingen and village of Gerresheim, both recipients of extended democratic agitation, revolutionary committees enforced the tax boycott, terrorizing helpless mayors, gendarmes, and tax collectors. The schoolteacher in Ratingen provided a nice touch by having the children write out copies of a tax boycott proclamation and post them on street corners. Across the Rhine in Neuss, the crowd seized control of the arsenal of the militia, to prevent it from being used by the army. On November 20, a great parade of the civic guard of Düsseldorf and neighboring cities and towns was held, ending with the guardsmen taking an oath from their commandant to fight to the last man for the assembly and the rights of the people. A congress of civic guards from the entire district was called to Düsseldorf for November 23.[61]

Such a step looked toward the creation of an insurrectionary authority all along the lower Rhine; yet it seemed the government was powerless against it. The Düsseldorf fortress commandant felt that he needed the entire strength of his garrison just to hold the civic guard in check; he could spare no troops to restore order in the vicinity. Under these circumstances, the district government suspended on November 18 any attempt to collect taxes by force and seems to have tacitly agreed not to collect the octroi if foodstuffs coming into the city were declared so that taxes could be paid later.[62]

More than that, as the movement grew in strength and intensity, some state officials themselves began going over to it. Düsseldorf's police commissioner let his superiors know that he regarded the adjournment of the assembly as an

[61] General accounts of the November crisis in Düsseldorf, *RhBA* 2/2, Nrs. 305, 310, 314, 329; Dowe, *Aktion und Organisation*, pp. 209–12; Lenger, *Zwischen Kleinbürgertum und Proletariat*, pp. 166–67. On events in Gerresheim and Ratingen, see HSTAD RD Pr. Nr. 815 ff. 15–28; HSTAD RD Nr. 8806 f. 335.

[62] HSTAD RD Pr. Nr. 700 f. 2; HSTAD RD Pr. Nr. 813 ff. 64–69. The octroi seems to have been collected in spite of this, ibid., f. 31.

unconstitutional "act of violence" and would not take measures to enforce it. Two days later, on November 20, speaking from the balcony of the city hall after the parade of the civic guard, he announced that he had come to Düsseldorf to "defend freedom" and would stand by the assembly and refuse to order the police to collect taxes. At just about the very same time, six of the thirteen councillors of the district government voted to issue a declaration suspending forced collection of taxes and the sending of funds to Berlin. The councillors later declared, perhaps not entirely falsely, that they advocated this measure in order to preserve order and prevent bloodshed, but they also admitted that, in their capacity as private citizens, they regarded the assembly as in the right against the king.[63]

On the evening of that remarkable day, District Governor von Spiegel personally informed a delegation of civic guard officers and municipal officials that as long as no violence occurred, he would not, as rumored, use the army and declare Düsseldorf in a state of siege. Just the opposite, he assured them, if things remained peaceful: "I quite agree with you, this ministry can not maintain itself, I will even say to you if it lasts longer than a week, all state agencies will refuse to obey it." This was not the language normally used by a high Prussian official.[64]

Although the evidence is not entirely clear, Spiegel was probably lying when he made the promise. After conferring with Spiegel, the provincial governor had, the morning of the day Spiegel promised not to use soldiers, requested and received troops from the Cologne fortress commandant to reinforce the Düsseldorf garrison, bringing it up to the strength needed to restore state authority. A state of siege was declared on November 22; the leaders of the left, naively believing Spiegel's promise, were caught by surprise and could offer no resistance. A familiar series of measures was carried out: dissolution and disarming of the civic guard and prohibition of the democratic clubs and of public meetings. The insubordinate officials were first suspended and eventually dismissed from state service. District Governor von Spiegel thought it prudent, after breaking his word to the citizenry, to move out of his apartment into the fortress, where he remained for a few weeks until he was pensioned off by the Interior Ministry for having let things get so out of hand.[65]

---

[63] The dossiers on the six councillors and their actions are in HSTAD RD Pr. Nr. 127 and LAK 403 Nr. 4148; for the police commissioner, see HSTAD RD Pr. Nr. 812 ff. 93–95; HSTAD RD Pr. Nr. 740 f. 1.

[64] Transcript of the conversation in *NRhZ*, 29 Nov. 1848, implicitly confirmed by Spiegel's public statement after the declaration of a state of siege, HSTAD RD Pr. Nr. 813 ff. 82–83.

[65] Besides the sources cited in notes 60–63, see HSTAD RD Pr. Nr. 813 ff. 39–40; LAK 403 Nr. 17332 pp. 281–84. The district government had made an attempt on 18 Nov. to provoke a clash between civic guard and troops, leading to the calling of a state of siege (HSTAD RD Pr. Nr. 740 ff. 1–5), but it is unclear whether Spiegel supported this or, as he claimed to the delega-

Things were even more out of hand in the Moselle Valley. In spite of the radical appeals of the citizens' committees of Koblenz and Trier, the inhabitants of the two cities themselves were held in check by the troops and artillery of their respective fortresses. Trier democrats had no success in getting peasants to boycott the octroi when the city resembled, as one newspaper correspondent noted, an "armed camp." An angry crowd in Koblenz did drive away the tax collectors from the city gates, and beat up the police sent to protect them; the district government then requisitioned the civic guard, which refused to turn out, proclaiming its loyalty to the Berlin assembly. Calling on the military for support, the authorities dissolved the civic guard, confiscated its weapons, and posted soldiers at the gates to collect the octroi.[66]

Between preserving order in Koblenz and Trier and restoring it in Kreuznach, all the available troops were used up, so for several days the central part of the Moselle Valley came under the de facto control of committees of safety formed by the democrats of Bernkastel and Cochem. These called for a tax boycott, intimidated the authorities into carrying it out, gained the support of the respective city councils, mobilized the civic guards and members of the militia to create an insurrectionary army, purchased gunpowder, forged bullets, and manufactured cartridges. Leading democrats of the two wine towns traveled up and down the valley holding mass meetings, their call for a tax boycott actively supported by the vintners. "In the Moselle villages from Cröv to Wintrich such excitement reign[ed] that any inspection of the district [for tax purposes] . . . [could] no longer occur." Tax collectors were mocked, cursed, and threatened; neither village mayors nor civic guards would lift a finger to protect them, even when a crowd in Pünderich tried to throw one official into the Moselle. The priest in Trittenheim tried to calm his parishioners when they brought a cat music to the tax collector. Instead, they turned on their pastor, throwing stones at him, chanting, "Republic, republic, our pastor is crazy."[67]

After repeated requests of the Trier district governor, reinforcements were sent from the border fortresses in Saarlouis and Luxemburg. The authorities could then take action against the mid-Moselle democrats, but when an attempt was made to arrest leftist leaders in Bernkastel, on November 26, the

---

tion, just signed whatever Councillor von Mirbach—the hard-liner in the district government—placed in front of him.

[66] *RhBA* 2/2, Nrs. 319, 321–22, 326, 335; *KnZ*, 26 Nov. 1848 (Zweite Ausgabe); Paul Schmidt, *Die Wahlen im Regierungsbezirk Koblenz 1849 bis 1867/69* (Bonn: Ludwig Röhrscheid, 1971), pp. 52–56.

[67] LAK 403 Nr. 6583 pp. 127–30, 136, 155–57, 220–25, 238–41; LAK 441 Nr. 3057 pp. 103–05, 115–17; Gendarme Briessen (Cochem) to LR Kr. Cochem, 24 Nov. 1848; LR Kr. Cochem to RKO, 4 Dec. 1848, both in LAK 441 Nr. 12929; Stahl, *1848/49 an der Mittelmosel*, pp. 20–23; Schmidt, *Wahlen im Regierungsbezirk Koblenz*, pp. 51–52. Cf. the account of the political orientation of the pastor in Trittenheim in LAK 442 Nr. 6659 pp. 143–52. As late as January 1849, a forced sale in Schweich, to collect money from tax boycotters, led to a riot. LAK 442 Nr. 2366.

whole town turned out to defend them. The storm bells were rung, and as had been prearranged, reinforcements poured in from the nearby villages Graach, Wehlen, and Zeltingen. Soon, the small corps of soldiers in Bernkastel—half of whom were absent, detached to protect the forests from the up-country peasantry—faced a crowd of six hundred–seven hundred insurgents, armed with some rifles, but mostly a miscellany of pitchforks, clubs, and improvised pikes made by tying, pruning knives, available in every vintner's household, to sticks. The soldiers were forced out of town.

Throughout the evening, reinforcements poured in from more distant villages, Rachtig, Kersten, Filzen, Uerzig, Cröv, Leiwen and Trittenheim, and from the neighboring county town Wittlich, perhaps 1,500 in all. However, the authorities also obtained reinforcements, including cavalry and mobile artillery, rather exceeding pruning knives in firepower, bringing the insurrection to an end. Bernkastel was declared in a state of siege; the civic guards there and in the insurgent villages were dissolved; their weapons, as well as privately owned firearms, were confiscated. Tax collection resumed, and the democratic leaders were forced to flee the country or face arrest.[68]

The special government commissioner directing the suppression of the insurrection—incidently, also the Trier correspondent of the constitutional monarchist *Kölnische Zeitung*—noted, with relief, that the up-country peasantry, Catholic as well as Protestant, had taken no part in the events. They had grievances enough concerning forest use, usually directed at the forest officials, but sometimes at Moselle villagers who stole their wood; however, unlike the latter's angry feelings about the must tax, the forest complaints of the mountain villagers had never been the subject of the democrats' political agitation.[69]

A few final military actions at the end of November, the occupation of Cochem and the sending of troops to guard the arsenals of the militia in Andernach and Neuss, completed the suppression of the tax boycott campaign, and the resolution of the November crisis. After briefly reconvening in the town of Brandenburg in early December, the Prussian National Assembly was dissolved; Count Brandenburg and his fellow reactionary ministers remained in office, determining government policy. The tax boycott had thus failed to protect the assembly or remove the ministry, but the powerful response it provoked in the Rhine Province revealed the distinctly limited base of support for Prussian rule and the feebleness of constitutional monarchism as a popular political doctrine. For the first time in the revolution, the democrats emerged as the main spokesmen for opposition to Berlin's rule in the Rhineland. Organizing a determined resistance to it, they came close to bringing it to an end.[70]

---

[68] Stahl, *1848/49 an der Mittelmosel*, pp. 20–27; LAK 403 Nr. 6583 pp. 138–39, 142–45, 149–50, 155–57, 159–63, 188–91, 205–209, 215–25, 229–32, 262–63. A small part of the archival material is printed in *RhBA* 2/2, Nr. 343.

[69] LAK 442 Nr. 6583 pp. 279–80, 288–91, 295–301; *NRhZ*, 30 Nov. 1848.

[70] Most general accounts of the revolution tend to see the tax boycott as evoking no response,

A WINTER OF DISCONTENT

A New Constitution and New Elections in Prussia

After sending the Constituent Assembly home, Count Brandenburg's ministry carried out a politically astute maneuver. The government decreed a constitution, and a relatively liberal one at that, containing guarantees for civil rights and establishing a legislature with power to approve taxes whose lower house was elected by universal, if indirect, manhood suffrage. Most important for the Rhineland, the constitution included major concessions to the Catholic Church, introducing "independence of the church from the state," as Cologne's Archbishop von Geissel wished it, with ecclesiastical administrative autonomy, free public exercise of religion, and a preference for confessionally segregated public schools.

The constitution was, on closer examination, not quite so liberal. The democratically elected lower house was equal in parliamentary power to an upper house chosen in elections with a stiff property franchise. Both houses together were weaker than the monarch, entitled "by the grace of God," who retained an absolute veto over legislation, full control over the army and foreign affairs, the right to name ministers without any responsibility to the parliament, and, in the shape of articles 105 and 108, the right to levy taxes and pass laws when the parliament was not in session. Such a constitution might have been broadly welcomed in 1847, but was less attractive a year later, especially to the democrats.[71]

Parliamentary elections under the new constitution were held at the end of January 1849. The election campaign itself was no more extensive than in April 1848, but the previous year's perception of elections as ceremonies of unanimity and the feelings of unity that had prompted it had vanished, a result of the bitter confrontations of the fall. Politics took the more familiar form of an open struggle between different, organized political tendencies. Although not possessing an organization comparable to those in the southern Rhineland—the Cologne Provincial Directory having for all practical purposes ceased to exist—the democrats had at least one club organized in every constituency, a provincewide newspaper, and journals in most major cities and many smaller towns. They could and did put up candidates in every single constituency.[72]

---

and much hostility. Cf. Wehler, *Deutsche Gesellschaftsgeschichte* 2:712; Valentin, *Geschichte der deutschen Revolution* 2:272–76; Botzenhart, *Deutscher Parlamentarismus*, p. 545; Hamerow, *Restoration, Revolution, Reaction*, pp. 185–87; Schwentker, *Konservative Vereine*, pp. 141–42. A contrary picture, which, for the Rhineland at least, conforms more to the actual events, can be found in *Illustrierte Geschichte*, pp. 263–68.

[71] Botzenhart, *Deutscher Parlamentarismus*, pp. 550–55; Valentin, *Geschichte der deutschen Revolution* 2:291–93; Siemann, *Die deutsche Revolution*, pp. 174–75; *RhG* 3:361–62.

[72] A "Central Electoral Committee for Popular Elections" in Berlin attempted to coordinate

As in May 1848, the state authorities were determined to see loyalist, constitutional monarchist candidates elected, but official action was better organized and coordinated as well. Acting on directives from Berlin, the provincial and district authorities officially endorsed and supported candidates—indeed, helped arrange their nomination—and printed and paid for leaflets and brochures on their behalf and attacking the democrats. The new election laws, allowing counties to be broken up and placed in different constituencies, or several to be combined into one constituency, which would elect several deputies, offered a rich field for gerrymandering. Officials made aggressive use of the provision preventing recipients of public charity from voting and attempted to define an ambiguous phrase in the law granting the vote only to "independent" adult males to exclude wage earners from the ballot, until the central government quashed such efforts.[73]

The authorities could count on the same groups that had been so loyal during the November crisis and, in fact, since the spring of 1848: the Protestant clergy and neoorthodox Protestants generally, especially the pious entrepreneurs of the Wuppertal, Bergisches Land, and the lower Rhine textile area. Additionally, they had an unexpected new ally. Frankly pleased with the new constitution, Archbishop von Geissel, after conferring on the forthcoming elections with the provincial governor, issued a statement to the Cologne Pius Association calling on its members to strive to elect men "who forthrightly mean well with the king and with the people, with church and state, with order and legality, with God and man, so that the happily completed work [the Prussian constitution] may bring honor to God and peace to man." This certainly sounds like, and the authorities understood it as, an endorsement of constitutional monarchism and the official position on the elections. Even more overt statements were issued by the bishop of Trier and the Westphalian bishop of Münster, part of whose diocese extended into the northern end of the Rhineland.[74]

Many priests and lay activists followed this lead. Attorney Otto Hardung of the Cologne Pius Association denounced, at an election rally in Eupen, the "unworthy intrigues of the left side of the now dissolved National Assembly." Another Cologne Pius Association speaker asserted in Mülheim a. Rhein that the forthcoming elections should be used to "strengthen the authority of the

---

the election campaigns of the left across the entire monarchy (Botzenhart, *Deutscher Parlamentarismus*, p. 607), but, as far as I can see, had no influence at all on elections in the Rhineland.

[73] HSTAD RD Pr. Nr. 557 ff. 38–40, 47; HSTAD RD Nr. 78 ff. 21–35, 46–54; HSTAD RA Pr. Nr. 705 f. 2; LAK 403 Nr. 9670 pp. 329–50, 371–76; LAK 442 Nr. 6696 ff. 23–25; LAK 442 Nr. 6506 passim.

[74] *KnZ*, 7 Jan. 1849 (quotation), 21 Jan. 1849; HSTAD RA Pr. Nr. 705 f. 55; ZSTAM Rep. 77 Tit. 505 Nr. 5 Vol. V ff. 252, 263–65; ZSTAM Rep. 77 CCXLV Nr. 4 ff. 113–21; *RhBA* 2/2, Nrs. 353, 363. For a similar opinion from laymen, ibid., Nr. 349. The election conference between archbishop and provincial governor apparently took place in the middle of December 1848; exactly what was said is unknown: LAK 403 Nr. 7531 pp. 5–6.

king as well as the servants of the church." The parish priest in Hessel "preached for a whole hour during the holy mass, consigning all the democrats to hell," an attitude particularly prevalent in the Rhine Valley around Cologne and Bonn, but found in the Ahr and Moselle valley as well. Rather more ingeniously, the pastor of St. Mauritius in Cologne had his parish council distribute municipal bread and rice certificates to five hundred of his parishioners, or their wives, thus qualifying them as charity recipients and preventing them from voting.[75]

Not all lay and clerical activists could endorse such outright support of the government. In Aachen, members of the Pius Association refused to accept its endorsement of the constitutional monarchists and went over to the democrats. The Catholic-clerical element in Koblenz split over the election. A minority, including the clergy and the leading lay activists, formed a Pius Association and entered into negotiations with the constitutional monarchists, while a larger group, with the support of the Catholic newspaper, endorsed the candidates of the democrats. The Catholic clergy of Jülich County and Düren County was also divided over the elections. The older priests supported the constitutional monarchists, while the younger ones followed the lead of one of their number, the area's deputy to the Berlin Assembly, Philipp van Berg, assistant pastor in Jülich, and supported the left. Political conflicts within the Neuss Pius Association were so great that its members voted not to take any stand on politics whatsoever, and confine the association's activities to religious affairs. After a debate late into the night of January 18, 1849, a majority of the Cologne Pius Association voted to endorse the constitutional monarchist ticket, only to have the group's election committee announce publicly a few days later that it had not entered into an agreement with any other group, but would propose its own candidates.[76]

The religious issue cut both ways for Catholic-clericals. On the one hand, the authorities who granted a constitution seemed to deserve Catholic support, since the constitution guaranteed the independence of the church from the state, the single most important civic freedom, as the *Rheinische Volks-Halle* in Cologne noted. The Koblenz *Rhein- und Moselzeitung*, a vehemently anti-Prussian and religiously neoorthodox newspaper, pointed out the other side,

[75] HSTAD RA Pr. Nr. 2229 ff. 82–83; Gernert, *1848/49 im Rheinisch-Bergischen*, p. 140; *NRhZ*, 27 Jan. 1849. For similar examples, see ibid., 19 (Beilage), 21, 25–26, 28, 31 Jan. 1849; *NKZ*, 30 Jan. 7, Feb. 1849; *KnZ*, 30 Jan. (Beilage), 4 Feb. 1849 (Zweite Beilage); LAK 442 Nr. 6659 pp. 143–51. On the actions of the pastor of St. Mauritius, and his and the parish council's unconvincing denials of any political intent, see *KnZ*, 27 (Beilage), 28 Jan. 1849 (Zweite Ausgabe); *FA*, 28 Jan., 8, 18 Feb. 1849.

[76] Schmidt, *Die Wahlen im Regierungsbezirk Koblenz*, pp. 78–81 (Koblenz); LAK 403 Nr. 9671 pp. 437–42; HSTAD RA Pr. Nr. 701 ff. 19–20 (Aachen, Jülich, Düren); *NKZ*, 17 Jan. 1849 (Neuss); Heinen, "Der Kölner Pius Verein," pp. 222–26; ZSTAM Rep. 77 CCXLV Nr. 4 ff. 113–21; *KnZ*, 21 Jan. 1849 (Zweite Beilage) (Cologne). For similar circumstances in Krefeld, cf. Röttges, *Die politischen Wahlen*, pp. 109–10.

that all these promises of religious freedom were being made by Protestants, whom no good Catholic could ever consider trusting. As this statement suggests—although the evidence on this point is scattered—Catholic political orientation tended to follow lines of intraconfessional division. Religious rationalists were more likely to be adherents of cooperation with the (largely Protestant) constitutional monarchists and the authorities; the anti-Prussian, anti-Protestant neoorthodox were more common among the adherents of supporting the democrats; and both groups found behind the prospect of independent Catholic candidacies.[77]

No less complicated were attitudes of other political tendencies competing for the Catholic vote. Constitutional monarchists and the authorities who supported them claimed that the democrats wanted to destroy religion and abolish the papacy (the Prussian elections occurred after Italian leftists had driven the Pope out of Rome). Protestant officials posing as defenders of the Catholic Church must have been a strange sight indeed. An even stranger one occurred at a constitutional monarchist election meeting in Siegburg, where a Jewish student from Bonn, an ex-democrat who had gone over to the right, gave a speech denouncing the leftists for their hostility to Catholicism. This provided the occasion for a group of peasants from nominally Catholic but strongly leftist rural Sieg County, led by a Bonn democrat, to burst into the meeting, denounce the speaker as a "renegade" and "Judas," and drive the constitutional monarchists out of the meeting hall and out of town.[78]

However, the democrats' position was no less problematic. The open hostility of many of the Catholic clergy and the Pius Associations—even when not supporting the authorities, most were by no means friendly to the left—frequently provoked an anticlerical response. Further, the democrats of Rhenish Prussia saw the election as an opportunity to reverse the voters' verdict in May 1848, when politics had centered around confessional identification and they had been badly defeated by the Catholic-clericals. As the democrats of Geilenkirchen announced, "The people's eyes have been opened. In regard to elections the old warning shots like 'purgatory, salvation, and danger to the faith' don't work any more." At the same time, the democrats wanted to mobilize the hostilities of Catholic Rhinelanders against the Prussian state for their cause, and had to reckon with the possibility of needing the support of organized Catholic politicians to win against the constitutional monarchists. This also led to peculiar politics, for example, the democratic election rallies in Gladbach County on the lower Rhine, where speakers attacked the Catholic

[77] On this point, cf. Weber, *Aufklärung und Orthodoxie*, pp. 156–67 (although his accounts of political events are not always accurate); Schmidt, *Wahlen im Regeirungsbezirk Koblenz*, p. 86 n.180 and p. 87 n.185; HSTAD RA Pr. Nr. 701 ff. 19–20; reports on the political opinions of the Catholic clergy, LAK 442 Nr. 6659.

[78] *NRhZ*, 22 Jan. 1849; LAK 403 Nr. 6582 ff. 29–30, 38–41; *KnZ*, 10 Jan. 1849; similarly, in Gladbach County, Röttges, *Die politischen Wahlen*, p. 118.

clergy for its right-wing political views, while simultaneously pointing out the danger to the Catholic religion posed by the Prussian state.[79]

Political alignments in predominantly Protestant areas were simplicity itself in comparison, pitting, as they had since the *Vormärz*, religious rationalists against the neoorthodox. The confrontations of November 1848 had resulted there in a substantial victory for the right; many freethinking bourgeois had given up on politics. Hermann Körner, teacher of draftsmanship and one of the leaders of the Elberfeld democrats, has left a marvelous account in his memoirs of how many of his middle-class friends took the black-red-gold ribbons out of their buttonholes and turned to playing whist at their club instead of attending political meetings. He had no high expectations when he and his remaining associates sponsored a public meeting in honor of the Declaration of Basic Rights for Germany, a sort of Bill of Rights for the German constitution, approved by the Frankfurt National Assembly in January 1849. To his astonishment, an enormous crowd appeared, not the "honest burghers," but the proletarian members of the Central Industrial Association of the Wuppertal. The democratic movement in the manufacturing regions of the right bank of the Rhine was passing from the freethinking bourgeoisie into the still-unsteady hands of the small-producing manufacturing outworkers and craftsmen.[80]

Election day was January 22, 1849, and even before the balloting was complete, it had become clear that the outcome of May 1848 would not be repeated. The democrats held on to their previous strongholds, electing 141 of 167 electors in Düsseldorf, and 62 of 67 in Trier, in spite of an aggressive campaign by the Pius Association there in favor of its own slate of electors. Leftists also made breakthroughs in areas where they had previously been defeated. They gained a substantial majority of the electors in Cologne and in the neighboring counties on the left bank of the Rhine from Neuss to Bonn, in the Moselle Valley, and in much of the Eifel uplands. Small, predominantly Protestant towns, such as Kreuznach and Simmern, chose democratic electors. Even in the previously conservative industrial areas, the democrats did unexpectedly well, gaining many electors—if probably still remaining in the minority—in Aachen and Elberfeld and taking a majority in some suburbs, like Stolberg and Velbert.[81]

---

[79] *NRhZ*, 19 Jan. 1849 (Beilage); "Aus dem Kreise Rheinbach," *KnZ*, 20 Jan. 1849 (Zweite Beilage); HSTAD RD Nr. 8806 ff. 270–76; similarly, HSTAD RD Pr. Nr. 557 f. 47.

[80] Körner, *Lebenskämpfe* 2:33–38.

[81] On election results, see the (occasionally overoptimistic) accounts in *NRhZ*, 24 Jan.–3 Feb. 1849. Trier election results from *Vbl*, 23–24 Jan. 1849 (confirmed, with small differences, by the authorities, cf. Schierbaum, *Wahlen in den Eifel- und Moselkreisen*, p. 49). Admissions of victories of the left by its adversaries, *KnZ*, 24, 26–27 Jan. 1849; HSTAD RA Pr. Nr. 705 ff. 15–16, 35–36; LAK 403 Nr. 9671 pp. 15–17, 39–42, 461–68; LAK 441 Nr. 8299 pp. 105–07, 111–13, 117; Lorenz, "1848/49 im Wuppertal," p. 260.

The only real question remaining after the selection of the electors was whether the deputies chosen by them would be almost unanimously democratic. In the two weeks between the election of the electors and their meeting to choose the deputies, the authorities and the constitutional monarchists worked at avoiding that prospect. One weapon they could use was an appeal to guild sentiments. This proved successful in the Wuppertal, where the voters had chosen a large number of outworkers as electors, defeating the candidacies of many of the devout, conservative manufacturers. Democrats were prematurely jubilant, envisaging a victory in the constituency Elberfeld-Düsseldorf, coming from an alliance of the Wuppertal proletarians with the Düsseldorf democrats.

They were outmanuevered by the constitutional-monarchists, who put up as a candidate the president of the Elberfeld weavers' guild. At a meeting of the Wuppertal electors in Vohwinkel, democrats who attempted to speak were shouted down with cries of "That's no craftsman! We want nothing to do with the democrats!" The democrats hastily nominated a weaver of their own and tried to mobilize support for him among the electors, but too late. While some 30–35 percent of the electors from Elberfeld County voted for the democratic candidates, they were not enough to put them through, and four Prussian loyalists were chosen to represent the constituency in Berlin.[82]

Constitutional monarchists tried the same manuever in Cologne, announcing that the electors should choose "practical men" who would discuss economic issues, not doctrinaire democrats. They floated the idea of nominating the master shoemaker Heinrich Schützendorf, a one-time leftist who had attended the Frankfurt Artisans' Congress and returned a convinced adherent of both guilds and conservative politics. However, when Schützendorf called a meeting of master craftsmen early in February, the audience greeted him with cries of "Down with the guild master! Down with the traitor! Down with the turncoat!" and drove him out of the hall. Outside, the journeymen were waiting, and they pursued Schützendorf and his followers for several blocks with curses and blows, putting an end to his candidacy and the chances of the constitutional monarchists in the Rhenish metropolis.[83]

The chief hope of the constitutional monarchists and the authorities supporting them rested in obtaining the cooperation of the Catholic clergy and the lay activists. Both the numbers of those elected and their political influence, however, were much smaller than in May 1848. Political organization had

---

[82] KnZ, 31 Jan. 1849; NRhZ, 25 Jan., 4, 6–7 Feb. 1849; NKZ, 7 Feb. 1849; LAK 403 Nr. 9671 pp. 471–73. Cf. Lorenz, "1848/49 im Wuppertal," pp. 259–60. Gerrymandering contributed to this result, a portion of Düsseldorf County having been detached from the rest and placed in another constituency.

[83] NKZ, 6 Feb. 1849; Seypel, "Die Demokratische Gesellschaft in Köln," pp. 357–67. It is interesting to note the greater strength of guild sentiment in the manufacturing districts than in Cologne, a city of small craft workshops.

been virtually nonexistent then; the priest had been seen as natural representative of the parish, the clergy dominating and directing the elections in Catholic areas. In January 1849, the elections were no longer representations of unanimity but battlegrounds for competing, organized political tendencies. Priests were forced to take sides politically, compete in election campaigns, and stand as candidates of one group against another, circumstances not well suited to the preservation of clerical authority. When the parish priest from Bedburdyck spoke up at a democratic election rally in the lower Rhine village of Fürth to defend the legitimacy of the constitution, the notary Hermens of Grevenbroich answered right back, "Herr pastor, you can preach in favor of absolutism day and night, but it will do no good."[84]

The results showed this weakening of clerical influence. At least 19 Catholic priests were chosen as electors in Gladbach County in May 1848, but only 2 in January 1849. No priests were chosen as electors in Koblenz or Andernach, both clerical strongholds the previous spring. Of the 39 electors chosen in the city of Neuss just 3 had been elected in the Catholic-clerical landslide in May 1848; 29 of the electors in January 1849 were supporters of the democrats. Even in pious Aachen, the number of priests chosen as electors declined from 18 of 97 in May 1848 to 10 of 188 nine months later.[85]

Particularly in the southern Rhineland, the voters seem to have judged the priests by political criteria. In four counties of the Trier District—Bitburg, Wittlich, Saarburg, and Trier (county)—for which lists of the electors and the authorities' November 1849 evaluations of the political opinions of the individual clergy are available, a very distinct picture emerges. Of 187 priests officiating in those counties, 41, or 22 percent, were chosen as electors, but of the 31 the officials noted as sympathetic to the democrats, 12 (39 percent) were chosen by the voters, whereas of the 156 noted as conservative or apolitical, 27, or just 17 percent, were elected. These results suggest that the Catholic voters preferred clergy on the left to those on the right.[86]

If no longer dominating the selection of deputies as they had in May 1848, the clerical electors, especially on the lower Rhine, remained a major political factor, and both democrats and constitutional monarchists strove to gain their support. Helped along by quarrels between Protestant constitutional monarchists and Catholic clericals in Aachen, the left obtained the votes of enough clergy and Pius Association members in the constituencies Aachen-Eupen and

[84] HSTAD RD Pr. Nr. 827 ff. 15–17.

[85] Röttges, *Die politischen Wahlen*, pp. 111–12, 114–15 (Neuss and Gladbach County); LAK 403 Nr. 9671 pp. 254, 524–28 (Koblenz and Andernach); HSTAD RA Pr. Nr. 705 ff. 22–23; Repgen, *Märzbewegung*, pp. 227–28 (Aachen).

[86] Clergy's opinions according to LAK 442 Nr. 6659 pp. 63–69, 87–90, 143–51, 192–97; lists of the electors in LAK 403 Nr. 9671 pp. 49–65, 171–77, 335–39; LAK 442 Nr. 6506 pp. 93–113. Two priests listed as electors were not mentioned in the reports on the political opinions of the clergy nine months later, perhaps having died or taken up a new parish in the interval.

Düren-Jülich to elect four of the five deputies chosen. In the lower Rhine constituencies of the neighboring Düsseldorf District, the situation was reversed. Quarrels between Protestants and Catholics among the supporters of the democrats and support by the clergy for the constitutional monarchists were exploited by the right to elect six of the seven candidates in the constituencies Duisburg-Rees and Kempen-Krefeld-Neuss.[87]

In a number of constituencies, the Catholic-clerical electors tried to elect a moderately oppositional figure, one not overtly in favor of Count Brandenburg's ministry but willing to accept the constitution, guaranteeing the interests of the church—as most democrats would not—and untainted by either anticlerical or republican ideas. They were successful in doing this for five of the six candidates elected in the constituencies at either end of the province, Kleve-Geldern and Saarbrücken–St. Wendel–Ottweiler, as well as in the Cologne suburbs. In Trier, on the other hand, the clergy and Pius Association, having failed to put through any of their own candidates, tried to prevent the election of Friedrich Simon, a German Catholic and father of the anticlerical Trier radical Ludwig Simon, but without success.[88]

Table 8.1 sums up the political opinions of the deputies elected. These results—a substantial majority of the deputies representing the Rhine Province sitting on the left in the new parliament, with the democrats the strongest po-

TABLE 8.1

Deputies Elected to the Prussian Parliament in the Rhine Province, January 1849

Political Viewpoint	Confessional Composition of Constituency	
	Majority Protestant	Majority Roman Catholic
Democratic	—	27
Moderate or clerical oppositional	—	11
Constitutional monarchist, governmental	13	8

Sources: Election results in NKZ, 9 Feb. 1849, supplemented and occasionally corrected by official reports on the outcome of the elections in LAK 403 Nr. 9671. The figures correspond roughly to the actual caucus affiliations of the Rhenish deputies in Berlin (for these, see Vbl, 13 Mar. 1849, or, slightly differently, Schwentker, Konservative Vereine, p. 264) but not exactly, since several candidates were elected in more than one constituency and by-elections were required.

[87] LAK 403 Nr. 9671 pp. 437–42; Röttges, Die politischen Wahlen, p. 114; NKZ, 16 Feb. 1849.

[88] Röttges, Die politischen Wahlen, p. 109; LAS 403 Nr. 9671 pp. 419–22, 489–93; LAK 442 Nr. 6506 ff. 81–83; Schierbaum, Wahlen in den Eifel- und Moselkreisen, pp. 51–55. Probably a similar event is described by Schmidt, Wahlen im Regierungsbezirk Koblenz, p. 98.

litical force—were among the best the left obtained anywhere in the Prussian state and a far cry from May 1848, when the deputies chosen in the Rhineland were among the most conservative. While the swing to the left occurred throughout the entire province, it was most pronounced in certain areas.

The Rhenish elections did not show, as historians have often asserted, a gap in political opinion between left-wing urban and industrial areas and a conservative countryside. The constituencies in the urbanized and manufacturing regions of the Wuppertal, Bergisches Land, and Ruhr basin sent deputies of the right to Berlin, while the rural, agricultural regions of the Eifel and Moselle Valley chose adherents of the left. If anything, the opposite was true: Two-thirds of the deputies in the rural, backward, and impoverished Koblenz and Trier districts were democrats, compared to just over one-third in the economically advanced and urbanized Cologne, Aachen, and Düsseldorf districts.[89]

The primary political distinction, as Table 8.1 shows, was a confessional one, leftist candidates obtaining majorities only in predominantly Roman Catholic constituencies, while all the deputies elected in predominantly Protestant ones stood on the right. This Protestant-Catholic contrast had characterized the elections of May 1848 as well, but then the Catholic voters had sent mostly right-of-center, clerical deputies to Frankfurt and Berlin. In January 1849, it was the democrats who were able to exploit confessional antagonism towards the Prussian state. Catholic voters often defied the clergy and Catholic-clerical politicians, who were only able to exercise their influence when they at least pretended to sympathize with the left. In that sense, the election is best understood as a confirmation, in peaceful, legal fashion, of the political alignments of the November crisis, a referendum on Prussian rule, with most votes cast in the negative.

TOWARD A SPRING OF LITTLE HOPE

The electoral success of the left in the west of Prussia was balanced by victories of the right in the eastern provinces, so that the composition of the new Prussian parliament was much like that of the dissolved National Assembly— roughly equal numbers of deputies on the left and right, with a small center group holding the balance. On the first roll calls the centrists voted with the right, giving forces favorable to the king and his ministers a working majority in the parliament. The democrats of the Prussian Rhine Province could now know the frustration their colleagues in Rhine-Hessen and the Palatinate had

---

[89] Both Schwentker, *Konservative Vereine*, p. 265, and Paschen, *Demokratische Vereine*, p. 126, assert that the rural voters were conservative in January 1849, while urban voters were on the left. Whatever the validity of this idea in other parts of the Prussian state, it does not apply to the Rhine Province.

learned the previous spring, of being in the majority regionally, but outvoted overall.[90]

An impotent militancy, a resigned frustration characterized the mood of the democrats in the entire Rhineland as the winter of 1849 moved towards spring. The celebrations of the revolutionary anniversaries in February and March showed the increasing radicalization of the left; its victories in the Prussian parliamentary elections and the expansion of the democratic clubs into the countryside of the southern Rhineland showed its growing popular support. Yet none of this could be translated into any political action. The radical provincials would move only on a signal from one of the capital cities, and the signals from Frankfurt, Berlin, and Vienna had already been given in the fall of 1848, resulting in the left's defeat.

Speaking before the Mainz Democratic Club at its session of March 14, 1849, Ludwig Bamberger proclaimed the revolution of the previous year dead, the German princes seeking systematically to destroy all it had accomplished. In a tone of defiant resignation, he concluded, "One thing has remained to the people: their spirit has powerfully awakened to a living political life and this no government can cripple or take from them." Within a few weeks, this popular spirit would receive a call to action from an unexpected source.[91]

[90] For political alignments in the Prussian parliament, see Botzenhart, *Deutscher Parlamentarismus*, pp. 607–21.

[91] *Der Demokrat*, 18 Mar. 1849.

PART THREE

Toward a Second Revolution:
The *Reichsverfassungskampagne*

> "There can be just one palace in Germany; [one] with the inscription, 'Here resides the President of the Republic.' "
>
> —Franz Haas, democrat of Alzey, at a mass meeting there,
> May 3, 1849.

CHAPTER NINE

Uprising on the Lower Rhine

FRANKFURT ELECTS AN EMPEROR

In March 1849, the Frankfurt National Assembly completed writing a constitution for a united German state. Following the outcome of the struggles of the previous fall, the Frankfurt parliamentarians were more acted upon than actors; decisions about crucial features of the constitution were forced upon the assembled deputies. The Austrian prime minister, Prince Schwarzenberg, appointed to office after the victory of the imperial armies over insurgent Vienna, rudely disrupted the final deliberations by announcing that only the entire Habsburg monarchy, complete with its Hungarian half and Slavic population, would affiliate itself with a united Germany. This declaration, coupled with a refusal to consent to any all-German legislature, was a scarcely veiled call for the restoration of the pre-1848 German Confederation. It would have meant an end to the whole movement for national unity, and was thus unacceptable to most of the deputies. The Austrian position left the way clear for the pro-Prussian element in the Assembly, consisting largely of Protestant constitutional monarchists from north Germany, the party of the hereditary emperor [die Erbkaiserlichen], as they called themselves, the "little Germans" [die Kleindeutschen], as they were dubbed by their enemies. They proposed to create a German national state without Austria, roughly with the boundaries of Bismarck's empire of 1870–1871, whose chief executive would be the king of Prussia, bearing the title Emperor of the Germans.

This idea had never previously found majority support in the assembly. It succeeded only because the "little Germans" reached an agreement with the deputies of the left, the latter reversing their alliance with the pro-Austrian element of just a few weeks previously. Most of the leftists accepted the king of Prussia as emperor, in return for which the pro-Prussian constitutional monarchists agreed to universal, secret, and equal suffrage in elections to the lower house of the future imperial parliament. All the horse-trading was concluded on March 28, 1849, with the election of the king of Prussia as emperor by a vote of 290 yeas and 248 abstentions.[1]

This election of an emperor is certainly the best known of all the events of the German Revolution of 1848–1849. Its dubious antecedents and even more

---

[1] Valentin, *Geschichte der deutschen Revolution*, pp. 296–373; Botzenhart, *Deutscher Parlamentarismus*, pp. 663–95. A preliminary test vote had succeeded by the even thinner margin of 267 to 263.

dubious outcome—the journey of a delegation of deputies from Frankfurt to Berlin to render the offer to Friedrich Wilhelm IV, and his celebrated refusal of a "crown from the gutter"—have, more than anything else, created the image of the revolution as farce. So it appears, if one's eyes are on the capital cities and the diplomatic and political maneuvering occurring in them, as most historians' have been. Looking away from Frankfurt and Berlin, however, a different picture emerges. Just as in September and November 1848, events in the revolutionary capitals sparked a response in the provinces, mixing *Vormärz* social grievances with the organized insurrectionary efforts of the democrats. Unlike the fall of 1848, however, the political struggles of April–June 1849, known as the campaign for the imperial constitution [die Reichsverfassungskampagne], with their mass meetings, threatening demonstrations, armed uprisings, and creation of revolutionary governments, occurred entirely in the provinces, where the political dynamics were often quite different from the familiar diplomatic and parliamentary alignments.[2]

DEMOCRATS AND THE FRANKFURT CONSTITUTION

To understand the nature of events, it is important to realize that the king of Prussia did not turn down the offer of the Frankfurt National Assembly all at once. Instead, he temporized, neither accepting nor refusing, saying he had to consult the other German princes, implying he might accept a modified, less democratic version. For most of April 1849, high officials and courtiers in Berlin argued with one another and for the king's ear about the Frankfurt constitution; a majority of the deputies in the Prussian parliament urged, in a very moderately worded statement, that the king accept the imperial crown. Twenty-eight of the smaller German states did consent to the constitution, and gradually the belief grew among those who followed public affairs that all this activity implied the king was going to accept the offer, perhaps in modified form.[3]

The whole idea of electing an imperial overlord for a united Germany was repugnant to the Rhenish democrats, and they had been denouncing the proposal since the beginning of 1849. Kaiserslautern democrats celebrated Frankfurt's proclamation of the Declaration of Basic Rights for Germany in January by bringing a toast that any future German emperor might perish. In a lighter vein, the Cologne Democratic Society's newsletter nominated the "jovial wineshop owner Dunker" for emperor, a choice it felt was at least as good as any of the princes the Frankfurt assembly was considering.[4]

---

[2] For a good general survey of the *Reichsverfassungskampagne*, with criticism of the usual viewpoint, see Christoph Klessmann, "Zur Sozialgeschichte der Reichsverfassungskampagne," *Historische Zeitschrift* 218 (1974): 283–337.

[3] Valentin, *Geschichte der deutschen Revolution* 2:376–92, 456–60.

[4] LAS H1 Nr. 1974 ff. 5–6; Seypel, "Die Demokratische Gesellschaft in Köln," p. 151 n.59; similarly, Ayçoberry, *Cologne*, p. 250; *NSZ*, 31 Mar. 1849; *NRhZ*, 31 Mar. 1849.

Far from reporting on the end of the constitutionmaking and the election of a head of state as a serious event, the democratic newspapers put the news from Frankfurt on the back pages or in small type, treating as a bad joke the idea that the king of Prussia, of all people, could be emperor. The leftist press was rather more serious about the Frankfurt representatives, the *Neue Kölnische Zeitung* referring to their decision as "the last link in a long chain of undemocratic decisions, by which the Frankfurt assembly has thrown a burning brand into the house of democracy." Democrats were particularly harsh on the left-wing deputies whose support had enabled the election of an emperor to proceed. They were "traitors to the people," or "wretched tailors, patching things together." Their "democratic diplomacy," had brought forth a "monstrous baby."[5]

Since national politics offered the disappointing prospect of a united Germany dominated by a reactionary Prussia, Rhenish democrats turned toward provincial or statewide issues. The Palatine People's Association launched a massive petition drive to place the Declaration of Basic Rights for Germany in the Bavarian constitution. Rhine-Hessian democrats began preparations for the forthcoming, long-delayed Hessian parliamentary elections and moved to consolidate their hold on the countryside by creating a democratic mediation service, to reconcile legal quarrels cheaply and efficiently, without the need to go to court.[6]

Even the long-dormant provincial democratic association in the Prussian Rhineland gave signs of life, although in this case, of decomposition. Frankfurt's election of an emperor seems to have provided the signal for Marx and his followers to secede from the provincial democratic association, nominally in their control, and set up their own organization. In mid-April, the committee of the Cologne Workers' Association asked all similar groups in the Rhine Province to send in their addresses. Shortly thereafter, it issued an appeal, claiming the clubs represented in the provincial democratic association were too heterogeneous in their composition for the "interests of the working class, or of the great mass of the people" to find proper consideration. Consequently, the association announced the creation of a new provincial organization, whose first congress would be held in Cologne, on May 6, 1849, to prepare for a nationwide congress of German workers, scheduled for Leipzig in June. All workers' associations and other groups of the Prussian Rhineland and Westphalia that "adhere with decisiveness to the principles of social democracy," were invited to send delegates.[7]

[5] *NRhZ*, 30 Mar. 1849; *NKZ*, 23, 30 Mar., 4, 20 Apr. 1849; *FBA*, 1, 9 Apr. 1849; *MZ*, 28 Mar., 19 Apr. 1849; *Der Demokrat*, 22 Apr. 1849; *NSZ*, 4, 7 Apr. 1849; Seypel, "Die Demokratische Gesellschaft in Köln," pp. 387–88; cf. *Vbl*, 19 Apr. 1849.

[6] *NSZ*, 5, 14 Apr. 1849; BHSTAM MInn Nr. 43865; *MZ*, 12 Apr 1849; *Der Demokrat*, 12, 29 Apr. 1849.

[7] *FBA*, 8, 22 Apr. 1849; *NKZ*, 12, 26–27 Apr. 1849; *NRhZ*, 26 Apr. 1849 (Beilage). Cf. Dowe, *Aktion und Organisation*, pp. 221–22.

This reemphasis on the proletarian track of his political activity was a sharp break for Marx from his previous commitment to the broader democratic movement—so sharp that the Cologne communists had to ask publicly for the addresses of the workers' associations to which they were appealing, lacking any previous contact with them. Such an abrupt change of political tactics calls for an explanation, and historians have usually looked to developments within the workers' movement. One was the growth of the Workers' Fraternization, a federation of German workers' associations, headed by the Berlin printer Stephan Born, a one-time member of the Communist League. The group was strongest in central and eastern Germany, and the *Neue Rheinische Zeitung* had reported with interest on some of its regional congresses in the preceding months.[8]

Affiliating with the Workers' Fraternization need not have meant a break with the democrats, since members of the two groups cooperated without difficulty elsewhere and joint memberships were common. Instead, one must look to problems specific to Cologne, in particular the suspicion of and hostility toward the democrats prevalent among members of the city's Workers' Association, dating from the ascendancy of Andreas Gottschalk, and never entirely driven out by the Marxist leadership. Gottschalk's trial and his triumphant acquittal in December 1848 gave these ideas new impetus. In murky factional struggles, he and his followers attempted to regain control of the association, demanding that it break its alliance with the democrats and put up independent workers' candidates—Gottschalk, for instance—in the January 1849 elections to the Prussian parliament. Since the association was not prepared to do this, such a last minute appeal would probably have resulted in an electoral fiasco similar to the one in May 1848.

The personal intervention of Marx, Engels, Schapper, and Karl Schneider II, president of the Democratic Society, convinced the committee of the Workers' Association to reject the proposal and retain the political alliance with the democrats. However, Gottschalk's followers gained control of the association newspaper, renamed it *Liberty, Labor*, and revived the moralistic language of the early days of the Workers' Association, by writing lead articles as open letters to prominent figures, denouncing their hostility toward and oppression of the poor. These articles did not condemn just evil capitalists, officials, and priests, but also prominent Cologne democrats, including Franz Raveaux, Karl Schneider II, and the Marxists who controlled the Workers' Association. While this was going on, Gottschalk was staying above the fray, studying socialism in Paris with the French revolutionary August Blanqui. On his return to Germany, he went to Bonn to live with relatives, but from behind the scenes

[8] This explanation has been advanced particularly by Marxist-Leninist historians, Becker, *Marx und Engels in Köln*, pp. 234–56; Strey and Winkler, *Marx und Engels 1848/49*, pp. 261–66, and is also propounded by Dowe, *Aktion und Organisation*, pp. 222–24.

he was advising his supporters and writing unsigned and savage polemics for their newspaper.[9]

Marx and his associates revived the previous newspaper, *Liberty, Fraternity, Labor*, but gave it a quite different content from the articles on political economy and dry reporting of political news that had dominated its columns the previous fall. The tone was set by the lead article of the first issue, which announced the newspaper would "expose in its nakedness the vice of oppression in its most awful evil." Continuing in this moralizing style, the newspaper published open letters attacking municipal officials who oppressed the poor, capitalists who refused to employ local craftsmen, and—something new for Marxist politics—the Catholic clergy. The paper even reprinted an attack on machines by Berlin handloom weavers, a position hardly associated with Marxism. This editorial policy was an obvious attempt to appease the followers of Gottschalk by imitating his style. The newspaper's masthead was an even more pronounced imitation, since it showed a smock-wearing proletarian brandishing a sword and bearing a red flag, a piece of kitsch unthinkable in the sober pages of the previous fall, but a direct copy of the proletarian and the flag on the masthead of *Liberty, Labor*.[10]

None of this helped mitigate the unpopularity of the alliance with the democrats. After proudly announcing its 640 adherents, the association stopped printing membership figures. Claims that membership was "steadily growing" were belied by the dispatch of busy Karl Schapper, not just the association's president but also its chief rural agitator, to "support" the sixth affiliated society, rather suggesting that it had never gotten off the ground.[11]

It is hard to avoid seeing the secession from the provincial democratic association and the call for a politically independent workers' movement as yet another step in the struggle against Gottschalk's influence by taking over his policies. The break with the democrats was accompanied by nasty personal attacks against Gottschalk, complete with anti-Semitic innuendoes—admittedly, something Gottschalk's followers had first used against Marx and, somewhat more peculiarly, against the eminently Gentile Engels. These maneuvers led a number of Gottschalk's followers to leave the Workers' Association, pointedly asking why the Marxists, who had in the past so vigorously

[9] Dowe, *Aktion und Organisation*, pp. 212–17; Becker, *Marx und Engels in Köln*, pp. 178–200. Minutes of the crucial committee session of 15 Jan. 1849 in *FA*, 21 Jan. 1849. Examples of the newspaper's polemics against prominent democrats, in the lead articles of *FA*, 14, 28 Jan., 11, 25 Feb. 1849, the last a vicious attack on Marx and his theory of history, written by Gottschalk personally. Although less given to polemics, Mathias Wessel's *Persecutor of Evil*, begun in February 1849, also supported Gottschalk.

[10] *FBA*, 8, 15, 22 Feb., 1, 4, 8, 11, 15, 22, 25, 29 Mar. 1849, and passim.

[11] *FBA*, 11 Mar., 8 Apr. 1849. On Schapper's activities in the countryside, see Kühn, *Der junge Hermann Becker*, p. 228.

opposed their leader's policy of noncooperation with the democrats, had now suddenly adopted it.[12]

Whatever the motives impelling Marx and his followers to break with the democrats, their decision required a lengthy political reorganization, which would not be concluded on a national level until June 1849 at the earliest. The Marxists thus perceived the near future as a period of relatively steady, crisis-free political development in which to carry out their reorganization. Marx himself was away from Cologne from April 14 to May 9, 1849, on a trip to north Germany, trying to raise funds for the always hard-pressed *Neue Rheinische Zeitung*, suggesting that he saw no dramatic events on the horizon. Like most Rhenish democrats, the Marxists expected the king of Prussia to come to some sort of agreement with the Frankfurt National Assembly, and continued to expect this to happen long after most others had changed their minds.[13]

Were this to occur, the united German state created as a result of it would provide a national framework for a politically independent workers' movement. More than that, it would also allow such a movement to take over the espousal of republicanism, seemingly abandoned by the left-wing deputies in Frankfurt, and by the Central March Association, which had also endorsed the monarchical Frankfurt constitution. Republicanism thus remained important to Marx's strategy, even when he was concentrating on the proletarian track of his political activity.[14]

A SUDDEN CHANGE OF POLITICAL SCENERY

All these long-range plans were destroyed, virtually overnight, at the end of April, when Friedrich Wilhelm IV finally decided against the Frankfurt constitution and in favor of the final suppression of the revolution. In quick succession, starting on April 26, the Prussian government took measures to that end. It dissolved the lower house of the newly elected parliament, which had not only declared in favor of the Frankfurt constitution, but had even sug-

---

[12] *FBA*, 29 Apr. 1849; *NRhZ*, 22 Apr. 1849; *FA*, 22 Mar., 6 May 1849. Cf. Dowe, *Aktion und Organisation*, pp. 224–25. The idea that the break with the democrats was designed to mollify Gottschalk's adherents was advanced by Hans Stein, in his pioneering work on the Cologne Workers' Association, *Der Kölner Arbeiterverein*, pp. 95–100. Marxist-Leninist historians have violently denounced this thesis (Becker, *Marx und Engels in Köln*, pp. 224–33, esp. p. 224 n.233), but they have no counterarguments to explain the changes in the association's newspaper, the stagnation of membership, the resignation of Gottschalk's supporters after the change in tactics (on this, see also *FA*, 3 June 1849), all of which support Stein's assertions.

[13] Hammen, *The Red '48ers*, pp. 386–87; *NRhZ*, 1 May 1849.

[14] Marxist-Leninist historians have pointed to Marx's expectation in the spring of 1849 that uprisings in France and the war between the Hungarians and Habsburg troops would lead to a new revolutionary crisis in Germany (Strey and Winkler, *Marx und Engels 1848/49*, pp. 278–79). Marx cannot have expected an immediate crisis, however, or he would not have embarked on his lengthy reorganization plans.

gested that the state of siege in Berlin, imposed since November, might be lifted. Then it announced it would oppose the Frankfurt constitution and offer armed assistance to those German states also opposing it—a scarcely veiled reference to events in Württemberg, where the crowd in Stuttgart, led by the democrats, had forced the king to accept the constitution. Finally, the ministry mobilized the militia to support such military intervention.[15]

These moves were greeted with disbelief and dismay in the Rhine Province. The dissolution of the parliament cost the ministry "all and every sympathy" of the inhabitants of Lennep County. In the woolens town of Werden, reported the acting county commissioner, "everyone is democratic," and even "the good Prussians express themselves vehemently [against the government]." The Aachen district governor feared the ministry's action would lead to the secession of the Rhine Province from Prussia. In Grevenbroich, on the lower Rhine, the inhabitants spoke with one voice: "[A]way with the ministry." Even conservatives in the Hunsrück county town of Simmern were depressed by the king's refusal of the imperial crown.[16]

The mayor of Neuss noted that the constitutional monarchists were "frightened then disconcerted" by the actions of the king and the ministry but the democrats were "filled with new hope." His observation was repeated throughout the entire province, from Geldern in the north to St. Goar in the south. The left launched the largest round of political agitation seen since the November crisis, holding mass meetings, denouncing the king and his ministers. As in November, the democrats made a special effort to gain armed supporters. The mobilization of the militia provided an ideal opportunity to do so, and everywhere the democrats implored militiamen to refuse to obey the "treasonous" ministers and to place themselves at the disposal of the representatives of the people, the Frankfurt National Assembly.[17]

Officially, the democrats were calling for support of the assembly and the

[15] Siemann, *Die deutsche Revolution*, p. 212; Valentin, *Geschichte der deutschen Revolution*, p. 461.

[16] Quotes: HSTAD RD Pr. Nr. 820 f. 2; HSTAD RD Pr. Nr. 821 f. 5; HSTAD RA Pr. Nr. 2229 ff. 101–103; LAK 441 Nr. 8317 pp. 57–58; HSTAD RD Pr. Nr. 827 f. 5. Similarly, ZSTAM Rep. 77 Tit. 505 Nr. 2 Vol. 4 ff. 221–24; RD to MInn, 1 May 1849, HSTAD RD Pr. Nr. 816; HSTAD RD Pr. Nr. 817 ff. 2–5, 12–13; HSTAD RD Pr. Nr. 818 ff. 15–16; HSTAD RD Pr. Nr. 819 ff. 29–32; HSTAD RD Pr. Nr. 821 f. 7–8; HSTAD RD Pr. Nr. 822 ff. 2–3; HSTAD RD Pr. Nr. 825 ff. 4–7; HSTAD RD Pr. Nr. 828 ff. 5–6; HSTAD RA Pr. Nr. 2229 ff. 114, 118–19, 138–39, 152–54; LAK 441 Nr. 3059 pp. 3–18; LAK 441 Nr. 8317 pp. 61–63, 75–77, 81–89.

[17] HSTAD RD Pr. Nr. 829 ff. 2–3; HSTAD RD Pr. Nr. 817 ff. 2–3, 11, 17; HSTAD RD Pr. Nr. 818 ff. 2–3; HSTAD RD Pr. Nr. 819 ff. 29–34, 42–47; HSTAD RD Pr. Nr. 820 ff. 5–7; HSTAD RD Pr. Nr. 821 ff. 5–6, 26; HSTAD RD Pr. Nr. 822 ff. 4–6; HSTAD RD Pr. Nr. 824 ff. 2–3, 7, 10, 12–13; HSTAD RD Pr. Nr. 825 ff. 14–16, 20–22; HSTAD RD Pr. Nr. 826 f. 4; HSTAD RD Pr. Nr. 827 f. 5; HSTAD RD Pr. Nr. 828 ff. 2, 7, 9; HSTAD RD Pr. Nr. 829 ff. 7, 10–11; HSTAD RA Pr. Nr. 2229 ff. 109, 136–37, 140–42, 182, 253–54; LAK 403 Nr. 2552 pp. 53–58; LAK 441 Nr. 3059 pp. 3–18, 39–42; LAK 441 Nr. 8317 pp. 61–63, 69–70, 75–77; ZSTAM Rep. 77 Tit. 505 Nr. 5 Vol. VI ff. 23–24; *KnZ*, 4–5 May 1849.

monarchical constitution it had written, naming the unwilling Prussian king emperor. But as the Kempen county commissioner noted, "[O]ut of the public eye they [were] working [to use the movement for the constitution] as a transition to the republic." Elsewhere, democrats openly admitted their republicanism. At a meeting of the Eupen Citizens' Association on April 30, 1849, democratic schoolteacher Theodor Hegener said that Germans would have to choose "between monarchy and republic." Democrats in Wittlich denounced their deputy in Frankfurt as a "manufacturer of emperors" and sent an address to the assembly reminding it that as the embodiment of popular sovereignty it "stood above the princes," and was both justified and obligated to persecute any who opposed its decisions as "traitors." Seven thousand to eight thousand participants at a mass meeting in Lüttringhausen (Lennep County) on May 2, 1849, heard Solingen democrats call for the republic, and then marched home singing republican songs.[18]

Most of the aspects of the situation at the beginning of May 1849—the conflict between king and assembly (in this case, two assemblies), the widespread distrust of the government, even by otherwise conservative men, the mass agitation, the attempt to gain armed support—were strongly reminiscent of the November crisis. One element, though, was different, in fact, completely reversed. While in November the Catholic clergy and lay activists strongly opposed the actions of Count Brandenburg and sometimes even supported the radical resistance of the democrats, a half-year later they were all in favor of the king and his ministers and strongly opposed to the Frankfurt National Assembly and the actions of the left.

The Cologne Pius Association issued an appeal announcing that it was not the will of the "Prussian people that violence be done to the king and government as happened in Württemberg." Quite the opposite, by turning down the imperial crown, Friedrich Wilhelm had "served well the German fatherland." Pius Associations in Aachen, Koblenz, Andernach, Neuss, Trier, and smaller towns issued similar statements, but when the leaders of the Catholic group in Eupen proposed such an address, the rank-and-file members shouted them down. The Trier Pius Association, in the past the most radical of the organizations, now went the furthest to assist the authorities, launching, at the height of the movement for the Frankfurt constitution, a school for the moral improvement of journeymen and apprentice artisans. Catholics explained the school was necessary because of the dangers of the "loosening of the ties between superior and subordinate, the manifold abuses of the ideas of freedom." The bigoted, anti-Catholic District Governor Sebaldt in Trier noted

---

[18] HSTAD RD Pr. Nr. 825 ff. 15–16; HSTAD RA Pr. Nr. 2229 ff. 115–16; Stahl, *1848/49 an der Mittelmosel*, p. 33; HSTAD RD Pr. Nr. 820 f. 5.; *KnZ*, 9 May 1849. Similarly, HSTAD RD Pr. Nr. 825 f. 14; HSTAD RA Pr. Nr. 2229 ff. 109, 124–25, 141–42, 253–54; LAK 403 Nr. 2552 pp. 53–58; LAK 441 Nr. 3059 pp. 23–25; Wegener, "Elberfeld," p. 145.

with some embarassment that the Pius Association was the only political force in the city supporting the authorities.[19]

The struggle between the confessions was topmost in the minds of Catholic activists. Their admiration for the Prussian king, not precisely in evidence in the recent past, stemmed from his refusal to become emperor of a Germany without Austria, one in which Catholics would be a permanent minority, as they were to become after 1870–1871. The newspaper of the Trier Pius Association suggested, "In written and spoken form they [Catholic associations] must everywhere instruct the people and say to them that the question of the constitution is really about whether Germany shall be Protestant or predominantly Catholic."[20]

As this last quote suggests, Catholic activists were in danger of being seen as overly sympathetic to the Protestant government. The Aachen Pius Association tried to avert this by asserting that its vote of confidence in the king did not extend to his ministers, the same people who had engaged in such unpopular actions in November. Rather more energetic in this respect were two young priests who called a mass meeting in the lower Rhine weaving village of Hüls at the beginning of May 1849 to demand that the Prussian government resign and that the Declaration of Basic Rights proclaimed by the Frankfurt National Assembly be incorporated into the Prussian Constitution. Their demands were chosen to divert popular anger against the Prussian authorities away from the dangerous goal of a predominantly Protestant united Germany, whether under a monarchical or republican form of government.[21]

If Catholic activists supported the Prussian government, however grudgingly and reluctantly, the Protestant constitutional monarchists, who had been so unreservedly loyal to their king and his chosen ministers in November 1848, could scarcely contain their incomprehension, disappointment, and outrage. From Moers, Mülheim a.d. Ruhr, Kettwig, Duisburg, Odenkirchen, Krefeld, Barmen, Elberfeld, and Lennep, that is, from the old regime possessions of the Prussian monarchy on the lower Rhine and the predominantly Protestant manufacturing cities, addresses of protest rained on Berlin, denouncing the false councillors who had refused to allow the king to become the Protestant emperor of Germany. Merchants, manufacturers, and city council members chaired protest meetings and put their signatures at the head of petitions. More than a few state officials openly agreed with them. The county Commissioner in Rees suggested that the best way to preserve order would be

---

[19] ZSTAM Rep. 77 Tit. 505 Nr. 2 Vol. 4 ff. 247–48; HSTAD RA Pr. Nr. 2229 ff. 134–35, 208; ZSTAM Rep. 77 Tit. 505 Nr. 5 vol. VI ff. 40–42; *Vbl*, 8 May 1849; sources cited in Chapter Six, note 29. Cf. ZSTAM Rep. 77 Tit. 505 Nr. 3 Vol. 4; HSTAD RA Pr. Nr. 2229 ff. 209–10.

[20] *Der Katholische Volksbote*, 9–10 May 1849, copy in ZSTAM Rep. 77 Tit. 505 Nr. 5 Vol. VI ff. 52–54.

[21] HSTAD RA Pr. Nr. 2229 f. 208; HSTAD RD Pr. Nr. 825 ff. 11, 15–16. The account of the Hüls meeting in Röttges, *Die politischen Wahlen*, pp. 122, 126, completely misses this context.

"the fastest possible resignation of the current government ministers." His counterpart in Lennep, reporting on the notables' demand for just this, informed his superiors that it would be good if the government did not close its ears to these expressions "of the public opinion of peaceful and reasonable men."[22]

But such men were getting harder to find as public opinion in predominantly Protestant areas shifted toward the left and the political initiative increasingly passed into the hands of the democrats. Constitutional monarchists in Kettwig, Mülheim a.d. Ruhr, and Wesel joined democrats in antigovernmental mass meetings and demonstrations. "Black-white Elberfeld has suddenly become black-red-gold," an astonished correspondent of a left-wing newspaper noted. Membership in the constitutional monarchist Citizens' Association fell to all of thirty-one, and the leftist Political Club, after a year of losing all its battles to Prussian loyalists and neoorthodox Protestants, had become the leading force in the city's political life. The only forthright adherents of the Prussian government remaining in the Wuppertal were the Protestant sectarians of the Association for the True Welfare of the Citizenry, led politically and religiously by the pious bankers the von der Heydt brothers.[23]

A mass meeting called by the Elberfeld Political Club on April 29 decided to send a delegation to Düsseldorf the following day to impress upon the district governor the demand that the Prussian government accept the Frankfurt constitution. Five hundred to eight hundred residents of Elberfeld made the trip, including militiamen and members of the sharpshooters' society, but observers thought that most participants were workers, who pushed onto the railroad train without paying their fare. Arriving in Düsseldorf, the protesters marched to the district governor's office to present their petition, accompanied by leading local democrats and an ever greater crowd. The return march to the railroad station was a true triumph, with thousands of astonished inhabitants of the district capital joining the demonstrators, calling out cheers for the red republic, and singing republican songs. Back in Elberfeld, the delegation closed its day by marching behind the black-red-gold flag from the railroad station to the city hall, stopping on the way to bring a cat music to reactionary banker Daniel von der Heydt.[24]

[22] Quotations: HSTAD RD Pr. Nr. 822 ff. 2–3; HSTAD RD Pr. Nr. 820 ff. 11–12. On public opinion in Protestant areas, ibid. ff. 2, 22–27; HSTAD RD Pr. Nr. 819 ff. 29–34; HSTAD RD Pr. Nr. 821 ff. 2, 6–8, 10; HSTAD RD Pr. Nr. 824 ff. 12–13; HSTAD RD Pr. Nr. 826 f. 9; HSTAD RD Pr. Nr. 828 f. 5; *KnZ*, 5 May 1849; Lorenz, "1848/49 im Wuppertal," p. 265; Körner, *Lebenskämpfe* 2:45–47. Similarly, if to a lesser extent, among the Protestants of the southern end of the province: *KnZ*, 6 May 1849; LAK 441 Nr. 8317 pp. 57–58; LAK 403 Nr. 2552 p. 107.

[23] HSTAD RD Pr. Nr. 821 f. 5; HSTAD RD Pr. Nr. 822 ff. 5–6; *NKZ*, 2 May 1849 (quotation); Illner, *Bürgerliche Organisierung*, p. 174; *KnZ*, 1 May 1849 (Außerordentliche Beilage); HSTAD RD Pr. Nr. 818 ff. 2–3; ZSTAM Rep. 77 Tit. 505 Nr. 3 Adh. I ff. 36–41.

[24] HSTAD RD Pr. Nr. 817 ff. 6–7; HSTAD RD Pr. Nr. 818 ff. 2–5, 9–12; LAK 403 Nr. 2553

It was, for contemporaries, an almost unbelievable event. The contrast between the nominally Catholic but strongly left-wing and republican Düsseldorf and the pious, Protestant, Prussian-loyalist Wuppertal had marked politics in the area throughout the revolution. Düsseldorf democrats even described Elberfeld as their city's "mortal enemy." The last time an Elberfeld delegation had visited Düsseldorf, during the visit of the king of Prussia, on August 14, 1848, its members had come to blows with the antimonarchical residents of Düsseldorf and stirred up the soldiers of the garrison to attack them. On seeing a delegation from the Wuppertal, with so different a purpose, Düsseldorf citizens expressed "their amazement . . . that such movement could originate in Elberfeld." The desire for national unity, expressed in a republican form of government, had overcome seemingly insurmountable barriers of culture and confession.[25]

Previously just the ideal of small groups of activists in the Wuppertal and the Bergisches Land, republicanism now obtained a mass following there for the first time during the revolution. After attending the mass meeting in Lüttringhausen at which speakers called for the republic, the amazed Lennep county commissioner reported that they were applauded for this, while just a few months previously they would have been chased out of town. By May 8, on the eve of an armed clash with the military, a gendarme stationed in Elberfeld could tell his superiors, with only a little exaggeration: "Many red ribbons are worn and red flags carried and the republicans are jubilant. Whomever one speaks with, he curses the government and many incline to the republic. There are those who still have proper sentiments but few in number and opinion here is almost unanimous."[26]

The republicanism of the Bergisches Land and the Wuppertal stemmed from a disappointed loyalty to the monarchy, not, as had previously been the case during the revolution, from hostility to it. The smiths and grinders of Solingen County had rioted against the state-supported manufacturers in the spring of 1848, while simultaneously expressing their monarchical loyalism. Slowly, over the following year, democratic agitation had impressed upon them the conviction that a resolution of their social grievances required political change. Now, for the first time, they fully accepted the radicals' contention that such a political change would mean the introduction of a republican form of government. Friedrich Wilhelm's refusal of the imperial crown had destroyed their monarchical loyalties once and for all.[27]

---

pp. 3–8; *NRhZ*, 3 May 1848; *KnZ*, 1 May 1849 (Außerordentliche Beilage), 3 May 1849; Lorenz, "1848/49 im Wuppertal," pp. 268–69; Körner, *Lebenskämpfe* 2:50–61.

[25] The two quotations, *NKZ*, 5 Jan. 1849; *KnZ*, 3 May 1849.

[26] HSTAD RD Pr. Nr. 818 f. 22; HSTAD RD Pr. Nr. 820 ff. 6–7.

[27] On this, see especially the insightful retrospective on the revolution offered by the mayor of Solingen, in HSTAD RD Nr. 8809 ff. 126–39. This growth of republicanism—or, one might say, this "demonarchization" of the Protestants—on the right bank of the Rhine was in many ways

TOWARD INSURRECTION?

As the movement in favor of the Frankfurt constitution grew in intensity, both in the Rhineland and throughout Germany, participants felt the need for some sort of centralized leadership that could set out tactics and strategy for the struggle. No less than five different provincial congresses were held in Cologne on May 6–8, 1849, four on Sunday, May 6, alone the date becoming known as Congress Sunday. Two of these meetings were sponsored by the constitutional monarchists; three, by the democrats.

On May 6, delegates of the constitutional monarchist citizens' associations of the Rhineland and Westphalia met in Cologne for their third regional congress during the revolution; two days later, representatives from 303 city, town, and village councils met there, following the appeal of the constitutional monarchist majority of the city council of Cologne. The citizens' associations petitioned the king to accept the Frankfurt constitution and dismiss the government ministers. The city councilmen, who met in defiance of an official prohibition of their congress, called for the same policy but in much stronger, more militant terms. Brushing aside attempts by the Pius Associations to endorse the king's actions, the councilmen issued a resolution demanding the acceptance of the Frankfurt constitution, the resignation of the Prussian government, and the revocation of the order to mobilize the militia. If these measures were not taken, they declared, then there could be no guarantee of the continued existence of the Prussian state in its present extent. When this, the final point of the resolution, was read out loud to the meeting, the presiding officer asked if the participants would rather be Prussian or German. The assembled city fathers replied, "German! German! Secession from Prussia!" and concluded by giving three cheers for Germany.[28]

The meetings of the democrats were, in contrast, far less straightforward, three different groups meeting both separately and together, doing little in public and much cloaked in secrecy. May 6 was the date set for the congress of workers' associations and allied groups of the Rhineland and Westphalia, called by Marx and his followers on their secession from the provincial democratic directory three weeks earlier. Twenty-one organizations from the Rhineland and five from Westphalia answered the summons. Following the

---

similar to the process of de-Christianization in eighteenth- and nineteenth-century Europe. Historians have argued that it became a mass phenomenon not because of anticlericalism but because of popular piety, the masses rejecting the church when it refused to sanction their religious customs and beliefs.

[28] Seypel, "Die Demokratische Gesellschaft in Köln," pp. 389–402; Becker, "Der Kongreß der Arbeitervereine," Doc. 2; ZSTAM Rep. 77 Tit. 505 Nr. 2 Vol. 4 ff. 228–36, 247–48, 250–51; *KnZ*, 9 May 1849; *NRhZ*, 10 May 1849 (Außerordentliche Beilage). The city council of Aachen, a majority of whose members were associated with the Pius Association, boycotted the congress altogether. HSTAD RA Pr. Nr. 2229 ff. 209–10.

Marxist secession, the rump provincial directory and the Cologne Democratic Society called their own congress for the same date, which was attended by delegates of twenty-five clubs, all from the Rhine Province. Finally, the Democratic-Constitutional Association of the Rhineland and Westphalia, formed at the time of the January 1849 elections by the secession of a number of left-leaning clubs from the constitutional monarchist federation, called its first congress for May 6. The number of clubs represented varied, according to different accounts, from thirty to twenty-five to six.[29]

The congresses showed, one last time, the poor state of organization of the democrats of Rhenish Prussia, since between one-third and one-half of the ninety-one clubs known to have existed in the province during the revolution were not represented. Saarburg's democratic club was the only one from the entire Trier district to send a delegate. Although at least two of the three congresses arose from Marx's plan to split off the more proletarian and socially revolutionary clubs from the rest of the democratic movement, a look at the clubs represented suggests that in this, as in all the other aspects of his political activities along the proletarian track, Marx was relatively unsuccessful.[30]

Attendance at the congresses showed no clear split in the democratic movement. Just the opposite happened—representatives of clubs from Bonn and Sieg counties had called for both congresses to be held jointly. If we add to these clubs the other organizations that sent delegates to both the workers' congress and the democratic one, we find that twelve clubs, about 30 percent of the participant associations in the two congresses, were represented at both of them. Delegates to the Marxist conference were not disproportionately from industrial areas. At the workers' congress, clubs from Aachen and several of its industrial suburbs were represented, as were groups from the manufacturing centers Solingen, Barmen, and Mülheim a. Rhein, but some two-thirds of the groups were from small county towns, such as Kreuznach or Heinsberg, or agricultural villages on both banks of the Rhine between Düsseldorf and Bonn. If anything, explicitly industrial areas were better represented at the democratic congress, with delegates coming from the factory towns Aachen, Eupen, Eschweiler, and Mülheim a.d. Ruhr and from the Lennep Workers' Association, the only group of its kind in the Rhineland definitely known to have included spinning-mill workers, genuine factory proletarians, in its ranks. Affiliation with one of the two congresses seems to have been based more on personal connections than on political principles or social structure.

[29] Most of the available material on Congress Sunday is in the excellent documentation of Becker, ''Der Kongreß der Arbeitervereine,'' with some additional details in Illner, *Bürgerliche Organisierung*, p. 174; Strey and Winkler, *Marx und Engels 1848/49*, p. 405 n.80; Dowe, *Aktion und Organisation*, pp. 226–27. The proceedings were mysterious, and many accounts, for example, Hammen, *The Red '48ers*, p. 389; Seypel, ''Die Demokratische Gesellschaft in Köln,'' pp. 389–402, are inaccurate, not even having the right number of congresses.

[30] List of associations present in Becker, ''Der Kongreß der Arbeitervereine,'' Doc. 1.

No contemporary account names the clubs represented at the congress of the democratic-constitutional associations, but since the group was founded by clubs from such manufacturing towns as Elberfeld, Mönchengladbach, Barmen, Werden, and Duisburg, it seems plausible that industrial areas were equally well represented at its meeting.[31]

The proceedings and decisions of the three congresses were more mysterious than the identity of the delegations attending them. Unlike the concurrent meetings of the city councils and the constitutional monarchists, the democrats did not publicize their proceedings and issued no widely circulated manifestoes or appeals. The democratic constitutionalists consulted with the democrats, one brief press report stated, and many of the more moderate organizations announced their intention of affiliating with the democratic provincial association. On the afternoon of May 6, delegates to the democratic congress met jointly with delegates from the congress of workers' associations (it is thoroughly unclear if the democratic constitutionalists also participated) to discuss the critical political situation, and then issued a statement asserting that they would not recognize the Frankfurt constitution or take any action in support of it, until the Frankfurt Assembly asserted its sovereignty. Only when the "liberal bourgeoisie" took up the struggle would the left join in.[32]

Strangely, the democrats seemed to lag far behind the city councilmen, and even the constitutional monarchists in both the militancy of their views and their willingness to make them known to a mass public. The joint statement calling for a wait-and-see attitude toward the Frankfurt constitution never appeared in any of the major democratic newspapers, and the statement itself was hardly compatible with the energetic, almost frantic political agitation over the issue of the constitution and the national unity it embodied, which the local clubs were so busy carrying out, both before and after Congress Sunday. It is hard to avoid the suspicion that something else was going on behind closed doors.

Something was, namely, planning for an armed insurrection. In his memoirs, Hermann Körner, delegate of the Elberfeld Political Club to the democratic constitutional congress, explained that after the public sessions, he held a secret meeting on the instructions of the Central March Association, to organize an uprising in all of western Germany. The Cologne communists were invited to this planning session, but they were not to be "moved away from the narrow standpoint of doctrinaire radicalism," and went so far in their "fanatical nihilism" as to oppose any movement for the Frankfurt constitution.

---

[31] On the Bonn wish for unity, see Dowe, *Aktion und Organisation*, p. 227 ns.849–50; founding clubs of democratic-constitutional association according to reports in *NKZ*, 12 Jan., 2 Mar. 1849. Under these circumstances, it seems not entirely accurate to describe the Workers' Association congress as the "first territorial workers' congress in Germany under communist leadership." Strey and Winkler, *Marx und Engels 1848/49*, p. 267.

[32] Becker, "Der Kongreß der Arbeitervereine," Doc. 2.

Only Friedrich Engels and the ex-artillery lieutenant Fritz Anneke would ultimately change their minds and join the uprising.[33]

Körner's memoirs are the only account of such plans, and critics have raised serious doubts about their reliability, the author of the most comprehensive work on Barmen and Elberfeld in 1848–1849 even claiming that Körner made the whole thing up. Some of what appears in the memoirs is false. Körner claimed that Marx, who was out of town when the congress took place, was one of the Cologne communists who refused to support an uprising, and that Gottschalk, who was neither in Cologne nor an associate of the Cologne communists by this time and was a fervent advocate of nonviolence to boot, was willing to participate. Körner, however, wrote his memoirs fifteen years after the event, so such slips might be expected.[34]

As usual, it is difficult to demonstrate the existence of a secret revolutionary conspiracy, since conspirators try not to leave documents around. Nonetheless, there is evidence to suggest that some sort of plotting was occurring in secret on Congress Sunday. On his return from Cologne, the chairman of the Kleve Democratic Club told the members that they should be prepared to meet force with force and be ready to march to other cities to help insurgents there. A debate between Eupen and Aachen democrats at a May 13, 1849, meeting of the Aachen Militia Association—a group formed by the democrats during the November crisis to gain armed supporters—centered around "definite decisions" [feste Beschlüsse], which had been taken in Cologne, calling on the population to choose between the king and Count Brandenburg, on the one hand, and the Frankfurt Assembly and the people, on the other. There were arguments about what would be the appropriate "time to strike" [Zeitpunkt zum Losbrechen]. One speaker explained that he could not be more explicit because police spies were present, and the eyewitnesses interrogated by the authorities gave vague testimony, but it would seem the debate was between the adherents of Körner's position, who expected an immediate uprising, and those of the Marxists, who did not.[35]

Körner's account of the unwillingness of the Marxists to become involved

---

[33] Körner, *Lebenskämpfe* 2:50, 68–72. Körner's memoirs are the only known source, and accounts tend to rely, directly or indirectly, on them. See, for example, Siemann, *Die deutsche Revolution*, pp. 208, 212; Valentin, *Geschichte der deutschen Revolution* 2:472. Valentin's version, taken from Gustav Mayer's classic biography of Engels, has Engels joining in the planning for the uprising, but Körner made no such assertion, just saying that Engels, Anneke, and Gottschalk could be convinced eventually to change their minds (not necessarily on Congress Sunday) and Engels and Anneke were the only ones ever to take up arms.

[34] The validity of the memoirs is harshly criticized in Lorenz, "1848/49 im Wuppertal," pp. 314–24. In contrast, I have found the memoirs reasonably accurate (when they can be cross-checked against other sources), although names and dates are sometimes confused and Körner had a strong tendency to exaggerate his own importance. Both of these traits were also found in the memoirs of his fellow Elberfelder, the constitutional monarchist Alexander Pagenstecher.

[35] HSTAD RD Pr. Nr. 823 ff. 8–9; HSTAD RA Pr. Nr. 2229 ff. 235–39.

in secret plans is plausible, since it corresponds to their public posture at the time. The *Neue Rheinische Zeitung* refused to endorse the movement for the Frankfurt constitution, claiming the movement's leaders had no sincere commitment to revolution. Even more explicit was the statement on the struggle over the constitution appearing in the May 6, 1849 issue of the Cologne Workers' Association newspaper. Seemingly militant, it called on the people to boycott taxes and arm themselves in preparation for insurrection. It also announced that the Frankfurt National Assembly, which had always betrayed the people, was not to be trusted and neither were the leaders of the democratic clubs. Behind them "lurked betrayal and self-interest"; the people should not allow them "to misuse you for overhasty, foolish actions." The appeal's last word was a warning against revolutionary action, against being "carried away, by the passions of your enemies, into struggles which will do you no good."[36]

Ironically, Gottschalk's remaining supporters in Cologne were taking a strikingly similar position to that of their Marxist rivals. Master baker Mathias Wessel was also for political passivity, the Persecutor of Evil telling the rustics in a tavern of the Cologne suburb of Frechen in early June 1849 that a struggle between the bourgeoise and the monarchy was in the offing "and the proletariat (the poor class of the people) would enjoy the fruits of it only by remaining quiet." This close alignment of political positions was no coincidence. Marx and his followers had adopted the position of their rival Gottschalk, trying to separate the workers from the broader democratic movement and using militantly revolutionary language to call for political passivity.[37]

The evidence is admittedly very scanty, but it would seem that the leaders of the democrats of Rhenish Prussia were divided into two political positions at the beginning of May 1849. One group, prominently represented by Marx's followers, but also including other, noncommunist democrats, was reluctant to join the movement for the Frankfurt constitution, fearing that the politically more moderate elements involved would drop out, as they had from the movement against the Malmö armistice of the previous September and from the tax boycott campaign of November 1848. Another group, which may or may not have been led by Hermann Körner, who may or may not have been acting on behalf of the Central March Asssociation, wanted to use the situation of great excitement prevailing in at least part of the province to plan for an insurrection. A sudden rush of events, outside the control or calculation of either

---

[36] Strey and Winkler, *Marx und Engels 1848/49*, pp. 300–01; *FBA*, 6 May 1849. Similarly, in the debates at the 13 May 1849 meeting in Aachen, the vice president of the militia association, who had attended the Marxist provincial congress, announced that the Frankfurt National Assembly was for the princes and the upper classes, not the lower classes. No revolutionary action could be taken until a delegation had been sent to Leipzig—presumably a reference to the planned national congress of the Workers' Fraternization.

[37] *VdB*, 30 June 1849.

group, would bring about this insurrection, encompassing the better part of the lower Rhine.[38]

INSURRECTION ON THE LOWER RHINE

The events leading to the insurrection began a week before Congress Sunday, at the mass meeting in Elberfeld called by the Political Club to demand the acceptance of the Frankfurt constitution. This meeting organized the delegation to Düsseldorf. The speaker who proposed the delegation, the "republican tavernkeeper" Hugo Hillmann, a most inventive agitator, had another, related plan for political mobilization. The key to Hillmann's second idea was the "Militiamen's Association," whose 180 members, although mostly outworkers, had been strong Prussian loyalists, regularly threatening to beat up Elberfeld democrats. Hillmann had founded sometime in the spring of 1849 a much smaller, politically competing "German Militiamen's Association," whose members marched as a group to Düsseldorf behind a large black-red-gold flag. On their return, they called for a meeting of all the county's militiamen, suspecting, not unjustifiably, that the king's refusal of the imperial crown had changed their opinions. The militiamen met in Elberfeld on May 3, 1849, and issued a declaration supporting the Frankfurt constitution and insisting that they would take the field only to fight foreign enemies, not their German fellow citizens.[39]

Their example was followed all along the lower Rhine over the next three days. Militiamen met, frequently under democratic leadership, or at least with left-wing participation, and issued similar declarations in Lennep, Mülheim a.d. Ruhr, Gerresheim, Werden, Mönchengladbach, Neuss, Krefeld, and surrounding villages. The militiamen and civic guard of Giesenkirchen (Gladbach County), gathered behind a red flag, and swore an oath of loyalty to the Frankfurt constitution. Under these circumstances, it hardly required great prescience to foresee that the actual mobilization of the militia would not go smoothly. A number of local and county officials suggested that it be put off, but the army insisted that it go on as planned. Since the fortress authorities in Düsseldorf were worried—with good reason—about the city's radical inhab-

---

[38] Friedrich Engels, another eyewitness, later denied that there was a plan for an uprising but did not deny the intent to plan one. It never came to pass, Engels claimed, because of the cowardice of the petit bourgeois local leaders, because "the organization of the democratic party and the workers' party . . . had fallen apart," and finally, because of lack of time before the uprising. If one ignores the polemics against the petit bourgeoisie, this sounds like a description of discussions of an insurrection on Congress Sunday being overtaken by events. Friedrich Engels, "Die deutsche Reichsverfassungskampagne," in *Karl Marx Friedrich Engels Werke*, ed. Institut für Marxismus-Leninismus beim ZK der SED, 3d ed. (East Berlin: Dietz, 1977), 7:111–97, here p. 124.

[39] HSTAD RD Pr. Nr. 818 ff. 9–12, 17; Lorenz, "1848/49 im Wuppertal," pp. 270–71; *Lebenserinnerungen . . . Alexander Pagenstecher* 2:55–56; Körner, *Lebenskämpfe* 2:62–67.

itants, they refused to detach any troops to ensure that the angry militiamen would appear for mobilization in orderly fashion.[40]

An Insurgency of the Militia

The actual mobilization, begun on May 6, proved just how right the official pessimists were. Roll call in Krefeld the following day was a disaster. Accompanied by about a thousand members of the city's lower classes, the men to be mobilized appeared on the parade grounds, shouting at the major calling the roll, "Down with that guy, Robert Blum is our man." The major was bombarded with manure, and other officers of the militia, trying to intervene, were beaten up. The militiamen marched off, calling out cheers to the republic. At a mass meeting on May 8, Krefeld reservists and militiamen announced their refusal to be mobilized. Eight hundred militiamen reporting to Neuss on May 9 held a meeting chaired by democratic tavernkeeper Lucas, with the result that only three reported for duty. Since Neuss was just across the Rhine from Düsseldorf, the fortress authorities were willing to send two companies of infantry to impose the mobilization, but by their arrival, the militiamen had all gone home.[41]

Events in Elberfeld far surpassed what happened elsewhere. Although the main leaders of the Political Club were all at the democratic-constitutional Congress on May 6, tavernkeeper Hillmann got the militiamen together, and they issued a powerful appeal condemning the Prussian government as "traitors to the people," acting on behalf of "the counter-revolution of the Prussian camarilla." They called on their comrades in the Duchy of Berg and the County of Mark—that is, roughly the area in the Düsseldorf District on the right bank of the Rhine and the neighboring regions of Westphalia—to gather, armed, in Elberfeld. Many did, and were joined by others with insurrection in mind, forming, by the morning of May 8, a camp of some one thousand at least partially armed men in one of the large beer halls in the hills overlooking the city. Over the next two days, similar mass meetings were held among the militias of the Solingen metalworking and the Krefeld/Mönchengladbach textile districts, reaching similarly insurrectionary decisions. Enthusiastic democrats began forging bullets, manufacturing cartridges, and sharpening scythes.[42]

---

[40] HSTAD RD Pr. 816 ff. 13, 133–37; HSTAD RD Pr. Nr. 817 f. 11; HSTAD RD Pr. Nr. 819 ff. 29–32; HSTAD RD Pr. Nr. 820 ff. 11–12; HSTAD RD Pr. Nr. 821 ff. 10, 14; HSTAD RD Pr. Nr. 823 ff. 8–9; HSTAD RD Pr. Nr. 825 ff. 7–9, 19; HSTAD Pr. 826 ff. 9, 22; HSTAD RD Pr. Nr. 828 ff. 2–4, 8; HSTAD RD Nr. 8810 ff. 14–19.

[41] HSTAD RD Pr. 826 ff. 8, 12–14; *KnZ*, 9 May 1849; HSTAD RD Pr. Nr. 829 ff. 12–14. Similar refusals in the Ruhr Basin and Lennep County: LAK 403 Nr. 2253 pp. 113–15; HSTAD RD Pr. Nr. 820 ff. 29–30.

[42] HSTAD RD Pr. Nr. 818 ff. 24–25; LAK 403 Nr. 2553 pp. 45–47; *KnZ*, 10 May 1849 (El-

This spontaneous outbreak of armed insurrection rendered irrelevant the plans made in secret on Congress Sunday, which had foreseen an uprising after ten days of preparation. However, the embarrassment of the democratic leaders was as nothing compared to the discomfort of the authorities, who once again lacked the means to control the situation. Although the district governor ordered the mutinous militiamen arrrested, the four gendarmes he sent to Elberfeld scarcely sufficed for that task, and the city's civic guard flatly refused to act in any way against the militia. When the rumor spread, on May 7, that the mayor had gone to Düsseldorf to summon troops—in reality, he had gone to plead with the district governor not to send them—an angry crowd of militiamen and workers assaulted the mayor and demolished the bourgeois social club where he had taken refuge, in spite of efforts by leftist leaders to calm them down.[43]

Both the tumultuous scenes and the mayor's trip were unnecessary since there were no troops in Düsseldorf to send, the fortress commandant insisting on keeping them all there to guard against the possibility of an insurrection. The acting commandant in Cologne was equally set on keeping all his soldiers in the fortress and refused repeated requests to send any of them to deal with the mutineers. The military was willing to allow some cavalry to be dispatched to Krefeld on May 8, forcing democratic leaders to flee, but not completely restoring order. When a few troops finally arrived in Düsseldorf from the Koblenz fortress, the district governor took a small force from the garrison—an infantry batallion, a cavalry squadron, and two pieces of field artillery—to Elberfeld on the afternoon of May 9, to suppress the insurrection.[44]

On their arrival at the railroad station in Elberfeld, they were met by a delegation, led by the mayor, the civic guard commandant, and seven or eight city councilmen, who requested that the troops not intervene. There ensued an almost surreal dialogue. Major von Mülbe, commander of the troops, ex-

---

berfeld militia meetings); HSTAD RD Pr. Nr. 819 ff. 42, 45–47; HSTAD RD Pr. Nr. 825 ff. 23–28, 33–36, 45; HSTAD RD Pr. Nr. 826 ff. 12–14; HSTAD RD Pr. Nr. 828 ff. 9, 11, 20 (actions taken elsewhere). Since the leaders of the Political Club were away at their provincial congress on 6 May, they could, justifiably, claim to have had nothing to do with the appeal. This, however, does not mean that it was the spontaneous action of overly excited Prussian patriots, as Lorenz, "1848/49 im Wuppertal," pp. 327–28, asserts, since one of the signatories of the appeal and the man responsible for the whole militia agitation, was the republican tavernkeeper Hillmann (HSTAD RD Nr. 8809 f. 14), politically to the left of the mostly democratic monarchist club leaders.

[43] LAK 403 Nr. 2553 pp. 51–53; ZSTAM Rep. 77 Tit. 505 Nr. 3 Vol. 4 ff. 120–27; HSTAD RD Pr. Nr. 818 ff. 22–25; *Lebenserinnerungen . . . Alexander Pagenstecher* 3:56–57; Körner, *Lebenskämpfe* 2:73–75 (with an explanation of how the plans for an insurrection were crossed up); *KnZ*, 10 May 1849; Carl Hecker, *Der Aufstand in Elberfeld im Mai 1849 und mein Verhältniß zu demselben* (Elberfeld: Julius Bädeker, 1849), pp. 10, 16–17; Lorenz, "1848/49 im Wuppertal," pp. 273–74.

[44] HSTAD RD Pr. Nr. 816 f. 21; LAK 403 Nr. 2553 pp. 45–48, 51; ZSTAM Rep. 77 Tit. 505 Nr. 3 Vol. 4 ff. 120–27.

plained that he had orders to enforce obedience to the municipal authorities of Elberfeld, and as a soldier, he had to follow orders. "But no one has refused to obey me," Mayor von Carnap told him. "I can't let that stop me," was the major's reply, and he led his troops into the center of the city.[45]

While the soldiers were marching, the insurgent militiamen and the Elberfeld workers were busy building barricades, breaking into the mayor's house to use his furniture for that purpose. Soon the entire inner city, in the narrow valley of the Wupper, was blocked off. The civic guard was called out and refused to appear, but insurgents from nearby Solingen County did, joining the barricade builders. Women approached the troops and begged them not to shoot at their men. The soldiers, native Westphalians, showed none of the pleasure at the prospect of shooting down Rhinelanders that the East Elbian regiments did. Accounts vary, but the troops apparently at first refused to obey the command to open fire, and later attacked the barricades at best half-heartedly. By nightfall, they had been driven out of or retreated from the center of the city, leaving it in the hands of the insurgents.[46]

The Uprising in Düsseldorf and the March on Neuss

The inhabitants of Düsseldorf, already in a state of high excitement over the turbulent political events of early May 1849, were further incited by the sight of a troop detachment taking the railroad to Elberfeld. On the evening of May 9 a courier from the democrats of the beleaguered city arrived at the house of Lorenz Cantador, the commander of Düsseldorf's civic guard before its dissolution in November 1848. A crowd gathered and marched through the streets, singing, "What is the German's fatherland?" Arriving at Cantador's house on the marketplace, it cheered him, and then offered cheers for the red republic and called on the city council to distribute weapons. The radical physician Joseph Neunzig from nearby Gerresheim spoke from the balcony, saying that Elberfeld had risen and the time had come to fight. The crowd moved off, singing, "Freedom, republic/If we were just rid of the Prussians," went to the houses of the fortress commandant and the state procurator, smashed their windows, and returned to the marketplace to build barricades. Neunzig hastened to Gerresheim for reinforcements, who arrived later that night, with red ribbons in their caps.[47]

[45] Hecker, *Der Aufstand in Elberfeld*, pp. 20–21; Körner, *Lebenskämpfe* 2:77–78; a somewhat different version in *Lebenserinnerungen . . . Alexander Pagenstecher* 3:58.

[46] The four main accounts, Körner, *Lebenskämpfe* 2:78–100; Hecker, *Der Aufstand in Elberfeld*, pp. 21–24; *Lebenserinnerungen . . . Alexander Pagenstecher* 3:58–63; and the report of the Düsseldorf district governor, in LAK 403 Nr. 2253 pp. 65–78, differ substantially in detail, but all give the same general picture. Cf. Lorenz, "1848/49 im Wuppertal," pp. 276–82.

[47] ZSTAM Rep. 77 Tit. 505 Nr. 3 Vol. 4 ff. 248–53; HSTAD RD Pr. Nr. 816 ff. 29–33; HSTAD RD Pr. Nr. 817 ff. 20–22; *KnZ*, 11 May 1849 (Beilage). These sources confirm in broad

The civilian and military authorities were in a state of panic. Fearing that the weakened garrison would not be able to hold all points against the crowd, the fortress commandant informed Councillor von Mirbach, in charge while the district governor was away in Elberfeld, that his troops would have to yield the city hall and either the jail or the district governor's own office to the insurgents. Both the bridge and the Rhine ferry were cut off, so the soldiers enforcing the mobilization of the militia across the river in Neuss could not join the fight. Troops stationed in Mülheim a.d. Ruhr included many Düsseldorf natives in their ranks and so were unreliable; in any event, the railroad lines had been cut, and they could not arrive in time. Messages were sent to the detachment outside Elberfeld to return on foot, since the railroad was too easy to sabotage. A last report of furious street fighting reached Cologne at 11:30 that night, then the telegraph line went dead.[48]

In retrospect, the officials were overly pessimistic. Since the dissolution of the civic guard and the confiscation of its weapons the previous November, Düsseldorf's civilians were largely unarmed, and although the six hundred soldiers were outnumbered by the thousands of insurgents, they had a decisive superiority in firepower. Using mobile artillery to destroy the barricades, the troops in the garrison were able to force a decision by the following morning, as the detachment sent to Elberfeld returned to their aid.[49]

In the meantime, couriers had been sent from Neuss to ask for armed assistance from the democrats of the lower Rhine. The messengers arrived in Mönchengladbach the afternoon of May 10, and the democrats there took steps to raise the whole region. The storm bells were rung, a prearranged signal for insurrection, and additional couriers were sent to the major textile centers of Krefeld and Dülken. From there, they went on to the smaller weaving, farming, and smuggling villages, most of these being informed by the following day.[50]

Even before the news from Düsseldorf arrived, the area had been in turmoil, with the militia asserting its loyalty to the Frankfurt constitution and its refusal to be mobilized, demanding weapons to carry out its resolve. Sometimes the response to the news of an insurrectionary outbreak remained at a symbolic level. The militia of Frimmersdorf (Grevenbroich County) gathered at a local tavern on May 11, heard a speech from their village councillor, who had attended the Cologne congress of municipal representatives, and then promised

outline, if not always in exact chronology, some of Körner's accounts of attempts by Elberfeld democrats to spread the uprising. *Lebenskämpfe* 2:73–74, 97–99.

[48] Besides the sources cited in the previous note, see HSTAD RD Pr. Nr. 816 f. 28; LAK 403 Nr. 2553 p. 55; HSTAD RD Pr. Nr. 817 ff. 31–33; HSTAD RD Nr. 200 pp. 260–65.

[49] Besides the sources cited in the two previous notes, see *NRhZ*, 13 May 1849 (Zweite Ausgabe), which describes how much of the crowd was unarmed.

[50] HSTAD RD Pr. Nr. 828 ff. 34–35; HSTAD RD Pr. Nr. 825 ff. 46–48; HSTAD RD Pr. Nr. 816 ff. 135–37; HSTAD RD Pr. Nr. 826 ff. 15–16.

to obey the orders of the Frankfurt National Assembly. After several glasses of schnapps, the militiamen took down the king's picture from the wall and burnt it, saying, "We will no longer recognize him as king; he has nothing more to say in this village."[51]

Many militiamen were more determined. They resolved to march on the arsenal of the militia in Neuss, storm it, and go to the rescue of "our hard pressed brothers in Düsseldorf." Local leaders, frequently village and small-town democrats, rang the storm bells, gathering the militia and civic guard. They went before the town and village councils, demanding from them weapons and financial support, and then organized insurgent columns, forcing every eligible man to march, yanking from their houses those reluctant to go.[52]

The few police or gendarmes, and the municipal authorities and county commissioners who commanded them, were completely helpless to stop the movement. Some Catholic priests stood up to the insurgents, the pastors in Mönchengladbach and Süchteln refusing to allow them into church to ring the storm bells. While the Süchtein pastor prevailed, a menacing crowd surrounded the Mönchengladbach one and eventually forced him to surrender the keys to one of the city's democratic leaders. In Hüls, where the clergy had been actively leading political meetings, against the Prussian government, but also against the Frankfurt constitution, there was little enthusiasm for the uprising. When insurgents from neighboring villages broke down the church door and rang the storm bells, just three or four people turned out to join them. Yet in spite of the attitudes of the clergy, insurgents came from the Catholic population of the region, the inhabitants of the Protestant manufacturing towns Rheydt and Odenkirchen keeping their distance from the insurrection. Just a few railroad construction workers temporarily quartered in the two cities were willing to fight.[53]

A column of several thousand insurgents left Mönchengladbach on the evening of May 10, marching southwards on the left bank of the Rhine, only to discover on nearing their destination that the army had triumphed over the people in Düsseldorf and troops were occupying Neuss. Discouraged by this news, some turned back, but others remained camped outside the walls of Neuss all night, attempting from time to time to force the troops from the city gates and also lighting fires, apparently as a signal for the Neuss democrats to take action. The commander of the two companies of infantry in Neuss withdrew all his patrols from the city, concentrating his men at the gates and the

---

[51] HSTAD RD Pr. Nr. 827 ff. 20–22. The declaration in favor of the Frankfurt Assembly was passed around in neighboring villages for signatures the following day.

[52] Besides the sources cited in the two previous notes, see HSTAD RD Pr. Nr. 828 ff. 19, 22–24; HSTAD RD Pr. Nr. 826 ff. 27–32; ZSTAM Rep. 77 Tit. 505 Nr. 3 Vol. 4 ff. 112–14.

[53] HSTAD RD Nr. 8810 ff. 14–19; HSTAD RD Pr. Nr. 816 ff. 133–34; HSTAD RD Pr. Nr. 577 ff. 6–10. This last, a retrospective account written twenty years later, describes the events in Süchteln as having happened in 1848, but almost certainly refers to the uprising of 1849.

threatened arsenal. At daybreak, the remaining insurgents returned home, weary and defeated.[54]

That afternoon, two further columns, counting together five hundred–one thousand men, left the weaving villages and the smugglers' capital of Breyell, further to the north in Kempen County. One column moved south through Viersen, while the other marched along the Rhine to Krefeld, to rendezvous with insurgents there. The silk-weaving center was in the hands of the revolutionaries; most of the civic guard had made common cause with the insurgent militia, and the remainder feared to act against them. The column requisitioned horses and wagons from the peasantry of the vicinity and marched south, only to receive news of both the victory of the army in Düsseldorf, and the failure of the previous day's march. Both columns halted, unsure of what to do, and then gave up and went home.[55]

Most insurgents disbanded peacefully, but a group of thirty weavers from Dülken went to the tavern at which the town's notables met, assaulted several manufacturers, and drove the others out into the night, shouting, "Rich people are the king's friends." Although this was the only overt incident of its kind during the uprising, the frequent threatening demands for money and ammunition from city and town councils by members of the militia, which directly preceded it, also suggest a certain class tension. The unequal municipal franchise with its stiff property qualification meant that most councilmen were property owners, many merchants and manufacturers among them, while the militia, recruited from the general male population, contained, like it, a large number of outworkers.[56]

The agitation spilled over into the neighboring Aachen District. Although the peasants of Erkelenz County refused the summons carried by messengers from Mönchengladbach to march on Neuss, the news of the street fighting in Düsseldorf brought the inhabitants of the county town Düren into a state of great excitement. At a mass meeting on May 10, also attended by peasants from the vicinity, they were making preparations to rush to the insurgents' assistance, when the area's deputy to the Prussian parliament, the left-wing priest Philipp van Berg, appeared and convinced them that they would be more successful with peaceful activities.[57]

The democrats held meetings of the militia—which was to be mobilized a week later than in the Düsseldorf District—in Monschau, Düren, and Jülich,

[54] HSTAD RD Pr. Nr. 816 ff. 133–34; HSTAD RD Pr. Nr. 829 ff. 15–17.

[55] HSTAD RD Pr. Nr. 825 ff. 46–48; HSTAD RD Pr. Nr. 826 ff. 15–16, 27–29, 32; HSTAD RD Pr. Nr. 816 f. 42.

[56] HSTAD RD Pr. Nr. 816 f. 136r; ZSTAM Rep. 77 Tit. 505 Nr. 3 Vol. 4 ff. 112–14. The account of the march on Neuss in Röttges, *Die politischen Wahlen*, pp. 124–26, denies the existence of any such social tensions, but the author did not use these sources. In general, Röttges' description is superficial and downplays the extent of the movement.

[57] HSTAD RA Pr. Nr. 2229 ff. 202–05.

the men announcing their refusal to serve. At mass meetings in Aachen's industrial suburb of Eschweiler on May 10 and 13, some thousand participants heard radicals denounce the king and his ministers and call for the people to arm themselves and await the call from Frankfurt. An equally large crowd of city- and countryfolk was present at the marketplace of Heinsberg on May 13, to hear the democratic leader Franz Joerissen, an unemployed intellectual, but also son of the former mayor, give a speech filled with antimonarchical invective: "the ministry Brandenburg-Manteuffel hated and despised by God and man"; the German princes, "the thirty-four headed hydra"; the king of Prussia as "chief stable-boy of the Czar"; "our tyrannical king, who had his mercenaries and officers who have forgotten their duty spill the blood of the noblest citizens of Dresden, Breslau, Elberfeld and Düsseldorf." Would the crowd obey such a tyrant, he asked, or place itself on the side of the National Assembly? All raised their hands in affirmation of their adherence to the people's cause. When Joerissen continued, asking, "Do you have weapons?", they replied yes, they did. It was the most revolutionary moment the peaceful little border town had ever experienced—or ever would.[58]

Weapons were indeed the problem, and Joerrissen touched on an issue that must have been felt keenly by an even larger crowd, once again of townspeople and countryfolk, at a mass meeting held in Jülich the same day. As the participants came to the meeting place, they could see soldiers turn the mobile artillery of the fortress on them. Democrats did indeed stockpile weapons: Police found barrels of gunpowder when they raided the house of the president of the Eschweiler Democratic Club. Particularly in Eupen and Eschweiler, leftists seem to have been waiting for a signal to go into action. All was quiet in the district's chief city, though. Democratic meetings in Aachen attracted small crowds, factory workers there, as always during the revolution, conspicuous by their absence. The brief left-wing moment in Aachen was now over, the dissidents from the Pius Association, whose support had been crucial to the election of democratic candidates in January 1849, reuniting with fellow Catholic-clericals and leaving the democrats once more a tiny, helpless minority. The vice president of the radical Aachen Militia Association was overheard saying that he "would rather have a small brave band than many and cowards, since he must then give up on everything," putting the best face on a bad situation.[59]

Although the democrats continued holding meetings in the countryside through the end of May, the situation gradually calmed down. The militia of both the Aachen and Düsseldorf districts reported for duty, a process smoothed by the generous granting of deferments, and order was restored on

[58] HSTAD RA Pr. Nr. 2229 ff. 255–56, 304–06.
[59] HSTAD RA Pr. Nr. 2229 ff. 189–90, 222–23, 231–32, 235–38, 255–56, 304–06, 334–35; HSTAD RA Pr. Nr. 701 ff. 19–20; Fischer, *Kreis Jülich*, pp. 55–57.

the left bank of the Rhine. The course of events shows the critical importance of the street fighting in Düsseldorf on the night of May 9–10, 1849. Had the badly outnumbered garrison been defeated by the crowd, which the officers themselves thought a real possibility, then the authorities would have been faced with a most unpleasant choice. They would either have had to cede Düsseldorf, and with it, the entire lower Rhine region, to the insurgents, or try to reconquer the city by taking troops from the fortresses in Cologne, Aachen, or Jülich. This would probably have led democrats in those areas to try their hand at an insurrection. As it was, the army was able to deal with the scattered uprisings and nonviolent protests separately, leaving the insurgents in Elberfeld and Solingen alone to meet their fate.[60]

Elberfeld and Solingen under the Committees of Safety

Repressing the scattered insurrections on the left bank of the Rhine and preventing others from breaking out took up all the available soldiers and kept troops out of the Bergisches Land and the Wuppertal for a week, allowing the revolutionary episode there to play itself out from May 10–17, 1849. As the confrontation between military and population was taking place in Elberfeld, Solingen was becoming a second insurgent center on the east bank of the river. Members of an angry crowd demanded weapons from civic guardsmen there on the evening of May 9, and on receiving about fifty rifles, marched off to Elberfeld. They joined the fight against the Prussian troops and also liberated from jail thirty-seven prisoners who had been arrested for their role in the destruction of the foundries in March 1848 and were about to be brought before the Elberfeld assizes.[61]

The next morning Solingen saw scenes similar to those in the weaving villages of the lower Rhine, only much amplified. A crowd of thousands gathered, from the city and the metalworking villages of the vicinity, going from house to house, insisting that everyone join them, threatening those reluctant to do so. Messengers from Elberfeld reached brewer Hermann Roese, one of the leading Solingen democrats, and he inspired the crowd to burst into the city hall and demand weapons from the city council: Either the civic guard should join a march to Elberfeld or turn its rifles over to those who would.

[60] On the gradual return to order on the lower Rhine during the second half of May, in spite of continued democratic agitation, see HSTAD RA Pr. Nr. 2229 ff. 243–49, 301–02, 310–11, 315, 325, 328–29; HSTAD RD Pr. Nr. 816 ff. 107–10; HSTAD RD Pr. Nr. 823 ff. 14–19, 30–31; HSTAD RD Pr. Nr. 824 ff. 25–28, 30–32; HSTAD RD Pr. Nr. 825 ff. 55–56, 59–61; HSTAD RD Pr. Nr. 826 ff. 34–35; HSTAD RD Pr. Nr. 828 ff. 38–39.

[61] HSTAD RD Pr. Nr. 818 ff. 37–38; HSTAD RD Pr. Nr. 819 f. 48; HSTAD RD Nr. 8809 ff. 57–70. The secondhand story of Engels, "Die deutsche Reichsverfassungskampagne" 7:121, according to which it was the liberation of the prisoners from Solingen that led the Prussian troops to open fire (uncritically accepted by Klessmann, "Sozialgeschichte der Reichsverfassungskampagne," p. 299), is contradicted by all published and unpublished eyewitness accounts.

During these turbulent scenes, word was received that the small detachment of troops guarding the arsenal of the militia in nearby Gräfrath had been withdrawn. The crowd, led by manufacturer Wilhelm Jellinghaus, president of the Democratic Club, marched there, seized the weapons, and proceeded, armed, to Elberfeld. They were joined by other insurgents from Lennep and Mülheim counties; by May 11–12, there were four thousand–six thousand at least partially armed outsiders camped in the insurgent city.[62]

Some Solingen insurgents were accompanied by their wives and women friends, wearing red scarves and carrying revolvers, with daggers in their girdles. The armed women from the Bergisches Land were a long-remembered feature of the revolution, probably growing ever more spectacular as the years went by. Contemporary reports, on the other hand, mentioned just a few, and saw them as a bizarre curiosity rather than a dangerous threat. It would seem that the female participants in the uprising were motivated by the same familial imperatives that brought women into more peaceful actions of the revolution. At least, this was what one older woman told an astonished burgher of Elberfeld: "Wherever my husband marches, I'll go with him, and if he dies there, then I want to die next to him."[63]

Whatever the sex of the insurgents, they had temporarily destroyed the authority of the Prussian state. On the night of May 9, the acting county commissioner fled the Elberfeld city hall by an underground tunnel and made his way to neighboring Barmen, whose civic guard announced its "neutrality" in regard to the uprising. He was joined by all the gendarmes and all but one of the municipal policemen. The Solingen county commissioner retreated to his rural estate, and remained there for a week, firing off letters to his superiors calling on the government ministers to resign, making no attempt to confront the insurgents. To replace the vanished authorities, the leaders of the Elberfeld Political Club formed, on the morning of May 10, a committee of safety. In spite of its name, it was not entirely a revolutionary body, since the club leaders requested the city council to approve the committee's creation and delegate several of its members to sit on it, which the council agreed to do. On the following day, such a committee was set up in Solingen by the democrats, the entire city council there joining as a corporate entity.[64]

[62] HSTAD RD Nr. 8808 ff. 46–55; HSTAD RD Nr. 8809 ff. 57–70; HSTAD RD Pr. Nr. 816 ff. 40–43; Gernert, *1848/49 im Rheinisch-Bergischen*, p. 161; *Lebenserinnerungen . . . Alexander Pagenstecher* 3:64.

[63] Cf. the dramatic retrospective of August Peiner, "Persönliche Erlebnisse während der Unruhen 1848/49 in Elberfeld und Solingen," *Monatsschrift des Bergischen Geschichtsvereins* 5 (1898): 3–18 (quotation, pp. 15–16), with the more prosaic account in *KnZ*, 13 May 1849 (Zweite Ausgabe), which talks of two young women bearing muskets "to the laughter of spectators." Neither Hermann Körner nor Alexander Pagenstecher, who deal with the Elberfeld uprising at length in their memoirs, mention any armed women.

[64] HSTAD RD Pr. Nr. 818 ff. 33–34, 41; HSTAD RD Pr. Nr. 819 ff. 50–54; HSTAD RD Nr.

Historians have often seen the formation of the committees as showing the incipient foundering of the uprising on the rocks of class conflict. While the radical proletarians, who fought on the barricades, wanted to go on to a social revolution, they assert, the Elberfeld democrats (events in Solingen, when discussed at all, are usually overshadowed by those in Elberfeld) were terrified of such a prospect and worked to calm the workers down, destroying their revolutionary élan. The main piece of evidence for these assertions is the Elberfeld committee's founding proclamation, also used in Solingen, which closed with the statement that the "slogan of the free people" should be "May Property be Holy [Heilig sei das Eigentum]." Also mentioned in this connection is the delegation of Elberfeld workers, who brought the democratic leaders a list of capitalists they wanted hanged, to the great dismay of the leftists.[65]

The source for both these incidents is the memoirs of the president of the committee of safety, Elberfeld radical Hermann Körner, but even a brief glance at this work shows that Körner described the events in ways incompatible with this interpretation. Körner recounted how the delegation from the Workers' Association (probably handloom weavers from the recently renamed Central Industrial Association of the Wuppertal) brought a list of "thirty-one dogs whom you must hang." There were capitalists on the list, but also neoorthodox clergy and lay supporters of revivalism, as well as miscellaneous reactionaries. The radical proletarians wanted to eliminate their enemies—many of whom, admittedly, were large merchant manufacturers, prominent on the right in the Wuppertal—as reactionaries, not as capitalists. Körner also remembered the workers' specific anger at the bourgeoisie. The weavers complained that they had fought on the barricades, while the "moneybags" and the "master manufacturers," who also wanted to force the king to accept the constitution, had not and, in addition, had closed down their businesses for the duration of the insurrection. "Where are we to get the money for our wives and children?" they asked.[66]

Much the same mood existed among the metalworkers in Solingen and vicinity. When the crowd charged into the city council meeting there on May 10, demanding weapons for a march on Elberfeld, it also insisted that the city councilmen, the merchant manufacturers, and the rich generally march at the head of the column. That way, if they refused to fight, they could easily be shot from behind. The insurgent manufacturing outworkers on the right bank of the Rhine did not want to eliminate the capitalists; rather, they wanted them

---

8808 ff. 46–53; HSTAD RD Nr. 8809 ff. 26–29, 57–70; Lorenz, "1848/49 im Wuppertal," pp. 283–85.

[65] Hamerow, *Restoration, Revolution, Reaction*, p. 194; Klessmann, "Sozialgeschichte der Reichsverfassungskampagne," pp. 299–300; Rudolf Stadelman, *Social and Political History*, p. 185.

[66] Körner, *Lebenskämpfe* 2:104–05. On the Elberfeld Workers' Association, see sources cited in Chapter Six, note 33.

to join in the struggle against the monarchy and for the nation. However, they strongly suspected that the capitalists would not, that they would engage in the same double-dealing in politics that the outworkers had experienced from them in economic affairs.[67]

In his memoirs, Körner went on to describe the effect of the committee of safety's appeal and its assurance to the rich that their property was safe. "Thanks to the effect of this proclamation . . . merchants and manufacturers came slinking in and personally handed over . . . thousands of Thaler 'to meet the needs of the freedom fighters,' [the contributions] accompanied by a sour-sweet smile, a trembling handshake and some hypocritical words of admiration for our perserverance.'' The same was true in Solingen, where the committee of safety raised substantial sums for the families of insurgents from the city and the metal-working villages of the vicinity. Even the county commissioner contributed, to his subsequent great embarrassment.[68]

The committees of safety thus enabled the democratic leaders to keep their proletarian following together and continue the insurrection in a manufacturing region where all economic activity had ceased. Perhaps a more appropriate question is why the other side agreed to cooperate with the democrats. It is not entirely obvious why the city councils of Elberfeld and Solingen joined the insurgent committees of safety. Nor is it clear why the two cities' civic guards, fully armed, and under constitutional monarchist leadership, seemed completely paralyzed, unlike the guard in neighboring Barmen, which upheld order and forced anyone interested in revolution to leave the city.[69]

When called to account by the Prussian government following the suppression of the uprising, the city fathers and civic guard officers claimed that they had no choice. With no gendarmes or soldiers present, they were helpless against the mob. Rather than oppose it, and allow the radicals to seize the reins of power, it seemed better to cooperate: to provide money to the unemployed insurgents so that they would not turn to looting, to use the civic guard to protect persons and property, since it could not suppress the insurrection. Of course, this cooperation to avoid the worst assisted and legitimated the uprising—not a point the local officials made in their apologia, but one the Prussian authorities saw right away. Collecting money for the insurgents allowed them to spend their time building more and stronger barricades. Escorting the crowd to the Gräfrath arsenal, as the Solingen civic guard did on its officers' command, may have helped prevent individual pillaging of the weapons, but it ensured that they would all be used for the uprising.[70]

---

[67] HSTAD RD Nr. 8809 ff. 92–93; similar accounts in ibid., ff. 26–20, 57–70.

[68] Körner, *Lebenskämpfe* 2:107–08; HSTAD RD Nr. 8808 ff. 22–25, 33, 46–53; HSTAD RD Nr. 8809 ff. 20–21, 57–70, 74–94. Similarly, Engels, "Die deutsche Reichsverfassungskampagne" 7:125.

[69] On Barmen during the insurrection, see Lorenz, "1848/49 im Wuppertal," pp. 309–10.

[70] HSTAD RD Nrs. 8808–09 passim contain these justifications of their behavior by the mayor,

While acting to avoid the worst was a genuine motive, not just a restrospective justification, it was not the sole motivation for the moderates' actions. They were in a position similar to that of the Catholic clergy and lay notables who were unhappy with the radical steps proposed by the democrats during the November crisis but were also strongly opposed to the policies of the ministry of Count Brandenburg that had prompted them. The Solingen city council, for instance, may have joined the committee of safety to preserve public order, but it had previously sent a delegation to the Cologne city council congress of May 8 and endorsed the strongly worded declaration against the government that the congress had issued.[71]

These mixed motives—fear of the uprising, yet a reluctant sympathy with the circumstances that gave rise to it—are documented in detail for one individual: Samuel Scheffler, the only municipal policeman who did not flee Elberfeld, but remained in the city and offered his services to the committee of safety. An administrative hearing on whether he should be dismissed for this action elicited his self-justification and brought many witnesses to testify to his opinions. A Protestant and veteran of the wars of liberation against Napoleon, Scheffler was a firm Prussian patriot. His fellow veterans testified to his loyalty to the monarch for whom they had fought together; his landlord noted that during the revolution he had "always shown the right sentiments." Scheffler insisted that he had remained at his post to protect Elberfeld's citizens from the outside insurgents, who were threatening their property and personal safety. He tried to stop workers from tearing up cobblestones and building barricades, but had to admit there was no way "to prevent these evil deeds [diesem Unwesen zu steuern]." At the very end of the uprising, he helped dismantle some barricades.

In doing this, Scheffler was certainly trying to avert the worst, but there was another side to his attitudes, one he was unwilling to admit later on. One witness testified that Scheffler had said that he "could not understand the king's not accepting the imperial crown; it could only be that his ministers were preventing him from it. The German constitution has been so thoroughly investigated by all the representatives of the nation." Another told of how he saw Scheffler enter a bar where some workers were drinking. They expressed their astonishment at seeing a policeman still in town, to which he replied, "[S]urely you know I'm no longer black-white." Scheffler's divided loyalties were probably shared by many of his fellow citizens, facilitating the radical steps taken by the democrats.[72]

---

city council, and civic guard officers of Solingen, with the comments of the Prussian authorities. Documents stemming from the time of the uprising itself, support this restrospective view: LAK 403 Nr. 2253 pp. 109–12, 187. Similarly, cf. Hecker, *Der Aufstand in Elberfeld*, pp. 25–38.

[71] HSTAD RD Nr. 8809 ff. 12–13. Similar feelings among members of the Solingen civic guard, ibid. ff. 95–122.

[72] HSTAD RD Pr. Nr. 220 ff. 41–43, 55–57, 65–69, 82–83, and passim. The reaction-era

The rule of the committees of safety was thus based on a tacit compromise between radicals and constitutional monarchists and between workers and capitalists, with all sides well armed. It was an unstable situation, and became even more so with the news of the suppression of the uprisings in Düsseldorf and on the lower Rhine. Even before they were ready to take direct military action, the Prussian authorities turned the screws on the insurgent manufacturing district, blockading its food supplies and cutting off its railroad connections. By May 14–15, the situation had become critical: Manufacturing had ceased, food and money were growing short, and thousands of people fled the barricaded city. More and more of the insurgent outworkers were drifting away from the rebellion, expressing a desire to give up and go back to work. Although the barricades were formidable, making a direct infantry assault on them and their armed defenders a difficult enterprise, the rumor began to spread that the military was planning instead to stand off on the heights overlooking the city and use its artillery to bombard it into submission.[73]

In these circumstances, differences between militants and moderates among the insurgent democrats became ever more pronounced. The moderates wished to preserve the tacit cooperation with the constitutional monarchists, the city councils, and the civic guards, which would have been difficult to achieve without dismantling the barricades and ending the uprising. In contrast, the radicals wanted, instead, to carry the revolution further by having the committees of safety replace the city councils altogether, by compelling the Elberfeld civic guard to take an oath to the Frankfurt constitution (and thus unambiguously join the uprising) or be disarmed, and by seizing the weapons of the civic guards of Barmen and other towns in the vicinity.[74]

The controversy between the two groups was brought to a head by the actions of Friedrich Engels. Appearing in Elberfeld on May 11, bringing with him two cases of cartridges from Solingen, Engels joined the Military Commission of the Committee of Safety, a body dominated by the radicals, and was appointed inspector of the barricades. Three days later, the committee asked him to leave, since his presence was giving rise to "misunderstandings"

---

authorities showed neither mercy nor willingness to recognize the profound ambiguity of Scheffler's motives: He lost both his job and his pension.

[73] ZSTAM Rep. 77 Tit. 505 Nr. 3 Vol. 4 ff. 66–68; HSTAD RD Pr. Nr. 220 ff. 4–6, 45–48; HSTAD RD Pr. Nr. 818 ff. 45–47; LAK 403 Nr. 2253 pp. 61–63, 109–12, 133–35; HSTAD RD Pr. Nr. 817 f. 26; HSTAD RD Nr. 8805 ff. 13, 20–30; Körner, *Lebenskämpfe* 2:115–18, 138, 141; *Lebenserinnerungen . . . Alexander Pagenstecher* 3:63–64; Engels, "Die deutsche Reichsverfassungskampagne" 7:126–27, 129.

[74] *Lebenserinnerungen . . . Alexander Pagenstecher* 3:67; Hecker, *Der Aufstand in Elberfeld*, pp. 41–43; Körner, *Lebenskämpfe* 2:125–26, 136–40; HSTAD RD Pr. Nr. 816 f. 56; HSTAD RD Pr. Nr. 820 ff. 36–37; HSTAD RD Nr. 8809 ff. 1–10; Engels, "Die deutsche Reichsverfassungskampange" 7:128–29. Engels's claim that he was the only one to advocate such measures, was made, as he explained, "for the safety of the Elberfeld insurgents held in jail under indictment," and so can be disregarded.

about the nature of the movement. By his own account, Engels had not acted as a communist, or even a republican. Aware that the uprising was a purely "black-red-gold movement," he had confined his participation to military matters, arguing vigorously for the more energetic measures proposed by the radicals on the committee of safety.[75]

Although eyewitness accounts of Engels's actions differed greatly, according to their witnesses' political opinions, they all agreed that he was a militant insurgent. The constitutional monarchist physician Alexander Pagenstecher remembered Engels as a rabid terrorist, gleefully boasting about taking the reactionary banker Daniel von der Heydt hostage. One of the moderate democrats on the Committee of Safety complained that Engels was a "fantasist, one of those people who are spoiling everything," (that is, taking militant measures and endangering the tacit alliance with the constitutional monarchists). Hermann Körner, who was on the left wing of the committee, saw Engels as capable of "noble, self-sacrificing devotion," but condemned his "always untimely, purely superficial socialist extravagances," which did more harm than good.[76]

Körner claimed that the pretext used for expelling Engels was his having replaced the black-red-gold flags on the barricades with red ones. Engels himself never explicitly denied having done this, and his position did take him around to all the barricades, so it is not impossible that he got a little overexcited in the heat of the moment and raised the symbol of the red republic. Whatever the truth of the matter, Engels's expulsion, with its rejection of any possible republicanism or drastic measures to expand the insurrection, was a victory for the moderates on the committee of safety and their program of cooperation with the constitutional monarchists. That same day, the moderates tried, without using coercion, to get the civic guard of Elberfeld to take an oath of loyalty to the Frankfurt constitution. The attempt ended in a fiasco when most guardsmen refused to appear. Both radical and moderate programs had failed, bringing the end of the uprising within sight.[77]

The final blow came the following day. Members of a delegation from Elberfeld to Berlin, led by the city's former deputy to the Frankfurt National Assembly, Alexander Pagenstecher, telegraphed that they had spoken with the government ministers. The latter had assured them that the king really did want German national unity. Regardless of the truth of this declaration (and it depended on one's definition of national unity), the delegates and their following in the Wuppertal were desperate to believe such promises as the best way out of an impossible situation. In both Elberfeld and Solingen, the civic guard

---

[75] Engels's declaration of his role in the uprising, published in *NRhZ*, 17 May 1849.

[76] *Lebenserinnerungen . . . Alexander Pagenstecher* 3:66–67; Körner, *Lebenskämpfe* 2:70–72, 137.

[77] Körner, *Lebenskämpfe* 2:137; ZSTAM Rep. 77 Tit. 505 Nr. 3 Vol. 4 ff. 66–68; Hecker, *Der Aufstand in Elberfeld*, pp. 38–39. Cf. Lorenz, "1848/49 im Wuppertal," pp. 268–69.

moved to disband the committees of safety; bloodshed was averted when last-minute negotiations allowed any insurgents who wished to leave to do so, taking their weapons with them. When Prussian troops finally arrived on May 17, they found the barricades in Elberfeld taken down and order restored throughout the entire manufacturing region on the right bank of the Rhine.[78]

The uprising had proceeded as far as it did only because conflicting loyalties had temporarily paralyzed the constitutional monarchists of the area, the wealthy merchants, bankers, and manufacturers and the neoorthodox Protestants of all social classes who supported them. When the uprising became bogged down, turning into a socially chaotic political stalemate, they recovered their initiative—in more conservative, pious Barmen they had never lost it—and brought the insurrection to an end, even before troops were sent. The uprising had shown, however, the support the region's democrats had built among the manufacturing outworkers.

The strongly antimonarchical and even openly republican sentiments they expressed, even though they were of the same confession as the ruling monarch, was something new in the revolution and set the stage for future developments. In May 1850, when almost all those brought before the assizes for their role in the uprising were acquitted, a jubilant crowd of thousands crowded the streets of Barmen and Elberfeld to celebrate. From the 1860s onward, the industrial area on the right bank of the Rhine, which had been so conservative for so much of 1848–1849, "marched along at the head of the Social Democratic movement."[79]

ABORTIVE UPRISINGS

While the most dramatic and violent events of early May 1849 in the Prussian Rhineland were taking place on the lower Rhine, the rest of the province was not passive. To be sure, the provincial metropolis was quiet. Seeing that the revolution was taking place without them, the Cologne communists quickly switched tactics, the *Neue Rheinische Zeitung* endorsing the Elberfeld uprising and a few of the activists on the Cologne Workers' Association following Engels to fight in the Wuppertal. Others, along with members of the Democratic Society, remained in town, forging bullets and manufacturing cartridges. The democrats agitated among the militiamen and called for the reforming of the civic guard. As long as acting fortress commandant Colonel

---

[78] *Lebenserinnerungen . . . Alexander Pagenstecher* 3:68–76; Körner, *Lebenskämpfe* 2:138–53; Lorenz, "1848/49 im Wuppertal," pp. 290–301. Events in Solingen were a bit more dramatic. Armed insurgents, returning from Elberfeld on 16 May, forced the civic guard to back down and briefly reinstated the committee of safety, intimidating the city council into rejoining it, only to give up and scatter later that same day. HSTAD RD Nr. 8809 ff. 57–70.

[79] LAK 403 Nr. 2253 pp. 398–405; quotation from Wittgenstein, "Die Entstehung der sozialen Frage," p. 165.

Engels refused to dispatch any of his troops to fight insurgents elsewhere, thus retaining the garrison at full strength, there was little that the left could do. A deportation order, long hanging over Marx's head (he had lost his Prussian citizenship while in exile in the mid-1840s), was finally issued, as was a warrant for Engels's arrest for his activities in Elberfeld. The two communists were forced to flee. As a parting shot, they printed the last issue (May 17, 1849) of the *Neue Rheinische Zeitung* in red ink, announcing that their concluding words were "the emancipation of the working class."[80]

Democrats in Bonn took decisive action, coming closest to creating circumstances like those on the lower Rhine. Starting at the end of April, Bonn leftists held mass rallies in the villages of Sieg County across the Rhine, calling on the peasants to prepare for armed insurrection and the creation of a republic. The mobilization of the militia seemed to provide the opportunity for an uprising, and the committee of the Bonn Democratic Club, meeting in permanent session, developed its plan. In posters and at meetings, the militiamen were called on to appear for their mobilization in Siegburg on May 11, 1849, but in order to fight for the Frankfurt constitution, not against it. The evening before, an armed column from Bonn would march to the arsenal of the militia in Siegburg, storm it with the help of the Siegburg democrats, and distribute its weapons to the insurgent militia.

Carl Schurz has told in his memoirs of how a small armed column, led by the ex-officer and Cologne communist Fritz Anneke, left Bonn on the evening of May 10, only to be dispersed by a detachment of dragoons it accidentally encountered. What usually does not appear in the retellings of his story were the hundreds, perhaps thousands, of peasants from the up-country of Sieg County who surrounded Siegburg that night, ready to join the insurrection. The following day they crowded the streets of Siegburg, while Schurz, who had evaded the cavalry and made his way to the original goal of the column, tried to organize an uprising. Democrats spoke to the peasants and the militia; the storm bells were rung; and the county commissioner was sure it would have come to the building of barricades and street fighting had not a company of infantry arrived from Bonn and dispersed the crowd.[81]

The southern end of the province was also the scene of political mobilization in conjunction with the Frankfurt constitution. Democrats held a series of mass meetings in Koblenz, one on May 9 issuing an appeal to support the Frankfurt constitution, "with the exception of the hereditary emperor, which is incompatible with the freedom of the people and has become impossible since the King of Prussia, elected to the post, refused it." All the meetings

---

[80] Hammen, *The Red '48ers*, pp. 394–99; Strey and Winkler, *Marx und Engels 1848/49*, pp. 304–05; Dowe, *Aktion und Organisation*, pp. 228–29; *Der Bund der Kommunisten* 1, Nr. 372; Kühn, *Der junge Hermann Becker*, pp. 235–38.

[81] Schurz, *Lebenserinnerungen*, pp. 188–97; Schneider, *Verfassungskämpfe der Jahre 1848–1849 . . . im Siegkreis*, pp. 19–20; LAK 403 Nr. 2552 pp. 53–58.

were marked by this anti-Prussian tone, officials seeing the speeches as designed to "incite people against the government, against the state servants and the military." The authorities expected some kind of action, perhaps in conjunction with the armed insurrections going on to the south in Rhine-Hessen and the Palatinate. Similar mass meetings, or meetings of the militia, were held in smaller towns known as strongholds of the left: Mayen, Münstermaifeld, Adenau, Kreuznach, and Saarbrücken, where two thousand people gathered on May 18, 1849, and took an oath of loyalty to the Frankfurt constitution.[82]

To dampen this political enthusiasm, the civilian authorities requested a mobile troop column be sent along the Moselle Valley and into the Eifel uplands. The commanding officers agreed, although they felt that fewer troops could be spared from the Koblenz fortress than the civilians wished. On learning of the approach of the soldiers, the civic guard of radical Cochem marched out fully armed to oppose them, and frightened inhabitants, fearing an armed clash, took steps to secure their persons and property. The soldiers were a day late on their march, and they arrived in Cochem unexpectedly and passed through the town peacefully, leaving behind a detachment to secure order there, as they did everywhere they went.[83]

Throughout all this, Trier remained quiet, just several smaller meetings of the democrats and the militia being held. The district authorities, who were convinced the democrats would have seized power in the metropolis of the Moselle Valley were it not for the fortress and the garrison, did not entirely trust the appearance of peacefulness and suspected, correctly, that something was going on behind the scenes. Following a mass meeting on the Marienburg, overlooking the south bank of the Moselle near the town of Zell on May 13, 1849, Trier democratic leaders gathered city councilmen and democrats of the Moselle Valley and the Eifel up-country to plan an uprising for the following week.[84]

The plan called for an armed column from Trier, Wittlich, and Bitburg to march to the Eifel town of Prüm on the night of May 18–19, 1849, storm the arsenal of the militia there, and return to the Moselle Valley, distributing the weapons they had captured. At first, all went as planned, the militiamen of Prüm making no effort to resist, and soon going over to the insurgents—for which three of them would later face a military firing squad. Simultaneously, there was a rising in Wittlich, a county town between the up-country and the

[82] LAK 441 Nr. 3059 pp. 23–72; LAK 441 Nr. 8317 pp. 131–33, 175–76; ZSTAM Rep. 77 Tit. 505 Nr. 4 Vol. III ff. 290–96 Vol. IV ff. 7–9; *NRhZ*, 13 May 1849; Noack, "1848/49 in der Saargegend," p. 117.

[83] LAK 441 Nr. 8317 pp. 121, 207–209, 213–15.

[84] Was this the uprising that had been planned in Cologne, on Congress Sunday? No one from Trier had been present at the congress, but according to Körner, *Lebenskämpfe* 2:68–69, a courier was sent there with the plans for the insurrection.

Moselle Valley. The town was ruled by "the lower class of people" during May 18–21, "no official being able to carry out his duties then." The insurgents marched from Prüm to Wittlich, stayed there overnight, and then, on the morning of May 19, went on to Bernkastel, center of events in the Moselle Valley during the November crisis. Explaining that they were there "to begin the revolution against Prussia," they began handing out arms to an enthusiastic crowd. The county commissioner was forced to flee town to seek military help. In contrast to the November uprisings, however, the city council and the notables showed little desire to become involved. When, later in the day, news was received that the rest of the Moselle Valley had not risen and that soldiers of the loyalist Twenty-Seventh Infantry Regiment were on the march, the insurgents collected their weapons and fled. A state of siege was declared in the mid-Moselle Valley and the neighboring Eifel up-country, bringing this very last phase of the movement in the Prussian Rhine Province to an end.[85]

AN UNEXPECTED INSURRECTION

The campaign for the Frankfurt constitution led to a major challenge to the authority of the Prussian state in its Rhenish province. Between ten thousand and fifteen thousand insurgents took up arms, and at least as many gathered weapons and prepared for an insurrection or participated in peaceful but illegal political protest: refusing as militiamen to be mobilized, attending mass meetings, and taking an oath to uphold the Frankfurt constitution. At several crucial turning points—the street fighting in Düsseldorf, the attempt to seize the Siegburg arsenal—the authorities narrowly averted insurgent successes, which undoubtedly would have brought many more people into the fight and greatly widened the extent of the uprising.[86]

Although all this activity was ostensibly in favor of the Frankfurt constitution, which named the king of Prussia emperor, monarchist sympathies were hardly to be seen within it. Everywhere, even in the previously strongly Prussian loyalist Wuppertal and Bergisches Land, the movement was accompanied by violent verbal assaults on monarchs in general, and Friedrich Wilhelm IV in particular, by the raising of red flags, and by cheers for the republic. At the local level, the campaign for the Frankfurt constitution looked more like the second, republican revolution that militant democrats had been demanding since the summer of 1848.

Much of what happened shows a continuity with previous political struggles

---

[85] LAK 403 Nr. 6583 p. 351; ZSTAM Rep. 77 Tit. 505 Nr. 5 Vol. VI ff. 30–35, 40–42, 60–69, 73, 93–95, 192–97; LAK 441 Nr. 8317 pp. 101–02, 313–17; Breuer, "1848/49 im Moseltal," pp. 191–92, 202–10; Stahl, *1848/49 an der Mittelmosel*, pp. 33–37.

[86] The county commissioner in Adenau, for instance, was sure that had the uprisings on the lower Rhine been more successful, "disturbances here would not have failed to occur." LAK 441 Nr. 1331 pp. 1–7.

and organizational efforts. Düsseldorf and Bonn, along with their rural hinter-
lands, had been centers of militant action during the November crisis and were
again six months later. Much the same could be said of Trier, Wittlich, Bernkastel, and Bitburg, although the magnitude of events in the mid-Moselle Valley had been much greater a half-year previously. The crucial tactic of the
democrats, appealing to the militiamen for armed support, had already been
tried out on a lesser scale in November 1848.[87]

Even the uprisings in the Bergisches Land and the Wuppertal, which genuinely surprised contemporaries, from the district governor to the Cologne
communists, would have been less of a shock, had closer attention been paid
to the political developments in the manufacturing districts on the right bank
of the Rhine. Forming clubs, and agitating in support of the outworkers' grievances, the democrats there had been slowly and gradually gaining popular
support since the summer of 1848. Their progress had been overshadowed by
their inability to overcome the conservative, loyalist forces in the area during
the two previous major political confrontations, the November crisis and the
elections to the Prussian parliament of January 1849. By May 1849, the leftists
were finally in a position to exploit their increasing political influence.

Nonetheless, contemporaries and, following them, most historians, have
tended to see the events of May 1849 as a break with the past political history
of the province during the revolution. In particular, the relationship between
confession and politics seemed to have been reversed: Previously, most noticeably during the November crisis, oppositional movements had occurred in
Roman Catholic areas, while Protestant ones had been loyalist; now, the eminently Protestant Wuppertal and Bergisches Land were in insurrection, while
the Catholic regions were quiet. This reversal is usually ascribed to a religiously based monarchical loyalism. Protestants supported a constitution making their king emperor, while Catholics vehemently opposed it, and saw no
reason to fight for it.[88]

There are two problems with this argument. First, Roman Catholics did
participate in the movement: Both Düsseldorf and the lower Rhine weaving
districts were heavily Catholic areas; in the latter, the Protestant minority explicitly refused to join the insurgency. The rural areas of Sieg and Mülheim
counties, where the peasants were actively involved in the insurrection, were
also heavily Roman Catholic, as were the county towns Wittlich and Prüm, in
the southern part of the province. Altogether, perhaps twice as many Catholics

[87] At the beginning of May 1849, the Solingen democrats sent threatening delegations around
to the mayors in their county, asking if they would support the government or the Frankfurt
National Assembly (HSTAD RD Pr. Nr. 819 ff. 29–45), a tactic reminiscent of, and probably
occasioned by, the appeal of the democratic provincial directory during the November crisis to
ask the municipal authorities if they stood with the king or the Prussian National Assembly.

[88] HSTAD RA Pr. Nr. 2229 ff. 209–10; ZSTAM Rep. 77 Tit. 505 Nr. 3 Vol. 4 ff. 47–50;
Valentin, *Geschichte der Deutschen Revolution* 2:471.

as Protestants were involved in an armed struggle. None of this includes more peaceful forms of political participation, such as the mass meetings on the lower or middle Rhine, in the Moselle Valley, or in the Eifel up-country. Nor does it take into account the democrats of Eupen, Eschweiler, and Cologne, who gathered rifles and ammunition, forged bullets, and manufactured cartridges, creating the danger of a potential uprising that could only be repressed by military force. If Elberfeld and Solingen became centers of insurrection, it was in part because the acting commandant of the Cologne fortress, fearing an uprising in the Rhenish metropolis, refused to allow any of his troops to march beyond the city walls.

Secondly, the movement was really not in favor of the Prussian king, but against him. In opposing the movement, the Catholic clergy and the lay notables of the Pius Associations were taking a pro-Prussian stance, not an anti-Prussian one. They were acting in favor of the Prussian constitution decreed in December 1848, with its guarantees for freedom of religion and confessionally segregated public education, wishing to hold on to these very tangible improvements for the church, rather than to plunge into a republican uprising, led by anticlerical leftists. This was an eminently sensible position from the Catholic leaders' point of view, but like a similar orientation in the January 1849 elections, it meant abandoning anti-Prussianism, thus limiting their influence over the mass of ordinary Catholics, allowing the democrats to exploit confessional antagonisms for their cause.

The Protestant constitutional monarchists were the one group in the Prussian Rhineland genuinely enthusiastic about the king of Prussia's becoming emperor. Their opposition to the policies of the Prussian government helped get the movement started in the Wuppertal and Bergisches Land, but it quickly passed out of their hands into those of the democrats, and they were soon faced with the unpleasant choice of supporting a government they disliked or supporting measures against it that they disliked even more. Only after the uprising had been isolated and contained, clearly doomed to failure, could they emerge from the political paralysis caused by being forced to choose between two such unpalatable alternatives.

In the end, the campaign for the Frankfurt constitution was the democrats' affair, and its results reveal both the strengths and weaknesses of the democrats of Rhenish Prussia. The rudimentary character of their provincial organization and the pronounced factional differences within the democratic movement worked against any effort at unified political action, whatever its nature. If there were plans for a general uprising—and it seems that something was afoot, although its exact nature, its adherents, and its connections with central, national organizations are extremely unclear—they seem to have been vague and provisional, quickly overtaken by events.

Political actions, whether violent or peaceful in nature, occurred in largely isolated fashion at the local level. In each of these local actions, the democrats played a leading role, exploiting social and confessional antagonisms, trying, and frequently succeeding, to guide the movement in a republican direction. When compared with the spontaneous but unorganized outbursts of popular anger and the feeble character of organized radicalism in March–May 1848, one can see how far the left had come in a year. In Rhine-Hessen and the Palatinate, where the democrats had always been stronger and better organized than further north, and the forces of order weaker, the events of the spring of 1849 would be more dramatic still.

CHAPTER TEN

Revolution on the Upper Rhine

ON THE WAY TO AN UPRISING

Maximilian II of Bavaria, and his statesmen, diplomats, and generals, were even less willing to accept the German constitution written by the Frankfurt National Assembly than their Prussian counterparts. But like Friedrich Wilhelm IV, the Bavarian monarch made no definitive statement for most of April 1849. He continued to refuse to call into session the Bavarian parliament elected in December 1848, knowing that its left-wing majority would demand the ratification of the Frankfurt constitution. Petitions flowed into Munich by the thousands during these weeks. Those from Alpine Old Bavaria, sponsored by the state authorities and the Catholic Church, called for the rejection of the constitution and a continuation of Bavarian independence; while those from the new Bavarian territories were heavily in favor of the constitution. Organized by the provincial committee of the People's Association, the hundreds of petitions from the Palatinate were almost unanimous in supporting the constitution; just one or two, the product of the Pius Associations, dared call for its rejection.[1]

When the king finally announced his refusal of the Frankfurt constitution on April 23, 1849, public opinion in the province, already considerably stirred up by the petitions, became ever more agitated. Outside the politically not very effective Palatine Pius Associations, Bavarian loyalism had few adherents; the constitutional monarchist enemies of the democrats, including many high state officials, were supporters of the Frankfurt National Assembly. The royal rejection of the Frankfurt constitution thus had at least as great an impact in the Palatinate as in Rhenish Prussia. "The excitment is immense," the county commissioner in Zweibrücken reported, not least because those who had always opposed "the spirit of revolution" were "bitterly disappointed in their expectations" by the action of the king and his ministers.[2]

From April 27 onwards, mass meetings were held throughout the Palatinate, where speakers debated what was to be done. There was general agreement that further petitioning was useless and that the most plausible next step

[1] Dietrich Thränhardt, *Wahlen und politische Strukturen in Bayern, 1848–1953* (Düsseldorf: Droste, 1973), p. 42 n.17; lists of petitions in BHSTAM MInn Nr. 43865 ff. 1–6, 13–31, 81–88.

[2] LK Zweibrücken to RP, 30 Apr. 1849, BHSTAM MInn Nr. 45531; similarly, RP to MInn, 28 Apr. 1849; LK Homburg to RP, 1 May 1849; LK Landau to RP, 1 May 1849, all ibid; LAS J1 Nr. 235 ff. 228–35.

was a great, provincial assembly on the model of the Hambach Festival of 1832. There, however, unanimity ended: "exalted" and moderate democrats had strongly opposed opinions about the purpose of such a meeting. Militants wanted an armed gathering, whose participants would announce the secession of the province from Bavaria and possibly proclaim the republic as well. Moderates, on the other hand, desired a meeting of the notables, which would demand that the king accept the constitution; otherwise, the province would place itself under the protection of the Frankfurt National Assembly. This tactic was modeled on the successful agitation of prominent rationalists in the Protestant Union Church—many of whom were also leading moderate democrats—the previous spring, which had forced the Munich Consistory to call a provincial synod.[3]

Directly related to the debate over the purpose of the meeting was the question of its venue. The most obvious one was Neustadt a.d.W., located in the most populous part of the province, where mass meetings had previously taken place—in 1832 and in March, June, and October of 1848. "Neustadt has always taken the lead," was how one speaker in Speyer put it. The wine capital was also the home base for the extreme left of the Palatinate, led by the German Catholic communists Johann Weber and Heinrich Loose; any mass meeting there would have been dominated by their followers. Consequently, the moderates preferred Kaiserslautern, the second-largest city in the province after Speyer, but isolated in the western uplands, conveniently accessible only by railroad. Such a location, they thought, might help cut down on both the number and radicalism of the participants. This logic was recognized by the radicals themselves, who had dominated the provincial congress of gymnastics societies, held in Kaiserslautern on April 29. The congress decided to create a central committee, which was to meet in permanent session to organize an insurrectionary armed corps, and would have its seat in Frankenthal in the forward Palatinate, "for in that region the people have more political education and are more courageous in action."[4]

The provincial steering committee of the Palatine People's Association in Frankenthal issued on April 27 an appeal for a provincial meeting, which, in its language seemed more on the radical side. Hostile to the National Assem-

[3] Sources cited in note 2; *NSZ*, 1–4 May 1849; Neustadt police commissioner to LK Neustadt, 25, 27–28 Apr. 1849; RP to MInn, 29–30 Apr. 1849; Gendarmerie Station Neustadt to Company Command Speyer, 28 Apr. 1849; LK Neustadt to RP, 29 Apr. 1849; Gendarmerie Brigade Zweibrücken to Company Command Speyer, 30 Apr. 1849; Gendarmerie Station Edenkoben to Company Command Speyer, 1 May 1849; LK Landau to RP, 1 May 1849; LK Kaiserslautern to RP, 2 May 1849; all in BHSTAM MInn Nr. 45531; Police Commissioner Speyer to LK Speyer, 27 Apr. 1849, LAS H1 Nr. 1975; LAS J1 Nr. 105 ff. 272–75; LAS J1 Nr. 242 ff. 98–101. Concerning the agitation over the church synod, see sources cited in Chapter Seven, note 74.

[4] On the gymnasts' congress, see LAS J1 Nr. 105 ff. 138–39; and report of Staatsprokurator Gogel, 3 May 1849, LAS H1 Nr. 1975; for the debate on the venue, see the sources cited in the previous note.

bly and firmly antimonarchical, the appeal described the Frankfurt constitution as "the only stunted fruit of the many flowers on the tree of revolution which has come to ripeness." Yet in spite of its moderation, the constitution was "threatened by princely lust for domination." Moving on to the Bavarian kingdom, the appeal denounced the "treason commmitted by an un-German government ministry against the German fatherland" and "the commands, backed by force, of a deluded princely family." It concluded with the powerful words, "If the members of the government have become rebels, then the free citizens of the Palatinate will enforce the law." For all the radicalism of the appeal's rhetoric, its substance supported the moderate position. The steering committee called for two meetings in Kaiserslautern. The first, on May 1, which would take the decisions, was to consist of the Frankfurt and Munich deputies, the members of the provincial parliament, the electors, mayors, city councillors, members of the provincial committee of the People's Association, and leaders of other political groups—in short, the notables. There would be a second meeting the following day, to which the entire male population of the Palatinate was invited, in order to ratify the decisions made by the first. The steering committee's appeal prevailed over radical efforts to hold the meeting in Neustadt, so both moderates and radicals rallied their followers to go to Kaiserslautern.[5]

At first, things seemed to go the moderates' way. Meeting on May 1, the notables voted down a proposal for yet another petition, but also condemned the idea of secession from Bavaria and the proclamation of the republic. Instead, they called for the creation of a "Provincial Defense Committee" [Landesverteidigungsausschuß], to be elected by the notables, which would meet in permanent session until the Frankfurt constitution had become law. Caucusing that evening, most of the radicals, apparently with the exception of the Neustadt communists, agreed to support this proposal.[6]

The following day, the streets of Kaiserslautern, a modest town of some ten thousand inhabitants, were filled with participants in the mass meeting, including many women, who appeared in spite of the steering committee's not having invited them. Most of those present were unarmed and carrying black-

---

[5] Copy of the appeal in BHSTAM MInn Nr. 45531. On the rallying of followers, besides the sources cited in the two previous notes, see LAS J1 Nr. 105 f. 173; LAS J1 Nr. 203 ff. 364–66.

[6] Although the Kaiserslautern mass meeting and the subsequent Palatine revolution have often been described in the literature, the two main investigations, on which most works are based (for example, RhG 2:402; Klessmann, "Zur Sozialgeschichte der Reichsverfassungskampagne," pp. 304–13), Fleischmann, Geschichte des Pfälzischen Aufstands; and Renner, "Die pfälzische Bewegung," are of little scholarly value; cf. the devastating criticism in Schwarzwälder, "Die Ursachen der Reichsverfassungskampagne," pp. 5–6. By far the best, if short, work, is Regina-Margarete Schneider, "Landesausschuß und Provisorische Regierung in Kaiserslautern 1849," JhGStLK 22/23 (1984/85): 91–117, the preliminaries to the meeting described on pp. 92–93. See also the report of Staatsprokurator Gogel, 3 May 1849, LAS H1 Nr. 1975; and LK Kaiserslautern to RP, 2 May 1849, BHSTAM MInn Nr. 45531.

red-gold flags, although there was one armed contingent from Göllheim, in the northern Palatinate, whose members marched behind a red flag, firing off their rifles as they went. Red scarves, sashes, and ribbons also bedecked many participants. Estimates of the size of the crowd varied from five thousand to twelve thousand; it was, in any event, too large to meet indoors at the Corn Hall, as had originally been planned, so a tribune, crowned with an enormous tricolor, was erected on the square behind the Protestant church.

Although the speakers denounced the princes as guilty of high treason, most held to the proposals of the previous day, only Johann Weber of Neustadt demanding secession from Bavaria and the creation of the republic. In the late afternoon, the crowd was asked to vote, by raising their hands, on the two opposing motions, the Provincial Defense Committee or the republic. The former won out by a narrow margin, but since the vote counters on the tribune were also the proponents of that proposal, some by no means left-wing observers thought that the extreme left had been cheated out of its victory. Frustrated, Weber and Heinrich Loose led some four hundred of their followers out of the meeting. Singing the Marseillaise, they marched to a neighboring square, where they gave three cheers for the republic and went home, with the intent of sponsoring a republican countermeeting in Neustadt, the following Sunday.[7]

The remaining radicals then took a quick step, confounding the moderates. The previous day, the notables had agreed that the members of the Provincial Defense Committee would be determined a week later, to give the Bavarian government a chance to respond to the Palatines' demands. Instead, the chair of the mass meeting, the Speyer republican notary Martin Reichard, called for an immediate gathering of the notables to elect the committee so that it might begin its work right away. Disgruntled moderates later suspected this move had been prepared in advance. In any event, the remaining notables who gathered in the Corn Hall that evening chose a committee most of whose ten members were advocates of the republic.[8]

The committee got to work immediately and promulgated several radical decisions the following day. It announced that state officials would have seventy-two hours in which to take an oath of loyalty to the Frankfurt constitution or be expelled from office. It called for the creation of a revolutionary army, a "people's guard" [Volkswehr], of all Palatine males from age eighteen to forty-five capable of bearing arms. To provide a corps of trained recruits, the committee asked the fathers of the province to prevail on their sons serving under the colors to go over to the people; to pay for weapons, it announced its

[7] Schneider, "Landesausschuß und provisorische Regierung," pp. 93–95; the reports of the LK and prokurator mentioned in the previous note; LAS J1 Nr. 105 ff. 187–97, 201–12; *NSZ*, 4 May 1849; *KnZ*, 5 May 1849; *NRhZ*, 6 May 1849.

[8] Besides the sources cited in the previous note, see LAS J1 Nr. 105 ff. 250–93, esp. ff. 258–59, 267–68.

intent to confiscate public moneys. A congress of officers of the Palatine civic guards, meeting on May 4, endorsed the decisions and called for the integration of the citizen militias into the revolutionary army. The Provincial Defense Committee announced its intent of approaching General Dufour, victorious commander of the radical troops in the Swiss Civil War of 1847, to act as commander in chief. To complete its series of revolutionary actions, on May 5 the Provincial Defense Committee issued an appeal to the province calling for the creation of similar committees in each of the thirty-one cantons of the Palatinate, to carry out its decrees. These committees were to be composed of the members of the cantonal committees of the Peoples' Association and the officers of the civic guard in the cantonal seat.[9]

These events in Kaiserslautern set a pattern for the Palatine revolution: Attempting to avoid the consequences of rash actions of the extreme left, more moderate members of the People's Associations, and even the constitutional monarchists, took the initiative themselves. But their actions, designed to pacify the population and steal the radicals' thunder, had the opposite effect. They stirred people up and allowed the more extreme element to press its demands, driving the uprising in an ever more militant direction. This pattern of events was in many ways similar to that occurring at the same time on the lower Rhine. In the Palatinate, though, the forces of order were weaker, and the whole political spectrum was shifted over to the left. The cycle of preemptive moderate action exploited by the radicals would be repeated several times over in the following two weeks, climaxing in the creation of a revolutionary regime.

THE RADICALIZATION OF THE PALATINE REVOLUTION

The ten days following the Kaiserslautern mass meeting were a period of rapid radicalization, proceeding on several different fronts. The meeting had done nothing to dampen the popular excitement prevailing at the end of April. Quite the opposite, its decision to set up a provincial defense committee and the latter's call for the arming of the people to enforce the Frankfurt constitution greatly heightened existing tensions. Civic guards met to swear an oath of allegiance to the Frankfurt constitution. In Neustadt a.d.W., the guardsmen were joined by all the adult males of the city, "burghers, day laborers and journeymen." Those not enrolled in the guard received sharpened scythes as weapons, so that they might be armed on taking the oath. Nearby, in Edenkoben, "young and old pressed onto the drill field [of the civic guard] and

<hr />

[9] Schneider, "Landesausschuß und Provisorische Regierung," p. 95 (not quite complete); Police Commissioner Kaiserslautern to RP, 3 May 1849, BHSTAM MInn Nr. 45531; LAS J1 Nr. 252 (alt) f. 567; LK Zweibrücken to RP, 3 May 1849; RP to Colonel von Xylander (Bavarian representative in Frankfurt), 4 May 1849; printed appeals of the defense committee, dated 5 May 1849, all in LAS J1 Nr. 1975.

demanded weapons. No one thought of their everyday occupations, the streets and taverns were constantly filled, everyone asked for the latest news; things happened so fast that no one could keep up with them.''[10]

Everywhere, money was gathered for the planned People's Guard, city and village councils voting appropriations, individuals contributing as well. If mayors or city councils were reluctant, as in Kandel, Pirmasens, and Lauterecken, activists of the People's Association led the crowd in forcing unwilling municipal officials to appropriate substantial sums. The books of the Provincial Defense Committee showed a total income for May 8–18 of 24,600 fl., almost all in the form of voluntary contributions, ranging from 2,400 fl. from the municipal treasuries of affluent Neustadt County to 13 French francs, contributed by the impoverished inhabitants of the border village of Sondernheim.[11]

The excitement spread into the countryside. On May 9, a member of the Dürkheim Cantonal Committee went to the nearby winegrowing village of Seebach, to administer the oath of loyalty to the Frankfurt constitution. He held a dagger aloft, and the vintners took the oath, amid tumultuous cheering and shouting. Trees of liberty were erected in several villages and small towns, especially of the western Palatinate, the largely drunken spectators cursing the government.[12]

Radicals were particularly active in these demonstrations, giving them a strongly republican tone. On May 6, members of the People's Associations of Bergzabern and the surrounding villages armed with muskets, pikes, and scythes, marched in a parade, behind a red flag. A mass meeting was then held on the marketplace of Bergzabern, the participants taking the oath to the Frankfurt constitution. The democratic monarchist Pastor Frantz of Ingenheim, tried to calm the crowd, but the one-time symbol of radical political opposition in the Palatinate, had been left behind by events. His denunciation of "illegal actions," and assertion that things had gone "too far" in Kaiserslautern, received just feeble applause, and a motion he proposed, calling for moderation, was voted down. The constitutive meeting of the Defense Committee in the

[10] Neustadt Police Commissioner to RP, 4 May 1849, BHSTAM MInn Nr. 45531; LAS J1 Nr. 205 ff. 417–30. Similarly, LAS J1 Nr. 205 ff. 232–34; or Gendarmerie District Command ZweibrÜcken to RP, 9 May 1849, LAS H1 Nr. 1975.

[11] LAS J1 Nr. 203 ff. 116–19, 121–22; LAS J1 Nr. 215 (alt) ff. 112–15; LAS J1 Nr. 243 (alt) ff. 55–56. Figures on contributions in LAS J1 Nr. 105 f. 469; and the reports on voluntary contributions, July 1849, BHSTAM KA Nr. B 771.

[12] LAS J1 Nr. 203 ff. 280–83 (Seebach). Similar actions by members of other cantonal committees: LAS J1 Nr. 235 f. 636; LAS J1 Nr. 215 (alt) ff. 121–24, 126, 132–37, 194–95; LAS J1 Nr. 147 f. 28; NSZ, 12 May 1849. Other rural disturbances: Gendarmerie Brigadier in Primasens to RP, 8 May 1849, BHSTAM MInn Nr. 45531; Gendarmerie Station Commander (Winnweiler) to RP, 9 May 1849, LAS H1 Nr. 1975; LK Frankenthal to RP, 4 May 1849; Controlbedienster Hammel (Bergazbern) to Königliches Hauptzollamt, 5 May 1849, both in BHSTAM MInn Nr. 45531; NSZ, 9 May 1849 (Homburg).

northwestern Canton Waldmohr was dominated by the chairman of the town's People's Association, who gave a strongly republican speech, culminating in the exclamation, "Death to the princes, a curse to the tyrants, let he who is with me swear."[13]

The high point of the agitation of the extreme left was the mass rally in Neustadt a.d.W. on May 6, 1849. Attendance estimates varied from five thousand to eight thousand, suggesting that the meeting was about the same size as the previous one in Kaiserslautern. In spite of the authorities' fears, the republic was not proclaimed on the spot, apparently because the Provincial Defense committee had reached an agreement with the Neustadt leftists. Nikolaus Schmitt of Kaiserslautern, one of the radical members of the committee, chaired the meeting. While the few speakers who called for moderation were shouted down and the many who spoke in favor of the republic, or the social-democratic republic, greeted with cheers, the rally broke up peacefully, calling on the defense committee to impose a progressive income tax, secede from the Bavarian monarchy and create the "rule of the people." Schmitt had the last word, concluding that the republic could not be "proclaimed" but had to be "won in struggle."[14]

Revolution in Rhine-Hessen

While the Palatinate was getting into an uproar, the democrats of neighboring Rhine-Hessen were acting in equally revolutionary fashion. They held mass meetings in Bingen, at the northern end of the province, on April 27, and in Alzey, to the southwest, on May 3. Although members of the constitutional monarchist Mainz Citizens' Association were present at both, and the meetings were officially in support of the Frankfurt constitution, the Rhine-Hessian leftists did not renounce their militant republicanism. Franz Zitz told the Bingen meeting that only "unity could bring victory over the princes," while Ludwig Bamberger, called on the spectators "at first to hold fast to the [monarchical] constitution of the *Reich* so that we can subsequently continue on to the republic." In Alzey, one Franz Haas said that all the "princes' palaces must be torn down. There can be just one palace in Germany; [one] with the inscription, 'Here resides the President of the Republic.' " Referring to the constitutional monarchists present, Haas said that the "moneybags" must

---

[13] LK Bergzabern to RP, 6 May 1849, BHSTAM MInn Nr. 45531; *NSZ*, 11 May 1849; LAS J1 Nr. 242 ff. 31–34; similarly, LAS J1 Nr. 245 f. 54. In Frankenthal, the crowd forced the city council to appoint radical democrats to the cantonal committee. LAS J1 Nr. 218 ff. 79–85, 121–26.

[14] LAS J1 Nr. 229 II (alt) f. 130; Police Commissioner Neustadt to LK Neustadt, 6 May 1849, BHSTAM MInn Nr. 45531; RP to MInn, 6 May 1849, LAS H1 Nr. 1975; *NRhZ*, 12 May 1849.

"give money" for the struggle, a demand also raised by Bamberger, although in more polite terms.[15]

In spite of their militant rhetoric, the leaders of the Rhine-Hessian leftists were intially at a loss for deeds to match their words. The grand duke of Hessen-Darmstadt was one of the twenty-eight German princes who had accepted the Frankfurt constitution, so their actions could not be directed against him. In any event, their real enemy was not the feeble Hessian authorities, but the Prussian army, firmly ensconced in the Mainz fortress. The disastrous attempt to throw it out by armed force a year previously was not an encouraging precedent for revolutionary action. People on the street in Mainz expected an uprising daily; Mainz democrats gathered weapons, molded bullets, manufactured cartridges; meetings at the editorial offices of the *Mainzer Zeitung* dealt with insurrection rather than lead articles; but no one could see how a successful uprising might be accomplished.[16]

The news from the Palatinate opened up a whole new range of possibilities for the democrats of Rhine-Hessen, and the provincial congress of democratic clubs, held in Oppenheim on May 6, 1849, like the meetings in Cologne that same day, was primarily concerned with planning an insurrection. Unlike the Cologne meetings, with their separation of innocuous public sessions and secret revolutionary planning, the Rhine-Hessian democrats set the regular agenda aside and discussed measures of armed resistance, calling on all town and village councils to appropriate money for weapons. August Vollmer of Oppenheim told the delegates, "It is time to come to the help of our Bavarian [that is, Palatine] brothers," and called for "the thunder of cannons on the rule of the princes and the damned priests [Fürsten- und Pfaffenwirtschaft]." At the mass rally following the meeting, Mainz democrat Philipp Wittmann gave a speech notable for its violent call for a second revolution, couched in a metaphor understandable to peasants who engaged in fruit growing: "The previous year we shook the princely caterpillars off the tree of liberty, but failed to trample them. Now they have crept up it again; this time we must make good what we neglected. . . . Smash their skulls in."[17]

The call to action was not long in coming: on the night of May 9, couriers set out from Mainz, and the following two days saw the revolutionary mobilization of the entire province. Two hundred democrats and gymnasts from the cantonal town of Oberingelheim and five nearby villages formed an insurgent

[15] *Vhdl*, pt. 1, pp. 93–95; *MZ*, 1 May 1849; *KnZ*, 3 May 1849 (Außerordentliche Beilage); BAF FN 7 Anhang 4 Gagern f. 96. The one sign of compromise with the constitutional monarchists was the Bingen meeting's voting down a proposal that the Badenese revolutionary Friedrich Hecker be named Prime Minister of the Provisional Central Power.

[16] Bamberger, "Erlebnisse aus der Pfälzer Erhebung," 3: 65–70; cf. "Die Volksversammlung in Bingen," *Der Demokrat*, 3 May 1849.

[17] *Vhdl*, pt. 1, pp. 95–98 (for an example of such preparation, ibid., pt. 2, pp. 83–84); *MZ*, 12 May 1849.

column. In Elscheim, the inhabitants proclaimed the republic and painted all the road signs red. The gymnasts of Budenheim met and mobilized all the young men of the village, dragging from their houses those reluctant to go. Their leader, farmer Heinrich Besant, wearing a red sash and red armband, drew them up threateningly in front of the village hall and demanded that the mayor and village council provide weapons and money. Led by a member of the Democratic Club and a German Catholic, a crowd surrounded the parish priest in the Mainz suburb of Bretzenheim, demanding his rifle. The priest refused, claiming that condoning violence was inappropriate for the servant of a religion of peace. After some pointed replies about how French and Spanish clergy bore arms for counterrevolutionary purposes, and how he would no doubt surrender his rifle if the princes called on him to do so, he found it prudent to turn over the weapon.[18]

There were turbulent scenes in Worms and Oppenheim, as democrats demanded that the civic guards be mobilized and that the municipal authorities provide money and ammunition for the uprising, which the latter eventually agreed to do. City council meetings in Worms had to be postponed because the council chambers were being used to manufacture cartridges and forge bullets. The Worms town fathers, many constitutional monarchists among them, did insist on a proclamation that the movement was exclusively in support of the Frankfurt constitution, which did not stop some of the insurgents from marching behind a red flag and wearing red ribbons in their hats.[19]

Mainz democrats made plans to leave the fortress city and place themselves at the head of the insurrection. A group of forty craftsmen from the Workers' Association went on ahead to the town of Wörrstadt on the evening of May 9, where they erected a cooperative armaments workshop, to manufacture weapons in the fight for the republic and national unity. The following day, several hundred armed gymnasts and mostly unarmed members of the Workers' Association prepared to march, under the direction of prominent leftists. To their leaders' dismay, they were joined by one hundred unorganized and disorderly proletarians, dock laborers and watermen, quite a different group from the disciplined craftsmen in the Workers' Association. Together, democrats, craftsmen, and laborers marched to Wörrstadt, rendezvousing with the insurgents from the northern part of the province.[20]

On May 10–11 two insurgent columns left Rhine-Hessen for the Palatinate on the invitation of the Provincial Defense Committee. A column of 1,000–1,500 men from Wörrstadt, under the command of Mainz democrats Franz Zitz and Ludwig Bamberger, headed southwest to take up positions in the

[18] BAF FN 7 Anhang 4 Gagern f. 95; *Vhdl*, pt. 2, pp. 89–107, 123, 337; similarly, ibid., pp. 79, 86.

[19] *Vhdl*, pt. 2, pp. 73–79, 191–209; LAS J1 Nr. 219 ff. 1012–19.

[20] *KnZ*, 13 May 1849 (Zweite Ausgabe); *Vhdl*, pt. 2, pp. 118–19; Bamberger, "Erlebnisse aus der Pfälzer Erhebung" 3:73–83.

Alsenz Valley on the border with Prussia. A second column of 500–1,000 men, mostly from the civic guard of Worms, but also including volunteers armed with sharpened scythes, commanded by the colonel of the Worms civic guard, wine merchant Ludwig Blenker, marched south along the Rhine toward the Bavarian border fortress at Ludwigshafen. The presence of these armed insurgents would heighten the revolutionary atmosphere and increase the strength of the revolutionary element in the Palatinate still further.[21]

The Collapse of the Forces of Order

The civilian and military authorities in the Palatinate watched the revolutionization of their province with a mixture of dismay at the Munich government's policy, which encouraged the trend, and frustration with their own inability to do anything about it. All officials were painfully aware of the Provincial Defense Committee's demand that they take the oath of allegiance to the Frankfurt constitution or be dismissed. This threat was most keenly felt by the tax collectors, customs agents, and foresters, placing them in an irresolvable dilemma. If they took the oath, defying their king, they were liable to be dismissed from their posts. If they refused, it would be "open season" on them; nothing could stop the people, stirred up by the democrats, from assaulting them and driving them off.[22]

Less exposed state servants, such as clerks, messengers, and the higher judicial and administrative officials, were not quite so fearful, but they still felt the pressure of the situation. While usually refusing to take the oath, they showed little willingness to stand up for government policy. Some bureaucrats made contributions to the People's Guard; groups of officials in Annweiler, Landau, Homburg, Zweibrücken, and Kaiserslautern met and issued strongly worded addresses to the king, demanding that he accept the Frankfurt constitution and thus restore order to the province. One such appeal was signed by all the justices of the provincial high court in Zweibrücken. Although the actions of the Provincial Defense Committee certainly met the legal criteria for the crimes of incitement to insurrection or even of high treason, the superior procurator in Zweibrücken refused to open proceedings against its members, since such a step would only serve as a pretext for a "long premeditated excess by the red republicans."[23]

---

[21] Besides the sources cited in the two previous notes, see LAS J1 Nr. 105 f. 636; LAS J1 Nr. 108 ff. 99–100; LAS J1 Nr. 219 f. 1017; "Präsenz-Liste der Mannschaft des Rheinhessischen Freischärler-Bataillons vom 16. Mai bis 14 Juni 1849,—Haupt-Quartier Kirchheimbolanden" (fly sheet, copy in Stadtbibliothek Mainz, sig. m: 4°/1558).

[22] Kgl. Forstamt Kaiserslautern to RP, 4 May 1849, LAS H1 Nr. 1975; LK Kaiserslautern to RP, 5 May 1849; reports of customs officials in Bergzabern and Neuburg, 5 May 1849, all in BHSTAM MInn Nr. 45531.

[23] LK Zweibrücken to RP, 8 May 1849; LK Kaiserslautern to RP, 8 May 1849; General-Staats-

The 188 gendarmes scattered across the province were of no use in preserving order; any serious step by the authorities would require the backing of the army. Officially, there were about 6,500 soldiers stationed in the province, a large proportion of whom, following Bavarian military policy, were on furlough, rather than with their units. They were all recalled to active service at the end of April, and two companies, which had been sent to Frankfurt after the September crisis to guard the National Assembly, were ordered back to their stations in the Palatinate.[24]

These should have been enough to restore order handily against at best half-armed insurgents, but some three-fourths of the troops were Palatine natives. Under heavy pressure from the civilian population, they showed increasingly less inclination to obey orders. Whole villages refused to let their furloughed soldiers return to their units. Other soldiers trying to report back were held up by the civic guard in Neustadt a.d.W., Bad Dürkheim, and Kaiserslautern. The Bavarian insignia was cut off their caps, to be replaced with tricolor or red ribbons. The soldiers were then told to go home or to enlist in the People's Guard.[25]

The two companies recalled from Frankfurt were particularly vulnerable. Even while stationed there, they had received letters from relatives at home imploring them not to fight for the king. When their train stopped in Darmstadt on the way back to the Palatinate, democrats placed subversive leaflets in the railroad cars. As they marched through Mannheim towards the bridge over the Rhine, crowds in this strongly left-wing Badenese city called out to them, "Stand by the people; don't shoot on your brothers." Stationed in Speyer, the citizens with whom they were quartered offered similar sentiments, and when the city's civic guard on May 8 took an oath to defend the Frankfurt constitution "with their fortunes and their lives" [mit Gut und Blut] the soldiers swore along with them.[26]

Although they tried, the officers could not keep their men away from the civilians. Soldiers in the fortress of Landau, where nearly half the troops in the province were stationed, "were propagandized hourly by the democratic party." Officers tore down placards calling on the soldiers to desert, but the democrats put them right back up with impunity. The radical villagers of neighboring Nussdorf invited the soldiers to drink the locally grown wine and

Prokurator (Zweibrücken) to RP, 8 May 1849, all in LAS H1 Nr. 1975; LAS J1 Nr. 104 ff. 10–11, 16–21; Kolb, *Lebenserinnerungen*, pp. 202–04. According to Kolb, Provincial Governor Alwens gave thirty fl. for the People's Guard.

[24] Calliess, *Militär in der Krise*, pp. 53–55, 183 n.178; MInn to King, 30 Apr. 1849, BHSTAM MInn Nr. 45531.

[25] Fortress Commandant Germersheim to Ministry of War, 7 May 1849; Oberst Bender to König. Brigade-Commando, 11 May 1849, both in BHSTAM KA A XXI Nr. 260; LC Homburg to RP, 11 May 1849, LAS H1 Nr. 1975; LAS H3 Nr. 154c ff. 7–9; LAS J1 Nr. 203 ff. 255–70.

[26] Hauptmann Ernst Keim to König. 2te Armee Corp Commando, 13 May 1849, BHSTAM KA A XXI Nr. 260.

talk about fighting for the people; when, on the other hand, officers came riding by, the vintners shouted, "You won't ride much longer; in a week we'll be the masters!" Soldiers openly refused orders, instead drinking in the off-limits "English Garden," whose owner was an "arch-republican." There, and in other such establishments, the inebriated warriors issued cheers to the red republic. When officers tried to inform them of their military duties, they replied, "Now things are different," or "I won't let myself be used against my countrymen."[27]

Under these circumstances, the question for the authorities was not whether the army could suppress the insurrection, but whether it would join it. This was precisely what the troops stationed in Ludwigshafen did, when the insurgent column from Worms appeared on the morning of May 11. Reinforcements sent from Speyer (the companies previously stationed in Frankfurt) also joined the insurgency, as did a steamboat load full of soldiers sent from trans-Rhenan Würzburg, the civilian crew of the steamboat taking service with the Provincial Defense Committee as well. Over the next several days a smaller detachment in Zweibrücken went over to the revolutionary forces, as did the soldiers stationed in Speyer, leaving the provincial government without any armed protection, at the mercy of the Cantonal Defense Committee.[28]

A steady stream of desertions so weakened the garrison in Landau that its commandant had his hands full keeping discipline and manning the fortress with his remaining troops, leaving none available to fight the insurrection. The only even partially reliable military force in the entire province were the 1,800 soldiers stationed in the fortress of Germersheim, on the Rhine near the French border, most of whom were natives of trans-Rhenan Bavaria. They broke up a mass meeting, held by the democrats in the fortress city on May 6, 1849, cheering King Max and whacking the leftists with their swords. Their commander, evidently convinced that they would not fight so well against armed opposition, appealed to Munich for reinforcements, which he felt were absolutely necessary if the province was to be saved for the Bavarian monarchy.[29]

The Germersheim fortress commandant was not alone in asking for reinforcements, his pleas repeated, in much more desperate tones, by his opposite number in Landau and by the provincial governor. Munich, however, had no troops to send. Franconia and Swabia, that is, the post-1800 possessions of the Bavarian state east of the Rhine, were, at the beginning of May 1849, in a state of uproar little short of that in the Palatinate. Franconian and Swabian soldiers refused to obey orders and were about to go over to the democrats.

---

[27] Fortress Commandant Landau to Ministry of War, 6–8, 12 May 1849, BHSTAM KA A XXI Nr. 260.

[28] Calliess, *Militär in der Krise*, pp. 179–82; LAS J1 Nr. 277 (alt) ff. 311–15; declaration of the Speyer Cantonal Defense Committee, 11 May 1849, LAS H1 Nr. 1975.

[29] Calliess, *Militär in der Krise*, pp. 184–86; Fortress Commandant Germersheim to Ministry of War, 7 May 1849, BHSTAM KA A XXI Nr. 260.

The reliable, loyalist regiments from Old Bavaria were fully occupied in brawling with the Swabian and Franconian troops and in trying to keep order in the kingdom's trans-Rhenan provinces. Munich statesmen's dreams of a Greater Bavaria seemed about to be replaced by their nightmare opposite: the secession of all of Bavaria's nineteenth-century acquisitions and the reduction of the monarchy to its Alpine, old regime core.[30]

Consequently, all that the Bavarian government could tell its hard-pressed officials in the Palatinate was to act firmly on their own, to arrest the members of the Provincial Defense Committee, and, in general, to proceed boldly and decisively against the troublemakers. The procurator in Landau had a sharp reply to such unrealistic demands. Munich, he wrote, seemed to view events in its Rhenish province as if they were a

> local putsch and the officials of the Palatinate both willing and able to suppress it with their bare hands—while soldiers go over almost by the company [to the insurrection] in Kaiserslautern and Neustadt, German ribbons rather than the royal insignia on their helmets, while in all the villages weapons are manufactured and bullets forged. Through all this one could reply to the government as once was said to the unfortunate Charles X: "C'est n'est plus une révolte, c'est une révolution!"[31]

The Intervention of the Provisional Central Power

While the unexpected election of the Provincial Defense Committee had allowed the extreme left to seize the initiative, more moderate elements in Palatine politics immediately attempted to regain control of the situation by calling on the Provisionial Central Power for assistance. This effort, actually two overlapping and contradictory plans, involved an attempt to placate public opinion and preempt the radicals' action, just as had been tried with the calling of the Kaiserslautern mass meeting. It accomplished, just as had happened in Kaiserslautern, the opposite of what was intended, radicalizing public opinion and pushing the movement in an even more revolutionary direction.

The main attempt stemmed from the more moderate element in the leadership of the People's Association. G. F. Kolb of Speyer, a major figure in the effort, described the members of the Provincial Defense Committee as "all unquestionably honorable, principled men, who passionately loved freedom." But they were also given to "completely imaginary hopes," failing to realize that the whole revolutionary enterprise had no means by which it could succeed, and that it would only be a provocation, playing into the hands of

[30] Calliess, *Militär in der Krise*, pp. 173–75; RP to MInn, 3 May 1849, LAS H1 Nr. 1975; MInn to RP, 6 May 1849, BHSTAM MInn Nr. 45531; Fortress Commandant Landau to Ministry of War, 6–7 May 1849, BHSTAM KA A XXI Nr. 260.

[31] Procurator in Landau to General State Procurator, 13 May 1849, LAS H1 Nr. 1975. Munich's orders, MInn to RP, 8 May 1849, ibid.

"reactionaries." To save the situation, steps had to be taken to ensure a "legalization of what had happened."

Acting on behalf of their moderate fellow provincials, several Palatine deputies to the Frankfurt National Assembly and to the Bavarian parliament approached Heinrich von Gagern, since December 1848 prime minister of the Provisional Central Power. On May 3–4, 1849, they asked him to send a commissioner of the Reich to the Palatinate, with instructions to calm things down and divert the struggle for the validity of the Frankfurt constitution into legal, noninsurrectionary channels. Any such representative would have to be, they insisted, a man of the left, since the radicals of the Provincial Defense Committee would only listen to a leftist. Gagern agreed and appointed as commissioner a center-left deputy to the Frankfurt Assembly, the Saxon attorney Bernhard Eisenstuck. Eisenstuck set out on his mission immediately, arriving in Speyer in the early morning hours of May 6.[32]

Just as the decision was being taken to send a commissioner, on May 4, 1849, the provincial governor and the commanding military authorities in Speyer and Landau were also turning to the Provisional Central Power. Fearful of a republican putsch, skeptical about the loyalty of the Palatine soldiers, and doubtful about receiving reinforcements from trans-Rhenan Bavaria in time, they requested that "troops of the Reich" be sent to reinforce the increasingly chaotic and undisciplined Landau garrison. Gagern and his minister of war agreed and requisitioned troops protecting the Frankfurt Assembly, Badenese dragoons, and, disastrously, Prussian infantry. These soldiers, sent without Commissioner Eisenstuck's knowledge and against his explicit request, arrived in the Palatinate forty-eight hours after he did, setting the stage for a dramatic confrontation.[33]

Before their arrival, Eisenstuck had not been idle. He had conferred with Provincial Governor Alwens on the morning of May 6, and then, accompanied by the Frankfurt deputies G. F. Kolb and August Culmann, two of the advocates of his appointment, set out for Neustadt to speak at the radical mass meeting there. His calls for moderation were apparently not well received, and the commissioner received some firsthand knowledge not only of the strength and anger of Palatine radical republicanism, but also of the attempts of members of the Provincial Defense Committee to calm and accommodate it. That evening he dashed off to Landau to confer with Major General von Jeetze, the fortress commandant, and, without breaking stride, went the next day to Kaiserslautern to meet the Provincial Defense Committee. There he made a fa-

---

[32] Kolb, *Lebenserinnerungen*, pp. 197–201; LAS J1 Nr. 105 ff. 670–73, 684–91; LK Neustadt to RP, 7 May 1849, BHSTAM MInn Nr. 45531. Eisenstuck's mission has been described many times in the literature, but, as will be seen below, almost invariably incorrectly, indeed, as the complete opposite of what it actually was.

[33] Fortress Commandant Landau to Ministry of War, 6 May 1849, BHSTAM KA A XXI Nr. 260; RP to MInn, 4 May 1849, LAS H1 Nr. 1975; BAF DB 54 Nr. 44 ff. 67–78.

mous and notorious decision, issuing a proclamation legalizing the committee in the name of the Provisional Central Power.[34]

Some historians have condemned this proclamation as an act of radical extremism, by which Commissioner Eisenstuck far exceeded his authority and contravened the terms of his mission, in doing so opening the floodgates to violent revolutionary action in a province whose inhabitants had a strong respect for legality and only wanted to see the Frankfurt constitution enforced. Others have praised the commissioner's initiative as the one single instance during the whole *Reichsverfassungskampagne* when the Frankfurt National Assembly, or at least a member of it, actually took a step to encourage the popular movement in support of that very assembly. Both interpretations, and virtually all historians who have studied the matter, agree that Eisenstuck was acting in revolutionary fashion when he legitimized the Provincial Defense Committee; in reality, his proclamation was designed to stop a revolution, not to encourage one.[35]

Justifying his actions to Prime Minster Gagern and Provincial Governor Alwens, Eisenstuck explained that the legitimation of the Provincial Defense Committee by the Provisional Central Power was the only way "to ensure the preservation of order." Munich, by refusing to accept the Frankfurt constitution, had created a situation that could "easily endanger general security and welfare," if the leadership of the movement for the constitution was "placed in the hands of those who do not possess the confidence of the province." In other words, to avoid the possibility of the Neustadt radicals' gaining control of the movement and using it to obtain the red republic—which, after the mass meeting there, seemed to the commissioner a real danger—he turned to the Provincial Defense Committee as the only force which could stop them.[36]

Eisenstuck took this action only after consulting with the Palatine deputies (who probably suggested it to him in the first place) and with Provincial Governor Alwens, obtaining the latter's tacit consent. The legitimation of the

---

[34] See sources cited in note 14; BAF DB 54 Nr. 44 ff. 67–68, 82–86; Gendarmerie Corps der Pfalz to König. Corps Commando, 6 May 1849; Commissioner Eisenstuck to RP Alwens, 7 May 1849, both in BHSTAM MInn Nr. 45531; Fortress Commandant Landau to Minister of War, 8 May 1849, BHSTAM KA A XXI Nr. 260. A copy of Eisenstuck's proclamation is in LAS H1 Nr. 1975.

[35] Examples of the first interpretation are Fleischmann, *Geschichte des Pfälzischen Aufstandes*, pp. 163–65; *Handbuch der Bayerischen Geschichte* 4/1:235; Renner, "Die pfälzische Bewegung," pp. 142–47. Examples of the second interpretation are Valentin, *Geschichte der Deutschen Revolution* 2:494–95; Siemann, *Die deutsche Revolution*, p. 214; Klessmann, "Zur Sozialgeschichte der Reichsverfassungskampagne," pp. 307, 337. One of the few exceptions to the view that the proclamation was a revolutionary act is the excellent account in Schwarzwälder, "Die Ursachen der Reichsverfassungskampagne," pp. 67–69. Schneider, "Landesausschuß und Provisorische Regierung," pp. 96–97, is vague on this point.

[36] BAF DB 54 Nr. 44 ff. 67–68, 80–82 104–07; RP to MInn, 9 May 1849, LAS H1 Nr. 1975; Eisenstuck to Alwens, 7 May 1849, BHSTAM MInn Nr. 45531.

Provincial Defense Committee, far from undermining the authority of the Bavarian officials, actually helped sustain it, since the commissioner's proclamation empowered the committee to take all actions necessary to defend the Frankfurt constitution "in so far as they do not interfere with the perogatives of the legally existing provincial authorities [in so weit sie nicht in die Befugnisse der zu Recht bestehenden Landesbehörden eingreifen]." The decree thus nullified the committee's threats to confiscate public money, or dismiss officials who refused to take the oath to the constitution.[37]

Quite understanding these implications, the Neustadt leftists had harsh words for the "Gagern-Eisenstuck doctrine of using different excuses to hold down any uprising by diplomacy until the people become annoyed and indifferent. . . ." State officials in the Palatinate, on the other hand, were grateful to the commissioner for protecting them from the crowd. Even Heinrich von Gagern, who in no way approved of Eisenstuck's legitimation of the Provincial Defense Committee, told the Bavarian representative to the Provisional Central Power that the commissioner's actions were devoted to moderating and calming tendencies toward violent action rather than to encouraging them.[38]

The commissioner's policy was put to the test on May 8, by the news of the arrival of Prussian troops. The presence in the province of soldiers of a monarch who did not support the Frankfurt constitution—who, indeed, was leading the action against it—raised the existing state of excitement to a fever pitch. Throughout the province, civic guards were called out to oppose the invaders. They occupied or made unusable railroads, bridges, roads, and border crossings. Thousands of men, armed with rifles, but also with sharpened scythes, pitchforks, and other agricultural implements, marched into Neustadt to join the fight. Democrats of the tiny cantonal town Dahn, nestled in the mountains on the French border, held a mass meeting calling on the people to take up arms and fight the Prussians.[39]

---

[37] The provincial governor's consent to these measures is mentioned in Eisenstuck to Alwens, 7 May 1849, BHSTAM MInn Nr. 45531, and in his report of 8 May to Heinrich von Gagern, BAF DB 54 Nr. 44 ff. 104–107. In his report to the MInn of 8 May 1849, Alwens claimed to be dismayed by Eisenstuck's legitimation of the defense committee, but by the following day he was endorsing it (both reports in LAS H1 Nr. 1975). Cf. also Kolb, *Lebenserinnerungen*, pp. 198–201.

[38] Neustadt radicals according to *Der Pfälzer Volksmann*, 20 May 1849, copy in LAS J1 Nr. 229 I (alt) f. 133; similar opinions of the radicals of Speyer, *Die Trompete von Speyer*, 12 May 1849, LAS J1 Nr. 252 II/1–2 (alt). Attitudes of provincial officials, LAS J1 Nr. 105 ff. 177–81, 201–12; those of von Gagern, Heinrich von Gagern, Reichsministerium, to König. Baierischen Herrn Bevollmächtigen von Xylander, 10 May 1849, BAF DB 54 Nr. 44.

[39] RP to MInn, 8–9 May 1849; LK Kaiserslautern to RP, 8 May 1849; König. Bau-Inspektor Zweibrücken to RP, 11 May 1849; LK Homburg to RP, 11 May 1849, all in LAS H1 Nr. 1975; LAS H3 Nr. 154c ff. 7–9; LK Neustadt to RP, 7 May 1849, BHSTAM MInn Nr. 45531; Depot Kommando Zweibrücken to Brigade Kommando in der Pfalz, 9 May 1849; Oberleutnant Jakob Bar (Ludwigshafen) to Festungs-Commando Landau 11 May 1849, both in BHSTAM KA A XXI

An armed clash seemed inevitable, and Commissioner Eisenstuck moved with speed and energy to avoid an incipient civil war. He rushed to Landau and requested that the fortress commandant order the Prussian troops (but not the Badenese, since their government recognized the Frankfurt constitution) out of the Palatinate. Major General von Jeetze, frankly afraid that his own men would shoot at the soldiers sent to "reinforce" them, but equally fearful of losing face by going back on his own actions, offered instead to send one of his officers to the Prussian troops with Eisenstuck's request they retreat, in the name of the Provisional Central Power. Eisenstuck accepted the offer, and the Prussians acceded to his request and left the province.[40]

These actions of a major general in the Bavarian army, above any suspicions of leftist sympathies, are the best proof imaginable of the conciliatory nature of Eisenstuck's mission. The government in Munich and its representative to the Provisional Central Power, however, could only see the commissioner's actions as revolutionary subversion (their interpretation being seconded by most historians) and demanded that he be recalled. The Provisional Central Power granted the request, and Eisenstuck's mission was terminated, just after he had prevented serious bloodshed. With his recall, the whole conciliatory aspect of his mission vanished, leaving behind an angered and embittered populace, a strengthened and legitimized Provincial Defense Committee, and an even more weakened Bavarian officialdom. Once again, actions aimed at calming the population and preventing its radicalization had had the opposite effect.[41]

Following Eisenstuck's recall, the Bavarian officials in the Palatinate were completely powerless, lacking any means of enforcing their authority or influencing events. They received no help from the central government in Munich, which informed the provincial authorities that if they could not suppress the insurrection, all state officials were to retreat to the fortress of Germersheim and await armed rescue. Since no Bavarian soldiers were available for that purpose, Munich instructed its representative to the Provisional Central Power to ask that the Central Power requisition troops to restore order in the province. If it could or would not send troops, he was to direct such a request to the provincial governor of the Prussian Rhine Province in Koblenz. It is surely an apt measure of the desperation of the Bavarian government that it was ready to turn to the Prussians to preserve its rule in the Palatinate.[42]

Nr. 260; LAS J1 Nr. 195 ff. 484–88; LAS J1 Nr. 200 ff. 55–58; LAS J1 Nr. 205 ff. 228–35; LAS J1 Nr. 247 ff. 374–78; LAS J1 Nr. 263 ff. 116–20; LAS J1 Nr. 228 (alt) ff. 323–38.

[40] BAF DB 54 Nr. 44 ff. 104–07; Fortress Commandant Landau to Ministry of War, 8 May 1849, BHSTAM KA A XXI Nr. 260; LAS J1 Nr. 108 ff. 309–14; cf. Calliess, *Militär in der Krise*, pp. 175–78.

[41] BAF DB 54 Nr. 44 ff. 95, 102–03; Staats Ministerium to Oberst von Xylander, 10 May 1849, LAS H1 Nr. 1975.

[42] MInn to RP, 8 May 1849; Staats Ministerium to Oberst von Xylander (Bavarian representative to the Provisional Central Power), 10 May 1849 (copy), both in LAS H1 Nr. 1975.

From Dual Power to a Revolutionary Regime

Referring to the Provincial Defense Committee, the provincial governor reported to the interior minister on May 8 that a "second power" existed in the Palatinate besides the Bavarian state authorities, thus anticipating by some decades Leon Trotsky's theory that the creation of a system of dual power characterizes the emergence of a revolutionary situation. The provincial governor's further reports showed that he also anticipated the next step in Trotsky's theory, namely, that the two powers could not coexist; if the state officials could not repress the institutions of revolutionary authority, they would be overthrown by them. This was precisely what happened in the week between the recall of Commissioner Eisenstuck and the proclamation of a provisional government.[43]

Kaiserslautern was not St. Petersburg, and the Palatine revolution showed a characteristically German twist on Trotsky's argument; the Palatine revolutionaries overthrew the Bavarian government out of fear of Prussia. From the moment of the proclamation of the Provincial Defense Committee, it had been threatened by Prussian intervention, a fear reinforced by (true) reports of the massing of soldiers in Kreuznach, at the southern end of the Prussian Rhine Province. The Provincial Defense Committee had requested of Commissioner Eisenstuck that troops from the smaller German states, which had endorsed the Frankfurt constitution, be sent to the Palatinate to protect it from the Prussians, but his recall cut short that prospect, not a very likely one in any event. Consequently, the committee was forced to raise, outfit, and pay for an army, tasks requiring compulsory measures, which only a government could carry out.[44]

The Palatine democrats thus found themselves with a problem similar to the one their conterparts in the Wuppertal and Bergisches Land were facing at the very same time. Initially successful at defying state authority, the leaders of the insurrection saw coming a powerful armed counterstroke on the part of the forces of order, and were faced with the choice of giving up and suffering whatever repressive measures the state authorities would bring to bear or going on to more drastic, revolutionary measures. Just as the debate over which course to take raged in the Elberfeld Committee of Safety, so it did in the Palatinate.

The vehicle for the debate was the election of the cantonal representatives, a sort of miniparliament for the Provincial Defense Committee, foreseen in its proclamation of May 5, and actually summoned on May 13, to meet in Kaiserslautern four days later. Everyone understood that the committee desired

---

[43] RP to MInn, 8, 10, 12 May 1849, LAS H1 Nr. 1975; Leon Trotsky, *The History of the Russian Revolution*, trans. Max Eastman, 3 vols. in 1 (Ann Arbor: University of Michigan Press, 1964), 1:206–15.

[44] BAF DB 54 Nr. 44 ff. 104–107; RP to MInn, 23 May 1849, LAS H1 Nr. 1975.

the representatives' endorsement for turning itself into a provisional government, with the power to raise money by taxation and an army by conscription. Debate on this issue dominated the cantonal representatives' elections, which were held in almost every canton of the province, although in different forms: sometimes in a public meeting held in the cantonal town, sometimes by secret ballot in every village.[45]

Convinced that the radicals would find a way to proclaim a provisional government, no matter how the elections of the cantonal representatives turned out, August Culmann, one of the Palatine deputies to the National Assembly, and also one of the prime movers behind the appointment of Commissioner Eisenstuck, attempted to repeat his maneuver. He rushed back to Frankfurt and implored Heinrich von Gagern on May 15 to forestall the radical action by appointing a provisional government in the name of the Provisional Central Power and naming only moderates as its members—something Eisenstuck seems to have had in mind before his recall. Gagern himself had been toying with such an idea, but by May 15 he was no longer in a position to do anything about it. His mild, nonviolent support of the Frankfurt constitution was too radical for the imperial regent, who had forced the Hessian constitutional monarchist to resign on May 10 and replaced his ministry, a week later, with a conservative one, appointed to liquidate the Provisional Central Power and the National Assembly.[46]

This second moderate attempt at outside intervention having failed, the elections for cantonal representatives were fought between those who wanted to preserve the Provincial Defense Committee in its existing form and those who wished to turn it into a provisional government. In effect, the voters were asked to choose between moderate and "exalted" democrats, and the moderates were the elections' clear winners, most of the representatives meeting in Kaiserslautern opposing the idea of a provisional governmenmt. However, the radical members of the Provincial Defense Committee were determined to carry through with their plans and found ways to induce the representatives to change their mind.[47]

The Provincial Defense Committee squeezed the cantonal representatives politically from both sides. On the one hand, it presented itself as a bulwark

[45] For an excellent brief account of the elections of the cantonal representatives and the creation of the provisional government, see Schneider, "Landesausschuß und Provisorische Regierung," pp. 97–103.

[46] LAS J1 Nr. 105 ff. 549–84, 631–32, 670–73; BAF DB 54 Nr. 44 ff. 67–68; Botzenhart, *Deutscher Parlamentarismus*, pp. 700–706.

[47] On the results of the cantonal elections and the victory, in most places, of moderates (admittedly, frequently with low turnouts), see LAS J1 Nr. 195 ff. 111–13; LAS J1 Nr. 205 ff. 228–35, 417–30; LAS J1 Nr. 235 f. 598; LAS J1 Nr. 203 ff. 395–99; LAS J1 Nr. 267 ff. 157–66; and esp. LAS J1 Nr. 106 I ff. 159–62.

against the left, Martin Reichard telling several representatives that the Bavarian officials lacked all authority and that the Palatinate was threatened by anarchy. If a provisional government were not formed, he continued, the movement would pass into even more radical hands—an obvious reference to the Neustadt communists. At the same time, the committee also pressured the cantonal representatives against acting too conservatively, refusing their request to meet behind closed doors, requiring them to debate the issue publicly in the Corn Hall, before an audience of Kaiserslautern radicals. The spectators in the gallery called for a provisional government and shouted at the cantonal representatives who spoke against it, "Pfui, down with the traitors, down with the moneybags," scenes reminiscent, on a miniature scale, of Jacobin intimidation of the deputies to the Convention, during the French Revolution.

The radicals also had a cogent argument on their side, namely the impossibility of going back and the lack of any way to continue the movement without taking stronger measures. Since the Bavarian government showed no signs of giving in to the Palatines' demands, how could it be forced to do so without more militant action? What would happen to the soldiers who had deserted from the army and gone over to the People's Guard, if the movement were abandoned? The moderates had no answer to these questions (not that the spectators would have let them express them if they had) or to the demand for a provisional government. All they could propose was to send one final ultimatum to Munich before taking any action, not a very convincing alternative. Many of the representatives previously opposing a provisional government were convinced or intimidated into supporting it, and they endorsed its creation by a vote of fifteen to thirteen, with two representatives absent and one arriving too late to vote. Even the defeated minority accepted the result, and stayed to vote for the members of the provisional government. They gave it a moderate cast by electing just one radical from the Provincial Defense Committee, Martin Reichard of Speyer, but three Palatine deputies to Frankfurt associated with the moderate democrats, August Culmann, Friedrich Schüler, and G. F. Kolb. The fifth member, Philipp Hepp of Neustadt a.d.W., a veteran of the Hambach Festival, stood politically between the moderates and the radicals. The representatives voted down three radicals, including Nikolaus Schmitt of Kaiserslautern, the leading Palatine republican, just naming these men substitutes.[48]

The Palatinate was now under the control of a revolutionary government, which would take drastic steps to prepare for war. Yet the more moderate elements among the cantonal representatives, in the People's Associations, and on the cantonal committees had not been purged or swept aside, but had been incorporated into the structure of the revolutionary regime. The regime

[48] LAS J1 Nr. 106 I ff. 96–162; Schneider, "Landesauschuß und Provisorische Regierung," pp. 99–103 (with some inaccuracies); LAS J1 Nr. 228 (alt) f. 61.

was, from its very beginnings, the result of a tacit compromise between moderate and radical democrats, and this initial condition continued through the entire month of its rule.

REVOLUTIONARY DIPLOMACY

While it may have been an honor, as the Provisional Government insisted, for the Palatinate to have taken on the "calling . . . of liberating Germany from its oppressors," it was also a heavy burden for a province of six hundred thousand in a nation of thirty-two million, especially as the shadow of a Prussian invasion lay over the revolutionary regime from the moment of its inception. If the Provisional Government were to survive, it would need allies. It searched diligently for help, but found little available.[49]

The Rhine-Hessian radicals were the best and closest friends of the Palatine revolution. The two insurgent corps that had marched into the Palatinate on May 10–11 placed themselves at the disposal of first the Provincial Defense Committee and then the Provisional Government, remaining on duty for the following six weeks, until the Prussian invasion. Zitz's and Bamberger's men in the Alsenz Valley, well organized and disciplined, possessing their own workshops for shoe, clothing, and weapons repair and manufacture in their headquarters, the county town, Kirchheimbolanden, were able to maintain themselves reasonably well over that long interval. Blenker's detachment in Ludwigshafen, on the other hand, fell into ever-greater chaos and disorder, reflecting the talents of its leader for inspiration but not organization.

No one had expected such a long campaign, and the frustrations of the Rhine-Hessians grew daily, as they found themselves involved in establishing order for the Provisional Government rather than fighting the enemies of the nation. Their irritation increased when the pay promised them by the initial invitation of the Provincial Defense Committee arrived late or not at all. After the eventual suppression of the revolutionary regime, these tensions between the Palatines and the Rhine-Hessians came to the surface in the memoirs of the participants and in testimony at court proceedings, but one should not exaggerate them in retrospect. Rhine-Hessian insurgents accepted the authority of the Palatine revolutionary government, followed its orders, if sometimes reluctantly, and worked with it to the very end.[50]

---

[49] Quotation from "An das Pfälzer Volk!" in *Amts- und Intelligenzblatt der provisorischen Regierung der Rheinpfalz*, Nr. 12, 11 June 1849. A complete run of this gazette of the revolutionary regime is available in LAS J1 Nr. 277 (alt).

[50] LAS J1 Nr. 106 II ff. 96–97; LAS J1 Nr. 110 ff. 42, 262, 361; LAS J1 Nr. 111 ff. 64–67, 142–52; LAS J1 Nr. 218 ff. 146–49; LAS J1 Nr. 267 ff. 85–86, 145–48; *Vhdl*, pt. 2, p. 131; Bamberger, "Erlebnisse aus der Pfälzer Erhebung" 3:107–08, 130–36. Bamberger's attacks in this work on the Provisional Government and the Palatine population in general, often taken at face value by historians, must be seen in the light of these ex post facto mutual recriminations.

Even though many of the militants of Rhine-Hessen had left for the Palatinate, the democrats remaining behind continued to make life difficult for the authorities. In Oberingelheim, admittedly one of the most radical towns in the province, they engaged in military drill during the daytime and gathered at night, on the sounding of the gymnasts' horn, to shoot at steamboats bringing Prussian troops downriver. When the mayor tried to post on the marketplace the government's address denouncing the movement for the Frankfurt constitution, the people attacked him, and he was forced to shut himself up in the city hall, not daring to leave for days on end.[51]

A Provincial Committee, which remained behind in Wörrstadt after the insurgent columns had left, acted as liason between the forces in the Palatinate and the democrats at home. It organized the purchase of such weapons as could be obtained in Mainz and elsewhere in the province, passed on information about Prussian troop movements, arranged for the transport of reinforcements to the Palatinate, or the return of soldiers home on leave. The women of Mainz gathered blankets and old clothing to send to their men in the field. This was more help and better support than the Provisional Government received from anyone else, including those with much more to offer, but it was hardly of the nature required.[52]

Greater hopes were raised by events in Baden, where the grand-ducal regime was overthrown and the grand duke was forced to flee. A revolutionary Provisional Government was declared there, at just the same time as one was proclaimed in the Palatinate. Unlike the Bavarian troops stationed on the left bank of the Rhine, who deserted individually or in small groups, only half the deserters taking service with the Provisional Government, the entire Badenese army, including the garrison of the great fortress of Rastatt, went over in a body to the revolutionary regime. The two revolutionary governments of southwestern Germany signed a mutual defense pact and eventually agreed to put their armed forces under a common command, so historians sometimes talk of the "Badenese-Palatine uprising."[53]

But relations between the two governments were never good, Baden refusing to send troops across the river to guard against the Prussians, or even to provide artillery for the People's Guard. Just the opposite was the case—the Badenese wanted military assistance from the Palatines. The government of Baden, in conjunction with leftist members of the Frankfurt National Assembly, including Franz Raveaux—this was the Cologne democrat's last major political action—planned an offensive north along the right bank of the Rhine through Hessen-Darmstadt towards Frankfurt, to protect the assembly from

[51] BAF FN7 Anhang 4 Gagern ff. 76–79, 84, 91–93.

[52] Ibid. ff. 82, 84; LAS J1 Nr. 110 f. 12; LAS J1 Nr. 106 II ff. 98, 105–12, 122; *Vhdl*, pt. 2, pp. 114–22; "Berichte aus Baden und der Pfalz," *Der Demokrat*, 31 May 1849; *MZ*, 31 May 1849 (Erste Ausgabe).

[53] Valentin, *Geschichte der deutschen Revolution* 2:509–16, 520–21.

the possibility of forcible dissolution by Prussian troops. Forces from the Palatinate were to invade Rhine-Hessen and provide a diversion on the left bank of the river.[54]

While the invasion was a total fiasco—its commander, Franz Sigel, beginning a long career of military incompetence, which would climax in the American Civil War—the diversion was enormously successful. Ludwig Blenker returned in triumph to Worms, leading a portion of the insurgents from there, reinforced by the civic guards of Frankenthal and Bad Dürkheim. The Hessian garrison withdrew across the Rhine, and Blenker was greeted with jubiliation by the population, his troops occupying the city from May 25 to May 29, 1849.

When the Hessian soldiers returned on May 29, announcing their imminent arrival by bombarding Worms from positions on the right bank of the Rhine, many inhabitants wanted to resist, ringing the storm bells of the cathedral and building barricades. Messengers were sent around into the countryside, and some young men from Bechtheim and Mettenheim—admittedly in a state of considerable inebriation—marched out to "defend the fatherland," sniping at the Hessians as they returned. It was all in vain, since the Badenese invasion on the right bank had failed, and Blenker, following orders, retreated back to the Palatinate. His incursion had demonstrated the radical sympathies of many of the Rhine-Hessians, suggesting that the revolutionary armies might have done better to organize an offensive to the west rather than to the east of the Rhine.[55]

The revolutionary regimes had one final card to play, a request for assistance from France, to which end a Badenese-Palatine delegation was sent to Paris at the end of May, asking for diplomatic recognition, weapons, and armed assistance. There was not much hope that the conservative regime of President Louis-Napoleon Bonaparte, and his ministers from the Party of Order, busy rooting out the revolution in France, would help it in Germany. As the French chargé d'affaires in the Badenese capital, Karlsruhe, put it, "All republicans are not necessarily brothers, thank God." The French government would not even meet with the envoys, much less offer them any assistance.[56]

[54] Ibid.; LAS J1 Nr. 110 f. 35; LAS J1 Nr. 111 ff. 65–67; "Franz Raveaux," *Allgemeine Deutsche Biographie* 27:465–70; Bamberger, "Erlebnisse aus der Pfälzer Erhebung" 3:113–15. Given the distance between the Palatine and Badenese governments, and the close relations between former and Rhine-Hessian insurgents, it seems more appropriate to speak of a "Palatine/Rhine-Hessian uprising."

[55] On Blenker's incursion into Worms, see *Vhdl*, pt. 1, pp. 114–18; ibid., pt. 2, pp. 183–268, 272–74, 283–319; LAS J1 Nr. 110 f. 63; LAS J1 Nr. 219 ff. 980–1322; *MZ*, 3 June 1849 (Zweite Ausgabe). Admittedly, the Mainz fortress, with its Prussian and Austrian garrisons, was a strong argument against any serious offensive into Rhine-Hessen by the revolutionary army.

[56] All sorts of strange conspiratorial theories have been advanced about this delegation (cf. Valentin, *Geschichte der deutschen Revolution* 2:517–19; or, still more bizarrely, Baumann, "Volkserhebung und Konspiration," pp. 312–16), but the recent excellent acount of Imma Mel-

Their real hope rested not with the French government, but with its left-wing opposition. Elections to the National Assembly, held May 13, 1849, had gone unexpectedly well for the democrats, and they formed the single largest caucus in the French parliament, although the different monarchist groups, when combined, could easily outvote the left. French leftists had demanded that their government cease supporting conservative regimes abroad and return to a policy of favoring republican and revolutionary ones. This demand, applied primarily to Italy, where French troops were about to intervene in favor of the Pope against the Roman Republic. In Alsace, where the democrats were strong, having taken all the seats in the May 1849 elections, and where family and business connections with Baden and the Palatinate were close, relations with the revolutionary governments in southwestern Germany were an important issue in domestic politics. Alsatian democrats held public meetings and formed committees to demand a new foreign policy: withdrawal of French troops from Italy and the sending of weapons and ammunition to the revolutionary regimes in Baden and Palatinate. A delegation of Alsatian democrats visited Speyer, issuing an appeal stating that in the unlikely[!] case that armed reaction should dare attack the Palatinate, the Palatines should not turn to the government in Paris, "which only knows how to suppress the freedom of other nations," but to "us, the French, the Alsatian people."[57]

The contact man between the German and French leftists was the Strasbourg democrat Joseph Savoye, a native of the Palatinate who had played a leading role in the organization of the Hambach Festival, and subsequently gone into exile in France and become a naturalized French citizen. It was on Savoye's invitation that the German envoys had come to France in the first place, and he introduced them to the leaders of the "Mountain," the left-wing, social democratic party in French politics. Following the refusal of the government, the envoys took their case to the leaders of the left.[58]

The leftists, however, were not willing to make any rash promises. Their leader, Ledru-Rollin, agreed that should the Mountain come to power, it would allow the export of weapons to the insurgent governments and permit volunteers from the Alsatian National Guard to join the struggle. He made no mention of official French involvement or of any support from the army. It is

---

zer, "Pfälzische Emigranten in Frankreich während und nach der Revolution von 1848/49," Parts 1, 2, *Francia* 12 (1984): 371–424; 13 (1985): 369–407, based on considerable research in French sources, sets the record straight.

[57] *Anklag-Akte*, pt. 2, p. 171; LAS J1 Nr. 235 f. 720. The Alsatian democrats explicitly rejected the idea of military intervention by the regular French army, or even by armed volunteers, but they did call on the government to send an observation corps to the Rhine. On politics in France in general and Alsace in particular in the spring of 1849, see Roger Price, *The French Second Republic: A Social History* (Ithaca: Cornell University Press, 1972), pp. 231–45; and Maurice Agulhon, *The Republican Experiment, 1848–1852*, trans. Janet Lloyd (Cambridge: Cambridge University Press, 1983), pp. 75–79, 168.

[58] Melzer, "Pfälzische Emigration," pt. 1, pp. 381–84, 409, 413–18.

hard to avoid the impression that the French radicals were interested in the cause of the German democrats primarily for its use in French domestic politics and might well have shown little inclination to honor their promises— which could easily have led to war with Prussia—had they come to power.[59]

Regardless of the ultimate utility of these promises, they were the best the Badenese-Palatine envoys could hope for. Continuing its counterrevolutionary foreign policy in Italy, the right-wing government provoked the left into a quasi-insurrectionary demonstration in Paris on June 13, 1849, the German envoys marching in it alongside prominent radical deputies. The army suppressed the movement in the capital without difficulty, in doing so destroying any hope of French intervention.[60]

A Diplomatic Alternative?

None of the three parliamentarians elected to the Provisional Government took their seats in it, as their friends in the Palatinate wished. Rather, leaving their portfolios to their radical substitutes, they made one final attempt to bring outside forces to the support of the Palatine revolution and save it from its confrontation with Prussia. When the Bavarian Parliament was finally called into session in mid-May, Schüler and Kolb (who were deputies to it as well as to Frankfurt) went to Munich, bringing an offer from the National Assembly. If the king of Bavaria would accept the Frankfurt constitution and agree to support it, the assembly would elect him emperor. Placing the German government most opposed to national unity at the head of the movement for the Frankfurt constitution was a desperate move, with little chance of success, as the Bavarian response showed. The Munich authorities declared the mandates of the Palatine deputies to the Bavarian parliament invalid, since the province was in a state of rebellion, and issued a warrant for Kolb and Schüler's arrest, forcing them to flee the capital.[61]

At about the same time, August Culmann was engaged in a parallel initiative. An activist of the Hambach festival, and generally regarded in 1848 as a republican extremist, Culmann had joined the caucus of the extreme left in the Frankfurt National Assembly, but in the course of the revolution his views had become steadily more moderate. In April 1849, when the the final fate of the Frankfurt constitution was still unclear, Culmann had given a speech to his constituents in Landau, explaining that a republic was impossible because

---

[59] LAS J1 Nr. 105 ff. 1085–93. These are copies of French police documents, sent to the Bavarian authorities via Prussia. Their authors were quite hostile to the leaders of the Mountain (Ledru-Rollin is described as the ''future dictator''), and had the latter made any more far-reaching promises, they would surely have been mentioned.

[60] Ibid.; Melzer, ''Pfälzische Emigranten,'' pt. 1, pp. 481–89; Agulhon, *The Republican Experiment*, pp. 78–79.

[61] Kolb, *Lebenserinnerungen*, pp. 152–54, 175–91.

most Germans did not want it, and that the election of the king of Prussia emperor had been a violation of Bavarian sovereignty. Radicals left the meeting shaking their heads, while officers and NCOs in the audience cheered wildly, one of the latter getting up and shouting, "For once there goes a true Bavarian."[62]

During the Palatine revolution, Culmann continued on the course outlined by his speech in Landau. He proposed to the Provisional Government that it negotiate for its return to Munich's authority, that the revolutionary regime in Baden recall the grand duke, and that Bavaria, Baden, and the other south German states then appeal to the French for protection against Prussia. Culmann was asked to head the Badenese-Palatine delegation to France; he refused to do so, but instead went to Paris on his own. Culmann's brother, Jacques, had been a deputy to the French National Assembly for the moderate French republicans, the party of General Cavaignac, until his death in April 1849, and Culmann wanted to use his connections with this party to change French policy. Culmann hoped for French intervention in southwestern Germany, albeit not for revolutionary purposes, but for the traditional diplomatic reason of opposing an increase in Prussian power. However, by the spring of 1849 the moderate republicans were already an increasingly marginal element in French politics, so even had they been willing to listen to Culmann's appeals, they would not have had the power to carry them out.[63]

The diplomacy of both moderates and radicals revealed a strong preference for France over Prussia. In the context of German national unification, as it occurred in 1870–1871, under Prussian hegemony by war against France, the actions of the upper Rhine leftists could only seem to be a treasonable betrayal of the national cause. For mid-nineteenth-century Rhenish democrats, who saw German and French nationalism as complementary rather than conflicting, and who regarded the Prussian monarchy as the enemy of the nation, as the close ally of the czar, an appeal to France to save the German national cause from the Prussians was a logical, if extreme, step. Rank-and-file Palatine democrats agreed with their leaders, many hoping during and even after the reign of the Provisional Government, for help from France.[64]

The problem was that the France to which they were appealing was a historical anachronism. Neither the Jacobin France of the 1790s, willing to offer

---

[62] LAS J1 Nr. 105 ff. 684–91. Culmann also asserted that a government created under the Frankfurt constitution would be dominated by north German free traders, hurting protectionist south German industry and agriculture.

[63] LAS J1 Nr. 105 ff. 531–47, 549–84; Melzer, "Pfälzische Emigranten," pt. 1, p. 419. It is unclear whether Culmann coordinated his actions with those of Kolb and Schüler, but their policy of placing a nonrevolutionary Bavarian regime behind the movement for the Frankfurt constitution, against the opposition of the Great Powers, Prussia and Austria, could have succeeded only with French help.

[64] LAK 403 Nr. 2554 pp. 167–69; LAS J1 Nr. 243 (alt) ff. 56–60; LAS J1 Nr. 252 (alt) ff. 99–102; Anklag-Akte, pt. 2, p. 118.

fraternal assistance to foreign republicans, on which the Palatine radicals placed their hopes, nor the Napoleonic France of the early nineteenth century, allied with the states of South Germany to limit Prussian power, basis of the moderates' plans, still existed in the Paris of 1849. Outside intervention to protect the Palatine revolution failed, and the Provisional Government remained set on its course leading to a final, fatal confrontation with the armed might of the Prussian state.

CHAPTER ELEVEN

The Revolutionary Regime and Society in the Palatinate, May–June 1849

SECURING REVOLUTIONARY RULE

Like other revolutionaries in a similar situation, the radical Palatine democrats discovered that their relationship to society changed following their seizure of power. Now they were exercising authority instead of denouncing it, collecting taxes rather than opposing them, suppressing opposition instead of expressing it. As a result, at least some of the resistance to the authority of the Bavarian state exercised by elements of Palatine society was now directed against the revolutionary regime, especially as that regime, facing the threat of a Prussian invasion, was forced to act more strictly than had the government it had overthrown. If the Provisional Government thus inherited the position of the Bavarian administration, it was also heir to the social dynamics of the oppositional democratic movement. Formerly oppositional radicals in towns and villages now turned their energies toward support of the revolutionary government; social and confessional differences that had previously characterized the supporters and opponents of the People's Associations also marked the friends and enemies of the regime. This simultaneous continuation and reversal of previous social and political antagonisms continued throughout the Provisional Government's one month of existence, from its proclamation to its overthrow by Prussian troops.

Creating Revolutionary Authority

Following Jacobin precedent, the Provisional Government appointed civil commissioners to represent it directly in each of the province's twelve counties. The official function of these commissioners was to coordinate the work of the cantonal committees in raising an army and securing the authority of the revolutionary regime. Their real task was to exercise political surveillance over the cantonal committees and, if necessary, to push them on to more vigorous action. The committees were composed of politically very heterogeneous elements, both radical and moderate democrats and even some constitutional monarchists—in different proportions and with different forces dominant in each of the Palatinate's thirty-one cantons. They could not necessarily be counted on to support the revolutionary government unreservedly.[1]

---

[1] The catalogue of basic measures taken by the government comes from its own account, a sort

The civil commissioners were men who had made a name for themselves previously as democratic activists, frequently with a legal background and some administrative experience. In Bergzabern, for example, the government appointed Philipp Bruch, a leader of the People's Association there, coeditor of the town's radical newspaper, and a democratic activist since the days of the Hambach Festival. While Bruch stood politically on the extreme left, other appointees did not. Karl Witt, judicial apprentice [Assessor] on the district court in Kaiserslautern and officer of the city's civic guard, was named civil commissioner in Homburg, but proved to be so moderate in his actions that the radicals on the Homburg Cantonal Committee demanded that the Kaiserslautern government replace him, which it did, but only after letting several weeks go by.[2]

One of the commissioners' first tasks was to enforce the Provisional Government's demand that all state officials, from the provincial governor down to village clerks, take an oath to the Frankfurt constitution and sign a statement agreeing to obey the revolutionary regime or face dismissal from office. This was simply a repetition of a measure proposed by the Provincial Defense Committee two weeks previously and foiled by the conciliatory actions of Commissioner Eisenstuck.

Now, with no outside moderate to save them, the officials were forced to confront the public hostility that had been an undercurrent of events since March 1848. During a mass meeting in the southeastern cantonal town of Kandel, at which the local leaders of the People's Association announced the formation of the Provisional Government, one speaker said, "The officials are now to be chosen by the people, and those who will not obey should be chased to the devil." His remarks were met with approval and shouts of "Better to drive them out right away."[3]

The citizens of the northwestern cantonal seat of Rockenhausen met on the marketplace to take the oath to the Frankfurt constitution, noticing, once they had gathered, that some of the officials were missing. A delegation brought them under threat of force, demanding their adherence. When the justice of the peace replied that he would later go to Kaiserslautern and take the oath directly from the Provisional Government, a wave of anger went through the assembled citizenry. A bricklayer shouted, "You've lied to us once already; we don't believe you any more"—a reference to the justice's promise, given

of apologia pro vita, issued toward the end of its rule, "An das Pfälzer Volk!" in *Amts- und Intelligenzblatt der provisorischen Regierung der Rheinpfalz*, Nr. 12, 11 June 1849, copies in LAS J1 Nr. 277 (alt). The decree naming the civil commissioners is ibid., Nr. 3, 25 May 1849.

[2] *Anklag-Akte*, pt. 2, pp. 213–14; LAS J1 Nr. 242 ff. 69–73, 141–44, 202–36. The commissioners for Landau, Pirmasens, Frankenthal, and Neustadt, like Bruch, came from the more radical wing of the People's Association (LAS J1 Nr. 205 ff. 202–04; LAS J1 Nr. 243 (alt) ff. 56–60, 74–82; LAS J1 Nr. 218 ff. 79–85; LAS J1 Nr. 229 (alt) I ff. 1–2), while those for Kirchheimbolanden, Speyer, and Germesheim counties had a more moderate reputation: LAS J1 Nr. 267 ff. 113–16; LAS J1 Nr. 252 (alt) ff. 140–45, 148–50; LAS J1 Nr. 263 ff. 250–53.

[3] LAS J1 Nr. 263 ff. 121–22, 130–32; similarly, LAS J1 Nr. 147 f. 70.

the previous spring, but soon revoked, to suspend trials for forest offenses. He was in physical danger until members of the cantonal committee intervened to protect him. At a similar meeting in Pirmasens, Civil Commissioner Diehl told the assembled officials, "Whoever does not take the oath will be handed over to the people, who will do with him what they will."[4]

Most officials who were summoned—not all were—took the oath and at least nominally subordinated themselves to the revolutionary regime. Among the more high-ranking ones who did so were the county commissioners in Kirchheimbolanden, Primasens, and Neustadt a.d.W. The only alternative was to flee over the border to France or Prussia or to the fortresses of Germersheim or Landau. The county commissioners of Zweibrücken and Homburg were the two highest-ranking officials to take refuge in Prussia.[5]

Flight was an option practiced above all by the gendarmes, following orders from their superiors to keep themselves, and their weapons and horses, out of revolutionary hands. The gendarmes of Canton Blieskastel, a stronghold of support for the Provisional Government, fled towards France, with the People's Guard in hot pursuit. They took the last steps of their retreat across the bridge from Palatine Habkirchen to Alsatian Frauenberg, under the protection of covering fire from French border guards and customs agents. The subprefect in Saarguemines then allowed them to take their weapons with them through French territory to Germersheim.[6]

Of the 188 gendarmes stationed in the Palatinate, 109 got away, but the flight of some of the others did not end so happily. The commandant of the gendarmerie station in Edenkoben was caught sneaking out of town in disguise. Suspecting him of spying, the crowd was about to lynch him, and he was only saved by members of the cantonal committee, who placed him under arrest. The gendarmes of Schweigen on their way to Landau were arrested in the radical county town Bergzabern. There they were disarmed and sent to Kaiserslautern in irons, this last on the explicit demand of the women of the city, who gathered to mock the paramilitary policemen as they were led off.[7]

---

[4] LAS J1 Nr. 249 (alt) ff. 127, 133, 137–37, 207–10; *Anklag-Akte*, pt. 2, p. 139. Similar instances of intimidation of public officials: LAS J1 Nr. 104 ff. 16–21, 24–27; LAS J1 Nr. 200 ff. 51–55, 113–14; LAS J1 Nr. 235 ff. 95–100, 278–79; LAS J1 Nr. 267 ff. 145–48; LAS J1 Nr. 104 ff. 24–27; Staatsprokurator Frankenthal to König. Armee Corps-Commando Speyer, 26 Aug. 1849, BHSTAM KA Nr. B778.

[5] LAS J1 Nr. 267 ff. 145–48; LAS J1 Nr. 243 (alt) ff. 83–85; LAS J1 Nr. 228 (alt) f. 92; LAS H1 Nr. 154c ff. 26–28; cf. LAK 441 Nr. 8317 pp. 357–58, 369–71. The county commissioner in Kirchheimbolanden eventually also fled to Prussia, his oath to the Frankfurt constitution notwithstanding.

[6] LAS J1 Nr. 195 ff. 187, 520–70; a similar incident in neighboring Canton Neuhornbach, *Anklag-Akte*, pt. 2, p. 118. The actions of the subprefect and the border guards (on his orders) show that the hostility toward the south German revolutionaries felt by the government in Paris was shared by provincial officials.

[7] Gendarmerie Hauptmann Sturz to König. Corps Commando Speyer, 25 June 1849, BHSTAM

It is hard to miss the strong element of hostility toward state officials in all these actions. Yet the revolutionary leaders did not so much want to destroy the structure of the state administration as to use it for their purposes. When the People's Guard made arrests for counterrevolutionary activity, they would often turn the arrestees over to the judiciary, usually the last thing the embarrassed judges and procurators wanted, since most of them had agreed to serve the new regime only under duress.[8]

The revolutionaries also wanted to use the state's executive bureaucracy for their regime. One of the first acts of the newly created Provisional Government was to go from Kaiserslautern to Speyer on May 19, and implore Provincial Governor Alwens to stay in office and administer the province for the new regime. The revolutionaries were even willing to drop the requirement that he take the oath to the Frankfurt constitution. Alwens refused, and the members of the Provisional Government made no effort to hinder his flight to the fortress of Germersheim, although they did insist that the office files of the provincial government be left behind.[9]

At the other end of the adminstrative structure was communal government, an equally crucial element to the revolutionary regime. While orders from Kaiserslautern went to the cantonal committees, sometimes directly, sometimes via the civil commissioners in the county towns, it was the village and town mayors who actually carried them out. Many communal officials, elected by a property owners' franchise and confirmed in office by the Bavarian authorities, did not possess the revolutionary enthusiasm necessary for such tasks. To strengthen its grip on the Palatinate's towns and villages, the Provisional Government ordered new local government elections, to be held under universal manhood suffrage.[10]

The results of these elections showed the extent to which the revolutionary regime was dependent on voluntary support from Palatine society. Where village democrats were active, especially when there was an organized People's Association, the elections could fulfill their revolutionary purpose, driving out the cautious local authorities and replacing them with "Hecker mayors," who would vigorously carry out the orders of the Provisional Government. When the mayor of Rodalben near Primasens, long an enemy of the People's Association, refused to obey the decrees of the Provisional Government, the local democrats forced him to resign and elected his former deputy, a close ally of

---

MInn Nr. 45532; LAS J1 Nr. 205 ff. 14–17, 204–07; *Anklag-Akte*, pt. 2, p. 215. The arrested gendarmes were eventually released and allowed to leave the province.

[8] LAS J1 Nr. 104 ff. 16–21, 28–32; LAS J1 Nr. 147 ff. 154–57; *Vhdl*, pt. 2, pp. 129–30; similarly, LAS J1 Nr. 205 ff. 202–04; LAS J1 Nr. 242 ff. 152–56; LAS J1 Nr. 246 ff. 100–05.

[9] RP to MInn, 19 May 1849 (draft), LAS J1 Nr. 1975. Since Speyer was close to the unsubdued fortress of Germersheim, the Provisional Government decided not to take its seat there but to return to Kaiserslautern.

[10] *Amts und Intelligenzblatt der Provisorischen Regierung der Rheinpfalz*, Nr. 5, 25 May 1849.

the founder of the village's People's Association. The new mayor promptly took steps to mobilize, drill, and outfit the People's Guard. Probably the most energetic village radicals were "several Heckers" in Münchweiler, near Pirmasens, who held elections for mayor on their own initiative, before the Provisional Government issued a decree to that end, replacing the existing one, who had refused to order the mobilization of the People's Guard.[11]

In villages lacking left-wing sympathizers, the peasants were usually reluctant to vote. If, after some prodding, such villagers did go to the polls, they would reelect their mayors and councilmen by large margins. A charming variation on this theme occurred in Frankeneck, to the west of Neustadt a.d.W., where the family of the mayor, paper manufacturer Johann Jacob Gossler, decided it was too dangerous for him to be reelected. He arranged for the business manager of his sister-in-law to be chosen in his place. Of course, if the village mayor was sympathetic to the revolution, his reelection would show that his fellow villagers supported it as well. In most cases, though, the reelection of the prerevolutionary communal regime was a sign that there was little enthusiasm for the revolutionary cause; measures demanded by the Provisional Government would be carried out reluctantly and grudgingly, only under threat of force.[12]

In the northwestern cantonal seat of Landstuhl and in the village of Berghausen, near Speyer, the voters turned out local officials sympathetic to the Provisional Government and replaced them with Bavarian loyalists. Such actions, going beyond political passivity to outright defiance of the revolutionary regime, were unusual ones, reflecting the activities of the Catholic clergy or Pius Associations. Neoorthodox Roman Catholics formed in this respect as in others, the mainstay of active counterrevolution.[13]

Two of the measures taken by the Provisional Government to establish its authority—naming civil commissioners, and calling new local elections—reveal the importance of preexisting political organization for the revolutionary regime. Both the civil commissioners and the revolutionary communal officials were activists in the People's Associations, which provided the cadre for the insurgent regime. Where People's Associations had not been founded, and no such activists were present, the revolutionary regime would find at

[11] LAS J1 Nr 172 f. 377, 421–22; LAS J1 Nr. 243 (alt) ff. 164–65, 180–81, 713–14, 750. Similarly, LAS J1 Nr. 178 ff. 169–70; LAS J1 Nr. 170 ff. 392–93; LAS J1 Nr. 200 ff. 63–64; LAS J1 Nr. 277 (alt) ff. 242–46; LAS J1 Nr. 243 (alt) ff. 30–35, 114–15; LAS J1 Nr. 242 ff. 170–72; LAS J1 Nr. 267 ff. 18–19, 123; LAS J1 Nr. 245 ff. 267–68; LAS J1 Nr. 252 (alt) ff. 99–102.

[12] LAS J1 Nr. 228 (alt) ff. 90–91, 93, 98–100; LAS J1 Nr. 229 I (alt) ff. 9–12; LAS J1 Nr. 202 I (alt) ff. 102–03; LAS J1 Nr. 242 ff. 159–61; LAS J1 Nr. 245 ff. 275–80; LAS J1 Nr. 267 ff. 157–66; LAS J1 Nr. 252 (alt) ff. 158–60, 168–71.

[13] LAS J1 Nr. 252 (alt) ff. 161–62; LAS J1 Nr. 242 f. 188. Similarly, in Weidenthal, to the west of Neustadt a.d.W., LAS J1 Nr. 246 ff. 100–05 and LAS J1 Nr. 229 I (alt) f. 11.

best an apathetic lack of sympathy, and sometimes open counterrevolutionary opposition.

The campaign to obtain the loyalty of the Bavarian state officials, or at least to intimidate them into not opposing revolutionary rule, shows another aspect of the regime: the importance of being able to draw on preexisting social tensions. The revolutionary government was able to intimidate the Bavarian officials with considerable success because it could count on popular hostility towards state officials, an underlying current of public opinion since the spring of 1848. Both these tendencies would shape society's response to the Provisional Government's other main task, raising a revolutionary army and the money to pay for it.

Taxes for the Cause

More than anything else, armies need money, and voluntary contributions would hardly suffice to pay for an armed force that could defend the Palatinate against the grave dangers threatening it. The Provisional Government revived the plans of the Provincial Defense Committee to seize public funds, only to discover that in the interval the authorities had emptied most of the treasuries, either by carrying out fictitious transactions or by physically taking the cash money and transporting it to the fortress of Germersheim. The revolutionary regime had no choice but to raise revenue on its own, levying a 25 percent surcharge on real estate taxes, payable immediately, and imposing a forced loan on all fortunes over the substantial sum of 40,000 fl.[14]

Of all the functions of government, the revolutionary authorities were least successful at raising money in compulsory fashion. Their broad-based source of revenue, the 25 percent tax surcharge, met with broad-based indifference: Virtually no one paid a kreutzer of it. Even the most radical Palatines, who were willing to attack and intimidate the Bavarian authorities or march fearlessly into battle with a vastly superior Prussian army, showed no inclination to pay taxes for the revolution. Especially in the countryside, as an amused but perceptive correspondent sent to the scene of the action by the *Kölnische Zeitung* noted, revolution meant not paying taxes. Understanding this, the revolutionary authorities only rarely made a token effort at tax collection, and even more rarely did they actually collect anything.[15]

[14] RP to MInn, 4 May 1849, LAS H1 Nr. 1975; LAS J1 Nr. 252 (alt) ff. 803–05; LAS J1 Nr. 205 ff. 476–79; LAS J1 Nr. 277 (alt) ff. 296–98; LAS J1 Nr. 243 (alt) ff. 99–107; LAS J1 Nr. 263 ff. 161–72; cf. Bamberger, "Erlebnisse aus der Pfälzer Erhebung" 3:91–94.

[15] *KnZ*, 3 June 1849 (Zweite Ausgabe). For just a few, of an enormous number of examples of nonpayment of the 25 percent surcharge, see LAS J1 Nr. 277 (alt) ff. 230–32; LAS J1 Nr. 218 f. 96; LAS J1 Nr. 205 ff. 442–43, 445–46, 472; LAS J1 Nr. 242 ff. 25–28, 63–64, 131–32. For examples of its collection, see LAS J1 Nr. 267 f. 123; LAS J1 Nr. 252 (alt) ff. 87–88. See also Franz Rink, "Die Eriegnisse im Kanton Otterberg während der Jahre 1848/49," *JhGStLK* 22/23 (1984/85): 349–75, esp. pp. 358–60.

The forced loan was a somewhat different story. Those bourgeois inhabitants liable to pay it understood why revolutions needed money; they just had no interest in its being their money. Familiar with a tax-collecting bureaucracy and how to evade it, they filed appeals, protesting that they had been overassessed, or tried to use their connections with individuals inside the regime to be exempted from payment. They asked for time, pleading that they were at the moment not liquid and generally twisted and turned, stonewalling the Provisional Government's tax collectors. It was not so much absolute defiance of the forced loan they had in mind as its reduction to a more modest amount.

No canton was wealthier and none had more individuals eligible for the forced loan than Dürkheim, in the Haardt mountain wine country, home to the "bourgeois aristocracy" of vineyard owners. Although the canton's wealthy inhabitants were assessed to pay some 80,000 fl., nothing made its way into the coffers of the Provisional Government, until one of its members made a special trip from Kaiserslautern. He summoned the cantonal committee and told its members that Zitz's Rhine-Hessian insurgent corps had not been paid for a long time. If some money was not forthcoming, he would suggest that all 1,400 of them march to Bad Dürkheim and collect their wages themselves. Liquidity was restored, as if by magic, but the 80,000 fl. assessment was reduced to 10,000 fl., of which only some 4,300 fl. were paid before the fall of the regime. As the wealthiest of the Palatine bourgeoisie, those of Canton Dürkheim were the most reluctant to part with their money, but this same pattern of attempted evasion, and revolutionary indignation followed by partial payment, was repeated, in less dramatic form, throughout the more affluent areas of the forward Palatinate.[16]

Largely unable to collect taxes, the Provisional Government was forced to rely on voluntary contributions and what it could seize from public treasuries, leaving it perpetually short of money. Resistance to fiscality was a popular cause in the Palatinate and throughout the entire Rhineland in 1848–1849; the democrats had everywhere exploited it as part of their campaign to oppose the existing regimes. Unlike the closely related issue of hostility to state officials, resistance to taxation played against the Palatine radicals once they were in power. However, the difficulties experienced by the revolutionary government in raising money for an army were much less than those it suffered in raising the army itself.[17]

[16] On events in Canton Dürkheim, see LAS J1 Nr. 203 ff. 164–74, 180–85, 187–90, 314–15, 336–55, 395–99; elsewhere, LAS J1 Nr. 218 ff. 104–05; LAS J1 Nr. 205 ff. 202–04, 442–43; LAS J1 Nr. 219 ff. 954–60; LAS J1 Nr. 267 ff. 121, 124–27; LAS J1 Nr. 229 I (alt) ff. 9–10; LAS J1 Nr. 252 (alt) ff. 349–50, 355–61. Since the wealth of the Palatine bourgeoisie was primarily in land, their claims of liquidity problems may not have been entirely a pretext.

[17] As of 7 June 1849, the books of the Provisional Government showed income of 33,060 fl. from voluntary contributions, 13,567 fl. confiscated from public treasuries, and 4,539 fl. from the tax surcharge, with no figures available on the forced loan. LAS J1 Nr. 105 f. 469.

RAISING A REVOLUTIONARY ARMY

Although attempts to raise, outfit, equip, and finance a revolutionary People's Guard had been under way for two weeks when the Provisional Government seized power, they had met with little success. Command, organization, recruitment, armaments, uniforms—none of these existed; all had to be created anew, in a crisis atmosphere, with the Prussians gathering menacingly, just across the border. It was a remarkable accomplishment of the regime that it was able to accomplish anything at all with the extremely meager resources at its disposal.[18]

Organization and Command

The government's problems began at the top rank of its projected army. Swiss General Dufour, the Defense Committee's original choice as commander in chief of the People's Guard, declined the dubious honor, leaving the incipient armed force without any guiding hand. The Provincial Defense Committee's interim solution, appointing as commander the Austrian political refugee Ferdinand Fenner von Fenneberg, one of the leaders of the barricade fighting in Vienna in November 1848, only worsened matters. While it may not have been true, as Fenner's enemies asserted, that he spent all day having his portrait painted, there is not much evidence that he did anything to organize a revolutionary army.[19]

After the Provisional Government came to power, it had Fenner briefly arrested, and then expelled from the country. A Military Commission was appointed, a revolutionary general staff composed mostly of radical Prussian ex-army officers fleeing their government's political repression, including the Cologne communists Friedrich von Beust and Fritz Anneke. They obtained armed assistance from the founder of their *Vormärz* communist circle, August Willich. The latter led into the Palatinate a group of insurgents, who had taken

[18] Two vivid descriptions of the desperate military situation at the beginning of the Provisional Government are in LAS J1 Nr. 106 II ff. 70, 165–66.

[19] A. Becker, "General Dufour und die Pfalz 1849," *ZGO* 86 (1935): 253–56; Fenner von Fenneberg, *Zur Geschichte der rheinpfälzischen Revolution*, pp. 34–87; *KnZ*, 30 May 1849; Bamberger, "Erlebnisse aus der Pfälzer Erhebung," 3:98, 111. Fenner claimed that he was foiled in his attempts to organize an army by the laziness and incompetence of the Palatines. The claim is accepted by the official Prussian military history, Wilhelm von Voß, *Der Feldzug in der Pfalz und in Baden im Jahre 1849* (Berlin: R. Eisenschmidt, 1903), p. 26, but contemporary documents, especially a report on the revolutionary armed forces right after his dismissal, LAS J1 Nr. 106 II ff. 165–66, show a very different picture. Like Bamberger's attacks on the Palatines, Fenner's denunciations of them contain a strong element of self-justification and should not be accepted at face value.

part in the republican uprising in Baden in April 1848 and had since then been in exile in France.[20]

The Military Commission reorganized the People's Guard into three separate groups, creating a "mobile guard," for which all single men between the ages of eighteen and thirty were made eligible. While the married and older men would stay at home, this younger, single group, also called the "first levy," would march into the field. More important, it was to be mobilized by conscription, the draft to be carried out, and the People's Guard organized, by military commissioners, appointed in tandem with the civil commissioners in each county. The military commissioners received administrative assistance from a "Student Legion," made up mostly of native Palatines at the Universities of Munich and Erlangen, recruited to return home and fight for their province and the nation.[21]

To act as supreme commander for these draftees, the Rhine-Hessian insurgent columns, and Willich's corps, the Provisional Government, through the good offices of German émigrés in Paris, obtained the services of a Polish officer, one Franz Sznayde, a veteran of Napoleon's army and the revolution of 1830. In late middle age and lacking energy and initiative, Sznayde reminded Ludwig Bamberger of a "pensioned off Austrian army officer." If far from the best possible choice, Sznayde at least had some idea of a general strategy, and he was certainly an improvement on Fenner von Fenneberg. Between his efforts and especially those of the Military Commission, a revolutionary army of sorts actually began to come into existence by June 1849.[22]

A commander in chief and a general staff do not make up an officer corps, and here the military weakness of the People's Guard was most apparent. Few Palatines sympathetic to the revolution had any experience as army officers, or even as NCOs. To be sure, August Willich, the one professional military man acting as a field commander in the Palatine army, was a very good one. All the witnesses of his men in action, even a Bavarian loyalist whom they sentenced to death, praised their discipline, organization, and fighting spirit

[20] On the commission's founding and Fenner's arrest, see Schneider, "Landesausschuß und Provisorische Regierung," p. 113; Schurz, *Lebesnerinnerungen*, pp. 208–09; LAS J1 Nr. 106 II ff. 165–66, LAS J1 Nr. 110 ff. 118–19, 146–47; and Fenner von Fenneberg, *Zur Geschichte der rheinpfälzischen Revolution*, pp. 101–05; the commission's activities are documented in LAS J1 Nr. 108–110. For Willich and his corps of insurgents, see *RhBA* 2/2, Nr. 130; and the documentation on their activity in the Palatinate in LAS J1 Nrs. 205 and 264.

[21] The decree of 19 May 1849 organizing the People's Guard and creating a draft is in LAS H1 Nr. 1975. On the student legion, see LAS J1 Nr. 105 ff. 878–940; LAS J1 Nr. 228 (alt) ff. 122–23.

[22] Schneider, "Landesausschuß und Provisorische Regierung," p. 113; Bamberger, "Erlebnisse aus der Pfälzer Erhebung" 3:108–10; Engels, "Die deutsche Reichsverfassungskampange" 7:154–55; a perhaps excessively nasty opinion in Schurz, *Lebenserinnerungen*, pp. 209–10; an example of Sznayde's strategic thinking in LAS J1 Nr. 110 f. 265. The often-repeated story that Sznayde was really a German named Schneider is untrue.

and Willich's abilities as a military leader. Willich was, however, far from typical. Commanding officers of the municipal civic guards taken over into the People's Guard and the commanders of outside insurgent columns, such as Zitz, Bamberger, and Blenker, were politicians or notables, not military officers. To borrow some twentieth-century terminology, they might have made good political commissars, but had no knowledge of tactics and no experience of command under fire.[23]

Unlike the civil commissioners, only three of the twelve military commissioners were Palatine natives, with most of the rest leftist Prussian ex-army officers or exiled Polish revolutionaries. While some of the German commissioners, such as Major Ehlert in Homburg, acted with energy and initiative—and, when needed, brutality—the Poles, like General Sznayde, recruited via Parisian émigré circles, spoke little or no German. They could communicate with their men only through an interpreter, if at all, making them a dubious addition to the revolutionary cause.[24]

The situation with regard to lower-ranking officers and NCOs was even more desperate. Most of these posts were taken by deserted Bavarian common soldiers, who, even when sober, had little knowledge of military command. Scenes on the drill field were comic or horrendous, depending on one's point of view. A journalist viewing the drilling of a corps of "scythe men" in Kaiserslautern concluded, "[I]t seemed to me the danger that these scythe bearers would cut each other's heads off was greater than any which they might pose to the Prussians."[25]

Arms for the Revolution

An army needs weapons, and even before the proclamation of the Provisional Government, the Provincial Defense Committee and several city councils had sent agents to France and Belgium, attempting to purchase rifles for the People's Guard. The conservative French government closed the borders to the export of weapons, enforcing this quarantine very strictly. While the Belgians did allow the revolutionaries to purchase rifles, the weapons shipments were confiscated by the Prussians at various points along the Rhine, as they passed

[23] For judgments about Willich and his corps, see LAS J1 Nr. 205 f. 461; LAS J1 Nr. 264 ff. 492–511, 563–73, 749–53.

[24] Schneider, "Landesausschuß und Provisorische Regierung," pp. 109–10; LAS J1 Nr. 108 ff. 133–36, 209; LAS J1 Nr. 109 f. 408; LAS J1 Nr. 110 ff. 130, 140, 163, 167, 171–77. The Polish military commissioners, insofar as they could act, were dependent on their German adjutants, local Palatine revolutionaries. Cf. LAS J1 Nr. 263 ff. 250–53.

[25] *KnZ*, 30 May 1849. On deserted soldiers as drill instructors, see LAS J1 Nr. 108 f. 206; LAS J1 Nr. 109 f. 404; LAS J1 Nr. 110 ff. 197–98; LAS J1 Nr. 195 ff. 108–09; LAS J1 Nr. 235 ff. 131–33, 136–38; LAS J1 Nr. 242 ff. 94–95; LAS J1 Nr. 245 f. 276; LAS J1 Nr. 243 (alt) ff. 187–89.

downstream. A last, desperate mission to Basel succeeded in obtaining 6,000 fl. worth of rifles, which arrived only after Prussian soldiers had conquered the Palatinate.[26]

A great store of weapons—including artillery, which the revolutionary army completely lacked—ammunition, and uniforms was free for the taking in the fortress of Landau, and one of the first acts of the Provisional Government was to attempt to capture this prize. The government asked Ludwig Blenker, commander of the insurgents from Worms, whose seizure of the small border fortress in Ludwigshafen on May 11 had been a major victory for the revolution, to repeat his triumph in Landau nine days later. Blenker was widely criticized by, among others, that eminent armchair general Friedrich Engels, for poor tactical judgment in his attack on the fortress, but such criticism rather misses the point. Blenker expected the garrison in Landau to go over to the insurgents, just as the troops stationed in Ludwigshafen had done, allowing him to take the fortress without firing a shot. Paradoxically, his attempt failed because the democrats' prior efforts to subvert the Landau garrison had worked too well. By May 20, 1849, all the soldiers who could be induced to desert had already done so; the officers and common soldiers remaining in the fortress, perhaps a third its normal complement, remained loyal and opened fire on the advancing insurgents, who retreated in disorder.[27]

Without artillery, which the revolutionary government of Baden refused to provide, the fortress could not be taken by assault. August Willich's insurgent corps placed Landau under siege, its 300–500 men, with a little help from the radical peasants in the vicinity, and occasional assistance from other revolutionary columns, containing the 1,800 soldiers stationed in Germersheim, as well as keeping the 1,500 soldiers in Landau bottled up. The latter emerged only on sorties to rustle cattle from neighboring villages. Food and water ran short in the besieged fortress, and the commandant was on the brink of surrender when the Prussians arrived, but the military cornucopia stored there remained tantalizingly out of the insurgents' reach throughout the uprising.[28]

---

[26] LAS J1 Nr. 170 f. 335; LAS J1 Nr. 229 I (alt) ff. 191–93, 248–52; LAS J1 Nr. 242 ff. 152–56; LAS J1 Nr. 245 f. 256; LAS J1 Nr. 277 (alt) ff. 261–63; HSTAD RA Pr. Nr. 2229 f. 297; LAK 441 Nr. 3059 pp. 87–88; material from 1851 on the disposition of weapons purchased by the city councils of Kaiserslautern and Zweibrücken but confiscated by the Prussians in BHSTAM MInn Nr. 45535. Although the individuals who purchased the rifles in Belgium have often been castigated as idiots, by both contemporaries and historians, for sending them through Prussian territory, the hostile attitude of the French government left them with no choice.

[27] LAS J1 Nr. 110 ff. 18–23; LAS J1 Nr. 111 ff. 89–93; LAS J1 Nr. 205 ff. 417–30; "Berichte aus Baden und der Pfalz," *Der Demokrat*, 3 June 1849; Calliess, *Militär in der Krise*, pp. 185–86; Bamberger, "Erlebnisse aus der Pfälzer Erhebung" 3:124–28; Engels, "Die deutsche Reichsverfassungskampagne" 7:157–58.

[28] On the siege of Landau, see LAS J1 Nr. 106 II ff. 165–66; LAS J1 Nr. 108 ff. 162–65; LAS J1 Nr. 110 ff. 71–73; LAS J1 Nr. 205 ff. 294–302; LAS J1 Nr. 263 f. 285; LAS J1 Nr. 202 I (alt) passim; Fortress Commandant Landau to Ministry of War, 18 June 1849, BHSTAM KA Nr. 735a;

The upshot was an appalling shortage of weapons, disastrous for the army's morale. From Speyer, the military commissioner wrote to Kaiserslautern, "Almost everywhere weapons are completely lacking, and unless they are procured, any attempt to firm up morale will be in vain." His opposite number in Bergzabern noted at the same time, "The troops want weapons and without them it is not easy to force them to take the field." Armed with straightened scythes, rusty flintlocks, and hunting rifles, the People's Guard was able to hold down internal enemies of the regime, even keep in check the intimidated Bavarian troops in the two besieged fortresses, but found the prospect of battle with the Prussian army so armed dubious indeed.[29]

Conscription and Opposition to the Revolutionary Regime

A jerry-rigged military administration, a lack of qualified personnel to serve as officers, a severe shortage of weapons and ammunition, and a powerful enemy just across the border—these were not ideal conditions in which to introduce conscription. Two further circumstances conspired to increase the difficulties of imposing a draft in the countryside. One was the season: Late May and early June were the time of the hay harvest, and the young men to be conscripted were badly needed for labor in the fields. This was a thoroughly apolitical coincidence of agrarian society; the mobilization of the militia in Rhenish Prussia, occurring at the same time, for the purpose of crushing the Palatine revolution, was unpopular for the very same reason.[30]

A second factor was more directly related to the specific situation in the Palatinate. There were far fewer weapons available than potential draftees, so the Military Commission ordered that only half the eligibles be drafted, the individuals chosen to be determined by drawing lots when the eligibles were mustered. This idea was unpleasantly similar to the unpopular Bavarian system of military conscription, which also used a lottery. It was particularly disliked in the countryside, where the unmarried young men of the village, following folkloric custom, formed a common group, and they felt that either all should go or none.[31]

Hanns Klein, "Wiederentdecktes Schriftgut der Pfälzer Revolutionsregierung von 1849," *JbwL* 12 (1986): 107–51, esp. pp. 143–44. The one time the troops in Germersheim attempted a major sortie, Willich's men advanced towards them, unarmed, waving the German tricolor, calling on them to desert. Some Bavarian soldiers began to do so, and their officers hastily called retreat, ending their military activity. *Der Demokrat*, 7 June 1849.

[29] These examples and others are in LAS J1 Nr. 108 ff. 121–22; LAS J1 Nr. 110 ff. 71–73, 167, 171–77, 197–98; LAS J1 Nr. 177 ff. 81–82; LAS J1 Nr. 109 f. 412.

[30] LAS J1 Nr. 109 ff. 355–56; LAS J1 Nr. 203 f. 651; LAS J1 Nr. 263 ff. 125–26; HSTAD RA Nr. 2229 ff. 243–44. The great rural uprising in the mid-century European revolutions, the 1851 revolt of French peasants against the coup d'état of Louis Napoleon-Bonaparte, occurred in December, the dead season of the agricultural calendar.

[31] LAS J1 Nr. 110 ff. 329–30; LAS J1 Nr. 218 ff. 126–28; LAS J1 Nr. 235 ff. 159–61; LAS

Conscription worked best in urban areas, where many of the eligibles were already enrolled in the civic guard, and so could be transferred without difficulty to the mobile guard. Most of the guards of the cantonal and county seats proved loyal to the Provisional Government, fought its internal enemies, and were willing to march (if not necessarily to fight) against the Prussians. There were some villages equally loyal to the revolutionary regime. The young men of Geralsheim marched to mustering in Frankenthal, led by their mayor—a Mennonite, whom one might have thought would have disapproved on religious grounds—and then went on to join the insurgent corps under Colonel Blenker in Ludwigshafen. Although there were a few exceptions, the military commissioner found that draftees from most villages of Frankenthal County, in the northeastern Palatinate, possessed a "good spirit."[32]

Much the same was the case at the other end of the Palatinate. The eligible young men of the village of Mittelbach were mustered in the schoolhouse by members of the student legion, representing the military commissioner in Zweibrücken. They drilled energetically, under the direction of the schoolteacher, who was the village democratic leader, and when called up to fight the Prussians, marched out against them, armed with scythes beaten straight. In the villages of Ingweiler and Einöd, the young men were mustered, and then elected one of their number, a day laborer who had previously served in the French Foreign Legion, to lead them in drilling and in the field.[33]

There were other villages scattered throughout the Palatinate whose young men showed a similar willingness to bear arms for the revolution, while their fellow villagers hammered scythes straight, cobbled boots, and sewed caps and tunics for them. More commonly, the peasants were less than enthusiastic about the cause. Two weeks after the institution of conscription, nothing had been done in Canton Dürkheim to raise the mobile guard: Village mayors had sent in lists of eligibles late, if at all; few or no young men had appeared for mustering. Inhabitants of most villages in Canton Kandel, in the southeastern Palatinate, were equally obstinate, their stubborn refusal to serve eventually being a factor in provoking the Polish military commissioner to hand in his resignation. In Heiligenstein, near Speyer, the mayor told the young men that they were not required to report, so they did not; in nearby Berghausen, many

---

J1 Nr. 252 (alt) ff. 163–64; LAS J1 Nr. 249 (alt) ff. 76–78, 95–96; LAS J1 Nr. 242 ff. 197–98; Klein, "Wiederentdecktes Schriftgut," p. 144; Calliess, *Militär in der Krise*, pp. 45–50. On the unmarried young men as a social group, cf. sources cited in Chapter Six, note 49.

[32] LAS J1 Nr. 108 ff. 133–34, 137, 160–63, 224; LAS J1 Nr. 110 ff. 361, 368, 395–96; LAS J1 Nr. 218 ff. 126–28, 646–47; similarly, ibid. ff. 103, 107–14. Quite a number of the Mennonites, who lived in villages around Frankenthal, seem to have sympathized with the revolution, perhaps because of the strong anti–Roman Catholic currents within it.

[33] LAS J1 Nr. 277 (alt) ff. 215–18, 242–44; LAS J1 Nr. 308 ff. 49–52; similar rustic enthusiasm in neighboring Canton Blieskastel, LAS J1 Nr. 195 passim, and parts of Canton Bergzabern, LAS J1 Nr. 177 ff. 81–82; LAS J1 Nr. 308 (alt) f. 13.

fled to the village of Lingenfeld, under the protection of the Germersheim fortress, thus avoiding the draft.[34]

Such boycotts were less disruptive of the People's Guard than the young peasants' actions when they did report for mustering. The eligible young men of Canton Kirchheimbolanden agreed in advance to refuse to draw lots, and to insist that all go or none, knowing that such a demand would disrupt the mustering because of the shortage of arms. The mustering, held in the cantonal seat, collapsed as planned, and the eligibles went home undrafted. The young men of neighboring Canton Rockenhausen, stirred up in advance by Bavarian loyalists, sabotaged conscription in a similar way. In Canton Lauterecken, the proceedings were disrupted by the bachelors of the village of Lohnweiler, who pounded on the floor with their walking sticks, demanding that the married men be taken too. The cry was taken up by the other eligibles, and the mustering was broken off.[35]

The drawing of lots for the eligibles of Canton Edenkoben was disrupted when the "lads" of the village of Rhodt, fortified by strong drink, beat up the members of the cantonal committee carrying out the mustering. The danger of the recruiters being beaten was particularly great in those cantons where they carried out the mustering isolated in the individual villages, and not in the cantonal seat under the protection of its mobile guard. Two student "legionaries" arrived several hours late for the mustering in the mountain village of Gossersweiler near the French border. The eligibles, waiting in the schoolhouse, had spent the time drinking and were in a bad mood. They assaulted the recruiters, throwing them bodily down the steps; the latter were lucky to escape with their lives.[36]

Such scenes were sometimes accompanied by counterrevolutionary demonstrations. When the young men of Canton Rockenhausen refused to draw lots, some of them broke out into cheers of "Long live King Max." Villagers of Jochgrim, coming to Kandel for the mustering, marched behind a blue-white Bavarian flag, brawling with the young men of the cantonal seat, who had a red one. The eligibles of Erlenbach, near Pirmasens, attacked the cantonal committee member come to administer the draft lottery, shouting at him, "Do you think you're the [legitimate Bavarian] County Commissioner, that you can make the young men draw lots?"[37]

[34] LAS J1 Nr. 203 ff. 574–83, 605; LAS J1 Nr. 308 f. 213; LAS J1 Nr. 109 f. 408; LAS J1 Nr. 252 (alt) ff. 160–62.

[35] LAS J1 Nr. 267 ff. 157–66; LAS J1 Nr. 249 (alt) ff. 90, 116–17, 119–20, 391; LAS J1 Nr. 215 (alt) ff. 112–15, 125, 137–38, 152–53. Similarly, *Anklag-Akte*, pt. 2, pp. 105–07.

[36] LAS J1 Nr. 205 ff. 281–82; LAS J1 Nr. 148 f. 7; similar incidents, LAS J1 Nr. 200 ff. 58–61, 88–90; LAS J1 Nr. 229 I (alt) f. 189.

[37] LAS J1 Nr. 249 (alt) ff. 90–93; LAS J1 Nr. 263 ff. 214–16; LAS J1 Nr. 200 ff. 88–90; similarly, LAS J1 Nr. 205 ff. 93–94.

Revolutionary Coercion

The supporters of the Provisional Government were not prepared to accept this disaffection; they acted firmly, energetically, and brutally to suppress opposition to the revolutionary regime, employing coercive measures to raise the People's Guard. First, they dealt with those who had openly opposed the regime. The quickest and most decisive action in breaking resistance to the draft came in Lauterecken, where the cantonal committee was composed of decidedly "exalted" democrats, with a strong following among the townspeople. On the very afternoon of the disrupted mustering, members of the town's civic guard surrounded the leader of the anticonscription demonstration, farm servant Carl Conrad of Lohnweiler, beat him unconscious with their rifle butts, and dragged him off to jail. They then picked up others who been involved in starting the disruption, taking them off to jail to jeers of "cowards, scoundrels" from the town's radicals. At that point, quite a number of young men came forth and "volunteered" to serve.[38]

When the news was received of the assault on the recruiters in Gossersweiler, the entire People's Guards—that is, not just the young men of the first levy, but their seniors as well—of the cantonal seat Annweiler, the county town Bergzabern, and six nearby winegrowing villages were mobilized and marched on the recalcitrant mountain peasants in a large-scale punitive expedition. It was a massive display of force, showing both the extent of popular support for the revolutionary regime, and the determination of its adherents to crush its enemies.[39]

After violently breaking open resistance, the cantonal committees and the civil and military commissioners went on to the next step, carrying out the mustering of the rural population by threat of force. Sometimes systematically, sometimes on a village-by-village basis, they made the communal authorities responsible for the mobilization of the first levy. If the young men did not appear, the mayor or village council would be fined or even arrested. In particularly stubborn cases, they threatened to quarter detachments of the People's Guard on the reluctant commune.[40]

These threats were quite successful. Where democrats were present but not strong enough to push the villagers into actively supporting the regime, the intervention of the urban revolutionaries changed the balance of power in the

---

[38] LAS J1 Nr. 215 (alt) ff. 139, 151–53. Similar violent intimidation of Bavarian loyalists in Canton Rockenhausen: LAS J1 Nr. 249 (alt) ff. 88, 90, 92, 115, 131.

[39] LAS J1 Nrs. 147–50 passim. The confrontation that arose out of this punitive expedition is very revealing of the characteristics of supporters and opponents of the revolutionary government, and will be discussed in some detail in the section on that topic, below.

[40] Just a few examples of this: LAS J1 Nr. 249 (alt) f. 391; LAS J1 Nr. 203 f. 605; LAS J1 Nr. 200 ff. 88–90; LAS J1 Nr. 228 (alt) f. 98; LAS J1 Nr. 229 I (alt) ff. 5, 7–8; LAS J1 Nr. 252 (alt) ff. 167–68, 170–71; LAS J1 Nr. 242 f. 172.

village. They allowed the democratic leaders—tavernkeepers, schoolteachers, rationalist Protestant pastors, or peasant "hotheads"—to mobilize the young men of the first levy for battle. More often, and this was the most common response, just the threat of coercion was enough to convince the young men, or, more correctly, to convince the village notables to convince the young men, to join the People's Guard. Even when it actually came to the use of revolutionary troops to bring in the conscripts, the show of force was often less than impressive. Ludwig Bamberger, whose Rhine-Hessian insurgents were involved in such actions on behalf of the military commissioner in Kirchheimbolanden while stationed in the Alsenz Valley, left a revealing description of the procedure:

> Into the recalcitrant villages, two men, that's right two men, were sent. These marched with pomp to the house of the mayor and ceremonially loaded their rifles. After this dangerous demonstration, the young men of the village capable of bearing arms submitted every single time. "Isn't it true," one called to the other, "I always said we would have to march out?" And frequently the two arms-bearers appeared, escorting fifty to seventy-five men into the camp [of the People's Guard].[41]

If the peasants of the Alsenz Valley, who were not quite so indifferent to the revolution as Bamberger would portray them, submitted to impressment without trouble, in villages where the peasants were more hostile to the regime, larger and more menacing detachments were needed to round up the young men. Once conscripted, they would desert at the first opportunity, or they would evade conscription altogether, fleeing into the forests, over the border to Prussia or France, or to the village of Lingenfeld, under the control of the garrison in Germersheim. Yet even this most determined resistance to the revolutionary government went little beyond the limits of political passivity: Many young peasants were willing to flee conscription in the revolutionary army, but just a handful felt strongly enough about the Bavarian regime to volunteer to fight with the king's troops against the revolution.[42]

[41] Quotation, Bamberger, "Erlebnisse aus der Pfälzer Erhebung" 3:112. For other examples, besides those cited in the previous note, see LAS J1 Nr. 267 ff. 157–66; LAS J1 Nr. 249 (alt) ff. 13–15; LAS J1 Nr. 203 ff. 183–85 (village democrats exploiting urban intervention); LAS J1 Nr. 110 ff. 193; LAS J1 Nr. 203 ff. 188–90, 216; LAS J1 Nr. 215 (alt) ff. 124, 154–56; LAS J1 Nr. 249 (alt) ff. 116–17, 119–20; LAS J1 Nr. 277 (alt) ff. 247–48; *Anklag-Akte*, pt. 2, pp. 102–03 (yielding to the threat of force); LAS J1 Nr. 168 ff. 7–10; LAS J1 Nr. 203 ff. 180–82, 187–95, 197–99; LAS J1 Nr. 218 ff. 97, 102, 104–05; LAS J1 Nr. 228 (alt) ff. 96; LAS J1 Nr. 229 I (alt) f. 189; LAS J1 Nr. 205 ff. 452–53 LAS J1 Nr. 277 (alt) ff. 220–21 (yielding to an actual military demonstration).

[42] LAS J1 Nr. 110 ff. 199, 282; LAS J1 Nr. 148 ff. 225–28; LAS J1 Nr. 195 f. 125; LAS J1 Nr. 203 ff. 185–88, 196–205; LAS J1 Nr. 205 ff. 93–94; LAS J1 Nr. 263 ff. 211–12, 243–44; LAS J1 Nr. 243 (alt) ff. 165–66; LAS J1 Nr. 249 (alt) ff. 92–94, 121–22; LAS J1 Nr. 252 (alt) ff. 160–62, 165–68; LAS J1 Nr. 277 (alt) ff. 235–36; LAK 403 Nr. 2554 pp. 63–68; LAK 441 Nr. 8317 pp. 369–71.

Along with their use of coercion, the officials of the regime offered certain concessions. Like many militias, the members of the People's Guard were reluctant to fight far from their homes. Their parents felt even more strongly about this, an attitude found even in otherwise left-wing towns and villages. Some military commissioners therefore allowed conscripts to drill at home, either under a leader of their own choosing or under an instructor from the Bavarian soldiers who had gone over to the revolution, rather than requiring them to march off to a central camp. This step certainly improved morale, but at the cost of weakening the army's ability to take the field.[43]

Major Ehlert, the energetic military commissioner in Homburg, found an additional way to facilitate the mustering process. Observing that the village officials administering the draft in his county were issuing exemptions to the sons of the better-off peasants, while insisting that the poor serve, he had the conscripts themselves decide on exemptions, obtaining in that way a remarkable increase in the number of recruits. Ehlert was even able to dismiss already-mustered recruits for this task, correctly confident that they would return with more soldiers.[44]

In all these ways, the Provisional Government succeeded in raising an army. On the eve of the Prussian invasion, it counted on paper some 12,000–13,000 soldiers: 1,500–1,800 Rhine-Hessians (down from a peak strength of 2,200–2,500), 500 under the communist August Willich, 700 other volunteer insurgents, the rest Palatine draftees of the first levy. The same record of troop strength showed that these 12,000–13,000 soldiers had only 4,200 rifles between them, many of which were hunting weapons or archaic flintlocks of Austrian manufacture, already rejected as useless by the Bavarian army. For all practical purposes, the army was untrained; morale of the conscripts brought in by force, or threat of force, was at best dubious; the prospect of confronting the Prussians essentially unarmed was not exactly encouraging, even to those insurgents with revolutionary sympathies.[45]

Camille Meuth, the constitutional monarchist cantonal physician in Kaiserslautern, who viewed the Palatine revolution with a jaundiced eye, had perhaps the best short description of the People's Guard. It consisted, he said, of ''some 10–12,000 mostly young men, without appropriate weapons, military spirit, drill, or the ability to bear up under hardship. In short, it lacked pretty

---

[43] LAS J1 Nr. 109 ff. 355–56, 404; LAS J1 Nr. 110 f. 386; LAS J1 Nr. 172 ff. 331–32.

[44] LAS J1 Nr. 110 ff. 165–66; LAS J1 Nr. 242 ff. 107–09; similarly, in Canton Kirchheimbolanden, LAS J1 Nr. 267 ff. 157–66.

[45] The original of the record of troop strength and list of weapons is attached to Commando 3er mob. Division (Steinen bei Lörrach) to General-Lieut. Prince zu Thurn und Taxis, 19 Sept. 1849, BHSTAM KA Nr. B771; another copy in Armee Corps Commando in der Pfalz (Speyer) to Gesammt Staats Ministerium, 1 Oct. 1849, BHSTAM MInn Nr. 45533. For the state of morale and armaments on the eve of the Prussian invasion, cf. LAS J1 Nr. 108 ff. 121–22; LAS J1 Nr. 110 ff. 64–65, 165–67, 171–77, 197–98, 214, 282, 395–96; LAS J1 Nr. 177 ff. 81–82.

much all the qualities needed to take the field." Accurately perceiving a Prussian invasion as the main threat to the regime, the Provisional Government was forced to raise an army. Largely because of factors outside its control, the People's Guard it managed to create was of no use against the Prussians and did more than any of its other measures to discourage its supporters, enhearten its enemies, and undermine its own rule.[46]

"Exalteds" and Moderates

The Provisional Government came to power in a tacit compromise between the moderate and "exalted" wings of the democratic movement in the Palatinate, and this compromise character continued to mark its official policy, as can best be seen by the ambiguous nature of its rule. All its decrees were issued "in the name of the Palatine people," and a week after its founding, the revolutionary government announced the Palatinate's secession from Bavaria, and ordered the royal insignia taken down from public buildings, to be replaced with the sign "Palatine Office." It always insisted, however, that its secession was provisional, lasting only until the Frankfurt constitution came into force. It never proclaimed the republic, either within the Palatinate or for all of Germany.

The regime's relationship to the Provisional Central Power and the Frankfurt National Assembly was similarly ambiguous. Officially, the revolutionaries seized power in order to fight for the realization of the Frankfurt constitution in all of Germany. For that reason, they even sent a formal notification of the creation of the Provisional Government to the imperial regent. Yet they went right on governing the Palatinate after Archduke Johann had condemned their regime as criminal, and the Frankfurt Assembly, unable to do much of anything to exert its authority, refused to recognize its legitimacy.[47]

The Provisional Government could exercise its authority across the Palatinate only because it had at its disposal a cadre of activists, politically trained in the People's Associations of the province, who filled positions as members of the cantonal committees, as officers of the People's Guard, and as revolutionary communal officials, or who acted informally, talking up the regime in taverns or on the streets. One such informal activist was the shopkeeper Xaver Bumiller of Edenkoben. Before the uprising, he had been a member of the executive committee of the town's People's Association. He held no official position in the revolutionary regime, but he demanded that its agents take the strictest possible measures, accusing the civil commissioner of laxity. Every market day Bumiller could be seen passing out the governments' printed fliers and appeals to the peasants, come to town for the market. He had the key to

[46] LAS J1 Nr. 105 ff. 177–88.

[47] Schneider, "Landesausschuß und Provisorische Regierung," pp. 105–08; BAF DB 54 Nr. 44 f. 89. Cf. LAS J1 Nr. 245 f. 140.

the storeroom in the city hall where the gunpowder was stored and directed the manufacture of cartridges.[48]

Whether or not they held any official position, such activists as Bumiller determined the character of the regime at the local level. For the "exalted" democrats—and they were the ones who put themselves to the fore—there could be no doubt of the antimonarchical goals of the movement. Before the revolutionary communal elections in the village of Dreiderslachen, in the southeastern Palatinate, the election commissioner, farmer Jacob Kraemer, gave a speech saying, "[W]e should hold together and chase all the princes to the devil." At a meeting announcing the formation of the Provisional Government, locksmith Krümmig told the peasants of Godramstein, near Landau, "[D]own with these princely dogs; down with the house of Wittelsbach."[49]

The Bavarian royal family came off especially poorly, a prominent leftist in Rheinzabern praising the new state of affairs, saying, "Now things are different, we don't need the kings and princes any more . . . we also don't have to pay for their whores, we have another government." King Max II was often called a "whore's son" [Hurenbub]. The epithet no doubt reflected memories of how his father had consorted with Lola Montez, but perhaps also expressed popular conceptions of honor and dishonor, and the rejection of a royal family whose members associated with whores. Speyer radicals took up this theme during the reign of the Provisional Government, denouncing princes as murderers, because they seduced the daughters of the poor, infecting them with venereal disease and destroying their future as happy wives and mothers.[50]

Radicals attacked monarchs more than they praised the republic, but they made no secret of what they wished to see replace monarchical rule. At a mass meeting in Steinwenden, in the northwestern Palatinate, designed to rally support for the Provisional Government, Philipp Schmidt of Kaiserslautern accomplished this task by denouncing the German princes as "rebels," closing his speech with the cry "Long live the republic!", all the spectators joining in. The cooper Michael Hoerner of Gleishorbach, near Bergzabern, a vigorous and brutal village democrat, said, "What do we need a Prussia or a Bavaria; we'll make Germany into a republic." Making the point in a nonverbal way, some officials of the revolutionary regime went around with red armbands or wearing a red sash.[51]

The decree ordering the removal of the royal insignia from public buildings

[48] LAS J1 Nr. 205 ff. 239–44.

[49] LAS J1 Nr. 263 ff. 121–22; LAS J1 Nr. 202 I (alt) ff. 103–04 Similarly, LAS J1 Nr. 263 f. 249; LAS J1 Nr. 148 f. 1; LAS J1 Nr 235 ff. 134–36, 138–42; LAS J1 Nr. 243 (alt) ff. 62–66.

[50] LAS J1 Nr. 263 f. 64; *Die Trompete von Speyer*, 19 May 1849, LAS J1 Nr. 252 II 1–2 (alt); similarly, LAS J1 Nr. 170 ff. 431–33; LAS J1 Nr. 180 ff. 609–10; LAS J1 Nr. 249 (alt) f. 98;

[51] LAS J1 Nr. 245 ff. 376–77; LAS J1 Nr. 180 ff. 611–12; LAS J1 Nr. 170 ff. 407–08; LAS J1 Nr. 180 ff. 611–12; LAS J1 Nr. 267 ff. 157–66.

offered militant leftists an opportunity to broadcast widely both their adherence to the republic and their hatred of monarchs. Taking down the Bavarian lion was sometimes a formal public ceremony, carried out by the civil commissioners, with spectators cheering and jeering. It could also be a spontaneous expression of radicalism. The inhabitants of Annweiler smashed the royal insignia one evening, and then went on to attempt to storm the gendarmerie station. Summoned to Rockenhausen for the mustering, the young men of the radical village of Katzenbach took the insignia from the office of the justice of the peace, dragged it through the dirt, and brought it home in triumph. Road signs and border posts in the blue-white colors were repainted red or black-red-gold. Pictures of the royal family and the Wittelsbach family tree were torn, burnt, or, in one instance, replaced with a picture of the Badenese republican revolutionary Friedrich Hecker.[52]

Through all these actions, the "exalted" democrats portrayed the Provisional Government as a Jacobin minirepublic. This was a less than welcome development for the Palatine moderates, to say nothing of the constitutional monarchists, but they found it difficult to counter the trend. On occasion, they could prevent the crowd from tearing down the Bavarian insignia, although sometimes only by taking them down themselves and hiding them. Civil Commissioner Müller of Kirchheimbolanden gave a speech on the marketplace of Rockenhausen on May 25, explaining that the Provisional Government did not intend to proclaim the republic, but "solely and uniquely to put through the constitution of the *Reich*." The reassurance of his speech was probably spoiled when he was followed on the tribune by one Kirchhofer from Rockenhausen, who spoke "very radically and cursed the princes and the damned priests." When public officials from part of Canton Bergzabern were called together to take the oath to the Frankfurt constitution, the democratic-monarchist Pastor Frantz of Ingenheim was willing to swear, but refused to add the required endorsement of the Provisional Government, saying, "[W]e are Bavarian and remain Bavarian." Civil Commissioner Bruch insisted that the Palatinate had seceded from Bavaria, and the meeting degenerated into a shouting match between the two.[53]

These incidents are revealing of the broader difficulties the moderate democrats of the Palatinate had in relating to the Provisional Government, whose creation they had opposed and whose policies they perceived as leading to disaster. They had several alternatives, none of which was very palatable.

---

[52] Schneider, "Landesausschuß und Provisorische Regierung," p. 108; *KnZ*, 30 May 1849; LAS J1 Nr. 174 f. 13; LAS J1 Nr. 218 f. 359; LAS J1 Nr. 242 ff. 69–73; LAS J1 Nr. 245 ff. 49–50; LAS J1 Nr. 200 ff. 51–58; LAS J1 Nr. 205 ff. 207–08, 220–21; LAS J1 Nr. 242 ff. 621–24; LAS J1 Nr. 249 (alt) ff. 8–11, 92–93, 107, 139–40; LAS J1 Nr. 277 (alt) ff. 27–30.

[53] LAS J1 Nr. 110 ff. 329–30; LAS J1 Nr. 203 ff. 395–99; LAS J1 Nr. 147 f. 13; LAS J1 Nr. 249 (alt) ff. 76–78; LAS J1 Nr. 170 ff. 45–47; cf. Schneider, "Landesausschuß und Provisorische Regierung," p. 108.

Some just refused to have anything to do with the whole movement as it became increasingly radical. The cantonal committee of Pirmasens, for instance, resigned from office upon the proclamation of the revolutionary regime. Its counterpart in Canton Annweiler, which contained an unusually large number of state officials (they had joined the People's Association there at the end of 1848 to prevent the radicals from dominating it), took a further step. It condemned the Provisional Government and its secession from Bavaria, announced that it would no longer obey orders from Kaiserslautern, and reconstituted itself a "Committee of Safety for the Protection of Property and Persons in the Canton."

These abdications backfired, opening the field to the radicals. In Pirmasens, Civil Commissioner Diehl responded to the resignation of the old cantonal committee by having a new one elected, composed entirely of radical republicans, willing to carry out the most extreme measures of the Provisional Government. Civil Commissioner Bruch of Bergzabern County (which included Canton Annweiler) dissolved the "Committee of Safety," annulled all its measures, and either took over its tasks himself or turned them over to the active and energetic radicals of Annweiler. Abdication might clear the moderates' consciences or, more important, prevent them from being thrown in jail when Bavarian rule was restored, but it did nothing to stop the radicals from acting.[54]

Little more successful were attempts to confront the Provisional Government directly, demanding that it change its policies. The most serious effort was undertaken by G. F. Kolb, following the collapse of his attempt to end the uprising by having the king of Bavaria elected emperor. Fleeing Munich, Kolb returned to Speyer, taking up his post of mayor there, rather than his portfolio in the Provisional Government. He chaired a meeting called by the city council of Neustadt a.d.W. at the beginning of June, also attended by several city councilmen from Speyer, which demanded that the revolutionary communal elections be postponed, that the civil commissioners be stripped of their powers, and that no new laws, in particular, no taxes, be levied without the consent of an elected representative assembly. In a similar but apparently not directly connected move, the city council of Zweibrücken demanded the repeal of the decrees calling for new communal elections and collection of taxes.

Had these demands been granted, they would have paralyzed the Provisional Government and prevented it from preparing for war. With the Prussians at the border, this would have been tantamount to beginning a liquidation of the revolutionary regime, which was probably what the moderates had in

---

[54] LAS J1 Nr. 104 ff. 16–21; LAS J1 Nr. 113 ff. 36–41; LAS J1 Nr. 148 ff. 233–40; LAS J1 Nr. 149 ff. 26–29, 239; LAS J1 Nr. 243 (alt) ff. 50–66. Similarly, on the part of the cantonal committee of Winnweiler, LAS J1 Nr. 110 ff. 79, 359–60; and of the city council of Kirchheimbolanden, LAS J1 Nr. 267 ff. 113–16.

mind, but was unacceptable to the Provisional Government and the radical democrats in general. The movement in Neustadt itself collapsed when the officers of the civic guard refused to support it, but in Speyer and Zweibrücken, where it enjoyed the support of the cantonal committees and the toleration of the politically moderate civil commissioners, more energetic steps were needed. The Provisional Government sent detachments of the People's Guard to both cities, and forced the city councils to back down. The forces sent to Zweibrücken were commanded by Gottfried Kinkel, the Bonn radical fleeing to the Palatinate and offering his services to the revolutionary regime, following the failure of the uprising in Siegburg. Kinkel not only intimidated the city council; he gave a powerful and fiery speech on the marketplace, ending with the spectators cheering wildly and endorsing his proposal that the Provisional Government not be bound by the Frankfurt constitution but act as a revolutionary dictatorship.[55]

Both withdrawal from public life and open opposition to the Provisional Government proving unsatisfactory, most moderates chose to cooperate with the revolutionary regime, hoping to avert the worst. Moderates on the cantonal committees of Edenkoben, Neustadt a.d.W., and Kaiserslautern, all points of concentration for the revolutionary army, devoted themselves assiduously to arranging quarters for the troops, trying to reduce the burdens of quartering on the townspeople as much as possible. Civic guard officers took up corresponding ranks in the People's Guard, using their positions to ensure discipline and order in the insurgent armed forces.[56]

Moderates actively participated in the revolutionary work of the cantonal committees, ensuring that these tasks were not carried out by extremists. The moderate democrat, merchant, and banker Friedrich Dacqué of Neustadt a.d.W., in charge of the mustering in Gimmeldingen, explained to the peasants that the task was a most unpleasant one for him. He was doing it because had he refused, then "perhaps another would have been ordered to, who would have been stricter and more inconsiderate." The cantonal committee of nearby Dürkheim, dominated by the moderates but under pressure from both the local radicals and the Provisional Government, was forced to confiscate the public treasuries in its canton, but chose someone to do it who would not take all the money, but leave enough to keep the government offices functioning.[57]

---

[55] Renner, "Die pfälzische Bewegung," pp. 180–84; *Anklag-Akte*, pt. 2, p. 116; *NSZ*, 30 May, 6, 8 June 1849; LAS J1 Nr. 106 I f. 46; LAS J1 Nr. 229 I (alt) ff. 134–35; LAS J1 Nr. 252 (alt) ff. 140–50. See also the self-justification of the Provisional Government, "An das Pfälzer Volk!" in *Amts- und Intelligenzblatt der Provisorischen Regierung der Rheinpfalz*, 10 June 1849.

[56] LAS J1 Nr. 109 f. 349; LAS J1 Nr. 205 ff. 316–25, 455–60; LAS J1 Nr. 228 (alt) f. 897; LAS J1 Nr. 229 I (alt) ff. 9–10; BM Watzenberg (Edenkoben) to LK Edenkoben, 26 July 1849, LAS J1 Nr. 113/2.

[57] LAS J1 Nr. 203 ff. 314–15; LAS J1 Nr. 229 (alt) I f. 180; similarly, ibid. f. 5; LAS J1 Nr. 218 ff. 318–27; LAS J1 Nr. 200 ff. 65–66.

As time went on, and both the character of the revolutionary regime and the likelihood of its destruction by Prussian invasion became ever more apparent, most moderates found themselves in a position from which they could see no way out. Mayor Wilhelm Sauerbeck of Bad Dürkheim, an active member of the cantonal committee, admitted to a forester on several occasions "that the whole business was repugnant to him," but if he and those who thought as he did resigned, the town's radicals would take power and carry out their drastic measures without any restraint. Sauerbeck's patience was rewarded when he and his fellow moderates succeeded in convincing the Provisional Government to remove their canton from the jurisidiction of the civil commissioner in Neustadt, a one-time ally of the Palatine communists, who had appointed a local radical to represent him in Bad Dürkheim. In his place, they received their own civil commissioner, who was not very strict about raising the People's Guard or, more important, about collecting the forced loan to pay for it, an issue dear to the hearts of the bourgeoisie of the Haardt Mountains.[58]

The lack of influence of the Palatine communists on the Provisional Government was also a victory for the moderates. Communist leaders Johann Weber and Heinrich Loose refused to take office under the revolutionary regime, since it was not radical enough for them. Instead, they set themselves up as a left-wing opposition, articulating their position in their newspaper, *Der Pfälzer Volksmann* [The Palatine Man of the People], planned in March 1849 as a provincial organ for the radical wing of the People's Associations, but first published during the uprising. The Neustadt communists demanded that the Provisional Government take such decisively revolutionary measures as conscripting young men into the People's Guard at gunpoint or declaring martial law and bringing enemies of the regime before military tribunals. A truly revolutionary regime, they asserted, would have to break politically with outdated "liberals" of the generation of the Hambach Festival, a description fitting most of the leading moderates in and around Neustadt. Tax reform was the only measure of social revolution they specifically proposed, but their visceral hostility toward the bourgeoisie appeared both in print and, more evidently, when they gathered in the Republic tavern in Neustadt, denouncing the "property-owning class" and saying that "when the time comes to strike, then the blood of the money-bags must flow."[59]

The Provisional Government rejected such a position as counterproductive, since it meant stirring up the hatred of the poor against the "self-sacrificing

---

[58] LAS J1 Nr. 203 ff. 164–74, 206–208, 222–23, 395–97. For similar situations elsewhere, cf. LAS J1 Nr. 218 ff. 35–36, 121–26, 314–15; LAS J1 Nr. 229 I (alt) ff. 175–76; LAS J1 Nr. 200 ff. 55–58.

[59] LAS J1 Nr. 228 (alt) ff. 254–56; LAS J1 Nr. 229 I (alt) ff. 128–29, 199–201; *Der Pfälzer Volksmann*, 20, 29 May, 3, 7, 11 June 1849; ibid. ff. 131–39. Interestingly, the extreme leftists imitated the moderates' call for elections to a provincial assembly, presumably hoping, as did the moderates, that such an assembly would enable them to control the Provisional Government.

property-owners'' who supported the revolution, and not just against the wor-
shippers of mammon who wanted nothing to do with it. This distinction was
reminiscent of attitudes expressed earlier in 1848–1849 by many democrats in
the southern Rhineland. It also suggested that radicals in the regime regarded
cooperation with the moderates, whose ranks included many large merchants
and estate owners, as more important for the revolution than the support of the
extreme left. A number of Neustadt leftists, former allies of the communists
in the Democratic Club and Workers' Association, agreed with this argument,
including the Neustadt civil commissioner, Karl Klein.[60]

A policy of cooperation with the Provisional Government was well suited
to the interest of the Palatine bourgeoisie, so prominent among the moderates'
leadership, in preserving their property throughout the revolutionary events.
We need not infer this; we have the word of vineyard owner Ludwig Heinrich
Wolf of Wachenheim, probably the richest man in the province. After the
suppression of the uprising, he praised the actions of Canton Dürkheim's civil
commissioner in keeping power out of the hands of the radicals, explaining
that the policy of cooperating with the revolutionary authorities and avoiding
any use of force was one he had personally advocated.[61]

Wolf made these remarks as part of a sworn deposition for the investigation
of the uprising's leaders on charges of high treason. Yet his comments show a
complete lack of loyalty toward the Bavarian monarchy. If the Palatine moderates opposed the Jacobin policies of the Provisional Government and feared
the war with Prussia it was preparing, they had little desire for the reassertion
of Bavarian authority, unloved by them at least since 1832. In many ways
their position was akin to that of the constitutional monarchist bourgeoisie of
Elberfeld and Solingen a few weeks earlier, during the regime of the committees of safety, except that the Palatine moderates were worse off, since they
had much less sympathy for the legitimate government and lacked any body
of armed supporters. Cooperation was thus the most sensible policy for them
to pursue, preferable to abdication or confrontation, but it also had its price:
Moderates could mitigate the actions ordered by the revolutionary government
in Kaiserslautern and keep politically more extreme elements from representing it at the local level only by carrying out themselves the revolutionary government's measures. In moderating the regime, they both legitimized it and
enabled it to function effectively.

ADHERENTS AND OPPONENTS OF THE PALATINE REVOLUTION

While the measures taken by the Provisional Government helped mobilize its
supporters, or, more often, dissipate their support, the basic identity of its

---

[60] LAS J1 Nr. 245 ff. 155–56; LAS J1 Nr. 229 I (alt) ff. 1–2, 5, 131–32.
[61] LAS J1 Nr. 203 ff. 211–14.

friends and enemies had stemmed from the structure of Palatine society and the political experiences it had gone through in the year preceding the revolutionaries' seizure of power. Two aspects of these experiences proved decisive in determining popular responses to the regime: inter- and intraconfessional conflict, so important to political life in the Rhineland, and the specific problems of the peasantry, the largest element in Palatine society.

Religion and the Revolutionary Regime

The largest religious conflict pitted the Catholic Church against the revolutionary movement. Hostility to the church, always a major feature of radicalism in the southern Rhineland, flared up again in the Palatinate at the beginning of the movement for the Frankfurt constitution. A mass meeting of the People's Association in support of the constitution in the religiously mixed but predominantly Roman Catholic village of Eppstein on April 29, 1849, led to a major riot between the village's Catholics, strong supporters of the Pius Association, and leftists from surrounding, predominantly Protestant villages and the nearby city of Frankenthal.[62]

The events in Eppstein, which were accompanied by similar ones elsewhere in the province, conflated religious and political conflicts. To neoorthodox Roman Catholics, the movement for the Frankfurt constitution was an attack on their religion, not an inaccurate perception, since many Palatine leftists found Catholicism and democracy incompatible. When the left seized power in the province, the stage was set for a confrontation between the activists of the revolutionary regime and the Catholic Church.

Catholic clergy and lay members of the Pius Association were decided enemies of the Provisional Government. Virtually all priests called on to take the oath of loyalty to the Frankfurt constitution refused firmly and openly. The pastor of Freinsheim announced that he would rather be led with a rope around his neck to Kaiserslautern than obey the Provisional Government, while his colleague in Schoenau, near Pirmasens, "cursed out" the revolutionary regime to anyone who would listen. Priests ordered the Catholic schoolteachers to sing the *Domine Salvum fac Regens* in church and to lead the children in praying for the king. The parish priest in Eppstein counseled furloughed soldiers to return to their regiments when recalled; his colleague in the village of Lingenfeld exhorted the not very warlike troops in the fortress of Germersheim to fight the insurgent columns besieging them. Many priests refused, publicly and angrily, to make any contributions for the People's Guard. The pastor in Schifferstadt told his flock that doing so would be falling into the snares of

[62] LK Frankenthal to RP, 30 Apr. 1849; Gendarmerie Station Frankenthal to Corps Command, Speyer, 30 Apr. 1849; RP to MInn, 4 May 1849, all in BHSTAM MInn Nr. 45531. A very similar, if more peaceful, confrontation occurred about the same time in villages of Canton Landstuhl, LAS J1 Nr. 242 ff. 55–57.

Satan; they should instead gather money for the Holy Father, driven out of Rome by republican revolutionaries.[63]

Lay activists of the Pius Association were equally hostile to the regime. The son of the chairman of the Pius Association of Leistadt led a cat music against the Protestant schoolteacher, the only official in the village to take the oath of loyalty to the Frankfurt constitution. A member in Breitenbach crossed the border and reported to the Prussians in St. Wendel on the positions and armaments of the People's Guard. The village clerk Ferdinand Maehrlein of Rülzheim, also chairman of its Pius Association, refused to post the decrees of the Provisional Government, corresponded with the Bavarian authorities in the fortress of Germersheim, and capped off his counterrevolutionary deeds by leading a security patrol, which captured a Bavarian soldier deserting from Germersheim and returned him to face a firing squad. This was only avoided when Willich's corps took Maehrlein hostage, announcing that if the deserter were shot, they would retaliate against the Bavarian loyalist responsible for his capture.[64]

Devout, neoorthodox Catholics were by far the largest group of true friends the Bavarian government had in the Palatinate, far more reliable than the bureaucracy or the army. Or were they? As the uprising went on, and the Bavarian state did nothing to stop it, some Palatine Catholics began to look for the defense of their religion to Germany's leading counterrevolutionary government, even if was headed by a Protestant monarch. Borrusophile sentiments began in some instances to replace or at least coexist with Bavarian loyalism. The parish priest in Kübelberg announced that "Russia, Prussia and Austria have formed an alliance to protect Catholicism." When Prussian troops marched into the Palatinate, the town of Landstuhl, stronghold of the Pius Association, was decked in black and white flags. A Prussian major, quartered in Speyer with the diocese's vicar-general, reported to his superiors the latter had told him that it would be a good thing if the Palatinate were annexed by the Prussian state.[65]

[63] LAS J1 Nr. 203 ff. 271–73; LAS J1 Nr. 200 ff. 92–93; LAS J1 Nr. 218 ff. 139–42; LAS J1 Nr. 205 ff. 396–97, 622–24; LAS J1 Nr. 228 (alt) ff. 99–100; LAS J1 Nr. 242 ff. 134–35; LAS J1 Nr. 252 (alt) ff. 99–102; *Die Trompete von Speyer*, 16 May 1849, LAS J1 Nr. 252 II/1–2 (alt); LAS J1 Nr. 264 ff. 567–73; LAS J1 Nr. 148 ff. 1, 212–14; LAS J1 Nr. 149 ff. 26–29, 235–37; LAS J1 Nr. 249 (alt) ff. 118, 125; *Anklag-Akte*, pt. 2, p. 84; Koch and Paul, "Die Ereignisse im Kanton Landstuhl," p. 336; Hanns Klein, "Gottfried Kinkel als Emissär der provisorischen Regierung der Pfalz im Frühjahr 1849 in Westrich," *JbwL* 8 (1982): 107–35, esp. pp. 118, 127–28. The few priests who did take the oath later explained that they feared—with good reason—that if they refused, they would be deposed from office and replaced by sectarian German Catholics. LAS J1 Nr. 235 f. 171.

[64] LAS J1 Nr. 203 ff. 385–92; LAS J1 Nr. 242 ff. 220–36; LAS J1 Nr. 264 ff. 490–523, 567–73, 593–98.

[65] LAS J1 Nr. 242 ff. 134–35; LAK 403 Nr. 2554 pp. 37–38, 149–53; cf. Schurz, *Lebenserinnerungen*, p. 214.

Whether pro-Bavarian or pro-Prussian, neoorthodox Catholics were certainly militant opponents of the Provisional Government. A few supporters of the revolutionary regime, including some of the most extreme radicals, were able to hold their tempers in the face of this position and separate religion from politics. Insisting that they had nothing against Catholicism as such, just opposing its use for reactionary purposes, they offered to guarantee the safety of individual priests or even to send detachments of the People's Guard to protect the Corpus Christi processions. For most Palatine revolutionaries, however, the political stance of the clergy and the Pius Associations offered an all too welcome opportunity to act out the worst of their anti-Catholic prejudices.[66]

During the rule of the Provisional Government, the whole province rang with cries of "We're going to get the damned priest" [Wir holen den Pfaff]. Those Catholic clergy who took a determined public stand against the regime—and some who did not—were victims of cat musics or were arrested by detachments of the People's Guard, led off to shouts of "You deserve to be hanged [or shot]," "man of darkness" [Finsterling], "rotten priest," and similar epithets. In some places, it was their own parishioners, following the lead of People's Association activists, who turned in or attacked the priests; elsewhere, schoolteachers got their long-awaited revenge. Stefan Lorenz, parish priest in Pirmasens, noting a Bavarian soldier who had gone over to the revolutionary government, said to a Catholic schoolteacher, "I see things have gone so far that people do not just want the republic, but the red republic." The teacher replied, "You blacks [that is, clericals, reactionaries] have been on top long enough; now it's the reds' turn." The teacher's reply was quoted throughout the city, and shortly thereafter the crowd assaulted the priest's house, smashing windows and furniture, leading him through the streets in his nightshirt, and screaming curses at him, until he was rescued by some compassionate inhabitants and democratic leaders calmed the crowd.[67]

Pirmasens was a predominantly Protestant city, and Father Lorenz's assailants were angry at him because of his long-term opposition to religiously mixed marriages, and not just because he had attacked the movement and publicly refused to contribute to the People's Guard. In the two areas of the Palatinate where relations between the revolutionary regime and the Catholic Church were at their worst, elements of interconfessional hostility, conflicts

---

[66] For such moderate attitudes toward the Catholic Church, see LAS J1 Nr. 110 ff. 59–60; LAS J1 Nr. 242 ff. 152–56; LAS J1 Nr. 264 ff. 543–48, 567–73, 762; LAS J1 Nr. 202 I (alt) ff. 95–96; LAS J1 Nr. 203 ff. 749–50. Cf. Schurz, *Lebenserinnerungen*, pp. 212–16. One of those expressing such an attitude was August Willich, like the other Cologne communists, desirous of avoiding a direct confrontation with the Catholic Church.

[67] LAS J1 Nr. 106 I ff. 304–08; LAS J1 Nr. 203 ff. 271–73; LAS J1 Nr. 264 f. 764; LAS J1 Nr. 243 (alt) ff. 30–35 (schoolteachers and own parishioners); LAS J1 Nr. 148 ff. 7–8; LAS J1 Nr. 203 ff. 271–73; LAS J1 Nr. 242 ff. 48–51, 55–57, 182–85, 627–30 (epithets); LAS J1 Nr. 243 (alt) ff. 120–22; LK Pirmasens to RP, 31 Jan. 1850, BHSTAM MInn Nr. 45615 (Pirmasens).

between rationalism and neoorthodoxy, and clashes between republicanism and Bavarian loyalism were all mixed together. Both these areas were in the western part of the province, Homburg County in the north and Bergzabern County in the south.

Some of the leading revolutionaries in Homburg County were anticlerical to an extent unusual even in the Palatinate. The bailiff Veit Zoeller of Waldmohr had left the Catholic Church but not joined another, his atheism a source of astonishment and horror to his contempraries. His counterpart in Landstuhl was a German Catholic who liked to say, "The princes are too strongly supported by the clergy. The latter must thus be overthrown first, before we can demand anything of the princes." Throughout 1848–1849 he denounced monarchs and priests, and enrolled peasants in the People's Association in the course of his official duties.[68]

He had his work cut out for him, since the cantonal town of Landstuhl was the stronghold of the Pius Associations in the Palatinate, the 336 Pius Association members outnumbering the organized democrats there about four and a half to one. The association's leader, the pastor Matthias Weber, was equally militant in his politically reactionary and religiously neoorthodox attitudes. In 1832, he had refused to put up exiled Polish revolutionaries, drawing the hostility of the local adherents of the democratic movement at the time of the Hambach Festival. Weber's "intolerant" sermons, denouncing Protestants (and, one presumes, the practice of Catholics' marrying them) drew the hostility of more rationalist and bourgeois members of his congregation, who in 1837 unsuccessfully petitioned the bishop to have him removed from his parish.[69]

The Landstuhl Cantonal Committee, sure that the strength of the Pius Association would make the mustering of the eligibles very difficult, applied to the Provisional Government for armed protection. The government sent the Kaiserslautern scythe men, commanded by the radical, violently anticlerical, and mentally unbalanced revolutionary Christian Zinn. His armed corps marched into Landstuhl on May 26, announcing their intention of "getting the damnned priest." Their presence in the canton did rather more harm to the regime's cause than good, and they were soon withdrawn, to be replaced by the mobile guards of Zweibrücken and the county town of Homburg. The revolutionary soldiers from these predominantly Protestant cities spent much of their time marching into Catholic villages and arresting lay and clerical opponents of the Provisional Government, or at least those who had not fled to safety in the nearby Prussian Rhine Province. Many of the Protestant villages of the area, on the other hand, were enthusiastic supporters of the

[68] LAS J1 Nr. 242 ff. 22–28, 186–88.
[69] Koch and Paul, "Die Ereignisse im Kanton Landstuhl," pp. 332–33; LAS J1 Nr. 242 ff. 141–44.

regime. Gottfried Kinkel, sent as a representative of the Kaiserslautern government to inspect military conditions on the border with Prussia, noted their fine fighting spirit and revolutionary dedication—something seemingly mixed up in their inhabitants' minds with anti-Catholicism.[70]

In Reichenbach, a heavily Protestant village, which was, however, the parish seat for surrounding Catholic communities, the peasants reacted with substantial hostility when the parish priest refused to contribute money to the People's Guard. They brought him a cat music and, several days later, on the night of Pentecost Sunday, attempted to storm the rectory. Pastor Heitzmann barricaded himself in the storeroom, and had the storm bells rung, bringing his parishioners from the nearby Catholic villages, armed with rustic implements, rushing to his defense. The rumor spread among the Protestants of the vicinity that the Catholics were planning to cut their throats, and they marched on Reichenbach, similarly armed, so that two religiously and politically contrary peasant militias faced each other the following day.

A detachment of the Homburg People's Guard came to Reichenbach and defused the situation, sending everybody home and taking the priest, at his own request, into protective custody. Rather than deliver him to a predominantly Catholic village of his parish, as he wished, they brought him to Homburg, amidst jeers and insults from the crowd, and sent him to Kaiserslautern as a prisoner. He was released, and allowed to go into exile in France.[71]

The restoration of Bavarian rule brought with it the victory of neoorthodox Catholicism over Protestantism and atheism. The women of the predominantly Roman Catholic mining town of Oberbexbach caught revolutionary Veit Zoeller attempting to flee, beat him up, and took him prisoner. Pastor Weber returned to Landstuhl in triumph from exile in Prussia to celebrate a high mass, leading the faithful in singing the *Domine Salvum fac Regens*, the altar decorated with the blue-white flag. Pastor Heitzmann also returned from exile to Reichenbach, escorted by a wagon convoy bearing the flags of Bavaria and the Mother of God. He later noted a historical peculiarity of the Protestants of his village: Every time there was a revolution—in the 1790s, in 1832, and again in 1849—they had attacked the Catholic priest living among them.[72]

[70] LAS J1 Nr. 108 ff. 224–27; LAS J1 Nr. 110 ff. 59–60; LAS J1 Nr. 242 ff. 12–17, 31–34, 55–59, 67–68, 134–35, 152–58; Rose Kermann, "Zwichen Revolution und Integration: Der Kaiserslauterner Bürger Carl Christian Julius Zinn (6.6.1821–1.4.1890)," *JhGStLK* 22/23 (1984/85): 223–52; Rink, "Ereignisse im Kanton Otterberg," pp. 369–70; Koch and Paul, "Die Ereignisse im Kanton Landstuhl," pp. 336–38; Klein, "Gottfried Kinkel as Emissär," p. 128. Kinkel also noted that on the other side of the border in Prussia, religious and political loyalties tended to be reversed (ibid., pp. 127, 133). There, the Protestant villages were conservative, while the Catholic ones supported the left—a wonderful example of the importance of religion-based monarchist loyalism in determining political attitudes in 1848–1849.

[71] LAS J1 Nr. 242 ff. 141–44, 179–85, 627–30; Koch and Paul, "Die Ereignisse im Kanton Landstuhl," pp. 335–37.

[72] LAS J1 Nr. 242 ff. 110–11, 627–30; Koch and Paul, "Die Ereignisse im Kanton Landstuhl," pp. 333, 336.

There was a similar clash between Catholics and Protestants in Bergzabern County, leading to two of the three deaths incurred in the otherwise largely bloodless Palatine revolution. Even before the uprising, politics in the county had been centered on the opposition between the two strongly left-wing towns, Bergzabern and Annweiler, supported by the mostly Protestant winegrowers, and the up-country Catholic villages in the Vosges Mountains to the west, devout and Bavarian loyalist, although situated in one of the poorest areas of the province. The Bergzabern democrats referred to these villagers as "Croatians," after the Catholic mountaineers of the Balkans, who had reconquered revolutionary Vienna for the Habsburg emperor.[73]

Led by their priests, the up-country villagers refused to recognize the authority of the Provisional Government. On June 4, Bergzabern democrat Valentin Borscht led a force of some seven hundred civic guardsmen from his city and seven nearby villages, six of them Protestant and viticultural, to the mountain village of Steinbach to force its officials to take the oath to the Frankfurt consitution and to compel the young men of the first levy to submit to conscription. Armed with pitchforks and flails, the peasants were at first planning to resist, but thought better of it and submitted, narrowly avoiding bloodshed.[74]

Blood did flow a week later, in the up-country village of Gossersweiler. After the two student legionaries sent to perform the mustering were beaten up by the eligible young men, rumor reached Annweiler and Bergzabern that they had been killed and the region was in insurrection against the Provisional Government. Great excitement reigned among leftist sympathizers; armed columns from Bergzabern, Annweiler, and several of the viticultural villages set out to suppress the uprising. The participants had no doubt who was responsible, the men from Annweiler announcing their intention to "get the damned priest" and telling an inhabitant of Gossersweiler they met on the way, "It's the fault of your damned priest that the peasants won't submit to the Provisional Government."

The storm bells were rung, and the villagers of Gossersweiler and neighboring Völkersweiler marched out to defend themselves and their religion. Badly outnumbered and outgunned, they soon surrendered, but only after one of their number had been shot and killed. The guardsmen of Annweiler marched into Gossersweiler, demanding a few loaves of bread and cups of wine—a small fortune to the totally impoverished mountain villagers. Then the column from Bergzabern appeared, and made straight for the rectory, bursting in and mocking the pictures of the saints on the walls, arresting the

---

[73] V. Borscht (Bergzabern) to G. F. Kolb, 3 Feb. 1849, BAF FN 9 Nachlaß G. F. Kolb; LAS J1 Nr. 104 ff. 16–21; LAS J1 Nr. 170 ff. 392–93, 421–22; LAS J1 Nr. 177 ff. 213–14; Wettengel, "Das liberale und demokratische Vereinswesen," pp. 86–88; Becker, *Die Pfalz und die Pfälzer*, pp. 425–32.

[74] LAS J1 Nr. 108 ff. 160–61; LAS J1 Nr. 168 ff. 7–10.

parish priest and his assistant. The latter was a Franciscan from the monastery in Oggersheim, whose abolition had been a demand of the Palatine left for years. Not content, both columns marched on another up-country village, Schwannheim, aiming to arrest the priest there, who had publicly refused to take the oath to the Frankfurt constitution. Forewarned, he was able to flee, but the armed men intimidated his housekeeper, turned everything upside down in search of him, and slashed all the leather holy water flasks they found in his bedroom.[75]

There was something sad, even to contemporaries, about this spectacle of the revolutionary intimidation and terrorization of some of the poorest and most wretched inhabitants of the Palatinate. The last column of armed men to reach Gossersweiler, composed of inhabitants of the winegrowing villages, seems to have perceived this, and the up-country peasants remembered them as the nicest and "most decent." One of their number, the Protestant school-teacher Edinger, commander of the People's Guard of Heuchelheim, gave a speech in front of the church, trying to explain the goals of the democrats. They did not want to suppress religion, as the "damned priests" said, but to defend the Palatinate from the Prussians and the Russians and to fight against the monarchy. The mountain villagers, the most oppressed and impoverished in the province, he asserted, should join the struggle, for, he told them, "You must eat potatoes and toil the whole year through, while others stuff themselves with tender veal and ox-meat."[76]

Sympathetic as it was, the speech had no political effect. Following the Prussian invasion and the fall of the revolutionary regime, but before the Prussian armies had reached the southwestern Palatinate, the leading revolutionaries in Bergzabern, including Civil Commissioner Bruch and Valentin Borscht, attempted to flee to France. They were captured by the peasants of Steinfeld, and as had happened a week before, after the incident in Gossersweiler, a wave of anger swept through the crowd in Bergzabern. The former civic guard, reinforced by neighboring vintners, gathered, armed, on June 17, 1849, and marched on Steinfeld to liberate their leaders. The parish priest fled, a good idea since one of the armed men from Bergzabern shouted at the villagers: "You cattle! Do you want to live another thirty years as slaves? Your damned priests have led you to this!"

The male villagers, most of whom were so drunk they could hardly stand up straight, refused to let the captives go, despite pleas from the women to be

[75] LAS J1 Nr. 147 ff. 73–74, 154–57; LAS J1 Nr. 148 ff. 1, 7–8, 15, 18–19, 23–30, 51, 66, 183–84, 189–90, 211–14, 283–85; LAS J1 Nr. 149 ff. 26–29. The death occurred when members of the armed columns wrestled with a villager—a Bavarian deserter who had not joined the insurgents—for his gun. Although the judiciary interrogated several hundred witnesses (depositions in LAS J1 Nr. 148), they could never determine whether the deceased was shot by a member of the Annweiler People's Guard or accidentally by the deserter, his own brother.

[76] LAS J1 Nr. 148 ff. 35–37, 47–48.

sensible and avoid violence. Instead, they requested (unsuccessfully) armed assistance from the commandant of the French border fortress at Weissenburg; then they theatened to kill their prisoners and shot at the armed townspeople, who returned the fire, killing one villager. The village mayor released the prisoners that evening, and promptly had to flee, so angry were the pious peasants at him for having liberated the revolutionaries.[77]

Political conflicts in Bergzabern County during the rule of the Provisional Government were reminiscent of those during the French Revolution, the armed sans-culottes of Bergzabern and Annweiler, supported by the wine-growing peasants, clashing with the impoverished, but devout and hence monarchist—or, as people said in both 1793 and 1849, "aristocratic"—mountain peasants. These conflicts were also a late episode of the Reformation. Protestant revolutionaries mocked images of the saints and slashed holy water flasks. They insulted and arrested priests and attacked Catholic villagers, who had themselves once been Calvinists, but had reconverted to Catholicism in the seventeenth century, under the influence of the Jesuits and the pressure of Louis XIV's soldiers. This opposition of Protestant Jacobinism and Catholic conservatism, typical of Palatine politics in the years 1830–1850, found its most violent expression in Bergazabern County in May–June 1849.[78]

By no means all Protestants were Jacobins. Adherents of neoorthodoxy were, if anything, even more faithful adherents of their king than devout Catholics. Revivalist pastor Johann Schiller of Iggelheim had so stirred up his parishioners against the Provisional Government that one democrat noted, calling for help, "[O]ur brothers, the true patriots, are in danger of being assaulted and beaten to death." The revolutionary authorities in Neustadt a.d.W. ordered Schiller arrested, but since his parishioners vigorously defended him, it took several detachments of insurgent troops to accomplish this, who were then quartered there for three days at the villagers' expense as punishment.[79]

Schiller's example was followed by other neoorthodox pastors, who refused to take the oath to the Frankfurt constitution, publicly said prayers for the king, and preached sermons denouncing the revolutionary regime, even if it meant facing arrest or a beating at the hands of their own parishioners. Devout Protestant laymen acted similarly, in the religiously mixed village Weidenthal,

---

[77] LAS J1 Nr. 168 ff. 7–10; LAS J1 Nr. 170 ff. 241–52, 257–58, 267–69, 289–90, 301–02, 307–09, 316–17, 332–33, 338–39, 360–61, 366–68; LAS J1 Nr. 171 ff. 17–24, 71–72, 102–03, 106–08; *Anklag-Akte*, pt. 2., pp. 223–26. A similar confrontation at the same time in Canton Pirmasens was avoided, when the Catholic, conservative peasants of Winzeln released the revolutionary leader they had arrested before the inhabitants of Pirmasens marched out to get him. LAS J1 Nr. 243 (alt) ff. 147–49.

[78] On the reconversion of the up-country peasants, cf. Becker, *Die Pfalz und die Pfälzer*, p. 430.

[79] LAS J1 Nr. 110 f. 56; LAS J1 Nr. 228 (alt) ff. 97–98, 254–56, 341, 397–99.

to the west of Neustadt a.d.W., even forming an alliance with the Catholic villagers. This united "party of the bigots" [Muckerpartei] terrorized the few village democrats, dominated the communal elections called by the Provisional Government, and brought a cat music to the rationalist Protestant pastor, an adherent of the revolutionary regime, calling out cheers for King Max and shouting, "we're no Heckers; we shit all over the Provisional Government."[80]

The radical commitment of the pastor of Weidenthal was typical of Protestant rationalists, and more than a few rationalist clergymen openly supported the revolutionary regime. The pastor of the border village Kirkel-Neuhäusel, president of the local People's Association, led his parishioners in barricading the roads leading to Prussia, exhorted the young men to enlist in the People's Guard, had a tree of liberty planted to celebrate the Palatine revolution, and crossed into Prussian territory to distribute revolutionary leaflets among the troops gathering there to crush it. His counterpart in Godramstein near Landau publicly called for the republic and had his daughters forge bullets for the People's Guard in the rectory kitchen. No doubt aiding the revolutionary mood in Canton Lauterecken was the preaching of "subversion" by the vicar in Odenbach and "mistrust of the princes" by Pastor Müller in the cantonal seat. Pastor Mathies in Homburg was a "big democrat," very active for the revolutionary cause. Although the opinions of lay rationalists are not so well documented as those of clerical ones, there is no reason to doubt that most of the Palatine Protestants who supported the revolutionary regime were religiously as well as politically radical, opponents of neoorthodoxy along with monarchy.[81]

On the face of it, one might have expected the small Jewish minority in the Palatinate to have been active supporters of the Provisional Government. Unlike either Catholics or Protestants, Jews had nothing to expect from the Bavarian state, while the Frankfurt constitution, on the other hand, was popular among them, since it guaranteed equality of all confessions before the law and abolished all discrimination on the basis of religion. The revolutionary authorities regarded such equality of religion as self-evident and in addition took firm steps against outbreaks of anti-Semitism. One Friedrich Sauberschwarz, in debt to Judas Oppenheimer, the district rabbi in Pirmasens, decided that the

[80] For other neoorthodox pastors, see LAS J1 Nr. 263 ff. 149–53, 234–46, 354–57; LAS H1 Nr. 2006 ff. 5–22. Events in Weidental according to LAS J1 Nr. 246 ff. 98–99, 100–05; LAS J1 Nr. 229 I (alt) f. 11; cf. also LAS J1 Nr. 228 (alt) f. 873. One particularly inventive pastor preached a sermon, not on the obvious "render unto Caesar," but on Matthew 6:25–34, "Sufficient unto the day is the evil thereof."

[81] LAS J1 Nr. 195 ff. 484–513; LAS J1 Nr. 202 I (alt) ff. 84–86, 105, 108–09, 154; LAS J1 Nr. 215 (alt) ff. 51–60; LAS J1 Nr. 242 ff. 114–17; similarly, LAS J1 Nr. 242 ff. 191–92, LAS J1 Nr. 178 ff. 213–14; and esp. LAS H1 Nr. 2006 ff. 34–37. The contention, long repeated in Palatine provincial historiography, that only three Protestant pastors supported the revolutionary regime (most recently in Scherer, "Zur Geschichte kirchlicher Parteien," p. 244) is not accurate.

revolutionary period was an ideal time to threaten his creditor with violence and force him to renounce his claims. The cantonal committee responded by ordering Sauberschwarz's own brother, a lieutenant in the People's Guard, to arrest him and bring him before them. They told Sauberschwarz in no uncertain terms to cease his threats, which he did and left town.[82]

Some Jews were active on the left, such as the Landau radical, merchant Emmanuel Deidesheimer, an official of the division of justice in the revolutionary government, or the rentier Moritz Eskales, the "reddest republican of [the very left-wing town of] Grünstadt." As a member of the cantonal committee, Eskales went around to all the villages, directing the revolutionary communal elections and giving fiery speeches praising the republic and denouncing princes who oppressed the people and "moneybags" who would not join the fight for freedom. Dr. Benjamin Maas of Neustadt a.d.W., a prominent member of the Workers' Association and the Democratic Club, called on his fellow physicians to serve in the People's Guard. When the moment came, he personally shouldered his rifle to fight for freedom. His fellow physician, A. Dreifuß of Edenkoben, if politically less prominent, had similarly radical views.[83]

Such radicals seem to have been outnumbered by Jewish moderates, who sought to curtail the actions of the revolutionary regime. Merchant Elias Liebmann of Neustadt a.d.W. "was not a member of the subversive party," and carried out his duties on the cantonal committee, reluctantly, if at all. When notary Schmitt of Kirchheimbolanden attempted to end the uprising by launching a petition to the king to issue an amnesty to all its participants, he turned to the merchant Leo Levi to carry out his plan. Merchants Wolf Isaak and Markus Bloch of Edenkoben were both employed in similar ways by the commandant of the Edenkoben People's Guard, leader of the moderate element among the revolutionary authorities there. If Julius Durlacher was chosen cashier for the forced loan by the Kirchheimbolanden Cantonal Committee, it was not for his politics—he was a "respectable, solid man"—but because the committee needed someone who knew how to keep the books.[84]

Certainly the most reluctant Jewish radical in the Palatinate was the merchant Bernhard Siegel of Dahn, a cantonal town in the mountains near the French border. Universally regarded as law-abiding and an opponent of radicalism, Siegel nonetheless was delighted to be on the cantonal committee, for it offered him the opportunity, which neither he nor any other Jew had ever

---

[82] LAS J1 Nr. 200 ff. 112–13 (Jewish enthusiasm for the emancipation promised by the Frankfurt constitution); LAS J1 Nr. 243 (alt) ff. 162–63, 312, 915 (Sauberschwarz).

[83] LAS J1 Nr. 202 I (alt) ff. 154–55; LAS J1 Nr. 215 (alt) f. 345; LAS J1 Nr. 218 ff. 41–51; LAS J1 Nr. 235 ff. 17–21, 131–36, 138–42; LAS J1 Nr. 228 (alt) ff. 256–58. LAS J1 Nr. 205 ff. 204–207. Other examples in Gerlach, "Juden in Kaiserslautern," pp. 207–08.

[84] LAS J1 Nr. 228 (alt) ff. 85–86; LAS J1 Nr. 105 ff. 771–72; LAS J1 Nr. 205 ff. 323–25, 339–41; LAS J1 Nr. 267 ff. 113–16. Similarly, LAS J1 Nr. 170 ff. 376–81.

had before, of associating as a social equal with the town's notables. When called upon to act in revolutionary fashion by confiscating a public treasury, he ran and hid in his neighbor's kitchen, proclaiming, "I would give much if things would return to the old ways and I could engage in my business deals again."[85]

Siegel's attitude hardly marked the right wing of Palatine Jewry, many of whose members were opponents of the revolutionary regime. Unlike their Christian counterparts, who could conduct their counterrevolutionary activities in a collective context, be it the parish, village community, or Pius Association, Jewish conservatives lacked both the numbers and institutional support to engage in effective or even perceptible resistance to the revolutionary regime. Their acts remained individualized and isolated, out of sight, both to contemporaries and historians, fueling the false notion that most Jews were on the left.[86]

Moses Brück of Odenbach harangued the eligible young men of the village, telling them that they were not required to serve in the People's Guard. The revolutionaries of Lauterecken planned to arrest him, and he was forced to flee the province. Jonas Levi of Bergzabern refused to participate in the June 4, 1849, march on Steinfeld, so the crowd assaulted his house and forced him to leave town. Rentier Moses Levi of Grossbrockenheim, a ninety-one-year-old family patriarch, fled to Mainz rather than pay the forced loan. When relatives arranged for him to return, on payment of a fraction of what he was assessed— as we have seen, a common practice among the Palatine bourgeoisie—Levi sent word that he would not pay a thing, remaining in Mainz until the Prussians conquered the Palatinate.[87]

Merchant Adolph Bär of Annweiler, in Pirmasens on business, denounced the Provisional Government in a tavern there; cattle dealer Abraham Dreifuß took some cattle to the fortress of Landau in defiance of the revolutionaries' blockade—or tried to, since his animals were confiscated on the road by the People's Guard of Leinsweiler. Merchant Isaak Isaak, Aron's son, of Edenkoben, attempted to prevent the town's civic guard from marching against the Prussian troops sent to reinforce the fortress of Landau in early May 1849, and again, ten days later, when the Provisional Government attempted to seize the fortress. Failing in these efforts, he fled to the fortress of Germersheim, placing himself under the protection of the Bavarian army—and just in time, for a

---

[85] LAS J1 Nr. 200 ff. 101–08, 112–17, 122–23, 125–28. Siegel's timorousness did not save him from being put on trial for high treason after the restoration of Bavarian authority. Like most of those accused, he was acquitted by the jury.

[86] Gerlach, "Juden in Kaiserslautern," pp. 307–08, for example, discusses only individual Jewish radicals, apparently never having searched for Jewish conservatives.

[87] LAS J1 Nr. 215 (alt) f. 143; LAS J1 Nr. 171 ff. 77–78; LAS J1 Nr. 235 f. 120. Similarly, LAS J1 Nr. 195 f. 114.

crowd gathered in front of his house, shouting, "The aristocrat should have his head chopped off and his house torn down."[88]

Such activities led to the one instance of what might be called anti-Semitic action on the part of supporters of the revolutionary regime. On the evening before the mustering of the eligibles was to take place in Canton Lauterecken, a crowd in the mining village of Odenbach placed all the Jews under house arrest, fearing that some of the Jewish young men were planning to flee the province to avoid the draft—as a number of them apparently were. This act, however, was not intended to exclude the Jews from the nation, as later anti-Semites wished, but to force their inclusion. One of the village revolutionaries explained this to merchant Jacob Kaufmann, when the latter's brother, Simon, eligible for the draft, was detained, stating, "everyone alike [einer wie der Andere] must defend the fatherland."[89]

Although the evidence is extremely scanty, it would seem that the chief difference between those Jews who were willing to defend the fatherland and those who placed their trust in the Bavarian king was their religious orientation. Advocates of a rationalist, reformed Judaism, such as the physician A. Dreifuß, stood on the left. Religious traditionalists, such as Dreifuß's fellow townsman, the merchant Isaak Isaak, Aron's son, who followed the old religious practice of referring to himself by his patronymic—a practice formally abolished in 1812 by the Napoleonic regime—were politically more conservative. If this was more generally the case, then the political orientation of the Palatine Jews resembled closely that of their Christian fellow citizens. Religious rationalists and anticlericals tended to support the revolutionary government; the neoorthodox, to oppose it, continuing a trend observable in the southern Rhineland throughout 1848–1849 and, indeed, since the early 1830s.[90]

The Peasantry and the Revolutionary Regime

The actions of the Provisional Government, taking the young men from the hay harvest into the army, or arresting clergy, while hardly intended to cost it the support of the peasantry, had very much that effect. A lack of understanding of peasant concerns and a certain antirural bias were apparent among many political activists, such as the Edenkoben wine merchant Adam Körber, who

---

[88] LAS J1 Nr. 243 (alt) f. 899; LAS J1 Nr. 148 ff. 344–48; LAS J1 Nr. 205 ff. 285–86, 332–33.

[89] LAS J1 Nr. 215 (alt) ff. 142–44.

[90] On the replacement of patronymics by surnames among Jews, cf. Hofmann, *Rheinhessische Volkskunde*, pp. 71–72. For Dreifuß's religious orientation, see LAS J1 Nr. 206 ff. 141–42; for an apparently similar attitude—a Jewish member of the Homburg People's Guard, sent to arrest a Catholic priest opposing the Provisional Government, announcing the reactionary rabbi would be next—see LAS J1 Nr. 242 ff. 55–57.

announced after the young villagers had disrupted the mustering of the People's Guard, "It's true, isn't it, that all you peasants are concerned about are your crops."[91]

Particularly revealing about the urban revolutionaries' lack of understanding of rural life was their attitude toward forest conflict. The collapse of Bavarian rule in May 1849 was a signal for the up-country peasants—all of them, whether radical or conservative, Protestant or Catholic—to engage in massive forest depredations. Forest officials, most of whom had taken the oath and accepted the Provisional Government, called on it for help. They were seconded by moderates on the cantonal committees, who saw this as a question of the protection of property. The regime responded favorably to their requests. The civil commissioners in both Pirmasens and Bergzabern were particularly active, dispatching units of the People's Guard to intimidate the peasants and force them to turn over their wood.

Civil Commissioner Bruch in Bergzabern regarded the wood thefts as counterrevolutionary activity, just one further proof of the hostility of the Catholic up-country villages to the revolutionary regime. A small unit of the People's Guard he sent to Schwannheim on June 7 was beaten up and driven out by the villagers, the hostilities engendered then an additional factor in the attitude of the armed townspeople in their punitive expedition to Gossersweiler and Schwannheim four days later. The urban leftists of Pirmasens tried to use persuasion rather than force on the peasants, the cantonal committee going to the village of Niedersimten to point out, "The forest is now ours, not the king's, and we are masters over it." In stealing from it, the villagers were stealing from themselves. Such abstract reasoning was not always well understood in the up-country, and where it was not, the Provisional Government appeared as the oppressive successor to the Bavarian regime.[92]

If these policies of the Provisional Government did not totally alienate the up-country peasantry, it was because they were creatively reinterpreted by some village activists, who continued under the revolutionary regime the democrats' campaign of linking leftist politics and forest use. When the village council of Alschbach in radical Canton Blieskastel met in May 1849 to discuss gathering wood in the state forest, the village mayor advised caution, pointing out that the king of Bavaria had recalled the parliament and that the "Basic Rights" of the Frankfurt constitution might yet be approved. Village councilman Johann Bauer, one of the founders of the local People's Association, and

[91] LAS J1 Nr. 205 ff. 281–82; similarly, LAS J1 Nr. 243 (alt) ff. 192–93.

[92] LAS J1 Nr. 243 (alt) ff. 115–16. See also ibid. ff. 183–85, 290, 344–45, 368–72, 632, 910–13; LAS J1 Nr. 108 f. 91; LAS J1 Nr. 147 f. 59; LAS J1 Nr. 148 ff. 58, 233–40; LAS J1 Nr. 149 ff. 20–22, 121, 158, 160–66, 332–33; LAS J1 Nr. 267 f. 460; LAS J1 Nr. 203 f. 216. Unaware of these disorders, Manfred Gailus asserts that spontaneous peasant uprisings ceased in April 1848 ("Soziale Protestbewegungen," p. 98), thus showing the weakness of his overly schematic categories.

an energetic supporter of the raising of the People's Guard, replied, "Today we no longer ask the king if he will accept the Basic Rights; today we demand his head."[93]

This example, along with the ones given in the sections above, suggest some of the different ways the peasantry could experience the revolutionary regime, and the variety of rural responses to it. Given the importance of the peasantry in mid-nineteenth-century Palatine society and, more broadly, in the events of 1848–1849 in the Rhineland and all of Europe, it seemed appropriate to ascertain more systematically the extent of different rural attitudes toward the Provisional Government and possible broad determinants of peasant actions and attitudes. I have studied the evidence from twenty-two of the thirty-one Palatine cantons, finding material for 370 villages, slightly over half the 700 in the entire province, and tried to determine the behavior of their inhabitants toward the revolutionary regime.[94]

If during May–June 1849 the inhabitants of a given village used violence against Bavarian state officials, supported enthusiastically the People's Guard—the young men serving voluntarily, other villagers providing them with arms or clothing—or voted out the mayor or village council in the communal elections called by the Provisional Government and replaced them with known leftists, I have referred to the village as revolutionary. If villagers acted only under the threat of compulsion, or actual armed demonstration, then I have called the village politically passive. Where the measures of the Provisional Government met with resistance, villagers assaulting revolutionary officials, publicly demonstrating Bavarian loyalism, or where the eligibles fled rather than serve in the People's Guard, then I have designated the village as counterrevolutionary. While most villagers showed political unanimity or virtually so, in a few places there was sharp division, both revolutionary and counterrevolutionary behavior occurring; I have described such villages as being in a state of internal conflict.

I have correlated these different positions with three possible determinants of political behavior: (1) political organization, the presence or absence of a local branch of the People's Association; (2) confessional composition; and (3) nature of village agriculture, distinguishing between the grain- and tobacco-growing of the Rhine plains, the viticulture of the areas along the Haardt Mountains and to the immediate north and south of them, and the

[93] LAS J1 Nr. 195 ff. 100–101. Similarly, LAS J1 Nr. 243 (alt) ff. 189–92; LAS J1 Nr. 277 (alt) ff. 244–45; LAS J1 Nr. 218 f. 117.

[94] The cantons are Annweiler, Bergzabern, Blieskastel, Dahn, Dürkheim, Edenkoben, Frankenthal, Grünstadt, Homburg, Kaiserslautern, Kandel, Kirchheimbolanden, Kusel, Landau, Landstuhl, Lauterecken, Neustadt, Pirmasens, Rockenhausen, Speyer, Waldmohr, and Zweibrücken. The sources did not always provide information on every single village in each canton, which is why the sample of two-thirds of all the cantons includes only about half the villages.

mountain and forest villages of the western Palatine up-country. The results of the analysis are summarized in Tables 11.1–11.3.

The single most important factor determining the political attitude of villagers during the reign of the Provisional Government was previous political organization (see Table 11.1). Villages with active People's Associations were far more likely to support the revolutionary regime and far less likely to oppose it than ones where no such democratic group existed. Areas with many village political clubs, such as the counties of Homburg and Zweibrücken in the western Palatinate, or the Canton Bergzabern to the south of them, were strongholds of rustic support for the Provisional Government, over half the villages in them acting in its favor. This conclusion is not without its tautological aspects—it says that revolutionary action occurred where there were organized revolutionaries—but it underscores once again the extent to which the Provisional Government was dependent for the effective exercise of its authority on activists organized by the democrats in the course of 1848–1849.

Not surprisingly, given the importance of confessional conflict in Palatine politics, the peasants' religion played a major role in determining attitudes toward the Provisional Government (see Table 11.2). Predominantly Protestant villages were somewhat more likely to support the regime than Catholic ones, and much less likely to actively oppose it. Protestant peasants without revolutionary enthusiasm responded to events in May–June 1849 with passivity, doing nothing unless forced to, while many more of their Catholic counterparts actively resisted revolutionary rule. The Provisional Government

TABLE 11.1

Political Orientation and Political Organization among the Palatine Peasantry

	Villages with:					
	Branch of People's Association		No People's Association		All Villages	
Political Orientation	N	%	N	%	N	%
Revolutionary	65	64	84	31	149	40
Passive	22	22	134	50	156	42
Counterrevolutionary	7	7	44	16	51	14
Conflict	7	7	7	3	14	4
Total	101	100	269	100	370	100

Sources: Political orientation of the villagers from the evidence gathered in the investigations for the high treason trial of 1851–1852 in LAS J1 Nrs. 104, 105–10, 147–51, 168–80, 195, 200, 203, 205–206, 218, 235, 242, 263–64, 267, 200 (alt), 202 I (alt), 215 (alt), 228–29 (alt), 243 (alt), 249 (alt), 252 (alt), 277 (alt). Presence of branches of the People's Association according to the sources cited in Chapter Five, note 3.

TABLE 11.2

Political Orientation and Confessional Composition among the Palatine Peasantry

	Villages with:			
	Protestant Majority		Catholic Majority	
Political Orientation	N	%	N	%
Revolutionary	107	45	41	31
Passive	107	45	47	36
Counterrevolutionary	18	8	33	24
Conflict	3	1	11	8
Total	235	99	132	99

Sources: Political orientation: same as Table 11.1. Confessional composition according to *Verzeichniß der Beamten . . . nebst . . . einer Gemeindestatistik der Pfalz*, pt. 2, pp. 2–50.

Note: Three villages in the sample, because of their large Jewish population, had neither a Protestant nor a Catholic majority.

came into open conflict with at least some of the inhabitants of a full third of predominantly Catholic villages.[95]

Prior political organization was necessary to overcome such religiously based Bavarian loyalism. People's Associations existed in over half the predominantly Roman Catholic villages that actively supported the Provisional Government (21 People's Associations in the 41 villages both predominantly Catholic and revolutionary) but in just three-eighths of the predominantly Protestant ones (41 of 107). Conversely, preexisting, neoorthodox, Catholic organizations stiffened the backs of the regime's opponents. My sample contains 14 of the 17 villages where Pius Associations existed. Of these 14 villages, 7 were either openly opposed to the regime or were scenes of conflict between revolutionary and counterrevolutionary elements—the highest proportion of counterrevolutionaries of any subgroup of the sample.[96]

Market relations were also important in peasant politics. The grain-growing villagers of the Rhine plain were noticeably less likely to support the regime and equally more likely to oppose it than either the mountain peasants of the western Palatinate or those of the wine country where the plains met the hills (see Table 11.3). Palatine revolutionaries were aware of the conservative

[95] I wondered if the presence of significant confessional minorities might have had an effect, so I broke down my sample further, comparing heavily (over 75 percent) Protestant or Catholic villages with those with larger confessional minorities, but found that the political behavior of villages that were 51–75 percent Protestant was virtually identical to that of villages that were over 75 percent Protestant; the same was true of villages with Catholic majorities.

[96] Location of Pius Associations according to Ziegler, *Die Jahre der Reaktion in der Pfalz*, p. 251; and LAS J1 Nr. 203 ff. 385–92.

TABLE 11.3
Political Orientation and Agriculture among the Palatine Peasantry

Political Orientation	Rhine Plains		Viticultural		Up-Country	
	N	%	N	%	N	%
Revolutionary	10	22	40	43	94	43
Passive	20	44	42	45	90	41
Counterrevolutionary	7	16	9	10	33	15
Conflict	8	18	2	2	4	2
Total	45	100	93	100	221	101

Sources: Political orientation: same as Table 11.1. Agriculture according to Müller, "Die Grundlagen der pfälzischen Landwirtschaft," in Becker, *Die Pfalz und die Pfälzer*; Becker, *Pfälzer Volkskunde*, p. 43; LAS H1 Nr. 2043 f. 67.

Note: The inhabitants of eleven villages in the sample engaged in weaving, fishing, metallurgy, or coal mining besides or instead of agriculture.

attitudes of the peasants on the plains of the Rhine, and they were to be expected when set in the context of *Vormärz* economic trends: Grain prices were rising, and peasants who could bring wheat or rye to market were in a favorable position and had, over the long run, less to be discontented about. The opposition to the combined efforts of the state and the capitalist market, so important in Rhineland radicalism, was lacking for them.[97]

A similar relationship between the market and political attitudes existed in the Palatine wine country. It can be divided into two subregions: a central area along the Haardt Mountains, containing large estates specializing in quality wine production, enjoying to the fullest extent the increase in wine prices apparent in the Palatinate since about 1840 (Canton Dürkheim, Canton Neustadt, and Canton Edenkoben), and the peripheral areas to the north and south, containing mostly smaller producers of poorer-quality wines (Canton Grünstadt, Canton Landau, and Canton Bergzabern). The vintners of the first area were much less likely to support the Provisional Government, just six of thirty-seven winegrowing villages (24 percent) doing so, while twenty-three remained politically passive, six were actively counterrevolutionary, and two were split by significant internal conflict. In the peripheral areas, where the vintners experienced less success in the market, twenty-seven of forty-four viticultural communes (61 percent) actively supported the revolutionary regime, fourteen were passive, and just three opposed it.

[97] Contemporary awareness of the conservatism of the Rhine plains peasants, "An das Landvolk der Vorderpfalz," *Der Pfälzer Volksmann*, 3 June 1849, LAS J1 Nr. 229 I (alt) ff. 134–35. To be sure, half the plains villages in the sample were predominantly Roman Catholic as against just one-third overall, but inhabitants of both predominantly Roman Catholic and predominantly Protestant plains villages were much less revolutionary and more counterrevolutionary than their coreligionists in villages with other kinds of agriculture.

The vintners of the Haardt Mountains had been supporters of the left at the time of the Hambach Festival, when Palatine wine prices were at their dismal nadir, and contemporaries occasionally observed that there had been much more enthusiasm for radical opposition among the winegrowers in 1832 than in 1849. A reverse generation gap, similar to the one among the Protestant clergy, seems to have developed among some of the vintners. Members of the older generation, who remembered the events of the 1830s, sympathized with the left, while younger vintners were less given to political opposition and perhaps more sympathetic to neoorthodox religion. When the young men of Flemmlingen, near Edenkoben, a stronghold of the Pius Association, drove off urban revolutionaries who wanted to speak in the village, the vintner Nicolaus Kern sadly remarked, "[T]he young people here are not for freedom," adding that they prevented its supporters "from agitating in its favor."[98]

The few villages where outworking or rural industry were practiced were politically very diverse. Lambrecht-Grevenhausen, to the west of Neustadt a.d.W., with its several hundred handloom weavers, was a stronghold of the left. Its inhabitants voted out their mayor, a woolens manufacturer, in the communal elections ordered by the Provisional Government, replacing him with a butcher. This may have reflected the aspirations toward social and political independence of the small-producing weavers, for in villages with actual factories, iron forges, or paper mills, politics was dominated by the factory owner's opinions. Where they were moderate, as in Franckeneck, near Neustadt a.d.W., or St. Ingbert, in the Palatine Saarland, the villagers kept their distance from the revolutionary regime. The manager of the ironworks in Schoenau, a mountain village near the French border, on the other hand, sympathized with the Provisional Government and simply deputized his workers into the People's Guard and sent them out after local enemies of the revolution, on pain of being fired.[99]

Most of the coal mines belonged to the Bavarian state, and one might have expected the miners to show their loyalty to it. This was the case in Mittelbexbach and Oberbexbach, where the director of the mines mobilized the miners to defend the treasury of the state mining office, and the money for their wages in it, against its seizure by agents of the revolutionary government. The Bexbachs were, however, predominantly Roman Catholic; in Protestant mining villages, such as Altenkirchen or Odenbach, the miners were enthusiastic radicals, willing to surrender at least part of the money of the state mining office to finance the revolution. As was the case with the state bureaucracy, Bavarian

---

[98] LAS J1 Nr. 205 ff. 101–02 (quotation); Becker, *Die Pfalz und die Pfälzer*, p. 363; LAS J1 Nr. 229 I (alt) f. 189.

[99] LAS J1 Nr. 228 (alt) f. 93, 97–98; LAS J1 Nr. 229 I (alt) f. 6; LAS J1 Nr. 195 f. 139; LAS J1 Nr. 200 ff. 75–77, 143–45; Klein, "Gottfried Kinkel als Emissär," p. 118.

authority among the coal miners rested more on religious loyalties than on ties of employment.[100]

Generalizing from the sample, it appears that inhabitants of about 40 percent of the villages in the Palatinate actively supported the revolutionary regime. A slightly greater number tried to stay out of the conflict between the legitimate authority and the insurgent government, concentrating on the hay harvest and wood theft, taking political action only under threat of force. Just a seventh were sufficiently opposed to the government to act against it. Since the leftist communes were disproportionately concentrated in the western Palatinate, with its less populous mountain villages, and the passive or counter-revolutionary ones more likely to be found in the more densely populated forward Palatinate, it may be that a slightly lower percentage of villagers, as opposed to villages, were adherents of the Provisional Government. Even so, these conclusions contradict the contention, which has now become a firm dictum, found in all the handbooks, that the entire Palatine peasantry was indifferent to or hostile toward the revolutionary movement.[101]

This judgment is largely based on a selective reading of the contemporary evidence, especially the memoirs of outsiders, come to the Palatinate to join the revolution. Most of them headed for Neustadt a.d.W. and vicinity, famous for its revolutionary activities in 1832 and center of the extreme left in 1848–1849. Radicalism in Neustadt and much of the forward Palatinate was, as we have seen above, concentrated in the cities and small towns. Few People's Associations were founded in the villages and the peasants kept their distance from the revolutionary regime. Outsiders were far less likely to find their way to the remote Westrich, into the vicinity of Bergzabern, Zweibrücken, Blieskastel, Pirmasens, or Homburg, where urban revolutionaries had agitated over forest issues and formed village political clubs and many of the peasantry—excepting, as always, Bavarian loyalist devout Catholics and neoorthodox Protestants—were supporters of the regime.[102]

Bonn radical Gottfried Kinkel, sent on a mission to the area by the Provisional Government, noted the peasant radicals, as did a Bavarian official fleeing the province, whose report on support for and opposition to the revolutionary government parallels almost exactly the results of the analysis of the sample of villages. We might leave the last word on the peasants to the Bavar-

---

[100] LAS J1 Nr. 242 ff. 55–57, 61–62, 65–66, 107–11; LAS J1 Nr. 215 (alt) ff. 140, 142–43, 154–56; ZSTAM Rep. 77 Tit. 505 Nr. 5 Vol. VI f. 142.

[101] Baumann, "Volkserhebung und Conspiration," pp. 298–302; *RhG* 2:462; Nipperdey, *Deutsche Geschichte*, p. 662. An exception to this is Klessmann, "Sozialgeschichte der Reichsverfassungskampange," p. 312.

[102] Cf. for instance, Fenner von Fenneberg, *Zur Geschichte der rheinpfälzischen Revolution*, p. 28, or Bamberger, "Erlebnisse aus der Pfälzer Erhebung" 3:54–55. In denying the Palatines' interest in revolution, both men were also attempting to justify their own failures—Fenner's in organizing the People's Guard, Bamberger's (as will be seen below), in commanding the Rhine-Hessians in battle with the Prussian army.

ian major general Theodor Prince von Thurn und Taxis, military governor of the Palatinate following the suppression of the uprising. A prominent figure in reactionary Munich court circles, the prince looked with a jaundiced eye on the formerly insurgent province, not excepting the peasantry from his criticism:

> The villages either took part in the revolution, or sent their young men fleeing into the forests, to keep them out of the hands of the Provisional Government. Usually, they bowed to force, let the law be dictated by a few audacious characters [verwegene Gesellen], and on their demand, drove out or tormented unwanted persons. Thus in the villages as well [the Bavarian government] can scarcely find a guarantee for the future.[103]

The Palatine Revolution: Homemade or Imported?

The prince was an exception among the Bavarian authorities, most of whom asserted that the Provisional Government was the creation of professional revolutionaries swarming into the Palatinate from across Germany and all of Europe to erect an outsiders' dictatorship with the armed support of the insurgent columns that had marched into the province in mid-May 1849. The officials claimed that the Palatines themselves—or at least the vast majority of them— had little to do with the revolution in their own province. Subsequent accounts have usually been based on these official contentions, the most elaborate version formulated in an influential article by the leading Palatine provincial historian, the late Kurt Baumann. He saw the entire uprising as the result of an international communist conspiracy, operating out of the German Democratic Committee in exile in Paris, working through Marx, Engels, and their Cologne comrade, the physician Karl D'Ester, who is said to have headed a "red camarilla" in the Provisional Government. Baumann's conclusions have made their way into the historical handbooks.[104]

It hardly seems likely that the Marxists would have sponsored the Palatine uprising, given their growing suspicions of "petit bourgeois" democrats in the spring of 1849 and their reluctance to become involved in the movement for the Frankfurt constitution. Marx and Engels's own activities in the Palatinate during the uprising are strong evidence against the idea that they were

---

[103] Prince von Thurn und Taxis to Gesammt Staats Ministerium, 1 Oct. 1849, BHSTAM MInn Nr. 45533; "Nachricht eines Kgl. Bayrischen Beamten in der Pfalz. Zustand der Provinz Juni 1849," BHSTAM KA Nr. B733c; Klein, "Gottfried Kinkel als Emmissär," p. 128.

[104] Baumann, "Volkserhebung und Konspiration," passim, which forms the basis for the account in *RhG* 2:402, 468–69. Similarly, Renner, "Die pfälzische Bewegung," pp. 180, 216–18; Fleischmann, *Geschichte des Pfälzischen Aufstandes*, pp. 107–08; *Handbuch der Bayerischen Geschichte* 4/1:235; Klessmann, "Sozialgeschichte der Reichsverfassungskampange," p. 309. For a vigorous criticism of this whole line of interpretation, see Schwarzwälder, "Die Ursachen der Reichsverfassungskampagne," pp. 5–6, 57, 81–94.

pulling the strings from behind the scenes. Fleeing from Cologne, Marx stopped briefly in Kaiserslautern on his way to France, letting the Provisional Government know that he found the whole movement premature: The further development of the mid-century revolution would come not from Germany but from the struggles of the French proletariat.[105]

Engels spent more time in the insurgent province. He avoided any association with the Palatine communists, but instead took service with the Provisional Government. Sent on a mission to Kirchheimbolanden, he spent so much time mocking the petit bourgeois leftists, asserting that their feeble armed forces would be destroyed by the invading Prussians, that everyone in the town decided he was a Prussian spy. The Rhine-Hessian insurgents stationed there arrested him and sent him off to Kaiserslautern, where he was released and left to join August Willich's troops. Ironically, Engels's arrest became one of the chief proofs for the Bavarian government's later assertion that the Rhine-Hessians had instituted a reign of terror in Kirchheimbolanden; it hardly suggests that he was a secret leader of the revolutionary regime.[106]

Karl D'Ester is a more plausible candidate for the role of revolutionary conspirator, since he was actively involved in a revolutionary conspiracy. Elected a member of the national democratic central committee by the Berlin Democratic Congress of November 1848, D'Ester moved his base of operations to Leipzig later that month, following the Prussian government's proclamation of a state of siege in the capital. In Saxony, D'Ester became involved with a strange group of conspirators, including the composer Richard Wagner, the Russian anarchist Mikhail Bakunin, exiled Czech and Polish revolutionaries, and former members of the Communist League, who opposed Marx's policy of open political agitation and wanted to engage in underground conspiracy. This group was planning an uprising in Saxony, which, like the similar but unrelated plans in the Prussian Rhineland, was crossed up, when an insurrection broke out spontaneously and prematurely. Seeing that the insurgent Saxon

---

[105] *KnZ*, 3 June 1849. In a later article, "Marx, Engels und die pfälzische Revolution im Sommer 1849," *Von Geschichte und Menschen der Pfalz*, pp. 333–47, Baumann notes that this source causes major problems for his interpretation, and cites a letter by Marx to Engels denouncing this report and asking Engels to let the public know that he, Marx, had left the Palatinate to go to Paris for revolutionary purposes. The letter (in *Marx-Engels Werke* 27:137–38), however, shows the complete opposite of Baumann's thesis, since Marx spends most of it denouncing the Palatine government for its confusion and lack of revolutionary activity. He points out that with the current conservative French government the Palatine envoys can accomplish nothing, but "one must make the Prussians believe that frightening intrigues are being spun out here." Marx himself thus testifies that the intrigues Baumann would have him involved in did not exist.

[106] Engels, "Die deutsche Reichsverfassungskampagne" 7:159–61; LAS J1 Nr. 267 f. 88; *Anklag-Akte*, pt. 2, pp. 25, 96–102. Baumann ingenuously asserts that Engels's arrest reflected the hostility of native Palatines to outside radicals, forcing the latter to be revolutionary ("Marx und Engels," pp. 344–46). He conveniently overlooks that Engels was arrested by the Rhine-Hessian insurgents, that is, by radical outsiders, not by Palatine natives.

regime had little hope of maintaining itself—it was quickly suppressed by Prussian troops—D'Ester fled to the German southwest and worked for the Palatine Provincial Defense Committee and later the Provisional Government.[107]

His work in Kaiserslautern, when seen from the inside, was anything but sinister. A clerk employed by the revolutionary government later testified about his activities:

> D'Ester, [working] in the Division of the Interior, was what one would call a *Chef de Bureau*. He opened the incoming correspondence, supervised the work of the personnel, and reported on all issues to [Prime Minister] Reichard, who worked in the office next door. It is also known to me that he was summoned to the discussions of the government members on important issues and that the decrees of the Provisional Government on military matters appeared in the official gazette after he had edited them.[108]

This witness, and other clerks, also attributed the decree on communal elections to D'Ester, since it was virtually identical to the draft law on local self-government he had proposed the previous year as a deputy in the Prussian National Assembly. All of this suggests that D'Ester was an important figure, a sort of senior revolutionary civil servant and confidential adviser to the regime, but hardly a puppet master of the Palatine radicals who formed the government.

The last link in Baumann's chain of conspiracy, the German Democratic Committee in exile in Paris, is an equally dubious candidate for the role of puppet master. First of all, the Marxists had nothing to do with it. From the spring of 1848 onwards, they had publicly and privately condemned its members as petit bourgeois fantasists playing at being revolutionaries. Connections between Andreas Gottschalk, and the committee during Gottschalk's stay in Paris, early in 1849, did nothing to improve relations.[109]

Although Marx was not in touch with the émigré committee, the Palatine radicals were, and it was through the German democrats in Paris that the Provisional Government obtained the dubious assistance of General Sznayde and the other Polish officers. These actions showed that the exiles were doing their best to help the movement in Germany, but are hardly proof that they were manipulating it. Among the documents later seized by the Bavarian authorities

---

[107] Weber, *Die Revolution in Sachsen*, pp. 277–86. One Czech participant in the conspiracy later claimed that D'Ester wanted military assistance from exiled Polish revolutionaries for an uprising in southwestern Germany, but this hardly proves that D'Ester planned the Palatine insurrection. The Polish help eventually obtained was, as we have seen, a dubious blessing for the revolutionary regime.

[108] LAS J1 Nr. 106 I ff. 243–44; similar testimony of other clerks, ibid. ff. 244–49.

[109] *Der Bund der Kommunisten* 1, Nrs. 210, 217, 229–30, 347. Cf. Hammen, *The Red '48ers*, pp. 201, 371.

was a letter from the Paris Committee, offering the services of an exiled German radical with military experience. The letter, dated May 20, 1849, was addressed to the Provincial Defense Committee. Three days after the Palatine revolutionaries had turned the Provincial Defense Committee into a Provisional Government, the Parisian exiles still had no knowledge of this revolutionary coup, a poor showing for the ostensible masterminds behind the scenes.[110]

If Baumann's conspiracy theory is untenable, a milder version of the outsider thesis might be maintained, namely, that the creation of the Provisional Government and the radical measures taken by it were largely, or at least disproportionately, the work of non-Palatines. The identities of the 333 defendants in the 1851–1852 trial for high treason committed during the Palatine uprising are frequently used as evidence to support this assertion, since one-third of the defendants were not natives of the province. This statistical argument loses a good deal of its luster when one observes that 579 individuals were placed on trial in civilian courts for lesser charges in connection with the uprising, some 1,100 came before military tribunals (731 in absentia), 1,200 individuals were granted a military amnesty, and 7,850 were granted a civilian amnesty. Virtually all of these 11,000 participants in the uprising were Palatine natives.[111]

The one area of the insurrection where outsiders did play a major role was in the revolutionary armed forces. However, the People's Guard was created by Palatine radical democrats—at the beginning with the assistance of the democratic moderates and even some constitutional monarchists—and if its high officers contained few Palatines in their ranks, it was because there were few leftist sympathizers in the province with military experience. The outside insurgents, two-thirds of whom were from neighboring Rhine-Hessen, did act in repressive fashion on behalf of the Provisional Government, rounding up draft evaders and arresting internal enemies of the regime. Such acts of political repression were far more frequently carried out by native Palatines: by the deserted Bavarian soldiers who had taken service with the Provisional Government or by the People's Guards of larger cities, such as Homburg, Kaiserslautern, Zweibrücken, Neustadt a.d.W., or Frankenthal, as well as those of smaller, radical towns, such as Bergzabern and Annweiler, or even of left-wing villages, such as Lambrecht-Grevenhausen. Even when outside insurgents took over repressive tasks, they could carry them out only with the help

[110] LAS J1 Nr. 110 f. 77.

[111] On the role of outsiders, besides the sources cited in note 104, see Schneider, "Landesausschuß und Provisorische Regierung," pp. 108–09. Judicial statistics according to LAS J1 Nr. 308 (alt) f. 219; Generalauditor to King of Bavaria, 6 Sept., 15 Dec. 1850; and Festungs Commando Landau to Zweite Armee Korps Commando (Würzburg), 27 Nov. 1850, both in BHSTAM KA Nr. B795. Memoranda attached to these statistics suggest that the Bavarian judiciary consciously chose to blame outsiders for the uprising.

of Palatine radicals. Willich's communist corps, for instance, which arrested enemies of the Provisional Government while besieging the fortress of Landau, knew whom to arrest only because village democrats had told them.[112]

The whole search for outside agitators is a futile one, because it starts from a false premise: namely, that until May 1849, the Palatinate was peaceful and its inhabitants nonrevolutionary. Such an assertion ignores the tradition of radical politics in the province dating back at least to 1832, and takes no notice of what had happened there between March 1848 and April 1849. The democrats had been victorious in the elections to the Frankfurt National Assembly, and had elected even more left-wing candidates to the Bavarian parliament, six months later. They had created a provincewide network of political clubs, whose activists would provide the cadre for the later revolutionary regime, and had formed dozens of civic guards, whose members would not take orders from the Bavarian government, but seemed ready to fight against it. Long before the final crisis of the revolution, the Palatinate had been conquered by the democrats; the authority of the Bavarian state had been reduced to a shadow. Once again, we can cite the crusty Prince von Thurn und Taxis, describing the province as a Bavarian conservative experienced it in the summer of 1848:

> [It was like] one huge madhouse; all law-abiding people, even state servants just spoke very softly among themselves . . . only the vice of arrogance, the armed proletariat, marched around, proud and noisy. All the streets were filled with idle people; all the public squares with Jacobin caps and muskets; from all the taverns there rang out day and night, wild republican songs. In short, if it was not already the revolution, it was the first taste of it.[113]

The one main difference between the events of April–June 1849 and those of the previous year was the steady loss of ground of the more moderate Palatine democrats to their "exalted" counterparts. This was primarily a reflection of the political, social, and confessional dynamics of the province, and only in small part attributable to radical outsiders. Both moderate and radical leaders tended to be bourgeois, usually local notables, but the latter were able to mobilize the mass of the urban population, especially master and journeymen artisans, to support their seizure of power and to ensure that the agents of the revolutionary regime acted in a revolutionary way. The moderates, many of whom were members of the "bourgeois aristocracy" of vineyard owners and veterans of the Hambach Festival, and of the campaigns of Protestant

---

[112] An informant's letter to Willich's corps, LAS J1 Nr. 264 f. 764. The sources cited in notes 38–41, 67, 70–71, 74–76, and 79 contain many examples of native Palatines used for the work of internal repression.

[113] Prince von Thurn und Taxis to Gesammt Staats Ministerium, 1 Oct. 1849, BHSTAM MInn Nr. 45533. For a trenchant critique of the literature on this point, see Schwarzwälder, "Die Ursachen der Reichsverfassungskampagne," p. 57.

rationalism, were forced to accommodate themselves to the revolutionary government.[114]

The moderates might feel that the peasantry, the large majority of the province's population, was on their side, but because of the distinct nature of rural politics they had difficulty making use of that support. Peasants understood little of factional struggles. Villages where People's Associations existed, even if they had been founded by moderate democrats, tended to support the revolutionary regime; peasants lacking enthusiasm for radical goals mostly did not oppose them, but tried to avoid politics altogether. The only active enemies of the revolutionary government in the countryside, devout Catholics and neoorthodox Protestants, were no allies for the freethinking, basically left-wing democratic moderates.[115]

Consequently, the radicals were able to seize power and create a regime with a network of supporters throughout the province, whether holding official positions within it or informally active. Once in power, the Provisional Government had the authority to command the outside insurgent columns and to call in further outsiders, mostly as military and administrative experts, while retaining native sympathizers who could work with them. The outsiders then increased the radicals' power, but they neither originated the revolutionary regime nor enabled it to sweep aside the Palatine moderates, who remained, often reluctantly, in alliance with it down to the very end.

The Prussian Invasion and the End of the Revolutionary Regime

By early June 1849, it was clear that end was not far off. Even revolutionary militants, to say nothing of the reluctant draftees of an unarmed People's Guard, lost their courage at the prospect of a full-scale Prussian invasion. The one thousand Bavarian deserters who had taken service with the Provisional Government were particularly affected. Fearing that they would face a firing

[114] Examples of radical democrats as local notables, LAS J1 Nr. 235 ff. 17–21; LAS J1 Nr. 170 ff. 228–33, 407–08. Lists of the participants in the marches of the armed inhabitants of Annweiler and Bergzabern on Steinfeld and Gossersweiler show a cross-section of Palatine small-town society, most involved being artisans. The documents do not distinguish between masters and journeymen, but since most of the eyewitnesses interrogated were between the ages of thirty and sixty, many masters were probably involved. LAS J1 Nr. 168 ff. 17–18 and passim; LAS J1 Nr. 149 ff. 74–75. Artisan members of the first levy of the People's Guard were mostly journeymen, but since they were conscripts between the ages of eighteen and thirty, it is improper to use such lists as evidence of the social composition of the supporters of Palatine radicalism in general, as does Renner, "Die pfälzische Bewegung," pp. 219–21.

[115] Wettengel, "Das liberale und demokratische Vereinswesen," pp. 83–85, uses the fact that most of the rural People's Associations were founded by moderates to explain why the peasants took no part in the uprising, unaware of the evidence showing that precisely these peasants were supporters of the revolutionary regime.

squad after the restoration of order, they began drinking heavily, becoming unruly and undisciplined.[116]

The Provisional Government tried every last resource, appealing on June 4, 1849, to the women of the province to join in the struggle, in the appropriately feminine way of sewing clothing for the People's Guard. The government's appeal for a sort of levee en masse against the Prussians on June 10, 1849, complete with the proclamation that "the fatherland is in danger," the ringing of the storm bells, and the mobilization of the entire population against the invaders, was a testimony to the failure of its attempts to raise an army that could actually go into combat. Its final appeal, in the last issue of the official gazette on June 11, 1849, contained elements of an *apologia pro vita*, suggesting that the leaders of the revolutionary regime had no illusions about what lay ahead.[117]

Two days later, the Prussians finally moved, sending thirty thousand troops into the province, following three routes of invasion: along the Rhine plains; from the north, through the Alsenz Valley; and from the Saarland to the west, along the "Emperor's road," the great military highway Napoleon had built connecting Paris and Mainz. The Prussians reached Kaiserslautern on June 14, forcing the Provisional Government to flee, and continued to march southwards to relieve the besieged fortresses of Landau and Germersheim. They accomplished this and completed their conquest of the entire province by June 18, continuing over the Rhine the following day into Baden, to destroy the remaining southwest German revolutionary regime.[118]

As the speed of the Prussian advance makes clear, the People's Guard posed little resistance. Its few attempts to offer battle were brief and militarily amateurish; many of the unarmed draftees broke and ran. Most of what opposition there was came from the outside insurgents, who had little left to lose, having already left their homes voluntarily or fled from them as political refugees. The Prussians among them may have been animated by the proclamation of General von Hirschfeld, commander of the Prussian troops, who announced that all his king's subjects, caught fighting against him, could expect the death penalty. While some native Palatines, in and out of the insurgent army, were

---

[116] LAK 403 Nr. 2554 pp. 149–53; LAS J1 Nr. 110 ff. 85, 124–25; LAS J1 Nr. 172 ff. 421–22; *Der Pfälzer Volksmann*, 11 June 1849, LAS J1 Nr. 229 I (alt) ff. 135–39.

[117] "Frauen und Jungfrauen der Pfalz!" and "An das Pfälzer Volk!" *Amts- und Intelligenzblatt der Provisorischen Regierung der Rheinpfalz*, Nrs. 10–11, 4, 11 June 1849; "Aufgebot zum Landsturm," LAS J1 Nr. 203 f. 60. Even before the government called on them, women of Bergzabern and Neustadt a.d.W. had volunteered to make or gather clothing for the army and tend the wounded. LAS J1 Nr. 178 ff. 255–57; LAS J1 Nr. 228 I (alt) ff. 929–30.

[118] The reader unwilling to wade through the official military history, Voß, *Der Feldzug in der Pfalz und Baden*, can turn to the short account of Jürgen Keddigkeit, "Das militärische Scheitern des Pfälzischen Aufstandes 1849," *JhGStLK* 22/23 (1984/85): 405–24, which, unfortunately, contains many errors when the author ventures outside of strategy and tactics, or the handy account of a participant, Friedrich Engels, "Die deutsche Reichsverfassungskampagne" 7:165–72.

willing to fight, rather more preferred to hang out a white flag, saving hearth and home from destruction at the price of surrendering their revolutionary aspirations.[119]

The Rhine-Hessian insurgent corps in the Alsenz Valley, better organized and disciplined than most of the People's Guard, skirmished with the Prussians and then fell back on Kirchheimbolanden. Its leaders wanted to build barricades there and resist, but the inhabitants, fearing the destruction of their town, convinced them to leave instead. In the confusion of the retreat, on the morning of June 14, 1849, a small detachment of thirty–forty men guarding the corps' headquarters was left behind. The Prussians marched in and killed seventeen who were unable to flee, some of whom were shot in cold blood as they were trying to surrender.[120]

The corps' commanders, Mainz radicals Franz Zitz and Ludwig Bamberger, did not march off with their men, but jumped into a carriage and left town by a different route. Their enemies accused them of cowardice under fire, of forgetting the soldiers guarding their headquarters and leaving them to their fate. This accusation was untrue—the retreat signal had been sounded, but the detachment apparently did not hear it—but the two leaders' actions did require explaining. They were on their way to the railhead at Frankenstein. From there, they took the train across the Rhine to Mannheim, to offer their corps' services to the revolutionary government of Baden, thus rescuing it from the collapse of the insurgent Palatine regime. Of course, they could have done this while staying with their followers, and a certain odium remained attached to their behavior.

Much of Ludwig Bamberger's reminiscences of the uprising, written a few months later, tried to justify his and Zitz's actions by denouncing the Palatines as passive, uninterested cowards, who had invited the Rhine-Hessians to do their political dirty work and placed them in the impossible situation of confronting a much larger and far better armed Prussian army. Both charge and countercharge were untrue. The Palatines had been involved in the revolution, although they became increasingly unwilling to fight the Prussians without

[119] General von Hirschfeld's proclamation, LAK 403 Nr. 2554 p. 44. Some eyewitness accounts of skirmishes between Prussian and revolutionary troops and of differences between Palatines and outsiders, ibid. pp. 37–38, 47–47, 63–73, 85–87; LAS J1 Nr. 123 ff. 4–5; LAS J1 Nr. 148 ff. 367–71, 375–78; LAS J1 Nr. 205 ff. 470, 559–63, 577–89; LAS J1 Nr. 267 ff. 157–66; Fleischmann, *Geschichte des Pfälzischen Aufstandes*, pp. 290–93; Roland Paul and Franz Rink, "Erinnerungen des Kaiserslauterer Seminaristen Ludwig Hartmann an die Tage des Pfälzer Aufstandes," *JhGStLK* 22/23 (1984/85): 383–404.

[120] Eyewitness accounts from various sides in LAS J1 Nr. 111 ff. 142–52; LAS J1 Nr. 267 ff. 86, 176–79; Roswitha Nagel, "Überblick über die Quellenlage in der Historischen Abteilung II des Zentralen Staatsarchivs zum Badisch-Pfälzischen Revolutionskrieg 1849," *Zeitschrift für Militärgeschichte* 13 (1979): 86–86, esp. p. 85; Fleischmann, *Geschichte des Pfälzischen Aufstandes*, p. 290. The official history, Voß, *Der Feldzug in der Pfalz*, p. 93, does not deny that some prisoners were shot on the spot.

weapons. Zitz and Bamberger were not cowards, but they were lawyers and politicians, lacking any experience of military command under fire.[121]

Only August Willich's corps, the one insurgent column commanded by a professional soldier, gave the Prussians a serious fight. Reinforced by some Badenese troops, and Palatine draftees from the vicinity of Pirmasens and Zweibrücken, Willich's men attacked the Prussians on June 17, 1849, at the village of Rinnthal in the southwestern Palatinate, near Annweiler. Although driven back, the attack delayed the Prussian advance long enough for the members of the Provisional Government and five thousand Palatines of the People's Guard—the other seven thousand having deserted—to cross the Rhine on June 17–18, and continue the struggle in Baden. Supported by Badenese regulars, and finally having some weapons, the Palatines fought well against the Prussians in several final encounters later that month, but the fate of the revolutionary movement in the Palatinate, in south Germany, and in all of central Europe had already been sealed.[122]

There is one last episode of the Palatine revolution to relate. Word of the battle of Rinnthal reached the isolated mountain region around Pirmasens in very distorted form. Rumor had it that the Prussians had been defeated and were being driven out of the province in disorder, and that a French army or armed French workers were on the way to help the revolutionary regime. Great excitement reigned throughout the area. In several villages, the storm bells were rung and peasants prepared to march to Pirmasens to join the fight. The villagers of Kröppen surrounded the customs agents shouting, "We must beat them to death today; it would be a shame if we allowed them to live."

Members of the cantonal committee sent word to the Pirmasens civil commissioner Gustav Diehl, who had fled across the border to France, to return. He did, meeting them on June 18, 1849, in the village of Schweix, where Diehl addressed a large crowd of peasants. He told them that the Prussians were in flight, and called on them to arm themselves with pitchforks and similar rustic implements "to drive them [the Prussians] out of the land, for their freedom was at stake, and their liberation from the yoke under which they had suffered." The armed men of Schweix and the neighboring villages of Hilst and Eppenbrunn did just that. Of course, they did not get very far before they learned the truth, but their rally and armed march was one more testimony to the strength of the spirit of freedom in the Palatinate and the role of the Prussian army in snuffing it out.[123]

[121] LAS J1 Nr. 267 ff. 86, 151–52; Fleischmann, *Geschichte des Pfälzischen Aufstandes*, pp. 290–93; Bamberger, "Erlebnisse aus der Pfälzer Erhebung" 3:146–48, 152–58. Bamberger also claimed that he could not accompany his men because his feet were too sore to march, but he was seen later that day walking from the village of Enkenbach to the railroad station in Frankenstein.

[122] LAS J1 Nr. 308 (alt) f. 219; Engels, "Die deutsche Reichsverfassungskampagne" 7:168–72; Fleischmann, *Geschichte des Pfälzischen Aufstandes*, pp. 340–41.

[123] LAS J1 Nr. 243 (alt) ff. 30–35, 56–60, 153–55, 181–83, 185, 189–92.

Conclusion

A TRIANGLE OF TENSIONS

Significant conflicts within Rhenish society, before and during the 1848–1849 revolution, had their origins in a triangle of tensions, whose vertices were the market, the state, and the church. Conflicts could and did occur around any one of the three vertices, but they were at their greatest when they were played out on a line connecting two of them. Such sources of conflict were hardly unique to western Germany in the mid-nineteenth century, but the exact nature of the tensions and their interaction did form a distinct pattern, each element of which played a specific role in shaping the democratic movement in the region and differentiating it from later versions of radical political opposition.

Toward the middle of the nineteenth century, much of the social and economic conflict in Germany centered around preservation or abolition of precapitalist market restrictions, such as feudal tenures or the guild system. In the Rhineland, where such institutions had long ago been replaced by an unlimitedly capitalist economic system and a bourgeois social order, the conflicts that did occur along these lines had more the character of rearguard struggles. Although capitalism was well established in the Rhineland, it was not the industrial capitalism of the later nineteenth and early twentieth centuries. In particular, it lacked the characteristic opposition between owners of the means of production and proletarians who worked them. Production was carried out primarily by nominally independent small producers, or those who could reasonably expect to aspire to such a status, such as journeymen artisans or young, rural day laborers, who were often the adult children of peasant smallholders. Their great grievance was their lack of access to the market, which was controlled by nonproducing mercantile and financial "capitalists." Reinforced by gradually declining standards of living, even before the subsistence crisis of 1845–1847, the social tensions engendered by this situation created a powerful impetus for change; it was among these aggrieved small producers that the democratic movement recruited the bulk of its members.

This specific locus of market tensions also helped shape the democrats' social and economic policies and their relations to spontaneous popular movements. The conflict between master and journeymen artisans, central both to the guild system and, reformulated as a clash between employers and workers, to the capitalist economy of the later nineteenth century, was less significant in the society of Rhenish small producer capitalism. Consequently, both journeymen and master artisans could be adherents of the same democratic movement. The numerical and intellectual dominance of small producers on the left and in society as a whole suggests some of the reasons for the appeal of producers' sales cooperatives, or of the slogan "the organization of labor," and why they should have been adopted by democrats seeking to gain support among urban artisans and manufacturing outworkers.

If the socioeconomic situation of the mid-nineteenth century was noticeably different from its precapitalist predecessors and industrial capitalist successors, the language used by leftists to discuss social and economic questions was not. Democrats denounced the bourgeoisie and capitalism in 1848–1849, as did later nineteenth-century socialists, although the two groups were using the same phrases to attack different economic systems in front of different audiences. This use of the same language to elucidate different social orders explains how some democrats could combine support of the free market with the advocacy of socialist ideas, or the otherwise puzzling lack of interest shown by most 1848–1849 workers' associations in wages, hours, and working conditions, the later staples of trade unionism. It provides a way to understand why many more communists could be found in the small, thoroughly nonindustrial town of Neustadt a.d.W. than in such factory cities as Aachen or Mülheim a.d. Ruhr.[1]

Since the state often controlled or influenced access to the market, it was frequently drawn into conflicts over market access, making them especially explosive. One need only think of events in Solingen, the Mainz railroad question, or the struggles of the Rhine watermen. Indeed, sometimes the issue of market access itself disappeared behind hostility to the state. Particularly in the countryside, the democratic social and economic program was directed almost entirely against the government. Democrats would resolve the market difficulties of the vintners by abolishing the must tax (or, outside of Rhenish Prussia, by lowering taxes in general); they would alleviate the poverty of the up-country peasants by granting them access to the state forests. Such an emphasis on state policy could help cover up differences over other aspects of social and economic questions, but it also reflected a broader feeling in mid-nineteenth-century European radicalism that the main cause of social and economic injustice was governmental misappropriation and maldistribution of economic resources. Even the leaders of the British Chartists, agitating in a far more advanced capitalist-industrial society than existed anywhere in mid-nineteenth-century Germany, saw poverty and exploitation as a result of state activity, to be remedied by a democratic suffrage.[2]

In and of itself, the expansion of the state was a major source of tension. Prussia, Bavaria, and Hessen-Darmstadt, like all the German states, had been reshaped in the first two decades of the nineteenth century. Their rule had

---

[1] In a similar way, if not to quite so great an extent, artisans and democrats used the language of the guild system to fight outworking merchants and promote producers' cooperatives.

[2] Gareth Stedman-Jones, "Rethinking Chartism," in his *Languages of Class*, pp. 90–178.

expanded externally, as they acquired new territories and the new subjects who lived in them. Their rule had expanded internally as well, the states making greater demands on their subjects for revenue, military service, and obedience to laws and administrative decrees that they had little or no role in formulating. Since most Rhinelanders, particularly those of the opposite confession to that of the ruling princely house, lacked ties of monarchical loyalty dating from the old regime, they were especially unlikely to accept such demands. Their opposition was in part obscured by censorship, lack of democratic, representative institutions, and military occupation, but it emerged with great clarity in the year of revolution.

Much of the conflict occurring in the Rhineland in 1848–1849, most of what made the revolutionary year revolutionary, was the clash between a minority, composed of adherents of the existing states, tied to them by religious or dynastic loyalties, economic self-interest, or guaranteed employment, and the majority of Rhinelanders without such allegiance and opposed, at least implicitly, to continued Prussian, Bavarian, or Hessian rule. Articulating this opposition to the rule of the core states was the single most important issue for the democratic movement; channeling it toward political radicalism—that is, toward opposition to monarchy and support for popular sovereignty and the republic—was the mainstay of the democrats' agitation.

The preceding discussion might be summed up by saying that support for the Rhineland democrats stemmed from their opposition to the power of the market and the state. By itself, this is a familiar theme of European history, hardly limited to western Germany in the middle of the nineteenth century. Charles Tilly, in his well-known typology of social conflict, points to the expansion of the national market and the national state as the chief causes of political discord and collective violence in Europe from the sixteenth through at least the middle of the nineteenth century. The word "national," however, points to one of the distinct peculiarities of mid-nineteenth-century German politics. Neither Prussia, Bavaria, nor Hessen were *national* states; in the Rhineland at least, opposition to their rule appeared as German nationalism. Contemporaries often understood political conflicts in 1848–1849 under the rubrics Prussian-German, Bavarian-German, or Hessian-German. Nation building and state building were contrary rather than complementary.[3]

This observation seems to return us to one of the stock themes of German history, the desire for a strong national state, which could create a unified national market and give Germany its appropriate place among the European powers. This criticism of the mid-nineteenth-century German states, at home among the contemporary bourgeoisie, expressed at length and in depth by articulate professors and journalists, needs to be set against a different critique

[3] Charles Tilly, Richard Tilly, and Louise Tilly, *The Rebellious Century, 1830–1930* (Cambridge: Harvard University Press, 1975), pp. 252–54.

of the German states. The main point of this alternate critique was that the states were too strong, not too weak. They demanded high taxes of a population whose standard of living was declining, drafted young men to serve in the army and then sent unfriendly outsiders to garrison the larger cities, imposed river tolls, restricted the use of the forests, subsidized dishonorable economic competition, supported an unwanted Christian confession and forced their subjects to tolerate it. The main adherents of this criticism were poorly educated peasants, artisans, and laborers; they did not express themselves in articulate or written form, but in jeers and catcalls on the streets, in slogans chanted during riots, and in acts of violence or hostility toward symbols of the state.

Democratic leaders, themselves well-educated or at least half-educated, shared the bourgeois critique of the existing governments and looked toward a future, powerful German national state. Their popular agitation, however, with its attacks on high taxes and on ''the standing army of soldiers and officials,'' its exploitation of confessional hostilities, and its secessionist undercurrent, suggests that support for their nationalist sentiments owed a good deal to an implicit acceptance of popular hostility toward the growing strength of the state. Paradoxically, much popular nationalism, ostensibly expressing a political loyalty transcending local or provincial identity, actually stemmed from precisely these identities and from hostilities against a state encompassing disparate groups.

This is especially apparent in the democrats' attitude toward Prussia, the one German state among the thirty-nine existing at the middle of the nineteenth century that could legitimately have aspired to the role of a strong national state and was supported in such aspirations by many constitutional monarchists and their disproportionately bourgeois supporters. Rhenish democrats, all firm German nationalists, were equally firm enemies of Prussia—whether they were Prussian, Hessian, or Bavarian subjects. This anti-Prussian German nationalism existed in a political universe very different from that of a quarter-century later, when the Prussian monarchy, under Bismarck's leadership, created a powerful German national state. It is important, however, not to project back the circumstances and political alignments of the years 1864–1871 onto 1848–1849. Just as much of the shared economic language of later socialists and mid-century democrats referred to different socioeconomic conditions, so the German nationalism of 1848 leftists had a very different political content. In particular it arose from a different attitude toward the Prussian state than did the nationalism of Bismarck's era.

If market conflicts created the recruiting ground for the democratic movement, and conflicts over the state provided the chief means of actually enlisting support, it was religious conflicts that were most important in determining whether tensions arising from the market and the state would be generalized and politicized and, if so, in which direction they would flow. Popular encounters with tax collectors, customs agents, foresters, or soldiers might well accumulate into a hatred of the monarch who employed them if the people encountering the agents of the crown were of the opposite Christian confession to that of the royal house. If they were of the same confession, such clashes would be fewer in number, and the people far more likely to separate the king and his rule from the servants he employed.

Confessional hostilities played a similar role in nationalist sentiment. Confessional rivalry was subsumed in nationalist sentiment, not, as both contemporaries and historians have sometimes charged, placed above the nation. Those Rhenish Catholics who strongly identified with their church just naturally assumed that their confession would be dominant in a united Germany—especially if they were subjects of a Prussian monarchy, in which they were subordinated to Protestants. Their Protestant counterparts assumed the opposite, in equally self-evident fashion.

These interconfessional rivalries were awkward for the democrats, whose leaders were mostly freethinkers, and many of whose local activists were schoolteachers and tavernkeepers, anticlerical by occupation. Ideally, Rhenish leftists did want to place nation over confession, and on rare occasions, such as the march of the Elberfeld democrats in Düsseldorf, on April 30, 1849—a crucial event for the uprisings on the lower Rhine that followed—they were able to accomplish this. Most of the time, however, they could not, and acted instead to politicize popular discontent within the existing framework of interconfessional hostility. They had varying degrees of success in their efforts, primarily because of the existence of additional, intraconfessional tensions, and the lack of social, political, and religious symmetry between Protestants and Catholics. The differences in the relationship between religion and politics in the Palatinate and the Prussian Rhine Province exemplify these circumstances.

As was the case everywhere in the Rhineland, the Palatine bourgeoisie was disproportionately Protestant, living along with a majority of its fellow provincials in a state with a Roman Catholic, that is, religiously alien, royal house. In addition, many of the Protestant bourgeoisie, like their fellow provincials from different social or confessional groups, were strongly inclined toward religious rationalism, coming into conflict with a trans-Rhenan Bavaria more sympathetic to neoorthodoxy. In such circumstances, where the wealthiest and most influential social group was, on inter- and intraconfessional grounds, opposed to the royal house, political opposition flourished. Radical religion and radical politics—combined among German-Catholics—found a congenial home, so congenial that the radicalism came to exceed what some of its bourgeois patrons might have wished.

In the Prussian Rhineland, by contrast, the comparable social, political, and religious alignments all told against the left. The bourgeoisie was still predominantly Protestant, which meant of the same confession as the royal family, so the same bourgeois influence that helped the democrats in the southern Rhineland worked against them in Rhenish Prussia. In addition, religious neoorthodoxy was clearly stronger and rationalism weaker in the northern Rhineland than further south. This strengthened the position of constitutional monarchism, Prussian loyalism, and outright reaction among Protestants, and it introduced additional difficulties for the democrats in agitating among the Roman Catholic majority of Prussia's Rhenish subjects.

While in the Palatinate, exploitation of confessional hostility against the royal house was exclusively the province of the left, this was far from the case in the Prussian Rhineland, where neoorthodox Catholic clergy and lay activists competed vigorously with the democrats for the anti-Prussian, anti-Protestant sympathies of the Catholic masses. Although Catholic-clericals and democrats were both enemies of Prussia, they were almost as hostile to each other. Catholic activists, who saw interconfessional public education as a fatal blow to their religion, and wanted their Hohenzollern prince replaced by a Habsburg one, had great difficulty coming to terms with the anticlericalism and republicanism prevalent on the left.[4]

Even the organized Catholics of the city of Trier, the most radical and anti-Prussian in the whole Rhineland, vacillated continuously throughout 1848–1849 between cooperating with the Prussian authorities and the (disproportionately Protestant) constitutional monarchist bourgeoisie and working with the democrats. Catholic-clericals celebrated the onset of the revolution as the overthrow of Prussian rule, only to support the constitutional monarchist election program in April 1848, but then to back away from it at the elections in May. They formed the Pius Association in September 1848, with the aim of splitting the Democratic Club, and then cooperated with the democrats during the Prussian tax boycott campaign. The Catholic-clericals drifted away from the democrats at the elections of January 1849, and ended the revolution by helping the authorities preserve order during the *Reichsverfassungskampagne*.[5]

Much of politics in the Prussian Rhine Province during the revolution consisted of a contest to see which version of opposition to Prussian rule, the democratic or the Catholic-clerical, would find the most support among the Roman Catholic majority of the province's inhabitants. At first, in April–May 1848, the clergy dominated almost everywhere, but the democrats, by dint of difficult agitation and tedious political organizing, began to make up ground. They were able to use outside events, in particular the November crisis, to gain the initiative, emerging rather ahead by the winter and spring of 1849.

---

[4] The comparable group in the Palatinate, Protestant religious revivalists, were firm adherents of the Bavarian monarchy, showing no interest in having their province annexed by a ruler of their confession.

[5] This political seesaw would continue after the end of the revolution, Catholic-clericals resuming their opposition to the Prussian government and their alliance with the (much weakened) democrats in fall 1849 and winter–spring 1850.

This competition for Catholic popular support was unique to the revolutionary period; the development of a political Catholicism and the firming up of clerical authority in the quarter-century after 1850 ensured that Catholic sentiments would flow exclusively to the support of Catholic politics.[6]

THE RHINELAND IN REVOLUTION

All the conflicts stemming from the triangle of tensions could be observed as early as the 1830s, and the various political groups that would attempt to exploit them were in place by the middle of the following decade. But the authority of the *Vormärz* German states sufficed to prevent the full expression of these conflicts and to repress attempts at their open and uninterrupted politicization. Both of these processes had to await the weakening of state authority and the creation of a more open political life, following the outbreak of revolution in February–March 1848. The course of the revolution in the Rhineland is best understood as a chain of explosions, triggered by events in the European revolutionary capitals, but occurring along the fault lines of preexisting tensions, and characterized by attacks on targets of long-suppressed popular anger. The largest of the explosions occurred in Solingen in March 1848; in Aachen, the lower Rhine manufacturing districts, and much of the countryside and waterfront in April; in Mainz and Trier in May; in Cologne, Worms, and Alzey in September; and in Düsseldorf, Bonn and vicinity, Koblenz, and the Moselle Valley in November. The last group occurred during May–June 1849, in Düsseldorf again, the Wuppertal and Bergisches Land, the lower Rhine textile districts, Prüm and Wittlich, a large part of Rhine-Hessen, and, above all, the Palatinate.

A chain of explosions is not an entirely appropriate metaphor, since it suggests a repetition of the same event, without any process of development. Considering the list of confrontations mentioned in the previous paragraph, it becomes apparent that they were increasingly organized by the democrats. It might be more exact to say that democrats increasingly put themselves forward as leaders of popular struggles, attempting to direct them toward left-wing political ends. In this sense, the history of the 1848–1849 revolution in the Rhineland is a story of the growing intersection between spontaneous popular movements and an organized democratic politics.

A chronology of this intersection would point to the summer of 1848 as the crucial period. The failures of the left in violent confrontations at the local and regional levels and the disappointing outcome of elections to the Frankfurt National Assembly made activists aware of the democrats' deficiencies in organization and agitation, and set them to work resolving them. Part of their

---

[6] On this process, see Sperber, *Popular Catholicism in Nineteenth Century Germany*, esp. chs. 2–4.

efforts involved shoring up their base of support: expanding their efforts among urban small producers, using the same tactics to organize manufacturing outworkers, forming democratic clubs in cities and towns where they had not previously existed, and organizing the clubs into provincial federations. The most interesting aspect of the democratic campaign, however, was the attempt to encompass groups previously shunned or even attacked: women, soldiers, and peasants.

Democrats achieved a fair success in their efforts to bring women into the movement, but largely because so little was demanded of them. Women's place on the left was women's place in society: as spectators, inspiring their men, and as representatives of the domesticity the armed male citizen sought to protect. This may not have changed women's position much, but it did a good deal for the radicals. Women organized as a democratic audience were still spectators, but spectators who applauded their men's taking militant action, rather than fearfully trying to hold them back.

The results of left-wing agitation and organization among the military were rather more mixed. Everywhere a line was drawn between Rhineland natives, accessible to the agitation of the left, and outsiders from East Elbian Prussia or trans-Rhenan Bavaria, deaf to the radicals' blandishments. The distinction between the two might be attributed to monarchical loyalism or—and these are complementary rather than conflicting explanations—to decades of verbal insults and brawling in taverns, at fairs, and in the streets between the Rhinelanders and the soldiers from distant regions who garrisoned their cities.

Agitation among soldiers was also far from organizing them and mobilizing them for political action. While the detachments of the Hessian and Bavarian armies stationed in the Rhineland were crippled by the actions of the radicals, unable to suppress insurgent movements, many Bavarian soldiers even going over to them, this was not the case for Prussian troops. The loyalist regiments remained true to their king, and followed their officers' orders. They held in check their politically unreliable Rhenish comrades, while simultaneously suppressing violent revolutionary movements, not just in the Prussian province, but throughout the entire Rhineland.

The most challenging group for the democrats was the peasantry. It was of all social groups the least politicized, the most heavily influenced by religion, and the most alien to urban ways of thinking. Yet it was also the most crucial to the success of the movement, since peasants made up a majority of the region's inhabitants. The results of the democrats' rural agitation can be considered in terms of the three main kinds of Rhenish agriculturalists: the farmers of the plains, the vintners of the valleys, and the peasants of the up-country.

The grain growers of the Rhine plains were the most prosperous of all the Rhenish peasants, beneficiaries of long-term price and production trends. Thanks to the work of village activists and the exploitation of grievances over the common lands and state forest policies, the left succeeded in organizing a minority of such peasants in spite of their favorable position in the market. This was about the best the democrats could have hoped to achieve.

Of all the types of farmers, vintners were most similar to urban small producers in their orientation toward the market, and their grievances about it and about the state. Urban leftists found their grievances easy to understand and were thus able to design an effective agitation. Taking the whole Rhineland into account, vintners were probably the most left-wing agriculturalists, particularly active in their support for the left in the Moselle Valley, Rhine-Hessen, and parts of the Palatinate.

The peasants of the uplands were the poorest and angriest of the inhabitants of the Rhenish countryside, but also the least familiar with politics, culturally the most alien to city democrats and so the hardest for them to organize. Where they made the effort, seeking ways to talk to these peasants, putting the question of forest use at the center of their rural agitation, leftists could have substantial success. Two areas in particular stand out. On the right bank of the Rhine between Düsseldorf and Königswinter and in the western Palatinate, the democrats enrolled thousands of upland peasants in the movement, organizing clubs and gaining rustic supporters ready to take up arms for the cause. One can only wonder if a comparable effort elsewhere might not have significantly expanded the ranks of organized democrats. For whatever reasons, such agitation was never seriously attempted, and this seems to me the greatest of the missed opportunities for the left in the Rhineland during the revolution.[7]

For all these qualifications, the democrats' campaign did result in a substantial expansion of their base of support. The expansion was so great that it seems appropriate to describe the fall of 1848 and the winter of 1848–1849 as a second phase of the revolution, characterized by the politicization of *Vormärz* social and political tensions in small towns and the countryside, as had occurred in larger cities the previous spring. It was at this time that a substantial majority of the democratic political clubs were organized. The unexpectedly strong resonance of the September and especially the November crises and the victories of the left in the elections to the Bavarian parliament in November 1848 and the Prussian parliament in January 1849 all showed the increasing influence of the left on the population. Although the revolutionary movement had been defeated in the capital cities—in Frankfurt in September, in Vienna in October, and in Berlin in November 1848—it expanded socially and geographically in the Rhineland, gaining new supporters in provincial small towns and villages. Seen in this light, the uprisings of May 1849 were not a farcical epilogue to a failed revolution but the culmination of a year of agitation and organization; their republican and anti-Prussian character was

[7] The Democratic Club in Trier had a particularly poor record in this regard, possibly reflecting the popularity of guildlike social restrictionism among its artisan supporters, and their hostility to the competition of part-time peasant craftsmen.

not an absurd contradiction of the Frankfurt constitution but consistent with previously espoused democratic ideology.

A Failed Revolution?

This course of events in one region cannot answer the broadest question posed by historians, namely, why the 1848 revolution failed. A more modest question might be asked: why the 1848 revolution, as Rhenish democrats envisaged it, failed. (Why the revolution as conceived by constitutional monarchists, such as Heinrich von Gagern, did not succeed, is altogether another story.) One answer is that within the confines of the Rhineland, the democrats' revolution was victorious. Already strong in the southern part of the region at the outset of events, the democrats successfully organized a mass following, gradually overcame or incorporated conservative and politically moderate elements, and emerged by early 1849 as the dominant political force in all of western Germany. The secret of the successful counterrevolution cannot be found in the social and political dynamics of the Rhineland itself; these ultimately worked in the revolutionaries' favor.

Provinces do not determine their own political destiny; the causes of the failed revolution lie beyond the Rhineland's boundaries. Contemporaries knew quite well why the democrats' efforts failed, the reason given in the celebrated slogan coined by the arch-conservative General von Griesheim, after his king sent troops to dissolve the Prussian National Assembly: "Gegen Demokraten helfen nur Soldaten," against democrats, only soldiers can help. The revolutionary movement in the Rhineland was suppressed by the loyal soldiers of the king of Prussia. Even they might not have prevailed, had all the explosive confrontations occurring between March 1848 and May 1849 taken place at once. They did not, and the army—in the end, relying on its ultimate weapon, the threat of destroying whole cities by artillery bombardment—was able to suppress each individual incident and in doing so usually intimidate the participants into not repeating their actions when the next crisis arose. Although at times pushed to their limits, the loyalist troops were always able to master the situation.

The 1848–1849 revolution, as Rhineland democrats conceived it, was more conquered than defeated. One might see the mid-century events as a victory of the seigneurial and agrarian world of East Elbia, conservative and royalist, over a more urbanized (including the rural areas) and egalitarian Rhenish society, profoundly shaped by the heritage of the French Revolution. Another, different but complementary regional interpretation might focus on the rural inhabitants of the north German plain, who seem to have been much less affected by the 1848 revolution than other central Europeans. The eastern portion of this plain, the heartland of the Prussian monarchy, was relatively unshaken by social and political turbulence; the peasants of this area manned the loyalist regiments, whose armed might destroyed the revolution in the Rhineland and much of the rest of Germany.[8]

1848–1849 IN THE RHINELAND AND ELSEWHERE

The conclusions reached in a regional study are, of course, not generally valid, and I have no intention of denying the many unique and atypical features of Rhenish society. Still, since general theories are supposed to explain particular cases, and since the Rhineland was an important center of the mid-century revolution, it is not without a certain interest to compare the conclusions reached here with some of the main explanations of the origins and nature of the German revolution of 1848–1849. Conversely, it might also be worthwhile to see if some of the characteristics of mid-century revolution in the Rhineland were found elsewhere in Germany, or for that matter, in other European countries. In that way new elements from this regional study might be introduced into more general accounts of the 1848 revolution.

General Explanations and a Particular Case

There are today three main explanations of the events of 1848, each containing many variations. One, following an older historiographical tradition, sees as central the attempt to create a German national state. This explanation focuses on the work of the Frankfurt National Assembly, especially on the politically moderate constitutional monarchists within it, and the responses to it of the German and other European Great Powers. While not denying the existence of extraparliamentary popular movements, the social and political tensions that caused them, or the political radicalism that came to be based on them, this explanatory variant tends to see them as irrelevant, subordinate to their leaders, who acted in the parliamentary and diplomatic arena. It was in this arena that the decisive questions of the revolution were posed and the fate of the revolution decided.[9]

---

[8] On the relative conservatism of the peasants of the north German plain, cf. Gailus, "Soziale Protesbewegungen," pp. 91–92.

[9] The most sophisticated version of such an explanation is in Nipperdey, *Deutsche Geschichte*, pp. 594–670, esp. 669; a recent textbook example is Günter Wollstein, *Deutsche Geschichte 1848/49. Gescheiterte Revolution in Mitteleuropa* (Stuttgart: W. Kohlhammer, 1986). Unsurprisingly, the parliament-centered studies of Manfred Botzenhart, *Deutscher Parlamentarismus in der Revolutionszeit*, and Frank Eyck, *The Frankfurt Parliamentg 1848–1849* (New York: St. Martin's, 1968), tend to this explanation. So does Konrad Repgen's work on the Prussian Rhine Province in the spring of 1848 (see Chapter Four, notes 19, 69; cf. other sources cited therein). Although Veit Valentin announced in the preface to his monumental study his intention of writing a "history of the people's movement of 1848/49" (*Geschichte der deutschen Revolution* 1:ix), his main sources, in accordance with the historians' practice of the time, were diplomats' reports, which tended to bring high politics and international relations back to the center of his work.

Although not empirically incorrect, this whole viewpoint tends to overlook what made the revolution revolutionary, namely, the enormous outpouring of popular political participation. Diplomacy certainly continued in 1848–1849, but in those years the diplomats had to take mass movements as well as *raison d'état* into their calculations. Parliamentary debates in Berlin, Frankfurt, or Vienna were followed with close attention all across central Europe, but without the results of street fighting these parliaments would never have met in the first place, and their destiny was ultimately decided in the streets.

Still more important, parliamentary-diplomatic activities did not cause the riots, barricade fighting, mass rallies, and political demonstrations or the political, social, and economic organizing typical of the revolutionary period. While some of the events of this mass movement were a response to parliamentary and diplomatic actions, they cannot be entirely understood in terms of them. In particular, this version of events has great difficulty explaining the divergence of mass movements and parliamentary-diplomatic maneuvering, as occurred during the *Reichsverfassungskampagne* in the Rhineland, when a strongly anti-Prussian movement was launched ostensibly in favor of a constitution naming the king of Prussia emperor. Some historians working in this tradition have had recourse to dubious conspiracy theories in order to fill this explanatory gap.[10]

A quite different tradition of explanation goes back to the retrospective accounts of Marx and Engels, elaborated by historians of the former German Democratic Republic. Unlike the previous version, in this one, mass movements hold center stage, explained by a Leninist analysis of class struggle. The revolution is said to have been begun by the liberal bourgeoisie, seeking to wrest power from the feudal-absolutist German states. The struggle was then abandoned by the bourgeoisie—a move either condemned as "betrayal" or, in more sophisticated fashion, seen as capitalists realizing their class interests could best be obtained by compromising with the feudal-absolutist element, rather than overthrowing it. Leadership in the revolutionary struggle passed some time in the summer of 1848 into the hands of the democrats, split into two wings: one socially and politically vacillating and petit bourgeois in social composition; the other militantly republican, committed to the class struggle, proletarian in character, and at least partly Marxist in leadership.[11]

Although much of the material for this theory of revolution is drawn from the Rhineland, where Marx himself was active, it fits Rhenish events poorly. There was a good deal of social struggle in the Rhineland connected to the democratic movement, particularly in the larger cities and manufacturing districts on the lower Rhine. This struggle, however, was not a Leninist one,

[10] Cf. sources cited in Chapter Eleven, note 104; or the critical remarks of Siemann, *Die deutsche Revolution*, pp. 13–14.

[11] A good summary version of the explanation can be found in *Illustrierte Geschichte der deutschen Revolution von 1848/49*, pp. 47, 102–07, 143–48, 167–71, 209–24, and passim.

pitting propertyless proletarians against capitalist owners of the means of production. The small group of Rhenish factory workers played at most a minor role in social and political struggles, whose main protagonists were nominally independent craftsmen and manufacturing outworkers pitted against financial and mercantile capitalists who controlled their access to the market.

Nor is it entirely clear that class struggle promoted revolutionary political struggle. The proclamation of a struggle against the bourgeoisie, as seen in the activities of the true socialists, especially their major political initiative, the Cologne Workers' Association during the presidency of Andreas Gottschalk, led away from political radicalism, not toward it. Muting the class struggle, as Marx and Marxists understood it, did not weaken the democratic movement. Whether measured by election results, the organization of democratic clubs, or the launching of insurrections, the Rhenish democrats were stronger in Rhine-Hessen and the Palatinate than they were in the urbanized factory and manufacturing districts of the lower Rhine. Yet in the democratic strongholds, factories were virtually nonexistent, outworking scarce, bourgeois and smallholding peasant participation in the democratic movement common, and an ideology of cross-class cooperation pronounced. There were many reasons for this democratic strength in the southern Rhineland, including the local prevalence of rationalist as against neoorthodox religion and the greater strength and repressive capacities of the Prussian state as against the Hessian and Bavarian ones, but it is hard to avoid the impression that political radicalism and class struggle, as Marx defined it, did not always go hand in hand.

Marx and Engels described their own followers as "proletarian," and generally wrote off the south German democrats as "petit bourgeois," beginning a long history of the Marxist use of that phrase as an all-purpose term of political abuse. There is no evidence, however, to support the assertion that factory workers formed a large portion of Marx's supporters, or even a disproportionate number when compared with other left-wing groups. The Cologne communists do not even seem to have devoted much time and energy to organizing the contemporary working class. Their lack of interest in the manufacturing outworkers of the lower Rhine, the Wuppertal, and the Bergisches Land is certainly striking.

The Marxist account does become plausible when the social categories used in it are translated back into the political ones from which they came: "bourgeois" to "constitutional monarchist," "petit bourgeois" to "moderate democrat," "proletarian" to " 'exalted' democrat." Marx and Engels themselves would then appear as particularly decisive and energetic "exalted" democrats, which seems closer to their actual political practice than does their self-description as leaders of proletarian revolution. This way of saving the Marxist version of the politics of the 1848–1849 revolution involves, however, abandoning the Marxist project of linking social and political struggles. If one wishes to keep this connection, of enormous worth for the study of present and past society, then it is necessary to approach critically Marx and Engels's own accounts of their revolutionary roles.

The third explanation of the revolutionary events has gained currency after 1945, particularly among historians in the former West Germany. This approach links the revolution to a crisis or crises of modernization. There are two crises usually cited, sometimes separately, sometimes together. One relates to the process of economic modernization, said to have produced a group of victims, especially artisans, socially backward looking, but ready for violent action and at least potentially politically radical. The other stems from a consideration of the total social process. While economic and social modernization in central Europe proceeded apace, political structures remained traditional. The revolution arose from the desire to replace them with a modern, parliamentary-democratic national state, appropriate to a modernizing society.[12]

Neither of these modernization crises was much in evidence in the Rhineland. There were spectacular instances of machine breaking at the outset of the revolution, but what seem to have been textbook cases of traditionalist opposition to economic modernity prove on closer examination to stem from a quite different dynamic of social and political tension. Many of the acts of ostensible agents of economic modernization—master manufacturers praising the guild system, capitalists seeking to profit from Malthusian shortages of goods rather than increasing production to overcome them, foresters cutting down oaks and planting spruce—were dictated by individual and group self-interest in ways that did not necessarily lead to economic growth via the capitalist free market. Popular opposition to such acts, often politically exploited by the left, involved a different attitude toward modernization rather than a refusal of it.

It is equally difficult to perceive the political goals of the Rhenish democrats and their supporters as examples of modernization. Radicals were certainly adherents of a regime of popular sovereignty, combining the politically "modernizing" factors of national unity, democratic suffrage, and parliamentary government, but the background to these positions tells another story. The importance of inter- and intraconfessional rivalries in political life, usually seen as a sign of "traditional" attitudes, hardly fits the modernization thesis. Moreover, much of the wish for national unity arose from a hostility to con-

---

[12] One of the first historians to consider some of these elements was Rudolf Stadelmann in his 1948 work, *Social and Political History of the Revolution of 1848*; they form the dominant theme of the major English-language study of the revolution, Theodor Hamerow's *Revolution, Restoration, Reaction*. For a particularly elaborate version of the revolution as a crisis of modernization, see Wehler, *Deutsche Gesellschaftsgeschichte* 2:660–779, esp. pp. 693–95. Siemann's *Die deutsche Revolution von 1848/49* also uses the modernization paradigm, although the author does not let it become a conceptual straitjacket.

fessional and provincial outsiders, not a modernizing interest in combining, through better communication, distant areas into one state. In this respect, a "modern" political demand seems inspired by "premodern," or "traditional," motives.

Additionally, both popular movements and democratic politics were shot through with a powerful hostility toward state officials. Vociferous agitation over this subject was the main theme of popular leftism. Since in Max Weber's work, from which all modernization theories descend, the state bureaucracy is the epitome of modernization, Weber defining modernization in terms of the practices of the Prussian bureaucracy, it is difficult to see how an antibureaucratic political movement could be an agent of modernization.

The problem with this whole approach is that it relies on a dubious conceptual apparatus. Modernization theory assumes, at least ideally, a direct and uniform march from "traditionalist" (that is, old regime) social, economic, administrative, and mental structures to "modern" ones (that is, those of the first half of the twentieth century). Whether this model really explains anything is a question that need not be considered here, but it certainly does not work well for understanding conflicts in the mid-nineteenth-century Rhineland, where social and economic structures were neither "traditional" nor "modern," and where elements of "tradition" and "modernity" could be found on both sides of most political and social struggles.

A Particular Case and a General Model

If the most prevalent general explanations of the 1848 revolution do not account for many of its features in the Rhineland, a look at other provincial histories suggests that at least some of these features could be found elsewhere in central Europe. Probably the single most prevalent one was the role of dynastic and confessional loyalties in determing political alignments. Prussian politics in 1848–1849 tended to break down along these lines, leftists finding many of their adherents among the Roman Catholic subjects of the crown or the inhabitants of conquered or annexed provinces, such as Posen, Silesia, and Prussian Saxony, while conservatism was strongest among the kingdom's Protestants and inhabitants of its older provinces east of the Elbe, long under Hohenzollern rule. Conservative political clubs, 40 percent of which were in the two East Elbian provinces, Brandenburg and Pomerania, were typically founded and led by state officials or neoorthodox Protestant pastors. Sporting names such as "Prussian Association" or "League of Loyalty to King and Fatherland," they denounced political and religious radicalism and promoted a confessionally tinged loyalism.[13]

[13] Schwentker, *Konservative Vereine*, pp. 78–86, 158, 214–22, 264–65, and passim. A large portion of the Roman Catholic population of the Prussian provinces of Pose and Silesia was ethnically Polish, which only increased hostilities towards the ruling dynasty.

Politically closest to the Prussian Rhineland was the neighboring province of Westphalia, where events during the mid-century followed similar confessional and dynastic dynamics. The neoorthodox Protestants of northeastern Westphalia, an area that had belonged to the Prussian kingdom under the old regime, were fervent monarchical loyalists. The extreme conservativism they supported was the dominant political force. Inhabitants of the heavily Roman Catholic western and southeastern portions of the province were strong supporters of Catholic-clerical politics at the outset of the revolution, but a democratic agitation campaign gradually won support in these areas, if to a lesser extent than in the Rhineland. Also as in the Rhineland, the outworkers of the predominantly Protestant Westphalian manufacturing district rose up in May 1849. Their radicalism, like that of the inhabitants of the neighboring Wuppertal and Bergisches Land, stemmed from a disappointed monarchism.[14]

These considerations by no means fully explain the course of the 1848–1849 revolution in the Prussian kingdom, since they do not account for the strength of the democrats in the royal capital of Berlin or for their partial successes in the old, East Elbian province of East Prussia. Even more than in Prussia, political alignments in Bavaria during the mid-century revolution followed closely on dynastic lines. The inhabitants of the Alpine provinces of Upper and Lower Bavaria and the Upper Palatinate, almost exclusively Roman Catholic, tied to the ruling dynasty for centuries, were hostile to democracy, and even more opposed to a national state, which might modify the social, political, and religious peculiarities of the Bavarian monarchy. The situation was completely turned around in the state's new provinces acquired at the beginning of the nineteenth century. Like the Palatines, the trans-Rhenan Franconians and Swabians had no love for the ruling house—an hostility expressed in adherence to a German national state and increasingly shading off into republicanism, if perhaps not quite so radically as west of the Rhine.[15]

Inter- and intraconfessional dynamics also interacted with dynastic loyalties in producing the political alignments in trans-Rhenan Bavaria during the revolutionary period. All in all, Protestants were more likely to support the left than the Catholics. The only conservative deputies to be elected from the new Bavarian provinces to the Bavarian parliament in December 1848 came from predominantly Roman Catholic constituencies in Swabia. Neoorthodox clergy and laity of both Christian confessions were the chief adherents of the Bavarian government, while religious rationalists, once again of both confessions, were usually to be found on the left.[16]

---

[14] See the excellent work of Schulte, *Volk und Staat*, passim.

[15] On the revolution in trans-Rhenan Bavaria, see Thränhardt, *Wahlen und politische Struktur in Bayern*, pp. 43–47; Nickel, *1848/49 in Augsburg und Bayerisch-Schwaben*; and Ludwig Zimmermann, *Die Einheits- und Freiheitsbewegung und die Revolution von 1848 in Franken* (Würzburg: Ferdinand Schöningh, 1951).

[16] Zimmermann, *Einheits- und Freiheitsbewegung*, pp. 380–84; Nickel, *1848/49 in Augsburg*

The connection of religious and dynastic conflict with political radicalism seems to break down when applied to the kingdom of Saxony. A major stronghold of the—ever more openly and militantly republican—left during the revolution, Saxony was confessionally homogeneous and had been ruled by the same princely family for centuries. The royal house, however, had converted to Catholicism in the eighteenth century. The resulting confessional opposition between a Catholic monarch and his Protestant subjects in this homeland of the Reformation had decisively weakened dynastic loyalty and helped promote, even in the *Vormärz*, and certainly during the revolution, movements of political and religious radicalism.[17]

Structures of dynastic and religious conflict were homogeneous throughout central Europe, their political ramifications correspondingly similar. Socioeconomic conditions and the conflicts arising from them were far less uniform, their politicization occurring in equally varied ways. Nonetheless, many of the patterns of social tension and political conflict found among Rhenish artisans and peasants existed elsewhere in Germany, although the presence of the guild system and feudal tenures altered the frequency with which certain positions were held.

The existence of guilds made conflicts between masters and journeymen more common outside the Rhineland. The Bavarian state's resolute attachment to a particularly retrogade and rigid version of artisan corporatism in its trans-Rhenan provinces won it the loyalty at least of those master craftsmen organized into artisans' associations. Journeymen—those affiliated with workers' associations at any rate—generally supported the democrats. A similar alignment was found in another stronghold of the guild system, the free city of Frankfurt a. Main. Guild masters there flocked into the conservative political associations, while the journeymen were heavily overrepresented among the participants of the September 1848 uprising. The connection master craftsman–supporter of the guilds–political conservative, although perhaps the most typical, was not universal. In the north German city-state of Bremen, it was the democrats who were the leading adherents of the artisanal corporations.[18]

In spite of the guilds, it was sometimes possible for masters and journeymen to unite under left-wing auspices behind a common program of small producer anticapitalism, as occurred more frequently in the Rhineland, where guilds were an increasingly distant memory. During the revolution, many associations of master artisans were founded in Württemberg, a south German state with a legally well established guild system. By early 1849 they had split into

---

und Bayerisch-Schwaben, pp. 160–62, 224–29, 243; Dieter Langewiesche, ''Die politische Vereinsbewegung in Würzburg und in Unterfranken in den Revolutionsjahren 1848/49,'' *Jahrbuch für fränkische Landesforschung* 37 (1977): 195–234, esp. pp. 222, 230–31.

[17] Weber, *Die Revolution in Sachsen 1848/49*, pp. 9–10 and passim.

[18] Lenger, *Sozialgeschichte der deutschen Handwerker*, pp. 68–86.

two separate groups. One supported the guilds, directed its efforts at holding down the journeymen, and aligned itself with the constitutional monarchists. The other, closely connected to the active and influential Württemberg democrats, cooperated with the journeymen, spoke out in favor of "association," and denounced as "our greatest enemy . . . the rule of capital."[19]

Journeymen also advanced similar economic and political positions. The founding congress of the Workers' Fraternization, a federation of workers' associations, whose initial members were mostly journeymen artisans in central and eastern Germany, rejected the idea of a "conflict between masters and journeymen" as belonging to the "medieval guild system." If masters and journeymen were not fundamentally in opposition, it was because of the "modern social antagonism of capitalists and workers," which brought together under the proletarian rubric journeymen and outworking masters. This point of view provided a basis for the Workers' Fraternization's projects of producers' cooperatives and its involvement in democratic politics.[20]

Although historians have pointed out the widespread rural disturbances in the spring of 1848, most have denied that these had political implications. Historians have suggested that generalizing in an abstract way from their own concrete experiences was difficult for the countryfolk and that governmental concessions, especially concerning grievances relating to feudal tenures, pacified the peasants, who lapsed into political passivity or manifested a royalist loyalism. The evidence presented in this work about the politicization of the Rhenish peasantry and the recruitment of thousands of peasants into the democratic movement calls this view into question and leads one to wonder how valid it is for other parts of Germany.[21]

A closer look suggests that this established version is most appropriate to the rural population of the north German plain, where the custom of impartible inheritance had produced sharp social divisions between larger, property-owning peasants on the one hand and smallholders, tenants, and landless laborers on the other. If they had any explicit political connotations, actions of the rural proletariat showed a conservative royalist loyalism. Landless laborers in Oldenburg, meeting to consider their grievances against their peasant employers, also announced their devotion to the grand duke, condemned the oppositional state parliament, and petitioned their prince "that he might, so far as possible,

---

[19] Carola Lipp, "Württembergische Handwerker und Handwerkervereine im Vormärz und in der Revolution 1848/49," in *Handwerker in der Industrialisierung*, pp. 347–80.

[20] Lenger, *Sozialgeschichte der deutschen Handwerker*, p. 84.

[21] Stadelman, *Social and Political History*, pp. 81–84; Siemann, *Die deutsche Revolution*, pp. 184–87; Nipperdey, *Deutsche Geschichte*, pp. 601–02. A good criticism of this point of view, although limited to examples from Saxony and Silesia, can be found in Helmut Bleiber, "Bauern und Landarbeiter in der bürgerlich-demokratischen Revolution von 1848/49 in Deutschland," *Zeitschrift für Geschichtswissenschaft* 17 (1969): 289–309; Bleiber's critique is followed in the differentiated account in Wehler, *Deutsche Gesellschaftsgeschichte* 2:706–15.

re-create the good old days.'' These actions helped fend off another possible politicization, encouraging the larger peasants to renounce the prosecution of their own grievances against noble landowners and the state, since to do so would be to set a dangerous precedent for their social inferiors.[22]

Elsewhere in central Europe, rural society was less sharply polarized and peasant politics took a different course. The Prussian province of Silesia, the one area in Germany where compulsory labor services still existed before 1848, was a center of antifeudal peasant uprisings, with disturbances continuing throughout all of 1848–1849. Silesian democrats were well organized and politically potent, dominating elections in May 1848 and January 1849 and taking militant action during the November crisis and the *Reichsverfassungskampagne*. Their peasant affiliates were grouped into ''Rustics' Associations,'' with a claimed—if probably exaggerated—membership of two hundred thousand.[23]

It would be easy to write off Silesia as a special case, but there is good evidence, admittedly often buried in obscure works of regional history, showing that the democrats were active in the countryside of Saxony, Franconia, Swabia, Hessen, Baden, and Württemberg. In all these areas, the liquidation of seigneurialism played an important role in leftist rural agitation, democrats demanding that feudal dues be abolished without the peasants' having to pay any compensation. However, other themes, familiar from the Rhineland, also surfaced in their efforts: demands for an end to state restrictions on forest use, violent attacks on state officials, calls for lower taxes, even the exploitation of religious controversies. The Protestant Vicar Kattmann of the village of Kirchbrombach, was a leading democrat in trans-Rhenan Hessen-Darmstadt. He left the Lutheran state church and founded a rationalist sect, which drew rustic supporters from the entire vicinity, who were prominent participants in the abortive Odenwald uprising during the *Reichsverfassungskampagne*.[24]

---

[22] B. Parisius, '' 'Daß die liebe alte Vorzeit wo möglich wieder hergestellt werde,' Politische und soziokulturelle Reaktionen von oldenburgischen Landarbeitern auf ihren sozialen Abstieg 1800–1848,'' in *Sozialer Protest*, pp. 198–211; Paschen, *Konservative Vereine*, p. 259. Similarly, Josef Mooser, *Ländliche Klassengesellschaft 1770–1848. Bauern und Unterschichten Landwirtschaft und Gewerbe im östlichen Westfalen* (Göttingen: Vandenhoeck & Ruprecht, 1984); generalizing, Gailus, ''Soziale Protestbewegungen,'' pp. 91–92. For a good summary, see Wehler, *Deutsche Gesellschaftsgeschichte* 2:711–13.

[23] Wehler, *Deutsche Gesellschaftsgeschichte* 2:713–14. There is no full-scale, modern history of the 1848–1849 revolution in Silesia; such a work is a scholarly desideratum.

[24] Zimmermann, *Einheits- und Freiheitsbewegung*, pp. 295, 300, 360–65, 384–85; Nickel, *1848/49 in Augsburg und Bayerisch-Schwaben*, pp. 140, 167, 184, 232; Roland Zeise, ''Bauern und Demokraten 1848/49. Zur antifeudalen Bewegung der sächsischen Landbevölkerung in der Revolution vom Sommer 1848 bis zum vorabend des Dresdner Maiaufstandes,'' *Jahrbuch für Regionalgeschichte* 4 (1972): 148–78; Langewiesche, ''Vereinsbewegung in Würzburg und in Unterfranken,'' pp. 229–32; Valentin, *Geschichte der deutschen Revolution* 2:407–08; 423. Most recently, Wettengel, *1848/49 im Rhein-Main-Raum*, pp. 286–304, has convincingly demonstrated the strength of the left in the Hessian countryside.

In these parts of Germany one can observe the same second wave of politicization, the same social and geographic expansion of the democratic movement in the fall and winter of 1848–1849 as occurred in the Rhineland. One form of this expansion was the founding of democratic clubs. The 75 Fatherland Associations (as the democratic clubs called themselves) existing in Saxony at the time of the elections to the Frankfurt National Assembly grew to 105 in September, and then almost tripled to some 280 by April 1849, their seventy-five thousand members constituting about 16 percent of the adult male population. Similarly, the 44 Fatherland Associations of Württemberg—also the local name for the democratic clubs—existing in the kingdom in September 1848 increased to 70 in December and to 181 by the following March. Badenese democrats, recovering from their two disastrous putsches in April and September 1848, succeeded in organizing 400 democratic clubs in the grand duchy during the fall and winter of 1848–1849. All these developments were a direct result of left-wing agitation among the rural and small-town population.[25]

Elections subsequent to those for the Frankfurt National Assembly tell a similar story of increasing democratic strength. Franconian voters sent politically moderate constitutional monarchists to Frankfurt in May 1848, such conflicts as existed during those elections, pitting Protestants against Catholics, not left against right. Seven months later, all the deputies elected from Franconia to the Bavarian parliament represented the left or the extreme left. Saxony had sent a full contingent of democrats to Frankfurt; at elections to the kingdom's legislature in January 1849, the left made a virtually clean sweep, many openly revolutionary republican candidates among them. Even the elections to the parliament's upper house, which were held under a property franchise, produced an overwhelming victory for the democrats, suggesting that they had substantial support from the Saxon bourgeoisie.[26]

It was precisely in those regions where the democratic movement had expanded and encompassed at least part of the rural population that the *Reichsverfassungskampagne* was at its most violent and militant. Events in the Rhineland were very far from unique. Mass demonstrations in Württemberg forced the king to recognize the Frankfurt constitution; there were local uprisings and mass demonstrations in the Prussian provinces of Westphalia, Sax-

---

[25] Weber, *Die Revolution in Sachsen*, pp. 250–51; Langewiesche, *Liberalismus und Demokratie in Württemberg*, pp. 111–13; Willy Real, *Die Revolution in Baden 1848/49* (Stuttgart: W. Kohlhammer, 1983), pp. 98–100. Similarly in Franconia and Swabia and trans-Rhenan Hessen: Zimmermann, *Einheits- und Freiheitsbewegung*, pp. 384–85; Nickel, *1848/49 in Augsburg und Bayerisch-Schwaben*, pp. 155–58; Langewiesche, "Vereinsbewegung in Würzburg und in Unterfranken," pp. 214–17; Wettengel, *1848/49 im Rhein-Main-Raum*, pp. 275–81.

[26] Weber, *Die Revolution in Sachsen*, pp. 43–50, 231–39; Zimmermann, *Einheits- und Freiheitsbewegung*, pp. 268–75, 367–70. Similarly in Württemberg: Langewiesche, *Liberalismus und Demokratie*, p. 223.

ony, and Silesia; similar demonstrations and abortive insurrections occurred in trans-Rhenan Hessen, Franconia, and Swabia. In both the kingdom of Saxony and the grand duchy of Baden, the royal government was overthrown and replaced with insurrectionary regimes, both suppressed by Prussian troops: the former within a few days, the latter only in July 1849. Seen on a map, these movements would trace a broad arc moving east to west through most of southern Germany, the northern extreme of which lay on the lower Rhine and in Westphalia.[27]

The entire course of the revolution suggests a broad north-south distinction in mid-nineteenth-century German politics. In the north, leftists were a distinct minority. The peasants were either politically passive or monarchist loyalists. Democratic support was limited to the inhabitants of larger cities and some manufacturing regions and there largely to the artisans, the bourgeoisie adhering to constitutional monarchism and early on in the revolution desiring a restoration of order. In south Germany, on the other hand, the democratic movement, if still disproportionately supported by artisans, enlisted a much broader range of social support. Some of the urban bourgeoisie stood on the left, and, most crucially, at least part of the rural population did as well. Some south German leftists had obtained majority support as early as the spring of 1848; others achieved it by the winter of the following year. In the south, support for conservatism or constitutional monarchism tended to be limited to those possessing confessional or dynastic ties to the ruling princely houses. The narrowness of the democrats' social base limited the extent of the revolution in north Germany, the victories of reaction in the capital cities of revolution, from June through November 1848, leaving the north German left without any further prospects. These same events strengthened the democratic movement in the south, encouraging the left to start a successful campaign of agitation and organization in small towns and the countryside, capitalizing on latent support and creating the organized basis for the uprisings of May 1849.[28]

Many of these same features of political and social movements characterized the 1848 revolution in France. This comparison goes against the prevailing practice of understanding the 1848 revolution as Germany's 1789. At the

---

[27] Klessmann's summary in "Zur Sozialgeschichte der Reichsverfassungskampagne," gives only the main points of the insurrections, but there were many additional events. For more details, see Kaschuba and Lipp, *Provinz und Revolution*, pp. 219–33; Schulte, *Volk und Staat*, pp. 294–318; Zimmermann, *Einheits- und Freiheitsbewegung*, pp. 393–433; Nickel, *1848/49 in Augsburg und Bayerisch-Schwaben*, pp. 183–98; Calliess, *Militär in der Krise*, pp. 163–71; Weber, *Die Revolution in Sachsen*, pp. 327–55; Wettengel, *1848/49 im Rhein-Main-Raum*, pp. 461–502; Valentin, *Geschichte der deutschen Revolution* 2:478, 496–509.

[28] Applying this distinction to the Rhineland, one would say that Rhine-Hessen and the Palatinate clearly belonged to leftist southern Germany, while the Prussian Rhine Province was a transitional region between north and south, with features of both.

national level, major issues of the German Revolution—the abolition of feudalism, the creation of a unified national state—were of no concern in mid-nineteenth-century France, having, indeed, been resolved in the turbulent decade following 1789. However, a view from below, focusing on the sources of social and political tensions and the development of popular support for radical politics, shows many similarities in the mid-century revolutions of the two countries. With these in mind, it might be more helpful to understand the 1848 revolution as Germany's 1848, not as its 1789.

French politics also showed the same north-south dichotomy as in central Europe. Rural northern France was politically conservative; leftist support was restricted to the artisans and skilled workers of the large cities and manufacturing or industrial areas. Their politics was marked by an antagonism toward a largely conservative (whether Legitimist, Orleanist, Bonapartist or republican) bourgeoisie. Social and political alignments were quite different in the "red" France of the center and south, where support for the left was socially more widespread. Bourgeois democrats supported rural agitation, exploiting grievances over forest use or excessive taxation, which helped to win large portions of the peasantry for the left. The same religious factors important to the movement in southern Germany could also be found there. Given France's religious homogeneity, interconfessional antagonisms were less significant (although the small Protestant minority in southern France strongly supported the radicals), but both rationalist religion and anticlericalism were keys to democratic political support.

The course of events during the revolution was also similar in both countries. Both revolutions began with barricade fighting in the capital cities and apolitical disturbances in the provinces. These preceded conservative victories in elections to constituent assemblies held under universal manhood suffrage, leading to subsequent confrontations between a disappointed left and the still-conservative postrevolutionary regimes—in France, concentrated in the Parisian June Days, the German equivalents scattered between April and November 1848. While these confrontations brought about, for all practical purposes, the end of the revolution in the capital cities and the northern part of the country, they led to a broad democratic organizing campaign in the south, whose successes could be seen in later elections and in the numerical growth of democratic clubs (in the France of 1850–1851, democratic secret societies) and their spread into the countryside.

Both these mobilizations climaxed in armed insurrections, the *Reichsverfassungskampagne* and the uprising against Louis Napoleon's coup d'état of December 1851. These were strikingly similar events, both occurring mainly in the provinces and in small towns and the countryside, while the capitals and larger cities remained quiet. Both were ostensibly for moderate political purposes, the installation of the Frankfurt constitution in Germany and the preservation of the bourgeois republic in France. Many of the one hundred thousand armed insurgents who participated in each of them had more radical goals in mind: the creation of the "red" or the "social and democratic" republic, proposed by the left-wing campaign of agitation and organization that had preceded the insurrection and made it possible.[29]

Going furthest afield, I would suggest this shift toward the provinces was characteristic of the 1848 revolutions in all of Europe. Whether in France, Germany, Italy, or Hungary, the revolution did not end in 1848. Rather, the revolutionary action of 1849—in France, of 1850 and 1851 as well—occurred away from the capital cities and many of the sites of the struggles of the previous year, encompassing new populations and new social groups. In this respect, the very expression "the revolution of 1848" is a misnomer, obscuring this second phase of revolutionary activity and its social and political preconditions.

FROM 1789 TO 1848 AND BEYOND

If the preceding section has suggested something of the place of the Rhineland democrats among the revolutionaries of mid-nineteenth-century Europe, I would also like to explore their relationship to preceding and subsequent left-wing activists. The events of 1848–1849 were not the first experience in political radicalism for the Rhineland. Fifty years previously, the region on both banks of the Rhine was one of the areas outside of France in which Jacobin clubs were formed and a democratic movement developed. The "Rhineland Jacobins" have become the object of prolonged scholarly polemics, which need not be reiterated here. Without being too unfair to either side, it might be reasonable to sum up the results of the controversy by saying that while the Rhineland radicals of the 1790s took their political cues from France, they were nonetheless a movement with roots in the indigenous society, able to mobilize a certain amount of popular support from it. However, they were, even at their greatest extent, only a relatively small minority. Outside their strongholds, such as the cities of Mainz and Cologne, they consisted of just scattered individual activists. Given this modest popular support, they were able to exercise political influence only because of the patronage of the occupying French revolutionary armies.[30]

---

[29] This description of the mid-century revolution in France is based on the two books of Agulhon, *Republic in the Village*; and *The Apprenticeship of the Republic*; Ted Margadant, *French Peasants in Revolt: The Insurrection of 1851* (Princeton: Princeton University Press, 1979); Edward Berenson, *Populist Religion and Left-Wing Politics in France, 1830–1852* (Princeton: Princeton University Press, 1984); John Merriman, *The Agony of the Republic: The Repression of the Left in Revolutionary France* (New Haven and London: Yale University Press, 1978), and especially on the first work emphasizing this line of interpretation, the marvelous study of Pierre Vigier, *La Seconde République dans la Région Alpine*, 2 vols. (Paris: Presses Universitaires de France, 1963).

[30] Conclusions along these lines, albeit with different nuances and from different political view-

The Rhineland democrats of 1848 made use of a Germanized version of the rhetoric of 1789 and 1793 to identify their ideals and denounce their enemies, obtaining a favorable response from a population in whom the memory of the revolutionary and Napoleonic years was still alive. The 1848 democrats strove to create cross-class coalitions in their struggle against monarchy and state bureaucracy—even, perhaps especially, Marx, the great protagonist of the class struggle. The Jacobin ideal of the armed male citizen played a substantial role in their social and political vision. In all these respects, they were very much the successors of the revolutionaries of the 1790s—sometimes biologically so, since many democratic activists of the southern Rhineland were descendants of the Rhenish Jacobins. When engaged in historical self-reflection, they understood themselves as such. Historians have usually treated the 1848 radicals as early socialists, but it might be at least as fruitful to understand them as late Jacobins.

Like the first Rhenish Jacobins, their mid-nineteenth-century successors were usually republicans, but they envisaged a different postrevolutionary regime: not a republic of virtue, but a republic of low taxes, easily available wood, and artisans' sales cooperatives. The creation of a democratic, preferably republican government was their answer to the social question. This orientation toward obtaining popular support was both cause and consequence of the far greater extent of the democratic movement at the time, marking the main difference between the Rhenish Jacobins of the 1790s and the Rhineland democrats fifty years later. There were still some areas in 1848, for example, parts of the lower Rhine plains or in the mountains of the Eifel, where democratic activists were isolated individuals, as they had been in the 1790s. In most places they were far more likely to have an organized body of supporters and a larger number of sympathizers, ready, at least on occasion, to take to the streets. To a much greater extent than the original version, the late Jacobinism of the 1840s was a popular, mass movement.

From this point of view, 1848–1849 appears more as a political endpoint than as a beginning. In comparison to France, where the broad political divisions created in the mid-century revolution remained present well into the twentieth century, the events of 1848–1849 had no comparable effect in central Europe. Large-scale emigration and the first wave of urbanization and industrialization transformed the social context of mid-nineteenth-century radicalism; the broad political repression of the 1850s, the growth of a political Catholicism, and the creation of a German national state under the leadership

---

points, in F. G. Dreyfus, *Sociétés et mentalités en Mayence au dix-huitième siècle* (Paris: Armand Colin, 1968); T.C.W. Blanning, *The French Revolution in Germany: Occupation and Resistance in the Rhineland, 1792–1802* (Oxford: Oxford University Press, 1983); and Axel Kuhn, *Jakobiner im Rheinland. Der Kölner Konstitutionelle Zirkel von 1798* (Stuttgart: Ernst Klett, 1976).

of the Prussian monarchy changed the political landscape beyond recognition. The democratic movement of 1848–1849 found no lasting, direct successor.[31]

Historians have often observed that the heritage of the mid-century revolution was preserved primarily in the German labor movement. In the Rhineland, as elsewhere in central Europe, veterans of 1848–1849 would be among the pioneering socialists and trade unionists of the 1860s. Republican tavernkeeper Hugo Hillmann, initiator of the 1849 Elberfeld uprising, forced to flee the country after its suppression, returned to Prussia under the terms of the 1861 amnesty. Two years later, he became a member of the executive committee of the first German labor party, the General German Workers' Association. It was founded by Ferdinand Lassalle, himself a leader of the left in Düsseldorf in 1848–1849; the association's agitation in Düsseldorf, the Wuppertal, and the Bergisches Land was supported by many revolutionary veterans.[32]

The labor movement, however, was just that, a movement of artisans and skilled workers, most of whom were Protestants from urban areas of northern Germany. It thus existed in a different social and geographic landscape from that of the mid-century democratic movement, lacking the latter's bourgeois and peasant supporters in the small towns and countryside of the south. To give a Rhenish example, one could compare the political attitudes of the inhabitants of Duisburg, Barmen, and Lennep on the one hand and Oberingelheim, Neustadt a.d.W., and Bergzabern on the other. In 1848–1849, it was self-evident that the latter towns were strongholds of radicalism, while the former were conservative and Prussian loyalist. Such a conclusion today, or even at the turn of the century, would seem perverse, leftism being closely associated with urban and industrial areas of northern Germany,

Mid-nineteenth-century Rhenish and, more broadly, central European radicalism found its most direct continuation in the United States, in the struggle against slavery, from the founding of the Republican party to the outbreak of the Civil War. While historians dissecting voting patterns have shown to be a myth the contention that all German immigrants, or even a majority of them, supported the antislavery cause at the ballot box, émigré radicals were prominent among those who did. Carl Schurz was the best known and politically most successful of the former Rhineland radicals active in the antislavery movement, but far from the only one. To take just a few examples, two former civil commissioners of the Palatine Provisional Government, Jakob Müller of Kirchheimbolanden and Georg Hillgärtner of Frankenthal, along with their

---

[31] On this last point, cf. Toni Offerman, *Arbeiterbewegung und liberales Bürgertum in Deutschland 1850–1863* (Bonn: Neue Gesellschaft, 1979), pp. 27–29, 32–33.

[32] For Hillmann's postrevolutionary activities, see ibid., p. 482 n.172; more generally, on the role of former 1848/49 activists in the formation of the 1860s labor movement, see ibid., pp. 91–92, 100, 305–06, 436, 468–69, 482–83 and passim.

superior, the interior minister of the revolutionary regime, Nikolaus Schmitt, were early Republican activists in Cleveland, Chicago, St. Louis, and Philadelphia.[33]

Like the German labor movement, if in different ways, left-wing North American politics involved adapting mid-century central European radicalism to new terrain. German democrats' vehement anticlericalism set them off from the Protestant Evangelicals of Anglo-Saxon descent who made up the bulk of the antislavery movement, to say nothing of their more religous fellow immigrants. Their Jacobin radicalism, expressed in its most extreme form by Karl Heinzen's condemnation of the office of the presidency as a monarchical institution, sat poorly in a political culture characterized by constitutionalism and the desire to preserve legal continuity. Carl Schurz has remained the best known of the émigré radicals in the United States because he was the most successful in adapting to a different political universe; many of his fellow exiled revolutionaries lacked his flexibility and ended their political careers in frustration.[34]

Their happiest moment came at the outbreak of the Civil War, when the American Union could be preserved only by extraconstitutional, quasi-revolutionary action. Veterans of the Palatine uprising, such as Ludwig Blenker and August Willich, once again raised corps of volunteers, many of whom came from immigrant members of gymnastics societies, and led them into battle. Willich's abilities as a field commander and Blenker's talents for political leadership coupled with the total chaos he made of military organization were as apparent in the Civil War as they had been in the Palatinate a decade previously. Of all these militias, the one in St. Louis was the most overtly revolutionary. Formed by émigré German democrats living in that city and manned by immigrant gymnasts, it disarmed secessionist forces, seized the St. Louis arsenal, and helped overthrow the pro-Confederacy governor of Missouri in April 1861, saving the state for the Union.[35]

Perhaps the last word on the 1848 democrats should be that they were able to overthrow the governor of Missouri, but not the king of Prussia. In the end,

[33] On refugee revolutionaries in the United States, see the two older but still useful works, Carl Wittke, *Refugees of Revolution: The German Forty-Eighters in America* (Philadelphia: University of Pennsylvania Press, 1952); and *The Forty-Eighters: Political Refugees of the German Revolution of 1848*, ed. Adolph E. Zucker (New York: Columbia University Press, 1950), esp. the biographical dictionary on pp. 269–357. German-American voting patterns are discussed in the essays in *Ethnic Voters and the Election of Lincoln*, ed. Frederich Luebke (Lincoln: University of Nebraska Press, 1971).

[34] On these issues, see Wittke, *Refugees of Revolution*, pp. 142–46, 161–76, and passim. Fritz Anneke's life in American exile is a particularly revealing chronicle of inability to adapt and subsequent frustration: Wilhelm Schulte, "Fritz Anneke," pp. 51–100.

[35] On the refugee radicals and the German-American gymnasts at the onset of and during the Civil War, see *The Forty-Eighters*, pp. 79–110, 182–210; Wittke, *Refugees of Revolution*, pp. 147–56, 221–43.

their revolutionary activism did more for the victory of republican and democratic ideals and the destruction of social and political oppression in the United States than in central Europe. As a most modest form of repayment, I have tried to illuminate their original struggles and their social, political, and religious background. In doing so I hope to have thrown some light on people and a cause they embodied, now deeply shadowed by the past.

Bibliography

MANUSCRIPT SOURCES

Bayerisches Hauptstaatsarchiv München
   Ministerium des Innern
   Kriegsarchiv
Bundesarchiv, Außenstelle Frankfurt am Main
   Deutscher Bund
   Nachlaß G.F. Kolb
   Dalwigk Papers in Nachlaß Gagern
Hauptstaatsarchiv Düsseldorf
   Regierung Aachen
   Regierung Düsseldorf
   Regierung Köln
Kölnisches Stadtmuseum
   Graphische Sammlung
Landesarchiv Speyer
   Regierung der Pfalz
   Oberlandesgericht Zweibrücken
Landeshauptarchiv Koblenz
   Oberpräsidium der Rheinprovinz
   Regierung Trier
   Regierung Koblenz
Stadtarchiv Aachen
   Oberbürgermeisterei-Registratur
Stadtarchiv Trier
   Bestand Tb
Zentrales Staatsarchiv der DDR, Dienststelle Merseburg
   Ministerium des Innern
   Geheimes Zivilkabinett

CONTEMPORARY PERIODICALS

Der Demokrat [Mainz].
Freiheit, Arbeit [Cologne].
Freiheit, Brüderlichkeit, Arbeit [Cologne].
Kölnische Zeitung.
Mainzer Zeitung.
Neue Kölnische Zeitung.
Neue Rheinische Zeitung [Cologne].
Neue Speyerer Zeitung.
Der Pfälzer Volksmann [Neustadt a.d.W.].
Die Trompete von Speyer.

Verfolger der Bosheit [Cologne].
Volksblatt [Trier].
Zeitung des Arbeitervereins zu Köln.

CONTEMPORARY PAMPHLETS AND FLIERS

"Demokratische Vereine oder Bürger-Vereine." Stadtbibliothek Mainz.
"Mittelrheinischer demokratischer Turnbezirks-Verband." Stadtbibliothek Mainz.
"Namens-Verzeichniß der Mitglieder des Demokratischen Vereins in Mainz. Im August 1848." Stadtbibliothek Mainz.
"Namens-Verzeichniß der Mitglieder des Mainzer Bürgervereins. (Aufgestellt aum 27. Juli 1848)." Stadtbibliothek Mainz.
"Präsenz-Liste der Mannschaft des Rheinhessischen Freischärler-Bataillons vom 16. Mai bis 14. Juni 1849—Haupt-Quartier Kirchheimbolanden." Stadtbibliothek Mainz.
"Protokoll über die Berathung und Beschlüsse der am 9. April 1848 zu Kaiserslautern in dem Fruchthallesaale stattgefundenen Versammlung . . . zum Zweck der Gründung eines Volks- oder Vaterlands-Vereins." Landesbibliothek der Pfalz, Speyer.

CONTEMPORARY HANDBOOKS, STATISTICAL PUBLICATIONS,
AND GAZETTES

Allgemeine Deutsche Biographie.
Amts- und Intelligenzblatt dr provisorischen Regierung der Rheinpfalz.
Amtsblatt der Königlichen Regierung zu Coblenz.
Beiträge zur Statistik des Grossherzogtums Hessen.
Tabellen und amtliche Nachrichten über den Preussischen Staat für das Jahr 1849. 6 vols. Berlin: A. W. Heyn, 1852–1855.
Verzeichniß der Beamten und Angestellten im Staats- und Gemeindedienste des Königlich Bayerischen Regierungsbezirks der Pfalz nebst . . . einer Gemeindestatistik der Pfalz. Speyer: Daniel Kranzbühler, 1857.

OTHER PUBLISHED PRIMARY AND SECONDARY SOURCES

Adelmann, Gerhard. "Die ländlichen Textilgewerben des Rheinlandes vor der Industrialisierung," *Rheinische Vierteljahrsblätter* 43 (1979): 260–88.
Agulhon, Maurice. *The Republic in the Village: The People of the Var from the French Revolution to the Second Republic.* Translated by Janet Lloyd. New York: Cambridge University Press, 1982.
―――. *The Republican Experiment, 1848–1852.* Translated by Janet Lloyd. Cambridge: Cambridge University Press, 1983.
Die Allgemeine Deutsche Arbeiterverbrüderung 1848–1850. Dokumente des Zentralkomittees für die deutschen Arbeiter in Leipzig. Edited by Horst Schlechte. Weimar: Hermann Böhlaus Nachfolger, 1979.
Anklag-Akte errichtet durch die K. General-Staatsprokurator der Pfalz . . . gegen Martin Reichard, entlassener Notär in Speyer, u. 332 Consorten wegen bewaffneter

Rebellion gegen die bewaffnete Macht, Hoch- und Staatsverrath etc. Zweibrücken: G. Ritter'schen Buchdruckerei und Buchhandlung, 1850.

Asmus, Helmut. "Die 'Rheinische Zeitung' und die Genesis des rheinpreußischen Bourgeoisliberalismus," in *Bourgeoisie und bürgerliche Umwälzung in Deutschland 1789–1871.* Edited by Helmut Bleiber. East Berlin: Akademie-Verlag, 1977. pp. 135–68.

Ayçoberry, Pierre. *Cologne enter Napoléon et Bismarck: le croissance d'une ville rhénane.* Paris: Aubier-Montaigne, 1981.

———. "Histoire sociale de la ville de Cologne (1815–1875)." 2 vols. Thèse: Univ. de Paris, 1977.

Bamberger, Ludwig. *Gesammelte Schriften.* 4 vols. Berlin: Rosenbaum & Hart, 1895–1897.

Banfield, T. C. *Industry of the Rhine. Series I. Agriculture.* London: Charles Knight & Co., 1846.

———. *Industry of the Rhine. Series II. Manufactures.* London: C. Cox, 1848.

Barkai, Avraham. "The German Jews at the Start of Industrialisation: Structural Change and Mobility 1835–1860," in *Revolution and Evolution 1848 in German-Jewish History.* Edited by Werner E. Mosse, Arnold Paucker, and Reinhard Rürup. Tübingen: Mohr, 1981. pp. 123–49.

Bassermann-Jordan, Friedrich. *Geschichte des Weinbaus unter besonderer Berücksichtigung der bayerischen Rheinpfalz.* 3 vols. Frankfurt a.M.: Heinrich Keller, 1907.

Baumann, Kurt. "Volkserhebung und Konspiration in der pfälzischen Bewegung von 1848/49," *Mitteilungen des Historischen Vereins der Pfalz* 68 (1970): 292–317.

———. *Von Geschichte und Menschen der Pfalz. Ausgewählte Aufsätze von Kurt Baumann.* Edited by Kurt Andermann. Speyer: Verlag der Pfälzischen Gesellschaft zur Forderung der Wissenschaften in Speyer, 1984.

Becker, A. "General Dufour und die Pfalz 1849," *Zeitschrift für die Geschichte des Oberrheins* 86 (1935): 253–56.

Becker, Albert. *Pfälzer Volkskunde.* Bonn und Leipzig: K. Schroeder, 1925.

Becker, August. *Die Pfalz und die Pfälzer.* Kaiserslautern: E. Lincks-Crusius, 1961.

Becker, Gerhard. "Der Kongreß der Arbeitervereine der Rheinprovinz und Westfalen am 6. Mai 1849," *Beiträge zur Geschichte der deutschen Arbeiterbewegung* 10 (1968): 373–83.

———. *Marx und Engels in Köln 1848–1849: Zur Geschichte des Kölner Arbeitervereins.* East Berlin: Rütten & Loening, 1963.

———. "Das Protokoll des ersten Demokratenkongresses von Juni 1848," *Jahrbuch für Geschichte* 8 (1973): 379–405.

Berenson, Edward. *Populist Religion and Left-Wing Politics in France, 1830–1852.* Princeton: Princeton University Press, 1984.

Bergmann, Jürgen. "Ökonomische Voraussetzungen der Revolution von 1848. Zur Krise von 1845 bis 1848 in Deutschland," in *200 Jahre amerikanische Revolution und moderne Revolutionsforschung.* Edited by Hans-Ulrich Wehler. Göttingen: Vandenhoeck & Ruprecht, 1976. pp. 254–87.

Biundo, Georg. *Die evangelischen Geistlichen der Pfalz seit der Reformation.* Neustadt a.d. Aisch: Degener & Co., 1968.

Blanning, T.C.W. *The French Revolution in Germany: Occupation and Resistance in the Rhineland, 1792–1802*. Oxford: Oxford University Press, 1983.

Blasius, Dirk. *Bürgerliche Gesellschaft und Kriminalität. Zur Sozialgeschichte Preußens im Vormärz*. Göttingen: Vandenhoeck & Ruprecht, 1976.

————. "Der Kampf um die Geschworenengerichte im Vormärz," in *Sozialgeschichte Heute Festschrift für Hans Rosenberg zum 70. Geburtstag*. Edited by Hans-Ulrich Wehler. Göttingen: Vandenhoeck & Ruprecht, 1974. pp. 148–61.

Bleiber, Helmut "Bauern und Landarbeiter in der bürgerlich-demokratischen Revolution von 1848/49 in Deutschland," *Zeitschrift für Geschichtswissenschaft* 17 (1969): 289–309.

Blessing, Werner K. *Staat und Kirche in der Gesellschaft. Institutionelle Autorität und mentaler Wandel in Bayern während des 19. Jahrhunderts*. Göttingen: Vandenhoeck & Ruprecht, 1982.

Boch, Rudolf. *Handwerker-Sozialisten gegen Fabrikgesellschaft. Lokale Fachvereine, Massengewerkschaft und industrielle Rationalisiserung in Solingen 1870 bis 1914*. Göttingen: Vandenhoeck & Ruprecht, 1985.

Bockenheimer, K. G. *Mainz in den Jahren 1848 und 1849*. Mainz: Mainzer Verlagsanstalt und Druckerei, 1906.

Boese, Heinz-Günther. "Ludwig Simon von Trier (1819–1872). Leben und Anschauungen eines rheinischen Achtundvierzigers." Diss. phil., Mainz, 1951.

Bonkhoff, Bernard H. *Geschichte der vereinigten protestantisch-evangelisch-christlichen Kirche der Pfalz*. Munich: C. H. Beck, 1986.

Botzenhart, Manfred. *Deutscher Parlamentarismus in der Revolutionszeit 1848–1850*. Düsseldorf: Droste, 1977.

Braun, Harald. *Geschichte des Turnens in Rheinhessen. Band 1: 1811 bis 1850*. 3 vols. Alzey: Verlag der Rheinhessischen Druckwerkstätte Alzey, 1986–.

Breuer, Karl. "Ursachen und Verlauf der Revolution von 1848 im Moseltal und seinem Randgebieten." Diss. phil., Bonn, 1921.

Broo, Hanno. "Die Anfänge der vereinsmäßig organisierten Arbeiter(bildungs)-bewegung in Mainz (1848–1853/54)," *Mainzer Geschichtsblätter* 3 (1986): 61–85.

Bruckner, Clemens. *Zur Wirtschaftsgeschichte des Regierungsbezirks Aachen*. Cologne: Selbstverlag Rheinisch–Westfälisches Wirtschaftsarchiv zu Köln e.V., 1967.

Buckler, Carlo. "Die politischen und religiösen Kämpfe in Mainz während der Revolutionsjahre 1848/50." Diss. phil., Gießen, 1936.

Der Bund der Kommunisten. Dokumenten und Materialien. Edited by Institutes for Marxism-Leninism, Moscow and East Berlin. 3 vols. East Berlin: Dietz, 1970–1984.

Buschbell, Gottfried. "Johann Anton Caspar Imandt, Begründer des ersten Krefelder Turnvereins, Deutschkatholik und Revolutionär von 1848," *Die Heimat* 19 (1940): 39–52.

Büttner, Siegfried. *Die Anfänge des Parlamentarismus in Hessen- Darmstadt und das du Thilsche System*. Darmstadt: Selbstverlag des Historischen Vereins für Hessen, 1969.

Calliess, Joerg. *Militär in der Krise. Die bayerische Armee in der Revolution 1848/49*. Boppard/Rh.: Boldt, 1976.

Canis, Konrad. "Der preußische Militarismus in der Revolution von 1848." Diss. phil., Rostock, 1965.

Chung, Hae-Bon. "Das Krefelder Seidengewerbe im 19. Jahrhundert (ca. 1815–1850)." Diss. phil., Bonn, 1974.

Clapp, Edwin J. *The Navigable Rhine*. Boston and New York: Houghton Mifflin, 1911.

Deutscher Liberalismus im Vormärz. Heinrich von Gagern Briefe und Reden 1815–1848. Edited by Paul Wentzcke and Wolfgang Klötzer. Göttingen, W. Berlin, and Frankfurt: Musterschmidt, 1959.

Diefendorf, Jeffrey M. *Businessmen and Politics in the Rhineland, 1789–1834*. Princeton: Princeton University Press, 1980.

Diehl, Anton. *Zur Geschichte der Katholischen Bewegung im 19. Jahrhundert. Das "Mainzer Journal" im Jahre 1848*. Mainz: Kirchheim & Co., 1911.

Doehn, Hans. "Eisenbahnpolitik und Eisenbahnbau in Rheinhessen 1835–1914." Diss. phil., Mainz, 1957.

Dowe, Dieter. *Aktion und Organisation: Arbeiterbewegung, sozialistische Bewegung und kommunistische Bewegung in der preußischen Rheinprovinz 1820–1852*. Hannover: Verlag für Literatur und Zeitgeschehen, 1970.

———. "Die erste sozialistische Tageszeitung in Deutschland. Der Weg der 'Trierschen Zeitung' vom Liberalismus über den 'wahren Sozialismus' zum Anarchismus (1840–1851)," *Archiv für Sozialgeschichte* 12 (1972): 55–107.

Dreyfus, F. G. *Sociétés et mentalités en Mayence au dix-huitième siècle*. Paris: Armand Colin, 1968.

Droege, Georg. "Zur Lage der rheinischen Landwirtschaft in der ersten Hälfte des 19. Jahrhunderts," in *Landschaft und Geschichte. Festschrift für Franz Petri zu seinem 65. Geburtstag zm 22 Feb. 1968*. Edited by Georg Droege. Bonn: Röhrscheid, 1970. pp. 143–56.

Droz, Jacques. *Les révolutions allemandes de 1848*. Paris: Presses Universitaires de France, 1957.

Düding, Dieter. "Das deutsche Nationalfest von 1814. Matrix der deutschen Nationalfeste im 19. Jahrhundert," in *Öffentliche Festkultur. Politische Feste in Deutschland von der Aufklärung bis zum Ersten Weltkrieg*. Reinbek: Rowohlt, 1988. pp. 67–88.

———. *Organisierter Gesellschaftlicher Nationalismus in Deutschland (1808–1847)*. Munich: Oldenbourg, 1984.

Eckert, Christian. *Rheinschiffahrt im XIX Jahrhundert*. Leipzig: Duncker & Humblot, 1900.

1832–1982. Hambacher Fest. Freiheit und Einheit. Deutschland und Europa. Edited by Joachim Kermann and Cornelia Foerster. Neustadt a.d.W.: D. Meininger, 1982.

Engel, Ernst. "Die Getreidepreise, die Ernteerträge und der Getreidehandel im preussischen Staate," *Zeitschrift des Königlich Preussischen Statistischen Bureaus* 1 (1861): 249–89.

———. "Der Weinbau im preussischen Staate vom 1819 bis mit 1860," *Zeitschrift des Königlich Preussischen Statistischen Bureaus* 1 (1861): 303–06.

Engels, Wilhelm. *Ablösungen und Gemeinheitsteilungen in der Rheinprovinz. Ein Beitrag zur Geschichte der Bauernbefreiung*. Bonn: Röhrscheid, 1957.

Ethnic Voters and the Election of Lincoln. Edited by Frederich Luebke. Lincoln: University of Nebraska Press, 1971.

Eyck, Frank. *The Frankfurt Parliament 1848–1849.* New York: St. Martin's, 1968.

Faber, Karl-Georg. "Rheinlande und Rheinländer 1814–1848. Umrisse einer politischen Landschaft," in *Landschaft und Geschichte. Festschrift für Franz Petri zu seinem 65. Geburtstag am 22. Februar 1968.* Edited by Georg Droege. Bonn: Ludwig Röhrscheid, 1970. pp. 194–210.

———. *Die Rheinlande zwischen Restauration und Revolution. Probleme rheinischer Geschichte von 1814 bis 1848 im Spiegel der zeitgenössischen Publizistik.* Wiesbaden: Franz Steiner, 1966.

Falck, Richard. *Germain Metternich. Ein deutscher Freiheitskämpfer.* Mainz: Verlagsbuchhandlung Krichtel, 1954.

Fenner von Fenneberg, Ferdinand. *Zur Geschichte der rheinpfälzischen Revolution und des badischen Aufstandes.* Zurich: E. Kierling, 1849.

Fenske, Hans. "Rationalismus und Orthodoxie. Zu den Kämpfen in der pfälzischen Landeskirche im 19. Jahrhundert," *Zeitschrift für die Geschichte des Oberrheins* 132 (1984): 239–69.

Fischer, Peter. *Das politische Leben im Kreise Jülich 1848- 1918. Erster Teil: Von der Revolution 1848 bis zur Reichsgründung 1871.* Jülich: n.p., n.d. [c. 1923].

Fleischmann, Otto. *Geschichte des pfälzischen Aufstandes im Jahre 1849.* Kaiserslautern: Emil Thieme, 1899.

Foerster, Cornelia. " 'Hoch lebe die Verfassung'? Die pfälzischen Abgeordnetenfeste im Vormärz," in *Öffentliche Festkultur. Politische Feste in Deutschland von der Aufklärung bis zum Ersten Weltkrieg.* Reinbek: Rowohlt, 1988. pp. 132–46.

———. *Der Preß- und Vaterlandsverein von 1832/33. Sozialstruktur und Organisationsformen der bürgerlichen Bewegung in der Zeit des Hambacher Festes.* Trier: Verlag Trierer Historische Forschungen, 1982.

The Forty-Eighters: Political Refugees of the German Revolution of 1848. Edited by Adolph E. Zucker. New York: Columbia University Press, 1950.

Franz, Eckhart G. "Die hessischen Arbeitervereine im Rahmen der politischen Arbeiterbewegung der Jahre 1848–1850," *Archiv für hessische Geschichte und Altertumskunde,* n.s., 33 (1975): 167–272.

Freilinger, Hubert. " 'Die Hambacher' Beteiligte und Sympathisante der Beinahe-Revolution von 1832," *Zeitschrift für bayerische Landesgeschichte* 41 (1978): 701–37.

———. "Die vorletzte Weisheit des Volkes. Der politische Aktionismus der Hambacher Bewegung und seine Grenzen," in *Hambach 1832: Anstöße und Folgen.* Edited by Alois Gerlich. Wiesbaden: Franz Steiner, 1984. pp. 31–59.

Frevert, Ute. *Krankheit als politisches Problem 1770–1880.* Göttingen: Vandenhoeck & Ruprecht, 1984.

Gagel, Hanna. "Die Düsseldorfer Malerschule in der politischen Situation des Vormärz und 1848," in *Die Düsseldorfer Malerschule.* Edited by Wend von Kalnein. Mainz: Philipp von Zabern, 1979.

Gailus, Manfred. "Soziale Protestbewegungen in Deutschland 1847–1849," in *Sozialer Protest: Studien zu traditioneller Resistenz und kollektiver Gewalt in Deutsch-*

land vom Vormärz bis zur Reichsgründung. Edited by Heinrich Volkmann and Jürgen Bergmann. Opladen: Westdeutscher Verlag, 1984. pp. 76–106.

Gatz, Erwin. "Kaplan Josef Istas und der Aachener Karitakskreis," *Rheinische Vierteljahrsblätter* 36 (1972): 207–28.

Gebhardt, Hartwig. *Revolution und liberale Bewegung. Die nationale Organisation der konstitutionellen Partei in Deutschland 1848/49*. Hamburg: Schünemann Universitätsverlag, 1974.

Gernert, Dörte. *Die Revolution von 1848/49 im Rheinisch-Bergischen (Landkreis Mülheim am Rhein)*. Remscheid: Kierdorf, 1984.

Gessner, Dieter. " 'Industrialisiertes Handwerk' in der Frühindustrialisierung. Ein Beitrag zu den Anfängen der Industrie am Mittelrhein und Untermain 1790 bis 1865," *Archiv für hessische Geschichte und Altertumskunde*, n.s., 40 (1982): 231–301.

————. "Metallgewerbe, Maschinenbau und Waggonbau am Mittelrhein und Untermain (1800–1860/65): Eine quantitative/qualitative Regionalanalyse," *Archiv für hessische Geschichte und Altertumskunde*, n.s., 38 (1980): 287–338.

Der gewerblich-industrielle Zustand der Rheinprovinz im Jahre 1836. Edited by Gerhard Adelmann. Bonn: Röhrscheid, 1967.

Goebel, Klaus. "Der rheinische Friedrich Engels," *Monatshefte für evangelische Kirchengeschichte des Rheinlandes* 22 (1973): 131–60.

Goeters, J. F. Gerhard. "Der Weg der reformierten Gemeinde Elberfeld in die Spaltung von 1847," *Monatshefte für evangelische Kirchengeschichte des Rheinlandes* 25 (1976): 133–43 .

Gothein, Eberhard. *Geschichtliche Entwicklung der Rheinschiffahrt im XIX Jahrhundert*. Leipzig: Duncker & Humblot, 1903.

Graf, Friedrich Wilhelm. *Die Politisierung des religiösen Bewußtseins. Die bürgerlichen Religionsparteien im deutschen Vormärz: Das Beispiel des Deutschkatholizismus*. Stuttgart-Bad Cannstatt: Frommannholzboog, 1978.

Grießinger, Andreas. *Das symbolische Kapitel der Ehre. Streikbewegungen und kollektives Bewußtsein deutscher Handwerksgesellen im 18. Jahrhundert*. Frankfurt, West Berlin, and Vienna: Ullstein, 1981.

Haan, Heiner. "Die bayerische Personalpolitik in der Pfalz von 1816/18 bis 1849," *Jahrbuch für westdeutsche Landesgeschichte* 3 (1977): 351–94.

Haasis, Helmut. *Morgenröte der Republik. Die linksrheinischen deutschen Demokraten 1789–1849*. Frankfurt, West Berlin, and Vienna: Ullstein, 1984.

Hahn, Dr. "Noch ein vierter Brief von Vincenz von Zuccalmaglio aus dem Jahre 1848," *Monatshefte des Bergischen Geschichtsvereins* 20 (1913): 91–93.

Hamerow, Theodore. *Restoration, Revolution, Reaction: Economics and Politics in Central Europe, 1815–1871*. Princeton: Princeton University Press, 1958.

Hammen, Oscar J. *The Red '48ers: Karl Marx and Friedrich Engels*. New York: Charles Scribner's Sons, 1969.

Handbuch der Bayerischen Geschichte. Edited by Max Spindler. 4 vols. in 5. Munich: Beck, 1968–1975.

Hasel, B. K. "Forstverwaltung und Jagd in der Revolution von 1848 und 1849," *Zeitschrift für die Geschichte des Oberrheins* 86 (1977): 297–313.

Hasenclever, Josua. *Josua Hasenclever aus Remscheid-Ehringhausen. Erinnerungen und Briefe*. Edited by Adolf Hasenclever. Halle/Saale: Karras, Kröber & Nietschmann, 1922.

Haupts, Leo. "Die Kölner Dombaufeste 1842–1880 zwischen kirchlicher bürgerlich-nationaler und dynastisch-höfischer Selbstdarstellung," in *Öffentliche Festkultur. Politische Feste in Deutschland von der Aufklärung bis zum Ersten Weltkrieg*. Reinbek: Rowohlt, 1988. pp. 191–211.

Hecker, Carl. *Der Aufstand in Elberfeld im Mai 1849 und mein Verhältniß zu demselben*. Elberfeld: Julius Bädeker, 1849.

Heinen, Ernst. "Piusverein 1848/49. Ein Beitrag zu den Anfängen des politischen Katholizismus in Köln," *Jahrbuch des Kölnischen Geschichtsvereins* 57 (1986): 147–242.

Helf, Wilhelm. *Die Revolutionsjahre 1848/49 im ländlichen Bereich der alten Landkreise Solingen und Lennep*. Opladen: Heggen-Verlag, 1968.

Henkel, Martin, and Taubert, Rolf. *Die deutsche Presse 1848–1850. Eine Bibliographie*. Munich: Saur, 1978.

Herberts, Hermann. *Alles ist Kirche und Handel . . . Wirtschaft und Gesellschaft des Wuppertals im Vormärz und in der Revolution 1848/49*. Neustadt a.d. Aisch: Ph.C.W. Schmidt, 1980.

Heukeshofen, Hans. "Die wirtschaftliche Entwicklung des Jülicher Landes seit seiner Zugehörigkeit zu Preußen unter besonderer Berücksichtigung des Kreises Jülich." Wirt.- und Sozialwiss. Diss., Cologne, 1934.

Hildebrandt, Gunter. "Die Liberalen um Heinrich von Gagern in der Phase der Vorbereitung und Konstituierung der Frankfurter Nationalversammlung," in *Bourgeoisie und bürgerliche Umwälzung in Deutschland 1789–1871*. Edited by Helmut Bleiber. East Berlin: Akademie-Verlag, 1977. pp. 267–98.

Hoefele, Karl Heinrich. "Die Anfänge des politischen Katholizismus in Trier (1848–1870)," *Trierer Jahrbuch* 2 (1939): 77–112.

Hoffmann, Alfons. "Franz Tafel als Mensch und Priester (1794–1869)," *Archiv für mittelrheinische Kirchengeschichte* 15 (1963): 180–207.

Hoffmann, Kurt. "Sturm und Drang in der politischen Presse Bayerns 1848–1850," *Zeitschrift für bayerische Landesgeschichte* 3 (1930): 205–65.

Hoffmann, Wilhelm. *Rheinhessische Volkskunde*. Bonn: Röhrscheid, 1932.

Hofmann, Jürgen. *Das Ministerium Camphausen-Hansemann. Zur Politik der preußischen Bourgeoisie in der Revolution 1848/49*. East Berlin: Akademie, 1981.

Hoth, Wolfgang. "Der Beginn der Arbeiterbewegung in Remscheid. Der Lenneper Arbeiterverein von 1848 bis 1850," *Zeitschrift des Bergischen Geschichtsvereins* 87 (1974/76): 110–15.

Husung, Gerd. *Protest und Repression im Vormärz. Norddeutschland zwischen Restauration und Revolution*. Göttingen: Vandenhoeck & Ruprecht, 1983.

Illner, Eberhard. *Bürgerliche Organisierung in Elberfeld 1775–1850*. Neustadt a.d. Aisch: Ph.C.W. Schmidt, 1982.

Jaeger, Harold. "Politische Lyrik im revolutionären 'Bote für Stadt und Land' aus Kaiserslautern," *Jahrbuch zur Geschichte von Stadt und Landkreis Kaiserslautern* 22/23 (1984/85): 161–88.

Jeuckens, Robert. "Die 48er Bewegung in Eupen unter Theodor Hegners Einfluß," *Zeitschrift des Aachener Geschichtsvereins* 64/65 (1951/52): 5–71.

Juillard, Étienne. *L'Europe rhénane. Géographie d'un grand éspace.* Paris: Armand Colin, 1968.

Kantzenbach, Friedrich Wilhelm. "Zur Geschichte des Deutschkatholizismus in Bayern und in der Pfalz im Vormärz," *Blätter für pfälzische Kirchengeschichte und religiöse Volkskunde* 39 (1972): 5–15.

Karch, Helga. "Die politische Partizipation der Juden in der Pfalz," in *Juden in der Provinz: Beiträge zur Geschichte der Juden in der Pfalz zwischen Emanzipation und Vernichtung*. Neustadt a.d.W.: Pfälzische Post, 1988. pp. 49–64.

Katz-Seibert, Mathilde. *Der politische Radikalismus in Hessen während der Revolution von 1848/49*. Darmstadt: Hessischer Staatsverlag, 1929.

Keddigkeit, Jürgen. "Das militärische Scheitern des Pfälzischen Aufstandes 1849," *Jahrbuch zur Geschichte von Stadt und Landkreis Kaiserslautern* 22/23 (1984/85): 405–24.

Keinemann, Friedrich. *Das Kölner Ereignis, sein Widerhall in der Rheinprovinz und in Westfalen*. 2 vols. Münster: Aschendorff, 1974.

———. "Die Unruhen bei Feier des Ursulafestes 1838 in Köln," *Annalen des Historischen Vereins für den Niederrhein* 174 (1972): 138–47.

Kermann, Joachim. "Die gesundheitliche, soziale, und wirtschaftliche Lage der pfälzischen Landbevölkerung in der Mitte des 19. Jahrhunderts nach Berichten der Kantonärzte und des Kreismedizinalrates," *Mitteilungen des Historischen Vereins der Pfalz* 74 (1976): 101–29.

Kermann, Rose. "Zwichen Revolution und Integration: Der Kaiserslauterner Bürger Carl Christian Julius Zinn (6.6.1821–1.4.1890)," *Jahrbuch zur Geschichte von Stadt und Landkreis Kaiserslautern* 22/23 (1984/85): 223–52.

Kern, Peter. "Kirche, Staat und geistliche Schulaufsicht. Schule als Terrain politischer Dilatorik," *Blätter für pfälzische Kirchengeschichte und religiösse Volkskunde* 45 (1978): 76–92.

Kersken, Hans. *Stadt und Universität Bonn in den Revolutionsjahren 1848–49*. Bonn: Röhrscheid, 1931.

Klein, Hanns. "Gottfried Kinkel als Emissär der provisorischen Regierung der Pfalz im Frühjahr in Westrich. Bemerkungen zu neuentdeckten Kinkel-Briefen," *Jahrbuch für westdeutsche Landesgeschichte* 8 (1982): 107–35.

———. "Wiederentdecktes Schriftgut der Pfälzer Revolutionsregierung von 1849," *Jahrbuch für westdeutsche Landesgeschichte,* 12 (1986): 107–51.

Klessmann, Christoph. "Zur Sozialgeschichte der Reichsverfassungskampagne von 1849," *Historische Zeitschrift* 218 (1974): 283–337.

Klutentreter, Wilhelm. *Die Rheinische Zeitung von 1842/43 in der politischen und geistigen Bewegung des Vormärz*. 2 vols. Dortmund: Ruhfus, 1966–1967.

Koch, Doris, and Paul, Roland. "Die Ereignisse im Kanton Landstuhl während der Zeit des Pfälzischen Aufstandes," *Jahrbuch zur Geschichte von Stadt und Landkries Kaiserslautern* 22/23 (1984/85): 313–48.

Kockerols, Wilhelm. *Das Rheinische Recht. Seine zeitliche und räumliche Begrenzung*. Hannover: Helwingsche Verlagsbuchhandlung, 1902.

Kolb, Georg Friedrich. *Lebenserinnerungen eines liberalen Demokraten 1808–1884*. Edited by Ludwig Merckle. Freiburg i.B.: Verlag Rambach, 1976.

Köllmann, Wolfgang. *Sozialgeschichte der Stadt Barmen im 19. Jahrhundert*. Tübingen: J.C.B. Mohr, 1960.

Körner, Hermann Joseph Aloys. *Lebenskämpfe in der Alten und Neuen Welt*. 2 vols. New York: L. W. Schmidt, 1865–1866.

Koselleck, Reinhart. *Preußen zwischen Reform und Revolution*. 3d ed. Stuttgart: Klett-Cotta, 1982.

Kriege, Wilhelm. *Der Ahrweinbau, seine Geschichte und wirtschaftliche Lage in der Gegenwart*. Trier: Paulus-Druckerei, 1911.

Kuhn, Axel. *Jakobiner im Rheinland. Der Kölner Konstitutionelle Zirkel von 1798*. Stuttgart: Ernst Klett, 1976.

Kuhn, Siegfried. "Der Aufstand der Kleineisenindustriearbeiter im Stadt- und Landkreis Solingen am 16. und 17. März 1848, seine Ursachen und seine Ergebnisse." Diss. phil., Munich, 1938. Teildruck: Solingen, Buchdruckerei B. Boll, 1938.

Kühn, Walter. *Der junge Hermann Becker: Ein Quellenbeitrag zur Geschichte der Arbeiterbewegung in Rheinpreußen*. Dortmund: Max Thomas, 1934.

LaCapra, Dominick. *History and Criticism*. Ithaca and London: Cornell University Press, 1985.

Langewiesche, Dieter. *Liberalismus und Demokratie in Württemberg von der Revolution bis zur Reichsgründung*. Düsseldorf: Droste, 1974.

―――. "Die politische Vereinsbewegung in Würzburg und in Unterfranken in den Revolutionsjahren 1848/49," *Jahrbuch für fränkische Landesforschung* 37 (1977): 195–234.

―――. "Republik, Monarchie und 'Sozial Frage.' Grundprobleme der deutschen Revolution von 1848," *Historische Zeitschrift* 230 (1980): 529–48.

Lavopa, Anthony J. *Prussian Schoolteachers: Profession and Office, 1763–1848*. Chapel Hill: University of North Carolina Press, 1980.

Lenger, Friedrich. "Die handwerkliche Phase der Arbeiterbewegung in England, Frankreich, Deutschland und den USA—Plädoyer für einen Vergleich," *Geschichte und Gesellschaft* 13 (1987): 232–43.

―――. "Polarisierung und Verlag: Schuhmacher, Schneider und Schreiner in Düsseldorf 1816–1861," in *Handwerker in der Industrialisierung: Lage, Kultur und Politik vom späten 18. bis ins frühe 20. Jahrhundert*. Stuttgart: Klett-Cotta, 1984.

―――. *Sozialgeschichte der deutschen Handwerker seit 1800*. Frankfurt a.M.: Surkahmp, 1988.

―――. *Zwischen Kleinbürgertum und Proletariat. Sozialgeschichte der Düsseldorfer Handwerker im 19. Jahrhundert*. Göttingen: Vandenhoeck & Ruprecht, 1986.

Lill, Rudolf. *Die Beilegung der Kölner Wirren 1840–1842*. Düsseldorf: Droste, 1962.

―――. "Kirche und Revolution. Zu den Anfängen der katholischen Bewegung im Jahrzehnt vor 1848," *Archiv für Sozialgeschichte* 18 (1978): 565–75.

Lipp, Carola. "Bräute, Mütter, Gefährtinnen—Frauen und politische Öffentlichkeit in der Revolution 1848," in *Grenzgängerinnen. Revolutionäre Frauen im 18. und 19. Jahrhundert*. Edited by Helga Grubitzsch, Hannelore Cyrus, and Elke Haarbusch. Düsseldorf: Schwann, 1986. pp. 71–92.

———. "Katzenmusiken, Krawalle und 'Weiberrevolution': Frauen im politischen Protest der Revolutionsjahre," in *Schimpfende Weiber und patriotische Jungfrauen. Frauen im Vormärz und in der Revolution 1848/49*. Edited by Carola Lipp. Moos and Baden-Baden: Elster, 1980. pp. 112–30.

———. "Württembergische Handwerker und Handwerkervereine im Vormärz und in der Revolution 1848/49," in *Handwerker in der Industrialisierung: Lage, Kultur und Politik vom späten 18. bis ins frühe 20. Jahrhundert*. Stuttgart: Klett-Cotta, 1984. pp. 347–80.

Lipp, Carola, and Kaschuba, Wolfgang. *1848—Provinz und Revolution. Kultureller Wandel und soziale Bewegung im Königreich Württemberg*. Tübingen: Tübinger Vereinigung für Volkskunde e.V. Schloss, 1979.

———. "Wasser und Brot. Politische Kultur im Alltag des Vormärz—und Revolutionsjahre," *Geschichte und Gesellschaft* 10 (1984): 320–51.

Lipp, Carola, Sabine, Kienitz, and Beate, Binder. "Frauen bei Brotkrawallen, Straßentumulten und Katzenmusiken—Zum politischen Verhalten von Frauen 1847 und in der Revolution 1848/49," in *Transformationen der Arbeiterkultur*. Edited by Peter Assion. Marburg: Jonas, 1987. pp. 49–60.

Lorenz, Gerd-Ekkehard. "Das Revolutionsjahr 1848/49 in Wuppertal. (Ein Beitrag zur Stadtgeschichte Elberfelds und Barmens im 19. Jahrhundert)." Phil. Diss., Marburg, 1962.

Lowenstein, Steven M. "The 1840s and the Creation of the German-Jewish Religious Reform Movement," in *Revolution and Evolution 1848 in German-Jewish History*. Edited by Werner E. Mosse, Arnold Paucker, and Reinhard Rürup. Tübingen: Mohr, 1981. pp. 256–97.

Luedtke, Alf. *"Gemeinwohl," Polizei und "Festungspraxis" Staatliche Gewaltsamkeit und innere Verwaltung in Preußen, 1815–1850*. Göttingen: Vandenhoeck & Ruprecht, 1982.

Margadant, Ted. *French Peasants in Revolt: The Insurrection of 1851*. Princeton: Princeton University Press, 1979.

Karl Marx Friedrich Engels Werke. Edited by Institut für Marxismus-Leninismus beim ZK der SED. 3d ed. East Berlin: Dietz, 1977.

Medick, Hans. " 'Missionare im Ruderboot'? Ethnologische Erkenntnissen als Herausforderung an die Sozialgeschichte." *Geschichte und Gesellschaft* 10 (1984): 295–319.

Meisenburg, Friedrich. "Die Stadt Essen in den Revolutionsjahren 1848/49," *Beiträge zur Geschichte von Stadt und Stift Essen* 59 (1940): 121–274.

Melzer, Imma. "Pfälzische Emigranten in Frankreich während und nach der Revolution von 1848/49," *Francia* 12 (1984): 371–424 and 13 (1985): 369–407.

Merriman, John. *The Agony of the Republic: the Repression of the Left in Revolutionary France*. New Haven and London: Yale University Press, 1978.

Meyer, Felix. "Zur Entwicklung des Moselweinbaues und Weinhandels im 19en Jahrhundert." Wirt.- und Sozialwiss Diss., Cologne, 1922.

Moenckmeyer, Friedrich. *Die Rhein- und Moselzeitung: Ein Beitrag zur Entstehungsgeschichte der katholischen Presse und des politischen Katholizismus in den Rheinlanden*. Bonn: Marcus und Weber, 1912.

Moldenhauer, Ruediger. "Die Petitionen aus den preußischen Saarkreisen an die deutsche Nationalversammlung 1848–49," *Zeitschrift für die Geschichte der Saargegend* 17/18 (1969/70): 31–111.

Monz, Heinz. "Der Waldprozeß der Mark Thalfang als Grundlage für Karl Marx' Kritik an den Debatten um das Holzdiebstahlgesetz," *Jahrbuch für westdeutsche Landesgeschichte* 4 (1977): 395–418.

Mooser Josef. *Ländliche Klassengesellschaft 1770–1848. Bauern und Unterschichten Landwirtschaft und Gewerbe im östlichen Westfalen.* Göttingen: Vandenhoeck & Ruprecht, 1984.

Muelhaupt, Erwin. "Die Union, ihre Freunde und ihre Gegner im Bergischen Land und am Niederrhein im 19. Jahrhundert," *Monatshefte für evangelische Kirchengeschichte des Rheinlandes* 14 (1965): 45–59.

Müller, Adolf. "Die Grundlagen der pfälzischen Landwirtschaft und die Entwicklung ihrer Produktion im 19. Jahrhundert bis zur Gegenwart." Rechts- und Staatswiss. Diss., Würzburg, 1912.

Müller, Alwin. "Das Sozialprofil der Juden in Köln (1808–1850)," in *Köln und das rheinische Judentum. Festschrift Germania Judaica 1959–1984.* Edited by Jutta-Bohnke Kollwitz, Willebad Paul Eckert, Frank Golczewski, and Hermann Greive. Cologne: J. P. Bachem, 1984. pp. 102–106.

Müller, Michael. "Die preußische Rheinprovinz unter dem Einfluß von Julirevolution und Hambacher Fest 1830–1834," *Jahrbuch für westdeutsche Landesgeschichte* 6 (1980): 271–90.

Nagel, Roswitha. "Überblick über die Quellenlage in der Historischen Abteilung II des Zentralen Staatsarchivs zum badisch-pfälzischen Revolutionskrieg 1849," *Militärgeschichte* 13 (1974): 84–86.

Ness, Peter. "Der Trier Versammlungs- und Petitionsstreit von 1845. Ein Beitrag zur Geschichte des Trierer Vormärz," *Neues triersches Jahrbuch* (1967): 39–45.

Nickel, Dietmar. *Die Revolution 1848/49 in Augsburg und Bayerisch-Schwaben.* Augsburg: Michael Seitz, 1965.

Nießner, Alois. *Aachen während der Sturmjahre 1848/49: Stimmungsbilder aus der deutschen Revolution.* Aachen: Gustav Schmidt, 1906.

Nipperdey, Thomas. *Deutsche Geschichte 1800–1860. Bürgerwelt und starker Staat.* Munich: Beck, 1984.

Noack, Richard. "Die Revolutionsbewegung von 1848/49 in der Saargegend." Diss. phil., Frankfurt a.M., 1930. Published as *Mitteilungen des historischen Vereins für die Saargegend, Heft* 18 (1929).

Noyes, P. H. *Organization and Revolution: Working-Class Associations in the German Revolution of 1848–1849.* Princeton: Princeton University Press, 1966.

Obenaus, Herbert. *Anfänge des Parlamentarismus in Preußen.* Düsseldorf: Droste, 1984.

O'Boyle, Leonore. "The Democratic Left in Germany, 1848," *Journal of Modern History* 33 (1961): 374–83.

———. "The Problem of an Excess of Educated Men in Western Europe, 1800–1850," *Journal of Modern History* 42 (1970): 472–95.

Offerman, Toni. *Arbeiterbewegung und liberales Bürgertum in Deutschland 1850–1863.* Bonn: Neue Gesellschaft, 1979.

Otto, Ulrich. *Die historische-politischen Lieder und Karikaturen des Vormärz und der Revolution von 1848/1849.* Cologne: Pahl-Rugenstein, 1982.

Pagenstecher, C. H. Alexander. *Lebenserinnerungen von Dr. med. C.H. Alexander Pagenstecher.* Edited by Alexander Pagenstecher. 3 vols. in 1. Leipzig: R. Voigtländer, 1913.

Palmer, Brian. *Descent into Discourse: The Reification of Language and the Writing of Social History.* Philadelphia: Temple University Press, 1990.

Parisius, Bernd. " 'Daß die liebe alte Vorzeit wo möglich wieder hergestellt werde,' Politische und soziokulturelle Reaktionen von oldenburgischen Landarbeitern auf ihren sozialen Abstieg 1800–1848," in *Sozialer Protest. Studien zu traditioneller Resistenz und Kollektiver Gewalt in Deutschland vom Vormärz bis zur Reichsgründung.* Edited by Heinrich Volkmann and Jürgen Bergmann. Opladen: Westdeutscher Verlag, 1984. pp. 198–211.

Paschen, Joachim. *Demokratische Vereine und preußischer Staat. Entwicklung und Unterdrückung der demokratischen Bewegung während der Revolution von 1848/49.* Munich and Vienna: Oldenburg, 1977.

Paul, Roland, and Rink, Franz. "Erinnerungen des Kaiserslauterer Seminaristen Ludwig Hartmann an die Tage des Pfälzer Aufstandes," *Jahrbuch zur Geschichte von Stadt und Landkreis Kaiserslautern* 22/23 (1984/85): 383–404.

Pauly, Heribert. "Zur sozialen Zusammensetzung politischer Institutionen und Vereine der Stadt Mainz im Revolutionsjahr 1848," *Archiv für hessische Geschichte und Altertumskunde* 34 (1976): 45–81.

Peiner, August. "Persönliche Erlebnisse während der Unruhen 1848/49 in Elberfeld und Solingen," *Monatsschrift des Bergischen Geschichtsvereins* 5 (1898): 3–18.

Pickering, Paul. "Class without Words: Symbolic Communication in the Chartist Movement," *Past and Present* 112 (1986): 144–63.

Price, Roger. *The French Second Republic: A Social History.* Ithaca: Cornell University Press, 1972.

Püschner, Manfred. "Die Rheinkrise von 1840/41 und die antifeudale Oppositionsbewegung," in *Bourgeoisie und bürgerliche Umwälzung in Deutschland 1789–1871.* Edited by Helmut Bleiber. East Berlin: Akademie-Verlag, 1977. pp. 101–34.

Quandt, Siegfried. "Eduard Colsman (1812–1876). Ein Beitrag zur Geschichte der sozialen und politischen Auswirkungen der rheinischen Erweckungsbewegung des 19. Jahrhunderts," *Zeitschrift des Bergischen Geschichtsvereins* 85 (1970/71): 129–69.

Radkau, Joachim. "Holzverknappung und Krisenbewußtsein im 18. Jahrhundert," *Geschichte und Gesellschaft* 9 (1983): 513–43.

Radtke, Wolfgang. *Die Preußische Seehandlung zwischen Staat und Wirtschaft in der Frühphase der Industrialisierung.* Berlin: Colloquium, 1981.

Real, Willy. *Die Revolution in Baden 1848/49.* Stuttgart: W. Kohlhammer, 1983.

Regula, Konrad. "Die Allmenden der Pfalz in Vergangenheit und Gegenwart, ein Beitrag zur Agrargeschichte Südwestdeutschlands." Staatswiss. Diss., Würzburg, 1927.

Renner, Helmut. "Die Bericht des Regierungspräsident von Zenetti über die politische Bewegung in der Pfalz 1848/49," *Mitteilungen des Historischen Vereins der Pfalz* 59 (1961): 138–78.

Renner, Helmut. "Die pfälzische Bewegung in den Jahren 1848/49 und ihre Voraussetzungen. (Ein Beitrag zur pfälzischen Geschichte des 19. Jahrhunderts)." Diss. phil., Marburg, 1955.

Repgen, Konrad. "Klerus und Politik 1848. Die Kölner Geistlichen im politischen Leben des Revolutionsjahres—Ein Betrag zur 'Parteiengeschichte von unten,' " in *Aus Geschichte und Landeskunde. Forschungen und Darstellungen. Franz Steinbach zum 65. Geburtstag gewidmet.* Edited by Ludwig Petry. Bonn: Röhrscheid, 1960.

———. *Märzbewegung und Maiwahlen des Revolutionsjahres 1848 im Rheinland.* Bonn: Röhrscheid, 1955.

Reulecke, Jürgen. *Sozialer Frieden durch soziale Reform.* Wuppertal: Peter Hammer, 1983.

Reuter, Fritz. "Johann Philipp Bandel (1785–1866). Ein Wormser Demokrat Altertümer- und Kunstsammler im 19. Jahrhundert," *Wormsgau* 8 (1967/69): 41–67.

Rheinische Briefe und Akten zur Geschichte der politischen Bewegung 1830–1850. 2 vols. in 3. Vol. 1 and vol. 2, pt. 1 edited by Joseph Hansen. Bonn: Peter Hanstein, 1919–1942. Vol. 2, pt. 2 edited by Heinz Boberach. Cologne and Bonn: Peter Hanstein, 1976.

Rheinsche Geschichte. 4 vols. in 6. Edited by Franz Petri and George Droege. Düsseldorf: Schwann, 1978–1979.

Ringel, Hermann. *Bergische Wirtschaft zwischen 1790 und 1860.* Neustadt a.d. Aisch: Verlagsdruckerei Ph.C.W. Schmidt, 1966.

Rink, Franz. "Die Ereignisse im Kanton Otterberg während der Jahre 1848/49," *Jahrbuch zur Geschichte von Stadt und Landkreis Kaiserslautern* 22/23 (1984/85): 349–75.

Roes, Jan. "Hierarchie und Demokratie. Die katholischen Bischöfe Deutschlands vor der demokratischen Frage während des Revolutionsjahres 1848/49," *Nederlands archief vour Kerkgeschiednis* 52 (1972): 178–238.

Rosdolsky, Roman. "Friedrich Engels und as Problem der 'Geschichtslosen' Völker (Die Nationalitätenfrage in der Revolution von 1848/1849 im Lichte der 'Neuen Rheinischen Zeitung')," *Archiv für Sozialgeschichte* 4 (1964): 87–282.

Rosenkranz, Albert. *Kurze Geschichte der Evangelischen Kirche im Rheinland bis 1945.* 2d ed. Neukirchen-Vluyn: Neukirchen Verlag, 1975.

Röttges, Otto. *Die politischen Wahlen in den linksrheinischen Kreisen des Regierungsbezirks Düsseldorf 1848–1867.* Kempen: n.p., 1964.

Rubens, Heinrich. *Forstgeschichte im Zeitalter der industriellen Revolution.* West Berlin: Dunckler & Humboldt, 1967.

Rupieper, Hermann-Joseph. "Die Sozialstruktur der Trägerschichten der Revolution von 1848/49 am Beispiel Sachsens," in Hartmut Kaelble et al., *Probleme der Modernisierung in Deutschland.* Opladen: Westdeutscher Verlag, 1978. pp. 80–109.

Schaberg, Rolf. "Die Geschichte der Solinger Arbeiterbewegung von ihren Anfängen bis zum Ausbruch des 1. Weltkrieges." Diss. phil., Graz, 1958.

Scharfe, Martin. "Zum Rügebrauch," *Hessische Blätter für Volkskunde* 61 (1970): 45–68.

Scherer, Karl. "Zur Geschichte kirchlicher Parteien in der Pfalz. Die 'Pfarrer Frantzische Parthey' 1848/49," *Blätter für pfälzische Kirchengeschichte und religiöse Volkskunde* 35 (1968): 231–52

———. "Zur pfälzischen Kirchengeschichte des 19. Jahrhunderts. Theologischer Rationalismus und politischer Liberalismus im pfälzischen Vormärz," *Blätter für pfälzische Kirchengeschichte und religiöse Volkskunde* 32 (1965): 146–74.

Schieder, Wolfgang. *Anfänge der deutschen Arbeiterbewegung. Die Auslandsvereine im Jahrzehnt nach der Julirevolution.* Stuttgart: Klett-Cotta, 1963.

———. "Kirche und Revolution. Sozialgeschichtliche Aspekte der Trierer Wallfahrt von 1844," *Archiv für Sozialgeschichte* 14 (1974): 419–54.

———. "Der rheinpfälzische Liberalismus von 1832 als politische Protestbewegung," in *Vom Staat des Ancien regime zum modernen Parteistaat. Festschrift für Theodor Schieder zu seinem 70. Geburtstag.* Edited by Helmut Berding. Munich and Vienna: Oldenbourg, 1978. pp. 169–95.

Schierbaum, Hansjürgen. *Die politischen Wahlen in den Eifel- und Moselkreisen des Regierungsbezirkes Trier 1849–1867.* Düsseldorf: Droste, 1960.

Schindler, Werner. "Franz Alwens, Regierungspräsident der Pfalz von 1846–1849," *Mitteilungen des Historischen Vereins der Pfalz* 78 (1980): 415–26.

Schmidt, Paul. *Die Wahlen im Regierungsbezirk Koblenz 1849 bis 1867/69.* Bonn: Röhrscheid, 1971.

Schmidt, Walter. "Der Bund der Kommunisten und die Versuche einer Zentralisierung der deutschen Arbeitervereine in April und Mai 1848," *Zeitschrift für Geschichtswissenschaft* 9 (1961): 577–614.

———. "Die Klassenkämpfe in Frankreich 1848/49 in der 'Neuen Rheinischen Zeitung'—ein Beitrag zum Ringen der Kommunisten um die Emanzipation der deutschen Arbeiterbewegung," *Beiträge zur Geschichte der deutschen Arbeiterbewegung* 10 (1965): 263–91.

Schmidt, Walter, Becker, Gerhard, Bleiber, Helmut, Dlubek, Rolf, Schmidt, Siegfried, and Weber, Rolf. *Illustrierte Geschichte der deutschen Revolution 1848/49.* 3d ed. East Berlin: Dietz, 1988.

Schnabel, Franz. *Der Zusammenschluß des politischen Katholizismus in Deutschland im Jahre 1848.* Heidelberg: Karl Winter, 1910.

Schneider, Benedikt. *Die Verfassungskämpfe der Jahre 1848/49 unter Berücksichtigung der Ereignisse im Siegkreise.* Honnef: Siebengebirgsbuchhandlung, 1929.

Schneider, Heinz Richard. "Bürgerliche Vereinsbestrebungen für das 'Wohl der arbeitenden Klassen,' in der preußischen Rheinprovinz im 19. Jahrhundert." Diss. phil., Bonn, 1966.

Schneider, Hermann. "Die Schule im Spannungsfeld zwischen Kirche, Staat und Gesellschaft im 19. Jahrhundert, dargestellt am Problem der Simultanschule in der Pfalz," *Blätter für pfälzische Kirchengeschichte und religiöse Volkskunde* 35 (1968): 253–63.

Schneider, Regina-Margarete. "Landesausschuß und Provisorische Regierung in Kaiserslautern 1849," *Jahrbuch zur Geschichte von Stadt und Landkreis Kaiserslautern* 22/23 (1984/85): 91–117.

Schöttler, Peter. "Die rheinischen Fabrikgerichte im Vormärz und in der Revolution von 1848/49. Zwischenergebnisse einer sozialgeschichtlichen Untersuchung," *Zeitschrift für neuere Rechtsgeschichte* 7 (1985): 160–80.

Schroers, Heinrich. "Hermesianische Pfarrer," *Annalen des Historischen Vereins für den Niederrhein,* 103 (1919): 76–183.

Schuetz, Friedrich. "Das Verhältnis der Behörden zur Mainzer Fastnacht im Vormärz (1838–1846)," *Jahrbuch für westdeutsche Landesgeschichte* 6 (1980): 291–31.

———. "Der Vormärz in Mainz und Rheinhessen," in *Hambach 1832: Anstöße und Folgen*. Edited by Alois Gerlich. Wiesbaden: Franz Steiner, 1984. pp. 77–99.

Schulte, Klaus H. S. "Die Rechtslage der Juden in Köln und am Niederrhein 1815–1847," in *Köln und das rheinische Judentum. Festschrift Germania Judaica 1959–1984*. Edited by Jutta-Bohnke Kollwitz, Willebad Paul Eckert, Frank Golczewski, and Hermann Greive. Cologne: J. P. Bachem, 1984. pp. 95–101.

———. "Zur gewerblichen Betätigung der Juden in Köln und im ländlichen Rheinland," in *Köln und das rheinische Judentum. Festschrift Germania Judaica 1959–1984*. Edited by Jutta-Bohnke Kollwitz, Willebad Paul Eckert, Frank Golczewski, and Hermann Greive. Cologne: J. P. Bachem, 1984. pp. 125–40.

Schulte, Wilhelm. "Fritz Anneke, geb. 1818 Dortmund-gest. 1872 Chicago. Ein Leben für die Freiheit in Deutschland und in den USA," *Beiträge zur Geschichte Dortmunds und der Grafschaft Mark* 57 (1960): 5–100.

———. *Volk und Staat. Westfalen im Vormärz und in der Revolution von 1848/49*. Münster: Aschendorff, 1954.

Schurz, Carl. *Sturmjahre. Lebenserinnerungen 1829–1852*. East Berlin: Verlag der Nation, 1973.

Schwarzwälder, Bernd. "Frühe 'Arbeiterbewegung' in Neustadt an der Haardt," *Mitteilungen des Historischen Vereins der Pfalz* 81 (1983): 371–405.

———. "Die Ursachen der Reichsverfassungskampagne in der Pfalz 1849. Politische Bewegung in Neustadt an der Haardt." Wissenschaftliche Hausarbeit für die Zulassung zur Prüfung für das Lehramt am Gymnasium in Bayern, Munich, 1982.

Schwentker, Wolfgang. *Konservative Vereine und Revolution in Preussen 1848/49*. Düsseldorf: Droste, 1988.

Sewell, William H., Jr. *Work and Revolution in France: the Language of Labor from the Old Regime to 1848*. Cambridge: Cambridge University Press, 1980.

Seypel, Marcel. "Die Demokratische Gesellschaft in Köln während der Revolution von 1848/49." Diss. phil., Cologne, 1988.

Shorter, Edward. *The Making of the Modern Family*. New York: Basic Books, 1975.

Siemann, Wolfram. *Die deutsche Revolution von 1848/49*. Frankfurt a.M.: Suhrkamp, 1985.

———. *"Deutschlands Ruhe, Sicherheit und Ordnung." Die Anfänge der politischen Polizei 1806–1860*. Tübingen: Max Niemeyer, 1985.

Sozialer Protest: Studien zu traditioneller Resistenz und kollektiver Gewalt in Deutschland vom Vormärz bis zur Reichsgründung. Edited by Heinrich Volkmann and Jürgen Bergmann. Opladen: Westdeutscher Verlag, 1984.

Sperber, Jonathan. *Popular Catholicism in Nineteenth Century Germany*. Princeton: Princeton University Press, 1984.

———. "State and Civil Society in Prussia: Thoughts on a New Edition of Reinhart Koselleck's *Preussen zwischen Reform und Revolution*," *Journal of Modern History* 57 (1985): 278–96.

Stadelmann, Rudolf. *Social and Political History of the Revolution of 1848/49*. Translated by James Chastain. (Athens, Ohio: Ohio University Press, 1975.

Stahl, Hermann. *Die Revolution von 1848/49 an der Mittelmosel*. Bernkastel: Buchdruckerei der Bernkasteler Zeitung, n.d. [1923].

Stearns, Peter N. *1848: the Revolutionary Tide in Europe*. New York: W. W. Norton, 1974.

Stedman-Jones, Gareth. *Languages of Class: Studies in English Working Class History, 1832–1982*. Cambridge: Cambridge University Press, 1983.

Stein, Hans. *Der Kölner Arbeiterverein (1848–1849). Ein Beitrag zur Frühgeschichte des rheinischen Sozialismus*. Cologne: Gilsbach & Co, 1921.

Sterling, Eleonore. *Judenhaß. Die Anfänge des politischen Antisemitismus in Deutschland (1815–1850)*. Frankfurt: Europäische Verlagsanstalt, 1969.

Stollenwerk, Alexander. *Der Deutschkatholizismus in den preußischen Rheinlanden*. Mainz: Gesellschaft für mittelrheinische Kirchengeschichte, 1971.

Stommel, Karl. "Der Armenarzt Dr. Andreas Gottschalk, der erste Kölner Arbeiterführer, 1848," *Annalen des Historischen Vereins für den Niederrhein* 165 (1963): 55–105.

Strauss, Leo. "Pre-Emancipation Prussian Policies towards the Jews," *Leo Baeck Institute Yearbook* 11 (1966): 105–36.

Strey, Joachim, and Winkler, Gerhard. *Marx und Engels 1848/49. Die Politik und Taktik der 'Neuen Rheinischen Zeitung während der bürgerlich-demokratischen Revolution in Deutschland*. East Berlin: Dietz, 1972.

Taubert, Rolf. *Autonomie und Integration. Das Arbeiter-Blatt Lennep*. Munich: Dokumentia, 1977.

Tenfelde, Klaus. *Sozialgeschichte der Bergarbeiterschaft an der Ruhr im 19. Jahrhundert*. Bonn-Bad Godesberg: Neue Gesellschaft, 1977.

Thränhardt, Dietrich. *Wahlen und politische Strukturen in Bayern, 1848–1953*. Düsseldorf: Droste, 1973.

Tilly, Charles, Tilly, Richard, and Tilly, Louise. *The Rebellious Century, 1830–1930*. Cambridge, Mass: Harvard University Press, 1975.

Tilly, Richard. "Zur Entwicklung des Kapitalmarkts im 19. Jahrhundert unter besonderer Berücksichtigung Deutschlands," *Vierteljahrsschrift für Wirtschafts- und Sozialgelschichte* 60 (1973): 145–61.

Titze, Hartmut. "Die zyklische überproduktion von Akademikern im 19. u. 20. Jahrhundert," *Geschichte und Gesellschaft* 10 (1984): 92–121.

Toury, Jacob. *Die politischen Orientierungen der Juden in Deutschland. Von Jena bis Weimar*. Tübingen: J.C.B. Mohr, 1966.

Trippen, Norbert. "Das Kölner Dombaufest 1842 und die Absichten Friedrich Wilhelms IV. von Preußen bei der Wiederaufnahme der Arbeiten am Kölner Dom," *Annalen des Historischen Vereins für den Niederrhein* 182 (1979): 99–115.

Trotsky, Leon. *The History of the Russian Revolution*. Translated by Max Eastman. 3 vols. in 1. Ann Arbor: University of Michigan Press, 1964.

Uhrig, Dorothea. "Worms und die Revolution von 1848/49." Diss. phil., Frankfurt a.M., 1934.

Valentin, Veit. *Geschichte der deutschen Revolution von 1848–49*. 2 vols. Berlin: Ullstein, 1930–1931.

Die Verhandlungen des rheinhessischen Hochverratsprozesses von 1850. Edited by S. Heinemann. Mainz: W. Pricken, n.d.

Vigier, Pierre. *La Seconde République dans la région alpine*. 2 vols. Paris: Presses Universitaires de France, 1963.

Volkmann, Heinrich. "Protesträger und Protestformen in den Unruhen 1830–1832," in *Sozialer Protest: Studien zu traditioneller Resistenz und kollektiver Gewalt in Deutschland vom Vormärz bis zur Reichsgründung*. Edited by Heinrich Volkmann and Jürgen Bergmann. Opladen: Westdeutscher Verlag, 1984. pp. 56–75.

———. "Wirtschaftlicher Strukturwandel und sozialer Konflikt in der Frühindustrialisierung. Eine Fallstudie zum Aachener Aufruhr von 1830," in *Soziologie und sozialgeschichtliche Aspekte und Probleme*. Edited by Peter Christian Ludz. Opladen: Westdeutscher Verlag, 1973.

Voß, Wilhelm von. *Der Feldzug in der Pfalz und in Baden im Jahre 1849*. Berlin: R. Eisenschmidt, 1903.

Wagner, Maria. *Mathilde Franziska Anneke in Selbstzeugnissen und Dokumenten*. Frankfurt a.M.: Fischer Taschenbuch, 1980.

Weber, Christoph. *Aufklärung und Orthodoxie am Mittelrhein 1820–1850*. Paderborn: Ferdinand Schöningh, 1973.

Weber, Rolf. *Die Revolution in Sachsen 1848/49*. East Berlin: Akademie-Verlag, 1970.

Wegener, Hans. "Elberfeld in den vierziger Jahren des 19. Jahrhunderts," *Monatsschrift des Bergischen Geschichtsvereins* 20 (1913): 1–15, 21–35, 41–49, 61–66, 81–91, 102–111, 125–31, 141–58.

Wehler, Hans-Ulrich. *Deutsche Gesellschaftsgeschichte*. 4 vols. Munich: Beck, 1987–.

Weidmann, Werner. "Schulbildung und Lehrerstand in der Pfalz um die Mitte des 19. Jahrhunderts und die 1848/49er Revolution," *Jahrbuch zur Geschichte von Stadt und Landkreis Kaiserslautern* 22/23 (1984/85): 269–98.

———. "Wirtschaftliche Probleme und sozialrevolutionäre Ansätze im Umfeld des Hambacher Ereignisses von 1832," *Mitteilungen des Historischen Vereins der Pfalz* 80 (1982): 23–67.

———. "Die wirtschaftlich-sozialen Hintergründe der Pfälzer Revolution von 1849 und die sozialrevolutionären Umsturzversuche," *Jahrbuch zur Geschichte von Stadt und Landkreis Kaiserslautern* 22/23 (1984/85): 19–58.

Weitz, K. Reinhold. "Die Preussische Rheinprovinz als Adelslandschaft," *Rheinische Vierteljahrsblätter* 38 (1974): 332–54.

Wende, Peter. *Radikalismus im Vormärz. Untersuchungen zur politischsen Theorie der frühen deutschen Demokratie*. Wiesbaden: Franz Steiner, 1975.

Wettengel, Michael. "Das liberale und demokratische Vereinswesen in der Pfalz während der Revolution 1848/49," *Jahrbuch zur Geschichte von Stadt und Landkreis Kaiserslautern* 22/23 (1984/85): 73–90.

———. *Die Revolution von 1848/49 im Rhein-Main-Raum. Politische Vereine und Revolutionsalltag im Großherzogtum Hessen, Herzogtum Nassau und in der Freien Stadt Frankfurt*. Wiesbaden: Selbstverlag der Historischen Kommission für Nassau, 1989.

Wickelhaus, Manfred. "Einheit und Freiheit im preußischen Kirchenkampf des 19. Jahrhunderts. Die Elberfelder Kirchenspaltung 1847," *Monatshefte für evangelische Kirchengeschichte des Rheinlandes* 25 (1976): 33–64.

Wilentz, Sean. *Chants Democratic: New York City and the Rise of the American Working Class 1788–1850*. Oxford and New York: Oxford University Press, 1984.

Wirtz, Rainer. *"Widersetzlichkeit, Excesse, Crawalle, Tumulte und Skandale: Soziale Bewegung und gewalthafter sozialer Protest in Baden 1815–1848."* Frankfurt, West Berlin, and Vienna: Ullstein, 1981.

Wittgenstein, Klara. "Die Entstehung der sozialen Frage und Bewegung im Wuppertal in den vierziger Jahren des 19. Jahrhunderts und ihre wirtschaftlichen Grundlagen," *Zeitschrift des Bergischen Geschichtsvereins* 54 (1923/24): 118–89.

Wittke, Carl. *Refugees of Revolution: the German Forty-Eighters in America*. Philadelphia: University of Pennsylvania Press, 1952.

Wollstein, Günter. *Deutsche Geschichte 1848/49. Gescheiterte Revolution in Mitteleuropa*. Stuttgart: W. Kohlhammer, 1986.

Zeise, Roland. "Bauern und Demokraten 1848/49. Zur antifeudalen Bewegung der sächsischen Landbevölkerung in der Revolution vom Sommer 1848 bis zum vorabend des Dresdner Maiaufstandes," *Jahrbuch für Regionalgeschichte* 4 (1972): 148–78.

Zenz, Emil. *Geschichte der Stadt Trier im 19. Jahrhundert*. 2 vols. Trier: Spee, 1979.

———. *Andreas Tont Karnevalist und Revolutionär*. Trier: K. G. Heuschreck 1848 e.v., 1979.

Ziegler, Hans. "Das Gefängniswesen in der Pfalz (1800–1862)," *Mitteilungen des Historischen Vereins der Pfalz* 62 (1964): 87–144.

———. *Die Jahre der Reaktion in der Pfalz (1849–1853)*. Speyer: Verlag der Pfälzischen Gesellschaft zur Förderung der Wissenschaften, 1985.

———. "Landau in der Vormärzzeit und im Jahre des pfälzischen Aufstandes 1849," *Mitteilungen des Historischen Vereins der Pfalz* 61 (163): 201–24.

Zimmermann, Ludwig. *Die Einheits- und Freiheitsbewegung und die Revolution von 1848 in Franken*. Würzburg: Ferdinand Schöningh, 1951.

Zucker, Stanley. "Female Political Opposition in pre-1848 Germany. The Role of Kathinka Zitz-Halein," in *German Women in the Nineteenth Century: A Social History*. Edited by John C. Fout. New York and London: Holmes & Meier, 1984. pp. 133–50.

Index